Memory

Handbook of Perception and Cognition
2nd Edition

Series Editors
Edward C. Carterette
and Morton P. Friedman

Memory

Edited by

Elizabeth Ligon Bjork
Robert A. Bjork

Department of Psychology
University of California, Los Angeles
Los Angeles, California

Academic Press

San Diego   London   Boston
New York   Sydney   Tokyo   Toronto

Find Us on the Web! http://www.apnet.com

This book is printed on acid-free paper. ∞

Copyright © 1996 by ACADEMIC PRESS, INC.

Academic Press, Inc.
A Division of Harcourt Brace & Company
525 B Street, Suite 1900, San Diego, California 92101-4495

United Kingdom Edition published by
Academic Press Limited
24-28 Oval Road, London NW1 7DX

Library of Congress Cataloging-in-Publication Data

Bjork, Elizabeth L.
    Memory / Elizabeth L. Bjork, Robert A. Bjork.
        p.   cm. -- (Handbook of perception and cognition)
    Includes bibliographical references and index.
    ISBN 0-12-102570-5 (alk. paper)
    1. Memory.   2. Mnemonics.   3. Human information processing.
    I. Bjork, Robert A.   II. Title.   III. Series: Handbook of perception
    and cognition (2nd ed.)
    BF371.B535   1996
    153.1'2--dc20   96-7674
                                                     CIP

PRINTED IN THE UNITED STATES OF AMERICA
96   97   98   99   00   01   BC   9   8   7   6   5   4   3   2   1

Contents

Overview of Human Memory

1 Structures, Processes, and the Flow of Information
Harold Pashler and Mark Carrier

2   *Conscious and Unconscious Forms of Memory*

Colleen M. Kelley and D. Stephen Lindsay

Transient Memories

3   *Sensory and Perceptual Storage:*
Data and Theory

Dominic W. Massaro and Geoffrey R. Loftus

4 *Short-Term/Working Memory*

James S. Nairne

Storing Information in Long-Term Memory

5 *Imagery and Visual–Spatial Representations*

Lynn A. Cooper and Jessica M. Lang

6 *Autobiographical Memory*

Martin A. Conway

Accessing Information
in Long-Term Memory

7   Retrieval Processes

Henry L. Roediger, III and Melissa J. Guynn

8 *Interference and Inhibition in Memory Retrieval*

Michael C. Anderson and James H. Neely

Monitoring and Controlling Our Memories

9 *Distributing and Managing the Conditions of Encoding and Practice*

Frank N. Dempster

10 Mnemonic Methods to Enhance Storage and Retrieval

Francis S. Bellezza

11 Metacognitive Processes

Janet Metcalfe

Differences across Individuals

Memory for Real-World Events and Information

14 Retrieval Processes and Witness Memory

Carla C. Chandler and Ronald P. Fisher

15 *The Long-Term Retention of Training and Instruction*

Alice F. Healy and Grant P. Sinclair

Contributors

Numbers in parentheses indicate the pages on which the authors' contributions begin.

Michael C. Anderson (237)
Department of Psychology
University of Oregon
Eugene, Oregon 97403

Francis S. Bellezza (345)
Department of Psychology
Ohio University
Athens, Ohio 45701

Douglas A. Bors (411)
Division of Life Sciences
University of Toronto
Scarborough, Ontario MIC 1A4
 Canada

Mark Carrier (3)
Department of Psychology
Florida State University
Tallahassee, Florida 32306

Carla C. Chandler (493)
Department of Psychology
Washington State University
Pullman, Washington 99164

Martin A. Conway (165)
Department of Psychology
University of Bristol
Bristol BS8 1TN, England

Lynn A. Cooper (129)
Department of Psychology
Columbia University
New York, New York 10027

Frank N. Dempster (317)
Department of Educational Psychology
University of Nevada, Las Vegas
Las Vegas, Nevada 89154

Ronald P. Fisher (493)
Department of Psychology
Florida International University
Miami, Florida 33199

Melissa J. Guynn[1] (197)
Department of Psychology
Rice University
Houston, Texas 77251

Alice F. Healy (525)
Department of Psychology
University of Colorado
Boulder, Colorado 80309

Colleen M. Kelley (31)
Department of Psychology
Macalester College
St. Paul, Minnesota 55105

Jessica M. Lang (129)
Department of Psychology
Columbia University
New York, New York 10027

Leah L. Light (443)
Department of Psychology
Pitzer College
Claremont, California 91711

D. Stephen Lindsay (31)
Department of Psychology
University of Victoria
Victoria, BC V8W 3P5 Canada

Geoffrey R. Loftus (67)
Department of Psychology
University of Washington
Seattle, Washington 98115

Colin M. MacLeod (411)
Division of Life Sciences
University of Toronto
Scarborough, Ontario M1C 1A4
    Canada

Dominic W. Massaro (67)
Program in Experimental Psychology
University of California, Santa Cruz
Santa Cruz, California 95064

Janet Metcalfe (381)
Department of Psychology
Columbia University
New York, New York 10027

James S. Nairne (101)
Department of Psychological Science
Purdue University
West Lafayette, Indiana 47907

James H. Neely (237)
Department of Psychology
The University at Albany–State
    University of New York
Albany, New York 12222

Harold Pashler (3)
Department of Psychology
University of California, San Diego
La Jolla, California 92093

Henry L. Roediger, III[2] (197)
Department of Psychology
Rice University
Houston, Texas 77251

Grant P. Sinclair[3] (525)
Department of Psychology
University of Colorado
Boulder, Colorado 80309

[1] Present Address: Department of Psychology, University of New Mexico, Albuquerque, New Mexico 87131

[2] Present Address: Department of Psychology, Washington University, St. Louis, Missouri 63130

[3] Present Address: Department of Psychology, Old Dominion University, Norfolk, Virginia 23529

Foreword

The problem of perception and cognition is in understanding how the organism transforms, organizes, stores, and uses information arising from the world in sense data or memory. With this definition of perception and cognition in mind, this handbook is designed to bring together the essential aspects of this very large, diverse, and scattered literature and to give a précis of the state of knowledge in every area of perception and cognition. The work is aimed at the psychologist and the cognitive scientist in particular, and at the natural scientist in general. Topics are covered in comprehensive surveys in which fundamental facts and concepts are presented, and important leads to journals and monographs of the specialized literature are provided. Perception and cognition are considered in the widest sense. Therefore, the work will treat a wide range of experimental and theoretical work.

The *Handbook of Perception and Cognition* should serve as a basic source and reference work for those in the arts or sciences, indeed for all who are interested in human perception, action, and cognition.

Edward C. Carterette and Morton P. Friedman

Preface

It would be hard to imagine a component of human cognition more fundamental than memory. Without a functioning memory, other cognitive
functions—such as perception, learning, reasoning, problem solving, and
language—would be impossible. For good reason, then, memory and its
role in other cognitive functions have long been of interest to researchers
and scholars. The past several decades, however, have seen a veritable explosion of research on human memory. During this period, the study of
memory has been approached from many directions by behavioral and
brain scientists employing a variety of methods to investigate normal and
abnormal memory phenomena in animals, children, adults, and the elderly.
The convergence and interaction of these efforts have been remarkably
fruitful, resulting in new and improved paradigms and methodologies, instructive empirical findings, promising theoretical developments, and potentially important applications to real-world contexts, such as law, education, and therapy. In short, these efforts have elevated our empirical and
theoretical understanding of human memory to a new level.

The principal goal of this handbook was to convey the present state of
our knowledge about human memory, and, happily, we were able to convince a distinguished group of researchers to summarize that knowledge. A
second goal was to arrange the contents of the volume in a way that would
make it useful not only as a resource for researchers and scholars, but also as
a textbook for students. Toward that end, we have organized and sequenced

the chapters in a fashion intended to provide a coherent picture of the field. Two overview chapters are followed by chapters on sensory storage and short-term memory, which are, in turn, followed by two chapters on different aspects of how we store information in long-term memory. Those chapters are followed by two chapters on how we access—or fail to access— information that exists in our long-term memories, and three chapters on how we monitor and control such storage and retrieval processes. The final four chapters comprise two chapters that review how our memory capacities and characteristics vary as a function of individual differences and aging, and two chapters that examine the implications of memory research for two real-world domains of strong current interest: witness interrogation and testimony and the long-term retention of skills and knowledge. For students new to the study of memory, the chapters are perhaps best read in order, although each can be read as a self-contained unit. To provide additional cohesion among chapters, we have also inserted frequent references within any given chapter to related content and discussions in other chapters.

The first overview chapter, "Structures, Processes, and the Flow of Information," by Harold Pashler and Mark Carrier, presents a framework for viewing different memory structures and the processes that regulate the flow of information between those structures. This chapter represents an updating of the information-processing approach, a theoretical perspective that has dominated the study of memory during much of the past several decades. The second overview chapter, "Conscious and Unconscious Forms of Memory," by Colleen Kelley and Stephen Lindsay, discusses the distinction between explicit and implicit memory; that is, between the influences of past episodes on our current perceptions, thoughts, and behavior that are and are not, respectively, accompanied by an awareness of the source of those influences.

The second section of this volume, "Transient Memories," consists of two chapters: Chapter 3, "Sensory and Perceptual Storage: Data and Theory," by Dominic Massaro and Geoffrey Loftus, and Chapter 4, "Short-Term/Working Memory," by James Nairne. In Chapter 3, Massaro and Loftus review the empirical and theoretical research that form the basis for our past and present conceptions of visual and auditory sensory stores, and they summarize the findings they believe provide evidence for multiple types of perceptual memories as distinct from sensory stores. Nairne, in Chapter 4, reviews the current characterizations of short-term or "working" memories, and the role such active but limited-capacity memories might play in the overall functioning of human memory.

The third section, "Storing Information in Long-Term Memory," contains two chapters: Chapter 5, "Imagery and Visual–Spatial Representations," by Lynn Cooper and Jessica Lang, and Chapter 6, "Autobiographical Memory" by Martin Conway. In Chapter 5, Cooper and Lang examine the state of research on visual–spatial representations in memory and the mechanisms by which these representations mediate performance, with a focus on imagery, object recognition, and memory for spatial layouts or cognitive maps. Conway, in Chapter 6, discusses recent research on autobiographical memory, addressing such questions as how autobiographical knowledge is represented in and retrieved from long-term memory; what happens when autobiographical memory becomes impaired, for example, as in amnesia; and what the relation of autobiographical memories is to the (sense of) self.

The fourth section, "Accessing Information in Long-Term Memory," includes Chapter 7, "Retrieval Processes," by Henry Roediger and Melissa Guynn, and Chapter 8, "Interference and Inhibition in Memory Retrieval," by Michael Anderson and James Neely. In Chapter 7, Roediger and Guynn adopt the view that remembering is best understood as a product of information from two sources: memory traces and retrieval cues. They then argue that the effectiveness of a retrieval cue is governed by two potent factors: (a) the extent to which the operations induced at the time memory is tested match those used in the initial encoding of that information or event, and (b) the extent to which a given cue is distinctive rather than "overloaded," that is, associated to a number of traces in memory. In Chapter 8, Anderson and Neely summarize both classical and contemporary evidence that implicates interference and inhibitory processes as the cause of forgetting (retrieval failure) in long-term memory.

The fifth section, "Monitoring and Controlling Our Memories," contains three chapters: Chapter 9, "Distributing and Managing the Conditions of Encoding and Practice," by Frank Dempster; Chapter 10, "Mnemonic Methods to Enhance Storage and Retrieval," by Francis Bellezza; and Chapter 11, "Metacognitive Processes," by Janet Metcalfe. In Chapter 9, Dempster examines the influence on memory of how and when information is studied or practiced, with an emphasis on the implications of such findings for optimizing learning and memory in educational settings. Bellezza, in Chapter 10, characterizes mnemonic techniques as the strategic manipulation of available knowledge to aid in the acquisition of new knowledge, and in the process he exposes many popular misconceptions about the nature and effectiveness of mnemonic devices and mnemonic learning. Metcalfe, in Chapter 11, analyzes the role of metacognitive processes in several domains of human cognition (problem solving, learning and skill acquisition, and judgment and decision making), highlighting the critical nature of metacognitive processes in cognition with a review of metacognitive impairments found in frontal-lobe patients.

The sixth section, "Differences across Individuals," contains two chapters: Chapter 12, "Individual Differences in Memory," by Douglas Bors and

Colin MacLeod, and Chapter 13, "Memory and Aging," by Leah Light. Bors and MacLeod, in Chapter 12, examine the basic findings on individual differences in memory abilities, with the goal of indicating how variations across individuals might inform theories of human memory. Light, in Chapter 13, presents a comprehensive survey of the nature of age-related changes in memory and evaluates the sufficiency of the alternate accounts that have been put forward to explain such changes.

The final section, "Memory for Real-World Events and Information," contains two chapters designed to illustrate the implications of modern research on memory for a variety of real-world contexts. Chapter 14, "Retrieval Processes and Witness Memory," by Carla Chandler and Ronald Fisher, focuses on a domain where understanding the capabilities and frailties of human memory is critical: witness memory in legal settings. Chapter 15, "The Long-Term Retention of Training and Instruction," by Alice Healy and Grant Sinclair, focuses on the long-term retention of knowledge and skills. Healy and Sinclair, drawing on what we know about human memory, include in their analysis a set of guidelines to optimize the conditions of training and instruction.

To the extent that this handbook, as we hope and expect, becomes an important resource for students of human memory, the primary credit belongs, of course, to our contributors, those distinguished investigators who created the chapters that compose this volume. We appreciate their effort and cooperation, and we admire their scholarship and expertise. As editors, we found their chapters provocative and instructive. Should you, as a reader of this volume, have the same reaction, we—and they—will be very pleased.

Elizabeth Ligon Bjork and Robert A. Bjork

Overview of Human Memory

Structures, Processes, and the Flow of Information

Harold Pashler
Mark Carrier

This chapter presents an overview of the structures and processes of human memory from an information processing perspective. The first section describes the memory systems that play an important role in our explicit memory for experiences (as manifested, e.g., in tasks like recall and recognition). It describes the characteristics of these systems and provides an overview of the various kinds of evidence that establish their separate identities. Section II reviews some major findings about how the flow of information between memory systems is regulated, including encoding and storage, rehearsal, and retrieval. It focuses on the demands these various processes place on limited capacity mechanism(s) and on how the flow of information between different memory systems is controlled. These phenomena are often subsumed under the heading "Attention and Memory." The use of the term *attention* as a theoretical construct will be avoided, however, because the concept is so sprawling and diffuse. Section III presents a tentative analysis of processes involved in copying information among different memory structures, postulating several distinct forms of "attention" with specifiably different properties.

The aim of this chapter is to provide the reader with a general framework for viewing different memory structures and the information processing operations that modify their contents. Some readers may be surprised to

Memory

find advocated in this chapter various concepts that some have claimed to be obsolete (e.g., iconic and echoic memory, short-term and long-term memory, central processing bottlenecks). The justification for this will emerge later: recent findings, far from rendering any of these concepts obsolete, have markedly strengthened their empirical support. On several other issues, however, especially those pertaining to attention and control, this chapter advocates some markedly unorthodox positions, and, questions certain traditional views.

I. STRUCTURES

A. Information Processing Approach to Memory

This chapter examines memory from an information processing perspective, which has dominated psychological studies of memory in the past thirty years. While the tradition is hardly monolithic, researchers adopting the information processing perspective have typically shared certain ideas and goals. One goal is to make sense of human memory with the help of the idea that when people have experiences, they form different kinds of memory representations of different aspects of the experience, sometimes referred to as "codes" (Posner, 1978) or "traces." Information processing theories assume that different codes dwell in different memory systems that have different temporal and other properties. Although memory traces and memory systems are in some sense "in the brain," the concepts are functional, not neurophysiological. To speak of moving information around between different systems is not to claim that anything in particular is moving from one spot to another within the skull. It has been known for some time that the trace of a single experience might not be stored in any single place in the brain (J. A. Anderson, 1973; Lashley, 1929), but even if this is the case, it would not invalidate the kinds of theories we are discussing. This fact notwithstanding, patterns of brain damage can provide crucial constraints for constructing information processing theories, because they can demonstrate that different structures are responsible for carrying out various functions (Caramazza, 1992).

As with any scientific tradition, there is little to be gained in debating the merits and deficiencies of the information processing approach in the abstract. If analyzing memory at the information processing level allows one to make sense of many important phenomena of memory, and leads to novel successful predictions, then it constitutes a useful scientific approach. If it cannot do these things, other approaches will need to replace it—perhaps ones that abandon the psychological or functional level of analysis entirely.

B. Distinct Memory Systems

For the last twenty-five years or so, many psychologists have postulated the existence of several different human memory systems. It is obviously more parsimonious to assume a single memory system rather than several. Why assume there is more than one? The existence of several memory systems is not something that can be proven by any one experiment or observation. It makes sense to propose different memory systems only if (1) doing so allows one to account in a natural way for a range of different findings, and if (2) these findings could be explained by a single-system model only if that model is burdened with implausible and ad hoc modifications. From a commonsense standpoint, several types of evidence offer strong arguments for positing separate systems: (1) if "filling up" one system leaves the capacity of other systems unaffected; (2) if brain damage sometimes destroys or damages one system while leaving others quite intact (ideally each can be selectively knocked out, yielding the "double dissociation" prized by neuropsychologists); and (3) if certain experimental variables have effects that can be sensibly interpreted by supposing that they affect one system and not others. If a multiple-systems model is supported by all of these types of evidence, then the model rests on strong ground. If only one or two are satisfied, however, the validity of the model becomes arguable, and it may be necessary to stop and reflect on exactly what one means by a separate system. This chapter argues that, fortunately, the evidence is clear enough to make this unnecessary here.

The first comprehensive attempt to divide human memory into different systems was proposed by Atkinson and Shiffrin (1968) and has come to be known as the "Modal Memory Model." The Modal Model postulated three broad sets of memory systems: sensory memory, short-term memory (STM), and long-term memory (LTM). This three-part division has been corroborated by evidence of each of the three forms noted above. The next sections describe the basic properties of sensory memory systems, STM, and LTM. The main evidence for the integrity of each memory system is discussed along with some recent arguments against these systems.

C. Sensory Memory Systems

When a visual stimulus is briefly presented, a sensory trace of that stimulus lasts several hundred milliseconds after its offset (at least with typical viewing conditions and a stimulus that is not followed by another stimulus of high intensity or contrast). Visual sensory memory is generally nicknamed *iconic memory*. Its existence was first suspected by researchers in the nineteenth century, who noted that very brief displays (say 1 ms or 100 ms in duration) did not seem to disappear instantaneously. Contemporary evidence corroborates these suppositions. First, subjects can successfully report subsets of a display of characters that have been cued by the experimenter *after* the offset of the display (e.g., by a tone cue indicating which row of a multirowed display to report). This partial-report advantage declines rapidly as the cue is delayed, demonstrating the existence of a rapidly fading trace that initially contains more information than can be reported before the trace fades away (Sperling, 1960). Another kind of evidence for iconic memory comes from experiments in which subjects indicate the duration of their phenomenal experience of the display. Examples include experiments in which subjects adjust auditory clicks to coincide with the moment at which a display subjectively disappears, or judge the continuity of intermittently flashed displays (Haber & Standing, 1969). These observations all argue for an iconic memory that lasts several hundred milliseconds after the offset of a stimulus and that is phenomenologically very much like a fading version of the stimulus itself.[1]

Some investigators have offered markedly longer or shorter estimates of iconic memory duration. However, these estimates should be regarded with suspicion. Claims that iconic memory lasts in excess of one-half second have usually come from experiments involving unusually intense displays (Sakitt, 1976). Estimates that iconic memory lasts under 100 ms, on the other hand, have usually been produced with tasks that are likely to index the time at which the subject first detects that iconic memory has *begun* to fade, rather than the point at which it has actually faded away (pointed out in Hawkins & Shulman, 1979). Other tasks yielding short estimates of iconic memory duration required observers to create a single percept out of the iconic memory from a preceding target *plus* a new stimulus (Di Lollo & Dixon, 1988). Even if iconic memory ordinarily produces a percept of a target that lasts several hundred milliseconds after the offset of the target if no other stimulus follows it, the visual system might nonetheless "resist" fusing this percept with new input arriving during that interval. (Indeed, the phenomenon of backward masking shows that the visual system often declines to fuse two successive stimuli, choosing rather to discard the first; Turvey, 1973.) In summary, then, traditional estimates of the duration of iconic memory in the several-hundred-milliseconds range appear well supported.

[1] Various researchers have argued that the persistence of information (e.g., identities of letters) has a wholly separate origin from persistence of the phenomenal experience of a display. The empirical evidence for this is far from compelling, and certainly not enough to overturn the commonsense presumption that if one can "see" something for a while one can also recognize it. For example, no one has reported conditions under which a normal observers reports a persisting clear image of some letters but is unable to report the identities of these letters; nor has the converse been reported. At most, it has been claimed that certain variables affect the two tasks in slightly different ways, but these arguments are open to various interpretations (Hawkins & Shulman, 1979; see also Massaro & Loftus, this volume, Chapter 3).

Rather little is known of the exact storage capacity of iconic memory beyond the fact that it substantially exceeds that of STM and can store at least a dozen or so letters (Averbach & Coriell, 1961) and large matrices of black-and-white squares (Phillips, 1974, 1983). If iconic memory is indeed like a fading image, it is likely to be limited in the precision with which it can represent visual features, rather than in the total amount of information it can hold.

Is iconic memory really separate from other memory systems? The partial-report studies described previously clearly distinguish iconic memory from short-term memory: the fact that people can transfer a cued subset of a display into a more durable form entails two different forms of storage with different temporal properties. Phillips (1974) has carried out several elegant experiments that reveal further differences between iconic memory and visual short-term memory (VSTM). First, iconic memory, but not VSTM, is severely disrupted by subsequent visual events in the same retinal location (i.e., backward masking). Second, patterns stored in iconic memory cannot readily be compared to patterns presented to different parts of the visual field (whereas VSTM *can* be used for such comparisons). These findings suggest that iconic memory may represent information in retina-centered coordinates, while VSTM may represent patterns in object- and/or viewer-centered coordinates.

Auditory sensory storage (also known as echoic memory) holds information for much longer than iconic memory, typically one or two seconds (Norman, 1969; but see Massaro & Loftus, this volume, Chapter 3, for a different estimate based on a distinction between sensory and perceptual auditory memory). The phenomenology of echoic memory is also different from that of iconic memory: one does not experience a fading auditory image, but rather the potential accessibility of sounds from immediately preceding time. Little is known of the capacity of echoic memory. Although it can hold more than verbal short-term memory, partial-report experiments using three location-defined channels have not demonstrated terribly impressive storage capacity (Darwin, Turvey, & Crowder, 1972).

Functional Role of Sensory Memory Systems

The preceding section argued that the classical picture of the properties of sensory memory systems is essentially correct. However, the traditional account of sensory memory as a way station for stimuli *en route* to more durable memory stores is problematic at best. Real-world scenes do not often disappear instantaneously;[2] usually, they remain present until the per-

---

[2] Actually, artificial illumination frequently produces periodic near-complete offsets at 60 Hz, but iconic memory cannot be an adaptation for dealing with this type of illumination, since it was not present in the environment in which *Homo sapiens* evolved.

son foveates a different part of the scene, producing new visual input. There is, therefore, no justification for regarding sensory memory as a *stage* in a serial progression of information from the stimulus to later memory systems. It is not clear what use iconic memory might have, except perhaps to bridge the temporal gap created by blinks (integration across eye movements now seems to be an unlikely function for iconic memory; see Irwin, 1992). In the case of echoic memory, on the other hand, many important events, especially in speech, are conveyed by acoustic patterns that unfold over considerable periods of time, and sensory memory may be essential for their recognition. Further research is needed, however, before one can say anything definitive about the functions of sensory memory.

D. Short-Term Memory Systems

Many textbooks still refer to a single STM or "working memory," sometimes implying that information in this system is always coded in a speech-like form. This unitary-STM view is often attributed to Atkinson and Shiffrin (1968). In fact, Atkinson and Shiffrin suspected that people have more than one STM system, and there is strong evidence that their suspicions were correct. Before considering evidence for multiple STMs, however, we consider the more basic question of why one should distinguish STM from any other form of postsensory memory. Why not simply speak of (postsensory) "memory," rather than distinguishing STM from LTM?

1. The STM/LTM Distinction

The most compelling evidence for a distinction between STM and LTM comes from patients with anterograde amnesia. These patients often perform normally on span tasks[3] as long as they are not distracted between study and test. One can have a conversation with an amnesia sufferer without suspecting any mental abnormalities—until one leaves the room and returns to find that one has been forgotten. Milner (1958) was apparently the first to interpret this syndrome as reflecting an inability to transfer (or, more precisely, *copy*) information into a distinct LTM system. Because these individuals retain the ability to hold onto information for a short period (in span tasks or in ordinary conversation), however, Milner proposed that they must have intact short-term memory system(s) that work over distraction-free intervals.

As every introductory psychology textbook describes, free-recall experiments with normals provide another prominent source of support for the STM/LTM distinction. In the free-recall task, people ordinarily remember

---

[3] Immediate serial recall of lists that are short enough to permit perfect recall on a large proportion of trials.

items early in the list and later in the list better than those in the middle (these excesses are termed the *primacy* and *recency* effects, respectively). According to the conventional account, recency arises because the last few items are likely to still be present in STM at the time recall begins (Watkins, 1974). This analysis, however, has been subjected to withering criticism in the past few years (see, e.g., Crowder, 1993; see also Nairne, this volume, Chapter 4, for an analysis of these effects). The main criticism hinges on the fact that recency effects are not confined to the conventional free-recall task. Recency, it turns out, also occurs in a very different sort of free-recall task that involves lists of word pairs. Here, the subject carries out mental arithmetic for 24 s between the presentation of each word pair and the following pair (Bjork & Whitten, 1974). Recency also shows up in recall of events that occurred weeks or months earlier (Baddeley & Hitch, 1977). The recency items can hardly have been lurking in STM in these cases. Critics have suggested, therefore, that it would be more parsimonious to attribute recency effects to the use of temporally based strategies for retrieving items from memory. Once that point is granted, the argument goes, there is no reason not to conceive of memory as unitary (Crowder, 1993).

This argument sounds reasonable but it fails to take account of several important facts. First, anterograde amnesics show an intact recency effect but typically recall little else from the list (Baddeley & Warrington, 1970)— a pattern predicted by the dual-memory account, if amnesics have intact STM but cannot get information into LTM. Administration of diazepam (Valium) to normals also tends to spare the recency portion of the list (Mewaldt, Hinrichs, & Ghoneim, 1983). Second, when a normal individual doing a conventional free-recall task performs mental arithmetic during a 10-s retention interval, recency is essentially abolished (Glanzer & Cunitz, 1966; see also Phillips & Christie, 1977a, for a close analogue with not-easily-verbalized visual stimuli). Because mental arithmetic is likely to displace the contents of STM, this finding is predicted by the dual-memory theory. It is not clear how a retrieval-strategy explanation of recency would account for either of these findings.

Even more compelling, though, is the behavior of patients who have suffered brain damage that leaves them with a digit span of only one or two items. According to the dual-memory theory, this result must reflect a defect in verbal STM. Sure enough, these patients also have a peculiarly shaped recency effect, shrunken down to little more than the last item in the list (Shallice & Warrington, 1970). Finally, consider what happens when these patients are tested in the situations that produce the *long-term* recency effects supposedly so problematic for the dual-memory view. In these tasks, the patients' performance seems indistinguishable from normals (Vallar, Papagno, & Baddeley, 1991). No one has yet shown how these findings can be explained without postulating a distinct short-term memory responsible for the conventional recency effect. Thus, the data as a whole provide rather compelling support for the traditional interpretation of recency in free recall and, along with that, the STM/LTM distinction. Long-term recency effects must have a different source than the conventional recency effect.[4] There are other important sources of evidence for the STM/LTM distinction beyond those described above; Phillips (1983) has provided an excellent summary of some of them.

2. Evidence for Distinct Forms of STM

There are at least two separate forms of STM, and there may possibly be many more. (See also Massaro & Loftus, this volume, Chapter 2; Nairne, Chapter 3; Cooper & Lang, Chapter 5, for further discussions of this issue.) The case for STMs that represent information in speechlike and visual forms, respectively, is especially strong. First, the patients described earlier who suffer from catastrophic verbal STM deficits are nearly normal at reporting *visually presented* characters (Warrington & Shallice, 1969). Furthermore, normal subjects suffer virtually no interference when they concurrently store spoken digits (presumably in a speechlike format) and visually presented letters (presumably in a visual format) for written report (Henderson, 1972; Scarborough, 1972; see also Frick, 1984, Margrain, 1967). Is the latter STM the same as the visual STM observed by Phillips (1974) in the studies with nonnamable visual patterns described earlier? There is no reason to doubt it, but it would be reassuring to have some positive evidence before assuming it is so. Baddeley (1986) reviews further lines of evidence for separating visual and verbal STM, and also discusses the rather intricate question of whether verbal STM should be conceived of as phonological, articulatory, or both (see also Howard & Franklin, 1993).

Are there further independent STMs beyond the verbal and visual? Few experimenters have required people to retain stimuli presented in modalities other than vision and audition, but a few that have done so provide some evidence for a haptic short-term memory (Bowers, Mollenhauer, & Luxford, 1990; Murray, Ward, & Hockley, 1975). There is also some evidence that *spatial* information can be stored in a memory system that is indifferent

---

[4] This is not the only beating the STM account of recency has taken. A more empirically grounded argument was offered by Baddeley and Hitch (1977). They noted that performing "articulatory suppression" (e.g., saying "the the the . . .") while reading a list did not wipe out the recency effect. As the reader can readily verify, however, one can do as reasonable job of reading a list of words and making rhyme judgments on each word while at the same time performing articulatory suppression (see also Besner, 1987). It seems, therefore, that articulatory suppression does not fully suppress articulation. Baddeley and Hitch also reported that people still showed a recency effect when they carried out a span task as the free-recall list was presented. This finding would be a real nail in the coffin for the dual-memory view of recency, except for the fact that their span list was presented as a *visual* display, which, as discussed below, makes it quite possible the recency items and the list occupied different STM systems, as in Scarborough's (1972) study.

to the sensory modality in which the information originated, and also independent of visual STM (Farah, Hammond, Levine, & Calvanio, 1988; Henderson, 1972). Intriguing studies suggesting that people can *acquire* a special-purpose "kinesthetic STM" were conducted by Reisberg, Rappaport, and O'Shaughnessy, (1984). They trained subjects to code digits in terms of sequences of finger movements, and this training allowed the subjects to increase their digit span performance by almost 50%. What about short-term storage of abstract or conceptual information, for example, ideas, propositions, plans, or intentions? Can a person maintain short-term memory for the abstract proposition—say, that a cat is on a mat—without rehearsing a sentence or image? These questions are potentially testable, but there seems to be rather little evidence either way (but see Saffran & Martin, 1990).

3. Forgetting in STM

As long as information in STM is regularly rehearsed, it can apparently be maintained indefinitely. The usual cause of information loss in STM is displacement by other stimuli. It turns out to be very tricky to determine whether information that is neither rehearsed *nor* displaced undergoes any sort of passive decay. The very fact that people do rehearse provides some hint that it probably does: otherwise, why not remember a phone number simply by sitting and doing nothing?[5] Reitman (1974) had subjects perform a tone detection task while holding onto some items in STM, assuming that detecting tones would prevent rehearsal and occupy the subjects' mental processes without displacing items from STM. He found that those subjects who did not rehearse showed modest evidence of STM decay. Shiffrin and Cook (1978) tried to improve upon Reitman's procedure by asking subjects to forget the items that were presented; their results also appeared to support STM decay.

There is evidence that the similarity of items in STM can speed up forgetting. This may support theories of STM forgetting that emphasize interference among items in STM and/or between these items and interpolated materials. However, it is difficult to assess the role of LTM in some of these effects (Crowder, 1976), and therefore difficult to assess the validity of these theories.

4. What *Is* STM?

The findings described above imply the existence of several, and perhaps many, subsystems for retaining information over relatively short time periods. These systems have certain commonalities: they retain information for only a short time after it has been input or refreshed, but, unlike sensory

---

[5] Of course, one might have the habit of rehearsing simply because interfering material often does arise, so this argument is not entirely compelling.

memory, storing an input in these systems protects it from being wiped out by new sensory stimulation (i.e., masked). The independence of different STM systems seems to be clearly documented by the neuropsychological and behavioral evidence summarized above. But distinguishing different systems raises, as well as answers, questions. One obvious question is whether these systems should be seen as *structures* that exist for the storage of information. Could STM simply reflect the fact that people can periodically refresh neural activity in many different neural systems—systems that are "designed" not for short-term retention but for specialized cognitive functions including language, visual and spatial problem solving, and motor control (Barnard, 1985)? If so, why not view STM as an activity or process rather than a set of neural/mental structures (Reisberg et al., 1984; see also Nairne, this volume, Chapter 4, for a discussion of this view of STM)?

There may not be much more than a semantic conflict here. Short-term storage may be vital for many activities, thus making it necessary for the brain to have *some* mechanisms capable of doing the job. However, evolution could, in its typical opportunistic fashion, have arranged for this function to be handled by systems that are primarily specialized for non-memorial functions. Even if this is so, talking about multiple STM systems would not be terribly misleading, as long as it is not inferred that some brain systems have the sole function of memory storage.

There is another idea, which sounds very similar to the view just considered, but which needs to be distinguished from it: the idea that what appears to be short-term memory merely reflects a certain kind of rehearsal strategy. On this view, all traces—whether we would normally describe them as being in LTM or in STM—are really of the same type, and they all gradually decay with time unless refreshed. Sometimes, however, a person may adopt the strategy of cycling through a set of traces and refreshing each trace just before it weakens to the point of being inaccessible. This set would correspond to the contents of STM. On this view, a person maintaining an STM set is very much like a juggler who keeps many balls in the air at the same time. This hypothesis is really a unitary memory model. While it seems to offer a pleasing parsimony, it is difficult to square with various data. Consider the amnesic patient who rapidly loses information that is not currently being rehearsed. On the trace-juggling model, the patient should have the same problem as the ordinary juggler placed in a high-gravity environment. Obviously, this would prevent a juggler from keeping as many balls in the air as he or she could normally. But recall that in span tasks, amnesics typically perform normally. The trace-juggling view also offers no ready explanation of what is going on with verbal STM-impaired patients who show normal long-term retention of verbal materials. Finally, it is difficult for this model to explain the fact that memory span for different types of material shows a close (inverse) relationship to pronunciation time for that class of item (Schweickert, Guentert, & Hersberger, 1990).

Where does the evidence leave us? There is strong support for multiple STM systems the contents of which are not to be identified with traces in LTM. One could still claim that although an item in STM is not represented by the presence of a trace in (episodic) LTM, it is represented by *activation* of long-term semantic memory (Cowan, 1988). This idea is close to Hebb's notion of reverberatory memory, but there is still a problem: why, then, should it be possible to fill different systems to their own respective capacity limits (as observed in Scarborough, 1972)? Together, these constraints seem to argue for the integrity of STM systems in a fairly strong sense. However, the actual neural tissue that supports STM need not have the sole function of storing information for short periods; it may do other things, as well.

E. Long-Term Memory

The evidence for a distinction between long-term memory and other memory systems has already been discussed. What are the properties of LTM? It has sometimes been suggested that information in LTM is coded in "semantic" form, but there is plenty of evidence that people can retain surface details of stimuli over indefinite time periods. The capacity of long-term memory is obviously vast, although exceedingly difficult to quantify (Landauer, 1986). How forgetting occurs in LTM poses something of a puzzle, as well. Associative interference can clearly make it harder to access information in LTM. What is less clear, however, is whether memories are also subject to passive decay. One argument that both decay *and* interference probably play a role in forgetting from LTM comes from the effects of delays on associative interference. The magnitude of associative interference on a target memory trace depends on both the age of the target and the age of the interfering memories. The nature of the dependency is just what one would predict if all memories (interfering memories as well as target memories) lose strength by passive decay (Baddeley, 1976, p. 95) and the potency of interference is proportional to the relative strength of interfering and target memories. More conclusive evidence about how information is lost from LTM—if it is lost—awaits discovery of more powerful methodologies. (For a discussion of interference and inhibition mechanisms in LTM, see Anderson & Neely, this volume, Chapter 8.)

II. PROCESSES

A. Attention and Memory: Basic Issues

The preceding sections described the main structures in episodic memory (as they show up in "standard" memory tasks like recall and recognition). We turn now to the processes that transfer (or, more properly, copy) contents from one memory system to another. Beginning with Waugh and Norman (1965) and Atkinson and Shiffrin (1968), it has been traditional to distinguish a number of processes for copying and maintaining information, chiefly including *rehearsal, encoding, elaboration,* and *retrieval.* Rehearsal refers to the overt or covert process that refreshes information in STM. Encoding refers to any mental operations performed on information arriving in the sensory systems that form memory traces of that information. Elaboration refers to the establishing of linkages between new information and previously stored information, a process that seems to be especially effective at promoting long-term storage of new information. Retrieval refers to the process of bringing information out of memory for current use.

These four concepts are useful in describing activities involved in the use of memory stores. More debatable is the utility of another concept that is widely used in this connection: the concept of attention. This term is used so frequently in ordinary discussion and in psychological theorizing that one is tempted to accept James's statement that "everyone knows what attention is" (James, 1890). When the goal is to understand mental phenomena at a mechanistic level, however, it may be better to assume that no one knows what attention is, and even to assume that there is probably no "it" there to be understood. The fact that our commonsense understanding of attention sprawls over so much of the mental landscape is particularly worrisome. On one hand, we talk about attention to refer to our selective control over the intake of information from the senses, as in the cocktail-party effect. On the other hand, we use the term attention to refer to just about any limitation on mental activity, including limits on how much information we can take in at any time, how many tasks we can carry out, and how long we can keep performing well in a single task. All of these things are routinely described and "explained" in terms of movement, shifts, depletions, or reductions in attention. There is no doubt that voluntary control over sensory input and capacity limitations are real phenomena. It seems very doubtful, though, that we have any privileged access to mental operations, especially as they occur on a rapid time scale. It is therefore a rather dubious undertaking to borrow the construct of "attention" from ordinary psychological discourse when the goal is to analyze our mental machinery.

The next section, therefore, discusses what has been learned about voluntary control and capacity limitations in the transfer of information between different memory systems without using the concept of attention (except occasionally as a verb to describe the subject's explicit and instructed goal, as in "pay attention to the left channel"). Rather than asking "does it take attention to get information into LTM?," for example, we will ask "to what degree can a person control transfer of information into LTM?" and "what concurrent activities interfere with transferring information into LTM and which do not?" Given the answers to these questions (insofar as they are available), one can then sensibly ask what kinds of processes and mechanisms must be postulated in accounting for these phenomena.

B. Control and Capacity Issues in the Transfer of Information

1. Stimulus Recognition

Does actively trying to ignore a stimulus reduce the extent or quality of the perceptual processing the stimulus undergoes? This question has been a preoccupation of selective attention researchers for several decades. While disagreements remain, many results, both behavioral and neurophysiological, now make quite a strong case that it does (e.g., Kahneman & Treisman, 1984; Yantis & Johnston, 1990). Does this mean that people can recognize only one object at a time, as some early attention theorists supposed? Probably not; people seem capable of parallel processing but are readily overloaded (e.g., people can probably recognize a handful of letters simultaneously, but reading several words seems inevitably to require serial processing; Duncan, 1987; Shiffrin & Gardner, 1972). These capacity limits are probably more severe within a given sensory modality than between different modalities (Treisman & Davies, 1973).

2. Getting Information into Sensory Memory

Stimuli are probably input into sensory memory even when a person tries to ignore them at the time they are presented. Furthermore, there is no sign that the input of information into sensory memory depletes capacity for other mental functions. One illustration comes from audition: if subjects shadow message A while ignoring message B, they can, if interrupted, access the last one or two seconds of message B (Norman, 1969). Shadowing message A interferes grossly with *detecting* events on message B (when the person is not permitted to abandon the shadowing), however (Rollins & Hendricks, 1980). Comparable experiments have not been performed with visual sensory memory, although in principle they could be.

3. Getting Information into Short-Term Memory

People ordinarily have voluntary control over what information gets stored in STM. This is seen, for example, in partial-report experiments using both auditory (Darwin et al., 1972) and visual modalities (Sperling, 1960), where people transfer information into STM on the basis of a cued attribute. Of course, saying that people have some voluntary control over what gets into STM does not deny that unwanted information may sometimes be inadvertently transferred, as well. The phenomenon of "conceptual masking" in picture memory may illustrate such involuntary transfer. When a target picture is followed after several hundred milliseconds by another novel picture, which the person tries to ignore, this impairs memory of the target, perhaps because it inadvertently replaces it in VSTM (Loftus & Ginn, 1984).

How do people exercise control over what information gets into STM? When a person selects a stimulus in order to make an immediate response to it, does this selection govern what gets stored in the (modality-appropriate) STM at that moment? Consider a task in which subjects see a display of letters (some of them colored and some of them gray) and make a rapid response to the color of the letters (Pashler, 1994a). Subjects can select and execute a response to the color of the letters and simultaneously store the forms of these letters in (presumably visual) STM with little interference. On the other hand, if subjects respond to the colored letters and try to store the forms of the noncolored letters, performance suffers greatly.

It seems, therefore, that one cannot simultaneously process some visual stimuli for one purpose and store other visual stimuli in STM at the same time. Such results suggest that "attending to" stimuli in a given modality is necessary to input those stimuli into STM. They do not, however, say whether it is *sufficient*. If it is, irrelevant stimuli, if attended, should regularly wipe out the contents of STM. Evidence is mixed about whether this happens or not. Reitman (1974) found that performing a discrimination task on syllables grossly disrupted short-term storage of verbal material. Phillips and Christie (1977b), on the other hand, found evidence that people could perceive and respond to a visual pattern without "flushing" the contents of visual STM. This issue, which has practical as well as theoretical importance, still needs to be sorted out empirically.

What kind of capacity limits govern the transfer of information into STM? Unrelated "central" mental operations, such as deciding on an action or retrieving some information from LTM, do *not* seem to prevent transfer of a stimulus into STM (although they might prevent a person from deciding to carry out such transfer). Consider experiments in which a list of words is presented (for later free recall) while someone performs a concurrent task requiring response selection and production. For example, Murdock (1965) played a spoken list while subjects sorted cards rapidly; subjects then free recalled the list. The recency effect, reflective of STM, was unaffected. The same was true when C. M. B. Anderson and Craik (1974) presented a list auditorily while subjects performed a concurrent task involving a visual/manual choice reaction-time task.

The notion that central processing does not interfere with storage in STM is also supported by experiments involving pairs of brief punctate tasks. Consider an experiment in which subjects make a rapid choice response to a tone—a task that sounds very easy, but that delays central processing in just about any speeded task regardless of input or output modality (Pashler, 1993b). When a single Phillips-type pattern (black and white squares) was briefly flashed at around the same time as the tone (and followed by a mask), subjects could store the visual pattern in VSTM without interference from the tone task (as shown by an immediately following recognition test; Pashler, 1993a).

What do these results tell us about control and capacity limitations with regard to inputting information into STM? On one hand, voluntary selection of stimuli seems to be necessary, but possibly not sufficient, for getting information into STM. On the other hand, *central* interference, although ubiquitous in human performance, does not prevent this transfer (at least when the person has prepared in advance to store a stimulus as soon as it arrives). The idea that STM storage does not suffer from central interference generates many as yet untested predictions: to pick an obvious example, can a person sort cards rapidly while listening to a phone number, and then immediately report the phone number?[6]

4. Maintaining Information in STM

Casual introspection suggests that when we try to hold onto a list of numbers, we generally repeat the numbers over to ourselves silently (rehearsal). Unless the number of items approaches the memory span, however, we do not need to rehearse the list continuously. Many researchers have investigated whether holding a subspan memory load affects performance on concurrent tasks. Some interference is typically found, but it is not great in magnitude. For example, a concurrent choice reaction-time task is slowed by only a few tens of milliseconds (Logan, 1978), and people can still carry out demanding thinking tasks (Baddeley & Hitch, 1974). Therefore, simply holding information in short-term memory does not impose much of a drain on "central mental resources" (e.g., as suggested in Shiffrin, 1976). On the other hand, *initiating* rehearsal of material shortly after it is first presented may interfere quite drastically with other central mental operations (Naveh-Benjamin & Jonides, 1984). It is hard to know if central interference recurs every time a new cycle of rehearsal is carried out. Whether or not there is recurrent interference, subjects can almost certainly schedule rehearsal so as to avoid any delays in central processing on other tasks. In view of the points raised in this paragraph, it is not surprising that memory load effects rarely produce much disruption.

Intermittently rehearsing a memory load may, however, prevent a person from preparing optimally for a concurrent task (during the interval prior to the arrival of the stimulus), even if it does not affect the actual execution of the task (Pashler, 1994b). This possibility may account for the typically mild interference that is observed between memory loads and concurrent speeded tasks (Logan, 1978). If this analysis is correct, using

---

[6] Our crude and informal observations suggest this is possible, but formal studies are needed.

concurrent memory loads as a tool to look at the effects of "depleting general mental resources" is misguided.

5. Getting Information into LTM

How is the flow of information into LTM controlled, and is the flow subject to capacity limits? The effects of voluntary control are at least as pronounced here as they are with STM. If a person deliberately ignores certain stimuli (e.g., the voice on the left channel, or the words written in green), little or none of the ignored information seems to find its way into LTM (Moray, 1959; Rock & Guttman, 1981).

How does information ordinarily find its way into LTM? As Atkinson and Shiffrin (1968) noted, voluntary elaboration seems to be one of the most effective strategies. The desire or intention to store information seems to make little difference, except insofar as it motivates the person to process the information in certain ways (Craik & Lockhart, 1972). Elaboration may often involve retrieval of associated information. Retrieval of information itself is also especially helpful in strengthening already-established long-term memory traces (e.g., Carrier & Pashler, 1992). Simply rehearsing information in STM results in a certain amount of LTM storage, but more rehearsal does not do much to increase LTM storage (at least as assessed by recall; recognition memory shows bigger effects; Greene, 1987). Information may not need to dwell in STM in order to end up in LTM, given that patients with grossly defective verbal STM can perform normally in delayed recall (Shallice & Warrington, 1970). In short, being in STM may be neither necessary nor sufficient for efficient copying into LTM. (See Nairne, this volume, Chapter 4, for additional discussion of rehearsal processes in STM and the relationship between STM and LTM.)

What concurrent activities prevent information from getting into LTM? Unlike with STM, concurrent tasks that make central processing demands produce large effects here. This is true even when the concurrent task and the memory set involve different sensory modalities, and when no overt responding is required in the memory tasks. For example, consider the studies described earlier that presented lists of words while the subject carried out concurrent speeded classification tasks. Free recall for items in the first two-thirds of the list was substantially reduced, while recency was unaffected (C. M. B. Anderson & Craik, 1974; Murdock, 1965).

This result is reinforced by studies in which subjects carried out concurrent choice tasks while items to be remembered were presented (Carrier & Pashler, in preparation). The concurrent tasks required speeded choice responses to tones, with a relatively short interval between the response to one tone and the presentation of the next tone. The material to be remembered was presented visually and testing occurred after delays (making LTM the relevant store). Delayed memory invariably suffered, whether the material to be remembered consisted of lists of words or sequences of faces, and whether the task was recognition or recall. (Furthermore, the results were essentially the same when memory was assessed with "implicit" tests such as word fragment completion [Carrier, McFarland, & Pashler, 1996], casting doubt on the common claim that implicit memory storage does not depend on attention; see Kelley & Lindsay, this volume, Chapter 2, for a review of differences between explicit and implicit memories.)

In short, the results of these studies imply that central interference reduces the flow of information into LTM. In contrast, there are many other studies reported in the literature where secondary tasks did *not* diminish LTM memory performance as assessed with delayed tests. Such results, however, seem to have occurred when the secondary tasks placed only very intermittent demands on central processing machinery. Tun, Wingfield, and Stine (1991), for example, found that a concurrent choice reaction-time task had little effect on recall of spoken prose passages, even though the prose passages were much too long to have been stored in STM. However, the secondary task used by these investigators involved responding to letters presented only once every three to seven seconds. If the demanding central-processing stages of the reaction-time task take, say, about 300 ms, then such a sparse secondary task would probably reduce the time during which central mechanisms are available for the memory task by no more than 5 or 10%

6. Retrieval from Long-Term Memory

Do concurrent tasks involving central processing interfere with retrieval from LTM? Studies present a mixed picture. For example, Park, Smith, Dudley, and Lafronza (1989) found that an auditory/manual concurrent task impaired free recall. On the other hand, Baddeley, Lewis, Eldridge, and Thomson (1984) found that the difficulty of a sorting task had little effect on concurrent memory retrieval, and concluded that there was no central interference with retrieval per se. Rather, they suggested interference may be confined to the production of responses in the two tasks.

We have recently carried out more fine-grained analyses of central interference in retrieval (Carrier & Pashler, 1996). The experiments used the psychological refractory period paradigm in which two speeded tasks are performed close together in time. Task 1 involved a manual response to a tone, and Task 2 involved cued recall to a visually presented cue word. The results—patterns of additivity in the effects of different factors on reaction times—provided strong evidence for central interference in retrieval, while arguing against response production as the locus of interference. Furthermore, they imply that central processing is a true bottleneck in this situation; that is, memory retrieval in Task 2 had to wait while a response was selected in Task 1.

III. FLOW OF CONTROL: A TENTATIVE ACCOUNT

The goal of this section is to try to make sense of the findings described in the preceding section and to point out implications of these results for some influential theoretical ideas about memory and the processes that govern it.

A. Attention as an Organizing Concept

As noted earlier, the term attention is commonly used to refer to processes involved in stimulus selection, to the source of capacity limitations of just about every kind, and to variation in cognitive resources over time. Can such a broad concept be helpful in explaining the facts described in the preceding section? To try it out, one can start by asking whether attention is necessary for getting information into STM. In one sense, the answer has to be "yes." What is transferred into STM is a function of selective attention, if anything is. On the other hand, as described earlier, what are widely regarded as "attention-demanding secondary tasks" do not seem to prevent a person from getting new stimuli into (modality-appropriate) STM as long as these tasks do not require the person to handle stimuli in the same sensory modality. What about copying information into LTM; is attention required for this? Apparently so, because, as described earlier, concurrent tasks often reduce storage a great deal. Here, central interference is also apparent: unrelated choice tasks prevent or at least reduce LTM storage. Clearly, then, one cannot make sense of all these phenomena without abandoning any insistence on using the term "attention" to refer to a putative unitary process.[7]

B. An Alternative Account

In constructing an alternative account for the facts reviewed in the preceding section, we must first postulate a *central* form of interference that arises when more than one central process is called upon at the same time. This type of interference seems to arise whenever both of the processes belong to a rather broad set of mental operations, including the following: (1) selection of responses; (2) retrieval from LTM; and (3) storage in LTM. This central interference seems to represent a true bottleneck: while one process of this kind operates, any other process of this type is apparently forced to wait (Pashler, 1994c, 1994d), as first proposed by Welford (1967). On the

---

[7] The idea that the concept of attention needs to be subdivided is by no means novel; see Treisman (1969).

other hand, although LTM storage is also plainly subject to central interference, there is no specific evidence that a true bottleneck is involved here:
the data cannot rule out the possibility that information dribbles into LTM
while other tasks are under way.

The simplest way to account for such a pattern of central interference is
to posit something like a central processor.[8] This central processor must not
be identified with all, or even most, senses of "attention," however. There
are several reasons *not* to identify this central processor with selective attention governing stimulus input. The most specific evidence against doing so
is that while response selection in one task evidently delays response selection in unrelated tasks, shifts of spatial selective attention triggered by a
visual cue are not so delayed (Pashler, 1991). Furthermore, the central processor cannot be associated with the capacity limitations observed when a
person tries to carry out difficult perceptual discriminations at the same
time; for example, trying to read two words simultaneously (for evidence
on this point, see Pashler, 1989).

Figure 1 provides a pictorial representation of our proposed alternative
account of information processing mechanisms for storage and retrieval of
information in episodic memory. Sensory memories are not represented as
stages of processing standing between the sense organs and later memory
systems. Rather, they are structures that sit *beside* the sensory pathways:
backup devices to keep stimuli available when needed, not way stations en
route to more permanent memory systems. Selective attention is conceived
of as a gate (although undoubtedly a porous and imperfect one) that controls
which stimuli are subjected to extensive perceptual analysis. The gate sits
after the sensory memories, but before the pattern recognition machinery.
Capacity limitations in pattern recognition reflect competition among only
those stimuli that pass this gate. This arrangement, which is reminiscent of
the earliest attention models, fits a wide range of recent behavioral, electrophysiological, and neurophysiological evidence (see, e.g., Kahneman &
Treisman, 1984; Yantis & Johnston, 1990).

If stimuli are permitted "access" to pattern-recognition machinery, they
may activate various representations in semantic long-term memory. They
may also activate representations in the appropriate STM without any involvement of the central processor (as noted above, it is not clear whether
passing through the selective attention gate is sufficient for this to happen
but it is surely necessary). However, as indicated by the various findings
previously described, the central processor *is* required (1) to get information
into LTM, (2) to recode information from one STM system to another,

---

[8] This assumption does not imply that any single brain structure carries out the functions of
the central processor; if different brain areas inhibited each other, this might be functionally
equivalent; see Pashler, Luck, O'Brien, Mangun, and Gazzaniga, M. (1994).

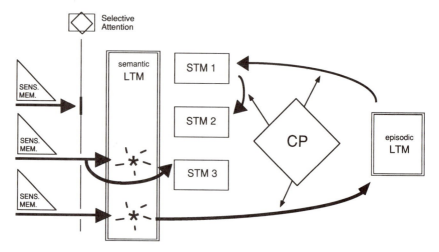

FIGURE 1   A possible overall structure for the flow of control between different memory systems. Information does not flow into sensory memory systems *en route* to short-term memory; rather, sensory memory effectively maintains input from the stimulus should the stimulus disappear. Selective attention gates the processing of stimuli. Once attended, stimuli simultaneously activate representations in semantic LTM (stimulus identification) and activate short-term memory representations in an STM system that depends on the input modality. The "central processor" (CP) is required for forming traces in episodic LTM, for retrieving from LTM (transfer into STM), and for transfer between different STMs ("recoding"), as well as other mental operations such as selecting actions. The CP could reflect a process of mutual inhibition, rather than an executive structure.

(3) to initiate rehearsal of information in STM, (4) to retrieve information from LTM (conceived of as recreating representations in STM), and (5) to select actions (Pashler, 1994d).

This proposal makes many predictions beyond those that have already been investigated and described above, so it could be tested much further. It also raises puzzling questions. Why, for example, should there be a single mental mechanism involved in such seemingly diverse mental operations as choosing actions and storing information in memory? At present, one cannot do much more than speculate. It may be that storing new information in LTM always involves retrieving related information from episodic memory. Similarly, selection of actions in simple tasks may constitute a simple form of memory retrieval. In that case, the mental operations that generate central interference may not be as diverse as they appear. Alternatively, the attempt to find a psychological feature these mental operations have in common may be futile; central interference may reflect facts about brain architecture devoid of psychological explanation.

C. A Selective Comparison with Previous Theories

It is instructive to consider how the proposal described above relates to various other proposed accounts of the flow of control between memory systems. One way the present proposed account differs from that of Atkinson and Shiffrin (1968) is in rejecting a serial arrangement of memory buffers (sensory memory → STM → LTM). In the present view, information can flow into STM without first residing in sensory memory, and it can flow into LTM without first residing in STM. One *could* probably contrive a situation in which the flow would be serial,[9] but it need not take that form.

Bjork (1975) presented a view of the flow of information in memory that addressed many of the issues considered here. His model was explicit and consistent with the great majority of results existing at the time, so it may be instructive to compare it with the present view. Bjork assumed the existence of a single STM that could code information in various different formats (e.g., speechlike, verbal). The present view postulates separate STMs, based chiefly on the fact that visual and articulatory/verbal STMs can be simultaneously filled up to their respective capacity limits. (Neuropsychological double-dissociations could probably be reconciled with either Bjork's position or the present view.) Bjork's account and the one described here both postulate a central processor or some functionally equivalent neural/cognitive architecture, with this processor playing a key role in initiating rehearsal and in transferring information into and out of LTM. Bjork's view differs from the present scheme in three important ways, however. First, Bjork suggested that STM was the output of the central processor. Second, Bjork equated the central processor with selective attention. Reasons for believing that selective attention and the central processor cannot be the same were described in preceding sections. Third, Bjork assumed that selective attention did not affect perceptual processing at all (making his a "late-selection" theory). As noted above, the past twenty years have seen a proliferation of evidence that selective attention *can* attenuate perceptual processing for ignored stimuli.

Another closely related account was suggested by Potter (1983; 1993), who focused on structures rather than processes. She postulated a fairly large number of memory systems to account for results of experiments in which observers see rapidly presented sequences of pictures. According to

[9] Here is one concrete (and highly contrived) example: present a high-intensity picture on a CRT display for 5 ms once every 2 s, and, at the same instant as the picture appears, sound a tone. The subject's task is to make a rapid choice response to each tone and to remember all the pictures. If the scheme presented in this chapter is correct, the picture must reside in iconic memory in order to be recognized (because the exposure is so brief). Next, it must reside in visual STM (because the tone task will prevent transfer to LTM during the brief lifetime of iconic memory). Only then could the transfer to LTM take place.

Potter, a rich conceptual representation of the contents of a picture is produced even when the picture is available for as little as 150 ms or so (at which time the next picture is flashed). This conceptual representation is created and destroyed without leaving any durable memory traces whatever, according to Potter. She termed it "conceptual very-short-term memory" and argued that it is distinct from either visual STM or verbal STM. The present scheme does not contradict this analysis in any substantive way; what Potter terms very-short-term memory is instead conceived of as transient activation in semantic LTM.[10]

Finally, the present proposal has much in common with the views of Baddeley (1986), and derives support from many of his empirical findings. One obvious point of agreement is the existence of independent visual and articulatory/verbal STM systems, for which Baddeley has amassed a great deal of evidence. Baddeley also postulates what he calls a "central executive" responsible for the control of attention. At first glance the idea of a central executive and the idea of a central bottleneck seem congenial (after all, if there is only one mechanism to do certain tasks, a processing bottleneck can readily result). However, a bottleneck need not imply a central executive; mutual inhibition or lockout among different processing mechanisms could also produce bottlenecks. In light of that fact and other evidence suggesting limited flexibility in control of cognition, the idea of a "central processor" is not meant to carry the connotations of intelligent planning or executive function. On the topic of memory retrieval, the account suggested here clearly disagrees with Baddeley. He argues that the central executive is not involved in retrieval from LTM, and furthermore, that the retrieval of information associated with a cue operates "automatically." The data described earlier suggest that retrieval is not automatic, for at least two reasons. First, without selective (perceptual) attention a retrieval cue would not be processed enough to allow retrieval to take place, and second, the retrieval itself is evidently subject to the same central bottleneck that arises in selection of motor actions (Carrier and Pashler, 1996).

IV. CONCLUSIONS

The point of the present chapter has been to suggest some fairly strong conclusions about the basic structures and processes involved in human information processing in simple sensorimotor and memory tasks. Obviously, all of the conclusions reached here need to be tested further, and some

---

[10] One reason for shying away from the notion of a conceptual memory is that the contents may not be as rich as that phrase would suggest. Everything in the scene may be analyzed sufficiently to allow a person to find a semantically defined target, but there may still be no maplike representation of the sort that would provide access to the identity of an object given a location probe (Pashler, 1984).

may be overturned by new evidence. Much work also remains to be done examining how these structures and processes function in more naturalistic tasks outside of the laboratory.

Acknowledgments

Address correspondence to H. Pashler at the Dept. of Psychology 0109, UC San Diego, La Jolla, CA, 92093, or hpashler @ ucsd.edu. The authors are grateful to the editors and to Gus Craik, Clark Fagot, James C. Johnston, Doug Rohrer, and John Wixted for very useful comments. Supported by NIMH (1-R29-MH45584-01).

References

Anderson, C. M. B., & Craik, F. I. M. (1974). The effect of a concurrent task on recall from primary memory. *Journal of Verbal Learning and Verbal Behavior, 13,* 107–113.

Anderson, J. A. (1973). A theory for the recognition of items from short memorized lists. *Psychological Review, 80,* 417–438.

Atkinson, R., & Shiffrin, R. M. (1968). Human memory: A proposed system and its control processes. In K. W. Spence (Ed.), *Psychology of learning and motivation: Advances in research and theory* (Vol. 2, pp. 89–195). New York: Academic Press.

Averbach, E., & Coriell, A. S. (1961). Short-term memory in vision. *Bell System Technical Journal, 40,* 309–328.

Baddeley, A. D. (1976). *The psychology of memory.* New York: Basic Books.

Baddeley, A. D. (1986). *Working memory.* Oxford: Oxford University Press.

Baddeley, A. D., & Hitch, G. (1974). Working memory. In G. Bower (Ed.), *Psychology of learning and motivation: Advances in research and theory* (Vol. 8, pp. 47–89). New York: Academic Press.

Baddeley, A. D., & Hitch, G. (1977). Recency reexamined. In S. Dornic (Ed.), *Attention & performance VI* (pp. 647–667). Hillsdale, NJ: Erlbaum.

Baddeley, A. D., Lewis, V., Eldridge, M., & Thomson, N. (1984). Attention and retrieval from long-term memory. *Journal of Experimental Psychology: General, 113,* 518–540.

Baddeley, A. D., & Warrington, E. K. (1970). Amnesia and the distinction between long-term and short-term memory. *Journal of Verbal Learning and Verbal Behavior, 9,* 176–189.

Barnard, P. (1985). Interacting cognitive subsystems: A psycholinguistic approach to short-term memory. In A. Ellis (Ed.), *Progress in the psychology of language* (Vol. 2, pp. 197–258). London: Erlbaum.

Besner, D. (1987). Phonology, lexical access in reading, and articulatory suppression: A critical review. *Quarterly Journal of Experimental Psychology, 39A,* 467–478.

Bjork, R. A. (1975). Short-term storage: The ordered output of a central processor. In F. Restle, R. M. Shiffrin, N. J. Castellan, H. R. Lindeman, & D. B. Pisoni (Eds.), *Cognitive theory* (Vol. 1, pp. 151–171). Hillsdale, NJ: Erlbaum.

Bjork, R. A., & Whitten, W. B. (1974). II. Recency-sensitive retrieval processes in long-term free recall. *Cognitive Psychology, 6,* 173–189.

Bowers, R. L., Mollenhauer, M. S., & Luxford, J. (1990). Short-term memory for tactile and temporal stimuli in a shared-attention recall task. *Perceptual and Motor Skills, 70,* 903–913.

Broadbent, D. E. (1989). Lasting representations and temporary processes. In H. Roediger & F. I. Craik (Eds.), *Varieties of memory and consciousness* (pp. 211–228). Hillsdale, NJ: Erlbaum.

Caramazza, A. (1992). Is cognitive neuropsychology possible? *Journal of Cognitive Neuroscience, 4,* 80–95.

Carrier, M., McFarland, K., Pashler, H. (1996). *Is implicit memory automatically encoded?* Manuscript submitted for publication.

Carrier, M., & Pashler, H. (1992). The influence of retrieval on retention. *Memory & Cognition, 20,* 633–642.

Carrier, L. M., & Pashler, H. (1996). Attentional limits in memory retrieval. *Journal of Experimental Psychology: Learning, Memory, and Cognition, 21,* 1339–1348.

Carrier, M., & Pashler, H. (in preparation). *Capacity limits in long-term memory storage.* Unpublished manuscript.

Cowan, N. (1988). Evolving conceptions of memory storage, selective attention, and their mutual constraints within the human information-processing system. *Psychological Bulletin, 104,* 163–191.

Craik, F. I. M., & Lockhart, R. S. (1972). Levels of processing: A framework for memory research. *Journal of Verbal Learning and Verbal Behavior, 11,* 671–684.

Crowder, R. G. (1976). *Principles of learning and memory.* Hillsdale, NJ: Erlbaum.

Crowder, R. G. (1993). Short-term memory: Where do we stand? *Memory & Cognition, 21,* 142–145.

Darwin, C. J., Turvey, M. T., & Crowder, R. G. (1972). An auditory analogue of the Sperling partial report procedure: Evidence for brief auditory storage. *Cognitive Psychology, 3,* 255–267.

di Lollo, V., & Dixon, P. (1988). Two forms of persistence in visual information processing. *Journal of Experimental Psychology: Human Perception and Performance, 14,* 671–681.

Duncan, J. (1987). Attention and reading Wholes and parts in shape recognition—A tutorial review. In M. Coltheart (Ed.), *Attention and performance XII: The psychology of reading* (pp. 39–61). Hillsdale, NJ: Erlbaum.

Fagot, C., & Pashler, H. (1992). Making two responses to a single object: Exploring the central bottleneck. *Journal of Experimental Psychology: Human Perception and Performance.*

Farah, M. J., Hammond, K. M., Levine, D. N., & Calvanio, R. (1988). Visual and spatial mental imagery: Dissociable systems of representation. *Cognitive Psychology, 20,* 439–462.

Frick, R. W. (1984). Using both an auditory and a visual short-term store to increase digit span. *Memory & Cognition, 12,* 507–514.

Glanzer, M., & Cunitz, A. R. (1966). Two storage mechanisms in free recall. *Journal of Verbal Learning and Verbal Behavior, 5,* 351–360.

Greene, R. L. (1987). Effects of maintenance rehearsal on human memory. *Psychological Bulletin, 102,* 403–413.

Haber, R. N., & Standing, L. G. (1969). Direct measures of short-term visual storage. *Quarterly Journal of Experimental Psychology, 21,* 43–54.

Hawkins, H. L., & Shulman, G. L. (1979). Two definitions of persistence in visual persistence. *Perception & Psychophysics, 25,* 348–350.

Henderson, L. (1972). Spatial and verbal codes and the capacity of STM. *Quarterly Journal of Experimental Psychology, 24,* 485–495.

Hoffman, J. E., Nelson, B., & Houck, M. R. (1983). The role of attentional resources in automatic detection. *Cognitive Psychology, 51,* 379–410.

Howard, D., & Franklin, S. (1993). Dissociations between component mechanisms in short-term memory: Evidence from brain-damaged patients. In D. E. Meyer & S. Kornblum (Eds.), *Attention and performance, Vol. 14: Synergies in experimental psychology, artificial intelligence, and cognitive neuroscience* (pp. 425–449). Cambridge, MA: MIT Press.

Irwin, D. E. (1992). Memory for position and identity across eye movements. *Journal of Experimental Psychology: Learning, memory, and Cognition, 18,* 307–317.

James, W. (1890). *Principles of psychology* (Vol. 1). New York: Holt.

Kahneman, D., & Treisman, A. (1984). Changing views of attention and automaticity. In R. Parasuraman & D. R. Davies (Eds.), *Varieties of attention* (pp. 29–62). New York: Academic Press.

Landauer, T. K. (1986). How much do people remember? Some estimates of the quantity of learned information in long-term memory. *Cognitive Science, 10,* 477–493.

Lashley, K. (1929). *Brain mechanisms and intelligence.* Chicago: University of Chicago Press.

Loftus, G. R., & Ginn, M. (1984). Perceptual and conceptual masking of pictures. *Journal of Experimental Psychology: Learning, Memory, and Cognition, 10,* 435–441.

Logan, G. D. (1978). Attention in character classification tasks: Evidence for the automaticity of component stages. *Journal of Experimental Psychology: General, 107,* 32–63.

Margrain, S. A. (1967). Short-term memory as a function of input modality. *Quarterly Journal of Experimental Psychology, 19,* 109–114.

Mewaldt, S. P., Hinrichs, J. V., & Ghoneim, M. M. (1983). Diazepam and memory: Support for a duplex model of memory. *Memory & Cognition, 11,* 557–564.

Milner, B. (1958). The memory defect in bilateral hippocampal lesions. *Psychiatry Research Reports, 11,* 43–58.

Moray, N. (1959). Attention in dichotic listening: Affective cues and the influence of instructions. *Quarterly Journal of Experimental Psychology, 11,* 56–60.

Murdock, B. B. (1965). Effects of a subsidiary task on short-term memory. *British Journal of Psychology, 56,* 413–419.

Murray, D. J., Ward, R., & Hockley, W. E. (1975). Tactile short-term memory in relation to the two-point threshold. *Quarterly Journal of Experimental Psychology, 27,* 303–312.

Naveh-Benjamin, M., & Jonides, J. (1984). Maintenance rehearsal: A two-component analysis. *Journal of Experimental Psychology: Learning, Memory, and Cognition, 10,* 369–385.

Norman, D. A. (1969). Memory while shadowing. *Quarterly Journal of Experimental Psychology, 21,* 85–93.

Park, D. C., Smith, A. D., Dudley, W. N., & Lafronza, V. N. (1989). Effects of age and a divided attention task presented during encoding and retrieval on memory. *Journal of Experimental Psychology: Learning, Memory and Cognition, 15,* 1185–1191.

Pashler, H. (1984). Evidence against late selection: Stimulus quality effects in previewed displays. *Journal of Experimental Psychology: Human Perception and Performance, 10,* 429–448.

Pashler, H. (1989). Dissociations and dependencies between speed and accuracy: Evidence for a two-component theory of divided attention in simple tasks. *Cognitive Psychology, 21,* 469–514.

Pashler, H. (1991). Shifting visual attention and selecting motor responses: Distinct attentional mechanisms. *Journal of Experimental Psychology: Human Perception and Performance, 17,* 1023–1040.

Pashler, H. (1993a). Dual task interference and elementary mental mechanisms. In D. Meyer & S. Kornblum (Eds.), *Attention and performance XIV* (pp. 245–264). Cambridge, MA: MIT Press.

Pashler, H. (1993b). Doing two things at the same time. *American Scientist, 81,* 48–55.

Pashler, H. (1994a). Divided attention: Storing and classifying briefly presented objects. *Psychonomic Bulletin & Review, 1,* 115–118.

Pashler, H. (1994b). Overlapping mental operations in serial performance with preview. *Quarterly Journal of Experimental Psychology, 47,* 161–191.

Pashler, H. (1994c). Graded capacity-sharing in dual-task interference? *Journal of Experimental Psychology: Human Perception and Performance, 20,* 330–342.

Pashler, H. (1994d). Dual-task interference in simple tasks: Data and theory. *Psychological Bulletin, 16,* 220–244.

Pashler, H., Luck, S., O'Brien, S., Mangun, R., & Gazzaniga, M. (1994). Sequential operation of disconnected cerebral hemispheres in "split-brain" patients. *NeuroReport, 5,* 2381–2384.

Phillips, W. A. (1974). On the distinction between sensory storage and short-term visual memory. *Perception & Psychophysics, 16,* 283–290.

Phillips, W. A. (1983). Short-term visual memory. *Philosophical Transactions of the Royal Society, London, Series B, 302,* 295–309.

Phillips, W. A., & Christie. D. F. M. (1977a). Components of visual memory. Quarterly Journal of Experimental Psychology, 29, 117–133.

Phillips, W. A., & Christie. D. F. M. (1977b). Interference with visualization. *Quarterly Journal of Experimental Psychology, 29,* 637–650.

Posner, M. I. (1978). *Chronometric explorations of mind.* Hillsdale, NJ: Erlbaum.

Potter, M. C. (1983). Representational buffers: The eye–mind hypothesis in picture perception, reading and visual search. In K. Rayner (Ed.), *Eye movements in reading: Perceptual And language processing* (pp. 413–437). New York: Academic Press.

Potter, M. C. (1993). Very short-term conceptual memory. *Memory & Cognition, 21,* 156–161.

Reisberg, D., Rappaport, I., & O'Shaughnessy, M. (1984). Limits of working memory: The digit digit-span. *Journal of Experimental Psychology: Learning, Memory, and Cognition, 10,* 203–221.

Reitman, J. S. (1974). Without surreptitious rehearsal, information in short-term memory decays. *Journal of Verbal Learning and Verbal Behavior, 13,* 365–377.

Rock, I., & Guttman, D. (1981). The effect of inattention on form perception. *Journal of Experimental Psychology: Human Perception and Performance, 7,* 275–285.

Rollins, H. A., & Hendricks, R. (1980). Processing of words presented simultaneously to eye and ear. *Journal of Experimental Psychology: Human Perception and Performance, 6,* 99–109.

Saffran, E. M., & Martin, N. (1990). Neuropsychological evidence for lexical involvement in short-term memory. In G. Vallar & T. Shallice (Eds.), *Neuropsychological impairments of short-term memory* (pp. 145–166). Cambridge: Cambridge University Press.

Sakitt, B. (1976). Iconic memory. *Psychological Review, 83,* 257–275.

Scarborough, D. L. (1972). Memory for brief visual displays of symbols. *Cognitive Psychology, 3,* 408–429.

Schweickert, R., Guentert, L., & Hersberger, L. (1990). Phonological similarity, pronunciation rate, and memory span. *Psychological Science, 1,* 74–77.

Shallice, T., & Warrington, E. K. (1970). Independent functioning of verbal memory stores: A neuropsychological study. *Quarterly Journal of Experimental Psychology, 22,* 261–273.

Shiffrin, R. M. (1976). Capacity limitations in information processing, attention and memory. In W. K. Estes (Ed.), *Handbook of learning and cognitive processes: Attention and memory* (Vol. 4, pp. 177–236). Hillsdale, NJ: Erlbaum.

Shiffrin, R. M., & Cook, J. R. (1978). Short-term forgetting of item and order information. *Journal of Verbal Learning and Verbal Behavior, 17,* 189–218.

Shiffrin, R. M., & Gardner, G. T. (1972). Visual processing capacity and attentional control. *Journal of Experimental Psychology, 93,* 78–82.

Sperling, G. (1960). The information available in brief visual presentations. *Psychological Monographs: General and Applied,* Whole No. 498, 1–29.

Treisman, A. (1969). Strategies and models of selective attention. *Psychological Review, 76,* 282–299.

Treisman, A., & Davies, A. (1973). Dividing attention to ear and eye. In S. Kornblum (Ed.), *Attention and performance IV,* (pp. 101–117). New York: Academic Press.

Tun, P. A., Wingfield, A., & Stine, E. A. L. (1991). Speech-processing capacity in young and older adults: A dual-task study. *Psychology and Aging, 6,* 3–9.

Turvey, M. T. (1973). On peripheral and central processes in vision. *Psychological Review, 80,* 1–52.

Vallar, G., Papagno, C., & Baddeley, A. D. (1991). Long-term recency effects and phonological short-term memory. A neuropsychological case study. *Cortex, 27,* 323–326.

Warrington, E., & Shallice, T. (1969). The selective impairment of auditory verbal short-term memory. *Brain, 92,* 885–896.

Watkins, M. J. (1974). The concept and measurement of primary memory. *Psychological Bulletin, 81,* 695–711.

Waugh, N., & Norman, D. A. (1965). Primary memory. *Psychological Review, 72,* 89–104.

Welford, A. T. (1967). Single-channel operation in the brain. *Acta Psychologica, 27,* 5–22.

Yantis, S., & Johnston, J. C. (1990). On the locus of visual selection: Evidence from focused attention tasks. *Journal of Experimental Psychology: Human Perception and Performance, 16,* 135–149.

CHAPTER 2

Conscious and Unconscious Forms of Memory

Colleen M. Kelley
D. Stephen Lindsay

Most people think of memory as the ability to recollect specific past experiences. You can remember what you had for breakfast this morning, what you did to celebrate New Year's Eve last year, or how you felt on your first day of school. However, past experiences can have pervasive effects on an individual's current behavior without that individual necessarily having a conscious recollection of those experiences. Perception, problem solving, thinking, and judgment can all be altered by the effects of specific past experiences in the absence of conscious remembering.

Such unconscious or implicit memory is illustrated most vividly in the behavior of anterograde amnesics. People who are profoundly amnesic seem unable to form new memories. If, for example, you introduce yourself to an amnesic person, leave briefly, and return, he or she will usually have no recollection of meeting you. On the other hand, there have long been anecdotes suggesting that amnesics are nonetheless affected by the past. One of the most famous stories involves the French neuropsychologist, Claparede, who concealed a pin in his hand and pricked the hand of an amnesic woman while shaking hands with her. She quickly forgot the incident, but on a subsequent occasion when he moved his hand toward hers, she withdrew hers reflexively. "When I asked for the reason, she said in a hurry, 'Doesn't one have the right to withdraw the hand?' and when I insisted, she said 'Is there perhaps a pin hidden in your hand?' " (Claparede, 1911/1951, p. 69). Claparede pointed out that although the patient did not recognize that thought or others as a memory, her reactions to people and objects changed as a function of experience. She walked around the institution without getting lost even though she did not recognize it after six years. She asked appropriate domestic questions of a nurse even though she did not recognize her and repeatedly asked to be introduced.

Warrington and Weiskrantz (1970) contrasted amnesics' performance on explicit or direct tests of memory (so called because the tests instruct subjects to report on memories of particular past experiences) with their performance on implicit or indirect tests (tests that do not instruct subjects to report on memories of past experiences but can nonetheless reveal the effects of the subjects' past experiences by changes in their performance on a task). Warrington and Weiskrantz's indirect test asked subjects to identify a word from a fragmented version of the word, or to report the first five-letter word that came to mind given the first three letters (e.g., METAL given MET_?). On the direct tests of recognition and free recall, the amnesics showed dramatic deficits compared to the control subjects. But on the indirect tests, the amnesics' performance was as much improved by prior study of a list as was the performance of the control subjects; for both groups, having previously studied a particular word, such as METAL, increased the likelihood of that word being identified in fragmented form or offered as a completion for a three-letter stem.

Dissociations between performance on direct and indirect memory tests can also occur in subjects with normally functioning memory (Graf, Mandler, & Haden, 1982; Jacoby & Dallas, 1981; Tulving, Schacter, & Stark, 1982). For example, Jacoby and Dallas manipulated levels of processing at study and then tested subjects with either a direct test (recognition memory) or an indirect test (perceptual identification of briefly presented words). As is typically found, recognition memory performance was better when study instructions oriented subjects to attend to the meaning of the words (considered deep processing) than when instructions oriented subjects to attend to their superficial characteristics (considered shallow processing). In contrast, the effect of having seen the words on the study list on the subjects' ability to later identify those words when they were briefly presented on the computer screen was the same regardless of how subjects had originally processed the words.

The differences between performance on direct and indirect tests as revealed by neuropsychological, developmental, and functional dissociations have posed a major puzzle for memory researchers. Do the two types of tests tap different kinds of memory, perhaps with different underlying brain structures and different encoding or retrieval mechanisms? Or do the two tests tap different aspects or uses of the same memory of an event? More generally, what do dissociations between direct and indirect tests tell us about the nature and function of human memory? This chapter reviews the empirical results, theoretical interpretations, and methodological issues that have arisen in recent work comparing direct and indirect tests of memory. Although it is not clear which of the current theoretical conceptions comes closer to reality, the dynamic tension between them has produced valuable insights into the nature of human memory.

Before reviewing this research, we briefly comment on the terminology used in this chapter. In a major review of the literature in this area, Richardson-Klavehn and Bjork (1988) advocated use of Johnson and Hasher's (1987) terms "direct" and "indirect" tests to refer, respectively, to tests that do or do not instruct subjects to use memories of particular past experiences as a basis for responding, and use of the terms "explicit" and "implicit" memory, respectively, to refer to effects of an episode that are expressed with or without awareness of remembering. This distinction between the nature of the test instructions (direct vs. indirect) and the nature of the subjective experience accompanying the use of memory (explicit vs. implicit) is frequently blurred in the literature, and the terms "implicit" and "explicit" have been variously applied to types of tests, mental states, and hypothetical memory systems or processes. In this chapter, we use the terms "direct" and "indirect" to refer, respectively, to tests that do and do not explicitly instruct subjects to respond on the basis of memories of studied materials. We use the terms "conscious" and "unconscious," as well as "explicit" and "implicit" to refer, respectively, to influences of the past that are and are not accompanied by awareness of remembering.

I. ILLUSTRATIVE FINDINGS AND EXPLANATIONS

The distinction between effects of the past on performance and the subjective experience of remembering has a long history in psychology and philosophy (see Schacter, 1987, for discussion of Ebbinghaus's studies of savings in relearning as an implicit memory measure; see also Roediger, 1990; Slamecka, 1985). The distinction was again brought into the mainstream of memory research with the publication of three papers in the early 1980s that we use below to illustrate three different indirect tests and three different theoretical interpretations.

A. Activation

Mandler (1980) proposed that recognition memory judgments were based either on retrieval of information about the context in which an item was presented or on the "familiarity" of the item. According to Mandler, retrieval depends on elaborative processing at study that creates relationships between items or between items and context. In contrast, simply perceiving an item activates its representation in memory and increases the integration of its constituent features, and that activation/integration can subsequently give rise to a feeling of familiarity when the item is later encountered. According to Mandler, activation/integration operates primarily on perceptual representations of an event, and the degree of subsequent familiarity is a function of the level of activation at study and the degree of perceptual match between study and test.

In a study supporting this two-component model of recognition, Graf et al. (1982) compared performance on the stem-completion task of War-rington and Weizkrantz (1970) to free recall as a function of study conditions that either required or prevented elaborative processing. Subjects studied a list of words by either deciding how much they liked each word, which would encourage elaborative processing, or deciding if each word shared any vowels with the previous word, which would effectively prevent elaborative processing. Subjects who did the vowel-checking task recalled very few words compared to subjects who made the liking decisions, but the likelihood of completing the stems with the studied words (as opposed to other possible words) was equivalent for the two groups.

B. Episodes and Procedures

Jacoby and Dallas (1981) compared the effects of a number of variables on the direct test of recognition memory and the indirect test of perceptual identification. In a perceptual identification test, words are presented briefly on a computer screen with instructions to identify the words, and the effect of prior study of the words is revealed in a higher probability of identification for studied compared to nonstudied words. They found some manipulations to affect one measure and not the other; others to affect both measures in the same direction; and yet others to affect the two measures in opposite directions. For example, varying the levels of processing during study affected recognition performance but not perceptual identification performance; spacing the repetitions of an item during study was better than massing the repetitions of an item for both tests; and reading an item versus solving an anagram of the item at study led to better performance on the perceptual identification test, but to worse performance on the recognition test.

Jacoby and Dallas (1981) accounted for the functional dissociations between recognition memory and perceptual identification by suggesting that the two types of tests rely on memory for different aspects of the study episode: perceptual identification tests depend more on memory for graphemic or physical/perceptual information, whereas recognition memory tests depend more on memory for elaborative processing and meaning.

Although the various aspects of the study episode are represented in a single integrated memory, the different types of tests draw on different aspects or attributes of that memory.

In support of the argument that perceptual identification depends on memory for physical information, a change from auditory modality at study to visual modality at test greatly reduced the effect of prior study on perceptual identification. To account for the parallel effects of some manipulations on recognition and perceptual identification, Jacoby and Dallas (1981) drew upon Mandler's (1980) dual-process model of recognition memory. Familiarity may reflect memory for physical or graphemic information and, thus, tap the same information used in the perceptual identification test. In fact, Jacoby and Dallas argued that the relative ease of perceptually identifying an item on a recognition memory test could be interpreted by subjects as being due to a past encounter with that item, and so give rise to a feeling of familiarity. In that case, enhanced perceptual identification—ostensibly an implicit memory process—could actually be a basis for conscious recognition. Thus parallel effects of variables on recognition and perceptual identification were interpreted as reflecting use of the same information on the two kinds of test.

Jacoby and Mandler differ primarily in that Jacoby attributes changes in perceptual identification performance to memory for a new episode, whereas Mandler proposes that familiarity arises from the activation and integration of pre-existing representations (Mandler, 1990). Both treat recollection and familiarity within a single framework and interpret dissociations as due to different processes.

C. Separate Systems

A very different theoretical approach was taken by Tulving et al. (1982). They studied the relation between recognition memory and the indirect memory test of fragment completion (e.g., complete a fragmented version of a word such as A__A__IN for ASSASSIN). Recognition memory declined more from one hour to seven days than did the effect of prior study on fragment completion (although it is difficult to interpret that particular interaction given probable differences in scale; Loftus, 1978). Tulving et al. also calculated the relation between performance on the two tests, using the subject–item as the unit of analysis. For items tested on the recognition test followed by the fragment completion test, stochastic independence was obtained between the two measures, that is, effects of prior exposure on fragment completion were the same whether subjects had recognized particular items or not. Tulving et al. suggested that the "priming" effect of studying words on later fragment completion reflects the operation of a separate memory system, different from the memory system that subserves recognition or recall. They argued against a view that priming reflects the temporary activation of nodes in a network structure because the effect is long lasting (e.g., seven days in their experiment) and is modality specific (Jacoby & Dallas, 1981; Morton, 1979).

II. TYPES OF EVIDENCE

As illustrated in the papers described in the preceding section, three forms of evidence have emerged for a distinction between whatever is being measured by direct versus indirect memory tests: (1) stochastic independence between performance on the repeated two types of tests; (2) functional dissociations, in which a variable has different effects on a direct versus an indirect test; and (3) dissociations among populations, including amnesics, children, the elderly, and "normal" controls (e.g., undergraduate students). A plethora of subsequent studies have made such comparisons across a range of direct and indirect memory tests, and have been interpreted in terms of three types of theories: activation models (Graf & Mandler, 1984); processing models (Jacoby, Kelley, & Dywan, 1989; Kolers & Roediger, 1984; Roediger, 1990); and multiple memory systems (Johnson, 1992; Squire, 1992a; Tulving & Schacter, 1990). Regardless of which of these three theoretical perspectives researchers were championing, the central claim for which they sought evidence was that the bases for responding on direct and indirect tests are different and hence independent. We next provide an illustrative, rather than exhaustive, review of these studies and the attendant theoretical developments, which we begin by describing and critiquing the three major types of evidence for differences between direct and indirect tests: stochastic independence, functional dissociations, and population dissociations.

A. Stochastic Independence

A number of studies have computed 2×2 contingency analyses between performance on a yes/no recognition memory test or a cued recall test versus an indirect test on the same items by the same subjects (Jacoby & Witherspoon, 1982; Tulving et al., 1982). If, in contrast to the dependence that is often found between pairs of direct memory tests, no significant association is found between a direct and indirect test, this pattern is sometimes taken as support for the hypothesis that the two tasks tap different processes or reflect the operation of different memory systems. For example, Hayman and Tulving (1989a) tested one group of subjects on two direct tests (recognition and recall cued with fragments) and another group on a direct and an indirect memory test (recognition and fragment completion). Whereas a strong correlation was obtained between performance on the recognition test and performance on the cued recall test using fragments, no significant relationship was observed between the recognition and fragment completion tests. Hayman and Tulving interpreted this result as evidence that different memory systems support performance on direct and indirect memory tests.

However, the interpretation of stochastic independence as evidence for different underlying memory processes or systems has been challenged on a number of grounds. Shimamura (1985) has argued that when a yes/no recognition test precedes an indirect test such as fragment completion, the recognition test can act as a study trial and thereby boost fragment completion probabilities for *all* items (whether or not they were consciously recognized by the subject), thus masking a dependent relationship. The reverse testing order allows successful fragment completion to act as an extra study trial for a word, which could produce a spurious dependent relationship.

Hintzman and Hartry (1990) have argued that lack of dependence between tests does not indicate independent processes or memory systems because suppressor variables can severely limit the degree of association that could be obtained. With materials such as those used in the fragment completion test in Tulving et al. (1982), the amount of variability in fragment completion due to prior study of items (the priming effect) is very small (5%) compared to the amount of variability due to item differences, which does not leave much room for a dependent relation to emerge. By contrast, the amount of variability in "yes" responses for the recognition of old and new items that is due to prior study of the items is large (92% in Hintzman and Hartry's experiment). Hintzman and Hartry also demonstrated that item differences can lead to wide variations in the strength of the relationship between direct and indirect tests with different subsets of items.

If performance on indirect tests is mediated by a single memory system or process, then successive indirect tests should reveal dependence. However, Witherspoon and Moscovitch (1989) found stochastic independence between fragment completion and a perceptual identification test, and Hayman and Tulving (1989b) reported independence between successive fragment completion tests that used different cues. Hintzman (1991) noted that these demonstrations of lack of dependence may stem from the small priming effect relative to the wide variability in item difficulty on such tests. In summary, lack of dependence between two tests does not afford unambiguous interpretation regarding the processes or systems underlying those tests.

B. Functional Dissociations

Cognitive psychologists and neuroscientists have searched for functional dissociations between tasks to argue for independent processes or systems subserving performance. If a variable has different effects on an indirect memory test versus a direct test, then the dissociation is often interpreted as reflecting some difference between memory systems or processes (see Richardson-Klavehn & Bjork, 1988; Roediger & McDermott, 1993; Schacter, 1987, for reviews). In general, indirect tests such as fragment completion, perceptual identification, and stem completion are far more sensitive to changes in perceptual aspects between study and test, such as modality, typeface, language, and mode (picture vs. word), than are standard direct tests. In contrast, direct tests are far more sensitive to manipulations such as depth of processing and amount of attention during study, delay between study and test, and proactive interference.

1. Problem of Confounded Variables

Roediger and Blaxton (1987; see also Blaxton, 1989) pointed out that comparisons of pairs of tests (e.g., yes/no recognition and fragment completion) often confound other variables with the direct/indirect test manipulation. In particular, indirect tests such as fragment completion, stem completion, perceptual identification, or lexical decision may involve more data-driven processing (analysis of physical features), whereas direct tests typically rely more on conceptually driven processing (analysis of meaning). Roediger and Blaxton also noted that it is possible to devise indirect tests that are likely to rely on conceptual processing and direct tests that are likely to rely on perceptual processing, thereby reversing the confounding between type of test and type of processing. They argued that patterns of dissociation between direct and indirect tests may arise from differences in the types of processing demanded by the tasks typically used in the two types of tests, rather than reflecting inherent differences between memory systems. Consistent with this idea, Blaxton (1989) found that a number of dissociations between direct and indirect tests could be attributed to the difference between conceptually driven tasks (free recall, semantic cued recall, and the indirect test of answering general knowledge questions) and data-driven tests (word fragment completion and recall using graphemic cues), rather than the difference between direct and indirect retrieval instructions. For example, regardless of whether subjects were given direct or indirect tests of memory, their performance on data-driven tasks was more enhanced by prior study when studied items had been read (XXX–COPPER) rather than generated from cues (TIN–C___), whereas the reverse was true for the conceptually driven tasks. Similarly, when subjects were given visually presented test cues, their performance on the data-driven tasks was enhanced more by visual study than by auditory study, whereas their performance on the conceptually driven tasks was equivalent across study modalities. Given that dissociations occur among indirect memory tests and among direct memory tests, one cannot draw conclusions about the difference between indirect and direct memory tests in general from the results of studies of a single example of each.

Roediger, Blaxton, and colleagues argued that many functional dissociations can be interpreted within a framework of "transfer-appropriate processing" (Jacoby & Dallas, 1981; Kolers & Roediger, 1984; Morris, Bransford, & Franks, 1977). The argument is as follows: Tasks performed during study and during test vary along a continuum from primarily data driven to primarily conceptually driven, and performance at test is better when the mental operations or procedures used during study are repeated at test. It should be noted, however, that the argument (see also Roediger, Weldon, & Challis, 1989) did not claim that tests are purely data driven or purely conceptually driven: for example, repetition of conceptual operations could contribute to priming in perceptual indirect tests (Bassilli, Smith, & Macleod, 1989; Challis & Brodbeck, 1992; Toth & Hunt, 1990; Weldon, 1991) and vice versa (Hunt & Toth, 1990).

2. The Interpretation of Functional Dissociations

Dunn and Kirsner (1988) argued that functional dissociations do not logically compel an inference of multiple processes or multiple systems and pointed out that associations between tests are as essential as dissociations for identifying different processes. Any form of a dissociation—single (a variable affects performance on Task A but not Task B), uncrossed double (one variable affects performance on Task A but not Task B, whereas a second variable affects performance on Task B but not Task A), or crossed double (a single variable has opposite effects on Task A and Task B)—*could* be accounted for by a single-process model. The two tasks could be differentially sensitive to the level of functioning of the same process at different levels of process efficiency. In contrast, a pattern of *reversed association* between two tasks does dictate rejection of a single-process model. A reversed association is any deviation from monotonicity in a plot of the levels of performance on one task against levels of performance on the second task, across a variety of conditions. A reversed association occurs when one variable affects two tasks the same way, and another variable affects those tasks in opposite ways. Such a finding would be strong evidence that different processes are involved in the performance of the two tasks, because if a single-process model were true one task would be a monotonic function of the other.

Dunn and Kirsner (1988) identified several instances of reverse associations between direct and indirect memory tests. For example, Graf and Schacter (1985) tested amnesic, matched controls, and undergraduate subjects on cued recall and stem completion of paired associates, using study of related (e.g., BUTTONED–SHIRT) versus unrelated (e.g., WINDOW–SHIRT) word pairs. Among the many potential comparisons, there are examples of both positive associations and negative associations. The probabilities of stem completion and cued recall were positively related across some conditions (i.e., prior study of related word pairs compared to unrelated word pairs increased the probability of a response on both tests). In contrast, the probabilities of stem completion and cued recall were negatively related across other conditions (i.e., comparing unrelated pairs for the student controls to related pairs for the amnesic patients, the probability of stem completion increased but the probability of cued recall decreased). Such a nonmonotonic relationship between cued recall and stem completion cannot logically be accounted for by a single-process model. Similarly, across several experiments comparing perceptual identification and recognition tests, Jacoby (1983a, 1983b) found instances of both positive relations and negative relations between the two tasks.

Dunn and Kirsner (1988) suggested that experimenters should move away from studies that attempt to demonstrate functional dissociations to studies that could reveal reversed associations between tasks, an approach that emphasizes associations as much as dissociations. There are often strong associations between performance on direct and indirect tests, a fact that is often lost in the search for functional dissociations. For example, Dunn and Kirsner (1989) plotted cued recall as a function of word fragment completion and found that the two correlated $r = .70$ for paired-associate recall and $r = .82$ for letter-cued recall (across 22 and 40 conditions, respectively), despite the fact that the data came from studies that focused on uncovering dissociations. Clearly, either both types of tests overlap in their reliance on memory systems or processes, or the separate systems or processes just happen to be influenced in the same way by a number of variables.

3. Tests Are Not Pure Measures

Memory tests are not pure measures of underlying processes. Even the simplest task relies on a number of component processes, and a given task may be solved in a variety of ways by different subjects. Dunn and Kirsner (1989) referred to the mistaken assumption that tasks are process pure as the "transparency assumption." One obvious counterexample to the transparency assumption arises when subjects spontaneously transform an indirect test into a direct test and so "contaminate" a supposedly pure measure of unconscious or implicit memory with conscious attempts to remember. Conversely, implicit processes may well play an important role in conscious uses of memory (Humphreys, Bain, & Pike, 1989; Jacoby & Dallas, 1981; Nelson, Schreiber, & McEvoy, 1992).

C. Population Dissociations

Differences between performance on direct and indirect memory tests have been investigated in a variety of populations, including anterograde amnesics, the elderly, children, and Alzheimer's patients. The underlying claim is that dissociations between populations and tests (e.g., the finding that amnesics and normals differ on direct tests but not on indirect tests) constitute evidence that different memory systems or processes are responsible for performance on the different kinds of tests.

The interpretation of population dissociations as reflecting separate modules or systems has been criticized on several grounds. One is that many population dissociations on direct and indirect tests are single dissociations, (e.g., anterograde amnesics exhibit normal priming on a perceptual identification test, but poor performance on a recall test). Single dissociations can occur simply because one test is harder than the other (Shallice, 1988; although "difficulty" cannot really be specified outside a theory of processing; Kosslyn & Intriligator, 1992). A second criticism of population dissociations is that comparisons of different populations do not always reveal clean dissociations between performance on direct and indirect tests. For example, in some studies older adults perform more poorly than younger subjects on direct tests but not on indirect tests; whereas, in other studies, the older adults perform more poorly than younger subjects on both kinds of test (Chiarello & Hoyer, 1988; Howard, 1988; Light & Singh, 1987). Even when the age difference on indirect tests is not statistically reliable, the direction of the difference is often the same as on direct tests. These problems may reflect contamination of the indirect test by uses of explicit memory or contamination of the direct test by influences of implicit memory. Lacking an independent means for measuring contamination, however, findings of associations across populations challenge the interpretation of dissociations across populations.

A third criticism of population dissociations is that they typically involve drawing conclusions about memory processes in normals from data concerning memory processes in brain-damaged people. It is always possible that the pattern of damaged and spared abilities in brain-damaged people emerges from the damage in complicated ways, rather than simply reflecting that everyone has two systems and one of them is damaged in the special population (cf. Kosslyn & Intriligator, 1992; Kosslyn & Van Kleeck, 1990).

III. CRITIQUES OF THEORIES

A. Activation

Theories proposing that priming on indirect memory tests is due to the activation of abstract representations have not been supported. First, the persistence of priming effects over long periods (days or weeks) seems inconsistent with a temporary activation process. Second, priming effects are often very specific, as shown by the decrease in priming when physical characteristics, such as modality or even font of words, are changed between study and test. Third, priming effects can reflect the use of new information, rather than just the activation of abstract, pre-existing representations.

Activation accounts have also had trouble accounting for findings concerning amnesics' ability to create new representations. An activation account of amnesics' preserved abilities and deficits would suggest that, although they benefit from the priming of existing representations, they should show no change in performance on indirect tests using novel items, nor should they be able to create new associations. Consistent with this prediction, Diamond and Rozin (1984) found that a group of amnesics did not exhibit priming in stem completion of nonwords formed by recombining the syllables of intact words (e.g., numby). On the other hand, a number of studies have demonstrated priming in amnesics for novel stimuli, including nonwords, novel line drawings, and objects (Haist, Musen, & Squire, 1991; Musen & Squire, 1991, 1992; Schacter, Cooper, Tharan, & Rubens, 1991).

Similarly, the evidence of amnesics' ability to form new associations on indirect tests is mixed. Schacter (1985) found that amnesics showed priming in free association for idioms (e.g., study SMALL–POTATOES, followed by a test on SMALL–?), but not for random pairs (e.g., SMALL–GRAPES), and argued that priming in amnesics depends on the presence at test of a part of a stimulus that has a pre-existing representation. Glisky, Schacter, and Tulving (1986) presented amnesic and control subjects with definitions of words related to computers and then tested for the defined word with stems as cues. Over repeated trials, the numbers of letters in the stems were gradually reduced, and the amnesics had an extremely difficult time moving from producing the word when given the definition and one letter to producing it when given only the definition. Similarly, Graf and Schacter (1985) noted that even three study trials on a pair of unrelated words (e.g., WINDOW–REASON) did not alter free-association probabilities (WINDOW–?) in normals as well as amnesics, whereas three study trials did alter the likelihood that the target word would be produced more often to a stem accompanied by the studied word (WINDOW–REA?) compared to an unstudied word (CAPTAIN–REA?), even in amnesics. In contrast, Shimamura and Squire (1989), using the same paradigm, found no evidence of new associations being formed in amnesics even when stems were provided at test, but they argued that the different results were due to their testing more densely amnesic subjects. However, an extremely dense amnesic learned new associations between words such as "RAYS softened

ASPHALT" after many repetitions (Tulving, Hayman, & Macdonald, 1991), which was interpreted as evidence that the amnesic had lost episodic but not semantic memory.

B. Processing Views

As described earlier, processing views hold that differences between direct and indirect tests reflect differences in the kinds of memory information on which the different tests rely. Studied items are thought to be stored in memory as unitary, multi-aspected representations, with some aspects being important for performing some kinds of tests and other aspects being important for other tests. The relationship between study conditions and test performance is said to be determined by the encoding specificity or transfer-appropriate processing principle: performance is best when processes at test are similar to processes at study.

One criticism of the transfer-appropriate processing (TAP) approach is that—lacking formal methods for specifying the processes that are involved in performing a task—the TAP account is circular and unfalsifiable: a large degree of transfer is predicted whenever processes at study and test are highly similar, and processes at study and test are said to be highly similar whenever a large degree of transfer is observed. As Tenpenny and Shoben (1992) have pointed out, at this point the nature and characteristics of "processes" are only vaguely specified. The usefulness of the TAP approach depends on the development of theories that specify what qualifies as different processes, and techniques for specifying, a priori, the processes that are involved in performing the tasks presented at study and at test.

A second criticism of processing views is that they do not provide a satisfying account of the problems amnesics have on direct memory tests. As Roediger, Weldon, and Challis (1989) noted, the most straightforward application of transfer-appropriate processing would suggest that amnesics have preserved data-driven processes and impaired conceptually driven processes. Amnesics do show priming on tasks classified as data driven, such as word stem completion (Graf, Squire, & Mandler, 1984), perceptual identification (Cermak, Chandler, & Wolbarst, 1985), lexical decision (Moscovitch, 1982), and picture naming latency (Cave & Squire, 1992); however, they also show priming on indirect conceptually driven tests, such as production of words cued by category labels or semantic associates (Gardner, Boller, Moreines, & Butters, 1973; Graf, Shimamura, & Squire, 1985; Shimamura & Squire, 1984). These findings of preserved conceptual priming challenge the hypothesis that amnesia reflects a general impairment in conceptual processing. Indeed, the well-established fact that amnesics are able to engage in conceptual thinking (e.g., have normal or near-normal IQ on subscales that do not require memorization of new material, and are able to engage in conversation about abstract topics) makes it clear that their memory deficits cannot be explained in terms of a general impairment of conceptual or "deep" processing. Therefore, a processing view must hold that amnesics have deficits in certain specific kinds of conceptual processing that are important for performance on direct tests. Thus, in a sense, this specific criticism of TAP arises from the more general criticism of TAP described above, regarding the lack of any formal method for specifying the nature and characteristics of particular kinds of processes.

C. Multiple Systems

Systems accounts explain dissociations between tests by positing that different tests reflect the operation of different memory systems (e.g., an episodic system that supports performance on direct tests and a variety of non-episodic systems that support performance on particular kinds of indirect tests). The concept of separate functional systems stems from neuropsychological analyses: For example, separate systems for language, memory, and visual perception are invoked to account for cases of patients with amnesia without aphasia or agnosia, using the criteria of double dissociations for invoking separate systems (Coltheart, 1989).

Historically, systems accounts have relied heavily (although not exclusively) on population dissociations. For example, the pattern of impaired and spared memory in amnesia has been interpreted as evidence for separate memory systems: A system that enables the recollection of individual episodes is damaged, whereas a variety of other perceptual and knowledge systems remain intact and are responsible for amnesics' memory as revealed by indirect tests (e.g., Squire, 1992a; Squire & Zola-Morgan, 1991; Tulving, 1985a, 1993; Tulving & Schacter, 1990; for recent reviews see Schacter, Chiu, & Ochsner, 1993; Squire, Knowlton, & Musen, 1993).

Systems accounts have been criticized for naming new systems without elucidating the processes performed by those systems. A second criticism is the lack of parsimony involved in invoking new systems to explain new findings of dissociations (Roediger, 1990). A third and closely related criticism concerns the question of what kinds of evidence are sufficient to justify the postulation of a new system. As noted earlier, functional dissociations can certainly happen within a "memory system," as in the many functional dissociations between recall and recognition, so findings of functional dissociations are not, in themselves, sufficient to invoke separate systems. Similarly, many population dissociations on direct and indirect tests are single dissociations (e.g., anterograde amnesics can exhibit normal priming on a perceptual identification test, but poor performance on a recall test). However, as also noted previously, single dissociations can occur simply because one test is harder than the other. To counteract the argument that direct tests are simply harder than indirect tests, proponents of systems accounts have pointed to the stochastic independence between tests, and the fact that subjects sometimes "pass" the harder test on an item (recognition) yet "fail" the easier test (perceptual identification). However, as we discussed previously, stochastic independence is not particularly valuable evidence. Hence, critics have argued that functional dissociations, population dissociations, and stochastic independence are inadequate bases for the postulation of separate systems.

IV. NEW DIRECTIONS

A. Specifying Systems

New formulations of the separate systems approach have attempted to specify further the processes underlying performance on indirect tests, rather than simply to give names to hypothetical memory systems. For example, Tulving and Schacter (1990) and Schacter (1990; 1992b) have proposed that perceptual priming effects reflect the operation of a perceptual representation system (PRS) that is independent of episodic and semantic memory systems. Schacter drew on the cognitive neuropsychology literature and proposed at least three separate components within the PRS: (1) a visual word form system (Warrington & Shallice, 1980) that represents information about the visual form of a word, independent of word meaning; (2) an auditory word form system; and (3) a structural description system that represents information about the form and structure of visual objects, independent of information regarding their meaning and function. In the neuropsychological literature, there are patients who have lost the ability to gain access to the meaning of words (as indexed by an inability to classify the words into semantic categories) and yet can read them aloud. In contrast, patients with surface dyslexia seemingly have lost that ability to access representations of the visual forms of words (as indexed by an inability to read irregular words such as "gone" and "through" accurately) and yet can understand the meaning of visually presented words. Similarly, a patient with visual agnosia is unable to name objects presented visually or describe their function, but nonetheless performs normally on tasks requiring information about object structure, such as deciding whether or not line drawings represent real objects.

Schacter, Cooper, and colleagues (see Cooper & Lang, this volume, Chapter 5; Cooper & Schacter, 1992) have found a number of functional and population dissociations between recognition memory and priming in a task involving judgments of whether or not line drawings could exist as three-dimensional objects. Some of the line drawings represented possible three-dimensional objects, whereas others did not. Priming occurred on the possible/impossible decision tasks following original encoding conditions that had involved analyzing the structure of the object (whether it faced mainly to the right or mainly to the left), but not following encoding that had involved local details (judging whether the object contained more vertical or more horizontal line segments) or that had asked subjects to report some familiar object of which the item reminded them. In contrast, recognition memory was highest after the semantic encoding condition (Schacter, Cooper, & Delaney, 1990; Schacter, Cooper, Delaney, Peterson, & Tharan, 1991). Furthermore, in all conditions priming was obtained only for possible, not impossible objects, yet recognition memory was only slightly higher for possible than for impossible objects. Changes of size and left/right orientation of the object between study and test affected recognition memory, but not priming on the possible/impossible objects test (Cooper, Schacter, Ballesteros, & Moore, 1992). Similarly, Biederman and Cooper (1991, 1992) found priming in repeated trials of an object naming task that was unaffected by size changes between the first and second presentation of an item, and unaffected by changes in position and orientation. In contrast, these changes in size, position, and orientation lowered performance on a recognition memory test. Furthermore, amnesics showed priming on the object decision task, even though they were severely impaired on the test of recognition for the objects (Schacter, Cooper, Tharan, & Rubens, 1991). Cooper and Schacter (1992) argued that these functional and population dissociations reflect the independence of episodic memory and priming in the structural description system.

Schacter (1992a) argued that cognitive neuroscience data provide constraints on processing accounts. For example, brain-lesion studies and single-cell recordings suggest that the inferior temporal cortex may be the locus for the structural description system (Plaut & Farah, 1990), but a posterior parietal area may be important for information about an object's location, size, and orientation in depth (Biederman & Cooper, 1992). However, as Srinivas (1993) pointed out, the cognitive neuroscience literature may be inconsistent or mute on the effects of some manipulations, such as changes in orientation in depth.

Sherry and Schacter (1987) specified an additional criterion for invoking multiple memory systems (see also Rozin, 1976; Rozin & Schull, 1988). They argued that modules might perform domain-specific computations and operate independently of one another, but the memory functions within the modules might nonetheless operate according to the same rules. That is, information about objects might be computed and primed within an object recognition module, whereas information about words might be computed and primed within a word identification module, but the priming effects could operate in the same way in both cases. Therefore, even though the two modules might be in separate places in the brain (and so double dissociations could occur in patients with damage to one or the other of these separate areas), the rules of operation might be the same across the modules. In contrast, if the two modules have different acquisition, retention, and retrieval processes, or different rules of operations of those memory processes, then it would make more sense to talk about separate memory systems, that is, they would be functionally distinct as well as located in different brain areas.

Sherry and Schacter (1987) suggested that separate systems evolve only if the functions the systems perform are mutually incompatible, such that the properties of one system cannot solve the demands of a novel problem. For example, functional incompatibility may have led to separate memory systems in birds for learning the song characteristic of their species versus where food was cached. To determine whether the functional demands of different memory tasks are incompatible would require a detailed understanding of the problem posed by a particular memory task, a description of an architecture that can handle that problem, and a description of the other architecture that specifies why it cannot handle the problem. Thinking about the functional considerations of systems may generate hypotheses for studies that will further specify their mechanisms.

B. Specifying Processes

The patterns of associations and dissociations between direct and indirect memory tests suggest that the tasks are complex and composed of multiple components. To understand those components, we need careful task analyses (Moscovitch, 1984) and theories that are more specific. As part of the trend to more specific task analyses, some researchers have begun to characterize differences in the results obtained across different types of indirect memory tests (Roediger, Srinivas, & Weldon, 1989; Roediger, Weldon, Stadler, & Riegler, 1992; Srinivas & Roediger, 1990; Tenpenny & Shoben, 1992; Weldon, 1991). Rajaram and Roediger (1993) compared visual word identification, stem completion, word fragment completion, and anagram solution within one experiment. These tests (which use visual presentation of test items) all exhibited the most priming from visual presentation of words at study, less from auditory presentation, and no priming from presentation of pictures at study. A change in typeface from handprinted to typed between study and test had no effects (but see Graf & Ryan, 1990; Jacoby & Hayman, 1987; see also review in Schacter et al., 1993, for a discussion of typeface effects on indirect tests). In contrast, free recall was best when pictures were presented at study, and equivalent for auditory versus visual presentation of study words and same versus different typefaces at study and test. Rajaram and Roediger interpreted these results as indicating that those indirect tests all primarily reflect the repetition of perceptual and lexical operations involved in identifying words or accessing specific visual word form representations (Kirsner, Dunn, & Standen, 1989).

A second approach to specifying processes has occurred in the development of formal memory models. Humphreys, Bain, and Pike (1989) proposed an associative theory of memory based on task analyses of seven different direct and indirect memory tests and familiarity judgments. They proposed that the tasks differ because some rely on a process of matching (recognition and familiarity judgments), others rely on retrieval (cued recall), and yet others rely on production (produce the first word that comes to mind). Their simulation implemented these processes in a distributed storage model that assumed two levels of memory representations: modality-specific and central representations. Word, part-word, or extra-list cues can be used singly, additively, or interactively combined with context cues. Humphreys, Bain, and Pike acknowledged that the distinction between peripheral and central memory codes, and the different ways cues can be used in their model are reminiscent of distinctions such as episodic, semantic, and procedural memory, but they preferred to view these distinctions as components in a single system, with a resulting emphasis on how the components worked together. Furthermore, they argued that the distinction between peripheral and central memory does not involve fundamentally different structures or operations.

Humphreys, Bain, and Pike (1989) argued that amnesics' deficits reflect an inability to use interactive cues during retrieval or matching, or an inability to reinstate a cognitive representation of the encoding situation. Humphreys, Bain, and Burt's (1989) task analysis of the Graf and Schacter (1985) findings regarding priming of new associations (described previously) illustrate their approach. They suggested that amnesics and control subjects, when tested on indirect production tasks such as stem completion and free association, produce the strongest associate of the cue. Prior study of an item or pair of items causes the associative strength to cumulate with any pre-existing associative strength, and the likelihood that such a change in associative strength can be detected at a later test depends on how much of an increment in associative strength is required to "tip the balance" in favor of the studied item. In stem completion with multiple solution words, each previously studied word will undoubtedly vary from subject to subject in how close it is to being the strongest associate to the stem presented at test, and if, for at least some subjects, the studied item was already the second highest associate, the increment in strength from a single exposure to the item would tip the balance. However, it might take many more study trials to make a new association between unrelated words (such as WINDOW–REASON in the Graf & Schacter study) the strongest association for even one subject. Therefore, indirect production tests may not be sensitive to a change in strength of a new association unless the pool of possible competing answers is restricted, perhaps by giving the first letter of the target item. This analysis thus obviates the need for proposing that priming occurs only for pre-existing associations.

Nelson et al. (1992) also proposed a single-system memory model that accounts for differences between performance on direct and indirect memory tests and points to the use of implicit memory on direct memory tests. Their PIER model (for Processing Implicit and Explicit Representations) assumes that study produces an explicit memory representation and also automatically activates meaningfully and phonologically associated words. At test, targets can be recovered by the mutually exclusive processes of searching through explicitly created memories or searching through implicitly activated memories, and direct memory test instructions increase the probability of a search of explicit memory. Nelson et al. noted that the search through explicitly encoded information could be identified with an explicit memory system, and the search of implicitly activated memories could be identified with various implicit memory systems, but the model does not require a multiple-systems view.

C. Convergence of Systems and Processes

The debate between systems views and processing views may well become unproductive as the two become less and less distinguishable. For example, Johnson's MEM model (a Multiple-Entry, Modular memory system; Johnson, 1992; Johnson & Hirst, 1993) is somewhere between an emphasis on systems versus processes, as the subsystems are sets of processes, and the primary units are cognitive actions that have memorial consequences. One set of functional subsystems (P1 and P2) is made up of processes that are important to perception, such as locating and tracking stimuli, or identifying objects and placing them in spatial relation to each other. The other major subdivision of functional subsystems (R1 and R2) is made up of processes that are important to reflective thinking and planning, processes such as noting relations, reactivating information, and discovering relations. MEM provides a more fine-grained analysis of processes than does the conceptually driven/data-driven distinction, and highlights the interaction of these subsystems in memory tasks.

We are hopeful that progress lies with the convergence between processes and systems, but we do not want to downplay the tensions between the two approaches. For example, Squire (1992b) insists that a brain-systems framework is the only one that will provide a complete account of memory. In contrast, Teitelbaum and Pellis (1992) forcefully argue that psychology must resist reductionism and aim to build a theory of function: "How can we adequately relate function to tissue when we don't understand the sub-components of function?" (p. 17).

D. Improved Evidence for Independent Processes: Separately Estimating Conscious and Unconscious Memory

One new direction centers on methodological advances. As mentioned above, performance on indirect tests of memory may sometimes be contaminated by conscious memory. Similarly, unconscious influences of memory of the sort that indirect tests are designed to measure may contribute to responding on direct tests such as cued recall. Thus, no test provides a factor-pure measure of memory with or without awareness. The fact that no test can serve as a process–pure measure of conscious or unconscious uses of memory is a major stumbling block for progress in attempts to understand the nature of these different uses of memory, because we can never be sure whether the effect of a variable on test performance is mediated by conscious or unconscious uses of memory. For example, several recent studies (Hamann, 1990; Toth & Hunt, 1990) have shown effects of manipulations of levels of processing during study on performance of indirect tests. As noted in our previous section on Roediger's (e.g., Roediger, Weldon, & Challis, 1989) notion of transfer-appropriate processing, such findings are important because they contradict the idea that implicit memory only reflects perceptual processing. However, a critic might argue that the only reason performance on these indirect tests was affected by levels of processing is that test performance was contaminated by conscious recollection, which is well known to be affected by such manipulations.

Several approaches to this problem of contamination have been explored. One approach has been to ask subjects, after performance on an indirect test, whether they had noticed the relationship between the study list and the test and whether aware uses of memory had contributed to their responding on the latter (Bowers & Schacter, 1991). The major problem with this approach, of course, is that it is less than ideal to rely on subjects' retrospective reports. A second strategy has been to use what Schacter termed the "retrieval intentionality criterion" (Schacter, Bowers, & Booker, 1989): When an indirect and a direct test differ only in the test instructions— that is, the retrieval cues are the same—and a test manipulation influences one test but not the other, then it is assumed that the indirect test paradigm must not be contaminated by explicit strategies of recall. As Schacter et al. noted, however, this approach does not address the issue of awareness and cannot distinguish between involuntary explicit memory and implicit memory.

Jacoby (1991) developed a method, termed the "process dissociation procedure," for separately estimating the contributions of conscious versus unconscious uses of memory to performance on a single task. He started with the assumption that conscious and unconscious uses of memory are independent. Then he argued that an important difference between the conscious and unconscious use of memory is that if people can consciously identify an idea as a memory, they can use that information as a basis for controlling a response. Conscious control is defined as the difference between performance when one is "trying to" versus "trying not to" perform some act. Performance in a condition in which subjects are trying to base their responses on memory for studied items (the "inclusion" condition) can be compared with performance in a condition in which subjects are trying *not* to base their responses on studied items (the "exclusion" condition) to obtain a measure of conscious memory. Once the estimate of conscious memory is obtained, one can solve for the estimate of unconscious memory influences in the same task.

The stem-completion experiments reported by Jacoby, Toth, and Yonelinas (1993) illustrate this approach. Subjects studied a list of words and were later given the first three letters of words as cues for recall (e.g., MOT_ for MOTEL). For inclusion test items, subjects were told to respond by recalling an item from the studied list and to guess with the first item that came to mind if they could not recall an appropriate studied item. For exclusion test items, subjects were told not to complete the item with an item from the studied list, but to use other words (e.g., MOTOR). Under the inclusion instructions, above-baseline use of studied items as completions (compared to responses to stems for which no completions were studied) can be due either to the subjects' conscious recollection of the items as having been on the studied list, or to the items coming to mind as unconsciously informed guesses due to the subject's prior study of the items. Thus, assuming independence of the contribution of conscious recollection and unconscious effects of prior study, the probability of producing studied items at an above-baseline rate under inclusion instructions is equal to the probability of conscious recollection, C, plus the probability of the word coming to mind due to unconscious memory when there is a failure of conscious recollection, U $(1-C)$. In equation form:

Probability of producing studied word in inclusion $= C + U(1-C)$.

Under the exclusion instructions, subjects should produce a studied word only if they fail consciously to remember that it was on the studied list, $1-C$. Subjects could nonetheless produce the studied item at a rate above baseline owing to unconscious influences of memory, U. Thus, in equation form:

Probability of producing the studied word in exclusion $= U(1-C)$.

The estimate of conscious recollection, C, is obtained by subtracting the proportion of studied items used as completions in the exclusion test, U(1−C), from the proportion of studied items used as completions in the inclusion test, C + U(1−C). This is the difference in the probability of using studied items as completions when subjects are trying to do so (the inclusion test) and when they are trying *not* to do so (the exclusion test). Given this estimate of recollection, an estimate of unconscious influences of memory, U, can be obtained using simple algebra.

These equations rest on the assumption that conscious recollection and unconscious influences of memory are independent processes. The equation for the inclusion condition can be rewritten to highlight the independence assumption as C + U − UC, or the probability of the two processes minus the overlap. Jacoby et al. (1993) sought evidence for this assumption in the form of "process dissociations." A process dissociation is obtained when a manipulation has a dramatic effect on the estimated contribution of one hypothesized process (e.g., C), but no effect on the other (e.g., U). The rationale for this approach is to use a manipulation that, on a priori grounds, would be expected to have a large effect on the contribution of one process but little or no effect on the other. If the obtained estimates reflect the predicted pattern (i.e., an effect of the manipulation on one estimate but not on the other), this outcome is taken as evidence that the two processes are indeed independent. Using these equations to compare stem-completion performance on the inclusion and exclusion tests, Jacoby et al. (1993; see also Jacoby, 1991) found that dividing attention at study dramatically lowered estimates of recollection but had no effect whatsoever on estimates of unconscious memory. Indeed, among subjects who had performed a demanding divided-attention task when the words were presented for study, the estimated contribution of recollection was driven to zero (as one would expect it to be in dense amnesia). In contrast, the divided attention task had no effect on the estimated contribution of unconscious influences of memory.

The findings reviewed here—that dividing attention impaired conscious recollection but had no effect on unconscious influences of memory—are consistent with previous theories and with findings from studies contrasting direct and indirect tests of memory (e.g., that direct tests of memory are greatly affected by dividing attention at study, whereas indirect tests are not; Eich, 1984; Parkin, Reid, & Russo, 1990). What is the advantage, then, of using the process dissociation procedure? The advantage is that, without the process dissociation procedure, one cannot compare the magnitudes of the effects of manipulations on conscious recollection or on unconscious influences of memory (e.g., cannot determine whether unconscious influences of memory are fully preserved in amnesia). Simply comparing direct and indirect tests of memory can lead one to conclude that a manipulation had no effect on memory when, in fact, it had offsetting effects on these two forms of memory.

This point is dramatically illustrated in Jacoby et al.'s (1993) Experiments 3 and 4. In those experiments, half of the study list items were presented as words to be read aloud and half were presented as anagrams to be solved (e.g., FIELR for RIFLE). Stems from these and other items were subsequently presented on a stem-completion task. For some subjects, the instructions for the stem-completion task were typical of studies using stem completion as an indirect test of memory, that is, subjects were simply instructed to complete each stem with the first word that came to mind. Other subjects were tested using the inclusion test instructions for half the items (i.e., try to complete the stem with a studied word) and the exclusion instructions for the other items (i.e., do not complete the stem with a studied word). An analysis of the probability of responding with studied words in the indirect and inclusion tests indicated no difference between items studied as anagrams and items studied as words to be read aloud. Inasmuch as the inclusion test is similar to a test of cued recall, this finding might be taken as evidence that the study manipulation had had no effect on recollection, which would be surprising because a host of studies on the generation effect (Slameka & Graf, 1978) suggest that solving anagrams should have produced better recollection than reading words. In fact, however, when the data were analyzed using the estimates derived with the process dissociation procedure, the estimates of U and C revealed that the study manipulation had had a dramatic effect on recollection, as also indicated by the fact that the difference between the inclusion and exclusion tests was greater for items studied as anagrams than for items read as words. The superior recollection of items studied as anagrams enabled subjects to follow the instructions and not use such words on the exclusion test. But the effect of the study manipulation on recollection was offset (and consequently masked on the indirect test) by an opposite effect of the study manipulation on unconscious influences of memory. Specifically, conscious recollection was greater for items studied as anagrams than for items studied as words, whereas unconscious influences of memory were greater for items studied as words than for items studied as anagrams.

The effect of the study manipulation on estimates of conscious recollection is consistent with the generation effect, and the effect on unconscious influences of memory is consistent with the transfer-appropriate processing hypothesis. Among subjects tested with a standard indirect test, prior exposure to words and to anagrams produced equivalent effects. This finding contrasts with that reported by Roediger et al. (1993). The fact that studying words as anagrams led to above-baseline use of those words on the indirect test might be taken as evidence for nonspecific transfer and, hence, as support for the idea that priming effects can be mediated by abstract representations. Furthermore, taken at face value, this finding might be taken as evidence against the transfer-appropriate processing view. Importantly, however, the estimates obtained with the process dissociation procedure revealed that the effect of prior exposure to anagrams on performance on the indirect test was due almost entirely to conscious recollection of studied items. In contrast, the effect of prior exposure to words on performance on the indirect test was mediated by unconscious influences of memory as well as by conscious recollection. Hence, the estimates indicate that the indirect test had been contaminated by aware uses of memory. As one would predict from the transfer-appropriate processing view, unconscious influences of memory were observed on the stem-completion test only when items had been presented as words to be read, not when they had been presented as anagrams.

In summary, the process dissociation procedure offers important advantages over task dissociations, which mistakenly treat tasks as process pure. For example, how can we interpret the above-chance performance of amnesics on cued recall tests? One interpretation is that if cued recall is a process-pure task assessing conscious recollection, then the amnesics have residual conscious memory. Using the process dissociation procedure, one could assess whether the cued recall performance reflects conscious recollection or unconscious uses of memory. When there are opposite effects of a manipulation on conscious and unconscious memory, those effects can be identified, and precise estimates can be obtained. Furthermore, one is not confined to investigation of conscious and unconscious influences in separate tasks, but can instead investigate tasks in which both processes contribute to performance.

E. Phenomenology of Memory

One defining difference between implicit and explicit memory has to do with subjective, phenomenal experience: Implicit memory refers to the influence of specific past experiences unaccompanied by subjective awareness of remembering, whereas explicit remembering refers to uses of memory that are accompanied by the subjective experience of remembering. Thus, a central aspect of the implicit/explicit distinction is conscious experience, and study of implicit memory can be viewed as part of cognitive psychology's renewed interest in consciousness (cf. Johnson's, 1988, "experimental phenomenology," and Tulving's, 1985b, discussion of forms of awareness).

Given that people can use memories from specific prior experiences without feeling that they are remembering (as on an indirect test), what is it that gives rise to the subjective feeling of remembering? For example, when an image comes to mind, what leads one to identify that image as a memory of a specific past experience, rather than as a product of current fantasy or perception? From the separate-systems viewpoint, this question has a simple answer: Use of the explicit memory system (e.g., Tulving's (1985b) episodic system) is accompanied by the subjective experience of remembering, whereas use of the implicit memory system (e.g., Tulving & Schacter's, 1990, PRS) is not. In contrast, according to proceduralist views, the same underlying memory system serves uses of memory with and without the subjective experience of remembering, and the feeling of remembering is the result of an unconscious decision-making process by which mental events are attributed to particular sources. The feeling of remembering is experienced when a current mental event is attributed to the use of memory (Jacoby et al., 1989; Johnson, 1988).

Gardiner and associates (e.g., Gardiner, 1988; Gardiner & Java, 1991; Gardiner & Parkin, 1991; see also Tulving, 1985b) have reported a series of studies in which subjects were asked to indicate, for each item on a recognition memory test, whether they (1) recollected encountering that item on the study list ("remember"); (2) felt they had encountered the item on the study list but did not remember the specifics of its presentation ("know"); or (3) did not believe the item was on the study list ("new"). Manipulations of factors associated with episodic memory (e.g., levels of processing) affected the number of "remember" responses but did not affect the number of "know" responses. Gardiner and his co-workers have interpreted such findings as evidence that the subjective experience of remembering accompanies use of an episodic memory system, whereas use of a semantic memory system gives rise to a less differentiated feeling of knowing or believing that one had recently encountered an item.

Although the dissociations between "remember" and "know" are consistent with a separate systems view, they do not compel it because other approaches would make the same prediction. For example, dual-process models of recognition propose that retrieval or recollection is dependent on elaborative processing, whereas familiarity is dependent on the repetition of operations. To the extent that recollection can be identified with reports of "remember" and familiarity can be identified with reports of "know," dual-process models would make the same prediction regarding the effects of levels of processing and other manipulations as does the separate systems view. Finally, as pointed out by Jacoby, Yonelinas, and Jennings (in press), Gardiner's approach assumes that remembering and knowing are mutually exclusive, that is, one cannot simultaneously know and remember. The assumptions of exclusivity versus independence dramatically change how one analyzes the data in a "remember"/"know" paradigm. Regardless of whether one takes a separate systems view or a proceduralist view, the two bases for responding are not necessarily mutually exclusive. Jacoby et al. presented a number of findings to support the hypothesis that conscious recollection and the memory effects that are tapped by performance on indirect tests operate independently, and that these processes underlie reports of remembering and knowing, respectively. By the independence assumption, the two processes can co-occur. In the terms used to describe the process dissociation procedure, a process of conscious recollection can lead one to have a memory of a studied item while simultaneously an unconscious process can lead the item to come to mind, although conscious recollection may dominate experience and so cause one to describe the experience as "remembering" rather than "knowing." (For a full explanation of the independence versus exclusivity relations between processes, see Jones, 1987.)

The proceduralist claim is that mental events that are based on the use of memories of prior experiences have characteristic qualities that serve to differentiate them from other kinds of mental events. For example, visual images based on retrieval of memories of past perceptions are generally more vivid and more easily generated than are visual images generated anew using imagination, a characteristic that Jacoby (e.g., Jacoby et al., 1989) termed "fluency." People also judge thoughts as memories when those thoughts can be placed in an ongoing context of events, what Johnson (1988) referred to as "embeddedness." Based on these qualitative characteristics and on the rememberer's current orientation and expectations, products of memory are identified as such, hence giving rise to the subjective experience of remembering. Generally, this attribution process is performed very quickly and automatically, without awareness of any decision-making processes. Moreover, most of the time such source-attributions are accurate: Products of memory are identified as memories and products of imagery or fantasy are identified as such. Sometimes, however, the products of ongoing cognitive processes such as thinking or imagining have qualitative characteristics that are typical of memories. For example, sometimes a newly generated image is unusually vivid, detailed, and easily generated. Such vivid and easily generated products of imagination may be misidentified as memories, particularly if the person is oriented toward the past when the image is generated. A vivid image that pops to mind during an attempt to remember some past event may, therefore, give rise to an illusory feeling of remembering. Experimental manipulations that cause nonstudied items to come easily to mind during a memory test can lead subjects to believe that they remember seeing those items in the study list (Lindsay & Kelley, in press). Similarly, manipulations that facilitate the perception of nonstudied items on a recognition memory test can lead subjects falsely to recognize those items as things presented in the study list (Jacoby & Whitehouse, 1989; Whittlesea, 1993; Whittlesea, Jacoby, & Girard, 1990).

By identifying the attributes that give rise to the subjective experience of remembering, the nature of the deficits found in amnesia could be pinpointed (see also Hirst, 1989; Johnson, Hashtroudi, & Lindsay, 1993). What is it that normals do, and amnesics do not do, that enables the former to have the subjective experience of remembering past experiences? Note that this question is important regardless of whether one conceptualizes amnesia as the result of an impaired episodic memory system or as the result of deficits in particular kinds of cognitive processing. The fact that even very densely amnesic people are able to have the subjective experience of remembering pre-onset experiences suggests that the deficit is in cognitive processes performed at acquisition rather than in the attribution-making processes themselves. One appealing possibility is that amnesics do not "knit together" or embed various aspects of their ongoing experience in the same ways that normal subjects do (Huppert & Piercy, 1978; Johnson, 1992; Mayes, 1992; Mayes, Muedell, & Pickering, 1985; but see Tulving et al., 1991). Thus, although capable of abstract conceptual thinking, amnesics may not integrate their ongoing conceptual, perceptual, and affective processing, and may not integrate current processing with prior and future processing, in the same ways that normals do. Thus, amnesics demonstrate transfer when the testing situation provides a close repetition of prior operations, yet are unable to retrieve memories of other aspects of a past experience when cued with some aspects (as on a recognition or cued recall test).

V. SUMMARY

Research on implicit and explicit memory has advanced substantially in recent years. Theorists oriented toward multiple-systems accounts have begun to specify the processes and functions performed by different hypothetical systems, and the evidence for such systems has become substantially more sophisticated and detailed. Advances in this direction have drawn on developments in neuroscience, and work in this area provides a model for the useful interaction between psychologists and neuroscientists. Similarly, proponents of processing views have begun further to define and specify the nature and characteristics of hypothetical processes and to explore in greater detail the relationships between tasks, processes, and memory performance. Progress along these lines has drawn on comparisons between multiple tasks and fine-grained task analyses.

Ultimately, the same questions must be answered by psychologists who favor the separate systems view and by those who favor the processing view. For example, to account for the pattern of impaired and preserved memory in amnesia, theorists oriented toward processing accounts must specify what kinds of cognitive processes are not performed by amnesics, and that explanation must be consistent with other features of amnesia (e.g., spared ability to perform a variety of conceptual processing tasks; spared ability consciously to remember pre-onset events; and spared ability to demonstrate memory on indirect tests). Similarly, proponents of systems views must ultimately specify the nature and operation of the systems. Thus, eventually, proponents of both approaches must grapple with the same issues.

References

Bassilli, J. N., Smith, M. C., & Macleod, C. M. (1989). Auditory and visual word-stem completion: Separating data-driven and conceptually driven processes. *Quarterly Journal of Experimental Psychology, 41A,* 439–453.

Biederman, I., & Cooper, E. E. (1991). Priming contour-deleted images: Evidence for intermediate representations in visual object recognition. *Cognitive Psychology, 23,* 393–419.

Biederman, I., & Cooper, E. E. (1992). Size invariance in visual object priming. *Journal of Experimental Psychology: Human Perception and Performance, 18,* 121–133.

Blaxton, T. A. (1989). Investigating dissociations among memory measures: Support for a transfer-appropriate processing framework. *Journal of Experimental Psychology: Learning, Memory, and Cognition, 15,* 657–668.

Bowers, J. S., & Schacter, D. L. (1991). Implicit memory and test awareness. *Journal of Experimental Psychology: Learning, Memory, and Cognition, 16,* 404–416.

Cave, C. B., & Squire, L. R. (1992). Intact and long-lasting repetition priming in amnesia. *Journal of Experimental Psychology: Learning, Memory, and Cognition, 18,* 509–520.

Cermak, L. S., Chandler, K., & Wolbarst, C. R. (1985). The perceptual priming phenomena in amnesia. *Neuropsychologist, 23,* 615–622.

Challis, B. H., & Brodbeck, D. R. (1992). Level of processing affects priming in word fragment completion. *Journal of Experimental Psychology: Learning, Memory, and Cognition, 18,* 595–607.

Chiarello, C., & Hoyer, W. J. (1988). Adult age differences in implicit and explicit memory: time course and encoding effects. *Psychology and Aging, 3,* 358–366.

Claparede, E. (1951). Recognition and "me-ness." in D. Rapaport (Ed.), *Organization and pathology of thought* (pp. 58–75). New York: Columbia University Press. (Reprinted from *Archives de Psychologie* (1911) *11,* 79–90)

Coltheart, M. (1989). Implicit memory and the functional architecture of cognition. In S. Lewandowsky, J. C. Dunn, & K. Kirsner (Eds.), *Implicit memory: Theoretical issues* (pp. 285–297). Hillsdale, NJ: Erlbaum.

Cooper, L. A., & Schacter, D. L. (1992). Dissociations between structural and episodic representations of visual objects. *Current Directions in Psychological Science, 1,* 141–146.

Cooper, L. A., Schacter, D. L., Ballesteros, S., & Moore, C. (1992). Priming and recognition of transformed three-dimensional objects: effects of size and retention. *Journal of Experimental Psychology: Learning, Memory, and Cognition, 18,* 43–57.

Diamond, R., & Rozin, P. (1984). Activation of exiting memories in anterograde amnesia. *Journal of Abnormal Psychology, 93,* 98–105.

Dunn, J. C., & Kirsner, K. (1988). Discovering functionally independent mental processes: The principle of reversed association. *Psychological Review, 95,* 91–101.

Dunn, J. C., & Kirsner, K. (1989). Implicit memory: Task or process? In S. Lewandowsky, J. C. Dunn, & K. Kirsner (Eds.), *Implicit memory: Theoretical issues* (pp. 17–31). Hillsdale, NJ: Erlbaum.

Eich, E. (1984). Memory for unattended events: Remembering with and without awareness. *Memory & Cognition, 12,* 105–111.

Gardiner, J. M. (1988). Functional aspects of recollective experience. *Memory & Cognition, 16,* 309–313.

Gardiner, J. M., & Java, R. I. (1991). Forgetting in recognition memory with and without recollective experience. *Memory & Cognition, 19,* 617–623.

Gardiner, J. M., & Parkin, A. J. (1991). Attention and recollective experience in recognition memory. *Memory & Cognition, 18,* 579–583.

Gardner, H., Boller, F., Moreines, J., & Butters, N. (1973). Retrieving information from Korsakoff patients: Effects of categorical cues and reference to the task. *Cortex, 9,* 165–75.

Glisky, F. L., Schacter, D. C., & Tulving, F. (1986). Learning and retention of computer-related vocabulary in memory-impaired patients: Method of vanishing cues. *Journal of Clinical and Experimental Neuropsychology, 8,* 292–312.

Graf, P., & Mandler, G. (1984). Activation makes words more accessible, but not necessarily more retrievable. *Journal of Verbal Learning and Verbal Behavior, 23,* 553–568.

Graf, P., Mandler, G., & Haden, P. E. (1982). Simulating amnesic symptoms in normal subjects. *Science, 218,* 1243–1244.

Graf, P., & Ryan, L. (1990). Transfer-appropriate processing for implicit and explicit memory. *Journal of Experimental Psychology: Learning, Memory, and Cognition, 16,* 978–992.

Graf, P., & Schacter, D. L. (1985). Implicit and explicit memory for new associations in normal and amnesic subjects. *Journal of Experimental Psychology: Learning, Memory, and Cognition, 11,* 501–518.

Graf, P., Shimamura, A. P., & Squire, L. R. (1985). Priming across modalities and priming across category levels: Extending the domain of preserved function in amnesia. *Journal of Experimental Psychology: Learning, Memory, and Cognition, 11,* 386–396.

Graf, P., Squire, L. R., & Mandler, G. (1984). The information that amnesic patients do not forget. *Journal of Experimental Psychology: Learning, Memory, and Cognition, 10,* 164–178.

Haist, F., Musen, G., & Squire, L. R. (1991). Intact priming of words and nonwords in amnesia. *Psychobiology, 19,* 275–285.

Hamann, S. B. (1990). Level-of-processing effects in conceptually driven implicit tasks. *Journal of Experimental Psychology: Learning, Memory, and Cognition, 16,* 970–977.

Hayman, C. A. G., & Tulving, E. (1989a). Contingent dissociation between recognition and fragment completion: The method of triangulation. *Journal of Experimental Psychology: Learning, Memory, and Cognition, 15,* 228–240.

Hayman, C. A. G., & Tulving, E. (1989b). Is priming in fragment completion based on a "traceless" memory system? *Journal of Experimental Psychology: Learning, Memory, and Cognition, 15,* 941–956.

Hinztman, K. L. (1991). Contingency analyses, hypotheses, and artifacts: Reply to Flexser and to Gardiner. *Journal of Experimental Psychology: Learning, Memory, and Cognition, 17,* 341–345.

Hintzman, D. L., & Hartry, A. L. (1990). Item effects in recognition and fragment completion: Contingency relations vary for different subsets of words. *Journal of Experimental Psychology: Learning, Memory, and Cognition, 16,* 955–969.

Hirst, W. (1989). On consciousness, recall, recognition, and the architecture of memory. In S. Lewandowsky, J. C. Dunn, & K. Kirsner (Eds.), *Implicit memory: Theoretical issues* (pp. 33–46). Hillsdale, NJ: Erlbaum.

Howard, D. V. (1988). Implicit and explicit assessment of cognitive aging. In M. L. Howe & C. J. Brainerd (Eds.), *Cognitive development in adulthood: Progress in cognitive development research* (pp. 3–37). New York: Springer-Verlag.

Humphreys, M. S., Bain, J. D., & Burt, J. S. (1989). Episodically unique and generalized memories: Applications to human and animal amnesics. In S. Lewandowsky, J. C. Dunn, & K. Kirsner (Eds.), *Implicit memory: Theoretical issues* (pp. 139–156). Hillsdale, NJ: Erlbaum.

Humphreys, M. S., Bain, J. D., & Pike, R. (1989). Different ways to cue a coherent memory system: A theory for episodic, semantic, and procedural tasks. *Psychological Review, 96,* 208–233.

Hunt, R. R., & Toth, J. P. (1990). Perceptual identification, fragment completion, and free recall: Concepts and data. *Journal of Experimental Psychology: Learning, Memory, and Cognition, 16,* 282–290.

Huppert, F. A., & Piercy, M. (1978). The role of trace strength in recency and frequency judgments by amnesic and control subjects. *Quarterly Journal of Experimental Psychology, 30,* 347–354.

Jacoby, L. L. (1983a). Perceptual enhancement: Persistent effects of an experience. *Journal of Experimental Psychology: Learning, Memory, and Cognition, 9,* 21–38.

Jacoby, L. L. (1983b). Remembering the data: Analyzing interactive processes in reading. *Journal of Verbal Learning and Verbal Behavior, 22,* 485–508.

Jacoby, L. L. (1991). A process dissociation framework: Separating automatic from intentional uses of memory. *Journal of Memory and Language, 30,* 513–541.

Jacoby, L. L., & Dallas, M. (1981). On the relationship between autobiographical memory and perceptual learning. *Journal of Experimental Psychology: General, 3,* 306–340.

Jacoby, L. L., & Hayman, G. A. (1987). Specific visual transfer in word identification. *Journal of Experimental Psychology: Learning, Memory, and Cognition, 13,* 456–463.

Jacoby, L. L., Kelley, C. M., & Dywan, J. (1989). Memory attributions. In H. L. Roediger & F. I. M. Craik (Eds.), *Varieties of memory and consciousness: Essays in honour of Endel Tulving* (pp. 391–422). Hillsdale, NJ: Erlbaum.

Jacoby, L. L., Toth, J. P., & Yonelinas, A. P. (1993). Separating conscious and unconscious influences of memory: Measuring recollection. *Journal of Experimental Psychology: General, 122,* 139–154.

Jacoby, L. L., & Whitehouse, K. (1989). An illusion of memory: False recognition influenced by unconscious perception. *Journal of Experimental Psychology: General, 118,* 126–135.

Jacoby, L. L., & Witherspoon, D. (1982). Remembering without awareness. *Canadian Journal of Psychology, 36,* 300–324.

Jacoby, L. L., Yonelinas, A. P., & Jennings, J. (in press). The relation between conscious and unconscious (automatic) influences: A declaration of independence. In J. Cohen & J. W. Schooler (Eds.), *Scientific approaches to the question of consciousness.* Hillsdale, NJ: Erlbaum.

Johnson, M. K. (1988). Reality monitoring: An experimental phenomenological approach. *Journal of Experimental Psychology: General, 117,* 390–394.

Johnson, M. K. (1992). MEM: Mechanisms of recollection. *Journal of Cognitive Neuroscience, 4,* 268–280.

Johnson, M. K., & Hasher, L. (1987). Human learning and memory. *Annual Review of Psychology, 38,* 631–638.

Johnson, M. K., Hashtroudi, S., & Lindsay, D. S. (1993). Source monitoring. *Psychological Bulletin, 114,* 3–28.

Johnson, M. K., & Hirst, W. (1993). MEM: Cognitive subsystems as processes. In A. Collins, M. Conway, S. Gathercole, & P. Morris (Eds.), *Theories of memory.* Hillsdale, NJ: Erlbaum.

Jones, G. V. (1987). Independence and exclusivity among psychological processes: Implications for the structure of recall. *Psychological Review, 94,* 229–235.

Kirsner, K., Dunn, J. C., & Standen, P. (1989). Domain-specific resources in word recognition. In S. Lewandowsky, J. C. Dunn, & K. Kirsner (Eds.), *Implicit memory: Theoretical issues* (pp. 99–122). Hillsdale, NJ: Erlbaum.

Kolers, P. A., & Roediger, H. L. (1984). Procedures of mind. *Journal of Verbal Learning and Verbal Behavior, 23,* 425–449.

Kosslyn, S. M., & Intriligator, J. R. (1992). Is cognitive neuropsychology plausible? The perils of sitting on a one-legged stool. *Journal of Cognitive Neuroscience, 4,* 96–106.

Kosslyn, S. M., & Van Kleeck, M. H. (1990). Broken brains and normal minds: Why Humpty-Dumpty needs a skeleton. In E. L. Schwartz (Ed.), *Computational neuroscience.* Cambridge: MIT Press.

Light, L. L., & Singh, A. (1987). Implicit and explicit memory in young and older adults. *Journal of Experimental Psychology: Learning, Memory, and Cognition, 13,* 531–541.

Lindsay, D. S., & Kelley, C. M. (1996). Creating illusions of familiarity in a cued recall Remember/Know paradigm. *Journal of Memory and Language, 35,* 197–211.

Loftus, G. (1978). On interpretation of interactions. *Memory and Cognition, 6,* 312–319.

Mandler, G. (1980). Recognizing: The judgment of previous occurrence. *Psychological Review, 87,* 252–271.

Mayes, A. R. (1992). Automatic memory processes in amnesia: How are they mediated? In A. D. Milner & M. D. Rugg (Eds.), *The neuropsychology of consciousness* (pp. 235–261). San Diego: Academic Press.

Mayes, A. R., Meudell, P. R., & Pickering, A. D. (1985). Is organic amnesia caused by a selective deficit in remembering contextual information? *Cortex, 21,* 313–324.

Morris, C. D., Bransford, J. D., & Franks, J. J. (1977). Levels of processing versus transfer appropriate processing. *Journal of Verbal Learning and Verbal Behavior, 16,* 519–533.

Morton, J. (1979). Facilitation in word recognition: Experiments causing change in the logogen model. In P. A. Kolers, M. E. Wrolstal, & H. Bouma (Eds.), *Processing of visible language* (Vol. 1, pp. 259–268). New York: Plenum.

Moscovitch, M. (1982). Multiple dissociations of function in amnesia. In L. Cermak (Ed.), *Human memory and amnesia* (pp. 337–370). Hillsdale, NJ: Erlbaum.

Moscovitch, M. (1984). The sufficient conditions for demonstrating preserved memory in amnesia: A task analysis. In L. R. Squire & N. Butters (Eds.), *Neuropsychology of memory* (pp. 104–113). New York: Guilford.

Musen, G., & Squire, L. R. (1991). Normal acquisition of novel verbal information in amnesia. *Journal of Experimental Psychology: Learning, Memory, and Cognition, 17,* 1095–1104.

Musen, G., & Squire, L. R. (1992). Nonverbal priming in amnesia. *Memory & Cognition, 20,* 441–448.

Nelson, D. L., Schreiber, T. A., & McEvoy, C. L. (1992). Processing implicit and explicit representations. *Psychological Review, 99,* 322–348.

Parkin, A. J., Reid, T. K., & Russo, R. (1990). On the differential nature of implicit and explicit memory. *Memory & Cognition, 18,* 507–514.

Plaut, D. C., & Farah, M. J. (1990). Visual object representation: Interpreting neurophysiological data within a computational framework. *Journal of Cognitive Neuroscience, 2,* 320–343.

Rajaram, S., & Roediger, H. L. (1993). Direct comparison of four implicit memory tests. *Journal of Experimental Psychology: Learning, Memory, and Cognition, 19,* 765–776.

Richardson-Klavehn, A., & Bjork, R. A. (1988). Measures of memory. *Annual Review of Psychology, 39,* 475–543.

Roediger, H. L. (1990). Implicit memory: Retention without remembering. *American Psychologist, 45,* 1043–1056.

Roediger, H. L., & Blaxton, T. A. (1987). Retrieval modes produce dissociations in memory for surface information. In D. Gorfein & R. R. Hoffman (Eds.), *Memory and cognitive processes: The Ebbinghaus Centennial Conference* (pp. 349–379). Hillsdale, NJ: Erlbaum.

Roediger, H. L., & McDermott, K. B. (1993). Implicit memory in normal human subjects. In F. Boller & J. Grafman (Eds.), *Handbook of neuropsychology* (Vol. 8, pp. 63–130). New York: Elsevier.

Roediger, H. L., Srinivas, K., & Weldon, M. S. (1989). Dissociations between implicit measures of retention. In S. Lewandowsky, J. C. Dunn, & K. Kirsner (Eds.), *Implicit memory: Theoretical issues* (pp. 67–84). Hillsdale, NJ: Erlbaum.

Roediger, H. L., Weldon, M. S., & Challis, B. H. (1989). Explaining dissociations between implicit and explicit measures of retention: A processing account. In H. L. Roediger & F. I. M. Craik (Eds.), *Varieties of memory and consciousness: Essays in honour of Endel Tulving* (pp. 355–389). Hillsdale, NJ: Erlbaum.

Roediger, H. L., Weldon, M. S., Stadler, M. L., & Riegler, G. L. (1992). Direct comparison of two implicit memory tests: Word fragment and word stem completion. *Journal of Experimental Psychology: Learning, Memory, and Cognition, 18,* 1251–1269.

Rozin, P. (1976). The psychobiological approach to human memory. In M. R. Rosenzweig & E. L. Bennett (Eds.), *Neural mechanisms of learning and memory* (pp. 3–48). Cambridge: MIT Press.

Rozin, P., & Schull, J. (1988). The adaptive-evolutionary point of view in experimental psychology. In R. C. Atkinson, R. J. Hernstein, G. Lindzey, & R. D. Luce (Eds.), *Handbook of experimental psychology* (pp. 503–546). New York: Wiley (Interscience).

Schacter, D. L. (1985). Priming of old and new knowledge in amnesic patients and normal subjects. *Annals of the New York Academy of Science, 444,* 44–53.

Schacter, D. L. (1987). Implicit memory: History and current status. *Journal of Experimental Psychology: Learning, Memory, and Cognition, 13,* 501–518.

Schacter, D. L. (1990). Perceptual representation systems and implicit memory: Toward a resolution of the multiple memory systems debate. In A. Diamond (Ed.), *Development and neural bases of higher cognitive functions. Annals of the New York Academy of Sciences, 608,* 543–571.

Schacter, D. L. (1992a). Understanding implicit memory: A cognitive neuroscience approach. *American Psychologist, 47,* 559–569.

Schacter, D. L. (1992b). Priming and multiple memory systems: Perceptual mechanisms of implicit memory. *Journal of Cognitive Neuroscience, 4,* 244–256.

Schacter, D. L., Bowers, J., & Booker, J. (1989). Intention, awareness, and implicit memory: The retrieval intentionality criterion. In S. Lewandowsky, J. C. Dunn, & K. Kirsner (Eds.), *Implicit memory: Theoretical issues* (pp. 47–65). Hillsdale, NJ: Erlbaum.

Schacter, D. L., Chiu, C.-Y., & Ochsner, K. N. (1993). Implicit memory: A selective review. *Annual Review of Neuroscience, 16,* 159–182.

Schacter, D. L., Cooper, L. A., & Delaney, S. M. (1990). Implicit memory for unfamiliar objects depends on access to structural descriptions. *Journal of Experimental Psychology: General, 119,* 5–24.

Schacter, D. L., Cooper, L. A., Delaney, S. M., Peterson, M. A., & Tharan, M. (1991). Implicit memory for possible and impossible objects: Constraints on the construction of structural descriptions. *Journal of Experimental Psychology: Learning, Memory, and Cognition, 17,* 3–19.

Schacter, D. L., Cooper, L. A., Tharan, M., & Rubens, A. B. (1991). Preserved priming of novel objects in patients with memory disorders. *Journal of Cognitive Neuroscience, 3,* 118–131.

Shallice, T. (1988). *From neuropsychology to mentral structure.* Cambridge: Cambridge University Press.

Sherry, D. F., & Schacter, D. L. (1987). The evolution of multiple memory systems. *Psychological Review, 94,* 439–454.

Shimamura, A. P. (1985). Problems with the finding of stochastic independence as evidence for multiple memory systems. *Bulletin of the Psychonomic Society, 23,* 506–508.

Shimamura, A. P., & Squire, L. R. (1984). Paired associate learning and priming effects in amnesia: A neuropsychological study. *Journal of Experimental Psychology: General, 113,* 556–570.

Shimamura, A. P., & Squire, L. R. (1989). Impaired priming of new associations in amnesia. *Journal of Experimental Psychology: Learning, Memory, and Cognition, 15,* 721–728.

Slamecka, N. J. (1985). Ebbinghaus: Some associations. *Journal of Experimental Psychology: Learning, Memory, and Cognition, 11,* 414–435.

Slameka, N. J., & Graf, P. (1978). The generation effect: Delineation of a phenomenon. *Journal of Experimental Psychology: Human Learning and Memory, 4,* 592–604.

Squire, L. R. (1992a). Memory and the hippocampus: A synthesis from findings with rats, monkeys, and humans. *Psychological Review, 99,* 195–231.

Squire, L. R. (1992b). Declarative and nondeclarative memory: Multiple brain systems supporting learning and memory. *Journal of Cognitive Neuroscience, 4,* 232–243.

Squire, L. R., Knowlton, B., & Musen, G. (1993). The structure and organization of memory. *Annual Review of Psychology, 44,* 453–495.

Squire, L. R., & Zola-Morgan, S. (1991). The medial temporal lobe memory system. *Science, 253,* 1380–1386.

Srinivas, K. (1993). Perceptual specificity in nonverbal priming. *Journal of Experimental Psychology: Learning, Memory, and Cognition, 19,* 582–602.

Srinivas, K., & Roediger, H. L. (1990). Testing the nature of two implicit tests: Category association and anagram solution. *Journal of Memory and Language, 29,* 389–412.

Teitelbaum, P., & Pellis, S. M. (1992). Toward a synthetic physiological psychology. *Psychological Science, 3,* 4–20.

Tenpenny, P. L., & Shoben, E. J. (1992). Component processes and the utility of the conceptually-driven/data-driven distinction. *Journal of Experimental Psychology: Learning, Memory, and Cognition, 18,* 25–42.

Toth, J. P., & Hunt, R. R. (1990). Effect of generation on a word-identification task. *Journal of Experimental Psychology: Learning, Memory, and Cognition, 16,* 993–1003.

Tulving, E. (1985a). How many memory systems are there? *American Psychologist, 40,* 385–398.

Tulving, E. (1985b). Memory and consciousness. *Canadian Psychologist, 26,* 1–12.

Tulving, E. (1993). What is episodic memory? *Current Directions in Psychological Science, 2,* 67–70.

Tulving, E., Hayman, C. A. G., & Macdonald, C. A. (1991). Longlasting perceptual priming and semantic learning in amnesia: A case experiment. *Journal of Experimental Psychology: Learning, Memory, and Cognition, 17,* 595–617.

Tulving, E., & Schacter, D. L. (1990). Priming and human memory systems. *Science, 247,* 301–306.

Tulving, E., Schacter, D. L., & Stark, H. A. (1982). Priming effects in word-fragment completion are independent of recognition memory. *Journal of Experimental Psychology: Learning, Memory, and Cognition, 8,* 336–342.

Warrington, E. K., & Shallice, T. (1980). Word-form dyslexia. *Brain, 103,* 99–112.

Warrington, E. K., & Weiskrantz, L. (1970). Amnesic syndrome: Consolidation or retrieval? *Nature, 228,* 628–630.

Weldon, M. S. (1991). Mechanisms underlying priming on perceptual tests. *Journal of Experimental Psychology: Learning, Memory, and Cognition, 17,* 526–541.

Whittlesea, B. W. A. (1993). Illusions of familiarity. *Journal of Experimental Psychology; Learning, Memory, and Cognition, 19,* 1235–1253.

Whittlesea, B. W., Jacoby, L. L., & Girard, K. (1990). Illusions of immediate memory: Evidence of an attributional basis for feelings of familiarity and perceptual quality. *Journal of Memory and Language, 29,* 716–732.

Witherspoon, D., & Moscovitch, M. (1989). Stochastic independence between two implicit memory tasks. *Journal of Experimental Psychology: Learning, Memory, and Cognition, 15,* 22–30.

Transient
Memories

CHAPTER 3

Sensory and Perceptual Storage
Data and Theory

Dominic W. Massaro
Geoffrey R. Loftus

Like William James's opinion that everyone knows what attention is, we all think we know what sensory storage is. Pashler and Carrier's introductory chapter in this volume set the foundation for the prototypical information processing model. Preperceptual (what we also call sensory) storage is usually designated as the first box in the information processing chain. The decade and a half beginning about 1960 was concerned with the properties of this initial storage structure. A variety of paradigms were brought to bear on the issue and a reasonable convergence of opinion was established. Neisser (1967) and many others to follow envisioned an iconic store of around a quarter of a second and an echoic store of several seconds.

Notwithstanding our understanding, one limitation was that the theorists were not clear about what they meant by sensory storage. Neisser (1967), for example, envisioned auditory sensory store as functional for the foreigner who is told, "No, not zeal, seal." The listener would not profit from this feedback if the /z/ was not maintained long enough to compare it to the /s/. If this were what was meant by sensory memory, however, then we should not have been so concerned with its time course. We must have an auditory perceptual memory that allows us to recognize not only the difference between the recently spoken "zeal" and "seal," but also a spoken word we have not heard for years. In this review, we make a clear

Memory

distinction between sensory storage and perceptual memory. Sensory storage is the initial maintenance of a stimulus event for immediate processing. Its duration sets the limit on how much time is available for processing. Perceptual memory is one of the outcomes of processing the sensory storage. Its life span is orders of magnitude longer than sensory storage.

In Section I in this chapter, we review the literature aimed at describing characteristics of initial visual storage and briefly sketch early conceptualizations of iconic memory. In Section II, we present an analogous treatment of initial auditory storage. In both domains, we use a semichronological organization to present findings from the three major tasks that have been used to study both visual and auditory sensory storage: partial report, backward masking, and subjective estimation of phenomenal presence. In Section III, we address how the early conceptions of the icon have changed over recent years in response to certain seemingly contradictory results about its nature and, in Section IV, we discuss a new linear-systems approach for thinking about iconic storage and visual information processing that reconciles these apparently contradictory results within a unitary framework. In Sections V and VI, we review the evidence for multiple types of perceptual memories as opposed to stores for more abstract or symbolic information and discuss the issue of how such perceptual memories or stores should be represented, if at all, within models of information processing.

I. VISUAL SENSORY STORE

It has been recognized for centuries that the perceptual experience of a briefly presented visual stimulus outlasts the stimulus itself. This phenomenon can easily be demonstrated in any perception laboratory; one need only present a visual stimulus very briefly (e.g., for 10 ms) and follow it by darkness. The resulting experience is that the stimulus fades away over a period of perhaps 300 ms. Indeed, naive observers believe it to be the physical stimulus that is fading, supposing perhaps that the bulb in the projecting device is extinguishing slowly rather than abruptly. Such an observer is surprised to learn that the fading is a mental rather than a physical event. Neisser's (1967) dubbing this visual sensory memory "iconic" was adopted by the field.

A. Visual Partial-Report Task

The first person to use this task was George Sperling in his seminal 1960 study. He realized that a whole report of a visual display of test characters was limited by the number of items that could be held in short-term memory (Miller, 1956). Bypassing this limitation using a partial report, Sperling could study the extraction of information from the iconic image and its placement into short-term memory. In a typical partial-report experiment, the stimulus might consist of a 4 (columns) × 3 (rows) array of letters in which only a single row was to be reported. The to-be-reported row (top, middle, or bottom) would be signaled by a tone (high, medium, or low frequency) that occurred sometime following stimulus offset. Total available information was estimated by multiplying the number of reported letters per row by the number of rows in the stimulus array. Sperling found that much more information was being held in a sensory store that decayed rapidly after stimulus offset. Before this hypothesis could be accepted, however, Sperling and other investigators realized that both short-term memory and loss of location information had to be eliminated as possible influences on the results.

As with any task, no matter how simple, performance in the partial-report task is multiply determined. Specifically, a performance decrease with a cue-delay increase could be a simple function of loss of information from short-term memory (STM). Sperling (1960) recognized this possibility and tested it with a different kind of partial-report cue. Two rows of four items each were presented with two digits and two consonants randomly mixed in each row. In this case the high or low tone cue indicated which category (letter or digit) to report. Performance in this condition was no better than that occurring in a whole report. This experiment and many to follow indicated that a decrease in partial-report performance with increases in cue delay could be demonstrated when a loss of STM was not responsible for the results.

There is no doubt that performance decreases with increases in the delay between the test display and the partial-report cue. Traditionally, it was assumed that the decrease in performance reflected the time to encode the test items in the display. When the partial-report cue came early, there would be plenty of time to switch attention to the cued row and selectively process the appropriate items while they were still in the visual sensory store. With increases in the delay of the cue, subjects become limited to what would normally be given in a whole report. In this interpretation, it is the identity of the letters that is critical for performance.

Mewhort and colleagues (Mewhort, Campbell, Marchetti, & Campbell, 1981) on the other hand, argue that most of the subjects were making errors on the location of the critical letters, not on their identities. This interpretation assumes that the letters have been recognized and that the delay in the cue presentation leads to poorer performance because of the participant forgetting the location of the test letters. The important influences that have been uncovered between identity and location information and the relationship between the two were not in the literature at the time of Sperling's (1960) and related investigations. We now know that location and identity are processed by somewhat independent channels in the visual system, and these two dimensions must be integrated (Treisman, 1986; Treisman & Gelade, 1980). Certainly, accurate performance given a partial-report cue requires that both of these dimensions be accurate.

Lupker and Massaro's (1979) study, however, showed that resolving the identity of the test letter is a time-extended process, and the partial-report advantage cannot simply be due to a loss of short-term memory or location information. They presented a display of four items positioned on the corners of an imaginary square centered around a fixation point. A single target letter, chosen from the set E, I, F, and T, was presented. The other three characters in the display were either all zero or all a hybrid letter highly confusable with the target letters. The 10-ms display was preceded or followed by a cue indicating the position of the target letter. The cue was either an arrow pointing to the target or a pattern mask positioned at the same location as the target.

The arrow cue improved performance if it was presented within 200 ms of the display. As often noted, the advantage of performance in the cuing condition could simply be due to less forgetting from short-term memory. Similarly, the location-forgetting hypothesis would state that this advantage is due to the forgetting of location information with increases in arrow cue delay. Given these alternative hypotheses, performance with the pattern mask cue is central to the experiment.

If the decreased performance with increases in cue delay were simply due to a loss of short-term memory or location information, the pattern mask cue should be an equally effective cue. Given that the items would be in a symbolic form, performance should be better with a shorter interval between the test display and the cue. However, the pattern mask cue was found to disrupt performance rather than to improve performance. The pattern mask cue actually produced a masking function: performance improved with increases in cue delay. Thus, it is reasonable to conclude that letter identification is a time-extended process that can be facilitated by an arrow cue but interfered with by a pattern mask.

B. Visual Backward Recognition Masking

Loftus and Hogden (1988) studied visual backward recognition masking (VBRM) in a picture memory task. Subjects studied naturalistic, colored pictures presented for 40 ms each. The pictures were presented alone or followed by a noise mask after some blank interstimulus interval (ISI). The mask was a jumble of black lines on a white background. Perceptual performance was assessed by memory performance in a later recognition test. Performance improved with increases in the ISI out to about 300 ms at which time it reached the level of the no-mask condition. These results replicated the findings from a plethora of studies carried out with alphanumeric test items, and they showed an impressive correspondence between their estimate of visual sensory memory and the estimate reached in the partial-report tasks. Even more striking is the fact that the results from these VBRM studies are exactly analogous to those from studies investigating auditory information processing, as detailed in the next section.

C. Estimation of Visible Persistence

The second perceptual event around which the concept of iconic store was intimately entwined was phenomenological appearance. Aside from an observer's ability to extract information from a stimulus, the stimulus appears consciously present to one degree or another, and stimulus appearance, like available information, fades gradually following stimulus offset. The duration of phenomenological presence following stimulus offset can be measured in various ways: the most simple and direct is a synchrony-judgment procedure in which a stimulus is followed after some ISI by a salient signal such as an audible click. The ISI is under the control of the subject, whose task is to set the interval such that the stimulus seems to have phenomenologically disappeared at the exact instant that the click occurs. The magnitude of the ISI is then taken to be the iconic image's duration.

D. Early Conceptions of Iconic Memory

The general conception of iconic memory that emerged from these three types of studies is presented in Figure 1, which assumes a visual stimulus presented for a (somewhat arbitrary) duration of 40 ms, and depicts what is referred to as "magnitude of perceptual event" as a function of time since stimulus onset. As is evident, the putative "perceptual event"—the perceptual response that occurs as a result of the physical stimulus presentation—is conceptualized to begin at stimulus onset, to remain at some constant level during stimulus presence, and then to decay following stimulus offset. The usual assumption was that decay is exponential; accordingly, exponential decay is incorporated in Figure 1.

   Implicit in the representation of Figure 1 is the idea that perception of a briefly presented stimulus invokes two sets of perceptual events. First, "normal" perception takes place "when it should," that is, while the stimulus is physically present. Second, perception also takes place during a brief period following stimulus offset, that is, during the iconic-decay period. Given this situation, a basic question addressed over the years is: Why did evolution provide this perceptual appendage; that is, why does perceptual activity continue past stimulus offset, and what role does such processing play in normal perceptual activity? A conclusion that we shall eventually reach in

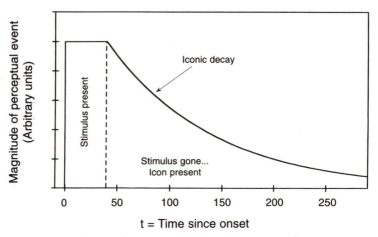

FIGURE 1   Assumed perceptual events surrounding a brief visual presentation.

this chapter is that this question is not a meaningful or interesting one. The ordinate of Figure 1, "magnitude of perceptual event," is deliberately vague, as it came to refer to two separate aspects of perception. When applied to information extraction, the "perceptual event" of Figure 1 would refer to "amount of information available to be extracted and placed into short-term store" (e.g., Averbach & Coriell, 1961; Sperling, 1960; see also Averbach & Sperling, 1961, who characterized available information as measured in bits). As indicated in Figure 1, all stimulus information was assumed to be available during stimulus presence, while available information decayed following stimulus offset. When applied to phenomenological appearance, the "perceptual event" of Figure 1 might be operationally defined as "apparent luminance" (e.g., Weichselgartner & Sperling, 1985), the implicit assumption being that a fading icon is literally equivalent to a physical stimulus fading in luminance. This early work resulted in a general conception of an iconic memory having the following characteristics.

1. Iconic memory constitutes the first mental representation of visually presented information.

2. Iconic memory is of large capacity (possibly including all information encodable by the initial stages of the visual system).

3. Iconic memory begins to decay immediately following stimulus off-set, disappearing entirely after approximately 200–300 ms.

4. Information in iconic memory is such that it can be assessed by physical characteristics. Thus, for example, a subject engaged in a partial-report task can select letters from a letter array based on the physical characteristic

of letter position (e.g., report letters in the third row). Letters can also be reported based on other physical characteristics, such as color (e.g., report all the blue letters) or size (e.g., report all the large letters). However, a subject cannot select letters by characteristics based on meaning (e.g., a subject cannot select all the vowels in a letter array). In this sense, information in iconic memory was thought to be precategorical, that is, information that had not yet been pattern recognized and assigned meaning.

5. The iconic image can be destroyed if the stimulus is followed not by a blank field but by a visual mask of some sort.

6. Various techniques for measuring iconic memory's duration (e.g., partial report and synchrony judgment) were all thought to measuring the same entity; that is, decaying available information and decaying phenomenological appearance were thought to issue from the same, unitary, internal event.

II. AUDITORY SENSORY STORE

Like visual experience, some auditory experiences appear to outlast the sounds producing them. One argument for an auditory sensory store is based on the fact that sound is continuously changing. How could we recognize the informative segments of speech if the system did not hold on to the earlier part of a segment until the later part occurred? Research in the 1970s was directed at measuring the duration of this storage. We briefly review the same three tasks used in the study of iconic memory and the results from each task.

A. Auditory Backward Recognition Masking

One of the most successful tasks in studying audition has employed auditory backward recognition masking (ABRM). As stated earlier, Neisser and others had claimed that the auditory sensory storage lasted on the order of seconds. Some tension existed in the empirical trenches, however, as the result of work by Massaro (1970a, 1972), who extended the backward masking paradigm from the visual world and from auditory detection to study the time course of auditory recognition. In auditory backward recognition masking, a brief target stimulus is followed after a variable ISI by a second stimulus (the mask), and the amount of time that the target information is available in preperceptual memory can be carefully controlled by manipulating this duration. Using this procedure, Massaro found the accuracy of target identification to increase as the ISI increased out to about 250 ms (see also Cowan, 1984; Hawkins & Presson, 1986; Kallman & Massaro, 1979, 1983).

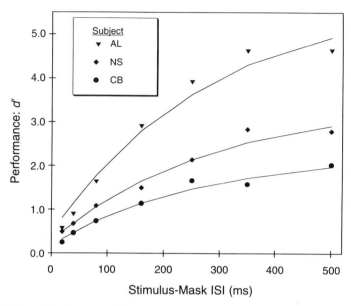

FIGURE 2   Identification of the test tone measured in *d'* units as a function of the silent interval between the test and masking tones. Results for three subjects. (Data from Massaro, 1970a.)

These backward masking results were explained within the framework of a model of auditory information processing in which the target sound is transduced by the listener's sensory system and stored in a preperceptual auditory store that briefly holds a single auditory event (Massaro, 1972, 1975a). Processing of the target sound is necessary for perceptual recognition. The mask replaces the target in the preperceptual auditory store and terminates any further reliable perceptual processing of the target, but it does not work retroactively. Masking does *not* reduce the amount of information that is obtained before the occurrence of the mask; it can only preclude further processing. Therefore, the terminology backward should be taken to mean only that the mask comes after the test stimulus.

In backward masking studies, performance typically asymptotes at an ISI of roughly 250 ms and this interval has been interpreted to reflect the duration of the preperceptual auditory store (Cowan, 1987; Kallman & Massaro, 1983). That is, the mask no longer affects performance after about 250 ms because the preperceptual trace is thought to no longer be available for processing. The three masking functions shown in Figure 2 represent the performance of three different young adults in an early study of auditory backward recognition masking (Massaro, 1970a). The two test alternatives were brief tones (20 ms) differing in frequency (770 and 870 Hz), the mask was another tone (820 Hz), and the subjects identified the test tone as high or low in pitch. Although there are individual differences in Figure 2, all three subjects asymptote at roughly the same interval of 250 ms.

Performance is measured in d' values rather than percentage correct because d' values have been shown to be less contaminated by decision biases in this task (Massaro, 1989). Larger d' values signify better discrimination between the two test tones, and the masking function shows the changes in this discrimination. The functions in Figure 2 can be described accurately by a negatively accelerated exponential growth function of processing time,

$$d' = \alpha(1 - e^{-\theta t}), \tag{1}$$

where the parameter α is the asymptote of the function and θ is the rate of growth to the asymptote. This function can be conceptualized as representing a process that resolves some fixed proportion of the potential information that remains to be resolved per unit of time. Thus, the same increase in processing time gives a larger absolute improvement in performance early relative to late in the processing interval. Zwislocki (1969) has offered a similar account (see Cowan, 1984, 1987).

Similar masking functions have been observed for a variety of auditory perceptual properties, including loudness, timbre, duration, and location, as well as speech distinctions (Massaro, 1975b; Massaro, Cohen, & Idson, 1976; Massaro & Idson, 1978; Moore & Massaro, 1973). In an unpublished study, subjects identified three properties of 20-ms test tones: pitch, loudness, and location (ear of presentation). The test tone could be followed by a masking tone after a variable ISI or no mask would be presented. For each property, the difference between the two alternatives was adjusted to give an average performance of 75% correct. The identification of all three properties showed the prototypical masking results. Performance improved with increases in ISI, reaching an asymptote at about 250 ms. Thus, these results provide additional evidence for an auditory sensory store of about 250 ms.

B. Detection versus Recognition

It should be noted that detection of the presence of an auditory signal versus recognition of the signal are not equally susceptible to backward masking. As shown by Bland and Perrott (1978), who contrasted detection and recognition masking, detection of presence versus absence can occur much more quickly and becomes immune from backward masking after only a few tens of milliseconds. In their detection task, a 10-ms pure tone was randomly presented on half of the trials, and nothing was presented on the other half. The subjects indicated whether or not a test tone had been presented. In the recognition task, a high or low test tone was presented on every trial. The subject's task was to identify the tone as high or low. In both tasks, the

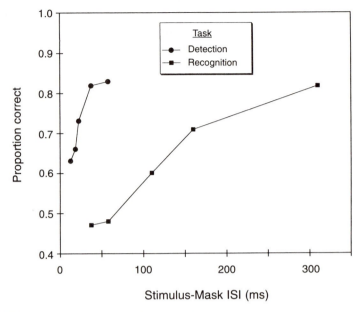

FIGURE 3   Percentage correct detection and recognition performance as a function of the silent interval between the test and masking tones. (Data from Bland & Perrott, 1978.)

observation interval was always followed by a 150-ms masking tone after a variable silent interval. Given two alternatives on both tasks, accuracy of performance can vary between 50 and 100%. As can be seen in Figure 3, detection and recognition were found to follow two different time courses. Detection performance reached asymptote (the highest level of performance) at around 50 ms, whereas recognition did not reach this level until there was at least three times as much silence between the test and target tones.

A similar distinction between detection and recognition exists in visual information processing. Breitmeyer (1984), summarizing the field of visual masking, provided evidence for different masking functions in detection and recognition. Detection is primarily a function of peripheral, energy-dependent, sensory integration and does not improve beyond a target mask asynchrony of about 100 ms. Recognition masking functions extend to longer intervals on the order of 200–250 ms and are influenced by more cognitive variables such as the allocation of central attention to the test items.

The masking results demonstrate the difference between detection and recognition. Detection of a change is sufficient for detection, whereas recognition of a pattern is necessary for recognition. Our perceptual world is rich, not because we detect change, but because we recognize patterns. The storage structures of echoic and iconic memory allow this recognition process to take place.

C. Auditory Partial-Report Task

The Bland and Perrott (1978) study and numerous other studies of auditory backward recognition masking have estimated the duration of echoic memory at around 250 ms. This number, however, conflicts with estimates from other paradigms, notably the partial-report and the suffix tasks. Perhaps the most famous partial-report task was carried out by Darwin, Turvey, and Crowder (1972), from which they estimated echoic memory to be on the order of about two seconds. Three lists of three items each were presented to the left, middle, and right of the subject's head, and following Sperling's procedure, subjects were cued to report the items in terms of either spatial location or category name (digits or letters). For some reason, however, spatial location information had to be reported as well in the category recall condition. The observed advantage of location recall over category recall, therefore, could have been due to this confounding and thus not indicate anything about the availability of information in echoic memory. (This single collaboration among these three superb researchers might have been unfortunate for the field. Each of the three seemed to have dissociated himself from the research almost immediately thereafter, but their erroneous conclusion has found its way into almost every introductory textbook in cognitive psychology; Greene, 1992, p. 11, is a recent example.)

Darwin et al. (1972) also found that partial report by spatial location was superior to whole report and decreased with increases in delay of the partial-report cue. However, the difference between the partial-report condition and the whole-report condition was embarrassingly small. Measuring performance in terms of items, the difference was actually less than half an item. For partial report, in terms of the number of items available, there were 4.9 items with an immediate cue and 4.4 with a 4-s cue delay. The whole report was 4.3 items correct. This small difference between the partial and whole report could easily have come from another process than sensory storage, most notably short-term memory. With a presentation of nine items, we can expect some forgetting from STM when subjects are waiting for the partial-report cue, or when attempting to recall all nine items. Furthermore, when the partial-report task was conducted without the earlier confounding present in the Darwin et al. study (Massaro, 1976), there was no evidence for a sensory holding of information on the order of seconds. Thus, we reach the intriguing conclusion that visual and auditory sensory storage both have a lifetime of about 250 ms.

D. Estimation of Auditory Persistence

If our auditory experience outlasts the sound producing it, then we should overestimate the perceived duration of the auditory event. This result has been documented in several experiments. Auditory persistence appears to function in an analogous way to visual persistence. An auditory stimulus is presented followed by the onset of a light and the participant states whether the light occurred before the offset of the sound. Efron (1970a) found that subjects estimated the duration of a tone that was actually shorter than 130 ms to be around 130 ms. Gol'dburt (1961) and Massaro and Idson (1978) found that the perceived duration of a short tone was decreased by a following tone, with the influence of the second tone decreasing with increases in the silent interval between the two tones. Von Bekesy (1971), influenced by similar results, stated that "If we assume that every stimulus starts a process in the brain which last perhaps 200 milliseconds, . . . and if we further suppose that this process can be inhibited at any moment during the 200-millisecond interval by the onset of the second stimulus" (p. 530). Thus, the results on auditory persistence are consistent with those on visual persistence.

E. Inverse-Duration Effect

These same experiments, however, also found an inverse-duration effect: subjects overestimated the duration of a short sound more than that of a longer sound (Efron, 1970a). If auditory sensory store is simply a fixed appendage tacked onto the end of an auditory stimulus, then we would not expect the overestimation of a sound's duration to vary with its duration. In order to describe this result, however, it is necessary to consider the perceptual processing of the sound stimulus, not simply its duration. One of the early themes of the ABRM research revolved around the assumption of continuity between processing during the test stimulus itself and during the silent interval afterward. That is, the processing time in Equation (1) was always defined as the total presentation duration plus the ISI. In an extreme test of this idea, Massaro (1974) contrasted two conditions. In the standard silent ABRM condition, a 26-ms vowel was presented and followed by a masking vowel after a variable ISI. In the continuous condition, the same processing intervals were used except that the test vowel was simply left on until the onset of the masking vowel.

Figure 4 shows that the time course of recognition is similar in the two conditions. The continuous condition benefits somewhat from the additional duration, but the masking function asymptotes at the same time as in the silent condition. The overall advantage of the continuous condition can be attributed to a difference of information. A vowel presented for a very

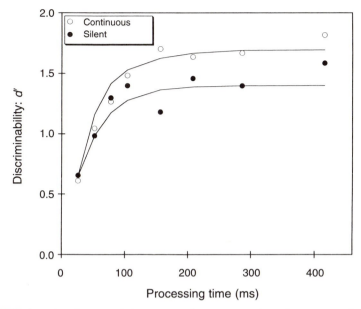

FIGURE 4 Identification of the test vowel /I/ (measured in d' units) as a function of processing time during the continuous vowel presentation or during the silent interval after a 26-ms vowel presentation. The points are the observations and the lines are the predictions given by Equation (1).

short duration necessarily has less information than a vowel presented for a somewhat longer duration because of temporal integration, the auditory system's capability of integrating sound across intervals of 50–60 ms. Independently of the stimulus information, however, the auditory system still requires time for perceptual processing. This processing can occur either during the test stimulus itself or during the silent processing time after its presentation. Thus, we obtain the similar masking functions in the silent and continuous processing conditions, as shown in Figure 4.

Zwislocki's (1969) model of auditory information processing (see Cowan, 1984) cannot predict the inverse duration effect. In this model, neural activity is integrated over time. An auditory stimulus triggers a peripheral neural response. The response is largest at onset, decreases to an asymptote at around 200 ms, remains at this level until the end of the stimulus, and then decays exponentially. This model predicts, as do the traditional models of iconic store, that the duration of the echoic store remaining after stimulus offset should be independent of stimulus duration. Both the inverse-duration effect and the ABRM results falsify this prediction.

These results illustrating the similarities in auditory information processing during the stimulus presentation and the silent interval afterward went mostly unnoticed by the students of iconic store. Thus, they continued to make a distinction between processing during the stimulus and during the period after its offset. However, as we discuss in the final section of this chapter, recent developments have brought the view of visual processing much closer to the existing one for auditory processing. This convergence on analogous mechanisms for auditory and visual processing can be considered to be an advance in our understanding of perceptual processing.

F. Conclusion

Auditory information processing, like visual information processing, is a time-extended process that can be interrupted by a new auditory event. Three different experimental paradigms converge on an estimate of about 250 ms for the duration of this process. The results are consistent with a model that assumes that properties of an auditory sound are represented in a central sensory storage. Perceptual processing involves extracting information from this representation and achieving a perceptual and perhaps an abstract representation. A second auditory event, occurring before the extraction is complete, will necessarily disrupt any additional processing. This conceptualization is rewardingly exactly analogous to the conclusions we reach in our discussion of recent advances in the analysis of iconic memory in the next section.

III. CHANGING CONCEPTIONS OF ICONIC MEMORY

The relatively simple conception of iconic memory that we have described began to change as a result of a number of influential articles that appeared in the early 1980s. In particular, some new empirical findings cast doubt on the icon as a passively decaying informational repository; a review by Coltheart (1980) questioned the unity of icon-as-information repository and icon-as-phenomenological experience; and a philosophical polemic by Haber (1983) questioned iconic memory as even being a suitable topic of scientific research. In this section, we discuss these issues in turn.

A. Inverse-Duration Effects

The counterintuitive phenomenon, known as the inverse-duration effect discussed earlier for auditory processing, was reported by a number of investigators including Bowen, Pola, and Matin (1974) and Efron (1970a, 1970b), who found that the duration of the iconic image, as measured by a synchrony-judgment task, decreased with increasing stimulus duration. Although this finding was rather at odds with the concept of a passively decaying iconic image, the prevailing concept of the icon went largely unchallenged until Di Lollo's (1980) research using an entirely different task, the temporal-integration task, first introduced by Eriksen and Collins (1967).

In this task, two visual stimuli, or frames, are shown in rapid succession, separated by some ISI. Each frame consists of 12 dots in 12 unique positions of an imaginary 5 × 5 grid, and the subject's task is to report the missing dot's position. If both frames are presented simultaneously, no matter how briefly, this task is trivially easy. Replicating previous studies, Di Lollo (1980) found missing-dot identification performance to decrease as the ISI between the two frames increased. The traditional interpretation of these results is that subjects need perceptually to integrate the two frames in order to perceive and report the letters: with a sufficiently short ISI, the iconic image of the first frame is still present when the second frame is presented; hence such integration is possible. As ISI increases, however, the first frame's iconic image presumably continues to diminish, thereby decreasing the probability that the two frames can be perceptually integrated. Creating problems for this interpretation, however, was Di Lollo's new result that performance also decreased as the duration of the first frame increased. This finding strongly disconfirmed the conception of the icon as a passively decaying store; instead, it appeared that iconic decay was also tied intimately to the onset, rather than to just the offset, of stimulus presentation. Based on these results, Di Lollo proposed that the visible persistence resulted not from a passive informational store, but from perceptual activity that began at the time of stimulus onset and diminished in magnitude as processing continued, as in our analysis of auditory processing. We return to this intriguing proposal in a later section.

B. The Splitting of the Icon

As part of an extensive review article, Coltheart (1980) strongly argued against the proposition (previously considered self-evident) that icon-as-information repository and icon-as-phenomenological experience issue from the same perceptual event. The central thrust of Coltheart's argument was that while some techniques for measuring the icon's duration (the synchrony-judgment task and the temporal-integration task) showed the just-described inverse-duration effect, the seminal measurement technique—the partial-report task—did not show such an effect. Accordingly, Coltheart argued, the two types of tasks must be measuring different entities. Coltheart suggested that the concept of an icon be split into (at least) two logically distinct phenomena. He suggested informational persistence as the term for icon-as-information repository, as measured by the partial-report task, and visible persistence as the term for icon-as-phenomenological appearance, as measured by visible-persistence tasks.

C. The Icon's Demise

Haber (1983) deftly finessed all extant difficulties having to do with investigating the icon by arguing that it was an inappropriate subject for scientific investigation to begin with. This unusual position issued from the "ecological validity" perspective (see also Neisser, 1976), a central tenet of which was that any alleged process should be studied only insofar as it had an obvious role in everyday, "real-life" activity. The icon, according to Haber, did not fulfill this criterion, being useful only for the ecologically infrequent activity of "reading during a lightening storm."

Haber's critique did leave investigators somewhat on the defensive, seeking, in an attempt to provide themselves with a worthwhile *raison d'etre,* a purpose for the object of their investigation. During a time of some excitement, for instance, it was believed that persistence was instrumental in maintaining the image obtained during a given eye fixation long enough for it to be integrated with images of subsequent fixations, thereby providing a solution to the mystery of how a stable perception of an ever-retinally-changing visual world was maintained. However, this idea was shown to be untenable (Irwin, 1991, 1992; Rayner & Pollatsek, 1983). The subsequent fixation functions as a masking event for the previous fixation in the same manner that a following stimulus can mask an earlier stimulus in the backward masking task. (If anything, this finding supports the ecological validity of masking experiments because normal successive eye movements can be thought of as successive masking events.)

D. Informational versus Visible Persistence

Despite Haber's broadside, research on persistence did not cease. In response to Coltheart's (1980) suggestion, however, several recent research endeavors have addressed the issue of whether the icon-as-informational repository and icon-as-phenomenological appearance should be viewed as unitary phenomena. Intuitively, the case for conceptualizing informational persistence and visible persistence as having a single basis seems quite compelling. Furthermore, Coltheart's (1980) arguments against this idea were not airtight. His principal reason for postulating informational persistence and visible persistence as different entities revolved around the difference between the effects of stimulus duration on partial report (duration seemed not to have an effect on partial report) versus duration's strong negative effect on visible persistence as measured by synchrony judgment or temporal integration. Recently, this central distinction has been challenged in two ways. First, evidence showing a lack of a duration effect in partial report had in fact been rather sparse, and recently Di Lollo and Dixon (1988, 1992; Dixon & Di Lollo, 1994) have shown that under appropriate conditions,

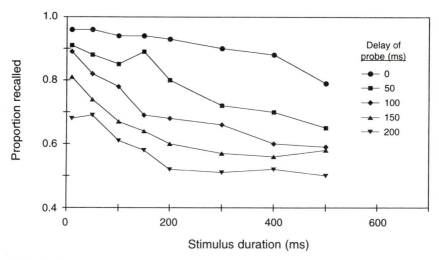

FIGURE 5 Results of Di Lollo and Dixon (1988). Performance in a partial-report task declines with increases both in stimulus-probe ISI and in stimulus duration.

there is a rather robust relation between stimulus duration and partial-report performance. Figure 5 shows results from a partial-report task in which Di Lollo and Dixon (1988) varied both (the usual) stimulus-probe ISI and also the stimulus duration. As expected, partial-report performance declined with increases in ISI; the new and unexpected result was that it also declined quite dramatically with increases in stimulus duration. Thus, contrary to Coltheart's original supposition, an inverse-duration effect is, at least in some circumstances, common to tasks measuring phenomenological appearance on one hand, and available information on the other.

The second difficulty with Coltheart's (1980) arguments is that they were based on the comparison of data from different experiments. This practice can lead to serious interpretational difficulties. To illustrate, suppose a partial-report task in which stimulus duration was varied (e.g., Sperling 1960) is compared with a synchrony-judgment task in which stimulus duration was varied (e.g., Efron, 1970b). While stimulus duration did indeed vary in both experiments, the experiments differed in many other ways as well: for instance, they involved different stimuli, observers, duration ranges, luminances, and contrasts. The consequences of these confoundings is that differences in the reported duration effects (Sperling's null effect vs Efron's inverse-duration effect) cannot be unambiguously attributed to any one element, namely, stimulus duration. For example, Sperling's null results come from a whole-report task in which performance could be data limited because of STM. Loftus and Irwin (in progress) attempted to address this difficulty by conducting experiments in which two tasks, temporal integration and partial report, were directly compared with all other factors held as constant as possible. They found (as did Di Lollo and Dixon) that partial-report performance, like temporal-integration performance, declined with both stimulus duration and ISI. Even so, the over-conditions correlation between the two tasks was far from perfect; briefly, the negative effect of stimulus duration was far more dramatic for temporal-integration performance than for partial-report performance.

Although stimulus duration affects temporal integration and partial report somewhat differently, this does not mean that icon-as-information repository and icon-as-phenomenological appearance must be viewed as entirely distinct and independent phenomena. Indeed, in the next section, we describe a new theory that integrates these phenomena.

IV. A LINEAR-SYSTEMS APPROACH TO PERSISTENCE

In this section, we describe a recent conceptual advance in the study of informational and visible persistence (Loftus & Ruthruff, 1994). We begin with the physical representation of a briefly presented stimulus. Suppose a stimulus (such as a black-on-white letter display) is presented for a brief time period, say 40 ms. The visual system's reaction to this physical stimulus can be described as a linear temporal filter that maps the stimulus wave form into what we shall call a sensory response (see Watson, 1986, for an excellent review of linear systems from a vision science perspective). Consider first the system's response to a very brief bright stimulus called an impulse. An impulse is assumed to produce what is referred to as an impulse–response function that relates the magnitude of some stimulus-signaling neural event to the time since the impulse's occurrence. A widely accepted form of the impulse–response function is shown in Figure 6A. Here, the impulse is shown as the vertical line on the left, while the system's response to it lags behind, rising to a maximum after about 50 ms, and then decaying back to 0 after about 250 ms.

Now consider a real stimulus (as opposed to an impulse), such as the 40-ms stimulus of Figure 6B. We can conceptualize this stimulus as divided into a series of four successive 10-ms impulses, starting at times 0, 10, 20, and 30 ms following stimulus onset. Now each impulse generates its own independent impulse–response function, starting at times 0, 10, 20, and 30 ms, respectively, as shown in Figure 6C. Finally—and this is the "linear" part—the individual "impulse–response functions" are assumed to sum to provide the overall sensory–response function, depicted by the heavy line in Figure 6C, and depicted again in Figure 6D.

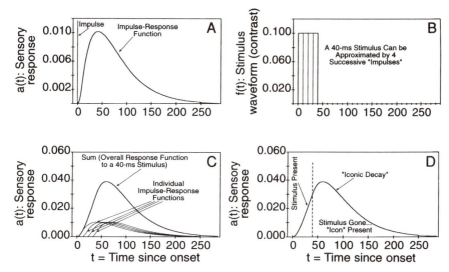

FIGURE 6   Generation of a sensory-response function. (A) Response to an "impulse." (B) A stimulus wave form can be conceptualized as a train of impulses. (C) Individual impulse–response functions sum to generate overall sensory-response function. (D) The sensory-response function generated by a linear temporal filter applied to the stimulus wave form. This curve should be compared to the corresponding curve of Figure 1.

A. The Diminished Status of "Iconic Decay"

The sensory-response function of Figure 6D is analogous to the curve originally shown in Figure 1 in the sense that it is meant to show the entire time course of some fundamental perceptual process that results from a brief visual presentation. Unlike the curve in Figure 1, however, this sensory-response function is derived from simple basic principles. In Figure 6D, the pre-stimulus-offset and post-stimulus-offset portions of the sensory-response function have been labeled analogously to Figure 1; again, the post-stimulus portion of the curve has been labeled "iconic decay." At this point, however, the entire concept of "iconic decay" starts to become somewhat moot. That is, the interest shifts to the entire sensory-response function; stimulus offset is not a particularly important event and accordingly it makes little sense to concentrate on only that portion of the sensory response that happens after stimulus offset. Earlier we noted that, since the time of Sperling's original work, psychologists have viewed the icon as a somewhat mysterious perceptual appendage, lurking around after stimulus offset, crying out to be "explained." With the conceptualization depicted in Figure 6, the icon's mystery evaporates: it occurs simply because the visual system, like most systems, has an output that lags behind and is temporally blurred relative to its input.

B. Consequences of Linearity

Any arbitrary stimulus wave form can be broken into a train of impulses, and the resulting impulse–response functions added to produce the overall sensory-response function. Figure 7 shows the sensory-response functions to six different stimuli ranging in duration from 20 to 480 ms. Several aspects of these functions are noteworthy.

1. A major difference between the Figure 7 curves and the original Figure 1 curve is that the magnitude of the sensory response does not leap to some greater-than-zero value instantaneously following stimulus onset; rather it rises gradually. This makes sense; virtually no physical system responds instantaneously to some input.

2. For a given intensity, the curve's maximum value increases with increasing stimulus duration.

3. Decay of the sensory response does not begin immediately at stimulus offset, but rather at some time following stimulus offset. This is most easily seen with short stimuli.

4. The sensory-response functions for longer duration stimuli appear similar to the original conception of iconic processing depicted in Figure 1:

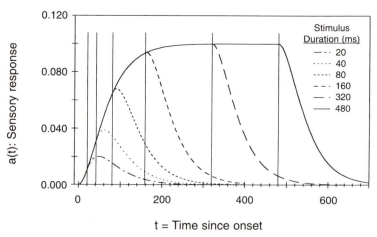

FIGURE 7   Sensory-response functions resulting from six stimulus durations. Vertical lines indicate stimulus offsets.

in both cases, the perceptual response remains at a relatively stable level until the stimulus ends and then starts more or less immediately to decay.

5. This view of "iconic memory" makes no distinction between perceptual events that occur before or after stimulus offset; rather, all that is important for subsequent processing is the height of the sensory-response function, regardless of whether it is established before or after the time of physical stimulus offset.

C. Applications of the Linear-Filter Model to Visible Persistence

We briefly describe the applications of the linear-filter model to visible persistence as measured by temporal integration and synchrony-judgment tasks. Earlier, we described the inverse-duration effect in a temporal-integration task by Di Lollo (1980) in which performance was found to decline dramatically as the duration of Frame 1 increased. More recently, however, Dixon and Di Lollo (1992, 1994) reported another new and surprising finding: Performance also declines as dramatically with increases in Frame 2 duration. Even more surprising, Dixon and Di Lollo (1994) found an analogous effect in a partial-report task. As in the earlier Di Lollo and Dixon (1988) partial-report experiment, Dixon and Di Lollo used a circular array of 15 letters presented for durations ranging from 20 to 320 ms. Immediately following the display's offset, a visual probe signaled which letter was to be reported. The probe's duration also varied from 20 to 320 ms. As in the temporal-integration experiment, partial-report performance declined with both array duration and probe duration.

To account for these various effects, Dixon and Di Lollo (1994) offered a theory that centered on the temporal similarity in the visual system's responses to each of two successively presented stimuli. Although this theory predicted the results from a variety of temporal-integration and partial-report tasks quite well, it is not clear how it would account for other visual phenomena, such as the inverse-duration effect obtained in a synchrony-judgment task. On the other hand, Loftus and colleagues (e.g., Loftus & Hanna, 1989; Loftus & Hogden, 1988; Loftus & Irwin, 1994) have applied the linear-filter model successfully to both synchrony judgment and temporal integration, as well as to partial-report tasks. To do so, they envisioned the subject to be extracting information at some instantaneous rate, where the magnitude of the information-extraction rate at time t is determined by the product of two things: the magnitude of the sensory response at that time and the amount of as-yet-to-be extracted information left in the stimulus at that time. The first influence dictates that rate depends on the sensory response. The second influence embodies a kind of "diminishing-returns" idea, as in Equation (1): the more information that has been extracted from the stimulus already, the less remaining new information. "Phenomenological appearance" is identified with this information-extraction rate: the assumption being that the slower the subject is extracting information, the less the subject will be consciously aware of the stimulus.

Figure 8 shows how these assumptions successfully account for the inverse-duration effect in a synchrony-judgment task. The general idea is that the subject will judge the stimulus as having phenomenologically disappeared at the time that the information-extraction rate falls below some criterion level. The 40-ms information-extraction rate function falls faster following its offset than does the 20-ms information-extraction rate function. This is because there is less yet-to-be-extracted information at the time of offset for the 40-ms than for the 20-ms stimulus. A consequence of this faster fall is that the 40-ms function crosses the same criterion sooner following its offset than does the 20-ms function. The times elapsing between stimulus offset and when the information-extraction rate functions fall below the criterion are indicated by the double-headed arrows in the figure (solid and dashed, respectively, for the 20-ms and 40-ms presentations). This time is obviously longer for the 20-ms presentation, thus accounting (at least qualitatively) for the inverse-duration effect in a synchrony-judgment task. This account also predicts that the perceiver would not become aware of the stimulus until some short time after its onset.

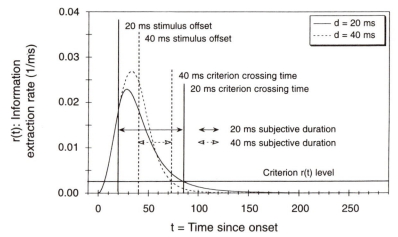

FIGURE 8   The information-extraction rate theory's explanation of the inverse-duration effect in a synchrony-judgment experiment. The two curves represent $r(t)$ functions for a 20-ms and a 40-ms stimulus. The two left-hand vertical lines represent time of stimulus offset, while the two right-hand vertical lines represent times that the $r(t)$ functions fall below the $r(t)$ criterion level. Two-headed arrows represent persistence duration, which is longer for the 20-ms stimulus than for the 40-ms stimulus.

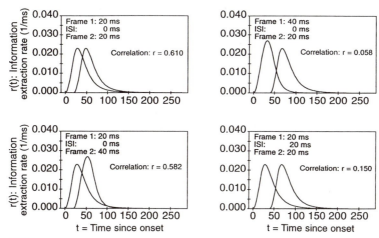

FIGURE 9   The correlation explanation of information-extraction rate theory of temporal-integration performance.

To account for the previously described temporal-integration effects, Loftus and Irwin (1994) borrowed the temporal similarity assumption from Dixon and Di Lollo's theory; however, Loftus and Irwin applied the technique to the information-extraction rate functions rather than to the sensory-response functions. Accordingly, their account of temporal integration is quite similar to Dixon and Di Lollo's. Figure 9 shows the result of this exercise. It is quite apparent that, as with Dixon and Di Lollo's theory, the correlation between the two information-extraction rate functions decreases with increases in Frame 1 duration, ISI, and Frame 2 duration.

Thus, the linear-systems approach can account for the visible-persistence phenomena. Now we describe the application of the approach to information extraction, and we also demonstrate a proposed theoretical relation between visible persistence and available information. In a picture-memory experiment, complex, naturalistic, colored pictures were shown, one at a time, in a "study phase" to a group of subjects (Loftus, in preparation). Each picture was shown in one of two conditions: Either it was shown once for 100 ms, or it was shown twice for 50 ms apiece with an ISI of 250 ms. For ease of exposition, these conditions are referred to as the "no-gap" and the "gap" conditions. The amount of information extracted from the pictures was assessed by memory performance in a later recognition test.

Two important results emerged. First, subjects were able to distinguish pictures in the gap condition from pictures in the no-gap condition with 100% accuracy. In the gap condition, the picture appeared to flash twice, while in the no-gap condition, the picture appeared to flash only once. Second, later memory performance was identical for the two study conditions. Although the two conditions were phenomenologically different, they produced the same degree of information extraction.

Figures 10A and B show the $a(t)$ sensory-response functions corresponding to the gap and no-gap conditions. As one would expect, the gap function has two distinct peaks resulting from the two separate presentations, while the no-gap function has only a single peak. Although it may not be immediately obvious, a consequence of linearity is that, although the gap and no-gap curves are of different shapes, the areas under them are identical (areas of 10.00 in both cases).

Figures 10C and D show the information-extraction rate functions. The gap function, like its sensory-response counterpart, is double peaked, which, according to the theory produces the experience of two flashes. Correspondingly, the single-peaked gap function produces the one-flash experience that occurs in the no-gap condition. Given that the areas under the two information-extraction rate functions are identical and that the total area under any extraction-rate function corresponds to the total amount of whatever it is that is being extracted, the amounts of extracted information are, according to the theory, identical in the gap and the no-gap conditions. Therefore, the theory correctly predicts memory performance to be identical in the two conditions.

The point of this discussion has been to underscore the idea that this information-extraction rate theory affords some degree of unity between the two important psychological events that we have been discussing: infor-

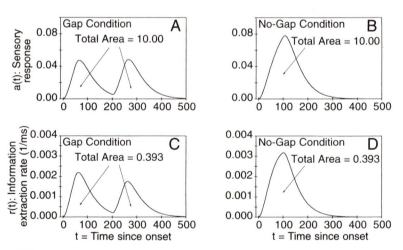

FIGURE 10   The information-extraction rate theory's explanation of the "gap" experiment described in the text. (A, B) $a(t)$ Functions for the no-gap and gap conditions. (C, D) Corresponding $r(t)$ functions. Phenomenological appearance is determined by the shape of the $r(t)$ functions, while extracted information is determined by the area under the functions.

mation extraction and phenomenological appearance. Within this theory, the two phenomena are both direct consequences of the same information-extraction rate function. Phenomenological experience corresponds to the shape of the function, while information extraction corresponds to the area under the function. Coltheart was correct that the two phenomena behave in somewhat different ways. According to the present theory, this occurs because the shape of a function and the area under the function likewise behave in somewhat different ways. But they are both aspects of, and predictable from, the same unitary sensory-response function. We now turn to the study of perceptual memory.

V. PERCEPTUAL MEMORIES

During the first decades of cognitive research, most of the field appeared to be intrigued by the loss of information from the initial iconic store. There was little concern for how the sensory information was processed and transferred to a more stable perceptual memory. The birth of the suffix effect and its cottage industry appears to have been due to John Morton's visit at Yale with the heretical hypothesis that the modality of a list of items would have important consequences for memory (Crowder & Morton, 1969). Perceptual and memory researchers tended to study either sensory storage or verbal (abstract) memory. Recently, only one investigator has stressed the importance of perceptual memory in accounting for information processing (Cowan, 1984, 1988). Massaro (1975a), on the other hand, devoted three chapters in his textbook to auditory and visual perceptual memory: After describing how familiarity in perceptual memory is central to the recognition of an event as one that has been experienced previously, the time course of the perceptual memory for auditory nonspeech and speech signals and visual events was presented. We shall briefly illustrate several prototypical results taken from these chapters because they are as relevant today as they were in 1975 (if not more so).

A. Auditory Perceptual Memory

Significant perceptual memory of a preceding auditory event can remain even after extended processing of a new event. This phenomenon has been illustrated in several memory-for-pitch tasks. For example, Wickelgren (1969), using a delayed comparison task in which a standard tone is followed by a comparison tone after a variable ISI (see Massaro, 1975a, p. 478), and an interference tone is presented during the ISI, found that forgetting of the standard tone followed a negatively decreasing exponential function but that significant memory remained after three minutes of the interference tone.

Another study illustrating the contribution of perceptual memory in verbal memory was carried out by McNabb and Massaro (described in Massaro, 1975a, p. 508). They presented a sequential list of one-syllable words on a memory drum, and subjects repeated the words as they were presented either subvocally or vocally. The list was followed by a visually presented test word and the recognition memory test required subjects to indicate whether the test word had occurred on the preceding list. Memory benefited from the vocal reading of the test list and this benefit was independent of the number of items between the original presentation and test. In this case, perceptual memory appeared to last at least 15 seconds or so. This result and a variety of other results (see Greene, 1992, chap. 2) appear to show that the life span of auditory perceptual memory is not limited to just a few seconds.

B. Visual Perceptual Memory

Perceptual memory is not limited to auditory and speech signals, but has also been demonstrated for visual information. The last two decades have witnessed a revival of the positive contribution of visual imagery on memory (Finke, 1989). Scarborough (1972) had previously found that less forgetting occurred in the Peterson and Peterson (1959) task when the test items were presented visually rather than auditorily. The interference task was counting aloud backward by threes so the advantage of the visual presentation mode is reasonable. Additional evidence for a variety of perceptual memories has been documented by Massaro (1975a) and Cowan (1984).

C. Models of Perceptual Memory

Massaro (1970a) had concluded that the evidence for perceptual memory and abstract STM could be described within the same information processing model. Baddeley and Hitch (1974) suggested that STM should be thought of as a working memory but with multiple subsystems controlled by a limited capacity executive (see also Baddeley, 1986; Nairne, this volume, Chapter 4). They pinpointed two important subsystems: a visuospatial scratch pad and an articulatory loop. However, there is nothing to preclude other subsystems, such as auditory and tactile memories. Furthermore, the evidence Baddeley and Hitch brought in favor of an articulatory memory cannot account for the advantage usually found for an auditory presentation relative to a visual one, as phonological or articulatory encoding should be equally engaged for both spoken and written language.

Cowan (1984, 1988), in a thorough review, has provided evidence for two types of sensory storage, which parallel the preperceptual and synthesized memories previously postulated by Massaro (1975a). The preperceptual store holds information for the initial stage of processing called perception. Perception, however, entails much more than simply an abstract categorization of the environmental event: It provides a perceptual representation that supports behavioral action. This perceptual representation can be exposed in a variety of ways as described in the previous section. Cowan (1988) has also acknowledged the modality-specific dimensions of STM. Contrary to abstract memory, modality-specific memories easily hold continuous information. The initial sensory store of roughly 250-ms duration differs from the modality-specific (perceptual) dimensions of STM. As pointed out by Cowan, the perceptual and abstract dimensions of STM have much more in common than either of these dimensions have with the initial 250-ms sensory store.

D. Implicit Memory

In some respects, this earlier research on perceptual memory anticipated the implicit memory paradigm shift of the last decade. It has shown that perceptual processing during study and the retention of these perceptual events influenced later recognition memory and recall. That is, this research had demonstrated that performance cannot be adequately described on the basis of only abstract symbolic representations. Rather, our sensory and perceptual interactions necessarily provide the groundwork for symbolic processing and memory.

The research on implicit memory during the last decade has awakened the field to the importance of perceptual memory (Crowder, 1993; Graf & Masson, 1993). Our perceptual experiences and perceptual memories provide the interface between sensory storage (our earlier visions of echoic and iconic memory) and some symbolic encoding. Roediger and Srinivas (1993) provide a nice demonstration of how previous perceptual experience is central to recognizing ambiguous figures, such as the famous dotted dalmation. Experience with ambiguous figures, such as the Street figures, the dotted dalmation, and the close-up view of a cow, makes these easier to see and recognize. Roediger and Srinivas (1993) describe these results in terms of transfer-appropriate processing. In extant memory research, participants show the largest influence of previous experience when the current situation most closely matches the earlier processing experience. The ambiguous figures and their recognition simply emphasize the important role of perceptual processing and perceptual memory in prototypical behaviors such as visual navigation, understanding speech and music, and reading.

E. Symbolic Representation and Perceptual Memory

Although it is difficult to impose historical rationality on previous work, it is reasonable to blame the computer metaphor for the neglect of perceptual memory. Computers do their most intelligent work with abstract symbols; why would not intelligent humans do the same? The prototypical information processing model was therefore directed at transforming the concrete stimulus information into an abstract form as quickly as possible. This perspective resulted in the notion of a sensory store interfaced to an abstract STM. Psychologists seemed to forget that our sensory grounding could provide valuable support for information processing. Even much of speech research was wedded to the symbol metaphor. Pisoni (1993) has recently criticized speech research for slighting modality-specific phenomena, such as the decrement in speech perception and memory when the perceiver is confronted with multiple speakers (talkers) relative to just one.

The relative contribution of perceptual and symbolic processes can be appreciated in an ingenious experiment carried out by Epstein and Rock (1960). Recency of experience and expectancy of events to come are factors consistently used to explain performance variations. The authors were interested in the relative influence of recency and expectancy in the perceptual interpretation of Boring's wife/mother-in-law figure. Subjects identified the two unambiguous forms presented one at a time in a sequence of alternations. Then at some point, the ambiguous version of this figure was substituted for one of the unambiguous figures. Given that the last presentation had been the unambiguous mother-in-law, would the participants identify the ambiguous figure in terms of what they had most recently experienced or in terms of what they expected? One might say there should be a symbolic anticipation of the wife but a perceptual memory of the mother-in-law. In favor of the perceptual over the symbolic, subjects identified the ambiguous figure as equivalent to what they had just perceived (the mother-in-law).

VI. MEMORY STORES AND INFORMATION PROCESSING

In his retrospective glance at iconic storage, Neisser (1976) asked the question whether it was in the observer or the environment. His justified complaint was that cognitive theorists treat the icon as if it were a picture, independent of the perceptual mechanisms that "look at it." With the hindsight of contemporary inquiry, we understand that any storage of information is inextricably bound up with the processing of that information. Sanders (1993) reminds us that delimiting a sequence of processing stages is only a preliminary heuristic. Given this start, one can proceed to develop more precise process models. Horst Mittelstadt (personal communication) advises that each box in the sequence contain a dynamic equation. By this view, information processing stage (box) models are acceptable as long as there is an equation yoked to each box. The equation would naturally describe the processing of the "stored" information.

A. Structure versus Process: Can We Do with Stores?

Simple studies of perceptual memory appear to be relevant to the structure/process issue. A well-worn psychophysical task that proved productive in the study of auditory perceptual memory was delayed comparison. A standard tone is followed after some intervening event or activity by a comparison tone (Massaro, 1970b; Wickelgren, 1969). The participant responds whether the comparison was the same or different from the standard. With a roving standard that fluctuates from trial to trial and a highly similar comparison tone to preclude any value of verbally encoding the standard, how do we describe performance without assuming some storage of the standard in memory? At some level, the current processing of the comparison must be compared to some representation of the standard. This simple task might convince most investigators of the need for structure as well as process in their description of perception and memory. Is it sufficient to say that a comparison tone is recognized as the same as the previous standard because the comparison is more easily processed?

As articulated by Freyd (1987), a structure process dualism remains central to many information processing theories. But she questions whether computation in real time utilizes structures distinct from processes. To clarify this dualism, consider the classical view of a preperceptual storage such as iconic or echoic memory. This view implies a temporary representation of a stimulus presentation (the proximal form of the distal event). The perceptual process, as described as some function of time, then "reads out" from this structure. For example, an exponential readout is commonly supported because the absolute gain in performance diminishes with increases in processing time. It appears to be more penetrating to describe both structure and process rather than to reduce the description to just process. The linear systems analysis of visual processing (described in the preceding section) provides a worthy example of the need for both structure and process. The magnitude of the sensory event serves as the structure for several different processes: information extraction and phenomenal appearance.

B. Stage Models and Multiple Representations

To justify the initial sensory storage as distinct from following processing stages and other perceptual representations, it is necessary to clarify the information processing framework. We have evidence that information can be maintained in memory at multiple levels and in various forms. This parallel storage of information does not negate the sequential stage model, however. What is important to remember is that transfer of information from one stage to another does not require that the information is lost from the earlier stage. Reading a word does not obliterate its visual representation. For our purposes, we now understand that the representation of an earlier processing stage maintains its integrity even after it has been "transformed" and transmitted to the following processing stage. Thus, it is entirely reasonable to have multiple perceptual and abstract representations within stage models of information processing (e.g., Baddeley, 1986; Massaro, 1975a).

Acknowledgments

The research reported in this chapter and the writing of the chapter were supported, in part, by grants from the Public Health Service (PHS R01 NS 20314 to DWM and NIMH MH413637 to GRL), the National Science Foundation (BNS 8812728 to DWM), and the graduate division of the University of California, Santa Cruz to DWM. GRL would like to acknowledge Tom Busey and Eric Ruthruff as collaborators on the linear-filter theory. The authors thank Nelson Cowan and Mary Sue Weldon for their comments.

References

Averbach, E., & Coriell, H. S. (1961). Short-term memory in vision. *Bell Systems Technical Journal, 40,* 309–328.

Averbach, E., & Sperling, G. (1961). Short-term storage in vision. In C. Cherry (Ed.), *Symposium on Information Theory* (pp. 196–211). London: Butterworth.

Baddeley, A. D. (1986). *Working memory.* Oxford: Clarendon Press.

Baddeley, A., & Hitch, G. J. (1974). Working memory. In G. Bower (Ed.), *Recent advances in learning and motivation* (Vol. VIII, pp. 47–90). New York: Academic Press.

Bland, D. E., & Perrott, D. R. (1978). Backward masking: Detection versus recognition. *Journal of the Acoustical Society of America, 63,* 1215–1220.

Bowen, R. W., Pola, J., & Matin, L. (1974). Visual persistence: Effects of flash luminance, duration and energy. *Vision Research, 14,* 295–303.

Breitmeyer, B. G. (1984). *Visual masking: An integrative approach.* New York: Oxford.

Coltheart, M. (1980). Iconic memory and visible persistence. *Perception & Psychophysics, 27,* 183–228.

Cowan, N. (1984). On short and long auditory stores. *Psychological Bulletin, 96,* 341–370.

Cowan, N. (1987). Auditory sensory storage in relation to the growth of sensation and acoustic information extraction. *Journal of Experimental Psychology: Human Perception and Performance, 14,* 204–215.

Cowan, N. (1988). Evolving conceptions of memory storage, selective attention, and their mutual constraints within the human information processing system. *Psychological Bulletin, 104,* 163–191.

Crowder, R. G. (1993). Auditory memory. In S. McAdams & E. Gigand (Eds.), *Thinking in sound: The cognitive psychology of human audition* (pp. 113–145). Oxford: Oxford University Press.

Crowder, R. G., & Morton, J. (1969). Precategorical acoustic storage. *Perception & Psychophysics, 5,* 365–373.

Darwin, C. J., Turvey, M. T., & Crowder, R. G. (1972). An auditory analogue of the Sperling partial report procedure: Evidence for brief auditory storage. *Cognitive Psychology, 3,* 255–267.

Di Lollo, V. (1980). Temporal integration in visual memory. *Journal of Experimental Psychology: General, 109,* 75–97.

Di Lollo, V., & Dixon, P. (1988). Two forms of persistence in visual information processing. *Journal of Experimental Psychology: Human Perception and Performance, 14,* 671–681.

Di Lollo, V., & Dixon, P. (1992). Inverse duration effects in partial report. *Journal of Experimental Psychology: Human Perception and Performance, 18,* 1089–1100.

Dixon, P., & Di Lollo, V. (1992). Effects of display luminance, stimulus type, and probe duration on visible and schematic persistence. *Canadian Journal of Psychology, 45,* 54–74.

Dixon, P., & Di Lollo, V. (1994). Beyond visible persistence: An alternative account of temporal integration and segregation in visual processing. *Cognitive Psychology, 26,* 33–63.

Efron, R. (1970a). The relationship between the duration of a stimulus and the duration of a perception. *Neuropsychologia, 8,* 37–55.

Efron, R. (1970b). Effect of stimulus duration on perceptual onset and offset latencies. *Perception & Psychophysics, 8,* 231–234.

Epstein, W., & Rock, I. (1960). Perceptual set as an artifact of recency. *American Journal of Psychology, 73,* 214–228.

Eriksen, C. W., & Collins, J. F. (1967). Some temporal characteristics of visual pattern perception. *Journal of Experimental Psychology, 74,* 476–484.

Finke, R. A. (1989). *Principles of mental imagery.* Cambridge, MA: MIT Press.

Freyd, J. J. (1987). Dynamic mental representations. *Psychological Review, 94,* 427–438.

Gol'dburt, S. N. (1961). Investigation of the stability of auditory processes in micro-intervals of time (new findings on back masking). *Biophysics, 6,* 809–817.

Graf, P., & Masson, M. E. J. (Eds.). (1993). *Implicit memory: New directions in cognition, development, and neuropsychology.* Hillsdale, NJ: Erlbaum.

Greene, R. L. (1992). *Human memory: Paradigms and paradoxes.* Hillsdale, NJ: Erlbaum.

Haber, R. N. (1983). The impending demise of the icon: A critique of the concept of iconic storage in visual information processing. *Behavioral and Brain Sciences, 6,* 1–54.

Hawkins, H. L., & Presson, J. C. (1986). Auditory information processing. In K. R. Boff, L. Kaufman, & J. P. Thomas (Eds.), *Handbook of perception and human performance: Vol 2. Cognitive processes and performance* (pp. 26-1–26-64). New York: Wiley.

Hogben, J. H., & Di Lollo, V. (1974). Perceptual integration and perceptual segregation of brief visual stimuli. *Vision Research, 14,* 1059–1069.

Irwin, D. E. (1991). Information integration across saccadic eye movements. *Cognitive Psychology, 23,* 420–456.

Irwin, D. E. (1992). Memory for position and identity across eye movements. *Journal of Experimental Psychology: Learning, Memory, and Cognition, 18,* 307–317.

Kallman, H. J., & Massaro, D. W. (1979). Similarity effects in auditory backward masking. *Journal of Experimental Psychology: Human Perception and Performance, 9,* 312–327.

Kallman, H. J., & Massaro, D. W. (1983). Backward masking, the suffix effect and preperceptual auditory storage. *Journal of Experimental Psychology: Learning, Memory, and Cognition, 9,* 312–327.

Loftus, G. R., Duncan, J., & Gehrig, P. (1992). On the time course of perceptual information that results from a brief visual presentation. *Journal of Experimental Psychology: Human Perception and Performance, 18,* 530–549.

Loftus, G. R., & Hanna, A. M. (1989). The phenomenology of spatial integration: Data and models. *Cognitive Psychology, 21,* 363–397.

Loftus, G. R., & Hogden, J. (1988). Picture perception: Information extraction and phenomenological persistence. In G. H. Bower (Ed.), *The psychology of learning and motivation* (Vol. 22, pp. 139–191). New York: Academic Press.

Loftus, G. R., & Irwin, D. E. (in press). Visible and informational persistence: Different tasks measure different things. *Cognitive Psychology.*

Loftus, G. R., & Ruthruff, E. (1994). A theory of visual information acquisition and visual memory with special application to intensity-duration tradeoffs. *Journal of Experimental Psychology: Human Perception and Performance, 20,* 33–50.

Lupker, S. J., & Massaro, D. W. (1979). Selective perception without confounding contributions of decision and memory. *Perception & Psychophysics, 25,* 60–69.

Massaro, D. W. (1970a). Preperceptual auditory images. *Journal of Experimental Psychology, 85,* 411–417.

Massaro, D. W. (1970b). Perceptual processes and forgetting in memory tasks. *Psychological Review, 77,* 557–567.

Massaro, D. W. (1972). Preperceptual images, processing time, and perceptual units in auditory perception. *Psychological Review, 79,* 124–145.

Massaro, D. W. (1974). Perceptual units in speech recognition. *Journal of Experimental Psychology, 102,* 199–208.

Massaro, D. W. (1975a). *Experimental psychology and information processing.* Chicago: Rand-McNally.

Massaro, D. W. (Ed.). (1975b). *Understanding language: An information processing analysis of speech perception, reading and psycholinguistics.* New York: Academic Press.

Massaro, D. W. (1976). Perceptual processing in dichotic listening. *Journal of Experimental Psychology: Human Learning and Memory, 2,* 331–339.

Massaro, D. W. (1979). Reading and listening [Tutorial paper]. In P. A. Kolers, M. Wrolstad, & H. Bouma (Eds.), *Processing of visible language* (Vol. 1, pp. 331–354). New York: Plenum Press.

Massaro, D. W. (1987). *Speech perception by ear and eye: A paradigm for psychological inquiry.* Hillsdale, NJ: Erlbaum.

Massaro, D. W. (1989). *Experimental psychology: An information processing approach.* Orlando, FL: Harcourt Brace.

Massaro, D. W., Cohen, M. M., & Idson, W. L. (1976). Recognition masking of auditory lateralization and pitch judgments. *Journal of the Acoustical Society of America, 59,* 434–441.

Massaro, D. W., & Idson, W. L. (1978). Target-mask similarity in backward recognition masking of perceived tone duration. *Perception & Psychophysics, 24,* 225–236.

Mewhort, D. J. K., Campbell, A. J., Marchetti, F. M., & Campbell, J. I. D. (1981). Identification, localization, and "iconic memory:" An evaluation of the bar-probe task. *Memory & Cognition, 9,* 50–67.

Miller, G. A. (1956). The magical number seven, plus or minus two: Some limits on our capacity for processing information. *Psychological Review, 63,* 81–97.

Moore, J. J., & Massaro, D. W. (1973). Attention and processing capacity in auditory recognition. *Journal of Experimental Psychology, 99,* 49–54.

Neisser, U. (1967). *Cognitive psychology.* New York: Appleton-Century-Crofts.

Neisser, U. (1976). *Cognition and reality.* San Francisco: W. H. Freeman.

Peterson, L. R., & Peterson, M. J. (1959). Short-term retention of individual verbal items. *Journal of Experimental Psychology, 58,* 193–198.

Pisoni, D. B. (1993). Long-term memory in speech perception: Some new findings on talker variability, speaking rate and perceptual learning. *Speech Communication, 113,* 109–125.

Rayner, K., & Pollatsek, A. (1983). Is visual information integrated across saccades? *Perception & Psychophysics, 34,* 39–48.

Roediger, H. L., III, & Srinivas, K. (1993). Specificity of operations in perceptual priming. In P. Graf and M. E. J. Masson (Eds.), *Implicit memory: New directions in cognition, development, and neuropsychology* (pp. 17–48). Hillsdale, NJ: Erlbaum.

Sanders, A. F. (1993). Performance theory and measurement through chronometric analysis. In D. E. Meyer & S. Kornblum (Eds.), *Attention and performance XIV: Synergies in experimental psychology, artificial intelligence, and cognitive neuroscience—A silver jubilee* (pp. 689–699). Cambridge: MIT Press.

Scarborough, D. L. (1972). Stimulus modality effects on forgetting in short-term memory. *Journal of Experimental Psychology, 95,* 285–289.

Sperling, G. (1960). The information available in brief visual presentations. *Psychological Monographs, 74* (11, Whole No. 498).

Treisman, A. M. (1986). Properties, parts, and objects. In K. R. Boff, L. Kaufmann, & J. P. Thomas (Eds.), *Handbook of perception and human performance: Vol. II. Cognitive processes and performance* (chap. 35). New York: Wiley.

Treisman, A. M., & Gelade, G. (1980). Feature-integration theory of attention. *Cognitive Psychology, 12,* 97–136.

Von Bekesy, G. (1971). Auditory inhibition in concert halls. *Science, 171,* 529–536.

Watson, A. B. (1986). Temporal sensitivity. In K. R. Boff, L. Kaufmann, & J. P. Thomas (Eds.), *Handbook of perception and human performance* (Vol. I, pp. 6-1–6-43). New York: Wiley.

Weichselgartner, E., & Sperling, G. (1985). Continuous measurement of visible persistence. *Journal of Experimental Psychology: Human Perception and Performance, 11,* 711–725.

Wickelgren, W. A. (1969). Associative strength theory of recognition memory for pitch. *Journal of Mathematical Psychology, 6,* 13–61.

Zwislocki, J. J. (1969). Temporal summation of loudness: An analysis. *Journal of the Acoustical Society of America, 46,* 431–440.

CHAPTER 4

Short-Term/Working Memory

James S. Nairne

One of the important properties of transient memories is that they allow us to prolong the immediate present. Through sensory memories, like the icon or the auditory echo, we preserve a relatively exact replica of the environmental message, for a brief interval, as an aid to on-line perceptual processing. But sensory memories play only a minor role in our conscious experience of the immediate moment. Instead, the conscious contents of mind—our internal thoughts and fleeting impressions (James, 1890/ 1983)—are represented as *short-term memories*. Short-term memories are the *active* contents of mind, and are typically conceived in psychological theory as the by-products, or end results, of a perceptual analysis (e.g., Bjork, 1975; Craik & Levy, 1976). A more inclusive term, *working memory,* is used to refer to the internal machinery that collectively selects short-term memo- ries, maintains them in an active state, and underlies most on-line psycho- logical functioning (Baddeley, 1986, 1992; Baddeley & Hitch, 1974).

   The development of internal machinery that keeps the by-products of perceptual analyses in an active state seems clearly adaptive. The interpreta- tion of spoken language, for example, requires us to remember the early part of an utterance, after it has receded into the past. Most mental tasks, like solving math problems, oblige us to retain intermediate bits of informa- tion as we work toward a solution. (We need to remember to carry the "one" if we are going to add 37 and 46 together successfully in our head.) It is probably not possible to read a story or comprehend a text without actively maintaining the theme of the material, or the particular situation that currently applies (Just & Carpenter, 1992; Kintsch & VanDijk, 1978). Working memory thus becomes an adaptive brain system that stores and manipulates information, as needed, for the performance of a variety of complex cognitive tasks (see also Baddeley, 1992).

Because this is a volume on memory, my chapter focuses on the creation, storage, and recovery of short-term memories, rather than on how short-term memories might be used in more complex cognitive skills like reasoning, problem solving, or comprehension (for reviews see Cantor, Engle, & Hamilton, 1991; Cowan, 1988; Daneman & Tardiff, 1987; Just & Carpenter, 1992). I begin by considering what it means to be part of the "active" contents of mind, including how the concept of activation is typically defined and measured as well as some of the logical implications of this notion for theory. Next, I review some specific short-term storage mechanisms that have been proposed, particularly Alan Baddeley's ideas about working memory, and I examine the interpretive tools that researchers typically employ for the analysis of short-term forgetting. I conclude the chapter with a brief discussion of retrieval processes in working memory and offer some speculations about the proper role of short-term memories in the current psychology of memory.

I. THE SHORT-TERM ACTIVITY TRACE

Most of the knowledge and experiences that accumulate in a lifetime lie dormant, undisturbed, in the human mind. Occupying the immediate "present," we find only fragments of knowledge—thoughts and images that subjectively appear to be in an active state. The technical meaning of the term "activation" can best be appreciated by appealing to what is perhaps the central tenet of modern brain science: namely, that all psychological processes are ultimately describable in neural terms. Memories, percepts, ideas—each is thought to be coded in the nervous system as a collection of active signals that move about in what are presumed to be large groups, or networks, of individual processing units (neurons). At a particular instant in time, these units have associated activation values (firing rates and graded potentials), and they communicate with one another based on these activation values and the unit-to-unit connections that exist in the network. The short-term memory trace is synonymous with *heightened* activation, relative to a baseline level, and is usually seen as a particular pattern of activity across a subset of the individual units (Gerard, 1949; Hebb, 1949).

Permanent knowledge is thought to be represented in terms of the unit-to-unit connection strengths, or weights, so it is common to describe short-term memory as that portion of permanent memory that is currently active (Cowan, 1988, 1993; Engle, Cantor, & Carullo, 1992; Shiffrin, 1993). Cue information in the environment stimulates the relevant portions of permanent memory (also called long-term memory) via perceptual processes, and the temporary remnants of this processing define the short-term memory trace. Note that the trace is defined as a *pattern* of activity; no one-to-one mapping is assumed between a memory and a particular unit. It is accepted that many individual units are involved, and that a given unit might, in fact, participate in the formation of multiple other memories (this kind of memory representation is often called *distributed;* see McClelland and Rumelhart, 1985).

A. Measurement Issues

Defining the short-term memory trace in terms of unit, or neural, activation raises some immediate concerns about how activation can best be defined and measured. Activation is often assumed to be a continuous variable, so at what point along the activation continuum does the short-term memory trace actually begin? To complicate the problem further, there are almost certainly multiple levels of "activated" traces. For example, short-term memories may comprise the set of activated portions of permanent memory, but only some of these traces occupy the focus of conscious awareness. Thus, there is the general set of active knowledge, short-term memories, and within this set there are activated traces that somehow map onto the elements of conscious awareness (see Potter, 1993, for a third, fleeting and conceptually based, kind of activation). Presumably, memories that are part of conscious awareness are more "active" than those outside the focus of awareness (Cowan, 1988), but there is, at present, no principled basis for a claim of this sort.

The idea that short-term memories may exist at or beyond the focus of awareness is motivated, in large part, by data demonstrating retrieval "priming" in the absence of conscious awareness. Our reaction time to the word NURSE is faster if DOCTOR has been presented to us moments before, even if DOCTOR was presented at perceptual levels where no conscious detection occurred (Merikle & Reingold, 1990). Moreover, our ability to identify a briefly presented word is significantly enhanced by its prior presentation, even if we consciously remember nothing about the prior occurrence at test (Jacoby & Dallas, 1981). Conscious awareness, then, is not a necessary precursor of increased accessibility. Priming effects, or enhanced retrieval times, have been offered as one way of defining activation operationally (Cowan, 1988), but there are reasons to doubt the ultimate usefulness of this approach. Retrieval priming has been detected after hours or even days (Tulving, Schacter, & Stark, 1982), so if we accept a definition of activation based on priming, we must reconsider the appropriateness of the term "short-term" for describing the set of activated knowledge.

A potentially more useful way of defining activation has been promised from those working in the areas of electrophysiological recording and brain imaging. The gross electrical activity emanating from the brain changes after presentation of an event, so-called event-related potentials, and it may be possible to correlate this activity with aspects of consciousness and remembering (Kutas, 1988; Paller, 1990). Work continues as well with single-cell recording techniques—groups of cells in the monkey brain, for example, show sustained activity during short retention periods; thus, there is hope that we may eventually be able to monitor short-term memories directly, or at least the units that comprise those memories (see Schneider, 1993, for a brief review). Finally, there are ever-increasing groups of researchers working with positron emission tomography and magnetic resonance imaging, which provide pictorial windows into brain activity; here again, the intent is to map out how activities in different brain regions correlate with a variety of conscious tasks (Kosslyn, 1992). Physiological indices are among the most direct of avenues for solving the measurement problem, but this work is still in its early stages.

It is worthwhile noting that information in the nervous system is often coded in terms of changes in activation (increases or decreases in firing rates) relative to a baseline (Carlson, 1991). Thus, defining short-term memory traces in terms of heightened activation, and then further delineating among levels of heightened activation, may be leaving out half of the important story. There is evidence from a variety of fronts that information can sometimes reside in a state of lowered activation: memories can become inhibited or less accessible than normal, perhaps as a consequence of the retrieval of other memories (Bjork & Bjork, 1992). This lowering of the activation of permanent knowledge, relative to its normal baseline, is presumably transitory, as well, and may constitute yet another class of short-term memories that need to be examined empirically. It seems likely that the field's recent emphasis on physiological indices of remembering may force a broadening of our views about what it means to be in an active state, that is, if we desire to bring our theories more into line with what we know about the operating properties of the nervous system.

B. Content Capacity and Forgetting

As the active contents of mind, short-term memories shoulder several important, but restrictive, properties. First, because one can be active only against a background of inactivity, it is logical to assume that the content capacity of working memory is limited. Only a portion of permanent knowledge can be in a *heightened* state of activity (otherwise the term "heightened" loses its meaning), so the set of short-term memories must be smaller than the set of long-term memories as a whole (Shiffrin, 1993). This assumption is driven by empirical as well as logical concerns, and it maps well onto subjective experience; we can certainly only be "aware" of a fraction of our ongoing experience at any instant in time. In a memory span task, where subjects are required to recall short lists of items immediately in their original order of presentation, performance tends to break down as list length reaches between five and nine items (Miller, 1956).

Besides these intrinsic capacity limitations, the short-term activity trace also suffers from inherent fragility. Short-term memories are transient in nature, and the conditions under which the activity trace returns from a heightened state to baseline (also known as forgetting) is a topic of major concern. It is common to assume that the activity trace naturally *decays,* that is, activity returns to baseline as a property of time, whenever the trace is not actively maintained by the machinery of working memory (Baddeley, 1992; Cowan, 1988, 1993). But decay is not the only interpretive tool available to analyze forgetting; indeed, as I discuss in a later section, there are empirical reasons to suspect that the passage of time per se may not be the critical factor controlling forgetting in most classical short-term memory environments.

Content capacity and forgetting are important components of working memory, but they should not be considered as *fixed* properties of the system, as was once believed (Atkinson & Shiffrin, 1968; Waugh & Norman, 1965). Instead, the characteristics of each are likely to be task dependent, arising from the interplay of what are perhaps fixed *resource* limitations in the system (how much attention we can direct to a task) and the inevitable presence of conditions that seem to promote forgetting. Think about a juggler trying to juggle a set of plates. The number of plates that can be maintained without a crash defines the content capacity of the juggling system, and it is roughly comparable to the number of items that can be successfully recalled in a memory span task. Clearly, the set of juggled items is limited—it has a content capacity—but the limit is not a fixed property of air. It is better seen as an equilibrium point between two opposing forces: the speed of the juggler's hand movements pushing the plates upward and the counteracting force of gravity constantly pushing things downward. In the same manner, a restricted memory span is best seen as a trade-off between the resources allocated to keeping short-term traces active and the opposing forces of forgetting. (The only place where the analogy breaks down with respect to forgetting. Gravity, for all intent and purposes, is fixed, but the rate of forgetting, as I illustrate later, depends on a variety of factors.)

This trade-off view of content capacity is compelling because it accounts for the individual differences that one often sees in immediate memory performance. The capacity of a juggler is going to depend on many factors: the juggling technique, the size of the plates, whether the juggler is distracted, and so on. Similarly, the size of the active set of short-term memories depends on the maintenance skills that the memorizer has acquired, the type of items that need to be maintained, and whether the necessary conditions are present to promote forgetting. In cases where subjects have received extensive skill training in short-term maintenance, for example, memory span has actually risen from the normal 5 to 7 items up to around 100 (Chase & Ericsson, 1982). Moreover, when the maintenance techniques are limited, as in young children who fail to rehearse spontaneously, memory span suffers accordingly (Gathercole, Adams, & Hitch, 1994).

C. Representational Format

The short-term activity trace arises as a by-product of perceptual processing, but the stimulus event that drives the processing need not originate directly in the environment. Anytime we recall something from long-term memory, in fact, we are internally generating a short-term activity trace. Memory performance arises from active contents of mind, whether subjectively experienced or not, so it is useful to consider all retrieval processes as related in one way or another to the working memory system. Moreover, the particular processing machinery that is used, either to perceive an external event or to retrieve a fact from permanent memory, helps to determine the coding, or representational format, of the final activity pattern (Craik & Levy, 1976; Craik & Lockhart, 1972).

In most immediate memory tasks, the short-term activity trace appears to consist primarily of activated features that are related to sound or speech (Baddeley, 1966; Conrad, 1964; Hintzman, 1967; Sperling, 1963). Conrad (1964) showed that subjects tend to make primarily phonetic confusion errors in immediate recall, even if the stimulus items are presented originally in a visual form (see also Sperling, 1963). Additionally, verbal distracter tasks either before or after presentation typically produce more forgetting than nonverbal ones (Wickelgren, 1966). It is easy to come up with reasons why a sound-based representation might be preferred. For instance, short-term memories are presumed to play an important role in the production and comprehension of speech, so it may be adaptive to maintain the active contents of mind in a primarily phonological form.

At one time, a sound-based representational format was accepted as a defining feature of the short-term activity trace; the active contents of mind were thought to be represented phonologically (or perhaps in an articulatory form), whereas long-term memory was coded semantically (Baddeley, 1966). In fact, in the 1970s it was popular for supporters of the dichotomous models of memory (those distinguishing short- and long-term memory as separate systems) to appeal to apparent coding-based peculiarities in the free-recall serial-position curve as fundamental evidence for the dichotomous position. Recall from the early portions of a memory list was observed to be sensitive to semantic dimensions (e.g., word frequency, or similarity in meaning), whereas end-of-the-list recall was affected by variations along a sound-based dimension. Because items from the early parts of a list had occurred further back in time, the reasoning followed, early list recall must be tapping long-term memory, whereas end-of-the-list recall must be tapping primarily short-term memories. In hindsight, this reasoning appears suspect given that all forms of recall must be mediated by short-term activity traces generated by the working memory system. One could just as easily have argued that recall-based sensitivity to semantic variables provides excellent evidence for the presence of semantic features in the short-term activity trace.

What became clear to researchers, however, was that under different task demands, a variety of trace representational formats could be detected in an immediate memory environment. It is relatively easy to demonstrate what appears to be visual coding under the right task demands (Cooper & Shepard, 1973; see also Cooper & Lang, this volume, Chapter 5), or even coding based on semantics (Shulman, 1972). Healy (1975, 1982) has shown that the immediate recall of spatial location may depend critically on the establishment of a visually based code, whereas the recall of immediate temporal order may benefit from a sound-based code. Coding format may also depend to some extent on one's dominant mode of communication (Shand, 1982); hearing-impaired subjects, for example, sometimes have trouble with immediate temporal order recall, which is assumed to be helped by phonetic-based coding (Hanson, 1990). Thus, a particular kind of coding format cannot be considered to be a defining feature of the class of short-term memories.

D. Chunking

There is another sense in which the representational format of the short-term activity trace is important, and that is with respect to chunking (Miller, 1956). Chunking is a processing component of working memory, perhaps related to perceptual processing, that allows the subject to rearrange incoming information in meaningful or familiar patterns (called chunks). A list of letters like *ca-tfl-ybu-g* becomes much easier to recall after one sees that the individual letters can be translated into the words *cat-fly-bug*. Why this is the case is easy to see from the perspective of the trade-off view of content capacity described earlier. Rather than having to maintain nine activity traces, corresponding to the nine individual letters, the working memory system needs to maintain only three, the activity patterns corresponding to the words *cat, fly,* and *bug.* Maintaining three patterns requires less resources, and so the system is better able to counteract the persistent effects of forgetting. Imagine that the juggler, faced with the task of having to keep nine plates aloft, binds the plates together into groups of three. It might be a bit harder to throw a three-plate unit aloft, but it is far easier to keep track of three falling units than nine.

II. THE MACHINERY OF STORAGE

One salient feature of research on short-term/working memory over the past two decades has been the steady emergence of sophisticated processing models of immediate retention. Whereas in the 1960s it was popular to propose sweeping distinctions among sensory, short-term, and permanent storage, today's models postulate vastly more complex modularized information processing systems. Rather than simple rehearsal buffers of fixed capacity and relatively fixed forgetting rates, today's researchers recognize myriad separable subsystems, each designed to handle the creation and control of modality-specific or task-specific short-term memories (Burgess & Hitch, 1992; Schneider & Detweiler, 1987).

Probably the most influential of these models, although by no means the most complex, is the working memory system of Baddeley and Hitch (1974). This approach has undergone substantial modification and refinement over the past twenty years, but in each of its sundry incarnations it has served as a useful heuristic for those interested in basic and applied research (for reviews see Baddeley, 1986, 1992). Currently, it is conceived as a tripartite system containing a main controller, or central executive, that handles and controls on-line attentional processing and two subsidiary slave systems: the articulatory "loop" and the visuospatial "sketch pad" (see also Baddeley, 1992). The central executive has received the least amount of theoretical attention, although it is assumed to be the device through which most cognitive tasks are performed. The brunt of the attention, presumably for reasons of tractability, has been directed toward the loop and sketch pad, which underlie the short-term storage of speech-based and visuospatial information, respectively.

A. The Articulatory Loop

The decision to treat the loop as a separate storage device, distinct from the storage capabilities of the central executive, was driven by Baddeley and Hitch's (1974) early finding that remembering short lists of digits typically has little damaging effect on concurrent cognitive tasks like reasoning or problem solving. Subjects can reason and learn just fine even with a near-capacity digit load, although things are slowed down a bit, and this fact encouraged Baddeley and Hitch (1974) to move forward with a modularized system. The loop was conceived as a short-term storage vehicle for speech-based material, perhaps as a backup system for speech comprehension, to be used as needed by the central executive. Over the years, the loop itself has been refined and modularized, and it now consists of an articulatory control process, acting like an "inner voice," and a phonological store corresponding to a kind of "inner ear." Information passively maintained in the phonological store is assumed to decay in approximately one to two seconds (a "fixed" property of the system), but it can be refreshed through subvocal rehearsal processes generated by the articulatory control process.

The articulatory control process serves two main functions in the working memory system. As just noted, it is the active part of the loop, controlling subvocal articulation, or rehearsal. Continued internal rehearsal improves storage time by acting to refresh decaying representations. The second function, or perhaps inevitable by-product, of the articulatory control process is the translation of visually presented material into phonological form. We noted in the previous section that the dominant coding format of the short-term activity trace tends to be phonological (sound based), even if the material to be remembered is presented originally in a visual form (Conrad, 1964). According to Baddeley, it is the articulatory control process that produces the modality translation, prior to registering the material in the phonological store. Evidence to support the translation function comes from studies in which the articulatory control process is subverted: subjects are asked to repeat an irrelevant sound (perhaps the word "the") during presentation and recall of material. This technique, known as articulatory suppression, produces activity representations that seem to lack the usual phonological attributes.

To illustrate, lists of items that sound similar typically lead to poor immediate recall (Conrad & Hull, 1964; Wickelgren, 1965). This result, known as the phonological similarity effect, occurs when list material is presented aloud or silently, and presumably results from confusions among the phonologically represented activity traces. Articulatory suppression eliminates the similarity decrement, but only for visually presented material (Baddeley, Lewis, & Vallar, 1984). Because the articulatory control process is not allowed to operate, no phonological code is created in the visual case and, hence, no sound-based confusions arise. For material presented aloud, however, the similarity remains because auditory material gains privileged access into the phonological store—no modality translation is required.

The articulatory nature of the loop receives its strongest support from studies examining the relationship between word length and memory span. Memory span is usually defined as the number of items in a list that can be correctly recalled in order, immediately after presentation, half of the time (Schweickert, 1993). Span turns out to be inversely proportional to the spoken durations of the items that need to be remembered. In general, long words lead to smaller spans than do short words; or, more precisely, words that take a long time to articulate lead to smaller spans than do words with short articulation times (this result is known generally as the *word length effect;* Baddeley, Thomson, & Buchanan, 1975). As a rule of thumb, span is roughly equivalent to the amount of material that can be spoken in about two seconds. It has been possible to account for a number of individual differences by appealing to this relationship with articulation time, including how span is affected by materials (Schweickert & Boruff, 1986), cross-cultural differences in span (Ellis & Hennelley, 1980), and how span length changes over age (Hulme & Tordoff, 1989).

According to the extant version of the articulatory loop, once information is deposited into the phonological store, it will decay in approximately two seconds. It is this fixed feature of the phonological store that produces span limitations, not the articulatory control process per se. The articulatory control process can refresh the decaying representation, through subvocal rehearsal, provided that the trace has not already been rendered unrecognizable by the processes of decay. (In juggling, it is gravity that causes the plates to fall; skilled jugglers can keep the plates aloft, provided that their quick hands reach the rapidly falling plates before they hit the ground.)

Long words produce smaller memory spans than short words because the to-be-remembered items take longer to articulate; more units, as a consequence, are likely to be lost through decay before they can be retrieved for covert articulation. One of the compelling features of this analysis is the prediction that the word length effect should disappear under conditions of articulatory suppression. Once the refreshing process has been removed from the equation, via the suppression, everything should decay in approximately two seconds, regardless of word length. A number of studies have confirmed this prediction (Baddeley et al., 1975). Thus, to re-emphasize, the fact that we forget at all is due to decay. But the word length effect, and other material-based differences in span, are attributable to the articulatory control process.

B. The Visuospatial Sketch Pad

Most of us can easily form a visual image of something in our heads: an apple, our pet cat, a hamburger. Visual images may not be the dominant coding format of the activity trace, at least under conditions where the comprehension and production of speech are required, but they are clearly an important subjective component of mind. Some tasks, in fact, may demand the formation of a visual code—perhaps remembering the position of an object on a map or remembering the details of someone's face. The visuospatial sketch pad is the short-term storage component of working memory that is assumed to handle visual and spatial information.

Most of the work that has been done on the visuospatial sketch pad has been concerned merely with demonstrating the existence of the system—documenting the presence of a visuospatial trace—rather than delineating its storage capacity or forgetting properties. In the prototypical experimental setting, subjects are asked to form and maintain a visual image while performing a concurrent task that taps visual, verbal, or spatial processing. For example, in one experiment subjects were instructed to learn a list of words using an imagery mnemonic (placing to-be-remembered items in locations along an imaginary walk through a college campus) while simultaneously tracking a moving spot of light (or not). Having to perform this concurrent tracking task disrupted memory performance relative to the control, but only when subjects were using the imagery mnemonic. If subjects learned the words by rote repetition, the concurrent tracking task had little negative effect on performance (Baddeley & Lieberman, 1980).

A number of studies have attempted to dissociate the visual and spatial components of the sketch pad representation. As Baddeley (1992) argues, there are reasons to assume that these components are controlled by separate systems in the brain. Patients with a particular form of brain damage might show a profound deficit in spatial processing (like following routes on a map), but no impairment on a task that taps purely visual processing (recognizing that guitars have round holes in the middle); other patients with different lesions might show the opposite pattern (Farah, 1988). In the laboratory it is possible to pick concurrent tasks that selectively disrupt the visual and spatial components of the image. Concurrent visuospatial tasks, like tracking the spot of light, typically produce the most impairment (Baddeley & Lieberman, 1980), but purely visual tasks can disrupt, as well (Baddeley, 1992; L. R. Brooks, 1968; den Heyer & Barrett, 1971).

C. Evaluating Working Memory

I have stressed Baddeley's version of working memory because of its broad appeal, and because Baddeley and Hitch (1974) were among the first researchers to recognize the need for multiple, perhaps independent, short-term storage systems. Baddeley has also expended enormous effort emphasizing applications of the system, particularly the role of working memory in understanding speech and reading, and an entire cottage industry of "working memory" advocates has emerged. But the scientific status of the system can be reasonably questioned, and further refinements are clearly needed.

One problem with the system is that alternative explanations for the basic data are possible. For example, considerable theoretical mileage is gained by the finding that articulatory suppression eliminates the word length and phonological similarity effects. It is not clear, however, exactly what effect suppression has on the retention process; specifically, it is not clear whether performance changes are best described in terms of the processes controlling storage or by appealing to representational format changes in the stored traces. For instance, I have shown elsewhere, through a computer simulation model, that the elimination of the phonological similarity effect under suppression (for visual but not auditory presentation) can be explained by simply assuming that suppression differentially affects the net trace similarity of phonologically similar and dissimilar materials. I was able to show not only why the phonological similarity effect is eliminated under some conditions, but also why suppression hurts immediate performance overall (Nairne, 1990).

Other work complicates the defined role of the articulatory control process in producing the word length effect. Time-limited spans, from the working memory perspective, arise from failures of the subvocal rehearsal processes to refresh active traces within the fixed decay window. But Cowan et al. (1992) have shown that the locus of the word length effect may actually be in the output stage, during the time that subjects are recalling the to-be-remembered items. In one experiment, subjects received random presentations of mixed lists in which word length was varied factorially in each half (i.e., there were four types of lists: short–short; short–long; long–short; long–long). Recall order was also varied randomly: A cue appeared at the beginning of the recall period indicating whether the list was to be recalled in a forward or backward direction. Long words produced lower performance, as expected, but only if the task required that long words be output first during recall. For forward recall, the short–long lists yielded better performance than that of the long–short lists, but the opposite pattern occurred in backward recall. Note that at the point of recall, subjects had no way of knowing whether forward or backward recall would be required; thus, the locus of the word length effect must be during the response output phase. Other evidence consistent with this conclusion comes from Avons, Wright, and Pammer (1994) who found that the word length effect is smaller in probed recall (which does not require the subject to output the entire list) than it is in spoken serial recall.

According to Cowan (1993), the critical determinant of time limits in span is the speed or efficiency with which subjects can reactivate items during the pauses that occur during the important recall output period. In work with children (Cowan, 1992), he found that silent interword pause times during recall increased as the length of the to-be-remembered list grew longer. He concluded that items are lost, presumably due to fixed decay, during the time that other items are being output, but they can be refreshed or reactivated (provided that they have not been completely lost) during the period separating one recalled item from the next. Final memory performance is therefore a function of pronunciation time, during which decay occurs, and the efficiency with which the remaining items can be reactivated during the response pauses. Most central to the present point, however, is that covert rehearsal of the type assumed to be controlled by the articulatory control process is unlikely to be occurring during these inter-response intervals. The pause times are simply too short for rehearsal of the list to be occurring, given what we know about covert rehearsal rates (Landauer, 1962). Instead, some kind of rapid search or scanning process may be operating (Cavanagh, 1972).

There is a collection of other results suggesting that memory span and the word length effect are actually rather complex phenomena, influenced by multiple factors. Gathercole and Adams (1993), for example, recently reported that young children's digit spans are unrelated to their articulation rates. Lapointe and Engle (1990) showed that the elimination of the word length effect under articulatory suppression may depend critically on whether lists are drawn from a large or small vocabulary. Work in my laboratory has shown that the word length effect may emerge only when some degree of proactive interference is operative; word length effects are not found for the first few trials in a session (Nairne, Neath, & Serra, 1996). These results, combined with the work of Cowan and colleagues, simply suggest that we are some distance from a complete understanding of time limitations in immediate memory performance. It is clear that some sort of trade-off between resource-limited reactivation processes (e.g., search or rehearsal) and forgetting underlies immediate memory performance, but the details remain to be worked out.

III. THE INTERPRETIVE TOOLS OF FORGETTING

The fact that the active contents of mind are fragile and easily forgotten is clear to anyone who has ever tried to remember a telephone number from its source to the phone. But what are the operative determinants of this trace fragility? Is forgetting a fixed feature of short-term memories—as activation-based definitions seem to imply—that can be only temporarily delayed by the internal machinery of working memory? As the preceding section demonstrated, many researchers working on the mechanics of immediate memory seem to assume as much: fixed decay is to the working memory system as gravity is to the struggling juggler. But there are several interpretive tools available to analyze forgetting, and the loss of memory in an immediate memory context may reflect all, one, or some combination of the factors that I consider in the following paragraphs.

A. Decay

Because forgetting is correlated with the passage of time, it is natural to assume that it is time per se that is responsible for the forgetting. Most neural network theories postulate, without controversy, that activation automatically decays with time, unless input from the environment (or from other internal units) counteracts this natural loss (McClelland & Rumelhart, 1985). But the early investigators of immediate memory were not so easily convinced. Theories of disuse—where impressions fade entirely as a function of time—were actually quite unpopular among researchers in the period leading up to the first investigations of short-term memory (McGeoch, 1942). Iron bars rust with time, it was common to argue, but it is not the passage of time that creates the rust; there are other factors, notably oxidation, that actually produce the change. In the case of forgetting, it was agreed that interference from other similar materials occurring during the retention period was responsible for the performance losses.

What convinced the early researchers that decay might be operating on the active contents of mind was the empirical finding that subspan material can be forgotten rapidly under conditions of minimal interference. In classic work by Brown (1958) and Peterson and Peterson (1959), subjects forgot short lists of consonants in under 20 s if a digit-counting distractor task immediately intervened between list presentation and recall. Because digits and letters are so dissimilar, it was reasoned that a distractor task like counting backward, although sufficiently taxing to prevent covert rehearsal, is unlikely to produce interference. This kind of argument continues to be a popular weapon in the arsenal of the modern decay theorist. Memory for unattended speech, for example, shows a regular loss function while a subject merely engages in silent reading, a task that is unlikely to interfere much with a sound-based activity representation (Cowan, Lichty, & Grove, 1990).

Most decay accounts of forgetting assume that information is simply lost as a function of time, but there are other ways to formulate time-based changes in retention. For example, Estes (1972) has argued that short-term memories are not lost per se; instead, short-term memories simply become less precise with the passage of time. When remembering temporal position over time, subjects' errors tend not to be random; they tend to be related systematically to the original input position. Response likelihood peaks at the correct input position, and declines gradually as distance from the true value increases (Bjork & Healy, 1974; Lee & Estes, 1977). The probability that an item will be remembered in its correct position changes systematically with time, but the original event is not lost in an absolute sense; there is always some probability that the item will return to its original state and be remembered correctly.

Absolute time-based models like the one proposed by Estes (1972) do an excellent job of accounting for the way that immediate memory performance changes as the retention interval increases. But all pure time-based models have trouble accounting for the variability that is found in forgetting rates across experimental contexts. Similarity among items in a list affects forgetting, for example, which is not easily accounted for by a decay model (although see Posner & Konick, 1966). Distractor paradigms like the Brown–Peterson task produce a characteristic forgetting function, but short-term forgetting can be substantially more rapid under conditions where subjects are not expecting an immediate memory test. In a task designed originally by Muter (1980), subjects received unexpected memory tests for material presented moments earlier, and forgetting appeared to be relatively complete in just a couple of seconds (see also Sebrechts, Marsh, & Seamon, 1989).

Perhaps more important, forgetting can be drastically reduced or it can even disappear altogether under the right conditions of testing. Keppel and Underwood (1962) showed that there is little or no forgetting in a Brown–Peterson task when performance is assessed after the very first trial in the experimental session. Performance is quite good on the first trial, but more important, recall does not depend on the length of the digit-counting distractor period. It is apparently necessary for subjects to have experienced several memory trials before variations in the retention interval begin to affect performance. This proactive effect of prior trials is exceedingly difficult for a pure decay theory to explain; the data suggest instead that short-term forgetting may be due to between-trial confusions that can arise, by definition, only after several trials have been presented (Bennett, 1975). Similarly, as noted earlier, the word length effect, which is usually presented as strong support for decay, may also depend critically on the proactive effects of prior trials.

B. Interference

The most popular alternative to decay is interference. Interference remains a commonly used tool for the analysis of short-term retention, although the term has had multiple meanings historically. In the dichotomous memory models of the 1960s (Waugh & Norman, 1965), interference was often synonymous with displacement; short-term/working memory was assumed to have a fixed capacity, so as new items arrived for processing, old items were displaced, or essentially kicked out of the system. Given that the content capacity of working memory is not fixed, pure displacement theories have fallen out of favor.

A second way that the term interference has been used is with respect to an overwriting or erasure process. Interference occurs when some or all of the active features of a short-term memory are rendered functionally lost by subsequently occurring material (see also Nairne, 1988). Event B interferes with or degrades the representation of Event A, usually to the extent that A and B share similar features. Note that time is not directly part of the equation; the appearance of new and similar material will, of course, be correlated with the passage of time, but time itself is not the causative factor behind forgetting. Strong support for this overwriting process comes from experiments demonstrating similarity-based retroactive effects on short-term retention. For example, a Brown–Peterson distractor task more effectively produces forgetting if it is presented in the same modality as the list items (Proctor & Fagnani, 1978).

Overwriting accounts do a nice job of handling similarity-based forgetting effects in immediate memory, but they have difficulties handling other aspects of the data. Similarity-based overwriting does not explain the word length effect, for example, unless one makes some gratuitous assumptions about similarity and its relation to articulation time. It is also unclear how overwriting explains the Keppel and Underwood (1962) data or, for that matter, proactive effects in general. Why should events that happened moments prior to the current trial erase components of currently active traces? Finally, similarity, by itself, cannot be used to predict when overwriting will occur. Ryan (1969) and others have shown that subjective grouping, based on temporal cues, is a critical determinant of whether retroactive interference effects will occur in immediate recall. Thus, although overwriting may be one source of forgetting in immediate memory, it is unlikely to be the sole source.

C. Deblurring

The third interpretive tool for short-term forgetting, deblurring, is actually related to a third meaning of the term interference. Deblurring (sometimes called redintegration) is the process through which the short-term activity trace is interpreted, or translated into a form that allows for an overt recall. Deblurring is required anytime the activity trace is degraded, or blurry, regardless of the original source of the degradation (e.g., overwriting, decay, poor encoding). In fact, it is possible to forget in an immediate memory environment without assuming any decay or overwriting, provided that the trace is incorrectly interpreted at the time of test.

To see how such a situation might arise, imagine that a subject simply encodes the sound of an item as part of the short-term activity trace. Further, assume that there is no decay or overwriting, so the sound-based activity trace is fully intact at the point of recall. Whether the subject will recall the original item is going to depend on whether the represented sound maps easily onto the correct response. If the original item was a homophone, like *pear,* then the deblurring process is likely to lead to an incorrect interpretation at test (that is, the subject could recall *pear, pair,* or *pare*). Forgetting, as measured through incorrect performance at test, can thus arise from the process of trace interpretation without assuming any loss in the represented information.

Numerous findings suggest that incorrect trace deblurring is an important source of forgetting in immediate memory environments. For example, memory span is typically greater for words than for nonwords, even when articulation times have been equated across items (Hulme, Maughan, & Brown, 1991); similar span differences are found for high- and low frequency words (J. O. Brooks & Watkins, 1990). These differences are assumed to result from the relative ease with which the blurry trace can be reconstructed; it is no doubt easier to reconstruct a meaningful word from a degraded fragment than it is to reconstruct a meaningless nonword. Trace deblurring is also clearly one important locus of similarity effects in immediate recall. If list members share many overlapping features, like vowel or consonant sounds, then it is likely that a subject will confuse the representation of a particular item in a sequence with other items that also occurred in the list (Nairne, 1990).

I mentioned earlier that the deblurring process is related to an additional meaning of the term interference. One historical interpretation of interference effects in memory is response competition—multiple responses become associated to a cue and competition among these responses at test produces forgetting (McGeoch, 1942). It is easy to conceive of the trace deblurring process in terms of response competition: the more distinctive the activity trace at the point of test, the less competition there will be from alternative plausible "interpretations." As with response competition, it is possible to use trace deblurring as one vehicle for explaining the proactive determinants of forgetting. For example, retention loss in the Brown–Peterson task depends on the occurrence of earlier trials because these earlier trials undermine the interpretation process. One possibility is that prior trials simply create more interpretation choices. Alternatively, if the same item is repeated across trials, then it might be difficult to determine whether the blurry trace represents the occurrence from trial N or the one from $N - 1$.

Obviously, the trick for memory theorists is to explain which of these numerous interpretive tools of forgetting (decay, interference, or deblurring) is responsible for performance loss in any particular experimental context. We are some distance from achieving such a measure of theoretical dexterity, although some current quantitative or simulation models have been successful using the different forgetting tools to account for data in restricted settings (Burgess & Hitch, 1992; Laming, 1992; Nairne, 1990; Scweickert, 1993). The problem is a sticky one because we are not sure at this point which of these tools is even psychologically valid, or whether data that appear to support a process like decay or overwriting might be more easily explained by some third, yet undiscovered, mechanism. The only conclusion that can be stated with reasonable certainty is that we have made some progress in delineating the range of possible mechanisms that might be involved.

IV. RETRIEVAL FROM SHORT-TERM/WORKING MEMORY

Once we accept that deblurring of the short-term activity trace might be an important component of forgetting, we commit to the position that retrieval from working memory is, at least in part, cue dependent. The degraded trace representation is used as a cue to decide on the most appropriate response, or to make decisions about whether an item, in fact, occurred moments earlier. Although the cue-dependent nature of retrieval is taken for granted in the study of long-term memory (Hintzman, 1988; Lewandowsky & Murdock, 1989; Raaijmakers & Shiffrin, 1981), the position remains somewhat controversial in the short-term memory literature. Some researchers have maintained that there might be a kind of "pure" recovery, at least of those elements maintained at the focus of conscious awareness (Wickens, Moody, & Dow, 1981).

Setting this issue aside, there has been a significant amount of interest in the retrieval dynamics of working memory. It has been popular over the years, for example, to address whether the recovery of information contained in the short-term activity trace is governed by a serial or parallel retrieval process. In classic work by Sternberg (1966), subjects were presented with short lists of items followed immediately by a single item probe. The task was to identify, as quickly as possible, whether the probe was a member of the just-presented memory set. Sternberg's main concern was with reaction time and, specifically, how reaction time might change as a function of the size of the memory set (i.e., list length). Across a number of experiments, he and others have found that reaction time is a roughly linear function of the number of studied items, and does not depend much on whether the probe is contained in the memory set (yielding a "yes" response) or not (a "no" response). Sternberg's original conclusion from these data was that the recovery of information from working memory is controlled by a serial process, where the probe is compared individually with each of the items maintained in the active memory set. This serial scanning process can be contrasted with a parallel one, where the probe is compared to all of the maintained items at the same time (Ratcliff, 1978).

As noted, the Sternberg task generated an enormous amount of research dedicated to understanding the nature of retrieval of short-term memories. Unfortunately, it turns out to be difficult to distinguish serial from parallel processing theoretically, at least when using mean reaction time (Townsend & Ashby, 1983; see also Ashby, Tein, & Balakrishnan, 1993). Consequently, researchers have turned to more elaborate devices, usually centering on a fuller analysis of the reaction time distributions. In work by Dosher and colleagues (Dosher, 1979; McElree & Dosher, 1993), for example, the entire time course of retrieval is measured by requiring subjects to respond immediately following a response cue that appears at various times after the probe. Using this procedure, one can map out how mnemonic information grows during the retrieval episode, from initial chance levels (where the response signal appears instantly after appearance of the probe) to asymptotic levels (where subjects have as much time as needed to make their responses). This kind of technique is useful because it allows the researcher to study how variables affect different aspects of the retrieval process—the rate of growth in availability of the mnemonic information, the final asymptotic level, and the intercept or minimal processing time (Gronlund & Ratcliff, 1989; McElree & Dosher, 1993).

Recent applications of this response-signal technique have led to dissociations in the retrieval dynamics of recovering item and order information from working memory. The classic Sternberg task requires decisions only about item information (did the probe occur before?), but immediate memory experiments often require knowledge about the order in which items occurred (did "cat" follow "bird" in the list?). When recovering item information, asymptotic reaction time depends importantly on the studied position of the item in the list (recent items are responded to more quickly), but the other indices of retrieval (rate and intercept) show no effects of studied position. If subjects are asked to make decisions about order, on the other hand, study position affects asymptotic reaction time as well as the other aspects of retrieval dynamics. According to McElree and Dosher (1993), these data compel one to conclude that the recovery of item information may be controlled by some kind of parallel process, whereas the recovery of order information involves a slower, serial retrieval process.

Of course, retrieval dynamics are likely to depend on the kind of retention test required. Recognizing that two items are appearing in the original presentation order may initiate different retrieval processes from those required to recall which two items went together in a list. We are only just beginning to apply microscopic analyses of processing to the study of memory, so much fruitful research awaits to be initiated. Of perhaps more importance, it will be interesting to see whether the analysis of retrieval dynamics will ultimately enable researchers to decide whether the recovery of short-term memories differs in any fundamental way from the recovery of permanent, or long-term, memories. As I discuss in the next section, there are reasons to question whether the short-term/long-term distinction is even necessary, that is, above and beyond the fact that retention is assessed at either a short or a long interval following initial presentation.

V. DO WE NEED SHORT-TERM/WORKING MEMORY?

Part of the appeal of transient memories to the psychologist is that they provide the only true window into the subjective experience of remembering. We all recognize the experience of the rapidly fading sensory icon or the lingering auditory echo; the same is true for the active contents of mind that we have been calling short-term or working memories. Permanent knowledge may be represented in our brains, but that knowledge is knowable, or experienced, only in the heightened form of activity that defines short-term memories.

But what are the data that compel us to draw theoretical distinctions between memories that are in an active versus inactive state? Are there really separate neurological systems in the brain, like the multiple pathways that are clearly present in the visual system, that underlie the recovery and maintenance of information over the short versus the long term? Such a question is difficult to answer for a number of reasons. First, as we noted earlier, most psychologists accept that all memory *performance* is mediated by the same general system—working memory, the system that controls retention over the short term. Long-term memories are expressed only after they have been transformed into an active state; as a result, how can we ever hope to disentangle the relative contributions of short- and long-term systems to performance?

It might be possible to distinguish between the recall of information that is still in an active state—like a telephone number heard moments before—and the recall of something that has left an active state (i.e., returned to baseline). In the former case, performance could be controlled by simple interpretation of the activity trace (Nairne, 1990), whereas recall of the latter might require alternative cuing—perhaps some process of sampling from long-term memory with a context cue (Raaijmakers & Shiffrin, 1981). But even here it is probably a lost cause; we are unlikely to be able to tell whether performance differences are due to the state of activity prior to recall, or to the use of different cues and cuing procedures. Moreover, as Crowder (1989) has emphasized, because we tend to represent information over the short term in a speechlike code, whereas permanent knowledge, or at least cue effectiveness in long-term recall, tends to be governed by semantic factors, there is an inherent coding confound present: we do not know whether performance is determined by the activity state prior to recall, or by the particular representational format that needs to be interpreted.

Another factor that compels one to question the idea that short- and long-term recall are governed by separate modularized processing systems is the fact that performance often seems to follow the same rules in the two cases. A good case in point is the immediate recall of temporal order. We noted earlier that immediate memory for order is characterized by a gradual and regular loss in precision; subject errors tend to be related systematically to the original input position and other aspects of the stimuli (Lee & Estes, 1977). Moreover, if recall is examined as a function of input serial position, the immediate recall curve is bow-shaped; performance is best at the beginning and end of the list. These two findings—systematic error gradients and bow-shaped serial position curves—were thought to be characteristic and defining features of immediate recall. But I have shown in a series of studies that exactly the same trends are found for the long-term recall of serial position, even if subjects are tested after 24 hours. Moreover, I was able to fit a short-term memory model, the perturbation model of Estes (1972), to the data without any changes in the model's basic assumptions (Nairne, 1991, 1992; see also Neath & Crowder, 1990; Schultz, 1955).

Thus, we are left with an enigma: is there something unique about the retention of short-term memories? Do the activity traces engendered by the machinery of working memory follow their own retention rules? Are they governed by specialized neurological structures in the brain that are exclusively designed to handle memory over the short term? Or, is immediate retention really nothing more than memory over the short term, controlled by the same mechanisms and rules that control all memories? There is little hope for an immediate resolution of this dilemma, even from those working in the area of brain science. It is possible to point selectively to populations of brain-damaged subjects who appear to have trouble with short- and long-term retention, respectively (see Martin, 1993, for a review); but, as before, it is difficult to know whether neurological data of this form are best interpreted as coding problems, storage problems, or cuing problems.

There is one additional piece of compelling data that remains, however—those thoughts, images, and feelings that occupy our awareness of the present. It is this subjective experience of awareness that originally drove Exner and James to the notion of primary memory (James, 1890/1983, pp. 607–608), where the current contents of mind are recognized and treated as a fundamentally distinct kind of memory. It is clear that neurons in the brain vary in level of activation, that experience changes the ease of transmission, and that different patterns of activity emerge from different experiences. But the link between neural activity and subjective experience remains purely correlational at this point. Whether we should treat these imaginal "specters" that define the subjective experience of remembering as anything other than epiphenomenal remains an open question.

References

Ashby, F. G., Jein, I.-Y, & Balakrishnan, J. D. (1993). Response time distributions in memory scanning. *Journal of Mathematical Psychology, 37,* 526–555.
Atkinson, R. C., & Shiffrin, R. M. (1968). Human memory: A proposed system and its

control processes. In K. W. Spence & J. T. Spence (Eds.), *The psychology of learning and motivation* (Vol. 2, pp. 89–105). New York: Academic Press.

Avons, S. E., Wright, K. L., & Pammer, K. (1994). The word-length effect in probed and serial recall. *Quarterly Journal of Experimental Psychology, 20,* 249–264.

Baddeley, A. D. (1966). Short-term memory for word sequences as as function of acoustic, semantic, and formal similarity. *Quarterly Journal of Experimental Psychology, 18,* 362–365.

Baddeley, A. D. (1986). *Working memory.* Oxford: Oxford University Press.

Baddeley, A. D. (1992). Working memory. *Science, 255,* 556–559.

Baddeley, A. D., & Hitch, G. (1974). Working memory. In G. H. Bower (Ed.). *The psychology of learning and motivation* (Vol. 8, pp. 47–89). New York: Academic Press.

Baddeley, A. D., Lewis, V. J., & Vallar, G. (1984). Exploring the articulatory loop. *Quarterly Journal of Experimental Psychology, 36,* 233–252.

Baddeley, A. D., & Lieberman, K. (1980). Spatial working memory. In R. Nickerson (Ed.), *Attention and performance VIII* (pp. 521–539). Hillsdale, NJ: Erlbaum.

Baddeley, A. D., Thomson, N., & Buchanan, M. (1975). Word length and the structure of short-term memory. *Journal of Verbal Learning and Verbal Behavior, 14,* 575–589.

Bennett, R. W. (1975). Proactive interference in short-term memory: Fundamental forgetting processes. *Journal of Verbal Learning and Verbal Behavior, 14,* 123–144.

Bjork, R. A. (1975). Short-term storage: The output of a central processor. In F. Restle, R. M. Shiffrin, N. J. Castellan, H. R. Lindman, & D. B. Pisoni (Eds.), *Cognitive theory* (Vol. 1, pp. 151–172). Hillsdale, NJ: Erlbaum.

Bjork, R. A., & Bjork, E. L. (1992). A new theory of disuse and an old theory of stimulus fluctuation. In A. F. Healy, S. M. Kosslyn, & R. M. Shiffrin (Eds.), *From learning processes to cognitive processes* (Vol. 2, pp. 35–67). Hillsdale, NJ: Erlbaum.

Bjork, E. L., & Healy, A. F. (1974). Short-term order and item retention. *Journal of Verbal Learning and Verbal Behavior, 13,* 80–97.

Brooks, J. O., III, & Watkins, M. J. (1990). Further evidence of the intricacy of memory span. *Journal of Experimental Psychology: Learning, Memory, and Cognition, 16,* 1134–1141.

Brooks, L. R. (1968). Spatial and verbal components of the act of recall. *Canadian Journal of Psychology, 22,* 349–368.

Brown, J. (1958). Some tests of the decay theory of immediate memory. *Quarterly Journal of Experimental Psychology, 10,* 12–21.

Burgess, N., & Hitch, G. J. (1992). Toward a network model of the articulatory loop. *Journal of Memory and Language, 31,* 429–460.

Cantor, J., Engle, R. W., & Hamilton, G. (1991). Short-term memory, working memory, and verbal abilities: How do they relate? *Intelligence, 15,* 229–246.

Carlson, N. R. (1991). *Physiology of behavior* (4th ed.). Boston: Allyn & Bacon.

Cavanagh, J. P. (1972). Relation between the immediate memory span and the memory search rate. *Psychological Review, 79,* 525–530.

Chase, W. G., & Ericsson, K. A. (1982). Skill and working memory. In G. H. Bower (Ed.), *The psychology of learning and motivation* (Vol. 16, pp. 1–58). San Diego: Academic Press.

Conrad, R. (1964). Acoustic confusions in immediate memory. *British Journal of Psychology, 55,* 75–84.

Conrad, R., & Hull, A. J. (1964). Information, acoustic confusion, and memory span. *British Journal of Psychology, 55,* 429–432.

Cooper, L. A., & Shepard, R. N. (1973). Chronometric studies of the rotation of mental images. In W. G. Chase (Ed.), *Visual information processing* (pp. 75–176). New York: Academic Press.

Cowan, N. (1988). Evolving conceptions of memory storage, selective attention, and their mutual constraints within the human information processing system. *Psychological Bulletin, 104,* 163–191.

Cowan, N. (1992). Verbal memory span and the timing of spoken recall. *Journal of Memory and Language, 31,* 668–684.

Cowan, N. (1993). Activation, attention, and short-term memory. *Memory & Cognition, 21,* 162–167.

Cowan, N., Day, L., Saults, J. S., Keller, T. A., Johnson, Y., & Flores, L. (1992). The role of verbal output time in the effects of word length on immediate memory. *Journal of Memory and Language, 31,* 1–17.

Cowan, N., Lichty, W., & Grove, T. R. (1990). Properties of memory for unattended spoken syllables. *Journal of Experimental Psychology: Learning, Memory, and Cognition, 16,* 258–269.

Craik, F. I. M., & Levy, B. (1976). The concept of primary memory. In W. K. Estes (Ed.), *Handbook of learning and cognitive processes* (Vol. 4, pp. 133–175). Hillsdale, NJ: Erlbaum.

Craik, F. I. M., & Lockhart, R. S. (1972). Levels of processing: A framework for memory research. *Journal of Verbal Learning and Verbal Behavior, 11,* 671–684.

Crowder, R. G. (1989). Modularity and dissociations in memory systems. In H. L. Roediger, III & F. I. M. Craik (Eds.), *Varieties of memory and consciousness* (pp. 271–294). Hillsdale, NJ: Erlbaum.

Daneman, M., & Tardiff, T. (1987). Working memory and reading skill reexamined. In M. Coltheart (Ed.), *Attention and performance XII* (pp. 491–508). Hillsdale, NJ: Erlbaum.

den Heyer, K., & Barrett, B. (1971). Selective loss of visual and verbal information in STM by means of visual and verbal interpolated tasks. *Psychonomic Science, 25,* 100–102.

Dosher, B. A. (1979). Empirical approaches to information processing: Speed-accuracy trade-off of reaction time. *Acta Psychologica, 43,* 347–359.

Ellis, N. C., & Hennelley, R. A. (1980). A bilingual word-length effect: Implications for intelligence testing and the relative ease of mental calculation in Welsh and English. *British Journal of Psychology, 71,* 43–52.

Engle, R. W., Cantor, J., & Carullo, J. J. (1992). Individual differences in working memory and comprehension: A test of four hypotheses. *Journal of Experimental Psychology: Learning, Memory, and Cognition, 18,* 972–992.

Estes, W. K. (1972). An associative basis for coding and organization in memory. In A. W. Melton & E. Martin (Eds.), *Coding processes in human memory* (pp. 161–190). Washington, DC: Winston.

Farah, M. J. (1988). Is visual imagery really visual? Overlooked evidence from neuropsychology. *Psychological Review, 95,* 307–317.

Gathercole, S. E., & Adams, A.-M. (1993). Phonological working memory in very young children. *Developmental Psychology, 29,* 770–778.

Gathercole, S. E., Adams, A.-M., & Hitch, G. J. (1994). Do young children rehearse? An individual differences analysis. *Memory & Cognition, 22,* 201–207.

Gerard, R. W. (1949). Physiology and psychiatry. *American Journal of Psychiatry, 105,* 161–173.

Gronlund, S. D., & Ratcliff, R. (1989). Time course of item and associative information: Implications for global memory models. *Journal of Experimental Psychology: Learning, Memory, and Cognition, 15,* 846–858.

Hanson, V. L. (1990). Recall of order information by deaf signers: Phonetic coding in temporal order recall. *Memory & Cognition, 18,* 604–610.

Healy, A. F. (1975). Coding of temporal-spatial patterns in short-term memory. *Journal of Verbal Learning and Verbal Behavior, 14,* 481–495.

Healy, A. F. (1982). Short-term memory for order information. In G. H. Bower (Ed.), *The psychology of learning and motivation* (Vol. 16, pp. 191–238). New York: Academic Press.

Hebb, D. O. (1949). *Organization of behavior.* New York: Wiley.

Hintzman, D. L. (1967). Articulatory coding in short-term memory. *Journal of Verbal Learning and Verbal Behavior, 16,* 312–316.

Hintzman, D. L. (1988). Judgments of frequency and recognition memory in a multiple-trace model. *Psychological Review, 95,* 528–551.

Hulme, C., Maughan, S., & Brown, G. D. A. (1991). Memory for familiar and unfamiliar words: Evidence for a long-term memory contribution to short-term memory span. *Journal of Memory and Language, 30,* 685–701.

Hulme, C., & Tordoff, V. (1989). Working memory development: The effects of speech rate, word length, and acoustic similarity on serial recall. *Journal of Experimental Child Psychology, 47,* 72–87.

Jacoby, L. L., & Dallas, M. (1981). On the relationship between autobiographical memory and perceptual learning. *Journal of Experimental Psychology: General, 110,* 306–340.

James, W. (1983). *The principles of psychology.* Cambridge: Harvard University Press. (Original work published 1890)

Just, M. A., & Carpenter, P. A. (1992). A capacity theory of comprehension: Individual differences in working memory. *Psychological Review, 99,* 122–149.

Keppel, G., & Underwood, B. J. (1962). Proactive inhibition in short-term retention of single items. *Journal of Verbal Learning and Verbal Behavior, 1,* 153–161.

Kintsch, W., & VanDijk, T. A. (1978). Toward a model of text comprehension and production. *Psychological Review, 85,* 363–394.

Kosslyn, S. M. (1992). *Wet mind: The new cognitive neuroscience.* New York: Free Press.

Kutas, M. (1988). Review of event-related potential studies of memory. In M. S. Gazzaniga (Ed.), *Perspectives in memory research* (pp. 181–218). Cambridge: MIT Press.

Laming, D. (1992). Analysis of short-term retention: Models for Brown–Peterson experiments. *Journal of Experimental Psychology: Learning, Memory, and Cognition, 18,* 1342–1365.

Landauer, T. K. (1962). Rate of implicit speech. *Perceptual and Motor Skills, 15,* 646.

Lapointe, L. B., & Engle, R. W. (1990). Simple and complex spans as measures of working memory capacity. *Journal of Experimental Psychology: Learning, Memory, and Cognition, 16,* 1118–1133.

Lee, C. L., & Estes, W. K. (1977). Order and position in primary memory for letter strings. *Journal of Verbal Learning and Verbal Behavior, 16,* 395–418.

Lewandowsky, S., & Murdock, B. B., Jr. (1989). Memory for serial order. *Psychological Review, 96,* 25–57.

Martin, R. C. (1993). Short-term memory and sentence processing: Evidence from neuropsychology. *Memory & Cognition, 21,* 176–183.

McClelland, J. L., & Rumelhart, D. E. (1985). Distributed memory and the representation of general and specific information. *Journal of Experimental Psychology: General, 114,* 159–188.

McElree, B., & Dosher, B. A. (1993). Serial retrieval processes in the recovery of order information. *Journal of Experimental Psychology: General, 122,* 291–315.

McGeoch, J. A. (1942). *The psychology of human learning.* New York: Longmans, Green.

Merikle, P. M., & Reingold, E. M. (1990). Recognition and lexical decision without detection: Unconscious perception? *Journal of Experimental Psychology: Human Perception and Performance, 16,* 574–583.

Miller, G. A. (1956). The magical number seven plus or minus two: Some limits on our capacity for processing information. *Psychological Review, 63,* 81–97.

Muter, P. (1980). Very rapid forgetting. *Memory & Cognition, 8,* 174–179.

Nairne, J. S. (1988). A framework for interpreting recency effects in immediate serial recall. *Memory & Cognition, 16,* 343–352.

Nairne, J. S. (1990). A feature model of immediate memory. *Memory & Cognition, 18,* 251–269.

Nairne, J. S. (1991). Positional uncertainty in long-term memory. *Memory & Cognition, 19,* 332–340.

Nairne, J. S. (1992). The loss of positional certainty in long-term memory. *Psychological Science, 3,* 199–202.

Nairne, J. S., Neath, I., & Serra, M. (1996). *Proactive interference as a determinant of the word length effect in immediate serial recall.* Manuscript in preparation.

Neath, I., & Crowder, R. G. (1990). Schedules of presentation and temporal distinctiveness in human memory. *Journal of Experimental Psychology: Learning, Memory, and Cognition, 16,* 316–327.

Paller, K. A. (1990). Recall and stem-completion priming have different electrophysiological correlates and are modified differently by directed forgetting. *Journal of Experimental Psychology: Learning, Memory, and Cognition, 16,* 1021–1032.

Peterson, L. R., & Peterson, M. J. (1959). Short-term retention of individual verbal items. *Journal of Experimental Psychology, 58,* 193–198.

Posner, M. I., & Konick, A. W. (1966). On the role of interference in short-term retention. *Journal of Experimental Psychology, 72,* 221–231.

Potter, M. C. (1993). Very short-term conceptual memory. *Memory & Cognition, 21,* 156–161.

Proctor, R. W., & Fagnani, C. A. (1978). Effects of distractor-stimulus modality in the Brown–Peterson distractor task. *Journal of Experimental Psychology: Human Learning and Memory, 4,* 676–684.

Raaijmakers, J. G. W., & Shiffrin, R. M. (1981). Search of associative memory. *Psychological Review, 88,* 93–134.

Ratcliff, R. (1978). A theory of memory retrieval. *Psychological Review, 85,* 59–108.

Ryan, J. (1969). Grouping and short-term memory: Different means and patterns of groups. *Quarterly Journal of Experimental Psychology, 21,* 137–147.

Schneider, W. (1993). Varieties of working memory as seen in biology and in connectionist/control architectures. *Memory & Cognition, 21,* 184–192.

Schneider, W., & Detweiler, M. (1987). A connectionist/control architecture for working memory. In G. H. Bower (Ed.), *The psychology of learning and motivation* (Vol. 21, pp. 54–119). New York: Academic Press.

Schultz, R. W. (1955). Generalization of serial position in rote serial learning. *Journal of Experimental Psychology, 49,* 267–272.

Schweickert, R. (1993). A multinomial processing tree model for degradation and redintegration in immediate recall. *Memory & Cognition, 21,* 168–175.

Schweickert, R., & Boruff, B. (1986). Short-term memory capacity: Magic number or magic spell? *Journal of Experimental Psychology: Learning, Memory, and Cognition, 12,* 419–425.

Sebrechts, M. M., Marsh, R. L., & Seamon, J. G. (1989). Secondary memory and very rapid forgetting. *Memory & Cognition, 17,* 693–700.

Shand, M. A. (1982). Sign-based short-term coding of American Sign Language signs and printed English words by congenitally deaf signers. *Cognitive Psychology, 14,* 1–12.

Shiffrin, R. M. (1993). Short-term memory: A brief commentary. *Memory & Cognition, 21,* 193–197.

Shulman, H. G. (1972). Semantic confusion errors in short-term memory. *Journal of Verbal Learning and Verbal Behavior, 11,* 221–227.

Sperling, G. (1963). A model for visual memory tasks. *Human Factors, 5,* 19–31.

Sternberg, S. (1966). High-speed scanning in human memory. *Science, 153,* 652–654.

Townsend, J. T., & Ashby, G. G. (1983). *The stochastic modeling of elementary psychological processes.* Cambridge: Cambridge University Press.

Tulving, E., Schacter, D. L., & Stark, H. (1982). Priming effects in word fragment completion are independent of recognition memory. *Journal of Experimental Psychology: Learning, Memory, and Cognition, 8,* 336–342.

Waugh, N. C., & Norman, D. A. (1965). Primary memory. *Psychological Review, 72,* 89–104.

Wickelgren, W. A. (1965). Short-term memory for phonemically similar lists. *American Journal of Psychology, 78,* 567–574.

Wickelgren, W. A. (1966). Phonemic similarity and interference in short-term memory for single letters. *Journal of Experimental Psychology, 71,* 396–404.

Wickens, D. D., Moody, M. J., & Dow, R. (1981). The nature and timing of the retrieval process and of interference effects. *Journal of Experimental Psychology: General, 110,* 1–20.

Storing Information in Long-Term Memory

Imagery and Visual–Spatial Representations

Lynn A. Cooper
Jessica M. Lang

Much of our remembrance of persons, situations, and occurrences from the past is accomplished by nonverbal thinking. Such thinking seems, phenomenologically, to be decidedly perceptual in character. Recalling the layout of rooms in the first house in which you lived, conjuring up an image of your grandmother's face, or remembering your first day at college all rely, in part, on evoking visual–spatial mental representations of the object, individual, or event being remembered. The functional role of mental images and of visual–spatial representations in memory has been documented since the time of the ancient Greeks (see Yates, 1966), and the contribution of such representations to creative discovery and problem solving has been noted by scientists, writers, and artists alike (for overviews see Miller, 1984; Roskos-Ewoldson, Intons-Peterson, & Anderson, 1993; Shepard, 1978a). However, the properties of visual–spatial representations and the mechanisms by which they mediate memory performance have been elucidated only recently, by research in cognitive psychology. Our goal in the present chapter is to provide a selected overview of this research, pointing to central issues and promising directions of current work.

Images and visual–spatial representations differ in important ways from verbal or abstract representations in memory. Consider, for example, your memory of a pet that you may have had when you were a child. You may

Memory

recall many things about this pet including its breed, name, disposition, shape, size, characteristic pattern of motion, and similarity to other people's pets. You may even remember contextual information, such as how old you were when you acquired the pet, and your parents' general attitude toward it. Note that this memory has many components, some that are visual–spatial in nature (shape, size, motion, similarity to other pets), some that are primarily factual (your age, your parents' attitude, the pet's breed and disposition), and at least one that is verbal (the pet's name). What distinguishes the visual–spatial aspects of this memory from other aspects, and, more generally, visual–spatial representations from semantic or verbal representations in memory, is that visual–spatial representations correspond in nonarbitrary ways to the external objects and events that they represent. More formally, there is some degree of isomorphism or structural correspondence between an object in the world and its visual–spatial mental representation. This correspondence may be schematic, embodying only salient features of an object or global information about an object's structure, or it may be more concrete, embodying metric information about object shape and size. Or, the isomorphism may be "second order" (cf. Shepard, 1978b; Shepard & Chipman, 1970), requiring that only relations of similarity among external objects be preserved in their corresponding internal representations. All of these types of correspondence can be distinguished from those that hold for verbal or semantic/factual representations, which bear arbitrary, conventional, or abstract knowledge-based relations to the objects or events for which they stand.

We divide our discussion of visual–spatial representations in memory into three sections: imagery, recognition of objects, and representation of information about spatial layouts or cognitive maps. Imagery can be distinguished from visual–spatial representation more generally in two primary ways. First, visual images have a phenomenal distinctiveness and concreteness that more abstract, schematic spatial representations often seem to lack. Second, and more important, are differences between the conditions required to evoke and to use images and other visual–spatial representations for a variety of cognitive functions. Imaginal representations of objects and events can be generated in the absence of any appropriate or corresponding external stimulus; visual–spatial representations used for processes of recognition are matched against relevant, externally available information, and are often derived in part from analysis of that information.

Our focus on imagery, object recognition, and memory for spatial layout prevents us from considering other fascinating issues concerning the use of visual–spatial representations in cognition. Some of the topics outside the scope of our discussion (with initial references for the interested reader) include: memory for patterns and alphanumeric characters that relies on visual or informational persistence and/or is controlled by low-level perceptual variables (Di Lollo & Dixon, 1988; Harvey, 1986; Irwin & Yeomans, 1986; Loftus & Ruthruff, 1994; Sperling, 1960; see also Massaro & Loftus, this volume, Chapter 3); the use of visual–spatial representations in short-term or working memory (Baddeley, 1992; see also Nairne, this volume, Chapter 4); memory for sequences of static visual patterns whose motion is implied (Freyd, 1987, 1993; Freyd & Finke, 1984; Freyd & Johnson, 1987); memory for spatial layouts in animals other than humans (Cheng, 1986, 1989); the use of visual–spatial representations in interpreting diagrams (Hegarty, Carpenter, & Just, 1990) and graphic displays (Kosslyn, 1994), in complex problem-solving tasks that involve memory components (Cooper, 1988, 1990; Hegarty, 1991; Novick, 1988, 1990), and in creative discovery (Finke, 1990; Roskos-Ewoldson et al., 1993).

I. IMAGERY

As noted above, there is abundant evidence that forming mental images can enhance performance on a variety of learning and memory tasks (for reviews see Bower, 1972; Paivio, 1971). This general finding holds for both direct (e.g., instructions to generate images) and indirect (e.g., the use of image-evoking stimulus materials) manipulations of imagery. Indeed, mental imagery is the basis of several commonly used mnemonic devices, including the method of loci (Bower, 1970; see also Bellezza, this volume, Chapter 10, for a discussion of mnemonic methods). During the past twenty years, research in cognitive psychology has turned from mere demonstrations of the functional role of imagery in memory to investigations and analysis of the properties, nature, or format of imaginal representations in memory, as well as the conditions under which images are likely to be used.

A. Properties of Images

In a now-classic experiment, Shepard and Metzler (1971) demonstrated the use of mental imagery in a cognitive task that simultaneously provided an indication of some properties of imaginal representations. Subjects in the Shepard–Metzler study were asked to compare the shapes of pairs of line drawings of unfamiliar visual objects, like those illustrated in Figure 1A. On half of the experimental trials, the objects were the same shape, and on the other half they were mirror images or stereoisomers. The objects in each pair could differ, as well, in their portrayed orientations in depth or in the plane of the picture. The important findings were (1) that the time required to make the "same–different" comparison increased in a strikingly linear fashion with the degree of angular difference between the objects in a pair (cf. Figure 1B), and (2) that the slope and the intercept of the reaction-time functions were nearly identical for angular differences in the picture plane and in depth.

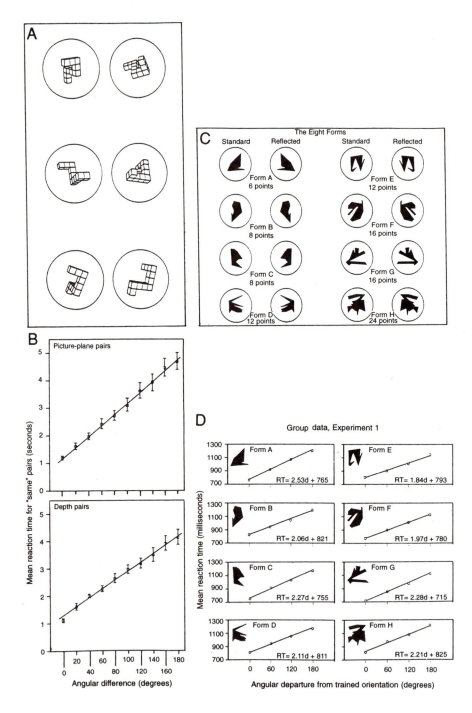

Shepard and Metzler (1971) interpreted these results as indicating that subjects accomplished the task by imagining one object in the pair rotated into congruence with the orientation of the other object, and then by comparing the two objects (one mentally transformed, the other visually available) for a match or mismatch in shape. This interpretation is consistent with the introspective reports of the subjects, who claimed to have done the task by a process of "mental rotation." This initial experiment was important in establishing that images could be transformed by a process that was a mental analogue of an external physical rotation, and that the imagined process was used spontaneously in accomplishing the "same–different" comparison task. The near equivalence of intercepts and slopes for object pairs differing by depth and by picture-plane rotations also suggested something about the properties of the representations being transformed; namely, that the images embodied information about the spatial structure of the corresponding three-dimensional objects, rather than simply representing information about the objects' two-dimensional retinal projections.

The initial Shepard–Metzler experiment inspired a great deal of subsequent and continuing research on the process of mental rotation and the nature of the underlying mental representations (for reviews see Cooper & Shepard, 1984; Shepard & Cooper, 1982). Cooper (1975; Cooper & Podgorny, 1976; Cooper & Shepard, 1973) extended this paradigm to a situation in which long-term memory representations of well-learned patterns (alphanumeric characters or random polygons) were compared with individual patterns presented in one of several rotated positions (cf. Figure 1C). As in the Shepard–Metzler experiment, response times increased linearly with angular departure of test shapes from the learned position; furthermore, the slopes and intercepts of the functions were quite similar for shapes differing in number of points or complexity (cf. Figure 1D). This finding suggests that rather detailed (in contrast to merely schematic) information about pattern structure is preserved in the mental representations undergoing rotational transformations (for qualifications see Bethell-Fox & Shepard, 1988; Folk & Luce, 1987; Hochberg & Gellman, 1977).

Mental rotation—as indicated by linear time functions with increasing stimulus disorientation—has also been reported for depictions of naturalis-

---

FIGURE 1   Stimuli and results from typical mental rotation experiments. (A) Pairs of line drawings of three-dimensional objects used by Shepard and Metzler (1971). (B) Results from the Shepard–Metzler experiment, expressed in terms of time required to determine that two objects in a pair are the same in shape as a function of the angular difference in their orientations, plotted separately for orientation differences in depth and in the picture plane. (C) Random, two-dimensional polygons differing in number of points, or complexity, used by Cooper (1975). (D) Results from the Cooper experiment, expressed in terms of time required to determine whether an individually-presented polygon is a "standard" or a "reflected" version, plotted separately for each of the test shapes.

tic objects including hands (Cooper & Shepard, 1975) and other body parts (Parsons, 1987), as well as for judgments other than mirror reversal (Corballis & Roldan, 1975; Hintzman, O'Dell, & Arndt, 1981; Shepard & Hurwitz, 1984). Variants of the mental rotation paradigm have been used more recently (Cave et al., 1994) to assess what form of location information is coded in mental images, and to ask whether single view-independent or multiple view-dependent representations of objects are employed for memory comparisons (Tarr & Pinker, 1989). Tasks requiring spatial operations other than rotation, including comparison of objects differing in size (Bundesen & Larsen, 1975), comparison of symbols on the faces of pairs of cubes (Just & Carpenter, 1985), synthesis of figures from parts (Palmer, 1977), and complex sequences of transformations (Shepard & Feng, 1972), have all yielded results similar in kind to those obtained with mental rotation. This body of research buttresses the idea that purely imagined, mental transformations on representations of objects and analogues of corresponding physical transformations on objects in space. Furthermore, the images of objects undergoing mental transformations apparently embody information concerning the spatial structure of their external counterparts.

A rather different experimental paradigm has been used by Kosslyn and associates to elucidate the properties of images in memory. In a typical study, subjects are instructed to memorize a set of drawings of objects (Kosslyn, 1973) or a set of locations on the map of an island (Kosslyn, Ball, & Reiser, 1978). They are then asked to form an image of one of the objects (or of the map), to focus mentally on one end of the object (or location on the map), and to verify whether a particular component is or is not present on the object (or to scan mentally to another location on the map). The outcome of interest is that the time required for property verification (or for scanning from one map location to another) increases linearly with the distance between the point of focus and the probed component (or between designated locations on the imagined map). These results with "mental scanning" are reminiscent of the mental rotation findings, and they suggest that information about spatial distance is preserved in images. Pinker (1980) has shown that the linear increase in response time with distance scanned mentally holds for images of three- as well as two-dimensional arrays, and Finke and Pinker (1982, 1983) have reported the same basic effect using a different procedure that does not rely on explicit instructions to form mental images.

B. Challenges to "Depictive/Analogue" Accounts of Images and Mental Transformations

The research described above has often been interpreted as demonstrating that images function like depictions or uninterpreted, though possibly schematic, pictures of the external objects that they represent; transformations on images function as analogues of corresponding perceived or physical transformations on objects in space. Pylyshyn (1973) and Anderson (1978) have challenged this view, suggesting instead that abstract, propositional data structures could serve as a format for representing all kinds of information in memory, including mental images. An adequate account of the complexities of this so-called "imagery debate" is beyond the scope of the present chapter. Suffice it to say that propositional accounts of imagery have never adequately addressed the striking regularity of the reaction-time results from mental rotation and mental image scanning experiments. However, prediction of linear time functions follows quite naturally from the notions that (1) images preserve information about shape and spatial distance in a depictive fashion, and (2) transformations on images correspond to analogous transformations on objects in three-dimensional space.

Aspects of the analogue/propositional debate have recently been revisited by investigators asking whether mental images are depictive (like pictures) or descriptive (tightly linked to and accessed by meaning) representations. Informal evidence against the depictive position includes Hinton's (1979) demonstration that people are limited in their ability to "read information off" of an image under conditions where the same information is immediately accessible from a picture. In this demonstration, people are asked to generate a mental image of a wire cube standing on one corner. They are then asked to point to the spatial locations of the other corners of the cube. This task turns out to be quite difficult when an image is used, but very easy to do from a picture or wire model of a cube. The more typical experimental situation for posing the depictive/descriptive question asks subjects to find multiple interpretations in images of ambiguous figures. The logic of the argument is as follows: if mental images of classic ambiguous or reversible figures (Jastrow's, 1900, duck/rabbit) are themselves ambiguous in that more than one interpretation can be reported, then the depictive view of imagery is supported. This follows from the fact that multiple interpretations can also be discovered in pictures of reversible figures. However, to the extent that images are unambiguous, allowing only a single interpretation when more than one exists, then the descriptive or meaning-linked view of imagery is supported.

The evidence on the depictive/descriptive question is conflicting. Chambers and Reisberg (1985) showed subjects one interpretation of the ambiguous duck/rabbit figure, and later asked them to form an image of the figure and to try to discover the alternative meaning from the image. Subjects were unable to attain the reconstrual, but they were able to reconstrue or reinterpret their own drawings of their images. This and other experiments by the same investigators (Chambers & Reisberg, 1992; Reisberg, in press) support the descriptive position, that is, the idea that not only spatial information but also information about meaning is encoded in images. However, subsequent work using similar (Brandimonte & Gerbino, 1993; Peterson, Kihlstrom, Rose, & Glisky, 1992) and quite different (Finke, Pinker, & Farah, 1989) stimuli and reconstrual tasks has placed limits on the generality of the Chambers/Reisberg findings. In the Finke et al. (1989) study, subjects were able to discover new information in images of geometric shapes or alphanumeric characters that were manipulated and recombined in memory; Peterson et al. (1992) have demonstrated convincingly that subjects can report multiple interpretations of standard ambiguous figures under a variety of different conditions. Thus, while the issue remains unresolved, the weight of evidence currently favors the depictive view of imagery (but see Reisberg, in press, for a critical discussion).

A second and quite different challenge to the depictive/analogue account of imagery has focused on potential methodological problems with the experiments themselves. In particular, Pylyshyn (1981) has argued that results of mental scanning experiments should not be interpreted as revealing operations on depictive representations; rather, these results reflect nothing more than the subjects' compliance with experimenter expectancies, coupled with their "tacit knowledge" of the temporal characteristics of transformations on physical objects. That is, subjects in mental scanning and mental rotation experiments deduce the experimenter's hypothesis and use their knowledge of how physical objects behave under transformation to reproduce the linear decision-time functions that the experimenter expects to obtain. While some data do lend partial support to the "experimenter expectancy" interpretation of mental scanning experiments (Intons-Peterson, 1983), the bulk of evidence (Denis & Carfantan, 1985; Goldstone, Hinrichs, & Richman, 1985; Jolicoeur & Kosslyn, 1985) continues to legislate against this possibility.

C. Functional Equivalence of Imagery and Perception

The chronometric studies and, to some extent, the experiments on image ambiguity establish that memory-images can code perceptual information and can be operated on like pictures of corresponding external objects. Another way of expressing this view is to claim that images are *functionally equivalent* to visual–spatial representations derived from perception. Finke and Shepard (1986) review considerable evidence supporting this idea, including findings from studies of imagined transformations, and parallels between the structure of similarity judgments for memory images and perceptual displays of stimuli of like colors (Shepard & Cooper, 1992) or shapes of states (Shepard & Chipman, 1970).

As Intons-Peterson and McDaniel (1991) and Baird and Hubbard (1992) have pointed out, there are weaker and stronger versions of the functional equivalence hypothesis. Weaker versions, consistent with empirical findings described thusfar, hold only that parallels exist between imaginal and perceptual processes. Somewhat stronger versions add the idea that correspondences exist between the structural properties of images and perceived objects, as well as between the processes that operate on both sorts of representations. Kosslyn's (1981) theory of images provides an example of this stronger version of functional equivalence. According to the theory, images and perceptual representations are constructed in a spatial medium called the "visual buffer," a data structure with an array format that functions like a coordinate space. Information about surface features or properties of images can be accessed from this buffer and operated on by processes that generate, inspect, and transform the image.

One of the testable predictions of this stronger form of the functional equivalence idea is that information should be equally accessible from perceptual and imaginal representations of visual patterns. Podgorny and Shepard (1978) have provided such a demonstration, using a task in which subjects were either shown or asked to imagine block letters filling a subset of the cells of a 4 × 5 matrix of squares (see Figure 2). A probe dot was then presented, and subjects had to determine as rapidly as possible whether the dot was on the (displayed or imagined) letter, or on one of the background cells. A number of structural features (e.g., figural compactness, proximity to a corner) influenced times to verify that a probe dot was contained in or outside of the cells filled by a letter. The important result is that structural variables that affected response times to displayed letters also affected response times to imagined letters in a strikingly similar fashion.

A form of the functional equivalence hypothesis even stronger than the "structural equivalence" view described here holds that images and percepts derive from a common set of underlying mechanisms. This proposal is extremely difficult to evaluate via behavioral experiments; however, one procedure based on the common-mechanism assumption has provided some limited support. The procedure is based on the following logic: if imagery and perception share common mechanisms, then tasks requiring both imaginal and perceptual processing should show mutual interference or facilitation, depending on the particulars of the experimental situation. Early demonstrations of selective interference documented impairment of performance on detection (Segal & Fusella, 1970) or classification (Brooks, 1968) tasks when stimuli were concurrently perceived and imagined in the same, relative to different, modalities (i.e., visual–spatial imagery interfered with performance on visual–spatial tasks, but not with performance on auditory–verbal tasks). More recently, Farah (1985) has shown pattern-specific facilitation effects on detection performance within the visual modality: namely, detecting a particular letter is facilitated by concurrent imagining of that same, as opposed to a different, letter.

PRESENTED   OR   IMAGINED

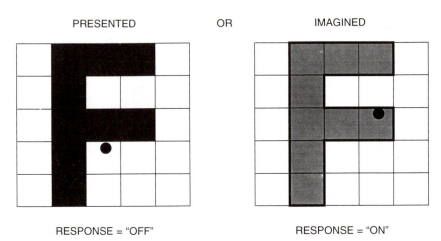

RESPONSE = "OFF"   RESPONSE = "ON"

FIGURE 2   Schematic illustration of the presented or imagined displays, test dots, and required responses from Podgorny and Shepard (1978). (Copyright © 1978 by the American Psychological Association. Reprinted with permission.)

D. Evidence from Cognitive Neuroscience

Results from selective interference and selective facilitation experiments are consistent with the idea that perceiving and imagining share common mechanisms and representations. But, this evidence is also consistent with a somewhat different, but related, possibility: that imagery and perception interact by virtue of different paths of access to a common representational system. By hypothesis, such common mechanisms and/or representational systems are instantiated in the human brain. Evidence concerning the brain systems engaged while people imagine, remember, and perceive external objects can help disentangle these and other hypotheses about forms of functional equivalence.

We consider four kinds of evidence from the emerging field of cognitive neuroscience about the nature of imagery and the relation between perception and imagery. One form of evidence comes from reports of specific imagery and visual–spatial processing deficits in patients who have suffered focal brain injury. The second and third techniques use noninvasive methods to measure electrophysiological correlates of brain activity or regional cerebral blood flow, respectively, while subjects perform imagery-based and corresponding perceptual tasks. The fourth type of evidence comes from experiments directly measuring the activity of neurons while nonhuman primates perform a mental transformation task.

In a well-known study, Bisiach and Luzzatti (1978) provided evidence that representation of information in images is disrupted by brain injury that produces neglect of corresponding regions in the visual field. Patients were asked to imagine a familiar outdoor area and to report the buildings that were "visible" in their mental images. Only buildings that would have been located in the nonneglected portions of visual space were reported; furthermore, when asked to image the area from a different vantage point, the formerly unavailable buildings "appeared" in the patients' mental images, while other buildings that had been reported previously now failed to "come into view." This intriguing study suggests not only that memory images and perceptual representations have functional similarities, but also that the same brain regions (presumably, the regions damaged in the patients) may give rise to both sorts of representations.

Other studies of brain-injured patients have presented a more conflicting picture of the extent of functional equivalence of imagery and visual recognition abilities. Part of the complexity may arise from the fact that brain damage in different locations produces dissociable effects on "visual" versus "spatial" aspects of imagery. Farah, Hammond, Levine, and Calvanio (1988) tested a patient with bilateral temporo-occipital damage, as well as damage to the right temporal and right inferior frontal lobe, on a group of tasks thought to tap spatial properties of imagery (e.g., spatial transformation and location tasks), and a cluster of tasks designed to assess visual information about object appearance. Relative to neurologically intact control subjects, the patient performed normally on the tasks requiring spatial operations on images, but he was severely impaired on the tasks that required visual information to be reported from images. A similar dissociation of imagery abilities, coupled with corresponding perceptual deficits, has been documented for two patients by Levine, Warach, and Farah (1985). One patient suffering parieto-occipital damage could identify objects and describe them from memory images, but was impaired on perceptual and imagery tasks requiring spatial localization. By contrast, the other patient with temporo-occipital damage performed the localization tasks normally, but experienced difficulty with tasks requiring objects to be perceptually identified or described and drawn from memory. These case studies provide support for the strong form of the functional equivalence view—that imagery and perception engage a common representational system deriving from a common neural substrate. However, in apparent contradiction to this view, Behrmann, Winocur, and Moscovitch (1992) have recently described a patient with profound deficits in object recognition who nonetheless performs well on a variety of tasks tapping visual aspects of imagery.

Studies measuring electrophysiological correlates and regional cerebral blood flow also present a somewhat complex picture of the relation between images and other visual–spatial representations. Farah, Peronnet, Gonon, and Girard (1988) measured event-related electrical potentials in the brain (ERPs) while subjects detected visual letters that were congruent or incongruent with letters they were instructed to imagine. Of considerable interest are the findings that (1) imagery had a "content-specific" effect on early stages of the ERP; that is, imaging a letter that was visually presented had a larger effect on the ERP than imaging a letter different than the one presented; and (2) the largest ERP effect was localized at electrodes recording occipital lobe activity. Together, these findings suggest that instructions to form visual images produce activity in the brain areas known to process external visual information, and also that images and visual–spatial perceptual representations of letters share a common representational locus.

A more sophisticated technique for gaining spatially precise information about affected brain areas involves measuring changes in regional cerebral blood flow in response to the presentation of particular stimuli and processing requirements of cognitive tasks. There are many methodological and theoretical assumptions underlying these techniques, one of which is that increases in regional blood flow are indicators of increased neural activity in the relevant brain area. Goldenberg et al. (1989) have provided confirmation of Farah, Peronnet, Gonon, and Girard's (1988) finding that imagery produces activity in occipital areas using a very different task (answering verbal questions that do or do not require the use of imagery), and employing single photon emission computed tomography (SPECT) to measure regional blood flow. A series of experiments recently reported by Kosslyn et al. (1993) used positron emission tomography (PET) to measure changes in regional cerebral blood flow while subjects performed the perceptual and the imagery conditions in a variant of Podgorny and Shepard's (1978) probe-dot task (cf. Figure 2). Although the precise pattern of results is complex, these experiments clearly indicate that regions of visual cortex are selectively activated in both the imaginal and perceptual conditions. Indeed, the imagery condition produced even greater activation than the perceptual version of the task.

Finally, we describe a provocative experiment by Georgopoulos, Lurito, Petrides, Schwartz, and Massey (1989) that provides neural evidence for the analogue nature of mental rotation, in the sense that the imagined transformation passes through intermediate states corresponding to intermediate positions in the rotation of an external object. These investigators trained a rhesus monkey to perform a version of a mental rotation task that required movement of a handle in the direction counterclockwise from and perpendicular to the position of a target light, whose position changed from trial to trial. While the monkey was doing the task, the activity of single neurons in its motor cortex was recorded. Based on previous work, Georgopoulos et al. (1989) reasoned that the direction of an upcoming movement is represented as a neuronal population vector in motor cortex, that is, as the weighted vector sum of the activity of neurons tuned to preferred directions of movement. If the handle movement task is accomplished by mental rotation of an imagined movement vector from the position of the light to the direction of actual movement, then the activity recorded in motor cortex during performance of the task should indicate that the neuronal population vector rotates through successive preferred movement directions in real time. Results of the experiment revealed such a rotation of the neuronal population vector, providing direct neural evidence for a process of imagined rotation of a movement.

II. VISUAL–SPATIAL REPRESENTATIONS IN OBJECT REPRESENTATIONS

Human perceivers are remarkably adept at recognizing the repeated occurrence of a visual object, even though the immediate information for recognition in the retinal image of an external object places a few constraints on which one of many memory representations might uniquely correspond to the object in question. One goal of most theories of object recognition is to explain how the perceptual system extracts information from the spatial distribution of intensity at the retina and develops representations of external objects at successive levels of abstraction from the retinal array. An equally important issue concerns how represented external information is compared with long-term memory representations of objects. In the next section, we focus on how several current theoretical approaches to object recognition characterize the nature of these long-term memory representations. (Pinker, 1985, provides an excellent discussion of the virtues and inadequacies of traditional models of object recognition.) We next present experimental and neuropsychological evidence supporting the various approaches, sampling quite selectively from the voluminous literature. We conclude with a brief discussion of the problem of face recognition.

A. Contemporary Theories of Object Representation

A landmark theory of object recognition advanced by Marr and Nishihara (1978; Marr, 1982) has influenced virtually every subsequent theoretical effort. The details of Marr and Nishihara's proposal—in particular, of how information is extracted from the retinal array and represented at succeedingly more abstract levels—are beyond the scope of our discussion. Of direct relevance is the Marr–Nishihara proposal of a format for representing information about object shape in long-term memory. Briefly, an object is represented as a three-dimensional model within a coordinate system centered on the object, as contrasted with a coordinate system defined with respect to a particular view of the object. Axes within this object-centered coordinate system are aligned with major object parts. The parts themselves are three-dimensional volumetric primitives, or generalized cones defined

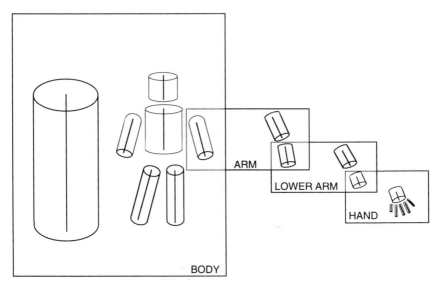

FIGURE 3   Schematic illustration of the representation of a familiar object, specified as hierarchically organized axis-based models of generalized cones. (After Marr, 1982.)

by the two-dimensional shape of the cone's cross section swept along an axis of particular shape, with a specification of how the area expands or contracts as it moves along the axis. It is important to note that the Marr–Nishihara object models are hierarchical, in that subordinate descriptions of object parts and their major axes are embedded within descriptions of superordinate parts and axes. Figure 3 provides a schematic illustration of how the Marr–Nishihara system would represent a familiar object. In summary, objects are represented in the Marr–Nishihara model in terms of their major axes of symmetry or elongation, with cylindrical parts defined in relation to the axes.

A very influential, somewhat related model has been proposed by Biederman (1987). Biederman's theory, like the Marr–Nishihara model, conceptualizes object parts or components as three-dimensional volumetric primitives derived from generalized cones. Object structure is defined by local relations between adjacent parts (e.g., on top of, to the right of), rather than by axis-based descriptions. The primitives in Biederman's system (called geons) comprise a limited vocabulary of 36 elements, generated by all combinations of three "nonaccidental" (Lowe, 1985) properties of two-dimensional images. These nonaccidental properties, which remain invariant over most changes in point of view, are used to specify the features (e.g., curved vs. straight) of the cross sections and axes of generalized cones.

Figure 4 presents some drawings of familiar objects, along with the geons from which they are constructed. According to Biederman, object recognition proceeds by the extraction of features from the retinal array that, in turn, activate intermediate-level geons and the local relations among them. Such intermediate-level representations of components and relations specify a complete object model that is matched against a similarly formated representation in memory.

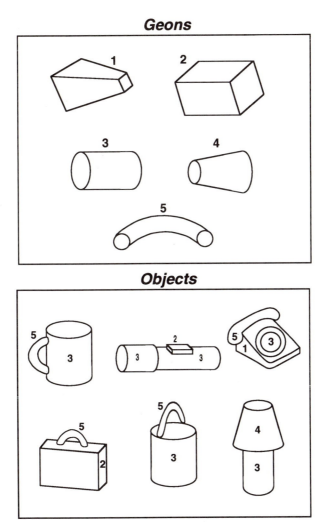

FIGURE 4   Examples of familiar objects and the corresponding geons from which they are composed. (From Biederman, 1990. Copyright © 1990 MIT Press.)

A rather different account of object representation and recognition has recently been offered by a number of investigators. The basic idea is that memory for visual objects is accomplished by the use of more than one representational system (or subsystem). The need for postulating multiple systems has come primarily from the desire to account for neuropsychological observations and behavioral data, reviewed below, showing strong dissociations between performance on different types of visual memory tasks. Schacter and Cooper (see Cooper & Schacter, 1992, for review) have proposed that dissociable systems represent information about an object's global shape and relations among its parts (the structural description system), and about semantic, functional, and individuating visual information (the episodic system). The Schacter–Cooper formulation thus combines the structural emphasis of the Marr–Nishihara model and the component-based approach of Biederman, but it organizes these elements in a different and more complex, yet flexible, fashion.

Another approach postulating separable subsystems for different aspects of visual recognition is Kosslyn's (1987; Kosslyn, Flynn, Amsterdam, & Wang, 1990) distinction between the representation and recognition of categorical versus coordinate spatial relations. By categorical relations, Kosslyn refers to abstract relations that specify general features of an object's spatial structure that are likely to remain invariant over a variety of spatial transformations. By contrast, coordinate representations specify precise metric information about the location of objects and their parts. Presumably, both types of representations of objects are stored in distinct subsystems in memory; information is accessed from the appropriate subsystem depending on the demands of particular recognition situations.

Finally, Treisman and Kahneman (Kahneman & Treisman, 1984; Kahneman, Treisman, & Gibbs, 1992; Treisman, 1992) have distinguished between the representation of object types, or stored symbolic descriptions of semantic and visual information about classes of objects, and the representation of object tokens, or stored information about the visual properties of particular objects. The format that they propose for object-specific representations is the "object file," a temporary storage medium in which information about view-specific properties of an object, as well as visual attributes like color and spatial location, can be assembled and updated as the momentary position of an object or a perceiver changes. Note that, unlike the models of object representation sketched earlier, this approach is essentially silent on the question of how object structure is represented in memory.

B. Evidence from Behavioral Experiments

While there is a staggeringly large body of psychological research on the topic of object recognition, little of the available evidence unequivocally supports a particular theory while infirming others. Furthermore, much of the evidence has been obtained in limited experimental situations, designed by researchers favoring a certain theoretical approach to provide outcomes supporting that view. However, many of the relevant behavioral phenomena are consistent with one or more of the models described above, providing some assurance that current theories are on the right track. Below, we review some results of just a few of the experimental techniques currently being used to understand how visual objects are represented in and accessed from memory. We focus much of our presentation on research using unfamiliar objects as stimuli. These studies enjoy the advantage of being able to examine how novel visual–spatial material becomes memorially represented without the uncontrolled and complicating effects of familiarity and associations to previously learned material.

Treisman and Kahneman (Kahneman et al., 1992; Treisman, 1992) have presented evidence from a variety of experimental paradigms that lend credence to their notion that visual–spatial information specifying an object token is represented, at least temporarily, in the form of an updatable file of the object's properties. In one kind of experiment, Kahneman et al. (1992) presented two boxes in which letters were briefly displayed. The boxes then moved to another spatial location, and a third test letter was flashed in one of the boxes. Subjects were then required to name the flashed letter as rapidly as possible. Naming times were most rapid when the test letter was identical to the letter previously presented in the same box, which had moved since the time of its initial presentation. This result is consistent with the idea that the contents of an object file, specifying the sequence of spatiotemporal coordinates of individual elements (boxes and letters) in the display, mediates performance. Using a different experimental technique, Treisman and DeSchepper (described in Treisman, 1992) showed that shapes defined as irrelevant to performance on an upcoming trial of a matching task could nonetheless affect speed of matching. Apparently, object files for shape tokens are formed even in the absence of attention.

Biederman and associates have amassed considerable experimental evidence consistent with his recognition-by-components (RBC) theory. Their experimental procedure requires subjects to name briefly presented line drawings of familiar objects; thus, reported effects tap levels of recognition up to, and including, the classification of an object as a member of an "entry-level" category (see also Biederman, 1990) and the retrieval of the name of the category to which the object is assigned. Initial experiments (Biederman, 1987) established that object naming is rapid and accurate when as few as three geons of a complex object are visible. Subsequent experiments have used the phenomenon of repetition priming—in this context, that speed and accuracy of object naming are facilitated by prior presentation of a picture identical to the test object—as evidence that object recognition is mediated by extraction and comparison of components. In one experiment (Biederman & Cooper, 1991a), both priming and test pictures had the complementary halves of their contours, corresponding to edges and vertices of components, removed. The magnitude of facilitation obtained when identical (deleted) pictures were presented in succession was roughly equivalent to that obtained when a complementary deletion followed the priming stimulus. This result suggests that the same intermediate-level representation (presumably, geon-like object components), as opposed to individual line segments forming contours, was activated by the drawings with complementary edges and vertices removed. Further properties of such geon-based representations of objects revealed by patterns of facilitation on the object-naming task include their insensitivity to changes in size (Biederman & Cooper, 1991b), spatial location (Biederman & Cooper, 1991c), left–right parity (Biederman & Cooper, 1991c), and rotation in depth (Biederman & Gerhardstein, 1993) between the priming and the test objects. While these results are clearly consistent with the RBC model, they would also be predicted by the Marr–Nishihara idea that volumetric primitives are related to an abstract axis-based object model.

Substantial evidence also exists supporting the Schacter–Cooper multiple representations approach, as well as Kosslyn's (1987) theory postulating separate subsystems for processing categorical and coordinate information about objects. Some of the evidence from experiments by Kosslyn and associates (Kosslyn et al., 1989) also suggests that judgments based on categorical information are performed most efficiently by the left hemisphere of the brain, whereas judgments requiring evaluation of metric information are faster when stimuli are presented to the right hemisphere. In a typical experiment, Kosslyn et al. (1989) presented unfamiliar two-dimensional shapes in either the right or the left visual field, and subjects were required to determine either whether a dot was "on or off" the shape contour (categorical judgment) or whether the dot was "near or far" from the contour (metric judgment). Response times exhibited an interaction between hemisphere of presentation and type of test judgment, suggesting that subsystems for processing categorical and coordinate information about shape are distinguishable and associated with hemispheric differences.

Schacter, Cooper, and collaborators have obtained strong evidence for a functional dissociation between systems specialized for representing global information about object structure and for representing episodic information about object meaning, function, and distinctive (nonstructural) visual properties. Their experiments draw on the distinction between "implicit" and "explicit" tests of memory (for review see Roediger, 1990; Schacter, 1987; Tulving & Schacter, 1990; see also Kelley & Lindsay, this volume, Chapter 2). By explicit memory, investigators refer to the conscious recollection of past experiences as measured by standard tests of recognition and recall. Implicit memory, by contrast, refers to unintentional retrieval of previously acquired information that does not require conscious recollection of the acquisition situation.

The experimental paradigm introduced by Schacter, Cooper, and Delaney (1990a, 1990b) to assess implicit and explicit memory for visual objects requires subjects to study a set of line drawings of novel three-dimensional structures. Following study, subjects engage either in an explicit "yes/no" test of recognition memory for the objects, or in an implicit "object decision task" that requires them to determine whether briefly presented test objects are possible or impossible in structure. Examples of stimuli used in the Schacter–Cooper experiments are shown in Figure 5A. Note that possible objects, while unfamiliar, could exist in the three-dimensional world, whereas impossible objects contain subtle surface or edge violations that would make it impossible for them to exist as connected three-dimensional structures.

A revealing twist in these experiments comes from manipulation of the conditions under which subjects are asked to study the objects. Presumably, such instructions influence how the objects are encoded in memory. In their basic comparison condition, Schacter et al. (1990a, 1990b) asked subjects to encode the global arrangement among object surfaces by determining whether each object in the study set faced primarily to the left or to the right. In other conditions, encoding instructions required elaborative semantic judgments (i.e., indicating some familiar object that each structure reminded subjects of) or judgments of object function (i.e., indicating whether each object would be used primarily for support or as a tool; see also Schacter & Cooper, 1993). When objects were encoded structurally, substantial priming or facilitation of accuracy on the implicit object decision task was obtained for possible objects (see Figure 5B). Under elaborative or functional encoding conditions, priming was dramatically reduced, whereas explicit recognition memory was enhanced relative to levels observed following the structural study task.

This dissociation between level of performance on the implicit and explicit tasks, attributable to how the objects were represented in memory, gives strong support to the idea that different representational systems were accessed by the different memory tasks. Cooper and Schacter (1992; see also Schacter, Cooper, Delaney, Peterson, & Tharan, 1991) refer to these systems as: (1) the structural description system, which represents the global structure and relations among parts of an object; and (2) the episodic system, which represents information including meaning and function that makes individual objects distinctive in memory. Other research (Cooper, Schacter, Ballesteros, & Moore, 1992) indicates that visual attributes like size and left–right parity are preserved in the episodic system, but not in the structural system. Presumably, this latter system is specialized to code in-

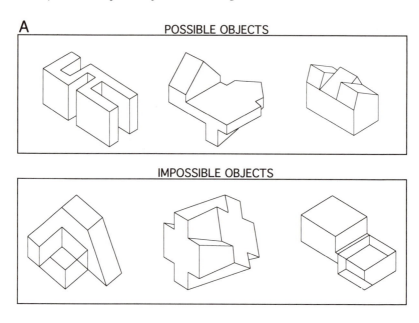

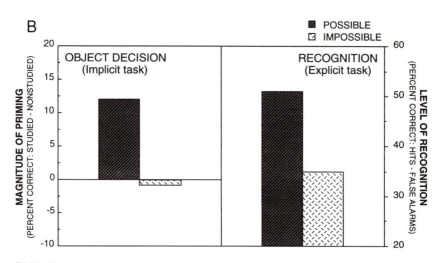

FIGURE 5   Examples of possible and impossible objects used in the experiments by Schacter and Cooper, and typical results on the object decision and recognition tasks (expressed as difference scores), following structural or "left/right" conditions of study. (From Cooper and Schacter, 1992. Reprinted with the permission of Cambridge University Press.)

variants of perceptual structure. Orientation of an object in the picture plane is apparently coded by both systems (Cooper, Schacter, & Moore, 1991), suggesting that structural representations of objects are axis based in the sense proposed by Marr and Nishihara (1978; see also Humphreys, 1983; Humphreys & Quinlan, 1987, 1988).

C. Evidence from Cognitive Neuroscience

As in the case of imagery, data from cognitive neuroscience has contributed centrally to our understanding of how visual–spatial information is represented in memory. By and large, evidence from electrophysiological and anatomical studies on nonhuman species, experimental studies of groups of patients with identifiable damage to the brain, and clinical case reports of individuals with selective visual–spatial impairments provide converging evidence that multiple neural systems exist for representing different kinds of visual–spatial information. Furthermore, distinctions among the properties of these neural systems often correspond well to the functional dissociations revealed in the behavioral experiments described previously.

Seminal research by Ungerleider and Mishkin (1982) introduced the widely held view that anatomically separate processing streams exist in extrastriate cortex for the analysis of object location and other object attributes, such as shape and color. The latter processing system, thought to subserve the function of object recognition, projects ventrally from primary visual cortex (area V1) to inferior temporal cortex. The other system also receives input from V1 and projects dorsally to posterior parietal cortex; functionally, this system is thought to mediate the localization of objects in space. In addition to the anatomical, electrophysiological, and behavioral evidence (the latter, from lesion studies with monkeys) reviewed by Ungerleider and Mishkin (1982), more recent findings provide support for their analysis (for review see Plaut & Farah, 1990). In particular, recordings from single neurons in inferior temporal cortex of monkeys (Bayliss, Rolls, & Leonard, 1987; Fujita, Tanaka, Ito, & Cheng, 1992) indicate selective responsiveness to visual features of complex shapes. Wilson, Scalaidhe, and Goldman-Rakic (1993) have provided evidence that the anatomical and functional separation of pathways for processing object identity versus object location information extends to prefrontal cortex.

Some behavioral evidence in humans for representational and processing dissociations corresponding to the "what" versus "where" distinction proposed by Ungerleider and Mishkin (1982) has been found (Kosslyn et al., 1989, studies cited earlier showing lateralization of judgments based on categorical and metric information; see also Kosslyn et al., 1990, as well as some of the variety of agnosia syndromes summarized in Farah, 1990), but the findings are mixed. Particularly notable is Biederman, Gehardstein,

Cooper, and Nelson's (in press) report that patients with unilateral temporal lobectomies, presumably a neural locus of object recognition processes, were nonetheless able to perform both "same–different" visual matching and object naming tasks at levels comparable to those of intact controls.

Goodale and collaborators (Goodale & Jakobson, 1992; Goodale & Milner, 1992; Milner & Goodale, 1993) have reinterpreted the Ungerleider–Mishkin "what/where" distinction as corresponding to separable systems for perceptual identification of, and directed action toward, objects in space. Behavioral evidence for this "what/how" distinction comes from observations of patients with visual agnosia who exhibit severe impairments in describing or naming common objects, but who are apparently able to make their way around in their immediate environments (see Farah, 1990, for descriptions). Goodale, Milner, Jakobson, and Carey (1991) provide a report of a patient with damage in occipital and occipitoparietal regions of the brain who performed poorly on tasks requiring the perceptual identification of objects' shapes or orientations, but who was able to achieve the degree of spatial analysis required to reach out for and grasp objects normally.

It is intriguing to speculate that the systems for representing the global structure of and episodic information about objects, functionally dissociated in the Schacter–Cooper experiments described above, subserve the action direction and perceptual identification functions proposed by Goodale and Milner (1992). That is, structural descriptions of objects may provide the basis for computing invariance under object or observer transformation that is crucial for locomotion in the environment and directing actions toward objects, whereas episodic representations of objects may provide the basis for determining their identities. Schacter, Cooper, Tharan, and Rubens (1991) have reported that amnesic individuals are severely impaired at explicit recognition of their possible and impossible objects, yet they exhibit the same level of priming on the implicit object decision task as matched and student control subjects. In addition, Schacter, Cooper, and Treadwell (1993) provide evidence that the system spared in amnesics has some of the same functional properties as the structural description system documented in intact individuals. In this study, amnesic patients showed intact priming despite study-to-test changes in the size of objects; and, the computation of size-invariant representations of objects is one striking characteristic of the structural description system (see Cooper et al., 1992). These and other demonstrations of spared priming, but impaired recognition, on visual–spatial tasks with amnesic patients (Gabrieli, Milberg, Keane, & Corkin, 1990; Musen & Squire, 1992) strongly suggest that the behavioral dissociations arise from distinct neural systems for representing different forms of information about visual objects. However, such results with amnesics do not shed light on the locus of the neural systems that are differentially spared and impaired.

In summary, evidence from clinical case reports and from behavioral, anatomical, and electrophysiological experiments supports the idea that multiple representational systems underlie memory for visual objects. Unfortunately, there exists as yet no satisfactory account of how the various systems and subsystems—both observed and postulated—might be related.

III. RECOGNITION OF FACES

We include a brief section on face recognition for two reasons. First, this class of visual stimuli has intrinsic interest and ecological significance. Second, it is widely believed that faces are represented and processed differently from other visual objects. Explicit suggestions about differences between faces and other visual stimuli come from the work of Farah (1992) and Carey (1992; Diamond & Carey, 1986). Farah points to the popular observation that faces have strong configural properties; thus, they are likely to be encoded and represented in memory as entire structures rather than as a series of parts or features. Tanaka and Farah (1993) provide evidence for this idea by showing that facial features were better recognized when presented in their appropriate context than when presented in isolation. Importantly, this effect of context did not extend to visual objects like houses and individual features of houses, in that features of a house were identified equally well whether they were presented alone or in context.

Diamond and Carey (1986) suggest that face recognition is unique in two ways. First, face recognition involves within-group discriminations. That is, all faces have the same basic configuration or "first-order relational properties": for example, the eyes are always set above the nose, and the mouth is always below the nose. Consequently, "second-order relational properties," for example, the distance between the eyes, must be used to differentiate between particular faces. Second, as we are able to recognize and distinguish among thousands of faces and are exposed to new faces constantly, people qualify as "experts" at face representation and recognition. This idea of expertise may explain a phenomenon in the face recognition literature known as the "inversion effect." Yin (1969) observed that subjects were more accurate at recognizing faces than at recognizing other types of objects. However, when the objects and the faces were inverted, recognition performance dropped more for faces than for the other objects. Thus, face recognition is differentially impaired by inversion, compared with recognition of common objects.

Diamond and Carey (1986) suggest that our expertise at using second-order relational properties to recognize faces explains this inversion effect. By hypothesis (Carey, 1992), second-order relational properties are orientation specific; thus, they are no longer useful for recognition when a face is inverted. In an empirical test of this hypothesized link between expertise and use of second-order relational properties, Diamond and Carey tested students' and expert dog judges' abilities to recognize upright and inverted pictures of dogs. The student novices performed equally well on recognition of upright and inverted dog pictures, whereas the dog experts exhibited the inversion effect. Moreover, the impairment of recognition for inverted pictures of dogs was specific to the particular breed of dog in which each expert specialized!

The phenomenon of prosopagnosia, the impaired recognition of faces in the absence of other cognitive impairments, is generally taken as evidence that faces are represented by a neural system separate from the system(s) that mediate recognition of other objects. However, Farah (1992) has recently proposed a general two-system account of object recognition that incorporates observations from prosopagnosic patients. One of the systems analyzes and represents objects as groups of parts; this system is responsible for recognizing words and some objects. The other system analyzes objects as wholes and is appropriate for faces, as well as certain other types of objects.

A survey of visual processing impairments in a population of agnosic patients generally supports this account (Farah, 1992). Several distinct subgroups emerged in the analysis: one group of patients showed recognition impairment specific either to faces or to both faces and objects. A second group exhibited impaired recognition for both objects and words. A third group showed recognition deficits for all three types of items, that is, words, objects, and faces. However, certain combinations of impairments were not observed in this population. For example, no patient was impaired at recognizing objects without also being impaired at recognizing faces or words; no patient exhibited impaired face and word recognition without also suffering impairment in object recognition. From these patterns of deficits, Farah concluded that one of the systems underlying object recognition decomposes objects into parts in order to facilitate recognition. This system is viewed as necessary for recognizing words and as useful for recognizing some objects. The second system analyzes objects as whole structures. This system is apparently necessary for face recognition and useful in some types of object recognition. Thus, prosopagnosia—while diagnostic of the operation of one of the two hypothesized recognition systems—does not necessarily imply that distinct neural mechanisms mediate face recognition and the recognition of other visual–spatial stimuli.

Sergent and collaborators have studied face recognition in normal subjects and prosopagnosic patients in an effort to elucidate the question of whether faces are represented and accessed differently from other visual–spatial material at the neural level. Their results indicate some specificity, but they are not entirely inconsistent with the general outline of Farah's analysis. In one study, Sergent, Ohta, and MacDonald (1992) employed PET scanning techniques while normal subjects performed both object and face recognition tasks. Their results indicated that some parts of the brain were activated during both object and face processing; however, some dissociation was observed. Certain areas in the right hemisphere (e.g., anterior temporal cortex) were activated during face processing, but not during object recognition, and the reverse pattern was obtained, as well. Thus, face and object recognition appear to share common neural processing mechanisms, as well as drawing on resources in specific brain areas. Sergent and Signoret (1992a, 1992b) also analyzed three prosopagnosic patients and discovered, consistent with Farah's (1992) population study, considerable variation in both the type and degree of impairment. Of particular interest was one patient who performed above chance at a task requiring a judgment concerning which of two faces was familiar. This patient apparently had little difficulty in encoding facial configurations, as he did exhibit covert recognition, but experienced difficulty in retrieving information related to faces.

Finally, Bruce and associates (Bruce, Burton, & Craw, 1992; Bruce & Valentine, 1985, 1986; Bruce & Young, 1986; Burton, Bruce, & Johnston, 1990) have developed a model of face recognition that consists of a series of information "pools" linked by two-way connectors. The first pool contains specifically visual information about each familiar face termed Facial Recognition Units (FRUs). When enough visual information has accumulated to activate an FRU at a level above threshold, the information is passed on to the next pool, consisting of items called Personal Identity Nodes (PINs). PIN units are not modality specific; they act as organizing stations where all forms of information (semantic, acoustic, visual, etc.) about a particular individual are connected. When a PIN reaches threshold, it activates items in the next pool called Semantic Information Units (SIUs). When an SIU reaches threshold, it activates each of the connected PINs. The model thus provides a mechanism whereby particular faces can be related to more abstract information about an individual. The model has been successful in accounting for various phenomena, including semantic priming of faces, in which presentation of one face facilitates recognition of a related face (Bruce & Valentine, 1986). It has also been used to provide a detailed account of face recognition impairments seen in prosopagnosics (Burton, Young, Bruce, Johnston, & Ellis, 1991), which apparently reflect either damage in links between pools or damage to the content of information in the pools.

IV. VISUAL–SPATIAL REPRESENTATIONS OF LAYOUTS

An obvious yet significant feature of our daily encounters with the visual world is our ability to navigate successfully in familiar environments. This ability is based on mental representations of environmental layouts, that is, on representations of relations among objects and their locations in the space around us. Such representations, often referred to as "cognitive maps," have been studied by cartographers, geographers, and urban planners (see also Downs & Stea, 1977), as well as by psychologists. As in the case of object recognition, an enormous literature on properties of cognitive maps exists. We consider below findings from just a small fraction of this literature, drawing primarily on results of recent experimental work. Our intent is to address two central issues in an effort to underscore differences between how information about visual objects and about layouts of objects are represented in and accessed from memory. The first concerns whether cognitive maps derived from different forms of external information share common functional properties. The second concerns the nature of the derived mental representations. In particular, do they code specifically visual information, as in the case of object representation, or do they embody more abstract knowledge about spatial relations?

A. Encoding Different Types of Information about Spatial Layouts

We obtain information about the structure, properties, and identities of objects primarily through our visual systems (but see Klatzsky, Loomis, Lederman, Wake, & Fujita, in press, for studies of conditions facilitating identification of objects through haptic exploration). Indeed, a cornerstone of James J. Gibson's (1979) theory of perception was that structured information in the optic array specifies objects' potential uses or affordances. By contrast, information about layouts often originates from nonvisual sources, as when we stop by the side of the road to ask directions to a target location. Taylor and Tversky (1992) examined whether mental representations of environments had functionally similar properties, despite differences in how information was acquired. Subjects studied two different types of descriptions of spatial layouts. One type, the route description, provided sequential information about what buildings and locations would be encountered while walking through a particular environment. The other type, the survey description, provided information as it would be encountered while observing an environment from an aerial view. Subjects were then asked questions about each environment, some of which were taken verbatim from the descriptions and some of which required inferences based on either route or survey information. When asked questions taken directly from a particular description, subjects who had studied that description responded more rapidly than did subjects who had studied the other type of description of the same environment. However, when asked questions that required inferences based on a spatial description, response time did not differ as a function of which type of description subjects had read. In a similar experiment, Ferguson and Hegarty (1995) showed a trend for superior performance when testing required the use of a visual–spatial representation, as compared with memory for the actual studied text. Results from both of these experiments support the ideas that some sort of cognitive map was formed by subjects in all conditions, and that this mental representation had similar functional properties regardless of how the information about a layout was studied.

The presentation of information about environments is not only varied, but also is often introduced in a linear fashion. We can learn much about an object in a single glance; however, we generally receive information about an environment over time, while exploring or while listening to a description. In order to form a coherent cognitive representation of a layout under temporally extended conditions of encoding, we must be able to connect and to integrate a series of discrete details about objects and locations. Montello and Pick (1993) have demonstrated such integration of two environments into a single cognitive map. Subjects learned two separate layouts by being guided through two different floors of the same building, without being told that the two routes were located one on top of the other. After learning the routes and landmarks in each environment, subjects were informed of the relation between the two and were asked questions about the locations of landmarks on either floor while standing at the beginning of a particular route. Location of objects on the same floor as the subjects were standing was faster than location of objects on the floor above or below, but performance achieved a greater than chance level in the latter condition. These results indicate some ability to integrate information from the distinct cognitive maps into a single, unified spatial representation.

Franklin, Tversky, and Coon (1992) have provided evidence that information from a series of points of view can be integrated into a single cognitive map. In this research, subjects studied verbal descriptions that provided information either about an environment from two distinct perspectives or about one environment at two different points in time. Although the pattern of results was complex, it is generally consistent with the conclusion that descriptions from different spatial or temporal perspectives can be integrated in a single internal model.

B. Abstract Nature of Encoded Layout Information

We have argued above that mental images can preserve visual properties of their corresponding external objects, and that memory representations supporting object recognition code information about object axes, parts, and other distinctive visual attributes. By contrast, there is converging evidence from several sources that mental representations of environments preserve only abstract relations about the spatial layout of objects.

One line of work (Hirtle & Jonides, 1985; Stevens & Coupe, 1978; Tversky, 1992) suggests that the spatial information in cognitive maps is organized hierarchically and affected by abstract semantic knowledge. The hierarchical nature of these representations leads to distortions in memory, revealed by errors in judgments about the relative locations of well-known places. For example, when asked which city is further north, Portland, Maine, or Portland, Oregon, subjects often erroneously answer Portland, Maine (Stevens & Coupe, 1978). Tversky (1992) claims that such errors result from hierarchical organization in cognitive maps. That is, rather than storing a mental image of a map of the United States, people store abstract information about where states are in relation to each other and where cities are within each state. In answering questions about the relative locations of cities, subjects may consider the fact that the state of Maine is adjacent to the Canadian border, whereas the state of Oregon is not. Therefore, Maine is further north than Oregon, so Portland, Maine, should be further north than Portland, Oregon. This type of erroneous inference indicates that the spatial organization of information in cognitive maps differs from mental images, in that the former do not obey principles of Euclidean geometry.

If mental representations of environments specify metric distance in a visual–spatial format, then we should expect information about any location in, or perspective on, an environment to be equally accessible. Franklin and Tversky (1990), however, showed that certain areas of cognitive maps, relative to the spatial orientation of an observer, are more easily accessed than others. Subjects read brief narratives that described the locations of objects around a reclining or standing observer. Questions about which objects in the environment were in different directions (in front of/behind, above/below, to the right/left) from the observer were then answered as rapidly as possible. Response times exhibited systematic variability; subjects were fastest to name objects above or below a standing observer, slower to name objects in front or behind, and slowest when asked to name objects to the left or to the right. Furthermore, the relative ordering of these response times changed when subjects answered questions about object locations relative to a reclining observer. This pattern of results clearly legislates against the idea that information about all positions and object locations is equally available from mental representations of environments. Rather, the results suggest that subjects locate objects in the mental representation along axes of the body. Certain axes, such as the front–back direction, may be more salient than others because of the way we obtain information about object locations while moving around in the world.

Still another line of work gives compelling evidence that mental models of the environment may specify only highly abstract, nonvisual information about the relations among objects in space. Indeed, previous experience with visual information is apparently not necessary for creating a useful representation of a spatial array. Landau and her collaborators (Landau, 1986; Landau & Spelke, 1985; Landau, Spelke, & Gleitman, 1984) have provided detailed accounts of how congenitally blind children learn about the environment and acquire representations of spatial layouts of objects. Loomis et al. (1993) reported that congenitally blind adult subjects can perform as well as blindfolded sighted subjects on a series of tasks requiring the formation of a spatial representation of a given area. Furthermore, congenitally blind and blindfolded sighted subjects achieved equal levels of performance on both simple and complex route acquisition tasks (Klatzky et al., 1990). These findings demonstrate that effective representations of layouts can be acquired without the use of vision, and that these representations preserve abstract, nonvisual information about spatial relations among objects.

V. CONCLUDING REMARKS

One of the central conclusions of this review is that visual–spatial representations provide a varied and flexible format for coding information about the world in memory. Moreover, such representations are used to accomplish many cognitive activities. The nature of the information accessed from representations of spatial objects and events is sensitive to the requirements of the task at hand. Mental images of visual objects preserve relational, structural, and sometimes metric information; they can be transformed internally in a fashion analogous to physical transformations on corresponding external objects. Recent research in cognitive neuroscience suggests that images of objects are not only functionally equivalent to perceptual representations, but also result in activation of some of the same areas of the brain used to perform perceptual tasks.

The type of visual information represented in memory for purposes of object recognition, as well as the nature of the recognition process, remain somewhat controversial. While theories differ in their emphasis, there is nonetheless agreement that representations of objects preserve information about components, along with a specification of global structure or relations among the primitive units. Considerable experimental and neuropsychological evidence suggests that multiple systems, designed to represent different forms of information about objects, are accessed by different cognitive tasks and are differentially affected by encoding requirements. Particularly dramatic are demonstrations of selective impairment and sparing of various memorial abilities following damage to the brain.

Finally, representations of spatial layouts of objects appear to preserve much more abstract and hierarchically organized information than do images or representations of individual objects. The variety of ways in which visual–spatial information is represented in memory, coupled with the fact that different aspects of those memory representations can be retrieved to accomplish different cognitive goals, help to account for the flexible and efficient manner in which stored information about the visual world guides our daily behavior.

References

Anderson, J. R. (1978). Arguments concerning representations for mental imagery. *Psychological Review, 85,* 249–277.

Baddeley, A. (1992). Working memory. *Science, 255,* 556–559.

Baird, J. C., & Hubbard, T. L. (1992). Psychophysics of visual imagery. In D. Algom (Ed.), *Psychophysical approaches to cognition.* New York: Elsevier/North-Holland.

Bayliss, G. C., Rolls, E. T., & Leonard, C. M. (1987). Functional subdivisions of the temporal lobe neocortex. *Journal of Neuroscience, 7,* 330–342.

Behrmann, M., Winocur, G., & Moscovitch, M. (1992). Dissociation between mental imagery and object recognition in a brain damaged patient. *Nature, 359,* 636–637.

Bethell-Fox, C. E., & Shepard, R. N. (1988). Mental rotation: Effects of stimulus complexity and familiarity. *Journal of Experimental Psychology: Human Perception and Performance, 14,* 1, 12–23.

Biederman, I. (1987). Recognition-by-components: A theory of human image understanding. *Psychological Review, 94,* 115–147.

Biederman, I. (1990). Higher-level vision. In D. N. Osherson, S. M. Kosslyn, & J. M. Hollerbach (Eds.), *Visual cognition and action.* Cambridge: MIT Press.

Biederman, I., & Cooper, E. E. (1991a). Priming contour-deleted images: Evidence for intermediate representations in visual object recognition. *Cognitive Psychology, 23,* 393–419.

Biederman, I., & Cooper, E. E. (1991b). Size invariance in visual object priming. *Journal of Experimental Psychology: Human Perception and Performance, 18,* 121–133.

Biederman, I., & Cooper, E. E. (1991c). Evidence for complete translational and reflectional invariance in visual object priming. *Perception, 20,* 585–593.

Biederman, I., & Gerhardstein, P. C. (1993). Recognizing depth-rotated objects: Evidence and conditions for 3D viewpoint invariance. *Journal of Experimental Psychology: Human Perception and Performance, 19*(6), 1162–1182.

Biederman, I., Gerhardstein, P. C., Cooper, E. E., & Nelson, C. A. (in press). High level objects recognition without an anterior temporal lobe. *Journal of Cognitive Neuroscience.*

Bisiach, E., & Luzzatti, C. (1978). Unilateral neglect of representational space. *Cortex, 17,* 129–133.

Bower, G. H. (1970). Analysis of a mnemonic device. *American Scientist, 58,* 496–510.

Bower, G. H. (1972). Mental imagery and associative learning. In L. W. Gregg (Ed.), *Cognition in learning and memory.* New York: Wiley.

Brandimonte, M. A., & Gerbino, W. (1993). Mental image reversal and verbal recoding: When ducks become rabbits. *Memory & Cognition, 21,* 23–33.

Brooks, L. R. (1968). Spatial and verbal components of the act of recall. *Canadian Journal of Psychology, 22,* 349–368.

Bruce, V., Burton, A. M., & Craw, I. (1992). Modeling face recognition. *Philosophical Transactions of the Royal Society of London, 335,* 121–128.

Bruce, V., & Valentine, T. (1985). Identity priming in the recognition of familiar faces. *Quarterly Journal of Psychology, 76,* 363–383.

Bruce, V., & Valentine, T. (1986). Semantic priming of familiar faces. *British Journal of Experimental Psychology, 38A,* 125–150.

Bruce, V., & Young, A. (1986). Understanding face recognition. *British Journal of Psychology, 77,* 305–327.

Bundesen, C., & Larsen, A. (1975). Visual transformation of size. *Journal of Experimental Psychology: Human Perception and Performance, 1,* 214–220.

Burton, A. M., Bruce, V., & Johnston, R. A. (1990). Understanding face recognition with an interactive model. *British Journal of Psychology, 81,* 361–380.

Burton, A. M., Young, A. W., Bruce, V., Johnston, R. A., & Ellis, A. W. (1991). Understanding covert recognition. *Cognition, 39,* 129–166.

Carey, S. (1992). Becoming a face expert. *Philosophical Transactions of the Royal Society of London, 335,* 95–103.

Cave, K., Pinker, S., Giorgi, L., Thomas, C. E., Heller, L. M., Wolfe, J. M., & Lin, H. (1994). The representations of location in visual images. *Cognitive Psychology, 26*(1), 1–32.

Chambers, D., & Reisberg, D. (1985). Can mental images be ambiguous? *Journal of Experimental Psychology: Human Perception and Performance, 11,* 317–328.

Chambers, D., & Reisberg, D. (1992). What an image depicts depends on what an image means. *Cognitive Psychology, 24,* 145–174.

Cheng, K. (1986). A purely geometric module in the rat's spatial representation. *Cognition, 23,* 149–178.

Cheng, K. (1989). The vector sum model of pigeon landmark use. *Journal of Experimental Psychology: Animal Behavior Processes, 15,* 366–375.

Cooper, L. A. (1975). Mental rotation of random two-dimensional shapes. *Cognitive Psychology, 7,* 20–43.

Cooper, L. A. (1988). The role of spatial representations in complex problem solving. In S. Steele & S. Schiffer (Eds.), *Cognition and representation.* Boulder, CO: Westview Press.

Cooper, L. A. (1990). Mental representation of three-dimensional objects in visual problem solving and recognition. *Journal of Experimental Psychology: Learning, Memory, and Cognition, 16,* 1097–1106.

Cooper, L. A., & Podgorny, P. (1976). Mental transformations and visual comparison processes: Effects of complexity and similarity. *Journal of Experimental Psychology: Human Perception and Performance, 2,* 503–514.

Cooper, L. A., & Schacter, D. L. (1992). Dissociations between structural and episodic representations of visual objects. *Current Directions in Psychological Science, 1,* 141–146.

Cooper, L. A., Schacter, D. L., Ballesteros, S., & Moore, C. (1992). Priming and recognition of transformed three-dimensional objects: Effects of size and reflection. *Journal of Experimental Psychology: Learning, Memory, and Cognition, 18,* 43–57.

Cooper, L. A., Schacter, D. L., & Moore, C. (1991, November). *Orientation affects both structural and episodic representations of three-dimensional objects.* Paper presented at the 32nd annual meeting of the Psychonomic Society, San Francisco.

Cooper, L. A., & Shepard, R. N. (1973). Chronometric studies of rotation of mental images. In W. G. Chase (Ed.), *Visual information processing.* New York: Academic Press.

Cooper, L. A., & Shepard, R. N. (1975). Mental transformations in the identification of left and right hands. *Journal of Experimental Psychology: Human Perception and Performance, 104,* 48–56.

Cooper, L. A., & Shepard, R. N. (1984). Turning something over in the mind. *Scientific American, 251,* 106–117.

Corballis, M. C., & Rodan, C. E. (1975). Detection of symmetry as a function of angular orientation. *Journal of Experimental Psychology: Human Perception and Performance, 1,* 221–230.

Denis, M., & Carfantan, M. (1985). People's knowledge about images. *Cognition, 20,* 49–60.

Diamond, R., & Carey, S. (1986). Why faces are and are not special: An effect of expertise. *Journal of Experimental Psychology: General, 115,* 107–117.

Di Lollo, V., & Dixon, P. (1988). Two forms of persistence in visual information processing. *Journal of Experimental Psychology: Human Perception and Performance, 14,* 671–681.

Downs, R. M., & Stea, D. (1977). *Maps in minds.* New York: Harper & Row.

Farah, M. J. (1985). Psychophysical evidence for a shared representation medium for mental images and percepts. *Journal of Experimental Psychology: General, 114,* 91–103.

Farah, M. J. (1990). *Visual agnosia: Disorders of object recognition and what they tell us about normal vision*. Cambridge: MIT Press.

Farah, M. J. (1992). Is an object an object? Cognitive and neuropsychological investigations of domain specificity in visual object recognition. *Current Directions in Psychological Science, 1,* 164–169.

Farah, M. J., Hammond, K. M., Levine, D. N., & Calvanio, R. (1988). Visual and spatial mental imagery: Dissociable systems of representation. *Cognitive Psychology, 20,* 439–462.

Farah, M. J., Peronnet, F., Gonon, M. A., & Girard, M. H. (1988). Electrophysiological evidence for a shared representational medium for visual images and visual percepts. *Journal of Experimental Psychology: General, 117,* 248–257.

Ferguson, E. L., & Hegarty, M. (1995). Learning with real machines or diagrams: Application of knowledge to real-world problems. *Cognition and Instruction, 13,* 129–160.

Finke, R. A. (1990). *Creative imagery: Discoveries and inventions in visualization*. Hillsdale, NJ: Erlbaum.

Finke, R. A., & Pinker, S. (1982). Spontaneous imagery scanning in mental extrapolation. *Journal of Experimental Psychology: Learning, Memory and Cognition, 8,* 142–147.

Finke, R. A., & Pinker, S. (1983). Directional scanning of remembered visual patterns. *Journal of Experimental Psychology: Learning, Memory, and Cognition, 9,* 398–410.

Finke, R. A., Pinker, S., & Farah, M. (1989). Reinterpreting visual patterns in mental imagery. *Cognitive Psychology, 13,* 51–78.

Finke, R. A., & Shepard, R. N. (1986). Visual functions of mental imagery. In K. R. Boff, L. Kaufman, & J. P. Thomas (Eds.), *Handbook of perception and human performance*. New York: Wiley.

Folk, M. D., & Luce, R. D. (1987). Effects of stimulus complexity on mental rotation rate of polygons. *Journal of Experimental Psychology: Human Perception and Performance, 13,* 395–404.

Franklin, N., Tversky, B. (1990). Searching imagined environments. *Journal of Experimental Psychology: General, 119,* 63–76.

Franklin, N., & Tversky, B., & Coon, V. (1992). Switching points of view in spatial mental models. *Memory & Cognition, 20,* 507–518.

Freyd, J. J. (1987). Dynamic mental representations. *Psychological Review, 94,* 427–438.

Freyd, J. J. (1993). Five hunches about perceptual processes and dynamic representations. In D. Meyer & S. Kornblum (Eds.), *Attention and performance XIV: Synergies in experimental psychology, artificial intelligence, and cognitive neurosciences*. Cambridge: MIT Press.

Freyd, J. J., & Finke, R. A. (1984). Representational momentum. *Journal of Experimental Psychology: Learning, Memory, and Cognition, 10,* 126–132.

Freyd, J. J., & Johnson, J. Q. (1987). Probing the time course of representational momentum. *Journal of Experimental Psychology: Learning, Memory, and Cognition, 13,* 259–268.

Fujita, I., Tanaka, K., Ito, M., & Cheng, K. (1992). Columns for visual features of objects in monkey inferotemporal cortex. *Nature, 360,* 343–356.

Gabrieli, J. D. E., Milberg, W., Keane, M. M., & Corkin, S. (1990). Intact priming patterns despite impaired memory. *Neuropsychologia, 28,* 5, 417–427.

Georgopoulos, A. P., Lurito, J. T., Petrides, M., Schwartz, A. B., & Massey, J. T. (1989). Mental rotation of the neuronal population vector. *Science, 243,* 234–236.

Gibson, J. J. (1979). *The ecological approach to perception*. Hillsdale, NJ: Erlbaum.

Goldenberg, G., Podreka, I., Steiner, M., Willmes, K., Suess, E., & Deeke, L. (1989). Regional blood flow patterns in visual imagery. *Neuropsychologia, 27,* 644–664.

Goldstone, D. B., Hinrichs, J. V., & Richman, C. L. (1985). Subject's expectation, individual variability, and the scanning of mental images. *Memory & Cognition, 13,* 365–370.

Goodale, M. A., & Jakobson, L. S. (1992). Action systems in the posterior parietal cortex. *Behavioral and Brain Sciences, 15,* 747.

Goodale, M. A., & Milner, A. D. (1992). Separate visual pathways for perception and action. *TINS, 15,* 20–25.

Goodale, M. A., Milner, A. D., Jakobson, L. S., & Carey, D. P. (1991). A neurological dissociation between perceiving objects and grasping them. *Nature, 349,* 154–156.

Harvey, L. O. (1986). Visual memory: What is remembered? In F. Klix & H. Hagendorf (Eds.), *Human memory and cognitive capabilities: Mechanisms and performance.* New York: Elsevier/North-Holland.

Hegarty, M. (1991). Knowledge and processes in mechanical problem solving. In R. J. Sternberg & P. A. Frensch (Eds.), *Complex problem solving: Principles and mechanisms.* Hillsdale, NJ: Erlbaum.

Hegarty, M., Carpenter, P. A., & Just, M. A. (1990). Diagrams in the comprehension of scientific texts. In R. Barr, M. L. Kamil, P. P. Mosenthal, & P. D. Pearson (Eds.), *Handbook of reading research* (Vol. II). New York: Longman.

Hinton, G. (1979). Some demonstrations of the effects of structural descriptions on mental imagery. *Cognitive Science, 3,* 231–250.

Hintzman, D. L., O'Dell, C. S., & Arndt, D. R. (1981). Orientation in cognitive maps. *Cognitive Psychology, 13,* 149–206.

Hirtle, S. C., & Jonides, J. (1985). Evidence of hierarchies in cognitive maps. *Memory & Cognition, 13,* 208–217.

Hochberg, J., & Gellman, L. (1977). The effect of landmark features "mental rotation" times. *Memory & Cognition, 5,* 23–26.

Humphreys, G. W. (1983). Reference frames and shape perception. *Cognitive Psychology, 15,* 151–196.

Humphreys, G. W., & Quinlan, P. T. (1987). Priming effects between two-dimensional shapes. *Journal of Experimental Psychology: Human Perception and Performance, 14,* 203–220.

Humphreys, G. W., & Quinlan, P. T. (1988). Priming effects between two-dimensional shapes. *Journal of Experimental Psychology: Human Perception and Performance, 14,* 203–220.

Intons-Peterson, M. J. (1983). Imagery paradigms: How vulnerable are they to experimenters' expectations. *Journal of Experimental Psychology: Human Perception and Performance, 9,* 394–412.

Intons-Peterson, M. J., & McDaniel, M. A. (1991). Symmetries and asymmetries between imagery and perception. In C. Cornoldi & M. A. McDaniel (Eds.), *Imagery and cognition.* New York: Springer-Verlag.

Irwin, D. E., & Yeomans, J. M. (1986). Sensory registration and informational persistence. *Journal of Experimental Psychology: Human Perception and Performance, 12,* 343–360.

Jastrow, J. (1900). *Fact and fable in psychology.* Boston: Praeger.

Jolicoeur, P., & Kosslyn, S. M. (1985). Is time to scan visual images due to demand characteristics? *Memory & Cognition, 13,* 320–332.

Just, M. A., & Carpenter, P. A. (1985). Cognitive coordinate systems: Accounts of mental rotation and individual differences in spatial ability. *Psychological Review, 92,* 137–171.

Kahneman, D., & Treisman, A. (1984). Changing views of attention and automaticity. In R. Parasuraman & D. A. Davies (Eds.), *Varieties of attention.* New York: Academic Press.

Kahneman, D., Treisman, A., & Gibbs, B. J. (1992). The reviewing of object files: Object-specific integration of information. *Cognitive Psychology, 24,* 175–219.

Klatzky, R. L., Loomis, J. M., Lederman, S. J., Wake, H., & Fujita, N. (1993). Haptic identification of objects and their depictions. *Perception & Psychophysics, 54,* 170–178.

Klatzky, R. L., Loomis, J. M., Golledge, R. G., Cincinelli, J. G., Doherty, S., & Pellegrino, J. W. (1990). Acquisition of route and survey knowledge in the absence of vision. *Journal of Motor Behavior, 22,* 19–43.

Kosslyn, S. M. (1973). Scanning visual images: Some structural implications. *Perception & Psychophysics, 14,* 90–94.

Kosslyn, S. M. (1981). The medium and the message in mental imagery: A theory. *Psychological Review, 88*, 46–66.

Kosslyn, S. M. (1987). Seeing and imagining in the cerebral hemispheres: A computational approach. *Psychological Review, 94*, 148–175.

Kosslyn, S. M. (1994). *Elements of graphic design*. New York: W. H. Freeman.

Kosslyn, S. M., Alpert, N. M., Thompson, W. L., Maljkovic, V., Weise, S. B., Chabris, C. F., Hamilton, S. E., Rauch, S. L., & Buonanno, S. (1993). Visual mental imagery activates topographically organized visual cortex: PET investigations. *Journal of Cognitive Neuroscience, 5*, 263–287.

Kosslyn, S. M., Ball, T. M., & Reiser, B. J. (1978). Visual images preserve metric spatial information: Evidence from studies of image scanning. *Journal of Experimental Psychology: Human Perception and Performance, 4*, 47–60.

Kosslyn, S. M., Flynn, R. A., Amsterdam, J. B., & Wang, G. (1990). Components of high-level vision: A cognitive neuroscience analysis and accounts of neurological syndromes. *Cognition, 34*, 203–277.

Kosslyn, S. M., Koenig, O., Barrett, A., Cave, C. B., Tang, J., & Gabrieli, J. D. E. (1989). Evidence for two types of spatial relations: Hemispheric specialization for categorical and coordinate relations. *Journal of Experimental Psychology: Human Perception and Performance, 15*, 723–735.

Landau, B. (1986). Early map use as an unlearned ability. *Cognition, 22*, 201–223.

Landau, B., & Spelke, E. S. (1985). Spatial knowledge and its manifestations. In H. M. Wellman (Ed.), *Children's searching: The development of search skill and spatial representation*. Hillsdale, NJ: Erlbaum.

Landau, B., Spelke, E. S., & Gleitman, H. (1984). Spatial knowledge in a young blind child. *Cognition, 16*, 225–260.

Levine, D. N., Warach, J., & Farah, M. J. (1985). Two visual systems in mental imagery: Dissociation in "what" and "where" in imagery disorders due to bilateral posterior cerebral lesions. *Neurology, 35*, 1010–1018.

Loftus, G. R., & Ruthruff, E. (1994). A theory of visual information acquisition and visual memory with special application to intensity-duration tradeoffs. *Journal of Experimental Psychology: Human Perception and Performance, 20*(3), 676–677.

Loomis, J. M., Klatzky, R. L., Gollege, R. G., Cicinelli, J. G., Pellegrino, J. W., & Fry, P. A. (1993). Nonvisual navigation by blind and sighted: Assessment of path integration ability. *Journal of Experimental Psychology: General, 122*, 73–91.

Lowe, D. G. (1985). Further investigations of inhibitory mechanisms in attention. *Memory & Cognition, 13*, 74–80.

Marr, D. (1982). *Vision*. San Francisco: W. H. Freeman.

Marr, D., & Nishihara, H. K. (1978). Representation and recognition of the spatial organization of three-dimensional shapes. *Proceedings of the Royal Society of London, 200*, 269–294.

Miller, A. I. (1984). *Imagery in scientific thought: Creating 20th-century physics*. Boston: Birkhauser Boston.

Milner, A. D., & Goodale, M. A. (1993). Visual pathways to perception and action. In T. P. Hicks, S. Molotchnikoff, & T. Ono (Eds.), *Progress in brain research*, Vol. 95. Amsterdam: Elsevier.

Montello, D. R., & Pick, H. L. (1993). Integrating knowledge of vertically-aligned large-scale spaces. *Environment and Behavior, 25*, 457–484.

Musen, G., & Squire, L. R. (1992). Nonverbal priming in amnesia. *Memory & Cognition, 20*, 441–448.

Novick, L. R. (1988). Analogical transfer, problem similarity and expertise. *Journal of Experimental Psychology: Learning, Memory, and Cognition, 14*, 510–520.

Novick, L. R. (1990). Representational transfer in problem solving. *Psychological Science, 1,* 128–132.

Paivio, A. (1971). *Imagery and verbal processes.* New York: Holt.

Palmer, S. E. (1977). Hierarchical structure in perceptual representation. *Cognitive Psychology, 9,* 441–474.

Parsons, L. M. (1987). Imagined spatial transformation of one's body. *Journal of Experimental Psychology: General, 116,* 172–191.

Peterson, M. A., Kihlstrom, J. F., Rose, P. M., & Glisky, M. L. (1992). Mental images can be ambiguous: Reconstruals and reference-frame reversals. *Memory & Cognition, 20,* 107–123.

Pinker, S. (1980). Mental imagery in the third dimension. *Journal of Experimental Psychology: General, 109,* 354–371.

Pinker, S. (1985). Visual cognition: An introduction. In S. Pinker (Ed.), *Visual cognition.* Cambridge: MIT Press.

Plaut, D. C., & Farah, M. J. (1990). Visual object representation: Interpreting neurophysiological data within a computational framework. *Journal of Cognitive Neuroscience, 2,* 320–343.

Podgorny, P., & Shepard, R. N. (1978). Functional representations common to visual perception and imagination. *Journal of Experimental Psychology: Human Perception and Performance, 4,* 21–35.

Pylyshyn, Z. W. (1973). What the mind's eye tells the mind's brain: A critique of mental imagery. *Psychological Bulletin, 80,* 1–24.

Pylyshyn, Z. W. (1981). The imagery debate: Analogue media versus tacit knowledge. *Psychological review, 87,* 16–45.

Reisberg, D. (in press). The non-ambiguity of mental images. In C. Cornoldi, R. Logie, M. Brandimonte, G. Kauffman, & D. Reisberg (Eds.), *Perception and mental representation.* New York: Simon & Schuster International.

Roediger, H. L. (1990). Implicit memory: Retention without remembering. *American Psychologist, 45,* 1043–1056.

Roskos-Ewoldson, B., Intons-Peterson, M. J., & Anderson, R. E. (1993). Imagery, creativity, and discovery: Conclusions and implications. In B. Roskos-Ewoldson, M. J. Intons-Peterson, & R. E. Anderson (Eds.), *Imagery, creativity, and discovery: A cognitive perspective.* New York: Elsevier/North-Holland.

Schacter, D. L. (1987). Implicit memory: History and current status. *Journal of Experimental Psychology: Learning, Memory, and Cognition, 13,* 501–518.

Schacter, D. L., & Cooper, L. A. (1993). Implicit and explicit memory for novel visual objects: Structure and function. *Journal of Experimental Psychology: Learning, Memory, and Cognition, 19,* 995–1009.

Schacter, D. L., Cooper, L. A., & Delaney, S. M. (1990a). Implicit memory for unfamiliar objects depends on access to structural descriptions. *Journal of Experimental Psychology: General, 119,* 5–24.

Schacter, D. L., Cooper, L. A., & Delaney, S. M. (1990b). Implicit memory for visual objects and the structural description system. *Bulletin of the Psychonomic Society, 28,* 367–372.

Schacter, D. L., Cooper, L. A., Delaney, S. M., Peterson, M. A., & Tharan, M. (1991). Implicit memory for possible and impossible objects: Constraints on the construction of structural descriptions. *Journal of Experimental Psychology: Learning, Memory, and Cognition, 17,* 3–19.

Schacter, D. L., Cooper, L. A., Tharan, M., & Rubens, A. B. (1991). Preserved priming of novel objects in patients with memory disorders. *Journal of Cognitive Neuroscience, 3,* 118–131.

Schacter, D. L., Cooper, L. A., & Treadwell, J. (1993). Preserved priming of novel objects across size transformation in amnesic patients. *Psychological Science, 4,* 331–335.

Segal, S. J., & Fusella, V. (1970). Influence of imaged pictures and sounds on detection of visual and auditory signals. *Journal of Experimental Psychology, 83,* 458–464.

Sergent, J., Ohta, S., & MacDonald, B. (1992). Functional neuroanatomy of face and object processing. *Brain, 115,* 15–36.

Sergent, J., & Signoret, J. (1992a). Implicit access to knowledge derived from unrecognized faces in prosopagnosia. *Cerebral Cortex, 2,* 389–400.

Sergent, J., & Signoret, J. (1992b). Varieties of functional deficits in prosopagnosia. *Cerebral Cortex, 2,* 375–388.

Shepard, R. N. (1978a). Externalization of mental images and the act of creation. In B. S. Randhawas & W. E. Coffman (Eds.), *Visual learning, thinking, and communication* (pp. 133–189). New York: Academic Press.

Shepard, R. N. (1978b). The mental image. *American Psychologist, 33,* 125–137.

Shepard, R. N., & Chipman, S. (1970). Second-order isomorphisms: Shapes of states. *Cognitive Psychology, 1,* 1–17.

Shepard, R. N., & Cooper, L. A. (1982). *Mental images and their transformation.* Cambridge: MIT Press.

Shepard, R. N., & Cooper, L. A. (1992). Representation of colors in the blind, color blind, and normally sighted. *Psychological Science, 3,* 97–104.

Shepard, R. N., & Feng, C. (1972). A chronometric study of mental paper folding. *Cognitive Psychology, 3,* 228–243.

Shepard, R. N., & Hurwitz, S. (1984). Mental rotation in map reading: Discrimination of right and left turns. *Cognition, 18,* 161–193.

Shepard, R. N., & Metzler, J. (1971). Mental rotation of three-dimensional objects. *Science, 171,* 701–703.

Sperling, G. A. (1960). The information available in belief visual presentation. *Psychological Monographs, 74,* 498.

Stevens, A., & Coupe, P. (1978). Distortions in judged spatial relations. *Cognitive Psychology, 10,* 422–437.

Tanaka, J. W., & Farah, M. J. (1993). Parts and wholes in face recognition. *Quarterly Journal of Experimental Psychology, 46A,* 225–245.

Tarr, M. J., & Pinker, S. (1989). Mental rotation and orientation-dependence in shape recognition. *Cognitive Psychology, 21,* 233–282.

Taylor, H. A., & Tversky, B. (1992). Spatial mental models derived from survey and route descriptions. *Journal of Memory and Language, 31,* 261–292.

Treisman, A. (1992). Perceiving and re-perceiving objects. *American Psychologist, 47,* 862–875.

Tulving, E., & Schacter, D. L. (1990). Priming and human memory systems. *Science, 247,* 301–306.

Tversky, B. (1992). Distortions in cognitive maps. *Geoforum, 23,* 131–138.

Ungerleider, L. G., & Mishkin, M. (1982). Two cortical visual systems. In D. J. Ingle, M. A. Goodale, & R. J. W. Mansfield (Eds.), *Analysis of visual behavior.* Cambridge: MIT Press.

Wilson, F. A. W., Scalaidhe, S. P. O., & Goldman-Rakic, P. S. (1993). Dissociation of object and spatial processing domains in primate prefrontal cortex. *Science, 260,* 1955–1958.

Yates, F. A. (1966). *The art of memory.* Chicago: University of Chicago Press.

Yin, R. K. (1969). Looking at upside-down faces. *Journal of Experimental Psychology, 81,* 141–145.

CHAPTER 6

Autobiographical Memory

Martin A. Conway

What are "autobiographical" memories? How is autobiographical knowledge represented in long-term memory? How are memories retrieved? What happens when autobiographical memory becomes impaired, for example, in amnesia? The purpose of the present chapter is to outline some of the answers memory researchers have provided to these questions. Other issues in the study of autobiographical memory, such as memory accuracy and the function of autobiographical memories in cognition more generally are also touched upon. For more wide-ranging reviews of autobiographical memory see Conway (1990a), Conway and Rubin (1993), or Robinson and Swanson (1990), and for collections of research chapters, see Conway, Rubin, Spinnler, and Wagenaar (1991), and Rubin (1986, in preparation).

I. CHARACTERISTICS OF AUTOBIOGRAPHICAL MEMORIES

Memory researchers have distinguished many different types of memories. In current use are classifications such as *episodic, semantic, declarative, procedural, implicit, explicit,* to name only some of the more prominent types of memory that have frequently formed the bases of recent research programs. Where, one might ask, does "autobiographical" memory fit in this typology? Consider the concept of "episodic" memory as originally proposed by

Tulving (1972). Tulving argued that the critical or defining feature of episodic memories was that they preserved knowledge of the spatiotemporal context in which an experience had taken place. In contrast to episodic memories, semantic memories did not have this characteristic; instead of preserving experiential aspects of events, they preserved factual and conceptual knowledge abstracted from the contexts in which that knowledge had been acquired. Episodic memory and autobiographical memory might then be equivalent and, indeed, Tulving (1983) comments that he considered using the term "autobiographical" rather than "episodic" (see also Conway, 1991).

Tulving, however, would have been incorrect to use the term "autobiographical" memory to refer to records of spatiotemporal aspects of experience because autobiographical memories cut across the episodic–semantic distinction. To see this, consider the following two accounts.

> We were going on holiday to France. I remember that we stayed at a boarding house in Dover and went down to the ferry very early the following morning. My brother and I were wildly excited. It was the first time we had been abroad and the first time we had been on a ship of any sorts. I have a vivid memory of looking back at the White Cliffs as the boat pulled out of the harbour—they seemed immensely tall.

> This happened early on at my Primary school. One year on sports day I won an egg-and-spoon race and the prize was a small toy car—"dinky" toys they were called—I remember I had an extensive collection of them and was highly delighted to have won one.

These verbal accounts were collected from subjects taking part in an autobiographical memory cue-word experiment (Conway & Bekerian, 1987; Crovitz & Schiffman, 1974; Galton, 1883; Robinson, 1976; Rubin, 1982). In cue-word experiments, subjects are presented with words naming common objects and activities (the two words that cued the memories in the verbal accounts were *ship* and *prize*) and are required to retrieve a memory of a specific event of which the cue word reminds them and that they themselves experienced. Usually additional instructions specify that the memory must be of some event that took place over a period of minutes or hours but not over a period of weeks or longer. Subjects are also required to respond with the first memory to come to mind. Both of these memory descriptions quite clearly show that the subjects had distinct spatiotemporal contexts in mind, but there is also some personal factual knowledge (first trip abroad, Primary school). As I discuss in the next section, autobiographical memories always contain both spatiotemporal knowledge *and* factual knowledge. The personal factual knowledge appears to contextualize the remembered event in terms of the rememberer's own personal history. Thus, one important characteristic of autobiographical memories is that they consist of multiple types of knowledge and, consequently, cannot easily be compartmentalized into classes of memory that are defined by a single knowledge type.

Another characteristic of autobiographical memories is their strong and direct relation to the self. Brewer (1986) has proposed that this self relation is the major distinguishing feature of autobiographical memories. Indeed, one possibility is that autobiographical memories are part of the self system, providing, as it were, a record of past selves and records of events that were at one time significant to the self. There seems little doubt that autobiographical memories are central to the self and that the self is critical in the encoding and retrieval of memories (Conway, 1992, in press), but the precise relations between self and memories have yet to be determined (but see Strauman, 1990, for a particularly interesting suggestion). Nevertheless, one interesting corollary of the "self" view bears directly on a central issue in memory research generally: namely, the accuracy of memories. In a much-discussed example, Neisser (1982) described his own highly vivid or "flashbulb" memory (Brown & Kulik, 1977) of learning of the news of the bombing of Pearl Harbor. Neisser relates that:

> For many years I have remembered how I heard the news of the Japanese attack on Pearl Harbor, which occurred on the day before my thirteenth birthday. I recall sitting in the living room of our house—we only lived in that house for one year, but I remember it well—listening to a baseball game on the radio. The game was interrupted by an announcement of the attack, and I rushed upstairs to tell my mother. This memory has been so clear for so long that I never confronted its inherent absurdity until last year: no one broadcasts baseball games in December!

Seemingly, autobiographical memory, even for unique and highly significant events, can be inaccurate. In a later study, however, Thompson and Cowan (1986) found that there had in fact been a radio broadcast of a football game on the eve of the attack on Pearl Harbor and, interestingly, both football teams had the same names as well-known baseball teams. Thompson and Cowan (1986) argued that Neisser's "incorrect" memory may, then, be basically accurate, containing only a comparatively minor error in the substitution of a baseball game for a football game. In a subsequent reply to Thompson and Cowan, Neisser (1986) agreed that he must have been listening to a commentary on the football game, yet argued that the substitution of baseball for football in his memory is significant in itself. Neisser (1986) pointed out that in his youth he had been intensely interested in the "all-American" game of baseball, far more so than in the then fledgling game of football. He argued that his earlier interest in baseball was part of a strong youthful identification with the adopted culture of his family and that the substitution error in his memory supported and furthered this identification. This "case" study of a single memory is revealing and illustrates an important characteristic of autobiographical memories: they are often basically accurate both in terms of what actually occurred and in terms of the goals, plans, and preoccupations of the self. As such, autobiographical memories should be viewed as personal *interpretations* of events rather than as literal or veridical records.

Autobiographical memories, then, contain multiple types of knowledge and are interpretations rather than true records of events. The fact that autobiographical memories can be incorrect and that errors are often explicable in terms of the influence of the self should not lead us to underestimate accuracy in autobiographical memories. For instance, in recent studies of flashbulb memories (Conway, Anderson, Larsen, Donnelly, McDaniel, McClelland, Rawles, & Logie, 1994; Pillemer, 1984), strikingly consistent accounts of the events in which a person learned surprising and consequential news have been observed. Conway et al. found that many of their subjects consistently recalled even minute event details one year after learning of a surprising news event (see Conway, 1994, for a review of the flashbulb memory literature). An impressive experimental demonstration of the accurate retention of event minutiae was reported by B. H. Ross (1984). In B. H. Ross's study, subjects learned how to use a word processor and some days later learned a new word processor that used slightly different word processing commands. The actual text processed was, however, held constant across the two training episodes. B. H. Ross (1984) found that when learning the second word processor subjects often spontaneously recalled the command they had previously executed on a specific item of text and could recall items of text previously manipulated in a different way. Autobiographical memories can then be remarkably accurate even when subjects recall event details. It does not, however, follow that autobiographical memories are complete or full accounts of events. It seems much more probable that autobiographical memories are inherently incomplete accounts of events, because in any event the self must direct attention and so determine, to at least some extent, which event features are strongly encoded and which are only weakly retained (Conway, in press). Thus, a further characteristic of autobiographical memories is that they may retain highly specific knowledge of event features (Tulving's, 1972, "spatiotemporal" knowledge), while at the same time be incomplete records of an event.

The retention of event minutiae in the form of sensory-perceptual details may also serve other purposes in autobiographical remembering. Johnson, Foley, Suengas, and Raye (1988) required subjects to recall an event they had actually experienced and an event they had only imagined. Subjects then completed a questionnaire that assessed such factors in the memories as the degree of perceptual details and the extent of emotion. The main finding was that memories of experienced events were judged to contain more specific knowledge of perceptual details than memories of imagined events. Overall, memories of experienced events were judged higher in visual detail, sound, smell, taste, and spatial array of objects than were memories for imagined events. In contrast, imagined events were judged to be more complex, more intense, entail more implications, and judged to be thought about more frequently than memories for experienced events.

Highly similar findings were obtained by Brewer (1988), who randomly sampled events by having subjects record an ongoing event in response to a randomly timed signal from a beeper. In latter sessions, subjects were cued to recall or recognize events they had previously recorded. In addition, subjects also rated their phenomenal experience when recalling on a seven-point "re-experience" scale. For example, a subject would rate how close their phenomenal experience of remembering approximated the actual visual experience of the original event. In the case of memories that subjects were highly confident were accurate, visual re-experience was rated extremely strong and to approximate the original visual experience closely. Also strongly re-experienced, but not as strongly as visual re-experience, were auditory and tactile aspects of the event. Moreover, both Brewer and Johnson et al. found that valence and specific emotions were well retained in autobiographical memories. Finally, other evidence for the retention of strong event-specific knowledge comes from a study by Whitten and Leonard (1981). In their study, subjects provided protocols while attempting to recall the names of their preuniversity school teachers. Analysis of these protocols indicated that a frequently used strategy was to bring to mind images of locations and routes through the school in the hope of "seeing" a teacher. Presumably, this strategy led to successful recalls of teachers by facilitating access to memories of event-specific knowledge cued by the visual information available in the images of locations.

In summary, several general characteristics of autobiographical memories have been outlined in this section. Autobiographical memories contain different types of knowledge. Some of this knowledge is sensory-perceptual in nature and can constitute a highly accurate record of at least some of the features of an event. In contrast, other knowledge is more abstract and decontextualized, relating more to an individual's personal history than to the features of any specific experience. Autobiographical memories can be accurate, but accuracy in this case means accurate both in terms of the self and in terms of the basic knowledge of the remembered event. In order to understand how autobiographical memories can have these characteristics, a detailed account of the nature of autobiographical knowledge in long-term memory is required as is an account of how this knowledge can be accessed and utilized. The next sections describe findings bearing on this structure of autobiographical knowledge and the retrieval of autobiographical memories.

II. THE AUTOBIOGRAPHICAL MEMORY KNOWLEDGE BASE

One assumption about the nature of autobiographical memories is that they come to mind fully formed in discrete "whole" units. Indeed, something like this assumption underlies the operational definition of autobiographical memories used in tasks such as cue-word retrieval, where subjects are explicitly instructed to bring to mind a memory of an event that occurred over a period of minutes or hours. But is this what happens when people access autobiographical knowledge?

Barsalou (1988) and colleagues examined this "holistic" assumption when they asked people returning to campus after summer vacation to describe events in which they had been involved that summer. The protocols revealed that subjects only rarely described specific events, despite the explicit instruction to do so. In fact, the subjects' responses largely consisted of *summarized events* and comments on aspects of events. Statements such as "we also went to the movies while we were there," "I watched a lot of TV," and "everyday we would leave our house," were very common in the protocols as were comments such as "the family is a friend of ours," and "we had a lovely apartment." This type of autobiographical knowledge accounted for 63% of all responses in comparison to mention of specific events (e.g., "we saw a play," "we went for a little picnic"), which accounted for only 21% of responses. Barsalou (1988) also noted that about 9% of responses named *extended events,* such as "I worked there for two weeks," "I took a trip to Italy," "I went on a diet" (see Barsalou, 1988, Table 8.1, p. 200). Thus, it appears that when a time period is sampled, people do not simply retrieve fully formed whole memories but, instead, access a variety of knowledge types only some of which might be classified as memories.

It seems possible that the multiple types of knowledge accessed during autobiographical memory retrieval may reflect the underlying organization of autobiographical knowledge in long-term memory. To explore this idea, Conway and Bekerian (1987) conducted a series of memory retrieval experiments using the cue-word procedure described earlier. Subjects were required to retrieve memories to cue words or phrases quickly and accurately, and the dependent measure was the time taken for retrieval. The critical variation was whether the memory cue was preceded by a word or phrase intended to prime memory retrieval. In one experiment, the cues named common objects and activities taken from semantic categories. Thus, on one trial the cue might be the word *chair* preceded by either the word *furniture* or the word *ready* (the no-prime condition). Because semantic category primes have been shown to facilitate semantic judgments, such as category membership (Rosch, 1975), we reasoned that, if autobiographical knowledge were also organized in terms of semantic categories, memory retrieval to *chair* preceded by *furniture* should be faster than memory retrieval to *chair* preceded by the neutral prime *ready*. However, no effects of semantic category primes on memory retrieval were found, indicating that autobiographical knowledge is not organized in long-term memory in terms of semantic categories.

Although this finding was useful in ruling out one form of potential organization (but see Conway, 1990b), it was problematic in raising another issue: namely, can autobiographical memory retrieval be primed at all? It seemed to us that everyday discourse provided good evidence of priming. Consider, for instance, a friend telling you about a holiday. Almost immediately memories of your own holidays come to mind, allowing the affirmation of shared experiences and supporting the dynamics of the interaction. Accordingly, we decided to conduct a further series of priming studies featuring personal knowledge rather than semantic categories. Initially, we asked a large group of subjects to list *lifetime periods*. Lifetime periods were described as periods from one's life that were usually of years and even decades in duration. They had identifiable beginnings and endings, although these could be fuzzy rather than discrete, and they often singled out some theme, set of goals, or other general aspect of a person's life. Subjects had no difficulty in following these instructions and listed a number of lifetime periods, which often took the form of periods such as "when I was at infant/primary/secondary school," "when I was at university," "when I lived with X," "when I lived in city Y," "when I worked at Z." Subjects then listed *general events* (Barsalou's summarized and extended events) that had occurred in each lifetime period. General events were described as covering a shorter period of time such as a holiday, business trip, period of illness, or as denoting a series of repeated events, and as being more event specific than lifetime periods. It was emphasized that general events did not include memory for specific incidents spanning a short period of time (i.e., hours).

Some months later, the subjects returned to the laboratory and took part in a cued memory retrieval experiment. In this experiment, individual cues were taken from the lifetime periods and general events that each subject had previously listed, with lifetime periods serving as primes, general events as cues, and the word *ready* as the neutral prime. Large priming effects were observed: memory retrieval times in the primed trials were, on average, over one second faster than retrieval times from the no-prime condition. Finally, it was found that the lifetime periods named by the subjects were not exclusive in the sense of referring to completely different periods of time. That is, most subjects named some overlapping lifetime periods: for example, "when the children were little" might partially or wholly overlap with"when I worked at Z," but each lifetime period indexed different sets of general events and different groups of memories.

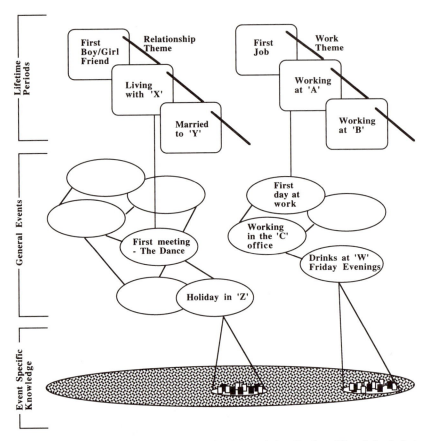

FIGURE 1   Organization of autobiographical knowledge for "work" and for "relationship" themes.

Conway and Bekerian (1987) proposed that autobiographical knowledge is organized into autobiographical memory organization packets or A-MOPS (after Kolodner, 1983; Schank, 1982) with each A-MOP consisting of a lifetime period with indices to a proscribed set of general events that, in turn, contain indices to highly detailed event-specific knowledge (ESK). Figure 1 illustrates this organization for two general themes, a relationship theme and a work theme, where the lifetime periods corresponding to each theme are shown in square boxes, the general events in ellipses, and the ESK is depicted by the large ellipse at the bottom of the figure. Lifetime periods are assumed to contain general personal knowledge that was highly related to the nature of the self when those periods were originally experienced (Conway, 1992, in press; Conway & Rubin, 1993; Strauman, 1990). For example, the lifetime period *first job* might contain knowledge about goal attainment relating to the goals of that period and, of course, significant others, locations, and even a few highly significant "whole" memories might be represented at this level. This "self" knowledge, or, as I call it, this *thematic* knowledge can be used to generate cues that access associated general events (see Conway, in press, for further discussion of themes in autobiographical memory). Of course, the cues available in the thematic knowledge of any individual lifetime period are limited and can directly access only a proscribed number of general events. General events contain more specific knowledge and index a pool of event features that constitute ESK. Thus, the *first job* lifetime period may contain knowledge relating to the goal of *being competent,* such as rewards for efficiently accomplished projects. Knowledge of a specific project may contain information that indexes general events related to that project, and such general event knowledge may, in turn, contain indices or cues to sets of ESK, including spatiotemporal and sensory–perceptual event features.

Similar suggestions concerning the organization of autobiographical knowledge have been put forward by Barsalou (1988), Linton (1986), and Schooler and Herrmann (1992). On the basis of an extended series of studies, Barsalou argued that autobiographical knowledge is organized into a series of partonomic hierarchical knowledge structures. In this scheme, ESK is part of a general event that, in turn, is part of a lifetime period, the highest level in the hierarchy. Linton (1986), in her diary study of her own memory, concluded that autobiographical knowledge was organized by themes and that themes accessed events and episodes. Similarly, Schooler and Herrmann (1992) identified what they called *periods, episodes,* and *moments,* corresponding to the concepts of lifetime periods, general events, and ESK, respectively. These independently conducted lines of research, each using different methodologies, have provided strikingly convergent evidence for the organization of the autobiographical knowledge base. In all these accounts, themes and temporal information are viewed as principles around which knowledge at different levels of abstraction is compiled into distinct knowledge structures, and it is these structures that constitute the autobiographical knowledge base.

Although structure in the autobiographical knowledge base might generally take the form of A-MOPs, other well-developed but more local organization may also be present. For instance, the organization of general events has yet to be extensively explored, and one possibility is that some general events may be linked together (within a lifetime period) and thus form an intermediate level of organization. Recent research by Robinson (1992) has provided some insights into this possible level of organization. Robinson (1992) investigated the organization of what he called "mini-histories" for episodes of skill acquisition and for first romantic relationships. He found that general events were organized around critical memories of goal attainment and that "first time" memories were central constructs in the organization of mini-histories. One domain of skill acquisition examined by Robinson (1992) was that of learning to drive a car. Autobiographical memory for this extended event was found to be structured around general self-evaluative knowledge relating to aspects of the skills acquired as well as to detailed memories for specific events. For example, many of Robinson's subjects recalled important moments when they succeeded or failed to master a particular skill component, such as reversing, signaling, or even keeping the vehicle in a straight line. Thus, knowledge of goal attainment appeared to be particularly central. Also frequently recalled were episodes featuring interactions with the driving instructor, particularly when these related to evaluation of the current status of goal attainment. Moreover, virtually all the subjects had highly detailed and vivid memories of the first time they drove a car alone and the changed sense of self this engendered. Sets of general events may thus be locally structured around self-relevant themes and so form coherent and identifiable mini-histories within the far larger pool of general events indexed by a lifetime period.

Anderson and Conway (1993) have investigated another area of local organization in autobiographical knowledge by exploring how knowledge within specific memories is organized. In a series of studies, subjects were required first to recall memories to cues and then to list details of the recalled memory as quickly as they could. Subjects were allowed 30 s to list memory details, and, for each memory, a particular detailing schedule was specified. For example, subjects were instructed to list memory details in the order in which they came to mind (free recall), in forward order (i.e., the actual order of their occurrence when the event was originally experienced), or in reverse order. It was reasoned that the recall schedule giving rise to the fastest memory detail production would be the one that most closely corresponded to the underlying organization of knowledge in specific memories (see also Barsalou & Sewell, 1985). If knowledge in specific memories was organized chronologically from first to last detail, then forward order should produce fastest production rates, whereas, if memory details were unorganized, then there should be no differences between any of the detailing schedules. Finally, it was expected that the free recall condition would act as a baseline in which memory details would be spontaneously listed in an order corresponding to their underlying organization in memory. Actual findings presented a more complex pattern. For example, although forward order was found generally to give rise to highest production rates, this listing schedule did not necessarily predominate in the free-recall condition. Additionally, although initial memory details were accessed more quickly in the free-recall condition, this initial advantage in memory detail access was somehow offset in the forward condition, with detail output, although initially slow, rapidly accumulating and eventually surpassing the free-recall level.

A key to these somewhat perplexing findings emerged when the distinctiveness of the memory details was examined. Subjects had rated which of the memory details were most distinctive and, specifically, had judged which of the memory details "made that memory what it is for you." Subjects had also been required to put into forward order details that had originally been free recalled. Using these measures, it was established that subjects in the free-recall condition initially accessed a small set of highly distinctive details and only then searched for other details. As these distinctive details frequently referred to event characteristics that had not occurred at the outset of the event, this strategy of listing memory details by rapidly accessing distinctive details was not available when the instruction was to list details in forward order. Anderson and Conway (1993) concluded that preferred access to memories is by way of distinctive or thematic details. However, details are actually organized in memory as chronologically ordered lists and, when full details of a memory are required, the head of the list must be located and a temporally ordered search conducted. Thus, in free recall, once a small set of distinctive details have been rapidly accessed, the search process must alter and the beginning details of the memory have to be located if the search is to proceed further. The additional time taken in the switch of search strategy slows down free-recall retrieval relative to a forward search strategy that is initially slow in locating the head of the memory but, once located, rapidly proceeds through a temporally ordered search of memory details. In summary, these findings indicate that memories are usually accessed by distinctive, thematic cues, but—because memory details are actually chronologically ordered—once a memory has been accessed, further processing must be undertaken if the majority of memory details are to become available.

In conclusion, the autobiographical knowledge base is structured, and at least three layers of knowledge have been identified. The first layer, lifetime periods, refers to lengthy periods of time typically measured in years and represents the goals, plans, and themes of the self during particular periods. Goals, plans, and themes are reflected in knowledge of significant others, records of goal attainment, and general knowledge of actors, actions, and locations characteristic of the period. The second layer, general events, is more specific and consists of records of extended and repeated events that occurred over periods of weeks and months. General events contain knowledge that can be used to access ESK sensory-perceptual details. In addition, general events may themselves be further organized into small sets of thematically related events. Specific memories are represented by chronologically ordered lists of memory details, and memory details may themselves consist solely of ESK knowledge. Indeed, Anderson (1993) found that subjects, when asked to list highly specific details of memories, responded by describing images, sensations, smells, thoughts, and other sensory-perceptual features associated with a given memory detail. Finally, across the three layers of knowledge, hierarchical knowledge structures may be formed such that cues available in a lifetime period index a particular, usually large, set of general events that in turn index other general events and ESK.

III. ACCESSING THE AUTOBIOGRAPHICAL KNOWLEDGE BASE: MEMORY "RETRIEVAL"

A striking feature of autobiographical memory retrieval is that retrieval times are slow and highly variable (Conway, 1990a, 1990b; Conway & Bekerian, 1987) compared to access times for other types of knowledge in long-term memory. Time taken to judge category membership or to verify factual statements, for example, typically varies around a mean of 1 s. Even the time taken to verify personal facts, such as the name of one's bank, college, or make of car, averages only 1.2 s across subjects (Conway, 1987). In contrast, autobiographical memory retrieval times, in cued retrieval tasks, often average 3 to 5 s and all subjects have some retrieval times longer than 6 s. Why? The answer appears to be that autobiographical memory retrieval is a constructive rather than a reproductive process (Alba & Hasher, 1983). The constructive nature of autobiographical memory retrieval was first illustrated in a protocol study by Williams and Hollan (1981) in which subjects attempted to recall the names of high school classmates. Consider the following extract from one of their protocols.

> The first thing that comes to mind is . . . I mean it's almost like images of different snapshots of our high school. You know, I can think of our general science class, and waiting in the lunch line, and halls. Umm, Sort of, Jeff Thompson! He was a friend of mine. Sort of pops into mind and I think, umm, we used to stand in the lunch line together, and he was in our general science class. That's where I first met him, our freshman year. There was, umm, let's see, I'm trying to think of people I interacted a lot with. And some of them . . . are sort of people I've known after high school. Like Bill Newell. I . . . I lived with him for a while, in Portland. Umm, after school. So he sort of comes to mind immediately too. Umm, let's see. I mean I guess it's almost easier for me to think of our home town, and think of people . . . that I've still run into on occasion, when I go back there. And then sort of check to see if they meet the requirements. Like were they in high school with me? And I can think of people like Buddy Collender, and John Trembel, who both live in our . . . Ah . . . home town. Umm . . . I guess it's. It also seems that I want to think of, sort of, it's clear that I have to think of some other situations. It's like I want to think of, sort of, prototypical situations and then sort of examine the people that were involved in those. And things like P.E. class, there was . . . Ah . . . Gary Booth. Umm, and Karl Brist, were sort of, we always ended up in the same P.E. classes, for some reasons. (Williams & Hollan, 1981, pp. 89–90)

This and the other protocols collected by Williams and Hollan clearly demonstrate the effortful nature of accessing information in the autobiographical knowledge base. Of particular interest is the way in which the memory search switches from cue to cue and how, as the search develops, different lifetime period cues (images of the school, hometown friends, prototypical school events) are used to probe different regions of the knowledge base. Williams and Hollan proposed that this type memory retrieval reflects the operation of a cyclic and staged retrieval process. In the first stage, a memory cue is elaborated into a *memory description* (Norman & Bobrow, 1979). The initial memory description is in the form of images of high school and high school activities, such as particular classes or waiting in line. In the second phase, the search phase, the memory description is used to access knowledge in long-term memory, and, in the third and final phase, accessed knowledge is evaluated in terms of the task demands (recalling the names of high school classmates).

The protocols collected by Williams and Hollan (1981) indicate that, in most searches of the knowledge base, retrieval is cycled through many times; that is, during the evaluation or verification stage, a new memory description is often generated that is then used to begin a new retrieval cycle. Conway (1992, in press; Anderson & Conway, 1993) have suggested that this cyclic aspect of retrieval is mediated by central control processes, such as the central executive of working memory (Baddeley, 1986; Norman & Shallice, 1980; Shallice, 1988). In the Norman and Shallice (1980) model, a central processor known as the Supervisory Attentional System (SAS) modulates knowledge access in long-term memory. Conway (in press) has applied the SAS to autobiographical memory retrieval and proposed that the SAS controls the process of cyclic retrieval. According to this view, a critical component of the SAS is a currently active and dynamic version of the self. The working self contains plan structures associated with the active goals of the self, and these include ongoing evaluation of goal attainment as well as general knowledge that can be used to index the autobiographical knowledge base. The SAS operates by building a temporary model of current task demands and, in the case of memory retrieval, evaluating the knowledge accessed in long-term memory in terms of constraints imposed by that model. A model of task demands specifies the criteria that must be met prior to executing a response. In autobiographical memory retrieval, the criteria may take the form of the specification of the nature of knowledge to be accessed. For example, the task model may specify that knowledge of a specific event must be accessed and that this knowledge must include ESK. In cue-word retrieval tasks, a further constraint is that the accessed knowledge must be conceptually related to the cue (memory description) that initiated the whole retrieval cycle. Thus, the SAS may directly influence the generation of memory descriptions and play a central role in the evaluation of accessed knowledge by providing constraints that the retrieval cycle must satisfy if a response is to be executed. Finally, although the SAS does not determine the spread of activation through knowledge structures in the knowledge base—the spread is channeled by the indices of the knowledge structures themselves—it may play a role in inhibiting the duration of activation of task-irrelevant knowledge and in maintaining the activation levels of task-relevant knowledge.

Consider how this process of memory construction might operate in, for instance, a cued memory retrieval task; recall that in this task subjects are instructed to retrieve a memory of a specific event of minutes or hours in duration. Figure 2 shows a coded protocol collected from a subject retrieving a memory to the cue word *chair*. In Cycle 1, the cue is elaborated into a memory description, the description is used to probe the autobiographical knowledge base, and lifetime period knowledge is accessed. The lifetime period knowledge is then used in Cycle 2 to access the general event of a particular shopping trip that, in turn, is used in Cycle 3 to access ESK in Cycle 4, at which point the retrieval process terminates. A stable, albeit temporary, pattern of activation has now been created across the knowledge structures in the knowledge base and a memory has been retrieved.

The resulting pattern of activation is, however, transitory and if it is to endure for any period of time must be effortfully maintained. Conse-

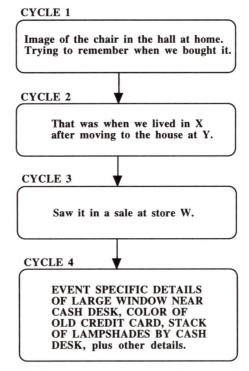

CYCLE 1

Image of the chair in the hall at home. Trying to remember when we bought it.

CYCLE 2

That was when we lived in X after moving to the house at Y.

CYCLE 3

Saw it in a sale at store W.

CYCLE 4

EVENT SPECIFIC DETAILS OF LARGE WINDOW NEAR CASH DESK, COLOR OF OLD CREDIT CARD, STACK OF LAMPSHADES BY CASH DESK, plus other details.

FIGURE 2   Retrieving a memory to the cue word *chair*.

quently, autobiographical memories are unstable temporary mental representations. Autobiographical memories are also unstable in other ways because their construction is wholly determined by the specific cues (memory descriptions) generated during retrieval. If memories are temporary patterns of activation established across lifetime periods, general events, and ESK, then when a memory is retrieved on successive occasions, establishing exactly the same pattern of activation in each episode of retrieval would seem unlikely. Instead, although the same memory may be constructed, the content and organization may vary slightly with each episode of retrieval. Anderson and Conway (1994; Anderson, 1993) investigated this possibility by requiring subjects to retrieve the same memory on two separate occasions. In one study, subjects listed details of memories recalled to cue words, marked the distinctive details, and also provided a title for each memory. Some days later, subjects returned to the laboratory and were provided with each cue word and corresponding memory title and asked again to recall and list memory details. It was found that about 70% of memory details were the same across the two episodes of retrieval and 30% were "new" details. Furthermore, for 40% of the memories, the distinctive details changed across the two episodes of retrieval. These findings show that the content of memories is variable to at least some extent and that memories can be accessed in different ways in successive retrievals; that is, different details may become distinctive in different retrieval cycles. In contrast to this flexibility in memory content across retrievals, a further study found highly accurate knowledge of memory content in a memory detail discrimination task. In this study, subjects were presented with memory details from two of their previously retrieved memories intermingled in random order and were required to sort the details into their separate memories. Subjects were surprisingly accurate, assigning over 90% of the details to the correct memory. In other studies, a 60% level of accuracy was observed when subjects repeatedly reordered memory details into forward order. Taken together, these findings lend further support to the view that memories are constructed rather than reproduced. Memory construction is, however, constrained both by central, executive processes and by the indices of the autobiographical knowledge base.

IV. AUTOBIOGRAPHICAL MEMORIES ACROSS THE LIFE SPAN

The preceding sections have considered what Conway and Rubin (1993) called the *microstructure* of autobiographical memory: the nature of the knowledge base and the retrieval processes that operate on that knowledge base. But autobiographical memory also has a macrostructure that is evident in studies that sample memory retrieval across the life span. In these studies, subjects retrieve memories to cue words and date each memory, or subjects simply free recall a number of memories and date them. Crovitz and Schiffman (1974), who reported the first of contemporary studies of life-span retrieval, plotted the age of the recalled memories across the life span of their subjects, who were 20-year-old college undergraduates. An idealized plot of the distribution they obtained, averaged over subjects, is shown in Figure 3. Clearly, most memories are recalled from the recent past and least from the remote past, and the number of memories recalled increases monotonically across the retention interval. This monotonic increase adequately describes the most recent 15-year portion of the retention interval shown in Figure 3, but it does not accurately describe the pattern of recall from 0 to 5 years of age. This period, often referred to as the period of *childhood amnesia,* is characterized by a rapid and terminal decrease in recall, with few subjects recalling events from below the age of 3 years and none from below the age of 1 year. Based on Figure 3, autobiographical memories seem to follow a retention function (Rubin, 1982) in which most memories are retained from the recent past and least from the remote past, with an additional period of exponential forgetting characterizing the period of childhood amnesia (Wetzler & Sweeney, 1986). In keeping with the earlier

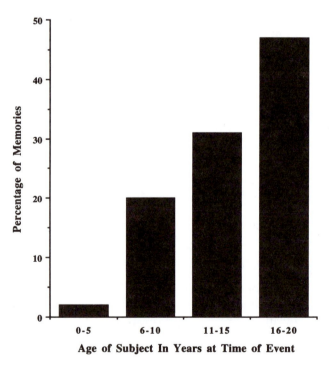

FIGURE 3   Distribution of memories in 5-year blocks for 20-year-olds.

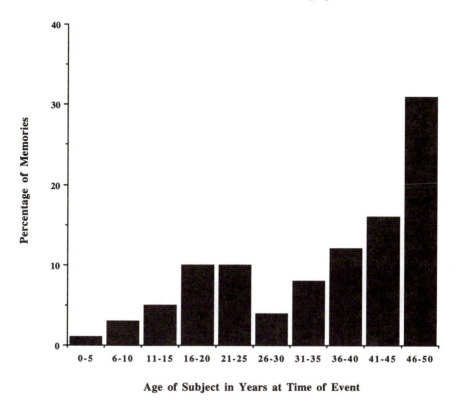

FIGURE 4   Distribution of memories in 5-year blocks for 50-year-olds.

account of the role of the working self in setting constraints on auto-biographical memory retrieval, the shape of this retention function might be taken to reflect the currently active plans, goals, and themes of the self associating most strongly with the recent past—thus providing potent cues to this period—and least strongly with the remote past. Indeed, the period of childhood amnesia might reflect an inability of the current self to generate any range of effective cues with which to access knowledge of this period. Maybe the goals, plans, and themes that were characteristic of infancy and central to the formation of autobiographical knowledge in that period simply cannot be regenerated by the adult self (see also Conway & Rubin, 1993).

Yet, patterns of life-span memory retrieval do not always take the form of a monotonic decreasing function and, interestingly, this is most evident in older adults. Consider the distribution of memories shown in Figure 4 (after Rubin, Wetzler, & Nebes, 1986) for a group of 50-year-old subjects. The retention function previously observed with younger subjects is again observed, but only for the most recent 20 years of the retention interval. Also present is the characteristic pattern of the childhood amnesia period. For the period when the rememberers were aged 10 to 25 years, however, there is an increase rather than decrease in recall, a period that has become known as the *reminiscence bump*. First observed by Franklin and Holding (1977), the reminiscence bump has since been reported in many studies using different experimental procedures, different patient and cross-national groups, and is even present in free recall, as long as subjects are older than about 40 years of age (see Conway & Rubin, 1993, for a review of these studies). One of the more interesting recent observations of the reminiscence bump comes from a sociological survey conducted by Schuman and colleagues (Schuman & Rieger, 1992; Schuman & Scott, 1989). In this survey, 1410 Americans over the age of 18 years were asked to list one or two particularly significant national or world events or changes. For each of the more commonly listed events, the number of subjects naming that event was plotted against their chronological age at the time of the event's occurrence. Figure 5 shows the resulting distributions for five of the more commonly named events. Note that zero and negative ages simply mean that those subjects were not alive at the time an event occurred, although they named that event in the survey. The regularity of the reminiscence bump is present for all five of the events shown in Figure 5, indicating that the majority of subjects spontaneously named events that had occurred when they were between 15 and 25 years of age.

Most of the more obvious explanations of the reminiscence bump have been rejected. For example, it might be argued that more significant events occur between the ages of 10 to 25 years than during other periods of life, and that these personally significant events are overrehearsed compared to other memories from both the same and other time periods. But examination of the events recalled from the reminiscence bump indicates that very few are actually significant life events (Fitzgerald, 1988; Fromholt & Larsen, 1992). Thus, the claim that the reminiscence bump is a product of the differential rehearsal given to significant life events is not supported. Other accounts suggesting differential encoding of events during the period between 10 and 25 years of age seem equally implausible as the same encoding mechanisms are presumably available after the age of 25 years, but recall actually decreases for some of the periods occurring after this age. One possibility, considered by Fitzgerald (1988), Conway (1992), and Conway and Rubin (1993), is that the reminiscence bump reflects a critical period in the formation of the self. If, during the period from 10 to 25 years of age, a stable self-concept comes to be formed (Erikson, 1978), it may be that the themes that endure across the life span are formed at this time. To the extent that the working self influences access of autobiographical knowledge and that themes formed during the period of late adolescence continue to consti-

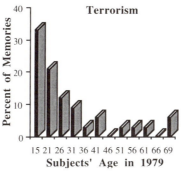

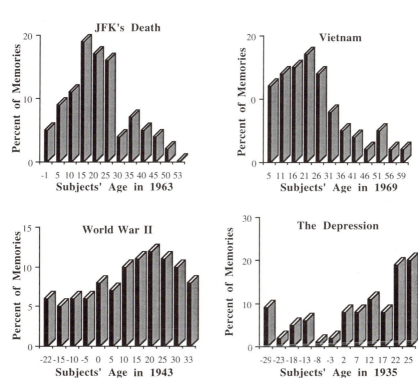

FIGURE 5 Recall of five significant public events plotted in terms of number of events by age of subjects at the time the events occurred. (Adapted from Schuman & Rieger, 1992.)

tute, albeit in changed form, parts of the adult self, then it may be that the self determines the pattern of life-span retrieval. Accordingly, the recency portion (the most recent 20 years in Figure 4) would reflect the diminishing effectiveness of the current plans and goals of the self to influence retrieval, whereas the reminiscence bump would reflect some form of privileged access by the self to a formative period—the period when a stable self-concept was first established, including elements such as enduring themes and the generational identity suggested by Schuman and Rieger (1992). The reminiscence bump is clearly a reliable phenomenon, and the account of memory retrieval outlined in the preceding section suggests how the role of the self in memory construction could potentially mediate this effect.

V. NEUROLOGICAL IMPAIRMENTS OF AUTOBIOGRAPHICAL MEMORY

Disruptions of both the macro- and microstructure of autobiographical memory have been observed across a wide range of brain injuries. The present section begins with a brief consideration of group studies of temporally graded amnesias, followed by more lengthy discussion of illustrative case studies.

Amnesic patients with retrograde amnesia are very often, but not always, most markedly impaired in remembering recent events (Albert, Butters, & Brandt, 1981; Albert, Butters, & Levin, 1979; Butters & Cermak, 1986; Cohen & Squire, 1980; Kopelman, 1985, 1989, 1991, 1992; Zola-Morgan, Cohen, & Squire, 1983). For example, the remote memory impairment of alcoholic Korsakoff patients typically takes the form of a retrograde amnesia extending back from the time of onset of the amnesia to the period of early adulthood or late adolescence. Memories of events from below the age of about 20–25 years, however, remain intact and can be recalled (cf. MacKinnon & Squire, 1989, and Squire, Haist, & Shimamura, 1989, for particularly clear patient examples). Temporally graded amnesias, then, tend to feature disruptions of the recency portion of the life-span retrieval curve that was illustrated in Figure 4, whereas the reminiscence bump and childhood amnesia regions of the curve appear to be spared.

One possible explanation of this form of temporal gradient in remote memory disorders is that it arises from a progressive impairment in the ability to form new memories (Butters & Albert, 1982; Cermak, 1984). Patients who eventually develop the brain damage characteristic of alcoholic Korsakoff's syndrome usually have a lengthy history of extreme alcohol abuse, and it may be that the alcohol abuse itself contributed to a developing impairment in the ability to encode stable new memories. If this were the case, however, then chronic alcoholics who have yet to develop Korsakoff's syndrome should show a fairly marked impairment for recent events, whereas such patients show only comparatively mild deficits and perform normally on some tests. Moreover, this suggestion cannot account for the temporally graded amnesias of other patients whose brain injury is not associated with chronic alcohol abuse (Kopelman, 1989). Alternatively, it may be that temporally graded amnesias arise primarily from a disruption of retrieval, rather than encoding. One speculative possibility, based on the earlier account of the role of the self in autobiographical memory construction, is that brain injury may lead to a disruption of the role of the self in remembering, such that the current plans and goals of the working self can no longer influence the retrieval process, although more enduring, and presumably more stable, aspects of the self continue to play a role in retrieval. Because stable aspects of self may have had their origin in processes that operated during adolescence and early adulthood, access to autobiographical knowledge from these periods could endure despite the severe impairments in accessing recent autobiographical knowledge. More generally, the observation that at least one empirically well established pattern of temporally graded amnesia corresponds in a systematic way to the pattern of intact life-span retrieval evident in non-brain-damaged subjects provides important convergent support for the proposed macrostructure of autobiographical memory.

More fine-grained and detailed studies of single amnesic patients demonstrate how the microstructure of autobiographical memory may be disrupted. For instance, one group of patients with very dense retrograde amnesias (Cermak & O'Connor, 1983; Stuss & Benson, 1984; Tulving, Schacter, McLachlan, & Moscovitch, 1988) show a general inability to retrieve memories. These patients, however, do have access to more general knowledge of their lives and can report some lifetime period information and, in the case of Cermak and O'Connor's patient S.S., can provide accounts of well-established stories or narratives of events. Despite these preserved abilities, however, the patients cannot retrieve memories and perform at floor on autobiographical memory cue-word retrieval tests. Given that these amnesics can access their autobiographical knowledge base and appear to be able to search lifetime periods and general events, to at least some extent, their problem relates to an inability to access ESK. This problem may arise because brain injury has led to a disconnection of ESK from the autobiographical knowledge base (Warrington & Weiskrantz, 1982) or because of some malfunction of the retrieval process. Perhaps the brain injury has reduced the processing resources available to the central control process; hence a sustained search of autobiographical knowledge cannot be made and a stable pattern of activation cannot be established in long-term memory.

Other patients suffering from impaired autobiographical memory following brain injury do not show such dense retrograde amnesia. For instance, McCarthy and Warrington's (1992) patient R. F. R. was able to access knowledge about famous individuals, family members, and friends. Under certain circumstances, R. F. R. could discriminate famous faces and the faces of people he personally knew. He could access knowledge about the occupations of the famous people and of his friends as well as other types of knowledge. However, R. F. R. could not recall events in which the famous people had been involved, even when a single event was the sole basis for an individual's fame. Moreover, he could recall virtually none of the events of his own life despite having preserved access to lifetime periods and some general event knowledge. Thus, R. F. R.'s autobiographical memory problem would seem specifically to relate to the ability to construct memories and, in particular, to integrate schematic knowledge of people with other more episodic types of autobiographical knowledge, that is, general events and ESK. An interesting counterpoint to the case of R. F. R. is the case of patient K. S. from Ellis, Young, and Critchley (1989). This patient, although apparently unimpaired on standard laboratory memory tests, nevertheless complained about the "mundane" quality of her memory. Although K. S. could recall specific autobiographical memories and appeared to have normal access to lifetime periods and general event knowledge for most of her life, she showed some problems with recent memories. In particular, K. S. could remember events in which she had been involved, but could not access knowledge about the other people who had been with her when a recent event had been experienced. Thus, she provided a full account of a lengthy trip to visit a consultant in another city and was able to provide a detailed account of the consulting room and her conversations with the consultant, but was unable to provide any details about the appearance of the consultant. She had a detailed memory for a recent holiday, but could not recall the people she had met on the holiday. K. S. then, unlike R. F. R., could recall event knowledge, but could not access knowledge of people. Again, it seems possible that the memory problem here might arise from an impaired ability to construct a memory and to integrate knowledge of people with general events and ESK.

Perhaps the most striking evidence of a disrupted ability to construct autobiographical memories comes from a recent study of patient P. S. by Hodges and McCarthy (1993), who had suffered a stroke featuring a bilateral paramedian thalamic infarction. The result was a dense retrograde amnesia in which P. S. was amnesic for most of his adult life and believed himself currently to be on active service in the Navy during the Second World War. Extensive testing of his autobiographical knowledge and memory revealed that he had some fairly consistent and accurate lifetime period and general event knowledge of his life during and prior to his Navy service, which covered the period 1941–1946. He also had some access to knowledge of his life after his Navy service, although this appeared to be intermittent and was associated with confabulatory reports of significant events such as the dates of birth of his children, his wedding day, and so on. However, on no occasion was P. S. able to retrieve a specific and detailed autobiographical memory. Hodges and McCarthy argued that the neurological damage to P. S.'s thalamus had led to a partial disconnection of autobiographical knowledge from central retrieval processes, and this problem was compounded by P. S.'s regression to a set of themes associated with a lifetime period from early adulthood. Because P. S. uses the themes of his Navy lifetime period, it is difficult for the retrieval process to verify outputs from long-term memory that, in any case, are degraded by the partial disconnection. P. S., then, confabulates by inappropriately interpreting accessed knowledge in terms of his Navy lifetime period.

Finally, consider the case of patients who have suffered damage to the frontal lobes but not to other areas of the brain. The frontal lobes have often been identified as a possible site of central control processes (see also Shallice, 1988); thus, damage to these areas should feature disruption of the retrieval process more than impaired abilities to access knowledge. This predicted characterization seems to be the case: Frontal lobe amnesia is characterized by confabulations and what Baddeley and Wilson (1986) call a "clouding" of autobiographical memory. In the series of frontal patients studied by Baddeley and Wilson, some showed striking confabulation and related long series of events that had not, in fact, occurred. For example, one patient related a long sequence of events concerning his brother's death in a road accident although, as it later transpired, his brother had been visiting him during his stay in the hospital. When confronted with this information, the patient denied that he had related the earlier account. From the present perspective, one of the most interesting features of such confabulations is that they are not delusional in the sense that they feature fantastic knowledge. The knowledge drawn upon is part of the individual's autobiographical knowledge base and is not imaginary; rather, it is the events into which this knowledge is compiled that are incorrect and confabulatory.

Many confabulations by patients with frontal lobe injuries are rather less complex, although equally striking. For instance, Dalla Barba, Cipolotti, and Denes (1990) described a patient, C. A., who could relate detailed autobiographical memories, many of which were verified, but who frequently assigned a recalled memory to an incorrect time. These dating errors were usually extreme. For example, C. A. dated her wedding day to 1964 when, in fact, she had married in 1943, but C. A. was both confident and persistent in such errors. Shallice (1988) described a confabulation by his patient R. W., who related a recent memory of his wife trying on a feather boa in a shop when, in fact, she had originally worn the boa at their home rather than a shop. The interesting feature of this memory was that R. W. accurately recalled the shop that had been visited as well as others who had been present, but was unaware that the shopping trip had taken place prior to the day his wife had tried on the feather boa. More recently, Dalla Barba (1993) described a patient, M. B., who, following brain injury, showed persistent and consistent confabulations featuring people, locations, and actions from his own autobiographical knowledge but configured in events that had not occurred or in events that occurred but not as described. Finally, Baddeley and Wilson (1986) reported that many of their frontal lobe patients, rather than confabulating, showed a "clouding" of autobiographical memories. Although they were able to recall specific episodes, these lacked the full range of detail usually observed in autobiographical remembering, and the patients seemed unable to establish full and elaborate memories, suggesting that the retrieval cycle was operating normally but terminating too rapidly. Taken together, the confabulatory responses and the clouded autobiographical memories implicate a failure in the retrieval cycle that may be related to the evaluation phase. Perhaps one consequence of injury to those parts of the frontal lobes that support cyclic retrieval is that processing resources become reduced, and this reduction leads to a degradation of the monitoring and modulating functions of the SAS on the complex retrieval cycle.

Clearly, the evidence from the impairment of autobiographical remembering in amnesia is particularly relevant to the view of autobiographical memory construction emerging from laboratory studies with neurologically intact subjects. At a minimum, the neurological data indicate that memory construction can be severely impaired such that only the top layers of autobiographical memory knowledge structures (lifetime periods) can be accessed. In less severe cases, it appears that more specific autobiographical knowledge can be accessed but cannot be formed into a complete memory. And last, findings from the study of amnesia associated with frontal lobe injury imply impairment of the evaluation phase of memory retrieval, rather than impairment of knowledge access. Frontal lobe confabulators can access the autobiographical knowledge base, but cannot establish patterns of activations that are constrained by the indices of the knowledge base or evolve an appropriate mental model for the retrieval task.

VI. CONCLUSIONS: SOME CAVEATS

Autobiographical memories are constructed by a centrally mediated, dynamic retrieval process that accesses a complex, layered, and structured knowledge base in long-term memory. By this view, memory retrieval is effortful and, once a memory is constructed, it must be maintained. Furthermore, as construction is critically dependent on the particular cues used during construction, memories vary in content and organization across separate instances of retrieval. The evidence reviewed in this chapter supports and converges on this general account of autobiographical memory construction. However, more specific accounts of the knowledge base and of retrieval processes remain open to revision and development. The study of autobiographical memory is comparatively recent (Conway, 1990a; Conway & Rubin, 1993), and the available data do not, as yet, impose strong constraints on specific implementations of the general model. Consider, for example, the depiction of ESK in Figure 1 as an undifferentiated pool of event features, some subset of which is activated by cues held at the general event level. Another possibility is that ESK is, in fact, a separate memory system, whereas lifetime periods and general events are part of some larger general purpose knowledge base (i.e., semantic memory). There is little evidence for this view from studies using neurologically intact subjects, but evidence from retrograde amnesia suggests that loss of, or disruption to, ESK is a common and almost characteristic feature of some types of amnesia. Maybe in these cases the memory system that represents ESK has become disconnected from the larger more general purpose knowledge base (Conway, 1992, 1993). Unfortunately, the evidence, although suggestive, does not compel a final decision either in favor of a separate memory system for ESK or against this conjecture.

In placing an emphasis on memory construction, it has been possible to develop an account of what autobiographical memories are and how they are generated in various processing tasks. Yet, the emphasis on memory construction tends to overlook the possibility that some memories may not be constructed. For example, the indices binding together certain types of autobiographical knowledge may be so specific and so well established that, when activation is directed at these knowledge structures, a fully detailed and stable memory automatically becomes available to the evaluation phase of memory construction and no further processing is required. Such memories would form a separate class of autobiographical memories, ones that did not require prolonged processing and maintenance. Indeed, Brown and Kulik (1977) have proposed such a separate class of autobiographical memories having these characteristics, which they named *flashbulb* (FBs) memories. According to Brown and Kulik, certain events are so unique and so personally relevant that they receive privileged processing at encoding, leading to the rapid formation of a "whole" and enduring memory. There has been much debate on the accuracy and creation of FB memories (Neisser, 1982; Neisser & Harsch, 1992; see also Conway et al., 1994; Conway, 1994, for reviews) and on whether such memories form a separate class of autobiographical memories (McCloskey, Wible, & Cohen, 1988). Although this debate raises many issues that are of central importance in memory research generally, they are not considered further here, except to note that the existence of "whole" memories that are accessed rather than constructed is not in itself a critical problem for the constructive view of autobiographical remembering. This view assumes that knowledge structures will be more or less well defined depending on the extent and types of processing in which they have featured. Just as there may be well-established local structures at the general event level (e.g., mini-histories), so there may be tightly structured stable sets of ESK. From this perspective, a central issue is the function of such structures within the autobiographical memory knowledge base. Possibly, FB memories act as reference points for existing knowledge structures, facilitate the ongoing creation of new knowledge structures by providing regions of stable and highly specific autobiographical knowledge, and/or representing knowledge central to the self, take a privileged role in the knowledge base. Currently, however, the function of FB and other types of vivid memories in autobiographical memory remains largely unknown and awaits further research (see also Conway, 1994).

Finally, there are a number of other important areas of autobiographical memory research that could not be covered in this chapter. For instance, although the role of the self in retrieval was touched upon, the elegant work of Barclay and colleagues (Barclay & DeCooke, 1988; Barclay & Smith, 1992; Barclay & Subramaniam, 1987; Barclay & Wellman, 1986) demonstrating strong effects of the self in retrieval was not discussed (see also M. Ross, 1989, for related work). Similarly, consideration of the accuracy of autobiographical memories was not given any extended treatment, although this issue is of increasing importance in certain areas of autobiographical memory research, particularly those dealing with childhood memories (see Loftus, 1993; Nelson, 1993; Usher & Neisser, 1993, for recent research and theory). It was not possible to include a whole range of issues pertaining to the phenomenological experience of autobiographical remembering, although intriguing findings have been reported by Nigro and Neisser (1983), the area is reviewed in Brewer (1992), and Conway (in press) discusses the nature of recollective experience in autobiographical remembering. The study of autobiographical memory is a rapidly developing area and many aspects of this type of memory are currently under investigation. The findings of future studies will certainly deepen our knowledge of this central area of human cognition and may even radically change our current understanding of human memory. For example, the notion that the self plays a central and significant role in all aspects of remembering has yet to be assimilated into our overall concept of human memory.

References

Alba, J. W., & Hasher, L. (1983). Is memory schematic? *Psychological Bulletin, 93,* 203–231.
Albert, M. S., Butters, N., & Brandt, J. (1981). Patterns of remote memory in amnesic and demented patients. *Archives of Neurology, 38,* 495–500.
Albert, M. S., Butters, N., & Levin, J. (1979). Temporal gradients in retrograde amnesia of patients with alcoholic Korsakoff's disease. *Archives of Neurology, 36,* 211–216.
Anderson, S. J. (1993). *Organization of specific autobiographical memories.* Unpublished doctoral dissertation, Lancaster University.

Anderson, S. J., & Conway, M. A. (1993). Investigating the structure of specific autobiographical memories. *Journal of Experimental Psychology: Learning, Memory, and Cognition, 19,* 1–19.

Anderson, S. J., & Conway, M. A. (1994). *Are autobiographical memories stable?* Manuscript submitted for publication.

Baddeley, A. D. (1986). *Working memory.* Oxford: Clarendon Press.

Baddeley, A. D., & Wilson, B. (1986). Amnesia, autobiographical memory, confabulation. In D. C. Rubin (Ed.), *Autobiographical memory* (pp. 225–252). Cambridge: Cambridge University Press.

Barclay, C. R., & DeCooke, P. A. (1988). Ordinary everyday memories: Some of the things of which selves are made. In U. Neisser & E. Winograd (Eds.), *Remembering reconsidered: Ecological and traditional approaches to the study of memory* (pp. 91–125). New York: Cambridge University Press.

Barclay, C. R., & Smith, T. S. (1992). Autobiographical remembering: Creating personal culture. In M. A. Conway, D. C. Rubin, H. Spinnler, & W. A. Wagenaar (Eds.), *Theoretical perspectives on autobiographical memory* (pp. 75–97). Dordrecht, Netherlands: Kluwer Academic Publishers.

Barclay, C. R., & Subramaniam, G. (1987). Autobiographical memories and self-schemata. *Applied Cognitive Psychology, 1,* 169–182.

Barclay, C. R., & Wellman, H. M. (1986). Accuracies and inaccuracies in autobiographical memories. *Journal of Memory and Language, 25,* 93–103.

Barsalou, L. W. (1988). The content and organization of autobiographical memories. In U. Neisser & E. Winograd (Eds.), *Remembering reconsidered: Ecological and traditional approaches to the study of memory* (pp. 193–243). Cambridge: Cambridge University Press.

Barsalou, L. W., & Sewell, D. R. (1985). Contrasting the representation of scripts and categories. *Journal of Memory and Language, 24,* 646–665.

Brewer, W. F. (1986). What is autobiographical memory? In D. C. Rubin (Ed.), *Autobiographical memory* (pp. 25–49). Cambridge: Cambridge University Press.

Brewer, W. F. (1988). Memory for randomly sampled autobiographical events. In U. Neisser & E. Winograd (Eds.), *Remembering reconsidered: Ecological and traditional approaches to the study of memory* (pp. 21–90). New York: Cambridge University Press.

Brewer, W. F. (1992). Phenomenal experience in laboratory and autobiographical memory tasks. In M. A. Conway, D. C. Rubin, H. Spinnler, & W. A. Wagenaar (Eds.), *Theoretical perspectives on autobiographical memory* (pp. 31–51). Dordrecht, Netherlands: Kluwer Academic Publishers.

Brown, R., & Kulik, J. (1977). Flashbulb memories. *Cognition, 5,* 73–99.

Butters, N., & Albert, M. S. (1982). Processes underlying failures to recall remote events. In L. S. Cermak (Ed.), *Human memory and amnesia* (pp. 257–303). Hillsdale, NJ: Erlbaum.

Butters, N., & Cermak, L. S. (1986). A case study of the forgetting of autobiographical knowledge: Implications for the study of retrograde amnesia. In D. C. Rubin (Ed.), *Autobiographical memory* (pp. 253–272). Cambridge: Cambridge University Press.

Cermak, L. S. (1984). The episodic/semantic distinction in amnesia. In N. Butters & L. R. Squire (Eds.), *The neuropsychology of memory* (pp. 55–62). New York: Guilford Press.

Cermak, L. S., & O'Connor, M. (1983). The anterograde and retrograde retrieval ability of a patient with amnesia due to encephalitis. *Neuropsychologia, 21,* 213–234.

Cohen, N. J., & Squire, L. R. (1980). Preserved learning and retention of pattern analyzing skills in amnesia. *Cortex, 17,* 273–278.

Conway, M. A. (1987). Verifying autobiographical facts. *Cognition, 25,* 39–58.

Conway, M. A. (1990a). *Autobiographical memory: An introduction.* Buckingham, England: Open University Press.

Conway, M. A. (1990b). Autobiographical memory and conceptual representation. *Journal of Experimental Psychology: Learning, Memory, and Cognition, 16,* 799–812.

Conway, M. A. (1991). In defense of everyday memory. *American Psychologist, 46,* 19–26.

Conway, M. A. (1992). A structural model of autobiographical memory. In M. A. Conway, D. C. Rubin, H. Spinnler, & W. A. Wagenaar (Eds.), *Theoretical perspectives on autobiographical memory* (pp. 167–194). Dordrecht, Netherlands: Kluwer Academic Publishers.

Conway, M., A. (1993). Impairments of autobiographical memory. In H. Spinnler & F. Boller (Eds.), *Handbook of neuropsychology* (Vol. 8, pp. 173–189). Amsterdam: Elsevier.

Conway, M. A. (1994). *Flashbulb memories.* Hove, Sussex, England: Erlbaum.

Conway, M. A. (in press). Autobiographical knowledge and autobiographical memories. In D. C. Rubin (Ed.), *Constructing our past: An overview of autobiographical memory.* Cambridge: Cambridge University Press.

Conway, M. A., Anderson, S. J., Larsen, S. F., Donnelly, C. M., McDaniel, M. A., McClelland, A. G. R., Rawles, R. E., & Logie, R. H. (1994). The formation of flashbulb memories. *Memory & Cognition, 22,* 326–343.

Conway, M. A., & Bekerian, D. A. (1987). Organization in autobiographical memory. *Memory & Cognition, 15,* 119–132.

Conway, M. A., & Rubin, D. C. (1993). The structure of autobiographical memory. In A. E. Collins, S. E. Gathercole, M. A. Conway, & P. E. M. Morris (Eds.), *Theories of memory* (pp. 103–137). Hove, Sussex, England: Erlbaum.

Conway, M. A., Rubin, D. C., Spinnler, H., & Wagenaar, W. A. (Eds.). (1993). *Theoretical perspectives on autobiographical memory.* Dordrecht, Netherlands: Kluwer Academic Publishers.

Crovitz, H. F., & Schiffman, H. (1974). Frequency of episodic memories as a function of their age. *Bulletin of the Psychonomic Society, 4,* 517–518.

Dalla Barba, G. (1993). Confabulation: Knowledge and recollective experience. *Cognitive Neuropsychology, 10,* 1–20.

Dalla Barba, G., Cipolotti, L., & Denes, G. (1990). Autobiographical memory loss and confabulation in Korsakoff's syndrome: A case report. *Cortex, 26,* 525–534.

Ellis, A. W., Young, A. W., & Critchley, E. M. R. (1989). Loss of memory for people following temporal lobe damage. *Brain, 112,* 1469–1483.

Erikson, E. (1978). *Adulthood.* New York: Norton.

Fitzgerald, J. M. (1988). Vivid memories and the reminiscence phenomenon: The role of a self narrative. *Human Development, 31,* 261–273.

Franklin, H. C., & Holding, D. H. (1977). Personal memories at different ages. *Quarterly Journal of Experimental Psychology, 29,* 527–532.

Fromholt, P., & Larsen, S. F. (1992). Autobiographical memory and life-history narratives in aging and dementia (Alzheimer type). In M. A. Conway, D. C. Rubin, H. Spinnler, & W. A. Wagenaar (Eds.), *Theoretical perspectives on autobiographical memory* (pp. 413–426). Dordrecht, Netherlands: Kluwer Academic Publishers.

Galton, F. (1883). *Inquiries into human faculty and its development* (1st ed.). London: Macmillan.

Hodges, J. R., & McCarthy, R. A. (1993). Autobiographical amnesia resulting from bilateral paramedian thalamic infarction. *Brain, 116,* 921–940.

Johnson, M. K., Foley, M. A., Suengas, A. G., & Raye, C. L. (1988). Phenomenal characteristics of memories for perceived and imagined autobiographical events. *Journal of Experimental Psychology: General, 117,* 371–376.

Kolodner, J. L. (1983). Maintaining memory organization in a dynamic long-term memory. *Cognitive Science, 7,* 243–280.

Kopelman, M. D. (1985). Rates of forgetting in Alzheimer-type dementia and Korsakoff's syndrome. *Neuropsychologia, 23,* 623–638.

Kopelman, M. D. (1989). Remote and autobiographical memory, temporal context memory, and frontal atrophy in Korsakoff and Alzheimer patients. *Neuropsychologia, 27,* 437–460.

Kopelman, M. D. (1991). Frontal dysfunction and memory deficits in the alcoholic Korsakoff syndrome and Alzheimer-type dementia. *Brain, 114,* 117–137.

Kopelman, M. D. (1992). Autobiographical memory in clinical research and practice. In M. A. Conway, D. C. Rubin, H. Spinnler, & W. A. Wagenaar (Eds.), *Theoretical perspectives on autobiographical memory* (pp. 427–450). Dordrecht, Netherlands: Kluwer Academic Publishers.

Linton, M. (1986). Ways of searching and the contents of memory. In D. C. Rubin (Ed.), *Autobiographical memory* (pp. 50–67). Cambridge; Cambridge University Press.

Loftus, E. F. (1993). The reality of repressed memories. *American Psychologist, 48,* 518–537.

MacKinnon, D. F., & Squire, L. R. (1989). Autobiographical memory and amnesia. *Psychobiology, 17,* 247–256.

McCarthy, R. A., & Warrington, E. K. (1992). Actors but not scripts: The dissociation of people and events in retrograde amnesia. *Neuropsychologia, 30,* 633–644.

McCloskey, M., Wible, C. G., & Cohen, N. J. (1988). Is there a special flashbulb-memory mechanism? *Journal of Experimental Psychology: General, 117,* 171–181.

Neisser, U. (1982). Snapshots or benchmarks? In U. Neisser (Ed.), *Memory observed: Remembering in natural contexts* (pp. 43–48). San Francisco: W. H. Freeman.

Neisser, U. (1986). Remembering Pearl Harbor: Reply to Thompson and Cowan. *Cognition, 23,* 285–286.

Neisser, U., & Harsch, N. (1992). Phantom flashbulbs: False recollections of hearing the news about *Challenger.* In E. Winograd & U. Neisser (Eds.), *Affect and accuracy in recall: Studies of "flashbulb memories"* (pp. 9–31). Cambridge: Cambridge University Press.

Nelson, K. (1993). Explaining the emergence of autobiographical memory in early childhood. In A. E. Collins, S. E. Gathercole, M. A. Conway, & P. E. Morris (Eds.), *Theories of memory* (pp. 255–386). Hove, Sussex, England: Erlbaum.

Nigro, G., & Neisser, U. (1983). Point of view in personal memories. *Cognitive Psychology, 15,* 467–482.

Norman, D. A., & Bobrow, D. G. (1979). Descriptions and intermediate stage in memory retrieval. *Cognitive Psychology, 11,* 107–123.

Norman, D. A., & Shallice, T. (1980). *Attention to action: Willed and automatic control of behaviour.* (Tech. Rep. No. 99). San Diego: University of California.

Pillemer, D. B. (1984). Flashbulb memories of the assassination attempt on President Reagan. *Cognition, 16,* 63–80.

Robinson, J. A. (1976). Sampling autobiographical memory. *Cognitive Psychology, 8,* 578–595.

Robinson, J. A. (1992). First experience memories: Contexts and function in personal histories. In M. A. Conway, D. C. Rubin, H. Spinnler, & W. Wagenaar (Eds.), *Theoretical perspectives on autobiographical memory* (pp. 223–239). Dordrecht, Netherlands: Kluwer Academic Publishers.

Robinson, J. A., & Swanson, K. L. (1990). Autobiographical memory: The next phase. *Applied Cognitive Psychology, 4,* 321–335.

Ross, B. H. (1984). Remindings and their effects in learning a cognitive skill. *Cognitive Psychology, 16,* 371–416.

Ross, M. (1989). Relation of implicit theories to the construction of personal histories. *Psychological Review, 96,* 341–357.

Rubin, D. C. (1982). On the retention function for autobiographical memory. *Journal of Verbal Learning and Verbal Behavior, 21,* 21–38.

Rubin, D. C. (Ed.). (1986). *Autobiographical memory.* Cambridge: Cambridge University Press.

Rubin, D. C., Wetzler, S. E., & Nebes, R. D. (1986). Autobiographical memory across the adult lifespan. In D. C. Rubin (Ed.), *Autobiographical memory* (pp. 202–221). Cambridge: Cambridge University Press.

Schank, R. C. (1982). *Dynamic memory.* New York: Cambridge University Press.

Schooler, J. W., & Herrmann, D. J. (1992). There is more to episodic memory than just episodes. In M. A. Conway, D. C. Rubin, H. Spinnler, & W. A. Wagenaar (Eds.), *Theoretical perspectives on autobiographical memory* (pp. 241–262). Dordrecht, Netherlands: Kluwer Academic Publishers.

Schuman, H., & Rieger, C. (1992). Collective memory and collective memories. In M. A. Conway, D. C. Rubin, H. Spinnler, & W. Wagenaar (Eds.), *Theoretical perspectives on autobiographical memory* (pp. 323–336). Dordrecht, Netherlands: Kluwer Academic Publishers.

Schuman, H., & Scott, J. (1989). Generations and collective memories. *American Sociological Review, 54*, 359–381.

Shallice, T. (1988). *From neuropsychology to mental structure.* New York: Cambridge University Press.

Squire, L. R., Haist, F., & Shimamura, A. P. (1989). The neurology of memory: Quantative assessment of retrograde amnesia in two groups of amnesic patients. *Journal of Neuroscience, 9*, 828–839.

Strauman, T. J. (1990). Self-guides and emotionally significant childhood memories: A study of retrieval efficiency and incidental negative emotional content. *Journal of Personality and Social Psychology, 59*, 869–880.

Stuss, D. T., & Benson, D. F. (1984). Neuropsychological studies of the frontal lobes. *Psychological Bulletin, 95*, 3–28.

Thompson, C. P., & Cowan, T. (1986). Flashbulb memories: A nicer interpretation of a Neisser recollection. *Cognition, 22*, 199–200.

Tulving, E. (1972). Episodic and semantic memory. In E. Tulving & W. Donaldson (Eds.), *Organization of memory.* New York: Academic Press.

Tulving, E. (1983). *Elements of episodic memory.* New York: Oxford University Press.

Tulving, E., Schacter, D. L., McLachlan, D. R., & Moscovitch, M. (1988). Priming of semantic autobiographical knowledge: A case study of retrograde amnesia. *Brain and Cognition, 8*, 3–20.

Usher, J. A., & Neisser, U. (1993). Childhood amnesia and the beginnings of memory for four early life events. *Journal of Experimental Psychology: General, 122*, 155–165.

Warrington, E. K., & Weiskrantz, L. (1982). Amnesia: A disconnection syndrome. *Neuropsychologia, 16*, 233–249.

Wetzler, S. E., & Sweeney, J. A. (1986). Childhood amnesia: An empirical demonstration. In D. C. Rubin (Ed.), *Autobiographical memory* (pp. 202–221). Cambridge: Cambridge University Press.

Whitten, W. B., & Leonard, J. M. (1981). Directed search through autobiographical memory. *Memory & Cognition, 9*, 566–579.

Williams, D. M., & Hollan, J. D. (1981). The process of retrieval from very long-term memory. *Cognitive Science, 5*, 87–119.

Zola-Morgan, S., Cohen, N. J., & Squire, L. R. (1983). Recall of remote episodic amnesia. *Neuropsychologia, 21*, 487–500.

Accessing Information in Long-Term Memory

CHAPTER 7

Retrieval Processes

Henry L. Roediger, III
Melissa J. Guynn

The key process of memory is retrieval.
—Endel Tulving (1991)

I. INTRODUCTION

Processes of learning and memory are typically conceptualized as involving at least three stages: encoding, storage, and retrieval (Melton, 1963). *Encoding* refers to initial learning or acquisition of information. Within the context of chapters in the present volume, encoded information would certainly have passed through sensory storage systems and in most treatments would also have been recoded into a short-term store (or primary memory, or working memory). *Storage* refers to maintaining information over time. The usual description of the information during the storage stage is in terms of *memory traces*. The idea is that encoding processes leave a residue in the nervous system—memory traces—that persist over time. The third stage, *retrieval,* refers to accessing stored information. Retrieval processes, then, refer to the means of using stored information; they are the topic of this chapter. However, as the foregoing should make clear, retrieval processes are inextricably bound to those of encoding and storage. Although we can focus on factors that are manipulated at the retrieval stage, we cannot ignore the other stages. How an event is encoded and stored determines how well it can be retrieved later, and what cues will effect its retrieval.

It is a curious fact that the retrieval phase of memory was largely neglected by researchers until the mid-1960s. One could find occasional mention of its importance by experimental psychologists (Köhler, 1947; Melton,

Memory

1963), but investigators rarely created conditions to study retrieval direct-ly. An unspoken assumption guiding much research was that responses produced on a memory test indicated the contents of storage. Failures to produce information were ascribed to problems in encoding or storage. For example, forgotten information might not have been transferred from a short-term store to a long-term store (Waugh & Norman, 1965), or it may not have been processed to a deep, semantic level (Craik & Lock-hart, 1972), or over time memory traces may have decayed or been over-written.

Tulving (1974) referred to theories, such as the original levels of process-ing ideas, as trace-dependent theories of memory: the critical determinant of performance on memory tests was thought to be the status of the memory trace at the time of testing. Little attention was paid to the idea that encod-ing and storage could have succeeded—the memory trace of the experience was robust—and that forgetting could still occur due to retrieval failure. The alternative to trace-dependent forgetting theories are those embodying the assumption of cue-dependent forgetting. Cue-dependent forgetting the-orists maintain that "memory for an event is always a product of informa-tion from two sources," the memory trace and the retrieval cue, the latter being "the information present in the individual's cognitive environment when retrieval occurs" (Tulving, 1974, p. 74). The key idea is that *both* the traces of past experience and the information or cues in the cognitive system during the test are critical determinants of remembering.

Although the retrieval phase of the learning and memory process has generally been neglected by psychologists until the past thirty years, early in the century Richard Semon, a German scholar, advanced ideas on the criti-cal role of retrieval processes in understanding memory (see Schacter, Eich, & Tulving, 1978, for a synopsis of Semon's thought). Semon coined the name *engram* for memory trace and it caught on and was widely used. He also advanced the term *ecphory,* defined as "the influences which awaken the mnemic trace or engram out of its latent state into one of manifested activ-ity" (Semon, 1921, p. 12). *Ecphory* is roughly the same as *retrieval* and in propounding The Law of Ecphory as one of two general laws of memory, he noted that successful ecphory requires "the partial return" of the original encoding episode (as we might put it today).

Semon's ideas were far ahead of their time and probably have not been completely mined by psychologists, even today. Tulving (1983) has cham-pioned use of Semon's terms for retrieval processes, but they have not been widely accepted. Schacter (1982) has written a fascinating book on the life and work of Richard Semon and speculates about why his work did not have more impact at the time.

The interesting point of this story for present purposes is that the impor-tance of retrieval processes was noted quite early in this century, yet it did not become the explicit object of study until much later (Tulving & Pearlstone, 1966; Weiner, 1966). However, by 1980, when Loftus and Loftus (1980) published a survey of psychologists interested in learning and memory, most of them said they believed that retrieval failures accounted for most cases of forgetting. Evidence presented in this chapter shows why so many psychologists came to believe that retrieval processes are critical determinants of recollection.

The purpose of the present chapter is to review what we know about retrieval processes in human memory. In Section II we review two basic ways of studying retrieval processes: giving retrieval cues during a test, and testing people repeatedly with the same cues. In Section III we describe one general principle that has been repeatedly emphasized as governing retrieval of memories and consider two other principles that seem to apply. We argue that understanding this small set of principles can provide considerable power in analyzing retrieval processes. In Section IV we introduce the encoding/retrieval paradigm (Tulving, 1983) and argue that it represents a fundamentally important method of studying retrieval processes and their interaction with encoding processes. In Sections IV–VI we (1) review how the encoding/retrieval paradigm has been applied to understand various phenomena; (2) discuss the effects of prior retrieval on later retrieval; and (3) briefly describe some related topics. Finally, we summarize the chapter's main points.

II. METHODS OF STUDYING RETRIEVAL

Psychologists interested in learning and memory have developed several distinct methods of studying retrieval. Indeed, in some sense, all methods of testing memory study retrieval, because a retrieval phase is involved in every memory test. However, we can single out some methods for special attention, given here or elsewhere in this volume. These are: (1) repeated testing (without intervening study opportunities); (2) presentation of cues at test; (3) judgments made during retrieval; and (4) comparison of different instructions at retrieval. In this chapter we cover results based on the first two techniques, repeated testing and presentation of retrieval cues (with greater emphasis on the latter). The method of requesting subjects to make judgments at test is covered by Metcalfe in Chapter 11 (about metacognitive processes). The use of different instructions at retrieval, as in Jacoby's (1991) process dissociation procedure or in the large number of techniques used to study implicit memory, is covered by Kelley and Lindsay in Chapter 2.

A. Repeated Testing: Reminiscence and Hypermnesia

One venerable method for studying the role of retrieval processes is to test subjects' memories repeatedly, without opportunities for intervening study. W. Brown (1923) conducted some of the first well-known experiments. He asked the fundamental question that formed the title of his paper, "To what extent is memory measured by a single recall trial?" Brown conducted two experiments to answer the question. In the first, he asked college students to recall as many of the 48 states as possible during a 5-min period. Half an hour later, without any warning, he gave them the same task again. The second experiment was similar, except in this case students were given 48 words to learn, with each word presented four times. Once again, the test involved an initial 5-min recall period immediately after learning and then a second test 30 min later.

The results from W. Brown's (1923) experiments are presented in Table 1. The first two rows indicate the total number of items recalled on the first and the second test, respectively, with the difference between them $(T_2 - T_1)$ in the third row. Brown discovered that subjects in both experiments, with either states or words in a list, recalled more items on the second test than on the first test. This increase in recall between tests is now called hypermnesia (Erdelyi & Becker, 1974). The finding is a surprise in some ways because the second test occurred a considerable amount of time after the first test. Thus, one would normally expect forgetting to occur between the two tests, at least in the case of list learning. Indeed, McGeoch (1932) used Brown's results as one prong in his attack on the law of disuse, or the decay theory of memory. How could memories decay with the passage of time, if more were recalled on a later test than on an earlier test?

W. Brown (1923) broke down performance into two components of interest in repeated testing, intertest forgetting and intertest recovery. Despite the fact that more items were recalled, overall, on the second test than on the first test, some items were actually forgotten between the two tests. That is, states or words recalled on the first test were forgotten on the second test, as shown in the fourth row of Table 1 (1.94 states and 3.04 words). The last row of the table shows the number of items recovered between the two tests, or items not recalled on the first test but recalled on the second test (5.29 states and 4.33 words). Obviously, the overall improvement between tests for states (and to a lesser extent for words) reflects the fact that intertest recovery exceeded intertest forgetting. This recovery component is often called reminiscence, after Ballard's (1913) definition: "the remembering again of the forgotten without re-learning" (p. v).

W. Brown's (1923) basic observations have been replicated many times. The results point out several basic facts about retrieval processes that will be repeatedly encountered in this chapter. A single test of memory is an imperfect indicator of knowledge. Give even the same test a few minutes later, and subjects will exhibit a different pattern of recall (sometimes remembering more, sometimes less—and different events will be recalled on the two occasions). Since the early experiments by Ballard (1913) and W. Brown (1923), many researchers have been intrigued by the observation that recall can improve across tests without intervening study opportunities. Reference

TABLE 1   Results from W. Brown's (1923) Experiments Using
Repeated Testing

	States	Word list	
Test 1	36.31	25.48	
Test 2	39.66	26.77	
Difference ($T_2 - T_1$)	3.35	1.29	Hypermnesia
Intertest forgetting	1.94	3.04	
Intertest recovery	5.29	4.33	Reminiscence

experiments by Tulving (1967) and Erdelyi and Becker (1974) impressed upon modern researchers the need to study reminiscence and hypermnesia, respectively. Throughout the 1970s and 1980s, many researchers were occupied with these topics, and summaries may be found in reviews by Erdelyi (1984), Payne (1987), and Roediger and Challis (1989).

Research on reminiscence and hypermnesia points out a fact that is sometimes overlooked: retrieval of a set of material extends over a period of time. The practice of many researchers is to give a fixed, often quite short, time period for a test. However, in experiments in which retrieval time has been extended up to 21 min, recall continues to improve, albeit at a negatively accelerated pace (Roediger & Thorpe, 1978). Curiously, the study of how recall changes over time under different experimental conditions has not been extensively studied and may hold considerable promise as a future area of inquiry. Wixted and Rohrer (1994) provide an overview of cumulative measures of recall and how they can be analyzed.

In attempting to answer the question of why recall improves across tests, Roediger and Thorpe (1978) suggested that people use subjective retrieval cues, or cues they generate themselves, to guide retrieval. That is, even though the task is nominally one of free recall, in which no cues are provided, subjects retrieve information by providing themselves with cues (Tulving, 1974; see also Conway, this volume, Chapter 6). The general idea is similar to Estes' (1955) stimulus sampling theory of spontaneous recovery in animal conditioning and has been embedded in more formal models by Mensink and Raaijmakers (1988). However, almost by definition, it is impossible to manipulate the nature of the cues used in free recall and therefore the theories can receive only indirect support. Perhaps for this reason more researchers have been interested in studying retrieval processes through manipulation of overt retrieval cues, in what are known as cued recall paradigms.

B. Cued Recall Paradigms

The logic behind cued recall techniques to study retrieval is straightforward and powerful. In the simplest case, two groups of subjects are exposed to the same set of material under identical study conditions and are treated in exactly the same way until the moment they are tested. Therefore, encoding and storage of the material can be assumed to be the same in the two groups. At the time of the test, the retrieval conditions of the two groups are manipulated in a systematic way (such as through the instructions given, the physical environment in which testing takes place, or the overt cues provided). Any differences in retention can then be attributed to differences in the retrieval processes invoked by the test conditions. Tulving and Pearlstone (1966) were the first to make this logic explicit and to provide an experiment to demonstrate it. We present only selected conditions to make their essential points.

Tulving and Pearlstone (1966) presented high school students with categorized word lists (items belonging to common categories such as articles of clothing, automobiles, or types of birds). In one of the study conditions, subjects were given lists of 48 words, with 2 words in each of 24 categories. Specifically, subjects heard lists such as "articles of clothing: blouse, sweater; types of birds: blue jay, parakeet," and so forth. Subjects were told to remember the 48 list words for an unspecified test.

Two test conditions were of interest. One was free recall, in which subjects were given a blank sheet of paper and asked to recall as many words as possible from the list. On average, they recalled 19.3 words correctly. We can then ask what happened to the other 29 or so? Were they not acquired? Not stored? Or was the failure one of retrieval? Absolute answers to these questions are not possible, but a companion condition in the Tulving and Pearlstone (1966) experiment indicates that retrieval difficulties likely were responsible for much of the forgetting. A second group of subjects, who had been given the same list of 48 categorized words, received a cued recall test in which they were presented with the 24 category names as recall cues. In this condition, subjects recalled 35.9 words. Therefore, with all encoding and storage conditions held constant, presentation of retrieval cues almost doubled the number of events recalled. This difference indicates that, for the free-recall subjects, information was *available* (i.e., stored) that was not *accessible* (i.e., retrievable) on a free-recall test. Tulving and Pearlstone emphasized this distinction between availability and accessibility of memories. Psychologists would like to have a method that could accurately tell what information is stored in memory, but such a technique is impossible. All we can ever know is what information is accessible under a particular set of retrieval conditions.

By the way, we should mention that an artifactual explanation of the Tulving and Pearlstone (1966) result in terms of guessing does not work. They had eliminated from consideration the most obvious associates to the category names and used other means to protect against guessing. Interestingly, in most cued and free-recall situations, subjects seem to guess very little unless instructed to do so. M. J. Watkins and Gardiner (1982) have discussed various precautions against guessing in cued recall experiments.

The basic procedure in providing people with specific cues to prompt or aid retrieval has become the dominant method of studying retrieval processes. The remainder of the chapter discusses results that have been obtained using this technique. First, however, we discuss some general principles that have guided research in this area.

III. PRINCIPLES GOVERNING RETRIEVAL

In his famous 1932 article attacking the law of disuse, McGeoch argued that two conditions increased forgetting. One was retroactive interference, which was heavily studied in the thirty years after his paper (see Anderson & Neely, this volume, Chapter 8, for a discussion of interference effects in memory). The other principle, mentioned only in passing, was "altered stimulating conditions" between learning and testing. The implication is that the opposite of such altered conditions would promote remembering: to the extent that the similarity between "stimulating conditions" during learning and testing was increased, good retention should result.

Even though McGeoch (1932) considered the stimulating conditions to be one of the critical factors, no one paid much experimental attention to this topic for over thirty years. Perhaps the reason is that the principle seemed obvious. After all, experimental psychologists of this era followed the animal conditioning literature closely, and McGeoch's principle seemed quite close to that of stimulus generalization, first noted by Pavlov (1927). In either classical or operant conditioning situations, if an animal is trained to respond in the presence of a particular stimulus, the closer a test stimulus is to that original training stimulus on some physical dimension, the greater is the responding. This principle of primary stimulus generalization may have been so ingrained in the thinking of experimental psychologists that they failed to investigate similar principles in human learning and memory, with but few exceptions (Pan, 1926; see Murdock, 1989, for discussion).

It was not until the late 1960s, when Tulving and colleagues announced the encoding specificity principle (Tulving & Osler, 1968; Tulving & Thomson, 1973), that interest in the match between properties of cues at test and those of "stimulating conditions" during study was aroused. As Tulving (1983, p. 223) put it, " . . . recollection of an event, or a certain aspect of it, occurs if and only if properties of the trace of the event are sufficiently similar to the retrieval information" provided in the retrieval cues. As we describe later, several lines of research can be interpreted under the broad framework of the encoding specificity hypothesis. Most of the research conducted within this framework has emphasized quite specific cues and how they matched (or did not match) the encoding of studied events.

A broadening of the encoding specificity ideas occurred in the notion of transfer-appropriate processing, endorsed by Bransford, Franks, Morris, and Stein (1979). The basic idea is that performance on a memory test can be considered a case of transfer, and that transfer will be affected by the match of processing activities during encoding and retrieval. The greater the match between encoding activities and retrieval activities, the greater positive transfer there will be. The emphasis is on mental processes and is similar to that embedded in Kolers' (1979) procedural approach to memory (see also Kolers & Roediger, 1984).

Roughly the same central idea is captured in the ideas of altered stimulating conditions, stimulus generalization, the encoding specificity principle, and transfer-appropriate processing. Maximizing the similarity (in overt stimulus conditions, in specific encoding, or in processing activities) between a study and a test occasion benefits retention. This general principle has guided much research in learning and memory and has been used to organize much of the rest of this chapter. However, there is one major difference between the encoding specificity and transfer-appropriate processing principles and the previous ideas. The ideas of stimulus generalization and altered stimulating conditions (or generalization decrement) focus completely on the external stimulus conditions, whereas encoding specificity emphasizes how the stimulus is coded. According to the latter idea, the properties of the stimulus *as coded* determine retention. For example, in some cases a cue that is different from the original studied event can provoke its recollection better than a literal copy of the event itself (Tulving & Thomson, 1973). Therefore, physical similarity of study and test events is not the crucial determinant of retention; rather, psychological similarity— the similarity of encoding and retrieval processes—is critical.

Other principles also are useful in understanding retrieval processes. One is the cue overload principle noted by Earhard (1967) and championed by O. C. Watkins and M. J. Watkins (1975; see also M. J. Watkins, 1979). The basic idea of this principle is that the more information that is subsumed under a single retrieval cue, the poorer will be the recall for any one piece of information. Consider Tulving and Pearlstone's (1966) situation using category name retrieval cues. The more items presented in a given category, the less likely that category name is to cue any particular item. The cue is said to be overloaded. For example, Roediger (1973) presented subjects with categorized lists with either four, five, six, or seven items per category. Probabilities of recalling words from a category, given its name as a cue, were .69, .65, .64, and .59 as the category size increased. Doubtless, probability of recall would have been even higher with only one or two items per category.

Another related principle governing retrieval is that of distinctiveness:

Events that are distinctive, or that stand out from a background of other similar events by being different, are generally well remembered. For example, you can probably remember the events you experienced on your most recent birthday better than you can the events that occurred either a few days before or a few days after your birthday. Unusual or distinctive events may be well remembered because they represent powerful retrieval cues that are not overloaded (i.e., relatively few events are subsumed under them, compared to other types of cues). We discuss this principle more fully later in the chapter.

Such general principles that govern retrieval may not be satisfying to those who seek molecular models to account for memory performance, but for purposes of a chapter reviewing a considerable body of research, this approach seems defensible. We turn next to the primary paradigm that has been used to study retrieval processes and their interaction with encoding conditions.

IV. THE ENCODING/RETRIEVAL PARADIGM

Consider the hypothetical arrangement of conditions in Figure 1. There are two encoding conditions (A and B) and two retrieval conditions (A' and B'). If we consider first the rows, and only one of the columns, we have an *encoding experiment.* That is, experimenters manipulate encoding strategies or material and examine performance on a single memory test. For example, the encoding dimension might be rehearsal versus imagery instructions, superficial versus meaningful processing requirements, pictures versus words, or high-imagery words versus low-imagery words. The important point is that encoding conditions are manipulated and test conditions are held constant. Consider next performance in the columns and only one of the rows. In this case, encoding conditions are held constant while test conditions are manipulated. This is a *retrieval experiment.* An example is the Tulving and Pearlstone (1966) experiment described earlier in which subjects studied a list of words and were then tested with either free recall or cued recall.

Both encoding experiments (the columns) and retrieval experiments (the rows) are quite common in the experimental study of memory and have yielded much useful information. However, simultaneous manipulation of both encoding and retrieval conditions permits a more powerful design, referred to by Tulving (1983) as the encoding/retrieval paradigm. Briefly, in this abstract case, we consider encoding conditions A and B to differ on some dimension, and retrieval conditions A' and B' to be similar on this dimension to encoding conditions A and B, respectively. If the principle of encoding specificity or transfer-appropriate processing holds, performance

Retrieval Condition

A'   B'

		A'	B'
Encoding Condition	**A**	A-A'	A-B'
	B	B-A'	B-B'

FIGURE 1   The encoding/retrieval paradigm. Minimally, two encoding conditions (A and B) are crossed with two retrieval conditions (A' and B'), often designed to be similar in some way to the encoding conditions. Retention should be enhanced in conditions represented by cells in which the best match exists between study and test conditions (A–A', B–B') relative to the other conditions (A-B', B-A'). (After Tulving, 1983, p. 220, with permission of Oxford University Press.)

in conditions A–A' and B–B' (where encoding and retrieval conditions match) should be better than performance in conditions A–B' and B–A' (where encoding and retrieval conditions match less well).

This basic paradigm has been used to investigate several problems in the psychology of memory and points out the critical interaction of encoding and retrieval processes. We consider below the following topics: (1) manipulating verbal context at study and test; (2) manipulating physical context or environmental context (locations) at study and test; (3) manipulating the subjects' internal context (their drug state or mood state) at study and test; (4) manipulating mental and physical operations applied to material at study and test; and (5) manipulating the type of information emphasized at study and test (relational or item specific). In each case, performance depends critically on the match of processes or information between study and test occasions.

A. Manipulation of Verbal Context

Much research on the effects of verbal context on remembering has employed the encoding/retrieval paradigm. People study the same nominal target (a word) in one or another context. Then, when they are tested later, cues are presented that instantiate either the same context as at study or a different context. Among the first such experiments were those reported by Tulving and Osler (1968) and Thomson and Tulving (1970). The authors were asking the critical question: Under what conditions is a retrieval cue effective? For example, prior research had shown that if people study a word like *black* in a list of otherwise unrelated words, they are much more likely to recall *black* in the context of a strong associate like *white* than they are under conditions of free recall (Bilodeau & Blick, 1965). Why are these strong associates effective retrieval cues?

Thomson and Tulving (1970, Experiment 2) presented subjects with target words such as *BLACK* with either no context word at study or with a weakly associated word (*train–BLACK*) as context at study. Subjects were told that their task was to remember the capitalized word, but they should also note its relation to the context word (when it was present) to aid later recall. These two study conditions were crossed with three test conditions: Subjects got either no cues (free recall), or the weak associates as cues (*train–???*), or the strong associates as cues (*white–???*).

Shown in Table 2 are the results of the experiment. Examine first the top row, which presents performance for words studied with no context cues. Under conditions of free recall, people could remember 49% of 24 target words; however, with strong associates as retrieval cues, they recalled reliably more, 68%. On the other hand, weak associates given at the time of test did not aid recall; indeed, these irrelevant cues seemed to hurt recall a bit (43% recalled). Now consider the second row, which presents performance for the same target words studied in the context of weakly associated words. Free recall of these words suffered relative to the no-context (at study) condition (after all, subjects studied twice as many words), but the real interest is in how the effectiveness of the weak and strong associate cues changed. Now, recall was quite good with weak associate cues (82%), but quite poor—even worse than in free recall—with the strong associate cues (23%)!

The results of Thomson and Tulving's (1970) experiment, combined with the earlier ones of Tulving and Osler (1968), led to the encoding specificity hypothesis as the principle governing the effectiveness of retrieval cues: A retrieval cue will be effective if and only if it reinstates the original encoding of the to-be-remembered event. When a word like *black* is presented without context, it is presumably encoded with regard to its dominant meaning (as associated with white). Therefore, *white* serves as an effective retrieval cue, and a weak associate like *train* does not. However,

TABLE 2 Results of Thomson and Tulving's Experiment 2 (1970)[a]

	Test context/cues		
Study context	No cues	Weak associates	Strong associates
No cues (Black)	.49	.43	.68
Weak associates (train–Black)	.30	.82	.23

[a]Subjects studied 24 target words (BLACK) without context or in the context of a weak associate (train-BLACK). Then they were provided with various test contexts: no cues (free recall), weakly associated cues (train-???), or strongly associated cues (white-???). Results are the proportion of words recalled in the various conditions. See text for explanation.

when *black* is encoded in the context of a weak associate like *train,* subjects are likely to engage in a more idiosyncratic encoding of the target word (e.g., they might imagine a black train). In this case, the weak associate could serve as an excellent retrieval cue, but now the strong associate is completely ineffective, even relative to free recall. So even a strong associate will not be an effective retrieval cue for a word if the study context led subjects to encode the word in a nonstandard manner.

One surprising aspect of Thomson and Tulving's (1970) experiment was that free recall could be superior to cued recall with strong associates as cues. Some later studies by Newman and Frith (1977), among others, questioned this finding, but more recent results have confirmed it and provided further support for the encoding specificity hypothesis (Roediger & Adelson, 1980; Roediger & Payne, 1983).

Another impressive demonstration of the role of encoding factors and the effectiveness of retrieval cues was provided by Barclay, Bransford, Franks, McCarrell, and Nitsch (1974). Their experiment used sentences rather than single words, although the target for recall was always a word in the sentence. For example, subjects studied sentences such as "The man lifted the piano" or "The man tuned the piano." A retrieval cue such as "something heavy" was predicted to promote better recall for the first sentence, whereas the cue "something with a nice sound" was predicted to promote better recall for the second sentence. The results bore out these predictions, as 47% of the target words were recalled to appropriate cues, but only 16% to inappropriate cues. As with other results of this ilk, their findings show that words are semantically flexible; depending on the context, different features of the word will be encoded and therefore different cues will be effective, even for the same nominal target (*piano* in this example).

The role of verbal context has been shown in dozens—and maybe even a hundred—experiments. However, the great bulk of these experiments make the same point: Matching of the verbal context between study and test in which a target event appears greatly determines its memorability. The "matching" in these cases is usually on some meaningful dimension (Roediger & Adelson, 1980). However, on other types of memory tests—perceptual implicit memory tests—manipulations of meaning play little role, and instead, matching of perceptual features between study and test produces better performance (see Kelley & Lindsay, this volume, Chapter 2; Roediger, 1990). However, for most explicit memory tests, or those invoking conscious recollection, matching of meaning of events between study and test largely determines their memorability.

B. Manipulation of Physical Context

Each of us has had the experience of returning to a place from some past time in our lives and being suddenly reminded of many of the events and people of that time. The place may be an elementary school, a former residence, or a city from which one has moved away. The experience is so compelling that we easily come to believe that location (and other physical features) serve as potent retrieval cues reminding us of these distant events. But is it the case that these physical cues actually enable us to remember more than we could without them, as compared, for example, to someone merely asking us to try to recall events from that particular time and place? That is, do the actual physical locations serve as better retrieval cues than would verbal cues designed to help us retrieve the original event? The anecdotes that we can all recount about sudden recollection after returning to familiar places do not answer this question.

Numerous experiments have been conducted in which subjects learn material in one of two distinct physical contexts and then are tested on it either in the same context or in a different context. Such experiments conform nicely to the encoding/retrieval paradigm. If physical context modulates memory, one would expect better retention when testing occurs in the same place as studying rather than in a different place. In the mid-1970s, two spectacular examples of such interactions were reported. Godden and Baddeley (1975) conducted an experiment in which skin divers heard a list of 36 words in one of two different contexts—under water or on land—and were later tested for recall in the same physical environment in which the list had been studied or in the other environment. The subjects wore wet suits in both contexts and recalled the words orally. The results are shown in Table 3, where it can be seen that a greater percentage of words was recalled when the context at study and test matched than when it did not match.

A second striking series of experiments reporting context dependency were conducted by S. M. Smith, Glenberg, and Bjork (1978). In their Experiment 3, subjects studied 80 words (from 10 categories, with 8 items per category) in one of two different rooms. The rooms were made distinctive on several dimensions (size, classroom or storeroom, the experimenter, equipment, scent in the room, time of day for the test) and subjects learned

TABLE 3   Results of Godden and Baddeley (1975)[a]

Study context	Test context	
	Land	Water
Land	.38	.24
Water	.23	.32

[a]Subjects studied 36 words on land or under water and recalled them in the same context or in the other context. The proportion of words recalled was greater when the test context matched the study context.

the list either in the same room in which they were tested or in the other room. Subjects were given a free-recall test 24 hr later. When subjects were tested in the same room in which they had studied, they averaged about 49 words correct; when they were tested in a different room, they averaged only 35 words correct. Once again, the results showed striking specificity of matching encoding and retrieval contexts. In a later experiment, S. M. Smith (1979, Experiment 2) showed that most of the disadvantage of being tested in a different context from the learning context could be eliminated if subjects imagined being in the room in which they had learned the material while taking the test.

Curiously, despite these impressive findings from the mid-1970s, the effects of physical context on memory have been difficult to replicate. Although there have been some successes, they have also been numerous failures. Fernandez and Glenberg (1985) conducted eight experiments examining context (room) dependency, varying numerous factors across the experiments, but in none of the experiments did an effect of context dependency appear. In one case, the experiment was conducted in even the same locations used by S. M. Smith et al. (1978), so the failure to replicate is especially puzzling. Averaging over all experiments (weighting each equally), the probability of recalling words in the same context was .29 and in the different context was .30.

Saufley, Otaka, and Bavaresco (1985) capitalized on a naturally occurring context manipulation present on many university campuses. Often at large universities, students hear lectures in large halls and then are assigned to take their examinations either in the same lecture hall or in small ancillary classrooms. Saufley et al. tested Introductory Psychology students over three years at the University of California at Berkeley in just such a situation, where students were randomly assigned to take their exams either in the main lecture hall (where they had been taught) or in smaller overflow rooms. Across 21 "experiments" in this classroom setting, they failed to find any difference between the performance of the 3613 students who took the test in the same room and the 2412 who took the test in a different room. Subjects recognized, on average, about 67% of the material in each context. Although this outcome may be comforting for students who might find themselves in this circumstance, the failure to find any effect of room dependency is disquieting, given the prior literature. However, all tests taken by students were multiple choice (recognition memory) tests, not free-recall tests, and, as we cover in the next section, sometimes encoding/retrieval interactions occur on free-recall tests but not on recognition tests.

Why does environmental context have such a puzzling relation to memory retrieval? Why do some researchers obtain striking effects and others none at all? Bjork and Richardson-Klavehn (1989) and S. M. Smith (1988) have considered a number of possible reasons. Some differences between the naturally occurring cases and the laboratory experiments are quite obvious. For one, many researchers use only very short retention intervals between study and test of material, whereas the most compelling examples from our lives occur when the retention interval is very great (when we return to a place from which we have been absent for years). In addition, the type of materials, conditions of learning, and many other factors differ between the naturally occurring cases and the laboratory experiments. These factors may explain differences between our experiences and laboratory experiments, but they certainly do not explain failures to replicate across relatively similar experiments.

Another possibility is suggested from experiments reported by Eich (1985). He had subjects study lists of 24 words in one of two rooms. Different groups of subjects were told to use different types of imagery during encoding. In one condition (integrated imagery), subjects were asked to generate an image in which the named object was seen as being conjoined with a particular feature in their environment (e.g., "I imagine a diamond-shaped *kite* lying on top of the table located in the corner of the room."). Other subjects were told to form isolated images in which the object was visualized as existing by itself (e.g., "I imagine a big blue *kite* sailing in the sky."). They were to rate the vividness of their images on a scale of 1 to 7 in both conditions. Subjects were tested 48 hr later, first on a free-recall test and then on a two-alternative forced-choice recognition test, and either in the same room or in a different room.

The results are shown in Panel A of Table 4, with free recall in the columns on the left and recognition in the columns on the right. We consider the recall results first. As can be seen, an effect of room context was obtained in free recall, but only in the case when integrated images were

TABLE 4   Results of Eich (1985)[a,b]

	Imagery condition	Free recall		Recognition	
		Context		Context	
		Same	Different	Same	Different
A	Isolated	.26	.24	.95	.93
	Integrated	.45	.31	.90	.91
		Free recall		Recognition	
B	Isolated	.25		.94	
	Integrated	.38		.90	

[a]Results in Panel B are collapsed across the Same and Different contexts.

[b]Subjects studied 24 words in one room and were tested on recall and on recognition in the same room or in a different room.

formed during the study phase (in the second row). Subjects recalled 45% when tested in the same room and 31% when tested in a different room. Presumably subjects associated their images of the target words to items in the room and then later these items served as effective retrieval cues when subjects were tested in the same room, which of course they could not do when subjects were tested in a different room. When studied events were imaged in isolation, a room context effect did not occur, with about 25% recall in each condition (in the first row). Also, note that, overall, subjects recalled words better in the integrated imagery condition than in the isolated imagery condition (see Panel B, on the left).

One possibility, then, is that the mixed evidence with regard to the effects of physical context on recall is due to subtle factors that determine whether studied items are associated with features of the room. Subjects may need to employ conscious strategies to relate target items to features of the room for the physical context to serve as a useful cue later. If this association occurs, then maintaining the same context or changing to a different context will affect performance. If associations are not made between the recall targets and features of the context, then maintaining the context or changing it will not affect performance (as in Eich's, 1985, isolated imagery condition). Although this interpretation is plausible, it is still unsatisfying in that there is no good reason to believe that instructions were actually varied in subtle ways across previous experiments in the literature in a way that would explain successes and failures to find context-dependency effects.

The recognition results appear on the right of Table 4. Although their interpretation is clouded by an apparent ceiling effect—subjects were very near perfect performance of 1.0—two other interesting findings emerge. First, in the recognition test, no hint of a context-dependency effect occurred in either study condition (Panel A). The second finding can be seen in Panel B, where results have been collapsed across the same and different context conditions. Now the experiment appears as an encoding/retrieval experiment in which isolated and integrated imagery were the study conditions and free recall and recognition were the test conditions. Interestingly, it can be seen that the integrated imagery condition led to better performance on the free-recall test than did the isolated imagery condition, but that the opposite effect occurred on the recognition test; that is, although performance is near the ceiling, the isolated imagery condition led to significantly better recognition than did the integrated imagery condition. Note that this outcome occurred despite the fact that the free-recall test occurred prior to the recognition test and probably differentially boosted recognition in the integrated imagery condition (i.e., recall was greater in the integrated imagery condition and the act of recall probably boosted recognition). The finding of an independent variable having opposite effects on free recall and recognition indicates that different processes operate in the two tests. We consider other results like these later in the section on effects of item-specific and relational encoding.

To return to the main question of why some experiments show effects of room context and others do not, perhaps the answer lies in subtle aspects of experimental instructions or manipulations that encourage subjects in some experiments to code the to-be-remembered items with regard to the room context, whereas others do not. These conditions would correspond to the integrated imagery and isolated imagery instructions, respectively, in Eich's (1985) experiment. Of course, Eich's experiment is only suggestive with regard to this point and by no means proves that this difference caused the discrepancies in the literature. However, at least Eich has identified a plausible candidate to explain these differences, which is a first step. McDaniel, Anderson, Einstein, and O'Halloran (1989) have alternatively proposed that if the original encoding was rich enough, subjects would be able to supply their own retrieval cues during the test and, accordingly, would not need to rely on environmental context. With weaker encoding strategies, however, greater reliance on environmental context at retrieval would lead to benefits of matching context at encoding and retrieval. S. M. Smith (1988) has proposed a similar idea. Despite the evidence from Eich (1985) and from McDaniel, Anderson, Einstein, and O'Halloran (1989), the effects of environmental context remain a puzzle.

One other experiment deserves mention before we leave this section, as it provides a convenient transition to the next topic. Schab (1990) asked whether presentation of a distinctive odor during learning and testing would aid memory. He presented adjectives under incidental learning conditions. During both the learning session and a later free-recall test, subjects were told to imagine the smell of chocolate, but in some cases they actually received a chocolate smell infused into the room and in other cases they did not. As shown in Table 5, when subjects experienced the chocolate odor during both the study phase and the test phase, their free-recall performance

TABLE 5   Results of Schab's Experiment 1 (1990)[a]

Encoding conditions	Retrieval conditions	
	Odor	No odor
Odor	.21	.17
No odor	.13	.14

[a] Subjects learned a list and were tested on it with a distinctive odor occurring both during study and test, during one occasion but not the other, or on neither occasion.

was better than when the odor occurred only at study, only at test, or not at all. This pattern was also replicated in later experiments and therefore represents another effect, albeit a rather small one, of environmental context on memory. In the next section, we consider somewhat more radical transformations of the subjects' internal context, created by introducing drugs into their systems.

C. State-Dependent Retrieval

Research on state-dependent retrieval involves manipulating the subject's internal state, usually in the form of changing the pharmacological state or the mood state of the individual. The literature on state-dependent retrieval is complex, but, at least in the case of manipulating drug states, some clarification has been gained. The business of how mood affects memory, however, is still rather uncertain.

The study of state-dependent retrieval arose from clinical observations. Psychologists and psychiatrists working with alcoholics occasionally noticed a curious phenomenon. Alcoholics would perform some act while under the influence of alcohol (e.g., hide a paycheck) and then, after becoming sober, forget where the paycheck was hidden. Of course, such alcoholic amnesia is not in itself surprising, because alcohol is known to have strong detrimental effects on memory and other cognitive processes. The curious event was that when the alcoholic fell off the wagon again, he could remember where the paycheck was hidden.

How can this phenomenon be explained? In line with the general principles of this chapter, the pharmacological state of the individual may serve as a retrieval cue; when intoxicated during an experience, the person will be better able to retrieve it later when intoxicated again than when sober. The surprising prediction is that retrieval under conditions of intoxication might actually surpass that in a sober state, at least when original learning occurred under conditions of intoxication. Retrieval depends on a match of the "state" of the person between study and test, in line with the general transfer-appropriate processing view of this chapter.

The early experimental literature on state-dependent retrieval was rather discouraging: Many experiments obtained the phenomenon (matching drug states at study and test led to better retention than mismatching states), but many experiments obtained null findings. Because of this disquieting state of affairs, many researchers concluded that state-dependent retrieval was not a reliable phenomenon. For example, Hilgard and Bower (1975, p. 547), in their influential textbook, stated that evidence for state-dependent retrieval in humans "rests on precarious grounds."

A seminal paper by Eich (1980; see also Eich, 1989) helped to straighten out the disparate findings. A hint to the solution was provided in an earlier paper by Eich, Weingartner, Stillman, and Gillin (1975). With the permission of appropriate government agencies, they tested the state-dependent memory effects of marijuana. Subjects served in four different conditions depending on their state (drugged or sober at the time of learning and testing of the material). To induce the drug state, people smoked a marijuana cigarette 20 min before they learned the material or were tested on it. In the nondrugged state, they smoked a cigarette that tasted like marijuana but from which the active ingredient had been removed. To insure that the drug was having an effect, the experimenters checked both objective measures such as heart rate (marijuana increases it) and subjective reports obtained from rating scales (asking, e.g., "How 'high' do you feel?"). Marijuana had a large effect on both measures relative to the placebo condition.

The volunteers who served in the experiment were tested in the four conditions shown in Table 6. They studied lists of words in either the placebo or drug condition and then were tested in either the placebo or drug state 4 hr later. The lists consisted of 48 words from 24 different categories, with 2 words per category (as in the Tulving and Pearlstone, 1966, experiment described earlier). Two types of test were given: either free recall or category-name cued recall, also like the Tulving and Pearlstone study.

Results of their experiment are shown in Table 6, for both free recall and cued recall. First examine the free-recall results on the left. Not surprisingly, performance was best for people who were sober both when they studied the material and were tested on it (11.5 words recalled). If the subjects learned the material when sober but were tested when under the influence of marijuana, they did not recall as many words (9.9 words recalled). Therefore, as in other studies, marijuana (and by extension, other depressant drugs) impedes retrieval of information. The subjects did even worse if they studied the material under marijuana and then were tested sober (6.7 words recalled), consistent with the usual impairment of learning and memory by depressive drugs when people are removed from the drug.

In the critical condition for the state-dependent retrieval hypothesis—

TABLE 6   Results of the Eich, Weingartner, Stillman, & Gillin (1975) Experiment on State-Dependent Retrieval[a]

Condition		Mean number of words recalled	
Study	Test	Free recall	Cued recall
Placebo	Placebo	11.5	24.0
Placebo	Drug	9.9	23.7
Drug	Placebo	6.7	22.6
Drug	Drug	10.5	22.3

[a]Subjects received marijuana or a placebo before learning and testing of materials under free recall and cued recall conditions.

where people studied information in a drug state and then were tested in the same state 4 hr later—people recalled the material better than those who also had learned while under the drug but were tested sober. As can be seen in the Drug–Drug condition in Table 6, when people acquired material in a drug state, they recalled more words when placed back in the drug state (10.5) than when tested sober (6.7). Of course, this is no recommendation to take depressive drugs to help remember, because even in the Drug–Drug condition, people recalled fewer words than in the Placebo–Placebo condition, when they were sober at both times.

Eich et al.'s (1975) free-recall results impressively confirmed the concept of state-dependent retrieval. Note, however, the cued recall results on the right, where no evidence of state-dependent retrieval occurred. When given category name retrieval cues, people in the Drug–Drug condition recalled no more words than those tested in the Drug–Placebo condition, unlike the free recall results. Of course, cued recall produced better performance in all conditions than did free recall, but the provision of cues also eliminated the state-dependent retrieval effect.

Eich (1980) examined many experiments conducted on the state-dependent retrieval phenomenon. He discovered that only about half of all studies showed a reliable state-dependent effect (i.e., performance better in the drug–drug state than in the drug–placebo state). However, when he separated the experiments into groups based on the type of test given, he discovered that almost all experiments that had used a noncued (free recall or serial recall) test had found the state-dependent retrieval phenomenon, whereas very few experiments that had used cued recall tests had found the effect. This general conclusion—that state-dependent retrieval occurs under conditions of free recall but not cued recall—has generally held up over the intervening years (Eich, 1989). Drug state can serve as a retrieval cue, but more powerful overt cues such as category names can overshadow the weaker state cues and eliminate their effect. S. M. Smith (1988) argued for a similar principle operating in place-dependent retrieval experiments.

D. Mood-Dependent Retrieval

Drugs obviously affect the internal state of the organism. A similar manipulation involves changing people's moods. If people learn something while they are happy, will they be able to retrieve the information better if they are happy—relative to being in a neutral or sad mood—during the test? Does mood also serve as an internal contextual cue similar to drug states? Readers will probably not be surprised at this point to learn that the literature on this topic is mixed, with some researchers finding mood-dependent memory effects (Bower, 1981) and others not (see Blaney, 1986, for a review of findings). In most of these experiments, subjects are induced into happy or sad moods by watching either comedy video tapes or sad or tragic video tapes, or by listening to uplifting music or dreary, depressing music. Typically, after the mood has been induced, subjects are presented with lists of words or other similar material to remember.

Eich and Metcalfe (1989) have reported an experiment that may help to unravel the puzzling effects of mood and memory. They had subjects either read words during study or generate them from a conceptual clue (e.g., either read *cold,* or generate it as the antonym of hot–???). Before the study phase, subjects listened to classical music that was designed to be either uplifting or depressing and they periodically rated their mood on a scale. Once subjects had met the experimenter's criterion for a mood change in the appropriate direction, the study material was presented. At a later point in time, subjects were reintroduced to the experimental setting, listened to classical music to induce either the same mood or the other mood, and then were given a free-recall test.

Eich and Metcalfe's (1989) results are shown in Table 7. The encoding/retrieval interaction for the read words, on the left, was not significant (although there was a slight tendency for recall in the matched mood cases to be a few percentage points higher than in the cases in which mood states were mismatched). However, the mood-dependency effect did appear, and in a striking fashion, for words that were generated during study, as shown in the data on the right of Table 7. Recall of generated words was almost twice as great when mood states matched between study and test as when they mismatched.

Eich and Metcalfe's (1989) results for the read words did not seem to represent a floor effect, because in later experiments they brought performance up by having subjects read words several times, and yet the mood-dependent effect still did not occur. The authors argued that mood-dependent effects might occur only for self-initiated activity on the part of the subjects, and not so powerfully for events presented externally. Subjects' moods may function as potent retrieval cues for their internally generated thoughts, but not for their externally produced reactions. Because most

TABLE 7   Results of Eich and Metcalfe (1989)[a]

	Test condition			
	Read words		Generated words	
Encoding condition	Happy	Sad	Happy	Sad
Happy	.09	.04	.32	.17
Sad	.05	.07	.17	.27

[a]Subjects read or generated words in a happy or sad mood and then were tested later in the same mood or the opposite mood.

prior experiments used external presentation of stimuli, perhaps mood-dependent effects were small and variable. This is an interesting hypothesis and its application to this field warrants further research. Eich, Macaulay, and Ryan (1994) provided additional evidence for its validity.

E. Manipulation of Mental and Physical Operations

Another means of implementing the encoding/retrieval paradigm is to require subjects to perform similar or different mental operations at encoding and retrieval. A classic experiment of this type reported by Morris, Bransford, and Franks (1977) introduced the transfer-appropriate processing approach. They were interested in how manipulations designed to influence the level of processing of studied stimuli affected performance on different types of memory tests. The usual expectation is that deeper, more meaningful processing should increase retention compared to more shallow or superficial processing (Craik & Lockhart, 1972; Craik & Tulving, 1975). Morris et al. (Experiment 1) had subjects study the same words in sentences that promoted either phonemic or semantic encoding of the words. For example, subjects studied words such as *Eagle* and answered questions like "_____ rhymes with legal" or "_____ is a large bird." Subjects responded *yes* or *no* to each statement, and we consider results based on tests of items to which subjects responded *yes* during study.

The subjects' memories were tested in two different ways, with the tests designed either to match or to mismatch the way the information was encoded. Half the subjects were tested on a standard recognition test in which studied words were intermixed with nonstudied words and the task was to identify the studied words. Morris et al. (1977) assumed that subjects accomplished this task by referring to the meaning of the test words, resulting in the typical levels-of-processing effect: better performance for words encoded semantically than phonemically. Indeed, as is apparent in the left column of Table 8, just this pattern occurred. The novel test condition involved a rhyme recognition test. Subjects were told that the test items included words that rhymed with studied words and that they should discriminate these rhyming words from distractors that did not rhyme with the targets. The results of this rhyme recognition test appear in the right column of Table 8, which shows that the standard levels-of-processing effect was reversed. Now phonemic encoding produced better performance than did semantic encoding, in general conformity with the principle of transfer-appropriate processing (or encoding specificity).

The Morris et al. (1977) experiment revealed two important lessons about retrieval processes that we have already met in other forms. First, even so powerful a variable as level of processing does not have a uniform effect across all types of test. On some tests, the levels-of-processing effect

TABLE 8   Results of Morris, Bransford, & Frank's Experiment 1 (1977)[a]

Encoding condition	Test conditions	
	Standard recognition semantic	Rhyme recognition phonemic
Semantic	.84	.33
Phonemic	.63	.49

[a]Study conditions encouraged phonemic or semantic processing and test conditions were designed to tap the two types of knowledge.

disappears (Fisher & Craik, 1977; McDaniel, Friedman, & Bourne, 1978) or even reverses (as in the Morris et al. results). Second, matching the processing required by study and test conditions enhances performance. It should be noted, however, that there was still a main effect such that semantic study and test processing produced better overall performance than did phonemic study and test processing (the upper left cell compared to the lower right cell in Table 8). Related observations that also document these points have been reported by Stein (1978), and this transfer-appropriate processing approach has been extended to differences between explicit and implicit memory tests (Blaxton, 1989; Roediger, 1990; see Kelley & Lindsay, this volume, Chapter 2).

Glisky and Rabinowitz (1985) have also shown that repetition of mental operations at test enhances memory performance (recognition in their case). In their study phase, subjects either read intact words (alcohol) or generated them from word fragments in which two letters were omitted (al—oho—). The words were easy to generate with letters missing so subjects made relatively few generation errors. When subjects took a later test, they either saw intact words or generated them from the same fragment, just as they had at study. The recognition test required subjects to decide if the words they were reading and generating on the test had appeared in the original study list (in either form). Results are presented in Table 9. The left column shows the standard generation effect (Jacoby, 1978; Slamecka & Graf, 1978): Generated words were recognized better than read words when the recognition test involved reading intact words. However, examination of the data in the right column reveals that the generation effect was enhanced by about 10% when the generation operations were reinstated at the time of test. Best recognition occurred when subjects generated words at study and test. Note that generating at test did not have a general advantage, but only enhanced recognition when subjects had generated the words during study. In companion experiments, Glisky and Rabinowitz showed that it was necessary for the same operations to be carried out at study and test (i.e., the same

TABLE 9   Results of Glisky and Rabinowitz (1985)[a]

	Retrieval condition	
Encoding condition	Read	Generate
Read	.60	.59
Generate	.76	.86
Difference (G − R)	.16	.27

[a]Subjects either read or generated single words at study and then during a later recognition test. False alarm rates were the same for Read (.18) and Generated (.19) words. Results shown are the proportion of hits.

letters to be omitted from the words) to see the whole advantage of generating items at test. In general, Glisky and Rabinowitz "found that the more closely the operations at retrieval matched those at encoding, the better [was] recognition performance" (p. 193).

A striking demonstration that corroborates the finding of Glisky and Rabinowitz (1985) has recently been reported by Engelkamp, Zimmer, Mohr, and Sellen (1994). They compared subjects' recognition of phrases that were either verbally encoded or self-performed. That is, subjects were given brief statements such as "close the book" and "pick up the pencil," and they either simply read the phrase or they actually performed the task with materials in front of them. Previous research had shown that subjects remembered the events better if they performed them than if they merely read about them. Engelkamp et al. wondered if this effect might be magnified if subjects were asked to perform the task again at test. (The standard test that had been used in prior research involved recognition of the verbal form of the item.) Therefore, during the study phase, they had subjects either read statements, or read them and perform the actions. On a later recognition test, subjects either read the statements, or read and performed them, before judging if they had been previously studied. Some test items referred to previously studied items and some were new, to measure the false alarm rate.

The results are presented in Table 10. The verbal test condition (reading the statement) showed a sizable advantage for self-performed tasks at study, 23% in Experiment 1 and 26% in Experiment 2, relative to verbal tasks (reading the statement at study), reflecting the typical advantage accruing to self-performed tasks. However, in both experiments, the advantage of self-performed tasks was increased if the tasks were also self-performed during the test, increasing the size of the effect by 7% in Experiment 1 and 12% in Experiment 2. Once again, recapitulating operations between study and test enhanced performance, although in this case the operations were actual physical movements and not mental operations. In another experiment,

TABLE 10   Results of Engelkamp, Zimmer, Mohr, & Sellen (1994)[a]

	Retrieval condition			
	Experiment 1		Experiment 2	
Encoding condition	Verbal	Self-performed	Verbal	Self-performed
Verbal	.64[b]	.64	.45	.40
Self-performed	.87	.94	.71	.78
Difference (SP − V)	.23	.30	.26	.38

[a]Subjects read phrases (verbal encoding) or in addition performed the action suggested by the phrase (self-performed encoding). The recognition test was composed of both old and new phrases that subjects read or performed.
[b]Data are corrected recognition (hits minus false alarms).

Engelkamp et al. (1994) showed that enhanced recognition of self-performed tasks was diminished if subjects performed the task with one hand at study and then with a different hand at test (e.g., opening the book with the right hand at study and then opening it with the left hand at test). Therefore, the motor component of recognition seems rather specific.

In general, the results reviewed in this section show quite clearly that the means of acquisition of material forms part of its representation in memory and that to the extent that the retrieval task recapitulates this original enactment, performance benefits. All these results are clearly in line with Kolers's (1979; Kolers & Roediger, 1984) procedural account of recognition performance.

F. Relational and Item-Specific Processing

At several points in the chapter we have written about the importance of distinctiveness, because, in general, distinctive events are well remembered. This effect has been known at least since the time of von Restorff (1933) and has been studied in many different paradigms since then (Guynn & Roediger, 1995; Tulving, 1969; Wallace, 1965; see Hunt & McDaniel, 1993, for review). The basic idea, embedded in many different theories, is that at least two different ways of encoding information exist (J. R. Anderson, 1972; Hunt & Einstein, 1981; Mandler, 1980). In one case, people can pay attention to the item-specific aspects of a particular event during encoding. This increases the likelihood that memory for that event will include features that differentiate the event from others in memory, thus making the event distinctive. The other type of processing is relational, which serves to interrelate events or to organize them according to some scheme. One basic idea is that item-specific processing will primarily enhance recognition, whereas both types of processing will benefit recall. In free recall, the interrelations or associations among events help to cue subjects so that recall of some events will cause people to remember more events later.

The basic importance of this distinction was illustrated in an important study by Hunt and Einstein (1981, Experiment 1). Subjects studied either a categorized list of 36 words (6 words from each of 6 categories), or a list of 36 words that subjects perceived to be unrelated (6 words from each of 6 ad hoc categories, e.g., liquids, things that are green, things that fly). Hunt and Einstein assumed that related words would automatically receive relational processing, but not necessarily item-specific processing; further, words that subjects perceived to be unrelated were assumed to automatically receive item-specific processing, but not necessarily relational processing. Subjects performed either a relational orienting task (sorting the items into specified categories) or an item-specific orienting task (rating the pleasantness of the items) on either the related or the unrelated words. Sorting the words into categories should require relational processing (for both the related and unrelated words), and rating the words for pleasantness should require item-specific processing (for both the related and unrelated words). The idea was that the most beneficial type of processing might be that which was different from the processing invited by the list structure; that is, the sorting task might primarily benefit memory for the unrelated words, because for the unrelated words, information gained from rating items for pleasantness is redundant with information from the list structure (i.e., both encourage item-specific information). Conversely, the pleasantness rating task might primarily benefit memory for the related words, because, for the related words, information gained from sorting is redundant with information from the list structure (i.e., both encourage relational information). Of course, the effects of these variables might well depend on the type of memory test. Thus, after either sorting or rating a related or an unrelated list, subjects were given tests of free recall (thought to depend on both relational and item-specific information) and recognition (thought to depend mainly on item-specific information).

The results appear in Table 11. First, consider recall results, shown on the left side of the table. As predicted, the item-specific task produced better free recall than did the relational task for the related list (.48 vs. .42 of the words recalled), but the relational task produced better free recall than did the item-specific task for the unrelated list (.47 vs. .33 of the words recalled). For the related list, information gained from rating (i.e., item-specific information) was not redundant with the information gained from the interrelations among list members, but relational information gained from sorting was somewhat redundant and thus less useful. For the unrelated list, information gained from sorting (i.e., relational information) was not redundant with the information gained from the list of unrelated words, but item-specific information gained from rating was perhaps redundant

TABLE 11   Results of Hunt and Einstein's Experiment 1 (1981)[a]

	Retrieval condition			
	Free recall		Recognition[b]	
	List type		List type	
Encoding task	Related	Unrelated	Related	Unrelated
Relational (sorting)	.42	.47	.73	.89
Item-specific (rating)	.48	.33	.93	.91

[a]Subjects studied 36 related or nominally unrelated words, sorted the words into categories (relational task) or rated the pleasantness of each word (item-specific task), and took tests of free recall and recognition.

[b]Recognition scores are AG scores. The AG score is a nonparametric signal detection measure (Pollack, Norman, & Galanter, 1964).

and thus less useful. These results show that both item–specific and relational processing are necessary for free recall.

The recognition results (on the right side of Table 11) differed somewhat from the recall results, however. For the related list, the item–specific task did produce better recognition than did the relational task (.93 vs. .73), the same pattern as in free recall. But for the unrelated list, the item–specific and relational tasks produced similar recognition (.91 vs. .89), with a slight benefit for the item–specific task, even though the words were nominally unrelated. However, this equivalence in performance should be treated cautiously, as performance is near the ceiling.

Hunt and Einstein's (1981) results provide another example of an encoding/retrieval interaction: The effect of a study variable (sorting or pleasantness rating) depended on the type of list (related or unrelated) as well as on the type of test (free recall or recognition). Sorting produced better free recall for the nominally unrelated list, and pleasantness rating produced better free recall for the related list. Rating the pleasantness of words produced better recognition for the related list, but for an unrelated list, rating and sorting produced similar recognition scores.

These ideas—relational and item–specific processing—are useful in explaining a number of phenomena in the literature. Relational processing can provide an account for organizational bases of recall (J. R. Anderson, 1972; Mandler, 1967; Tulving, 1968). For present purposes, item–specific or distinctive processing can be understood in terms of cue overload; that is, a distinctive event, such as a picture embedded in a list of words, is well remembered because subjects trying to retrieve items from the category "pictures" have only one item to retrieve. The same mechanism may be at work to produce what are called flashbulb memories (R. Brown & Kulik,

1977), which are believed to be extraordinarily vivid memories associated with a particular cataclysmic event. Most of us remember vividly (or at least *believe* we remember vividly) events surrounding a particularly emotional event, whether personal (the birth of a child), or a national tragedy, such as the explosion of the space shuttle Challenger or the assassination of a president. These distinctive events are unique and, therefore, serve as powerful retrieval cues, with no other memories associated to the event. We can thus understand how these memories continue to stand out and be retrievable even when more recent memories have suffered interference from over-loaded cues.

G. Reprise

This chapter has emphasized principles of transfer-appropriate processing (or encoding specificity) and distinctiveness (or absence of cue overload). We culminate this section with an apt experiment showing how good re-trieval can be if a situation maximizes both principles. Mäntylä (1986) re-ported several experiments in which he presented subjects with 500–600 words, under incidental learning conditions, with subjects showing 90% retention on a later test of recall! How did his subjects achieve this level of performance on such a huge amount of material? In Mäntylä's experiments, the subject's encoding task was to generate either one property or three properties that described or defined each word. So, for example, when given the word *marmalade,* subjects might write that it is *sticky, sweet,* and *can be eaten.* Of course, it took subjects considerable time to generate these properties. During the later test, subjects were given either a single cue or all three cues that they had generated. Mäntylä showed that subjects given a single cue could remember about 50% to 60% of the words, and those given three cues could remember about 90% on a test given the same day as the study phase. This level of performance was not achieved by guessing because an appropriate control group, who did not receive the encoding phase but who were given cues and told to generate the words, performed at the level of 5% with one cue and 17% with three cues. Guessing may have played some role in the subjects' spectacular performance, but the greater part seems due to other factors powerfully aiding their memories.

Mäntylä (1986) argued for two factors. One is cue/trace compatibility, which embodies the logic of the encoding specificity hypothesis or transfer-appropriate processing. The retrieval cues were highly effective because they were quite compatible with the subject's mode of encoding the mate-rial: The subjects themselves had constructed the cues during encoding. The second principle was cue distinctiveness: The cues subjects generated were quite different from one another, each tailored to the particular word-event to be remembered. Because the cues precisely identified the targets, the item–specific cues had little or no overlap with other cues, and were thus distinctive. Therefore, Mäntylä's study serves as a powerful demonstration of the importance of the two principles guiding this chapter: transfer-appropriate processing (or encoding specificity) and distinctive, item-specific processing. If factors in a situation maximize the effectiveness of both these principles, retention will be outstanding, as it was for Mäntylä's subjects.

V. EFFECTS OF PRIOR RETRIEVAL

Tests of memory are not neutral events that merely assess the state of a person's knowledge; tests also change or modify memories (Bjork, 1975; McDaniel & Masson, 1985; see also Dempster, this volume, Chapter 9, for a discussion of test effects). Changes can be either positive, aiding later retention, or negative, causing forgetting, interference, and even false recollections. We consider some positive effects here and negative effects in a later section of the chapter.

A. Effects of One Test on Another

How does one test of memory affect performance on another test given later? Does a recall test improve later recognition? Does a recognition test improve later recall? The answer to this last question is relatively easy, because the recognition test also serves as another study opportunity: The *old* words on a recognition test are presented again, and thereby benefit subsequent recall of those words. Although the evidence is not entirely consistent, a recall test also generally improves subsequent recognition, at least for the last few items in a list (Jones & Roediger, 1995; Lockhart, 1975). Other researchers have asked more subtle questions with regard to the influence of one test on another, and the results are complex (McDaniel, Kowitz, & Dunay, 1989). These questions reflect the fact that tests differ on dimensions other than whether they require recall or recognition. For instance, as illustrated in the Morris et al. (1977) study described earlier (as well as in McDaniel et al., 1978), tests differ on the kind of information required for successful performance. For example, depending on how it is constructed, accurate responding on a recognition test might require access to meaning, to phonemic features (Morris et al., 1977), or to graphemic (visual appearance of letters) features (McDaniel et al., 1978). In line with the notion of levels of processing, prior tests that require use of semantic information tend to benefit later tests more than do prior tests that require use of nonsemantic (e.g., phonemic) information (Bartlett, 1977; McDaniel, Kowitz, & Dunay, 1989; McDaniel & Masson, 1985).

The pattern becomes more complex, although understandable from the retrieval principles already presented, when one considers the nature of the information tested on the later test. McDaniel, Kowitz, and Dunay (1989, Experiment 2) varied whether the initial test focused on semantic or phonemic information by providing subjects with meaningful associates or rhymes, respectively, of studied words (i.e., a cued recall test was used). On a later test, subjects were provided with either identical cues from the earlier test, different cues directed at the same level of information as the cues from the earlier test, or different cues directed at a different level of information from the cues used on the earlier test. The initial test most improved performance on the later test (relative to conditions in which the words were not tested initially) to the degree that the later test focused on information that matched the information used in the earlier test. That is, identical cues were better than different cues directed at the same level of information, which in turn were better than different cues directed at a different level of information. This pattern reflects a transfer-appropriate processing effect, and suggests that memory testing induces additional processing of already-encoded information. As a general conclusion, then, there is a benefit from taking a prior test on taking a later test of whatever sort, although the amount of benefit will differ depending on the nature of the two tests (McDaniel, Kowitz, & Dunay, 1989).

B. The Testing Effect: Taking the Same Test Twice

From the perspective of transfer-appropriate processing, and the results just discussed, we might expect that the greatest facilitation on a later test would occur if subjects had taken the same test previously and successfully retrieved the events. What could be better practice for retrieving information on a later test than having retrieved it earlier? Indeed, often a prior test has a greatly facilitating effect on a later test, even better than another study opportunity for the material. This finding has a long history in experimental psychology (Spitzer, 1939), but its importance for educational settings seems overlooked (but see McDaniel & Fisher, 1991). The testing effect, as it is called, occurs both for meaningful prose materials and for lists of words in laboratory settings (Glover, 1989). To provide but one example, Wheeler and Roediger (1992) had subjects study a series of 60 pictures under one of two conditions, either in the context of a story presented auditorily (the pictures popped up as the appropriate words occurred in the story), or simply in a list where the names of the pictures were heard as the pictures were presented. After the pictures were presented in one of the two encoding conditions, subjects filled out a brief questionnaire and then took either zero, one, or three successive free-recall tests on the studied pictures (subjects wrote down the names of the pictures on the test). For present purposes, the critical test of interest occurred when subjects returned to the laboratory a week later and took one last free-recall test.

The results of this last test are shown in Figure 2, where it can be seen that the pictures embedded in the story were generally remembered better than pictures presented only with their names. That is, the story did promote better recall. However, this later benefit required an earlier test to bring it out. The number of prior tests given a week before greatly affected memorability on the delayed test, with the more powerful effect occurring for pictures that were recalled in the context of the story rather than presented in a list. Because the three groups of subjects in each of the two encoding conditions (pictures plus story or pictures plus names) had been treated identically up to the point of the first test, the large differences in retention a week later must have been a direct consequence of the number of tests taken. In general, the retrieval practice induced by taking a prior test provided great transfer or benefit to taking a later test. Indeed, many experiments have shown that retrieval practice from taking a test actually produces greater gains in later retention than does another presentation of the material for study (Hogan & Kintsch, 1971; McDaniel & Masson, 1985; Thompson, Wenger, & Bartling, 1978; Tulving, 1967). Runquist (1986) showed that a test can actually eliminate forgetting in some conditions.

A final example of the power of testing comes from a study by Landauer and Bjork (1978), who examined different schedules of testing in recall of

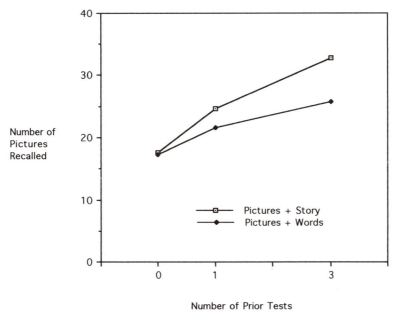

Number of Prior Tests

FIGURE 2   The testing effect. The number of tests taken soon after studying pictures greatly affected recall one week later. (Data from Wheeler and Roediger, 1992.)

name–face pairs. Is it better to have a test (with feedback) shortly after a pair has been presented, or is it better to wait? Landauer and Bjork tested several variations and discovered that a schedule of temporally expanding tests produced the best performance on a delayed retention test. That is, in remembering name–face pairs, subjects benefited most when they were first tested after a short delay (before they had forgotten the pair), then after a bit longer delay, then after a still longer delay, and so on. Because the eventual test of retention occurs at a great delay (hours, days, or weeks later), this expanding test procedure helps to shape eventual retention under transfer-appropriate conditions: The best practice for a long delayed retention test is being able to retrieve the pair after increasingly long delays.

VI. RELATED TOPICS

In a brief chapter on retrieval processes, we cannot hope to cover in full all the topics falling under its purview. Yet we would be remiss if we did not deal, however superficially, with some other miscellaneous topics.

A. Repression

Early in this century, Freud (1914/1957) popularized the idea that some memories are too painful and traumatic to be permitted into consciousness. Such memories are banished to an unconscious state, where they may nevertheless disrupt ongoing behavior in the form of neurotic symptoms, slips of the tongue, or expression in dreams. The concept of repressed memories existing in the unconscious is firmly embedded in the folk psychology of our times, but experimental evidence for it is slight. Indeed, we know of no strong evidence for the existence of unconscious memories from repression, at least in the strong sense. If, instead, repression is defined simply as people's trying to avoid thinking about unpleasant topics (Erdelyi & Goldberg, 1979), then certainly it exists. On the other hand, the notion of traumatic memories being banished to an unconscious state and then suddenly reappearing is supported only by anecdotes that cannot be experimentally evaluated. In fairness, however, experimental tests of the repression idea are notoriously difficult to undertake. Nonetheless, those who believe in repression and repressed memories do so as an article of faith rather than as a tested proposition having an experimental basis in fact (Loftus, 1993).

An idea akin to that of repression is that of retrieval inhibition (Bjork, 1989). One idea is that people can inhibit material that is no longer necessary—they can tell themselves to forget it or be so instructed by an experimenter—and this material will then not create interference with other material. Some researchers have specifically linked retrieval inhibition as studied in the laboratory with other forms of inhibited or repressed memories

(Geiselman, Bjork, & Fishman, 1983). Such inhibitory processes are considered more fully by Anderson and Neely in Chapter 8 of this volume. However, the link between retrieval inhibition as studied in the laboratory and the Freudian concept of repression remains tenuous at best.

B. Hypnosis and Memory Retrieval

A companion idea to that of repression is the notion that there exist psychological means of unlocking repressed memories and bringing them to the surface. Hypnosis is considered by some practitioners to be one of these means. Hypnotized subjects are placed in a relaxed state and encouraged to visualize the original event. On some occasions, hypnotized subjects do recall information that they could not previously recall in an awake state, but at the expense of increased guesses (Dywan & Bowers, 1983). Many laboratory experiments have been carried out, both with word and picture lists and with materials that more realistically approximate natural events, but with the same outcome: There is no good evidence that hypnosis can aid memory retrieval (M. C. Smith, 1983). Gains that are seen under hypnosis in some experiments would likely occur merely from the act of repeated testing (Nogrady, McConkey, & Perry, 1985). In other cases where hypnosis appears successful, the outcome is likely due to the instructions and cues given during hypnosis on how to retrieve information, rather than on hypnosis per se (Geiselman, Fisher, MacKinnon, & Holland, 1985). Although some psychological techniques may enhance retrieval from memory, hypnosis does not seem to have this power.

C. Spontaneous Recovery

In classical conditioning experiments, a conditioned stimulus (CS) can be made to elicit a conditioned response (CR) through repeated pairings with an unconditioned stimulus (US). After conditioning, if the conditioned stimulus is repeatedly presented in the absence of the unconditioned stimulus, the conditioned response declines, and eventually disappears altogether (extinction). However, if the researcher waits for a period of time and then re-presents the conditioned stimulus, the conditioned response recovers. Such recovery occurs even in the absence of any additional CS–US pairings and, therefore, is called spontaneous recovery. Pavlov (1927) first discovered this phenomenon, and researchers in human learning and memory have sought analogues ever since.

In humans, the question becomes: Can memory improve over time in the absence of repeated testing? (We have already seen—through the phenomena of reminiscence and hypermnesia—that subjects will often be able to remember more on a later test than on an earlier test; the question with regard to spontaneous recovery is whether the increase can occur over time without intervening testing.)

The evidence on spontaneous recovery is mixed, but it does seem to occur. The necessary condition in humans is to have a large amount of interference that blocks retrieval of events. In a typical paradigm, subjects learn paired associates (A–B pairs, such as *radio–hammer*) and then later they learn other pairs (A–D, *radio–dictionary*) with the same stimuli and different responses. After the interpolated A–D learning, subjects are then given the stimulus (A, or *radio*) and asked for the response from the first list. If the test is given immediately after learning the interpolated list, subjects show great amounts of retroactive interference, and recall of B (*hammer*) is poor. If an interval elapses between the interpolated learning and the test of the first list association, however, then recall of B (*hammer*) is better (at least in some experiments). This improvement is also referred to as spontaneous recovery and seems at least analogous to the process occurring in Pavlovian conditioning. Barnes and Underwood (1959) presented evidence for such spontaneous recovery, although other researchers have had difficulty replicating the effect. In a thorough review of this literature, however, A. S. Brown (1976) concluded that the bulk of the evidence supported spontaneous recovery. In addition, Wheeler (1995) has also reliably obtained spontaneous recovery in several paradigms in a recent series of experiments. Thus, the phenomenon does seem to exist, but it remains poorly understood.

D. Retrieval of False Memories

Other chapters in this volume are concerned with effects of misleading information on memory, but here we pause to note that the act of retrieval can itself cause forgetting and false memories in several ways. The phenomenon of output interference (Tulving & Arbuckle, 1963) indicates that the process of recalling some events may interfere with recall of later events. This process has been most thoroughly studied in categorized list recall, where recall of early categories seems to inhibit recall of later categories (Roediger, 1978; see also M. C. Anderson, Bjork, & Bjork, 1994) and recall of the contents of those categories (Roediger & Schmidt, 1980).

Retrieval of events can modify memory in other ways, too. If subjects retrieve an event from memory—even if they are in error and know it at the time—then often they will falsely recollect this event as a "true" memory later on. Roediger, Wheeler, and Rajaram (1993) reported an experiment in which subjects were forced to guess items on a first test and then, unexpectedly, were tested again a week later. They discovered that subjects often falsely recalled their guesses from the first test as items actually appearing in the study list. This sort of error indicates a reality monitoring problem of the type studied by Johnson and Raye (1981). The general point of this section is that the act of retrieval does not always enhance performance (as in the testing effect discussed earlier), but may harm memory through output interference and in other ways. These harmful effects are discussed further by Anderson and Neely and by Chandler and Fisher in Chapters 8 and 14, respectively.

VII. CONCLUSION

Tulving (1974) emphasized that remembering is a product of information from two sources: encoded information or "memory traces" and retrieval information. *Product* is to be taken literally in this treatment: Relatively weak traces may be accessed by powerful retrieval cues, but with strong traces, weak cues may suffice. The study of retrieval processes cannot occur in isolation any more than can the study of memory traces. Memory traces must be actualized through retrieval, and retrieval without memory traces is confabulation.

We have argued in this chapter that consideration of two principles helps us, at our current primitive level of understanding, to organize and systematize knowledge of memory retrieval. One principle, stated in various ways by different investigators, is that performance on a retention test will benefit to the extent that the operations required by the test match those used in initial encoding or learning of the event (the encoding specificity principle, or the principle of transfer-appropriate processing). The second principle is that a cue will be effective to the extent that it is distinctive or not overloaded by numerous memories (the cue overload principle).

Acknowledgments

Preparation of this chapter was supported by Grant AF 49620-92-J-0437 from the Air Force Office of Scientific Research to Henry L. Roediger, III, and by a National Science Foundation Graduate Research Fellowship to Melissa J. Guynn. Any opinions, findings, conclusions, or recommendations expressed in this publication are those of the authors and do not necessarily reflect the views of the National Science Foundation.

We thank Mark A. McDaniel for his aid in preparing the chapter and Elizabeth Bjork, Robert Bjork, Eric Eich, Dawn Macaulay, and Endel Tulving for helpful comments.

References

Anderson, J. R. (1972). FRAN: A simulation model of free recall. In G. H. Bower (Ed.), *The psychology of learning and motivation: Advances in research and theory* (pp. 315–378). New York: Academic Press.
Anderson, M. C., Bjork, R. A., & Bjork, E. L. (1994). Remembering can cause forgetting: Exploring the retrieval dynamics of long-term memory. *Journal of Experimental Psychology: Learning, Memory, and Cognition, 20*, 1063–1087.

Ballard, P. B. (1913). Oblivescence and reminiscence. *British Journal of Psychology Monograph Supplements, 1,* 1–82.

Barclay, J. R., Bransford, J. D., Franks, J. J., McCarrell, N. S., & Nitsch, K. (1974). Comprehension and semantic flexibility. *Journal of Verbal Learning and Verbal Behavior, 13,* 471–482.

Barnes, J. M., & Underwood, B. J. (1959). "Fate" of first list associations in transfer theory. *Journal of Experimental Psychology, 58,* 97–105.

Bartlett, J. C. (1977). Effects of immediate testing on delayed retrieval: Search and recovery operations with four types of cue. *Journal of Experimental Psychology: Human Learning and Memory, 3,* 719–732.

Bilodeau, E. A., & Blick, K. A. (1965). Courses of misrecall over long-term retention intervals as related to strength of preexperimental habits of word association. *Psychological Reports, 16,*1173–1192.

Bjork, R. A. (1975). Retrieval as a memory modifier. In R. Solso (Ed.), *Information processing and cognition: The Loyola Symposium* (pp. 123–144). Hillsdale, NJ: Erlbaum.

Bjork, R. A. (1989). Retrieval inhibition as an adaptive mechanism in human memory. In H. L. Roediger & F. I. M. Craik (Eds.), *Varieties of memory and consciousness: Essays in honour of Endel Tulving* (pp. 309–330). Hillsdale, NJ: Erlbaum.

Bjork, R. A., & Richardson-Klavehn, A. (1989). On the puzzling relationship between environmental context and human memory. In C. Izawa (Ed.), *Current issues in cognitive processes: The Tulane-Floweree symposium on cognition* (pp. 313–344). Hillsdale, NJ: Erlbaum.

Blaney, P. H. (1986). Affect and memory: A review. *Psychological Bulletin, 99,* 229–246.

Blaxton, T. A. (1989). Investigating dissociations among memory measures: Support for a transfer appropriate processing framework. *Journal of Experimental Psychology: Learning, Memory, and Cognition, 15,* 657–668.

Bower, G. H. (1981). Mood and memory. *American Psychologist, 36,* 129–148.

Bransford, J. D., Franks, J. J., Morris, C. D., & Stein, B. S. (1979). Some general constraints on learning and memory research. In L. S. Cermak & F. I. M. Craik (Eds.), *Levels of processing in human memory* (pp. 331–354). Hillsdale, NJ: Erlbaum.

Brown, A. S. (1976). Spontaneous recovery in human learning. *Psychological Bulletin, 83,* 321–338.

Brown, R., & Kulik, J. (1977). Flashbulb memories. *Cognition, 5,* 73–99.

Brown, W. (1923). To what extent is memory measured by a single recall trial? *Journal of Experimental Psychology, 6,* 377–382.

Craik, F. I. M., & Lockhart, R. S. (1972). Levels of processing: A framework for memory research. *Journal of Verbal Learning and Verbal Behavior, 11,* 671–684.

Craik, F. I. M., & Tulving, E. (1975). Depth of processing and retention of words in episodic memory. *Journal of Experimental Psychology: General, 104,* 268–294.

Dywan, J., & Bowers, K. (1983). The use of hypnosis to enhance recall. *Science, 222,* 184–185.

Earhard, M. (1967). Cued recall and free recall as a function of the number of items per cue. *Journal of Verbal Learning and Verbal Behavior, 6,* 257–263.

Eich, J. E. (1980). The cue-dependent nature of state-dependent retrieval. *Memory & Cognition, 8,* 157–173.

Eich, E. (1985). Context, memory, and integrated item/context imagery. *Journal of Experimental Psychology: Learning, Memory, and Cognition, 11,* 764–770.

Eich, E. (1989). Theoretical issues in state-dependent memory. In H. L. Roediger & F. I. M. Craik (Eds.), *Varieties of memory and consciousness: Essays in honour of Endel Tulving* (pp. 331–354). Hillsdale, NJ: Erlbaum.

Eich, E., Macaulay, D., & Ryan, L. (1994). Mood dependent memory for events of the personal past. *Journal of Experimental Psychology: General, 123,* 201–215.

Eich, E., & Metcalfe, J. (1989). Mood dependent memory for internal versus external events. *Journal of Experimental Psychology: Learning, Memory, and Cognition, 15,* 443–455.

Eich, J. E., Weingartner, H., Stillman, R. C., & Gillin, J. C. (1975). State dependent accessibility of retrieval cues in the retention of a categorized list. *Journal of Verbal Learning and Verbal Behavior, 14,* 408–417.

Engelkamp, J., Zimmer, H. D., Mohr, G., & Sellen, O. (1994). Memory of self-performed tasks: Self-performing during recognition. *Memory & Cognition, 22,* 34–39.

Erdelyi, M. H. (1984). The recovery of unconscious (inaccessible) memories: Laboratory studies of hypermnesia. In G. H. Bower (Ed.), *The psychology of learning and motivation: Advances in research and theory* (Vol. 18, pp. 95–127). New York: Academic Press.

Erdelyi, M. H., & Becker, J. (1974). Hypermnesia for pictures: Incremental memory for pictures but not for words in multiple recall trials. *Cognitive Psychology, 6,* 159–171.

Erdelyi, M. H., & Goldberg, B. (1979). Let's not sweep repression under the rug: Toward a cognitive psychology of repression. In J. F. Kihlstrom & F. J. Evans (Eds.), *Functional disorders of memory* (pp. 355–402). Hillsdale, NJ: Erlbaum.

Estes, W. K. (1955). Statistical theory of spontaneous recovery and regression. *Psychological Review, 62,* 145–154.

Fernandez, A., & Glenberg, A. M. (1985). Changing environmental context does not reliably affect memory. *Memory & Cognition, 13,* 333–345.

Fisher, R. P., & Craik, F. I. M. (1977). Interaction between encoding and retrieval operations in cued recall. *Journal of Experimental Psychology: Human Learning and Memory, 3,* 701–711.

Freud, S. (1957). The history of the psychoanalytic movement. In J. Strachey (Ed.), *The standard edition of the complete psychological works of Sigmund Freud* (Vol. 14). London: Hogarth Press. (Originally published 1914)

Geiselman, R. E., Bjork, R. A., & Fishman, D. L. (1983). Disrupted retrieval in directed forgetting: A link with posthypnotic amnesia. *Journal of Experimental Psychology: General, 112,* 58–72.

Geiselman, R. E., Fisher, R. P., MacKinnon, D. P., & Holland, H. L. (1985). Eyewitness memory enhancement in the police interview: Cognitive retrieval mnemonics versus hypnosis. *Journal of Applied Psychology, 70,* 401–412.

Glisky, E. L., & Rabinowitz, J. (1985). Enhancing the generation effect through repetition of operations. *Journal of Experimental Psychology: Learning, Memory, and Cognition, 11,* 193–205.

Glover, J. A. (1989). The "testing" phenomenon: Not gone but nearly forgotten. *Journal of Educational Psychology, 81,* 392–399.

Godden, D. R., & Baddeley, A. D. (1975). Context-dependent memory in two natural environments: On land and underwater. *British Journal of Psychology, 66,* 325–331.

Guynn, M. J., & Roediger, H. L. (1995). The impact of distinctive events on implicit and explicit tests of memory. *Psychological Research, 57,* 192–202.

Hilgard, E. R., & Bower, G. H. (1975). *Theories of learning.* Englewood Cliffs, NJ: Prentice-Hall.

Hogan, R. M., & Kintsch, W. (1971). Differential effects of study and test trials on long-term recognition and recall. *Journal of Verbal Learning and Verbal Behavior, 10,* 562–567.

Hunt, R. R., & Einstein, G. O. (1981). Relational and item-specific information in memory. *Journal of Verbal Learning and Verbal Behavior, 20,* 497–514.

Hunt, R. R., & McDaniel, M. A. (1993). The enigma of organization and distinctiveness. *Journal of Memory and Language, 32,* 421–445.

Jacoby, L. L. (1978). On interpreting the effects of repetition: Solving a problem versus remembering a solution. *Journal of Verbal Learning and Verbal Behavior, 17,* 649–667.

Jacoby, L. L. (1991). A process dissociation framework: Separating automatic from intentional uses of memory. *Journal of Memory and Language, 30,* 513–541.

Johnson, M. K., & Raye, C. L. (1981). Reality monitoring. *Psychological Review, 88,* 67–85.

Jones, T. C., & Roediger, H. L. (1995). The experiential basis of serial position effects. *European Journal of Cognitive Psychology, 7,* 65–80.

Köhler, W. (1947). *Gestalt psychology.* New York: Liverwright.

Kolers, P. A. (1979). A pattern-analyzing basis of recognition. In L. S. Cermak & F. I. M. Craik (Eds.), *Levels of processing in human memory* (pp. 363–384). Hillsdale, NJ: Erlbaum.

Kolers, P. A., & Roediger, H. L. (1984). Procedures of mind. *Journal of Verbal Learning and Verbal Behavior, 23,* 425–449.

Landauer, T. K., & Bjork, R. A. (1978). Optimum rehearsal patterns and name learning. In M. M. Gruneberg, P. E. Morris, & R. N. Sykes (Eds.), *Practical aspects of memory* (pp. 625–632). London: Academic Press.

Lockhart, R. S. (1975). The facilitation of recognition by recall. *Journal of Verbal Learning and Verbal Behavior, 14,* 253–258.

Loftus, E. F. (1993). The reality of repressed memories. *American Psychologist, 48,* 518–537.

Loftus, E. F., & Loftus, G. R. (1980). On the permanence of information stored in the human brain. *American Psychologist, 35,* 409–420.

Mandler, G. (1967). Organization and memory. In K. W. Spence & J. T. Spence (Eds.), *The psychology of learning and motivation* (pp. 327–372). New York: Academic Press.

Mandler, G. (1980). Recognizing: The judgment of previous occurrence. *Psychological Review, 87,* 252–271.

Mäntylä, T. (1986). Optimizing cue effectiveness: Recall of 500 and 600 incidentally learned words. *Journal of Experimental Psychology: Learning, Memory, and Cognition, 12,* 66–71.

McDaniel, M. A., Anderson, D. C., Einstein, G. O., & O'Halloran, C. M. (1989). Modulation of environmental reinstatement effects through encoding strategies. *American Journal of Psychology, 102,* 523–548.

McDaniel, M. A., & Fisher, R. P. (1991). Tests and test feedback as learning sources. *Contemporary Educational Psychology, 16,* 192–201.

McDaniel, M. A., Friedman, A., & Bourne, L. E. (1978). Remembering the levels of information in words. *Memory & Cognition, 6,* 156–164.

McDaniel, M. A., Kowitz, M. D., & Dunay, P. K. (1989). Altering memory through recall: The effects of cue-guided retrieval processing. *Memory & Cognition, 17,* 423–434.

McDaniel, M. A., & Masson, M. E. (1985). Altering memory representations through retrieval. *Journal of Experimental Psychology: Learning, Memory, and Cognition, 11,* 371–385.

McGeoch, J. A. (1932). Forgetting and the law of disuse. *Psychological Review, 39,* 352–370.

Melton, A. W. (1963). Implications of short-term memory for a general theory of memory. *Journal of Verbal Learning and Verbal Behavior, 2,* 1–21.

Mensink, G. J., & Raaijmakers, J. G. W. (1988). A model for interference and forgetting. *Psychological Review, 95,* 434–455.

Morris, C. D., Bransford, J. D., & Franks, J. J. (1977). Levels of processing versus transfer appropriate processing. *Journal of Verbal Learning and Verbal Behavior, 16,* 519–533.

Murdock, B. B. (1989). The past, the present, and the future: Comments on section 1. In H. L. Roediger & F. I. M. Craik (Eds.), *Varieties of memory and consciousness: Essays in honour of Endel Tulving* (pp. 93–98). Hillsdale, NJ: Erlbaum.

Newman, S. E., & Frith, U. (1977). Encoding specificity vs. associative continuity. *Bulletin of the Psychonomic Society, 10,* 73–75.

Nogrady, H., McConkey, K. M., & Perry, C. (1985). Enhancing visual memory: Trying hypnosis, trying imagination, and trying again. *Journal of Abnormal Psychology, 94,* 195–204.

Pan, S. (1926). The influence of context upon learning and recall. *Journal of Experimental Psychology, 9,* 468–491.

Pavlov, I. P. (1927). *Conditioned reflexes* (G. V. Anrep, Trans.). London: Oxford University Press.

Payne, D. G. (1987). Hypermnesia and reminiscence in recall: A historical and empirical review. *Psychological Bulletin, 101,* 5–27.

Pollack, I., Norman, D. A., & Galanter, E. (1964). An efficient nonparametric analysis of recognition memory. *Psychonomic Science, 1,* 327–328.

Roediger, H. L. (1973). Inhibition in recall from cueing with recall targets. *Journal of Verbal Learning and Verbal Behavior, 12,* 644–657.

Roediger, H. L. (1978). Recall as a self-limiting process. *Memory & Cognition, 6,* 54–63.

Roediger, H. L. (1990). Implicit memory: Retention without remembering. *American Psychologist, 45,* 1043–1056.

Roediger, H. L., & Adelson, B. (1980). Semantic specificity in cued recall. *Memory & Cognition, 8,* 65–74.

Roediger, H. L., & Challis, B. H. (1989). Hypermnesia: Improvements in recall with repeated testing. In C. Izawa (Ed.), *Current issues in cognitive processes: The Tulane–Floweree symposium on cognition* (pp. 175–199). Hillsdale, NJ: Erlbaum.

Roediger, H. L., & Payne, D. G. (1983). Superiority of free recall to cued recall with "strong" cues. *Psychological Research, 45,* 275–286.

Roediger, H. L., & Schmidt, S. R. (1980). Output interference in the recall of categorized and paired associate lists. *Journal of Experimental Psychology: Human Learning and Memory, 6,* 91–105.

Roediger, H. L., & Thorpe, L. A. (1978). The role of recall time in producing hypermnesia. *Memory & Cognition, 6,* 296–305.

Roediger, H. L., Wheeler, M. A., & Rajaram, S. (1993). Remembering, knowing and reconstructing the past. In D. L. Medin (Ed.), *The psychology of learning and motivation: Advances in research and theory* (Vol. 30, pp. 97–134). New York: Academic Press.

Runquist, W. N. (1986). The effect of testing on the forgetting of related and unrelated associates. *Canadian Journal of Psychology, 40,* 65–76.

Saufley, W. H., Otaka, S. R., & Bavaresco, J. L. (1985). Context effects: Classroom tests and context independence. *Memory & Cognition, 13,* 522–528.

Schab, F. R. (1990). Odors and the remembrance of things past. *Journal of Experimental Psychology: Learning, Memory, and Cognition, 16,* 648–655.

Schacter, D. L. (1982). *Stranger behind the engram.* Hillsdale, NJ: Erlbaum.

Schacter, D. L., Eich, J. E., & Tulving, E. (1978). Richard Semon's theory of memory. *Journal of Verbal Learning and Verbal Behavior, 17,* 721–744.

Semon, R. (1921). *The mneme.* London: Allen & Unwin.

Slamecka, N. J., & Graf, P. (1978). The generation effect: Delineation of a phenomenon. *Journal of Experimental Psychology: Human Learning and Memory, 4,* 592–604.

Smith, M. C. (1983). Hypnotic memory enhancement of eyewitnesses: Does it work? *Psychological Bulletin, 94,* 387–407.

Smith, S. M. (1979). Remembering in and out of context. *Journal of Experimental Psychology: Human Learning and Memory, 5,* 460–471.

Smith, S. M. (1988). Environmental context-dependent memory. In G. M. Davies & D. M. Thomson (Eds.), *Memory in context: Context in memory* (pp. 13–34). Chichester, England: Wiley.

Smith, S. M., Glenberg, A. M., & Bjork, R. A. (1978). Environmental context and human memory. *Memory & Cognition, 6,* 342–353.

Spitzer, H. F. (1939). Studies in retention. *Journal of Educational Psychology, 30,* 641–656.

Stein, B. S. (1978). Depth of processing reexamined: The effects of precision of encoding and test appropriateness. *Journal of Verbal Learning and Verbal Behavior, 17,* 165–174.

Thompson, C. P., Wenger, S. K., & Bartling, C. A. (1978). How recall facilitates subsequent recall: À reappraisal. *Journal of Experimental Psychology: Human Learning and Memory, 4,* 210–221.

Thomson, D. M., & Tulving, E. (1970). Associative encoding and retrieval: Weak and strong cues. *Journal of Experimental Psychology, 86,* 255–262.

Tulving, E. (1967). The effects of presentation and recall in free recall learning. *Journal of Verbal Learning and Verbal Behavior, 6,* 175–184.

Tulving, E. (1968). Theoretical issues in free recall. In T. R. Dixon & D. L. Horton (Eds.), *Verbal behavior and general behavior theory* (pp. 2–36). Englewood Cliffs, NJ: Prentice-Hall.

Tulving, E. (1969). Retrograde amnesia in free recall. *Science, 164,* 88–90.

Tulving, E. (1974). Cue-dependent forgetting. *American Scientist, 62,* 74–82.

Tulving, E. (1983). *Elements of episodic memory.* New York: Oxford University Press.

Tulving, E. (1991). Interview. *Journal of Cognitive Neuroscience, 3,* 89–94.

Tulving, E., & Arbuckle, T. Y. (1963). Sources of intratrial interference in paired-associate learning. *Journal of Verbal Learning and Verbal Behavior, 1,* 321–334.

Tulving, E., & Osler, S. (1968). Effectiveness of retrieval cues in memory for words. *Journal of Experimental Psychology, 77,* 593–601.

Tulving, E., & Pearlstone, Z. (1966). Availability versus accessibility of information in memory for words. *Journal of Verbal Learning and Verbal Behavior, 5,* 381–391.

Tulving, E., & Thomson, D. (1973). Encoding specificity and retrieval processes in episodic memory. *Psychological Review, 80,* 352–373.

von Restorff, H. (1933). Uber die Virkung von Bereichsbildungen im Spurenfeld. *Psychologie Forschung, 18,* 299–342.

Wallace, W. P. (1965). Review of the historical, empirical, and theoretical status of the von Restorff phenomenon. *Psychological Bulletin, 63,* 410–424.

Watkins, M. J. (1979). Engrams as cuegrams and forgetting as cue overload: A cueing approach to the structure of memory. In C. R. Puff (Ed.), *Memory organization and structure* (pp. 347–372). New York: Academic Press.

Watkins, M. J., & Gardiner, J. M. (1982). Cued recall. In C. R. Puff (Ed.), *Handbook of research methods in human memory and cognition* (pp. 173–195). New York: Academic Press.

Watkins, O. C., & Watkins, M. J. (1975). Buildup of proactive inhibition as a cue-overload effect. *Journal of Experimental Psychology: Human Learning and Memory, 104,* 442–452.

Waugh, N. C., & Norman, D. A. (1965). Primary memory. *Psychological Review, 72,* 89–104.

Weiner, B. (1966). Effects of motivation on the availability and retrieval of memory traces. *Psychological Bulletin, 65,* 24–37.

Wheeler, M. A. (1995). Improvement in recall without repeated testing: Spontaneous recovery revisited. *Journal of Experimental Psychology: Learning, Memory, and Cognition, 21,* 173–184.

Wheeler, M. A., & Roediger, H. L. (1992). Disparate effects of repeated testing: Reconciling Ballard's (1913) and Bartlett's (1932) results. *Psychological Science, 3,* 240–245.

Wixted, J. T., & Rohrer, D. (1994). Analyzing the dynamics of free recall: An integrative review of the empirical literature. *Psychonomic Bulletin & Review, 1,* 89–106.

CHAPTER 8

Interference and Inhibition in Memory Retrieval

Michael C. Anderson
James H. Neely

I. INTRODUCTION

In memory research, interference refers to the impaired ability to remember an item when it is similar to other items stored in memory. Consider, for example, the deceptively simple task of recalling where you parked your car at a local shopping center. If you have never before been to that shopping center, recalling your car's location may be fairly easy. If you park there frequently, however, you may find yourself reunited with the spot where you parked yesterday or, if you are like the present authors, standing befuddled at the lot's edge. Further, if asked where you parked on previous visits, you would almost certainly fail to recall the locations, as though your intervening parking experiences had overwritten those aspects of your past. These examples illustrate typical cases of retrieval failure arising from interference. Understanding the causes of such interference has been a central goal of research on forgetting since the inception of experimental psychology.

Research on interference has generated a variety of conceptions of how forgetting occurs. This variety may be illustrated intuitively in terms of our previous parking situation. For example, sometimes our ability to recall our current parking location seems blocked by the intrusion of similar episodes. When this occurs, we often feel confident that we know where we parked, but that recall of the location demands that we penetrate through memories that get in the way. On other occasions, particularly when retrieving older parking episodes, we feel less confident that we retained the information, as though subsequent episodes disrupted or overwrote prior experience. Additional possibilities are suggested by different examples. For instance, we often experience difficulty recalling our new telephone number after a recent change in residence, because our old number keeps coming to mind, disrupting recall of the new one. With time, however, we typically suppress the outdated number. In terms of our earlier parking example, this intuition suggests that ensuring the recallability of today's parking spot involves the suppression of earlier parking memories in that same lot. Each of these intuitions has motivated theorizing at some point in the history of interference research.

The present chapter reviews what experimental research has revealed about the causes of memory interference and the breadth of situations in which these mechanisms operate. We describe this research in four main sections. First, we discuss some widely held assumptions about the situation of interference, focusing on the idea that such effects arise from competition for access via a shared retrieval cue. This notion is sufficiently general that it may be applied in a variety of interference settings, which we illustrate briefly. Having introduced these basic assumptions, we review the classical interference paradigms from which these ideas emerged, as well as the variety of particular conceptions of forgetting developed in the context of these procedures. Many of these ideas remain relevant today, influencing how we conceive interference in modern terms. In the next section, we move outside of the classical arena to review more recent phenomena that both support and challenge classical conceptions of interference. These phenomena provide compelling illustrations of the generality of interference and, consequently, of the importance of our understanding its mechanisms. We close by highlighting a recent perspective on interference that builds upon insights from modern work, while validating intuitions underlying several of the classical interference mechanisms. According to this new perspective, forgetting derives not from acquiring new memories per se, but from the impact of later retrievals of the newly learned material. After discussing findings from several paradigms that support this retrieval-based view, we illustrate how forgetting might be linked to inhibitory processes underlying selective attention.

II. BASIC ASSUMPTIONS OF INTERFERENCE RESEARCH

Most approaches to interference share basic assumptions about the representations and retrieval processes at work in interference situations. For example, many approaches characterize retrieval as a progression from one or more retrieval cues to items stored in memory by way of associative links. Retrieval cues can be anything from components of the desired memory to incidental concepts associated with that item during its encoding. Thus, recalling where we parked our car might involve the activation of many concepts, including features of the car, the act of parking, the layout of the lot, or the time of day, any of which might reasonably have been encoded when we parked. The success of this progression from cues to the target memory hinges on many factors, including the number of cues used and the strengths of the associations linking cues to the memory items, both of which are influenced by the amount and character of attention paid during encoding. Under normal circumstances, retrieving a target item is thought to occur when the cues available at the time of recall are sufficiently related to that target to identify it uniquely in memory.

By the foregoing analysis, the essential problem in interference is that the retrieval cues available at the time of recall fail to access the target memory. Why might such failures occur? Figure 1 illustrates one general approach to this question. In this approach, interference arises when the retrieval cue normally used to access a target (Figure 1A) becomes associated to additional memory items (Figure 1B). Successfully progressing from a retrieval cue to a target memory thus depends not only on how strongly that cue is related to the target, but also on whether the cue is related to other items in memory as well. When a cue is linked to more than one item in memory, those items are assumed to compete with the target for access to conscious awareness—what M. C. Anderson, Bjork, and Bjork (1994) have referred to as the *competition assumption*. In the present chapter, we refer to any negative effect on memory performance associated with this competition as *interference*. Interference owing to the mechanisms of competition is generally thought to increase with the number of competitors, a notion supported by the observed tendency for recall performance to decrease with the number of items that are paired with the same cue. This generalization has come to be known as the *cue-overload principle* (see, e.g., Watkins, 1978).

How might the notion of competition among items associated to the same retrieval cue capture interference arising from the acquisition of new memories similar to those already stored? The basic approach to this question can be illustrated in terms of our previous parking example. During your visit to the shopping center, you encoded aspects of your parking experience into a mental representation of that event. Other parking experiences that are similar to this visit will also contain characteristics that are stored in the target event, including, for instance, the fact that you drove the car, the type of car you drove (e.g., a 1989 blue Honda), and perhaps your goal of doing shopping at the supermarket. If components of the target event (e.g., your concepts of yourself, parking, and your Honda) serve as the primary retrieval cues by which you access your car's location, other memories sharing those features will also be evoked during retrieval. Figure

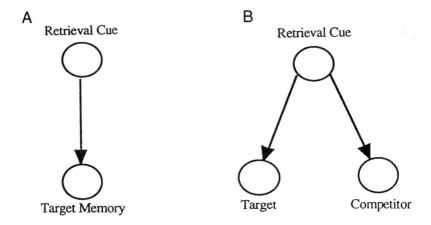

A Retrieval Cue

Target Memory

B Retrieval Cue

Target   Competitor

C Retrieval Cues

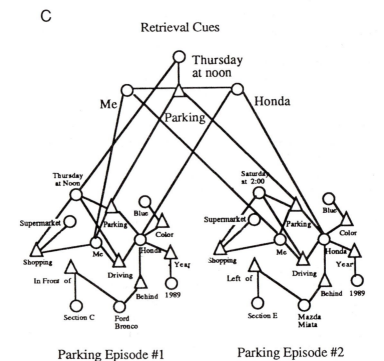

Thursday at noon

Me   Honda

Parking

Thursday at Noon

Supermarket   Parking   Blue
                          Color
Shopping   Me   Honda
In Front of   Driving   Year
              Behind 1989
Section C   Ford
             Bronco

Saturday at 2:00

Supermarket   Parking   Blue
                          Color
Shopping   Me   Honda
Left of   Driving   Year
              Behind 1989
Section E   Mazda
             Miata

Parking Episode #1   Parking Episode #2

FIGURE 1 Illustration of the notion of competition among items sharing the same retrieval cue. (A) A retrieval cue that is associated to only one target item in memory. (B) The basic situation of interference, in which a retrieval cue becomes associated to one or more additional competitors that impede recall of the target, given presentation of the shared retrieval cue. (C) How the basic situation of interference illustrated in (B) may be applied to understand a more complex example of interference in which two episodes of having parked at the supermarket interfere because they share the retrieval cues "Me," "Honda," and "Parking" at the time of retrieval. Circles and triangles in the representations of Episodes 1 and 2 in (C) depict concepts and relations, respectively.

1C illustrates this point by showing how the general logic advanced in the case of one cue (Figure 1B) may be scaled up to the many cues available in the more naturalistic example of remembering where one parked (e.g., "Me," "Parking," and "Honda"). If retrieval cues become less effective as they acquire new associations, then similar memories should compete with one another to the extent that the sets of cues useful in accessing those memories overlap. Thus, competition among items that share the same retrieval cues provides a useful way of viewing the problem of interference, even for complex episodes.

The notion of competition among items that share retrieval cues is even more general than the previous example. For instance, items in memory need not be episodes to compete with one another. Consider the task of retrieving, from general knowledge, the particular exemplar *banana* given the cue *fruit*. This simple retrieval should be impeded by competition from other fruits that one might know, such as *orange* and *lemon*. Furthermore, items need not be semantically similar to compete, provided that they share a common cue. For instance, competition might ensue among items grouped by mere co-occurrence in time, as in the problem of recollecting, from the morning conversation with one's spouse, the items one is supposed to buy at the market. Although the items to be remembered may be quite dissimilar, they might compete with one another if the memory for the morning episode serves as the primary cue. A recurring theme of this chapter is the far-ranging generality of retrieval competition as a mechanism for interference.

III. CLASSICAL APPROACHES TO INTERFERENCE

Much of modern thinking about the causes of interference has been shaped by the substantial body of research completed during what has come to be known as the "classical interference era" (approximately 1900–1970). Indeed, the basic insight that interference arises from the competition of memory items for a shared retrieval cue originated early in this period (McGeoch, 1936, 1942). In this section, we review the basic paradigms of classical interference research because these paradigms provide a clear specification of the conditions of interference. We then discuss the wealth of findings and theoretical concepts emerging from these paradigms. These ideas remain relevant to contemporary theorizing and to our intuitions about the causes of forgetting. (The reader is referred to Postman, 1971; Postman & Underwood, 1973; Crowder, 1976, for more detailed reviews of the classical interference literature.)

A. Methodology of Classical Interference Research

If interference arises from competition for a shared retrieval cue, an experimental paradigm for studying this phenomenon should allow control over three things: (1) the cues to which people associate target memories; (2) the cues by which people retrieve the target at the time of test; and (3) the relations of those cues and targets to other items in memory. Control over these factors has been achieved in the classical paired-associate paradigm. We now describe this paradigm and the basic methodologies and designs of classical interference experiments.

1. The Paired-Associate Paradigm

According to the classical interference perspective, the participant's task in the paired-associate paradigm (and in learning more generally) is to acquire memory *responses* to verbal *stimuli*. In this paradigm, a person studies unrelated pairs of verbal items (typically words), one pair at a time, for a later memory test. For example, people might be shown the pair *dog–rock* and be instructed to study this pair so that when the stimulus term *dog* is later provided as a cue, it can elicit the relevant response term, *rock*. Typically, repeated study–test trials would be given until participants achieved a certain criterion level of learning on these responses (a practice not generally observed in modern research using paired associates). Learning paired associates in this fashion is typically thought to induce the encoding of various associations between the verbal items, including forward associations linking stimuli to responses (i.e., the association linking *dog* to *rock*), backward associations linking the responses back to their stimuli (i.e., the association linking *rock* to *dog*), and contextual associations linking each item to the general representation of the list context. Most of our discussion focuses on forward associations, although other kinds of associations are considered when relevant.

Interference is studied in the paired-associate paradigm by having people learn a first list of critical target pairs (e.g., *dog–rock*) and then a second list of pairs that bear any one of a number of different relations to the critical target pairs, with the aim of examining the effect of such new learning on recall performance for the initial target item (e.g., *rock*). The relation between the new paired associates and those previously learned are described in a standard notation in which a cue–target pair from the first list (e.g., *dog–rock*) is designated as an A–B item, with the first letter of this notation referring to the stimulus term and the second letter to the response. Following this notation, the items on the second list can be related to those on the first list in a variety of ways, four of which are illustrated in Figure 2A. Note that all four groups of participants depicted in this example study the same initial A–B list (List 1), but the content of the second list they study (List 2) varies. In the A–B, A–B paradigm (the leftmost group), the pairs on the second list (A–B) share both the stimulus and the response terms of the first-list (A–B) pairs (e.g., *dog–rock*) and are thus merely repetitions of those

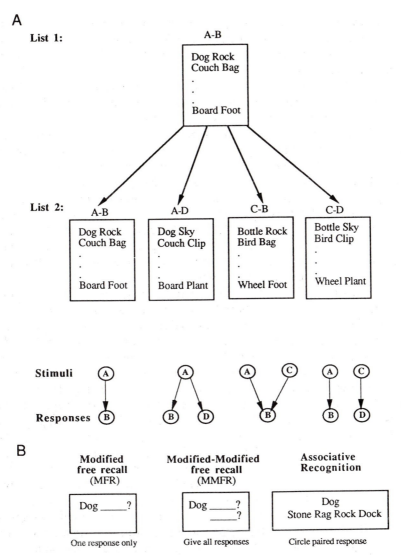

FIGURE 2   Classical interference methodology. (A) The four most common interference designs used in classical interference research, in which an initial A–B list (List 1) is followed by another list (List 2) that presents either A–B, A–D, C–B, or C–D associates (see text for elaboration). The boxes in this figure do not imply that items were presented together on a page; they denote only that the items appeared on the same list of individually presented associates. The stimulus–response relations resulting from such consecutive presentations are depicted schematically below each condition, with the forward associations between the various retrieval cues and memory responses represented. (B) Three common testing procedures employed in paired-associate research.

pairs; in the A–B, A–D paradigm, the second-list (A–D) pairs share the stimuli of the first-list (A–B) pairs but differ in their responses (e.g., *dog–sky*); in the A–B, C–B paradigm, the second list (C–B) pairs share the response terms of the first-list (A–B) pairs, but differ in their stimuli (e.g., *bottle–rock*); finally, in the A–B, C–D paradigm, the second-list (C–D) pairs share neither the stimuli nor the response terms with the first-list (A–B) pairs (e.g., *bottle–sky*). These critical relationships between the first-list and second-list associates are depicted schematically in Figure 2A, immediately beneath the groups studying those relationships. (Note that only forward associations are depicted.) Other relationships may also be constructed by manipulating stimulus or response similarity, introducing additional stimuli or responses, and re-pairing the same stimuli and responses in different ways (Postman, 1971). For present purposes, the most important relationship is found in the A–B, A–D design. This design represents the classical situation of interference in which memory targets (B and D) share a retrieval cue (A) that induces competition when presented as the cue on later tests (i.e., *rock* and *sky* should compete when *dog* is presented).

After two lists of paired associates have been studied, memory for the target responses from one or both lists can be assessed in a variety of ways. Several of the most typical testing procedures are depicted in Figure 2B. The leftmost diagram in Figure 2B depicts the test, used in many studies conducted prior to 1959, in which the experimenter provided the stimulus for each pair and asked the subject to retrieve the first response that came to mind—a procedure called *modified free recall* (Underwood, 1948; hereafter, MFR). This procedure was a change from earlier recall tests in which participants were *directed* to retrieve one response from a particular list (e.g., List 1). To the right of the MFR procedure is depicted the test used in most studies conducted after 1959—the *modified modified free-recall* (hereafter, MMFR) procedure (Barnes & Underwood, 1959)—in which the experimenter asked for all responses associated with the stimulus and allowed participants as much time to recall as needed. Finally, the experimenter can also test a person's ability to recognize having seen a particular target response paired with a stimulus by providing the stimulus and a set of items, including the response, and asking the person to match the appropriate response paired with that stimulus (illustrated in the rightmost diagram). Although such associative recognition tests were explored late in the history of interference research, they have proven important as a means of discriminating among various theories of interference. Performance on all of these tests can be assessed by a number of dependent measures, but here we focus on the percentage of requested responses that are correctly recalled or recognized. (See Postman, 1971, for a discussion of other measures such as relative recall.)

2. Interference Designs

The paired-associate methodology just described can be used in numerous ways to study interference phenomena. Here, we describe the designs used to examine two of the most important and widely studied phenomena in classical interference research: retroactive interference and proactive interference. Findings from these paradigms have proven informative with respect to the mechanisms of forgetting.

a. Retroactive Interference

Retroactive interference refers to impaired memory performance on target items caused by learning new material between the initial encoding of those target items and their final test. For example, we suffer retroactive interference when we can no longer recollect where we parked last week because we have parked in the same lot on several subsequent occasions. This crucial phenomenon was the primary focus of classical interference theory for over six decades and was primarily studied using the classic retroactive interference design (G. E. Mueller & Pilzecker, 1900) illustrated in Figure 3A. In the experimental condition (left side of 3A), people study a first list of paired associates (upper box) and then a second list, the pairs of which may be

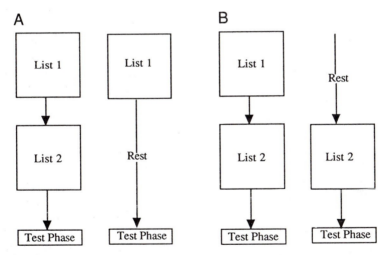

FIGURE 3   The generic procedure for the classical retroactive (A) and proactive (B) interference designs. The left portion of each panel depicts the experimental group, which always receives two lists of items, and is tested either on the first list (A) or on the second list (B). The right portion of each panel depicts the control group, which only receives one list, either at the same point as List 1 in the case of retroactive interference designs, or at the same point as List 2 for proactive interference designs. As noted in both panels, control participants rest (or perform irrelevant activity) in place of receiving an additional list.

related to first-list items in any of the ways discussed in our previous section on paired associate methodology (note that this procedure can also be used with stimuli other than paired associates). Following these two lists, people are tested with either an MFR, MMFR, or recognition test for the List 1 A–B responses. In the control condition, people also study a first list of responses, but either rest or engage in irrelevant activity during the interval in which people in the experimental condition study List 2. Thus, these conditions allow us to ask the crucial question "What is the effect of learning new information (i.e., List 2) on the ability to remember information that was previously studied (i.e., List 1), relative to a situation in which no additional information was learned at all (i.e., Control List 1)?"

A great number of studies using this paradigm have consistently demonstrated that memory performance on first-list A–B items suffers greatly when a second list of responses must be learned. The magnitude of this retroactive interference effect varies dramatically as a function of the stimulus conditions and the method of testing, with the greatest forgetting of A–B items found in the A–B, A–D paradigm with MFR tests. This generalization reinforces the notion that interference effects reflect competition among items sharing the same retrieval cue. However, some interference is often observed in the A–B, C–D procedure, as well (McGovern, 1964), although in dramatically reduced amounts. Interestingly, even when severe deficits in recall are demonstrated, our ability to recognize the older information often remains intact: recognition tests often show little or no retroactive interference in the A–B, A–D paradigm relative to the A–B, C–D paradigm (Postman & Stark, 1969). This finding suggests that recognition tests eliminate or greatly reduce the retrieval competition that occurs in the MFR and MMFR tests.

b. Proactive Interference

Proactive interference refers to previously learned materials hurting our memory for more recently learned items. For example, we suffer proactive interference when we fail to recall our new phone number momentarily because our old number intrudes during the recall process. Figure 3B depicts the design that allows us to examine proactive interference. The proactive interference paradigm resembles the retroactive interference design except that (1) it tests people's memory for the List 2 responses rather than the List 1 responses, and (2) in the control condition, the rest (or performance of irrelevant activity) replaces List 1 learning rather than List 2 learning. Thus, this design allows us to explore how previously acquired knowledge (i.e., List 1) might impair our ability to recollect new information (i.e., List 2), relative to a situation in which the previous knowledge had not been learned (Control, List 2).

Many studies using the proactive interference procedure have demonstrated that people are more likely to forget items from a list when a prior list has been studied. The magnitude of this proactive interference effect varies as a function of the stimulus structure and test conditions in the same way that retroactive interference does, with proactive interference being most severe when lists share retrieval cues. Furthermore, the effect of proactive interference is far more severe when recall is tested rather than recognition. In addition, the relative magnitudes of proactive and retroactive interference effects vary in interesting ways as the retention interval between List 2 and the final memory test increases. Whereas retroactive interference is more pronounced at short retention intervals, proactive interference dominates at longer delays (Postman, Stark, & Fraser, 1968), a finding that has proven important in arguments about the mechanisms of interference.

B. Classical Conceptions of Interference

The insight that interference might result from the competition of memories sharing the same cue provides only a starting point for understanding the causes of forgetting. Why might associating many memories to the same cue hinder our ability to recall items that were once accessible? As we noted in the introduction to this chapter, a variety of answers to this puzzle have been explored. We now review some of these ideas, highlighting both their classical origins and modern incarnations. This review is organized according to a general tripartite division of theories, within which retrieval failures are attributed to one of three components of the memory representations: (1) the retrieval routes (associations) linking cues to target memories; (2) the retrieval cues used to access targets; and (3) the activation levels in the memory targets themselves. (For a more detailed discussion of these and other theories, see M. C. Anderson & Bjork, 1994.) For the remainder of the present chapter, the more current terms *cue* and *target* are used synonymously with the classical terms stimulus and response, respectively.

1. Ineffective Retrieval Routes

Sometimes we discover that an item that we failed to recall on an earlier occasion was in memory all along. These failures to retrieve available information even occur when we use familiar methods to retrieve the information. For example, looking at the dial of a gym locker combination lock may fail to elicit the desired combination, no matter how many times one has opened the lock in the past, and no matter how intently one stares. In such cases, retrieval failure might derive from some breakdown in the retrieval method by which we normally access the desired information. In the aforementioned tripartite approach to interference, these intuitions suggest that the association between the cue and the target memory is degraded. This general approach is the oldest and most popular means of explaining forgetting. Theories that explain interference in terms of ineffective associations may be categorized in at least two different classes: occlusion and unlearning.

a. Occlusion

Failures to retrieve an item are sometimes accompanied by persistently intrusive memories that are similar to the target item. These situations are characterized by a distinctive feeling: Intrusive memories seem to get in the way or occlude the target item, and we feel confident that if we could only get past the intruding memory, we would access the target. The clearest examples of this experience occur during the tip-of-the-tongue state, in which our ability to name a particular person, place, or object seems thwarted by a persistently intrusive word. Such persistent alternates are typically similar to the target item on both semantic and linguistic dimensions, such as the competing words' lengths and initial sounds (R. Brown & McNeill, 1966; see A. S. Brown, 1991 for a review). The existence of situations analogous to occlusion in nonlanguage contexts—as when we sometimes visit yesterday's parking spot rather than today's—suggests that occlusion may cause interference more generally.

To understand how similar memories might occlude target retrieval, consider how such blocking might impair the recall of B items (i.e., produce retroactive interference) in the A–B, A–D paradigm. In this paradigm, presentation of the A cue should induce B and D to compete for access to conscious awareness, with the induced competition being greater the more strongly D is associated to A. When the D item is sufficiently strong, it may win this competition, displacing the retrieval of the B target item. Note that this view need not assume that anything has happened to the target memory B itself or to its association to the cue A. Rather, the *effectiveness* of the association linking A to B is presumed to decrease as the associations for competitors become more effective, inducing greater competition during retrieval. The notion that the amount of interference exerted by an item increases with its memory strength—which M. C. Anderson et al. (1994) have called the *strength-dependence assumption*—forms the cornerstone of classical and modern approaches to explaining interference phenomena (Gillund & Shiffrin, 1984; McGeoch, 1942; Mensink & Raaijmakers, 1988; Raaijmakers & Shiffrin, 1981).

The notion that competition is strength dependent—indeed, the more basic notion of competition for a shared retrieval cue itself—originates from McGeoch's (1942) classical analysis of the conditions of interference. According to McGeoch, interference is most strongly instantiated in the A–B, A–D paradigm, because in this paradigm people must acquire mutually incompatible responses to a common retrieval cue. Responses thus related were assumed to impede each other's accessibility in a process that McGeoch called *response competition*. For example, when people were provided with an A stimulus in a List 1 recall test, both the B and D responses were assumed to compete with one another until one response attained momentary dominance and was reported. Because a List 1 recall test (and the subsequent MFR test) requested only one response for each cue, the ultimate resolution of this competition precluded participants from reporting the competing item. McGeoch assumed that the magnitude of this memory impairment or *reproductive inhibition* on a target response varied as a function of its competitor's strength of association to the shared cue. Thus, McGeoch's proposal was an early (perhaps the first) instance of an occlusion theory. (For clarity, in the remainder of the present chapter, we use the term response competition when referring to the general proposal that items sharing a cue compete, and occlusion when referring to models in which this competition is strength dependent and causes forgetting. Historically, however, McGeoch's theory of forgetting has been called the response-competition theory.) In support of these ideas regarding strength–dependent competition, McGeoch cited the tendency for the D responses to intrude on final memory tests for the B targets, and for retroactive interference to increase as competition from the D response was increased through greater amounts of A–D learning (but see the discussion of Melton & Irwin's, 1940, results later). Finally, this account provides a natural explanation for both proactive and retroactive interference because the tendency for items to compete with one another at the time of the final recall test should not depend on the order in which these items were initially learned.

The assumptions about competition and strength dependence proposed by McGeoch (1942) permeate modern mathematical and computational thinking with regard to the causes of interference. Clear examples of this influence can be found in the relative strength retrieval assumptions typically adopted in modern memory architectures (J. R. Anderson, 1983; Raaijmakers and Shiffrin, 1981). According to relative strength models, the likelihood of retrieving B, given the retrieval cue A, is determined by the absolute strength of the A–B association, relative to the strengths of all associations emanating from A. Such behavior is captured with what is called a *ratio-rule equation*. To illustrate, suppose we wished to compute the probability of recalling the item *rock*, given the cue *dog*, and given that there are N items in total associated to *dog* (including, for example, the item *sky*). A simple ratio-rule equation expressing this recall probability might be written as follows:

p (recall *rock*, given *dog*) = Strength (*dog–rock*)/Strength (*dog–rock*) + Strength (*dog–sky*) . . . Strength (dog–Nth item).

Note that as the associations between the cue and other competing items (e.g., *dog–sky*) become stronger, the probability of recalling the target (*rock*) should decrease, because the denominator of this recall probability equation should increase. Similar effects should occur when additional items become associated to the same cue. Modern theoretical work with architectures using relative strength retrieval assumptions (J. R. Anderson, 1983; Gillund & Shiffrin, 1984; Mensink & Raaijmakers, 1988; Raaijmakers & Shiffrin, 1981; Rundus, 1973) has accommodated a broad array of memory phenomena (see also, Luce, 1959, for a more general treatment of "choice" models). Thus, McGeoch's elementary ideas of competition and strength dependence might provide a general account of interference in the form of an occlusion process (see, e.g., Mensink & Raaijmakers, 1988).

b. Unlearning

Is it possible to forget permanently experiences that have been stored in long-term memory? Consider the following scenario, which does not seem altogether uncommon. An acquaintance visits you and, in the course of reminiscing, describes a conversation that you had at a party several years ago. You may recall, in respectable detail, elements of the party, including your friend's attendance, your various conversations, as well as several amusing events that occurred. However, you may fail to remember having discussed a certain topic specifically with your friend, despite your friend's most confident confirmations, and even when you may clearly recollect both your friend's attendance and having discussed the topic. Subjectively, it seems as though your memory for that past event has become fragmented, impairing your ability to judge how elements of the experience (e.g., your friend and the discussion) go together. One approach to explaining this apparent fragmentation would be to assume that the originally encoded associations between the elements of that event have been disrupted or damaged in permanent fashion by subsequent experience.

Research relevant to the previous intuitions was conducted in the classical interference era in the context of Melton and Irwin's *unlearning hypothesis* regarding retroactive interference (Melton & Irwin, 1940). According to Melton and Irwin, the impaired recall of A–B items typically observed in the retroactive interference paradigm was not merely the result of occlusion of those responses by A–D items; those A–B items were also recalled less well because the associative connections linking As to Bs were weakened during the learning of A–D items. The process of associative unlearning was considered analogous to the extinction of conditioned responses in animal learning—that is, the decrease in the probability of a response, previously conditioned by repeated reinforcements in the presence of some stimulus A, that occurs when that response is subsequently followed by repeated nonreinforcements in the presence of that A stimulus. Melton and

Irwin's idea was that whenever the B item intruded inappropriately during practice on the new D target in the A–B, A–D paradigm, the earlier learned A–B association that mediated the offending B intrusion would be unlearned so as to reduce the likelihood of its subsequent intrusion. Because Melton and Irwin combined their unlearning mechanism with the occlusion mechanism postulated by McGeoch, their theory came to be known as the *two-factor theory* of interference.

Melton and Irwin proposed the addition of a separate unlearning mechanism based on perplexing findings observed in a study in which they examined retroactive interference as a function of the degree of interpolated learning. A natural prediction following from McGeoch's occlusion approach is that increases in retroactive interference should be accompanied by increases in overt intrusions of stronger, second-list memory items. Melton and Irwin discovered, however, that as the number of learning trials on a second list was increased to extreme levels (e.g., 10, 20, or 40 learning trials), the frequency of intrusions from the second list decreased, even though retroactive interference continued to increase. Because retroactive interference continued to grow—that is, fewer and fewer of B responses were recalled—even as the frequency of competitor intrusions diminished, Melton and Irwin reasoned that some additional factor, a factor X, must be contributing to retroactive interference. They tentatively identified this factor as unlearning of the A–B association.

Subsequent tests for unlearning yielded supportive results. Because retroactive interference should be produced by both unlearning and occlusion, whereas proactive interference should be produced by only the latter, the theory correctly predicts Melton and von Lackum's (1941) finding that retroactive interference is more pronounced than proactive interference on an immediate test. Support also came from two additional findings. One was that B items suffering from retroactive interference exhibited spontaneous recovery (i.e., the recall of these items got better over time; see Roediger & Guynn, Chapter 7, this volume) as the retention interval between List 2 and the MFR test increased (Underwood, 1948). This finding bolsters the claim that unlearning is analogous to extinction, which also yields spontaneous recovery of the previously conditioned response with increasing delays between extinction and retesting. See, however, Crowder, 1976, for a critique of spontaneous recovery as a signature of unlearning.) The second supportive result was the observation of retroactive interference on the MMFR test (Barnes & Underwood, 1959). This result was initially viewed as especially compelling evidence for unlearning because the MMFR test allowed people generous time to recall both items associated with a stimulus; most researchers presumed such conditions would eliminate the effects of occlusion thought to be at work on tests directing participants to recall only one response (see previous discussion of occlusion).

Investigations of the role of unlearning in retroactive interference that employed recognition memory measures produced less clearly supportive results. According to early theorizing, recognition tests should totally eliminate occlusion because they provide the correct targets, obviating the need for actively retrieving those items from memory (but see our later section on fan effects). As emphasized in our earlier party example, however, unlearning predicts that some retroactive interference ought to be observed even when people are given both the cue and intact target item on a recognition test. Retroactive interference should occur because people's recognition performance depends on their memory of the supposedly unlearned cue–target *associations*. Evidence against the unlearning prediction was obtained by Postman and Stark (1969), who failed to find a statistically significant retroactive interference effect when the nontarget distractor items in the recognition test were other B targets from List 1. Subsequent work demonstrated significant retroactive interference, however, when distractor items on the recognition test were the D targets that had been paired with the tested A cues on List 2 (R. C. Anderson & Watts, 1971). Additional studies favored unlearning, suggesting that intact recognition performance in Postman and Stark's (1969) study may have reflected genuine unlearning of A–B associations masked by participants' use of intact backward associations (B–A, instead of A–B) to match the correct target item with the cue (Greenberg & Wickens, 1972; Merryman, 1971). These studies demonstrated retroactive interference on a recognition test when the backward B–A associations were unlearned as well as the forward A–B associations by including both B–E and A–D learning during List 2. (See, however, Postman & Underwood, 1973, for an interpretation of these findings that discounts unlearning.) Because of the complexity of the arguments highlighted above, it remains an open question whether recognition tests eliminate competition effects, and, as important, whether unlearning actually occurs. (See, however, Wickelgren, 1976, for a systematic listing of studies favoring the unlearning view; see also Loftus, 1979b; Loftus & Loftus, 1980, and our later section on Related Research Areas for discussion of a related view proposed in the context of eyewitness memory research.)

2. Ineffective Retrieval Cues

Suppose that your car breaks down, and you are forced to go to the market in your neighbor's car. If you are like most people, when it comes time to return, you will initially try to remember where you parked your own car. That failing, you will likely realize that you did not, in fact, drive your own car. The failure to recall the target memory in this case arises because your frequent experience of driving your own car to the market led you to use the wrong retrieval cue on this exceptional day. Similar failures might arise for more remote past events as well. That is, after acquiring considerable experience with a new car, answering queries about prior parking occasions with your old car would be difficult if you failed to recollect that on those occasions you were driving your old car. These are examples of retrieval failures resulting from the use of ineffective retrieval cues—cues that are simply not associated to the target memory. The initial proposal that such failures might account for some instances of interference was called the Variable Stimulus Encoding theory.

Variable Stimulus Encoding Theory

Variable stimulus encoding (VSE) theory was developed by E. Martin (1968, 1971) as an alternative account for the retroactive and proactive interference effects observed in the classical A–B, A–D paradigm. A central assumption of Martin's VSE theory is that two memory responses cannot be simultaneously associated to the same stimulus element (see also Estes, 1955). Because of this restriction, asking people to learn a new set of A–D responses after having learned an initial A–B list forces participants (to the extent that they wish to remember both B and D responses) to encode the repeated A stimuli differently from how they were encoded during A–B learning (hereafter, the List 1 encodings), and to then associate these new encodings of A stimuli (hereafter, the List 2 encodings) with the new D responses. Thus, in a final MMFR test for a given A stimulus, both B and D responses can be given only if the A test stimulus elicits both its List 1 and List 2 encodings, and if both encodings are then used to search memory. If only the List 2 encoding is used, the B response will not be found, resulting in retroactive interference; if only the List 1 encoding is used, the D response will not be found, resulting in proactive interference. Martin assumed that the List 2 encoding of a given A stimulus would be the most accessible encoding immediately after A–D learning, but that the List 1 encoding would become more accessible with increasing delays. Thus, Martin's VSE theory accounts for retroactive interference being greater at short retention intervals, and for proactive interference being greater at long retention intervals.

To illustrate how variable stimulus encoding might produce interference outside the laboratory, consider the following situation. In one of your college classes you meet a casual acquaintance, Sally, with whom you played on a softball team for two years in early grade school, but whom you have not seen since. You once again become casual friends and confine your conversations to college-related activities. Treating Sally as the A stimulus, what you learned about her in grade school can be considered A–B learning, and what you learned in college, A–D learning. Now assume that a mutual college acquaintance asks you for the name of Sally's brother, which you had learned about in grade school—that is, you are asked to recall an A–B association. To retrieve this A–B association, upon being given the A stimulus "Sally," you first use the memory representation that corresponds to your current "image" of her as a young adult and fail to retrieve the earlier learned B response (i.e., "has a brother named Fred"). However, when you then think of Sally as a youngster in her softball uniform, you correctly retrieve her brother's name. In this case, the process of maturation has more or less forced you to have two different encodings of the A stimulus Sally. Martin's VSE theory says that a person in the A–B, A–D paradigm spontaneously shifts from how A was encoded in A–B learning to a different encoding of A during A–D learning. By creating these two different functional encodings of A, the person is able to learn two different responses to the same nominal stimulus.

The early evidence that people can indeed switch stimulus encodings from List 1 to List 2 was somewhat mixed. The theory was supported by results from experiments (Merryman & Merryman, 1971; Richardson & Stanton, 1972; Schneider & Houston, 1968; see Rudy, 1974, for review) that introduced a new stimulus X into each pair in List 2 of the A–B, A–D paradigm (yielding an A–B, AX–D paradigm). For example, *dog–rock* learning would be followed by *dog arm–desk* learning. The results indicated that learners shifted their encoding away from the A stimulus (*dog*) to the X stimulus (*arm*). This resulted in better learning of the X–D (*arm–desk*) association than in a control condition in which the AX–D (*dog arm–desk*) learning was preceded by A–D (*dog–desk*) learning. This shift toward encoding X (*arm*) also resulted in less retroactive interference, that is, better retention of the A–B (*dog–rock*) association than in the standard A–B, A–D paradigm in which no X cue was provided to which encoding could be shifted. Although these results from the A–B, AX–D paradigm indicate that variable stimulus encoding might, in principle, also be operating in the A–B, A–D paradigm, they are not directly relevant to that paradigm. In the A–B, A–D paradigm, no new stimulus component (X) or new encoding of A is explicitly provided by the experimenter during List 2 A–D learning, but must be generated by the learners themselves. To avoid this problem of the A–B, AX–D paradigm, Williams and Underwood (1970) employed trigrams (e.g., three-letter strings, such as XRM) as stimulus terms in a paradigm highly similar to an A–B, A–D paradigm (e.g., XRM–*rock* learning, followed by XRM–*desk* learning). Immediately after XRM–*rock* learning and immediately after XRM–*desk* learning, each individual letter in the XRM stimulus was tested alone. They found that if X was the letter most likely to elicit the B response *rock* after XRM–*rock* learning, it was also the letter most likely to elicit the D response *desk* following XRM–*desk* learning. Hence, contrary to VSE theory, no evidence was obtained to indicate that, in learning a new D response to XRM, the learner shifted to a new letter that had not been associated with the old B response.

Although research directly relevant to VSE theory has largely lain dormant since the mid-1970s, Chandler and Gargano (1995) recently reported a result supporting VSE theory. In their experiment, Chandler and Gargano examined how well people could recall a paired associate such as *child–apple,* given the retrieval cue *child–app__,* after also studying either *child–cookies* or *child–bicycle* in an A–B, A–D paradigm. Compared to a control condition in which only *child–apple* had been studied, studying *child–bicycle* produced the typical retroactive interference effect in the recall of *apple.* However, studying *child–cookies* facilitated recall of *apple!* One interpretation of this finding is that the encoding of *child* during the learning of *child–cookies* was similar to, but not identical with, the encoding of the stimulus term *child* that had occurred in List 1. For example, one aspect of the encoding of *child,* common to both lists, might be "has teeth." This commonality should facilitate *child–apple* to the extent that the persistence of the List 2 encoding encourages an interpretation of the test cue *child* more appropriate for retrieving the List 1 response. During *child–bicycle* learning, on the other hand, *child* might be encoded as *child–*"has legs." This inappropriate encoding of *child* might perseverate into the test, causing people to forget (suffer retroactive interference for) *child–apple.* An additional experiment yielded further support for this VSE interpretation of retroactive interference. In this additional experiment, *child–bicycle* interfered more if it was presented at the time of testing *child–apple* than if it had been studied.

In summary, part of the forgetting that occurs in retroactive and proactive interference paradigms may be mediated by people using the wrong retrieval cue to access memory. Under this analysis, retroactive and proactive interference would occur even though the ability to use the A–B and A–D associations to access responses in memory remains unimpaired (once the appropriate encoding of the A stimulus is selected for searching memory) and even though the availability of the target representation itself remains unaffected by the learning of competing responses. Moreover, the general idea that forgetting may be induced by using different encodings of the cue at study and at test has been applied with good success to many other memory procedures besides the standard interference paradigms (see, e.g., Tulving & Thomson, 1973; Chandler & Fisher, Chapter 14, this volume, and Roediger & Guynn, Chapter 7, this volume).

3. Impaired Target Memories

Sometimes we simply draw a blank when trying to recall something and we have very little confidence that the memory will ultimately be recallable. Such forgetting seems to occur even in the absence of intruding memories, and in the context of a highly appropriate set of retrieval cues. In such cases, the most straightforward explanation of forgetting seems to be that the target memory itself has been lost, disrupted, or otherwise impaired. We consider one such interference mechanism that was postulated in the last stages of the evolution of classical interference theory. This mechanism was called response-set suppression.

Response-Set Suppression

Upon arriving at work, you discover that the management switched your old computer with a new one, which, of course, runs a word processor different from the one you normally use. At first, this shift to a new way of doing things may be difficult. Not only must you learn new commands and procedures for editing your documents, but you must also prevent yourself from trying to do things the old way. This lesson was impressed on one of the present authors, who in hitting the keystroke designating "save" for his old editor lost a document because that keystroke happened to match "quit" in the new software. As time progresses, however, you gradually master the new word processor, and you seem to forget about the old one, including those older features that have no competing function in the new program. It almost seems that one can suppress entire sets of "responses" if their sustained activity substantially interferes with performance on a current task. The proposition that our need to shift "response sets" in this fashion might underlie some forms of interference is known as response-set suppression (Postman et al., 1968).

To see how the idea of response-set suppression can account for retroactive interference, consider the classical retroactive interference procedures from the learner's point of view. The learner must first learn to produce the prescribed set of responses to first-list retrieval cues and is given repeated study–test trials until some level of mastery is achieved at producing those responses. Then, the experimenter gives the learner a second list of items and the task of learning begins all over again. It seems reasonable that people would require a little time to reorient to the new task, particularly if the second list presented the same retrieval cues with different responses. Under these conditions, the tendency inadvertently to provide one of the already "prepared" responses during second-list learning may hinder performance on that task, until the person learns to suppress items from the earlier set and to facilitate second-list responses. Postman et al. (1968) proposed that the facilitation of current responses and suppression of past ones were achieved by a general-purpose "selector" mechanism that operated on the entire class of responses associated with each list. This process was thought to be separate from other mechanisms of associative interference, such as occlusion or unlearning, and to affect the representations of the responses. Thus, response-set suppression attributes some decrement in performance observed in interference studies to changes in the target memories themselves.

The response-set suppression hypothesis was proposed as a means of explaining the conditions under which items suffering retroactive interference would exhibit spontaneous recovery, that is, an absolute increase in their availability with increasing delays (see our earlier section on Unlearning). After its initial demonstration, however, spontaneous recovery proved to be an irregular and variable phenomenon, the conditions of which were unclear (Crowder, 1976). In a detailed analysis of the literature concerning this phenomenon, Postman et al. (1968) proposed that items suffering retroactive interference will exhibit spontaneous recovery when testing procedures favored the maintenance of a "List 2" set, that is, a set that favored the selection of second-list responses and the suppression of the first-list responses. Maintenance of a List 2 set could be enhanced, for example, if testing procedures reminded participants of List 2 responses during tests of List 1 items (e.g., if List 2 responses were presented at test). A List 2 set would be maintained under such conditions, according to Postman et al., because the hypothetical selector mechanism exhibited an inertia that (even without the experimenter's intervention) led people to maintain the most recent response set after it was no longer relevant. According to Postman et al., however, this inertia dissipated over time, allowing earlier responses to recover. Postman et al. showed that when test conditions were manipulated so as to vary the person's tendency to maintain the List 2 response set, the predicted variation in spontaneous recovery could be induced (see also Wheeler, 1995, for a recent and very convincing demonstration of spontaneous recovery).

The response-set suppression hypothesis was consistent with certain recognition memory findings that we discussed earlier. For example, consider Postman and Stark's (1969) demonstration that retroactive interference in the MMFR procedure nearly disappears in a multiple-choice recognition test. Such a finding is readily accommodated by the notion that the List 1 response terms that were being suppressed in the MMFR procedure were now being made available by their presentation in the recognition test. (However, see our section on Unlearning for an alternative interpretation.) Second, response-set suppression can account for the retroactive interference observed in the A–B, C–D procedure. If the previous B response set must be suppressed to facilitate the availability of the D response set during List 2 learning, the perseveration of this List 1 suppression should produce retroactive interference. Furthermore, because no common stimulus terms are shared in the A–B, C–D procedure, neither competition nor unlearning assumptions can account for this finding in a straightforward way (see McGovern, 1964; Mensink & Raaijmakers, 1988, for alternative explanations of this effect).

No theory is perfect, however. Toward the end of the classical interference era, a number of empirical phenomena arose that appeared to be inconsistent with the response-set suppression hypothesis, as initially formulated. For example, when a mixed-list design was used (i.e., both experimental A–D items and control C–E items were randomly intermixed on the same List 2 following A–B learning, rather than having separate A–D and C–E lists studied by different groups of people), retroactive interference was observed only for those A–B pairs for which a corresponding A–D pair was learned on List 2. If retroactive interference is produced solely by a perseverating suppression of the entire List 1 response set, forgetting should have been observed for all of the A–B pairs, not just those for which there was a corresponding A–D competitor. Indeed, Postman and Underwood (1973) conceded that these findings were problematic for the response-set suppression hypothesis and modified their theory to allow for the possibility of stimulus-specific response suppression as well. Crowder (1976), however, justifiably criticized this modification, as it seemed merely to be the unlearning mechanism in disguise, predicting effects virtually identical to those predicted by unlearning. Nonetheless, recent evidence from a new interference procedure, the retrieval practice paradigm, suggests that Postman and Underwood may have been on the right track after all (see later section on retrieval-induced forgetting).

IV. INTERFERENCE IN EPISODIC AND SEMANTIC MEMORY

According to the classical interference perspective, the act of retrieving an item from memory was a matter of eliciting a memory "response" to a "stimulus" cue. This research tradition did not differentiate among qualitatively distinct forms of memory responses. Shortly after the classical interference era, however, Tulving (1972) proposed a distinction between two different varieties of memory, which he argued might be governed by different laws of operation. According to Tulving, answering questions about general knowledge, such as "Who are five people who have received the Nobel Peace Prize?" "How do you pronounce the word *tear*?" and "What are the different meanings of the word *ring*?" taps what he calls *semantic memory*. This form of memory differs from what he referred to as *episodic memory,* which is the type of memory one uses to make temporal/spatial discriminations among episodes that one has experienced, such as the most recent parking of one's car or the presentation of a particular pair of words in a particular list in a psychology laboratory. In this section, we review findings from episodic and semantic memory paradigms that have furthered our understanding of both the mechanisms of interference and the breadth of situations in which interference effects occur.

A. Interference Effects in Episodic Memory

As noted previously, episodic memory refers to one's memory for particular episodes or events that one has experienced at a particular point in the past. A typical laboratory procedure for examining episodic memory presents people with a list of items to be studied for a later memory test. Items are usually either words or pictures and are often presented only once for a brief period. The later memory test may then be assumed to tap participants' memory for the episode of having seen the items on the study list. (This procedure contrasts with that typically used in the classical interference literature in which people were given an initial training phase composed of repeated study–test trials, designed to ensure participants' ability to elicit the appropriate verbal "responses.") Such episodic memory paradigms have been the primary tools used to explore three more recent interference phenomena that we now describe: part-set cuing inhibition, directed forgetting, and output interference.

1. Part-Set Cuing Inhibition

Most of us have forgotten the name of someone, or something, and have been offered assistance by a well-meaning friend who supplies guesses about the word we are seeking. Unless the friend is lucky and guesses correctly, it often feels as though his or her suggestions make matters worse. Sometimes recall fails until a much later point when, unencumbered by the clutter of incorrect guesses, your mind yields the delinquent name. If you have had this happen, you have experienced, firsthand, the puzzling phenomenon of part-set cuing inhibition.

Part-set cuing inhibition refers to the tendency for target recall to be impaired by the provision of retrieval cues drawn from the same "set" (e.g., category) of items in memory as the target (C. W. Mueller & Watkins, 1977). First, we describe this phenomenon and discuss its core empirical characteristics. (For more comprehensive coverage, see Nickerson, 1984; Roediger & Neely, 1982.) We then present a popular theory that accounts for many of these basic findings and illustrate how this theory, although constructed on the principles of classical interference theory, contributed to a general movement away from the unlearning postulate prevalent in the classical interference era.

a. Basic Findings

The basic phenomenon of part-set cuing inhibition was first nicely illustrated in findings reported by Slamecka (1968). Slamecka had people study lists composed of six words from each of five semantic categories (e.g., trees, birds), which were randomly ordered in the study list. On the final recall test, some people were given some of the members from each category as cues to help them recall the remaining items; others were given no such cues. Of critical concern was people's ability to recall the remaining noncue items in the experimental condition relative to their ability to recall those same items in the condition in which no cues were given. Quite naturally, Slamecka expected that the cues would help recall of the remaining noncue target items. However, when recall was scored for only the noncue target items, people who received the cues performed worse than did people who received no cues! This phenomenon has become known as part-set cuing inhibition (C. W. Mueller & Watkins, 1977) because providing part of the set (which was defined by each semantic category) as cues inhibited performance on the remaining items from that set.

Since Slamecka's initial discovery, several characteristics of part-set cuing inhibition have been consistently observed. In general, as the number of cues given to the subject at recall increases, the ability to recall remaining noncue targets decreases. For example, in an experiment by Roediger (1973), people listened to lists containing varying numbers of exemplars from 16 semantic categories (e.g., Fruits, Trees), blocked by category, and were then given an immediate-recall test in which they were provided with the 16 category names. A critical manipulation concerned whether people received, as additional recall cues, either zero, one, three, or five exemplars from the six-exemplar categories. As the number of these additional exemplar cues increased from zero, one, three, to five cues, the probability of recalling the remaining noncue targets decreased from .66, .63, .59, to .53, respectively. Analogous findings have been observed in a variety of other studies (M. Q. Lewis, 1971; Rundus, 1973; Slamecka, 1968, 1972; Watkins, 1975).

The phenomenon of part-set cuing inhibition is not confined to items selected from the same semantic category. Indeed, in some of Slamecka's (1968) experiments, people heard 30-item lists composed of noncategorized words, varying in their frequency of occurrence in the language and their degree of interrelatedness. At test, they were cued with from 0 to 29 of the list words. A part-set cuing inhibition effect was obtained regardless of word frequency and interrelatedness, presumably because these items merely occurred together in the same experimental context. Part-set cuing inhibition has also been observed by Roediger, Stellon, and Tulving (1977) using unrelated words, and by C. W. Mueller and Watkins (1977) using a variety of "set" definitions, including sets defined by rhyme, by subjective organization, and even by an arbitrary shared cue, as in the paired-associate procedure. Roediger (1978) even demonstrated that cuing people with varying numbers of category names from an earlier-studied categorized word list impaired their free recall of other categories from that list, suggesting that the categories themselves functioned as a set in memory. Thus, a crucial factor underlying part-set cuing inhibition is whether the cues and targets share a common retrieval or "set" cue.

Although part-set cuing makes recall of noncue targets more difficult, it appears to have little or no effect on people's ability to recognize those items. This finding was first demonstrated by Slamecka (1975), who gave people varying numbers of exemplars as cues during forced-choice recognition tests for critical target exemplars. Slamecka found that these cues had no effect on target recognition, irrespective of the number of cues provided. A similar failure to find impaired recognition was observed by Todres and Watkins (1981), although they did find a small effect when nonstudied exemplars served as cues. Because part-set cuing impairs recall more seriously than recognition, it would seem that the deficit reflects a problem in retrieval rather than impairment of the noncue target memories themselves.

b. A Popular Account of Part-Set Cuing Inhibition

On the face of it, part-set cuing inhibition is an extremely puzzling and counterintuitive finding. Why might the presentation of information that is clearly related to the items to be retrieved hurt recall rather than help it? Although a number of factors are likely to contribute to part-set cuing inhibition (see Nickerson, 1984, for a review), the one receiving the greatest attention was proposed in a model by Rundus (1973). In the Rundus model, cuing recall with part of a set impairs performance on the remaining noncue items by inducing retrieval competition between cues and the noncue targets. Thus, Rundus's model applies classical notions of interference (McGeoch, 1942) to explain this intriguing phenomenon.

According to Rundus (1973), people studying a categorized word list encode items in hierarchical fashion with respect to their experimental categories, and those categories with respect to the experimental context. This representation is illustrated in Figure 4, which depicts a potential encoding for the items *orange, banana, grape,* and *apple.* On a recall test, a person first recalls the experimental categories by recalling categories via contextual associations (unless the categories are provided), and then recalls exemplars using each category in turn as a cue. Note here that Rundus assumes that people's memory search is thus guided by a separate *set cue* (or, in his terms, a *control element,* after Estes, 1972)—in this case, a category—in addition to whatever exemplar cues the experimenter may overtly provide. The retrieval process is presumed to be susceptible to strength-dependent competition and is thus modeled in terms of a ratio-rule equation: the probability of recalling an item (e.g., *orange*) to a retrieval cue (e.g., *fruit*) is determined by that item's associative strength to that cue, divided by the strengths of all associations (e.g., *orange, banana, grape,* and *apple*) emanating from that same cue. According to Rundus, presentation of exemplar cues (e.g., *orange, banana*) strengthens those cue items' associations to their shared set cue (i.e., category), reducing the relative strength of noncue targets (e.g., *grape* and *apple*). By this analysis, the strength advantage of cues over noncues causes exemplar cue items to intrude persistently during attempts to retrieve the noncue targets. Impaired recall of noncue targets arises when the number of exemplar cue intrusions exceeds the person's "stopping criterion" for

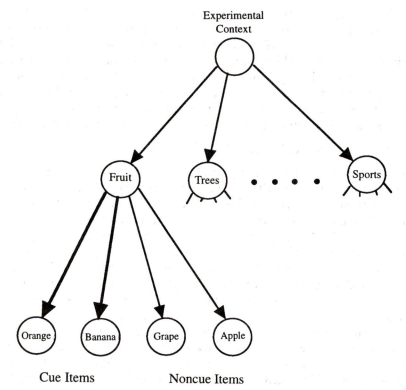

FIGURE 4   A typical representation of a categorized word list that would be assumed by the Rundus model of part-set cuing inhibition. Exemplars of a category are associated to their shared set (category) cue, and categories are associated to a representation of the general experimental context.

recall—essentially the continued intrusion of cue items leads people to give up their memory search. Thus, Rundus's model of part-set cuing inhibition is another example of an occlusion theory (see previous section on occlusion).

The Rundus (1973) model provides a straightforward account of the major empirical findings of part-set cuing inhibition. For example, increasing the number of part-set cues should reduce recall performance for noncue targets because more competitors will have had their relative strengths increased by being presented as cues. The nature of the set should make no difference as long as the members of the set are associated with a shared set cue (indeed, this seems to be the defining characteristic of "set"). Finally, recognition accuracy should remain unimpaired by part-set cuing because providing the intact target item eliminates the presumed source of impairment: competition for retrieval access. Because the Rundus model provides such a natural account of these findings in terms of classical principles of competition, it has retained considerable popularity as a means of accounting from this intriguing effect.

The Rundus (1973) model accounts for part-set cuing effects by adapting classical notions of occlusion to this new paradigm. An important contribution of this adaptation was the demonstration that forgetting on unpaced MMFR tests (which is essentially what category-cued recall is) need not reflect unlearning. Recall from our previous discussion of unlearning that the initial observation of retroactive interference on an MMFR test was considered strong evidence of unlearning, because such tests were believed to eliminate occlusion effects (Barnes & Underwood, 1959). The Rundus model illustrated how forgetting on MMFR tests could arise form occlusion alone if one simply assumed that people adopted a "stopping criterion" for memory search, which was exceeded in cases when competitors intruded frequently enough (see also Ceraso & Henderson, 1965, 1966, for earlier challenges of the Barnes & Underwood argument, based on the observation that proactive interference occurs in the MMFR procedure). The ability to account for interference data with occlusion alone, together with the growing body of research showing that interference disappeared (or at least was greatly reduced) on recognition tests, led to a general disenchantment with the unlearning postulate of the two-factor theory of interference. Rather, interference came to be seen as *retrieval inhibition,* that is, a deficit in the ability to retrieve otherwise available memory items. Thus, the discovery of part-set cuing inhibition and its later explanation in terms of occlusion contributed to an important shift that has shaped mathematical and computational thinking about the causes of forgetting. (Later, we discuss a new approach to interference that questions the general viability of occlusion as an account of interference.)

2. Directed Forgetting

So far, we have treated forgetting as a flaw of the cognitive system, an involuntary result of both the structure of our experiences and the properties of memory. In recent decades, however, some work has focused on the benefits of forgetting and on the possibility that memory lapses often arise from voluntary, intentional processes. Consider R. A. Bjork's (1970) example of a short-order cook who during a typical morning breakfast shift must process dozens of highly similar orders. Having completed a particular order such as "Scramble two, crisp bacon, and an English" the cook's performance can suffer only to the extent that the prior orders have not been forgotten. Similarly, we have all experienced times, after completing a memory-demanding activity such as an exam or a well-rehearsed speech, when we wish to "let go" of the information so that our minds may shift to new thoughts and endeavors. When we return to the "dropped" material later, we are often surprised that the material that was so readily accessible only a short time ago now eludes us. These two examples suggest that forgetting may often be an intentional act initiated to reduce the tendency of past experience to impede concentration on some more current activity.

In this section, we highlight basic findings from empirical work on intentional forgetting. Much of this work has been done with what has come to be known as the directed forgetting paradigm (see, e.g., R. A. Bjork, 1972; 1989; Epstein, 1972; Johnson, 1994, for reviews). Other work not discussed here, but relevant to the issue of intentional forgetting has been pursued in research on hypnotic amnesia (Coe, Basden, Basden, & Fikes, 1989; Geiselman, Bjork, & Fishman, 1983; Geiselman, MacKinnon, et al., 1983; Kihlstrom, 1977; 1980; 1983; Kihlstrom & Barnhardt, 1993; Kihlstrom & Evans, 1979); repression (Erdelyi, 1985; 1993; Erdelyi & Goldberg, 1978; Holmes, 1990); thought suppression and mental control (Wegner, 1994; Wegner & Pennebaker, 1993); and on the effects of instructions to disregard certain information in the formation of social judgments (see Johnson, 1994, for a review).

a. Basic Findings

The two most basic, consistently observed findings in the study of directed forgetting are that directing people to forget a set of previously learned items (1) greatly reduces proactive interference from those items on subsequent material, often bringing the level of recall for subsequent information up to the level observed when no prior items are studied, and (2) impedes access to the to-be-forgotten items on a final memory test. These basic findings are nicely illustrated in an early experiment by Reitman, Malin, Bjork, and Higman (1973), who adapted a procedure first introduced by R. A. Bjork (1970). In the Reitman et al. procedure, people received lists of one to eight paired associates, with each associate presented on a computer screen for 2.2 s. During some of these lists, people received a signal to forget all list pairs presented prior to the signal. Following presentation of the list, people received a stimulus member from one of the pairs and were asked to recall the associated response. On most of the forget-cue trials, the test item was drawn from the set of associates appearing after the forget cue. On a smaller number of trials, the test item was drawn from the to-be-forgotten set. Participants were forewarned that such tests of to-be-forgotten items would occur infrequently, and that they would be signaled by an asterisk next to the stimulus member during the tests of those items.

Two features of Reitman et al.'s results are striking. First, recall of items studied prior to the forget cue was impaired by approximately 20%, relative to comparable items on lists in which no forget cue was given. Thus, directing people to forget causes a substantial performance deficit for to-be-forgotten associates. Second, recall of list items presented *after* a forget cue no longer exhibited the typical proactive interference present when people had to remember those same precue items: On lists in which either zero, one, two, or three paired associates were presented prior to a forget signal, people were able to recall 73, 73, 76, and 72% of the postcue associates, respectively—even though performance on those postcue items should have decreased by approximately 8% per precue item without the forget cue (see Reitman et al., Figure 1, for support of this estimate). These data suggest that low recall of to-be-forgotten information was not caused solely by the participants' conforming to the experimenter's forget instructions at the time of retrieval. If such intentional response withholding were the sole cause, it would not have eliminated the typical proactive interference effects of those items when the to-be-remembered items were tested. Thus, when people are directed to forget previous items, they, like Bjork's short-order cook, are able to intentionally forget those items, reaping considerable benefit in the process.

Because people can voluntarily inhibit information they wish to forget so that they may focus on more current tasks, early work on directed forgetting emphasized its potential relationships to repression (Weiner, 1968; Weiner & Reed, 1969). However, most of the early theoretical accounts of directed forgetting attributed the effect to processes that had little to do with inhibition or even forgetting per se (see R. A. Bjork, 1970; 1972; Epstein, 1972, for reviews of these ideas). For instance, evidence suggests that the two main components of the effect—forgetting of to-be-forgotten items, and the consequent reduction in proactive interference on later material—can be explained by factors such as: (1) encoding deficits for "forget" items arising because participants, in anticipation of a forget cue, perform only shallow rehearsal of early items until they know that they will be responsible for remembering them; and (2) differentiation or segregation of to-be-remembered and to-be-forgotten items into discrete sets in memory (see, e.g., R. A. Bjork & Woodward, 1973; Jongeward, Woodward, & Bjork, 1975; D. W. Martin & Kelly, 1974; MacLeod, 1975; Tzeng, Lee, & Wetzel, 1979; Wetzel & Hunt, 1977; Woodward & Bjork, 1971, for evidence bearing on these factors). For example, the case that low recall performance on to-be-forgotten items might simply reflect their poor encoding seems especially plausible in procedures that cue participants to remember or forget *individual words* (as opposed to whole lists)—a conclusion supported by the finding that final recognition performance for individually cued, to-be-forgotten items is consistently inferior to that of to-be-remembered items (Davis & Okada, 1971; MacLeod, 1975; Wetzel & Hunt, 1977; see Basden, Basden, & Gargano, 1993, for a thorough treatment). However, recent work argues that these accounts do not tell the whole story.

b. Evidence for Retrieval Inhibition in Directed Forgetting

Several findings argue that at least part of the impairment observed in studies of directed forgetting derives from a process that impairs access to items successfully encoded into long-term memory. Consider, for example, a classic study by Geiselman, Bjork, and Fishman (1983). Geiselman et al. presented people a list of 48 four-letter nouns, auditorally, with each word preceded by one of two instructions: an instruction either to learn the word in preparation for a final recall test (e.g., learn *hand*) or to judge the word for its pleasantness (e.g., judge *rake*). Midway through the list of 48 words, half of the participants were told that "What you have done thus far has been practice; therefore, you should forget about all of the to-be-learned words that you heard." The remaining participants were also stopped, but were instead told that the first half of the list had been presented and that they should continue to try to remember the to-be-learned words they heard. After the entire list had been presented and a 3-min distractor task had been given, people were given either a recall test for all items—both to-be-learned and to-be-judged words—or a yes–no recognition test containing all learn and judge words together with 48 new distractor items. Geiselman et al. reasoned that if the forget cue caused poorer recall of to-be-forgotten items simply because it induced people to stop rehearsing those items during the second half of the list, then there should be no effect of the forget cue for "judge" words, which the participants were presumably not rehearsing during either half of the list.

People's performance on the "learn" words in Geiselman, Bjork, and Fishman's (1983) experiment showed the typical two-component directed forgetting pattern: participants instructed to forget the initial "learn" words midway through the list recalled fewer first-half learn words (56%) than did people instructed to continue remembering those words (73%), but people instructed to forget recalled more second-half learn words (72%) than did people not allowed to forget the first half (55%). More surprising, however, was the finding that the incidentally encoded "judge" words showed precisely the same two-component pattern, even though participants had no reason to rehearse these items during either half of the list: That is, people directed to forget the initial "learn" words recalled fewer of the judge words from the first list half (30%) than did people instructed to remember first-half learn words (45%), but people instructed to forget recalled more judge words from the second list half (40%) than did those not allowed to forget the first list half (30%). These results indicate that impaired recall performance on to-be-forgotten items in the directed forgetting procedure is more than a failure to rehearse (and thus encode) those items to the same extent as participants instructed to remember those items. This interpretation is supported by the observation that participants in both the forget and remember conditions, given a final recognition test for all types of words (learn words and judge words from both list halves) recognized all classes of items extremely well, with performance falling between 80 and 85% in all cases. The finding of comparable recognition for forget and remember items argues that to-be-forgotten words are actually encoded into long-term memory, but are rendered inaccessible through some intentional forgetting process, a process that Geiselman et al. referred to as retrieval inhibition. (See Horton & Petruk, 1980, for further evidence, using a levels-of-processing encoding manipulation, that semantically encoded material is subject to directed forgetting; see also Basden et al., 1993, for a replication of the finding of intact recognition memory for to-be-forgotten material when people are cued to forget whole lists of words instead of individual words.)

Additional support for Geiselman et al.'s view comes from an intriguing series of studies examining the circumstances under which this inhibition might be "released." These studies are motivated by the idea that re-exposure of to-be-forgotten material might cause a "rebound" effect in the accessibility of the inhibited information—that is, re-exposure of the information might "release" it from its inhibited state, restoring its accessibility as well as its tendency to interfere with people's ability to recall subsequent material. Findings from a study by E. L. Bjork, Bjork, and Glenberg (1973) support this release-of-inhibition hypothesis. People were presented with word lists (each with 32 items) of three different types: (1) lists with a midlist cue to forget the first list half; (2) lists with a midlist cue to remember the first list half; and (3) lists without a first half, in which the presentation of initial items was replaced by a shape judgment task. After each list, people's memory for the second list half was assessed under one of three conditions: immediate recall, recall delayed by an arithmetic task, or recall delayed by a recognition test for second list half items. E. L. Bjork et al. found performance to be quite similar when recall was tested immediately and when it was delayed by a simple arithmetic task: An instruction to forget the first list half brought people's performance on the second list half (54%) up to the level exhibited by people with no first half (55%), as compared to the clearly inferior performance exhibited by people not allowed to forget those initial items (43%).

More interesting, however, was what E. L. Bjork et al. (1973) found when recall was delayed by an interpolated recognition test for some second list half items. On this interpolated eight-pair recognition test, people were asked to select the item that had appeared on the second list half. On four trials, the distractor item paired with the second list half target was an item from the to-be-forgotten set, instead of a novel, nonexposed item. When recall of the second list half was delayed by this recognition test, people given an instruction to forget the first list half recalled only 35% of postcue second list half items, about as many items as recalled by people required to remember the first list half (33%), and clearly fewer items than were re-called when no initial list half was given (51%). It appears that the mere re-exposure of the four first-half distractor items on the recognition test was sufficient to "release" the inhibition of the entire first half list, as measured by the tendency for those items to cause proactive interference during the recall of the second half items. This conclusion was reinforced by the results of a study by E. L. Bjork, Bjork, and White (1984), who replicated the findings of E. L. Bjork et al. (1973), but also found that a recognition test not including first list half distractors did not by itself reinstate proactive interference from the first list half (see R. A. Bjork, 1989, for a discussion of these studies).

Conceptually related work on the "release" of inhibition was reported by Geiselman and Bagheri (1985). They represented both to-be-forgotten and to-be-remembered items for a second study trial (on which all items were then designated as "remember" items). Final recall of to-be-forgotten items benefited more from this representation (39%) than did final recall of the to-be-remembered items (7%). Differential improvement for "forget" items would be expected if those items benefitted both from their repeated encoding and from their "rebound" from their previously inhibited state. When taken together with the E. L. Bjork et al. results, there appears to be intriguing support for the notion of inhibition release.

c. Necessary Conditions for Directed Forgetting

Although the evidence reviewed here suggests that it is possible inten-tionally to forget previously learned items, there appear to be several limita-tions on this ability. First, evidence indicates that an instruction to forget is most effective when it follows immediately after the to-be-forgotten items. When a cue to forget is delayed until after additional material has been interpolated, less forgetting is observed for the to-be-forgotten material, and the reduction of proactive interference for later-studied items is smaller or even absent (see, e.g., R. A. Bjork, 1970; Epstein, Massaro, & Wilder, 1972; Epstein & Wilder, 1972; Timmins, 1974, for data bearing on this issue; see also Roediger & Tulving, 1979, for related experiments).[1] A second precondition for effective directed forgetting, suggested by R. A. Bjork (1989), is that new study material must be acquired after the forget instruc-tion is given. Support for this claim comes from a study by Gelfand and

---

[1] Whether a forget cue can be "aimed" at material farther back in time (e.g., the list that appeared immediately before the most recently studied list) remains to be established. Al-though some evidence suggests that such delayed forget cues are ineffective, most studies that have examined this issue seem to have confounded this delay with the omission of additional to-be-learned material after the delayed forget cue. Gelfand and Bjork (1985) provided strong evidence that such postcue learning may be a necessary condition for directed forgetting to occur, even under immediate conditions.

Bjork (1985, as reviewed in R. A. Bjork, 1989), in which an initial study list was followed by either (1) an unfilled interval, (2) an unrelated verbal activity, or (3) a second study list. Gelfand and Bjork found that directing people to forget the first list did not impair their final recall of the items in that list when this instruction was followed by an unfilled interval or by unrelated verbal activity (with deficits of 3 and 2%, respectively). When a second study list was given, however, people instructed to forget the first list recalled 17% fewer items from that list on the final recall test, compared to control participants directed to remember those items. These findings suggest that reorientation to new material that substitutes or "replaces" to-be-forgotten items may be necessary intentionally to forget that information. To the extent that the acquisition of new material is essential for the impairment of to-be-forgotten items, the finding of directed forgetting and its interpretation in terms of inhibition begin to resemble the finding of retroactive interference and the hypothesis of response-set suppression (see R. A. Bjork, 1989; Wheeler, 1995, for discussions of this point).

Whatever the relationship between directed forgetting and retroactive interference may be, research on directed forgetting demonstrates that the magnitude of the forgetting observed under conditions of interference depends, in some situations, on people's disposition toward that material. That the magnitude of forgetting depends so strongly on participants' intention to remember (or to forget) suggests that such factors may have played a far greater role than was realized in many classical studies of interference. At the very least, work on directed forgetting provides a precedent illustrating that forgetting may sometimes be intentional and controllable, and that such forgetting may have significant advantages for the current focus of cognition. We return to a related perspective in our later discussion of retrieval-induced forgetting.

3. Output Interference

If you are fond of constructing lists—such as a list of things to do, items to buy, or people to invite to a party—you have probably experienced the sensation that generating new items for your list gets more difficult as you proceed. The most natural interpretation of this sensation is that you are, in fact, running out of things to list, and that if you leave something off, it must not be particularly important. Although there is some truth to these intuitions, we often do omit important things. Such omissions are likely to be a product of what is known as output interference.

Output interference refers to the gradual decline in memory performance as a function of an item's position in a testing sequence. For example, a person's ability to recall the word *sky* in response to the cue *dog* will decrease if that item is tested later rather than sooner in a testing sequence. This decline in recall performance with testing position was first observed in a study using paired associates (Tulving & Arbuckle, 1963) and was originally attributed to the loss of information from short-term memory over the interval of testing. However, a number of findings show that output interference occurs even when the contribution of short-term memory to performance is eliminated. For example, giving people an unrelated task to occupy their short-term memory in the interval between the initial study and the final recall test does not affect the degree of output interference (A. D. Smith, 1971). Further, output interference does not depend on the position of a category in the study list (or even on the position of an item within a category set; see Roediger & Schmidt, 1980). If the loss of items from short-term memory were responsible for output interference, the drop-off in recall should have been worse when analyses focused on the recall of later (more recent) learned categories rather than earlier-learned categories (if one assumes that short-term memory contributes more to recall performance for later categories). Thus, the crucial variable modulating output interference appears to be the amount of prior retrieval, not the passage of time.

An intriguing characteristic of output interference is that it appears to violate the widely held idea, recurring throughout this chapter, that interference is initiated by competition for a shared retrieval cue. In the output interference procedure, recall of a target item is impaired by the previous retrieval of other items whether or not the target shares cues with those retrieved items. Consider a study by A. D. Smith (1971), in which people studied seven items from seven unrelated semantic categories. On a final recall test in which the people were cued with each category name in turn, the average number of items recalled per category dropped systematically from approximately 70% for the first category tested to 45% for the seventh category tested. Roediger and Schmidt (1980) obtained analogous findings with paired associates. After studying 20 pairs, people were given the stimulus term of each associate as a cue for the recall of its target. Across the five sequential test blocks (each block containing four test cues), there was a systematic decline in the probability of correct recall (.85, .83, .80, .76, and .73, respectively.) Thus, the decline in recall caused by prior output is nonspecific in that it extends across "sets" and does not depend on set type (to use the language of part-set cuing). This cross-cue impairment resists straightforward interpretation in terms of competition for a shared cue, although one might appeal to a more generalized competition for an experimental context cue (see, however, M. C. Anderson & Spellman, 1995, reviewed later, for evidence against this interpretation).

Although most studies of output interference have employed recall tests, the phenomenon has also been observed in recognition. For example, A. D. Smith (1971) had people study a list containing seven categories and assessed recognition memory for targets from those categories, as a function of the category's position on the final recognition test. The test provided each category name together with seven studied target exemplars and seven nonstudied distractors, requiring people to decide whether each item had appeared on the initial study list. Correct recognition declined across the first three test positions, leveling off for the remaining positions. Similar findings have been observed in other studies (see, e.g., Ratcliff, Clark, & Shiffrin, 1990; Ratcliff & Murdock, 1976). Thus, output interference does not appear to be specific to the task of cued or free recall.

Output interference has also been demonstrated in a procedure that measured participants' recognition time in addition to recognition accuracy. In an experiment by Neely, Schmidt, and Roediger (1983), people studied a categorized list with five exemplars per category (targets) and then made speeded recognition judgments to targets and distractor exemplars taken from those categories. Neely et al. varied whether the critical target item was preceded by (1) a test item from the same category or from a different category, and (2) two or six test items from the same category as the item immediately preceding the target. In addition, Neely et al. equated the nonspecific cross-category output interference effects discussed previously by measuring performance on critical test items occupying the same overall positions in the test list. The foregoing manipulations had only small effects on recognition accuracy, but clearly influenced how fast people made recognition judgments: People were faster when the preceding item was from the same category (as compared to an unrelated category), but were slower when the critical test item was preceded by six rather than two same-category test items. This result illustrates that, holding generalized output interference effects constant, one can observe category-specific output interference on recognition speed.

Two general implications of output interference are important. First, output interference clearly demonstrates a case of interference among items that do not share retrieval cues. Such interference appears inconsistent with straightforward accounts of the impairment in terms of competition among items that share the same retrieval cue—a point to which we return in our later discussion of cue-independent forgetting. Second, output interference shows that the retrieval situation itself might be a source of forgetting. To understand the importance of this observation, one need only consider the ubiquity of this basic cognitive process in our daily cognitive experience. That is, any cognitive act that makes reference to representations stored in memory (which is likely to be all processes) employs retrieval. If retrieval is a source of interference, then accessing what we already know might contribute to forgetting, independent of the encoding of new experience. This implication was first emphasized by Roediger (1974), although its ramifications were not fully appreciated by others. However, this observation forms the starting point for the most recent perspectives on the nature of interference, described in the final section of this chapter.

B. Interference Effects in Semantic Memory

The distinction between episodic and semantic memory led to a large body of research exploring the characteristics of people's memory for very well established, general knowledge. A typical procedure for examining such general knowledge might measure how fast people can make various judgments about an item in semantic memory, such as judgments about the truth of a fact (e.g., deciding whether birds have wings), or about the status of an item as a word (e.g., deciding whether *dog* is a word). Often, the aim of this research is to examine *how* (as opposed to *whether*) retrieval is performed, with considerable analysis given to the on-line dynamics of retrieval such as the rate, extent, and longevity of spreading activation within the semantic network. In this section, we discuss research demonstrating that interference effects occur even in tasks such as these that tap very well learned general knowledge. We discuss two areas of research in semantic memory that illustrate the breadth of situations in which such effects occur: Interference in retrieving facts and interference in our ability to understand a word's meaning.

1. Fact Retrieval, Fan Effects, and the Paradox of Interference

As E. E. Smith, Adams, and Schorr (1978) pointed out, if semantic memory for facts were as susceptible to interference as episodic memory, one would be confronted with what they called the paradox of interference. Specifically, as an expert learned more and more facts about a given topic area, he or she should develop more and more difficulty in remembering any one of them. Although this does not seem to happen in real life, early studies on the speed of verifying "facts" learned in the laboratory showed interference effects (J. R. Anderson, 1974). After students intensively studied many "facts" about various people being in various locations such as "A hippie is in the park," "A hippie is in the church," and "A lawyer is in the school," they were asked to verify "A hippie is in the park" was true or "A lawyer is in the church" was false. An interference effect was observed in that the more different facts that were learned about a person or location, the longer it took for the students to verify a statement about that person or location.

To account for this interference, J. R. Anderson (1976) assumed that the facts the students learned were stored in memory as a network of associations, such as the example depicted in Figure 5. When a test sentence such as "A hippie is in the park" was presented, the memory nodes corresponding to *hippie* and *park* would be activated, and this activation would spread down the links emanating from these nodes. If the activation spreading from one node intersected with activation spreading from the other node down the associative link connecting them, a "true" response would be made. Under the assumption that a node's capacity for sending out a wave

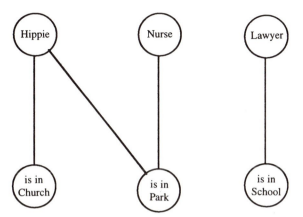

FIGURE 5   A simplified network representation depicting the facts "The hippie is in the church," "The hippie is in the park," "The nurse is in the park," and "The lawyer is in the school." The concept "hippie" is associated to (i.e., fans out to) two locations, and "park" fans to two people, decreasing the effectiveness of both of these concepts as cues, relative to either "lawyer" or "school" or "nurse," each of which is associated to only one thing. These representations are simplified from those proposed by J. R. Anderson (1974).

of activation is resource limited, the speed at which activation spreads down an associative link emanating from that node would be slower the greater the number of other associative links fanning out of that same node. The more different facts the person learns about someone, such as the hippie, the more links there are fanning out from the node for hippie, and the longer verification times become, a phenomenon known as the *fan effect*. Thus, Anderson's model of the fan effect assumes that associations emanating from concepts in semantic memory compete for activational resources, consistent with the broader competition assumption sketched earlier.

Of course, J. R. Anderson's (1974) "fact"-retrieval experiment might not really have tested semantic memory rather than episodic memory. That is, students might have performed this memory task not by "verifying facts" but rather by determining whether the test sentence had been studied at a particular time and place, namely, in the memory experiment. To examine this issue, C. H. Lewis and Anderson (1976) had students study both true facts ("Teddy Kennedy is a liberal senator") and up to four fantasy facts (e.g., "Teddy Kennedy wrote Tom Sawyer") about well-known people. Even when the students knew that they were being tested only on true facts and hence did not need to refer to what they had learned in the experiment to perform well, a fan effect occurred as the number of fantasy facts learned about the famous person increased. If the learning of only four additional facts about someone about whom many facts are already known produces memory interference, then the number of facts learned by an expert should produce massive interference. Yet experts retrieve facts quickly. How can this paradox be resolved?

a. Resolving the Paradox of Interference

McCloskey and Bigler (1980) and Reder and Anderson (1980) were able to provide a partial resolution of the paradox of interference. Their experiments showed that by focusing memory search on only information specifically relevant to a memory query, one can restrict the source of interference to only the small number of other directly relevant facts and greatly reduce or eliminate interference from all of the other facts stored about that general topic. To borrow an example from McCloskey and Bigler (1980), an expert on Richard Nixon might have stored different subcategories about Richard Nixon, such as his foreign policy views, his family life, and his Watergate actions. If asked a question about Nixon's wife, this expert would not search through all of the facts she or he knows about Nixon, but rather would search only through those facts relevant to his family, with only the facts stored under that subcategory producing memory interference. McCloskey and Bigler (1980) and Reder and Anderson (1980) independently proposed and tested this idea in a series of clever experiments and obtained similar results. (See also Bower, Thompson-Schill, & Tulving, 1994, for a similar type of experiment using an MMFR test in the classical A–B, A–D paired-associate paradigm.)

To create different "subcategories" on which memory search could be focused, Reder and Anderson (1980) used narrative materials in which named people (e.g., Alan) performed a series of actions relevant to different scenarios, such as taking a train trip or going skiing. Figure 6 displays how these materials were presumed to have been stored. People who studied the materials in (C–F) learned about Alan participating in both scenarios, whereas people who studied the materials in (A) and (B) learned only about Alan taking a train trip. The foils (test items that were false) were always related to the true test items in that they were always related to the scenario(s) in which Alan had participated. For true facts, such as "Alan checked the weekend Amtrak schedule," verification times revealed a fan effect as the number of facts learned about Alan's train trip increased (A vs. B; C vs. D; E vs. F), but not as the number of facts learned about Alan skiing increased (C vs. E; D vs. F). However, verification times for statements

---

FIGURE 6   Simplified network representations for the materials in each of the conditions of the Reder and Anderson (1980) fan-effect experiment. Subjects studied either zero, one, or three facts about a fictional person named Alan going on a ski trip (spanning top to bottom), and either one or three facts about Alan going on a train trip (spanning left to right). Subjects are assumed to represent facts about each of these separate trips in distinct "subcategories" (depicted in the figure as nodes lying intermediate between Alan and scenario facts) that reduce memory search complexity.

Number of Facts About Train Trip

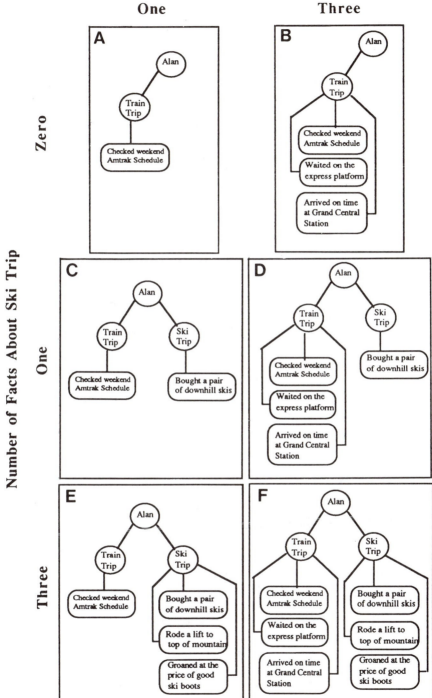

about Alan's train trip were slower if Alan had also participated in the skiing scenario (C–F) than if he had not (A and B). These results imply that people first select the relevant subcategory, and the time it takes to do this is affected by the number of irrelevant subcategories but not the number of facts learned within those irrelevant subcategories. Once the relevant sub-category is selected, only the number of facts within that category influences search time. McCloskey and Bigler (1980) obtained similar fan effects when search could be restricted on the basis of whether the grammatical object of a to-be-verified fact was an animal or a country, and all of the foils were related to the true test items, that is, were about animals or countries.

It is important to note that the fan effects produced by items within the relevant scenario were obtained when all of the foils were related to the true test items, as was described earlier. However, Reder and Anderson (1980) showed that even a fan effect from items within the relevant scenario can be reduced when the foils are unrelated to the true test items. Reder and Ander-son argued that with unrelated foils, a person can accurately verify a test item merely on the basis of its plausibility. To understand this, consider the conditions represented in (C–F) of Figure 6, in which all of the true items are about Alan's taking a train ride and going skiing (which he did) and all of the foils are unrelated to these scenarios (e.g., are about Alan going to the circus, which he did not do). To respond accurately to a "true" item, such as "Alan arrived on time at Grand Central station" or "Alan groaned at the price of good ski boots," or to a false item, such as "Alan liked the trapeze artists the best" one would need to decide only if each statement is plausibly true about Alan (i.e., is related to taking a train ride or going skiing) and would not need to look up that particular fact. Under such circumstances, one must still determine in which general scenarios Alan had participated, such that two scenarios (C–F) would lead to slower verification times than only one scenario (A and B). Indeed, this effect was still observed.

However, once people determined that one of the studied scenarios was or was not the one being tested, they could immediately respond "true" or "false," respectively, without searching for the specific fact within that sce-nario. Thus, the fan within that relevant scenario would no longer slow down verification times, thereby accounting for the greatly reduced fan effect within the relevant scenario. Indeed, under some circumstances in which plausibility judgments can be used, and especially when the retention interval is long, verification times for "true" statements are faster, not slow-er, the more facts that have been learned about the tested subcategory or scenario (Reder & Ross, 1983; Reder & Wible, 1984). This speed up (nega-tive fan effect) occurs because the more facts that have been learned about the relevant subcategory or scenario, the greater is the total activation level of the category node that is being retrieved in making the plausibility judg-ment, thereby speeding its access. (See Myers, O'Brien, Balota, & Toyofuku, 1984; Reder, 1982, for the roles that the use of integrated causally linked facts and plausibility, respectively, play in producing negative fan effects. See also Radvansky & Zacks, 1991, who have shown that fan effects from relevant facts may be eliminated even when a plausibility judgment cannot produce accurate performance. This result can occur when learners can create a representation of many objects residing in the same location, what Johnson-Laird, 1983, has called a mental model. Finally, see Conway & Engle, 1994, for evidence that fan effects in long-term memory do not vary as a function of an individual's short-term working-memory capacity; see also Nairne, Chapter 4, this volume.)

b. Implications of Fan-Effect Research

What are the implications of fan effects for our present discussion of interference? First, they illustrate clearly that interference effects occur in both semantic and episodic memory. Thus, although Tulving's (1972) speculations about the differences between semantic and episodic memory may be true for other aspects of these systems, the basic properties of interference appear similar for these two forms of memory. However, interference effects that occur in tests of "semantic" memory can be greatly reduced in at least two ways. Interference may be reduced when memory is compartmentalized into subcategories that allow for a focused search that restricts the source of interference to only those items within that subcategory (but see Whitlow, 1984, for potential limitations of this analysis); or interference may be reduced when correct responses can be made merely on the basis of the test item's plausibility. In fact, when plausibility judgments suffice for responding correctly, response times can be faster the more different facts have been learned about the topic—a negative fan effect. Such findings help explain how experts avoid interference and retrieve information so quickly. A second implication is that fan effects in semantic memory demonstrate that interference can occur in recognition tests. Recall that according to classical interference theory, recognition tests should eliminate response competition effects. By that analysis, either unlearning or response suppression would be the source of these interference effects. However, this implication does not hold in the context of more recent theories (e.g., J. R. Anderson, 1976) in which multiple associative links emanating from the same memory node compete for the flow of a resource-limited spread of activation from that node.

C. Interference in Word Meaning Retrieval

The research on fan effects discussed in the previous section illustrates how considerations of interference enter into the ostensibly simple task of judging the truth of a fact. Interference effects can occur on an even more basic level than this, however. For instance, in the English language, many sources of interference can be found even in apparently effortless, highly practiced tasks like retrieving information about a word's pronunciation, spelling, or its meaning. Retrieving the pronunciation of a word is potentially subject to interference when, for example, whole words like *tear* are associated with two distinct pronunciations (one associated with an action that can rend cloth and the other associated with crying). Similarly, interference can arise in retrieving a word's spelling when a sound like /dō/ is associated with more than one spelling, that is, *doe* and *dough*. Because two different "responses" must be associated with the same linguistic stimulus in each of these cases, the learning that occurs for such items represents the perfect semantic memory analogue of a randomly intermixed A–B, A–D paradigm.

An important example of interference in language processing occurs in the retrieval of word meanings, particularly in the case of homonym meaning retrieval. Homonyms are words with at least two distinct meanings associated with the same spelling and pronunciation (e.g., the word *ring*, with one of its meanings being related to jewelry and the other to a bell's sound). In both speeded lexical (word vs nonword) decision and pronunciation tasks, response times to homonyms are typically faster than to words having only one meaning (Balota, Ferraro, & Connor, 1991; Joordens & Besner, 1994). However, because one need not discriminate between the homonym's different meanings to perform these two tasks, this facilitative effect of semantic ambiguity may be viewed as analogous to the negative fan effect observed for plausability judgments. More relevant to potential interference effects is how a person retrieves the appropriate meaning from a homonym's multiple semantic interpretations. To determine which of the homonym's two meanings is activated at various times after meaning retrieval has begun, researchers have used the *semantic priming paradigm*. In this paradigm (Neely, 1976), people are asked to respond as quickly as possible to a target word (e.g., *cat* by either pronouncing it or making a lexical decision to it. Immediately preceding this target, a word (called the prime) is presented. Not surprisingly, people respond more quickly to the target when it follows a semantically related prime (e.g., *dog*) compared to an unrelated prime (e.g., *wall*).

The semantic priming paradigm has been used to examine the time course of activation for dominant (frequent) and subordinate (less frequent) interpretations of homonyms. For example, Burgess and Simpson (1988) presented homonyms (e.g., *ring*) as visual primes. Either 35 or 750 ms after a prime, a target was presented to the left or to the right of a fixation point to manipulate which cerebral hemisphere of the brain would process the target first (see Springer & Deutsch, 1993, for review). For present purposes, the most interesting result occurred for targets that were first processed by the left hemisphere. For targets related to the homonym's dominant meaning (e.g., *diamond*), priming occured at both delays. For targets related to the nondominant meaning (e.g., *bell*), however, priming was restricted to the 35-ms delay, with the 750-ms delay exhibiting an inhibitory priming effect: Responses were now slower to a target related to the homonymic prime's nondominant meaning than to a target preceded by a totally unrelated prime. These data suggest that when a homonym is recognized, the left hemisphere selectively focuses attention on its dominant meaning and actively suppresses its nondominant interpretation. (See Marcel, 1980; Simpson & Kang, 1994, for evidence of similar suppression effects that occur when the homonymic prime and target word are presented at visual fixation.)

These studies of the dynamics of homonym meaning retrieval illustrate two important points about memory interference. First, they show that interference can occur even for the highly overlearned and seemingly effortless memory retrieval involved in accessing an individual word's meaning. These findings make it abundantly clear how ubiquitous interference phenomena are in cognition, influencing performance across a variety of cognitive tasks. Second, these data on the time course of meaning retrieval support the proposal that suppression mechanisms contribute to changes in the accessibility of knowledge in semantic memory. If such retrieval processes influence the accessibility of items in semantic memory, the possibility arises that similar mechanisms may influence the accessibility of items more generally. This issue is the concern of our next section.

D. Retrieval-Induced Forgetting: A New Perspective on Interference

Studies of episodic and semantic memory have yielded a number of important insights and findings that pertain to the mechanisms of interference. At least two of these insights have contributed to a recent perspective on the causes of forgetting. First, studies of output interference and part-set cuing have highlighted how the act of recall itself might be a source of forgetting in episodic memory (see Roediger, 1974, 1978, for clear proposals of this view). Second, the more detailed analysis of the retrieval process that accompanied research on semantic memory has emphasized how retrieval was not simply a matter of "responding" to a stimulus, but was a complex process the dynamics of which could be examined empirically. These insights form the foundation of a new perspective on interference in which fluctuations in the accessibility of information in both semantic and episodic memory derive from suppression mechanisms that are tied to the retrieval process itself. To take the example offered in the introduction to the present chapter, you do not forget where you parked yesterday because storing subsequent parking memories alters the representation of yesterday's epi-sode; rather, such forgetting stems from your suppressing yesterday's park-ing episode while retrieving where you parked today. Thus, the impairment associated with the learning of interfering materials is seen as a problem of *retrieval-induced forgetting*.

What are the dynamics of the retrieval process that might be responsible for the impaired recall observed in studies of interference? Consider the following analysis of the functional circumstances often faced during re-trieval tasks. Retrieval ordinarily begins with a cue that is necessarily in-complete as a specification of the target memory. For instance, remember-ing that we are supposed to buy some fruit is a helpful start to an outing at the market, but *fruit* is overly general as a cue if we wish to remember to buy oranges. Such general cues will necessarily be consistent with many potential targets in memory (e.g., *lemon, banana*) that, we might assume, also become active in response to that cue. When activation spreads broadly in this manner, retrieval competition will ensue and access to the target item will be momentarily impeded. If the resolution of such competition in favor of the target item were achieved by a suppression process that focused activation to target items, the consequences of that inhibition should be observable as a decrement in the performance on the inhibited item on subsequent tasks. That is, accessing target items may entail suppression of competitors that can be seen as retrieval-induced forgetting of those com-petitors on later recall attempts. In this section, we review recent work on retrieval-induced forgetting in both semantic and episodic memory para-digms that supports the operation of a special retrieval-based suppression process causing interference effects in subsequent retrieval.

E. Retrieval-Induced Forgetting in Semantic Memory

Have you ever tried to retrieve a word, fact, or name from semantic memo-ry and felt on the verge of being able to do so, only to fail because some other related item comes to mind and seems to block your retrieval of the item you are trying to recall? As noted earlier when we introduced occlu-sion, R. Brown and McNeill (1966) have called this experience the tip-of-the-tongue state, a state that apparently occurs rather frequently (at least as reported in Reason & Lucas, 1984, who had people keep track of and classify the tip-of-the-tongue states they had in their everyday lives; see also A. S. Brown, 1991). We now discuss experimental data indicating that such retrieval-induced forgetting in semantic memory may be produced not by a retrieval block induced by the conscious retrieval of related interlopers, as the subjective experience associated with the tip-of-the-tongue state sug-gests, but rather by an active suppression mechanism that operates when retrieval is difficult.

1. Evidence for Impairment Specific to Retrieval

Perhaps the earliest demonstration of retrieval-induced forgetting in semantic memory may be found in a study of part-list cuing inhibition by J. Brown (1968). Brown had one group of people study a list of 25 American states for a period of five min, while a control group did light reading. On an immediate recall test, he instructed both groups to list all 50 of the American states. Of critical concern was participants' ability to recall the remaining noncue states from semantic memory in these two conditions. The people who received the cues recalled the remaining noncue states more poorly than did those who received no cues, even though the recall period for both groups extended for a full 10 min. One might argue that the impaired recall of noncue items by the cued group reflects retrieval-induced forgetting because the cued group recalled more of the cue states earlier in the output sequence than did the noncued group. Evidence supporting this speculative interpretation of Brown's data comes from Karchmer and Winograd's (1971) demonstration that the cuing inhibition effect was accentuated when people were explicitly instructed to retrieve the states that had served as cues first. Thus, these findings may be taken as early evidence that prior retrieval of items from semantic memory impairs retrieval of related items.

A more systematic examination of retrieval-induced inhibition in semantic memory was undertaken by A. S. Brown (1981), who attempted to control the nature of people's prior retrievals. In Brown's experiment, people were presented with a category name and a letter (e.g., *fruit–g*) and asked to report an exemplar of that category beginning with that cued letter (e.g., *grape*). Each category name was followed by five exemplar trials, one at a time, at about 5-s intervals, with each exemplar cued by its own first letter. The time to retrieve an exemplar increased from the first to the fifth retrieval within that category, suggesting that prior retrievals from a semantic category induce "forgetting" (as represented by slower retrieval times) of a subsequently retrieved target item from that same category. However, it is unclear from this result whether it was the attempt actively to retrieve the prior "cuing" items or their mere (albeit self-) presentation that was responsible for slowed target retrieval.

To determine whether or not the prior cued retrievals were responsible for the impairment in A. S. Brown's (1981) experiment, Blaxton and Neely (1983) directly compared the effects of prior retrieval and prior presentation of competitors on target retrieval speed. In Blaxton and Neely's study, people either actively generated or read aloud a category exemplar on each of the "cuing" trials preceding the critical target trial. On the target trials of interest here, people were to generate a category exemplar in response to a letter cue, as in the Brown study. As the number of cue exemplars preceding the target trial increased from one to four, retrieval times for the target increased, but only when cues were actively retrieved and were from the same semantic category as the target item. Thus, retrieval of the cue items appears to be directly responsible for the impairment of target items in this paradigm because the mere presentation and reading of cues did not hinder the generation of the target item.[2]

Although Blaxton and Neely's (1983) study clearly illustrates a case of retrieval-induced forgetting in semantic memory retrieval, one might still argue that these data do not necessitate the postulation of retrieval-based suppression processes of the sort relevant to the present discussion. Indeed, Blaxton and Neely suggested two explanations of their findings. First, the slowed recall of target exemplars might arise from the blocking of those critical items by the highly available exemplar competitors that had just been retrieved on prior cue trials. For example, given the target trial *fruit–g*, people might retrieve *apple* and *banana* before retrieving the target *grape*. To explain the absence of the hypothesized blocking when primes were merely presented, one might assume that actively generating cue items makes those items more strongly competitive than merely reading them aloud. Thus, impairment might not have been observed in the reading condition because competition from cue items was not strong enough. Alternatively, the slowed recall of target exemplars might reflect the suppression of those target items that occurred during the previous retrievals of cue exemplars. Under this account, *grape* might have covertly intruded during the previous *fruit* cuing trials, rendering *grape* vulnerable to retrieval-based suppression processes. The slowdown in target retrieval as the number of cue trials increased follows naturally if one simply assumes that *grape* would have been suppressed more often with four previous *fruit* cuing trials than with one. However, because both of these explanations can account for the Blaxton and Neely findings, these data only support, but do not demand, the postulation of an active suppression process.

[2] It is important to mention that the interference effect that Blaxton and Neely (1983) reported depended on there being multiple retrievals from the same semantic category. When only one item had been actively generated from the same semantic category as the target, target retrieval was facilitated, relative to when there was active generation of one item from an unrelated category. This facilitation effect conceptually replicated earlier results by Loftus and Loftus (1974). Moreover, a similar facilitation effect occurs in a definition answering paradigm, in which people are asked to retrieve a relatively rare word (e.g., banshee) from its definition (e.g., female spirit whose wail portends death), when a single semantically related cue (ghoul) is read before or after the definition. (See Roediger, Neely, & Blaxton, 1983, and Meyer & Bock, 1992, the latter of whom also showed that the related cue induced more tip-of-the-tongue states.) However, this latter facilitation effect occurs only if the cue that is read is never the correct answer to the definition. When the cue sometimes is the correct answer, the semantically related cue slows target retrieval (A. S. Brown, 1979; Roediger, Neely, & Blaxton, 1983).

2. Evidence for Impairment Caused by Suppression

Recent work by Carr, Dagenbach, and colleagues (Carr & Dagenbach, 1990; Dagenbach & Carr, 1994a; Dagenbach, Carr, & Barnhardt, 1990; Dagenbach, Carr, & Wilhelmson, 1989) argues more clearly in favor of a suppression mechanism mediating retrieval-induced forgetting in semantic memory. In the Dagenbach et al. (1990) study, people learned the meanings of obscure vocabulary items such as accipiter (i.e., hawk) and subsequently participated in a lexical decision task in which these newly learned words served as primes. For the lexical decision task, people were asked to try to retrieve the meaning of the prime word during its 2-s presentation, and to use this meaning to predict what the lexical decision target would be. After the lexical decision test, Dagenbach et al. both tested people's ability to recall the meaning of the primes and administered a recognition accuracy test. They then limited their analysis of lexical decision performance to those trials containing primes for which people could correctly recognize but could not recall the meanings. The presumption was that if the prime's meaning could not be recalled in the unpaced recall test, retrieval failure would have occurred during the 2-s interval allowed during the lexical decision task.

Dagenbach et al.'s (1990) analysis of their lexical decision data clearly supports the notion that a retrieval-based suppression process may be invoked when retrieval is difficult. When people failed to retrieve the meaning of a prime word, such as *accipiter,* lexical decisions for a related target, such as *eagle,* were markedly slower, relative to decisions made for an unrelated target such as *clam* under those same conditions. When people could successfully recall the prime word's meaning, however, lexical decisions on related targets were facilitated. Thus, when people struggled (and failed) to retrieve the meaning of an item from memory, information related to the sought-after item suffered an increase in reaction time, consistent with the notion that those related items were suppressed when they interfered with the difficult retrieval. Dagenbach et al. (1989) obtained a similar result when well-known words (e.g., *cat*) served as primes, provided that meaning retrieval was impeded by making the prime hard to see through brief presentations and masking. As in the Blaxton and Neely (1983) study, when conditions encouraged people actively to retrieve the prime's meaning, related primes produced inhibition; when conditions encouraged passive processing of the prime, related primes yielded facilitation. Neither of the present findings is easily accommodated by blocking mechanisms, because target impairment occurred even when the putative blocking items were never successfully retrieved.

To account for why retrieval failure might impair the subsequent retrieval of related information, Carr and Dagenbach (1990) postulated that when one fails to retrieve a word's meaning under arduous conditions (e.g., when the meaning is only weakly learned or when the word is extremely difficult to see), attention is so centered on the representation of the word itself that the representations of other surrounding words related to that meaning are actively suppressed. Support for this center/surround hypothesis, which is similar to lateral inhibition in perception, was obtained in an additional study by Carr and Dagenbach (1990). Carr and Dagenbach showed that when people attempted to retrieve the meaning of a word that was quickly masked, a large facilitation effect resulted when that priming word itself (the center) was presented as a target. This facilitation was observed even though the same masked prime produced substantial inhibition for related targets (the surround). Thus, these results imply that items in semantic memory may be impaired by an active suppression mechanism when a related retrieval target is sufficiently difficult to retrieve. (It should also be mentioned that such inhibition effects can occur even in the simple task of silently reading a clearly presented priming word when this task is made difficult by virtue of the person having suffered from brain trauma; see, e.g., Blaxton & Bookheimer, 1993; Bushell, in press.) Thus, the results reviewed in this section are congruent with the idea that an item-specific suppression mechanism (akin to that suggested by Postman and Underwood, 1973) can produce retrieval-induced "forgetting" in semantic memory when the retrieval conditions are arduous.

F. Suppression and Retrieval-Induced Forgetting in Episodic Memory

To what degree might retrieval-induced forgetting akin to that observed in semantic memory occur in episodic memory? We have already discussed output interference, in which the retrieval process seemed to cause forgetting (Roediger, 1974). Now we turn to more recent research that specifically examines whether a retrieval-based suppression mechanism might provide a general account of forgetting in episodic memory. Three issues relevant to establishing suppression mechanisms as a cause of long-term episodic forgetting are discussed: (1) the dependence of a target's impairment on its previous tendency to interfere with retrievals of related information; (2) the localization of the impairment to the representation of the previously interfering target item itself; and (3) the durability of episodic retrieval-induced forgetting. Each of these issues has been addressed with the retrieval-practice paradigm (M. C. Anderson, et al., 1994), which we briefly describe next.

1. The Retrieval-Practice Paradigm

The retrieval-practice paradigm was devised as a means of examining the effects of episodic memory retrieval on the subsequent ability to retrieve competing items (M. C. Anderson et al., 1994). In the retrieval-practice paradigm, people take part in three main phases: a study phase, a retrieval-practice phase, and a final test phase. In the study phase, people study several semantic categories, each composed of several exemplars presented in category–exemplar format (e.g., *fruit–banana*). Next, they perform directed "retrieval practice" on only some of the items that they just studied by completing category-plus-exemplar stem cue tests (e.g., *fruit–ba____*). This retrieval practice is then followed by a final test in which people are cued with each category name and asked to free recall any exemplars of that category that they remember having been presented at any point in the experiment.

Of central interest is the impact of retrieval practice on people's ability to recall the remaining unpracticed exemplars of practiced categories on the delayed-recall test. If retrieving an item renders related items less accessible, performing retrieval practice on some category exemplars should impair recall of the remaining unpracticed exemplars of those categories, relative to the recall of unpracticed exemplars from unpracticed baseline categories. This outcome is indeed what M. C. Anderson et al. found. Whereas performance on practiced items improved rather dramatically relative to the baseline condition (as expected), such facilitation appeared to come at the cost of performance on unpracticed exemplars of practiced categories.

2. Dependence of the Impairment on Concurrent Interference

The impairment observed in the retrieval practice paradigm clearly supports the idea that retrieval causes the forgetting of related episodes. The question arises, however, whether such retrieval-induced forgetting reflects the operation of a suppression mechanisms. For example, the impaired recall performance for unpracticed competitors might instead reflect occlusion (McGeoch, 1936, 1942; Mensink & Raaijmakers, 1988; Raaijmakers & Shiffrin, 1981; Rundus, 1973) from exemplars that were strengthened by retrieval practice. M. C. Anderson et al. (1994) addressed this possibility by examining whether the likelihood of an item suffering retrieval-induced forgetting depended on its tendency to interfere during retrieval practice of its competitors.

According to the suppression account of retrieval-induced forgetting, unpracticed competitors undergo suppression because presenting the shared category cue during retrieval practice leads unpracticed items to interfere during the retrieval of the practice targets. If these assumptions are correct, the more interfering an item can be made, the more likely it will be to suffer from retrieval-induced forgetting. Importantly, and contrary to a competition account, these variations in impairment need not rely on the degree to which practiced items are strengthened. Indeed, if unpracticed competitors are sufficiently noninterfering, no impairment may result at all, even given considerable strengthening of practice competitors.

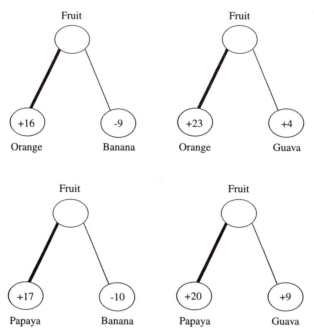

FIGURE 7   Design and results of the retrieval-practice experiment of M. C. Anderson, Bjork, and Bjork (1994) in which they manipulated the taxonomic frequency (high vs. low) of practiced exemplars (left side of each category diagram) and unpracticed competitors (right side of each diagram). Results are depicted in each node as a difference between performance for that item and the corresponding baseline item, with positive numbers designating facilitation and negative numbers designating impairment. The amount of benefit due to retrieval practice may be seen by examining the left side of each node diagram, and the amount of retrieval-induced forgetting on competitors by examining the right side of each diagram.

Figure 7 illustrates some examples of the materials used by M. C. Anderson et al. (1994) to examine the relationship between retrieval-induced forgetting and the degree of interference caused by unpracticed competitors. This figure illustrates four conditions, with the categories and exemplars in each condition depicted as nodes connected by associative links (items that people practiced are depicted on the left of each diagram and unpracticed competitors are depicted on the right). The four conditions differed according to the materials people studied—either high-frequency exemplars (e.g., *orange*) or low-frequency exemplars (e.g., *guava*)—and according to the materials on which people performed retrieval practice. People in both of the top two groups were given retrieval practice on high-frequency members of their categories (e.g., *orange*), but the unpracticed exemplars of their categories were either also high-frequency members (e.g., *banana,* top left) or were instead low-frequency members (e.g., *guava,* top right). People in both of the bottom two groups were given retrieval practice on low-frequency members of their categories (e.g., *papaya*), but the unpracticed exemplars of their categories were either high-frequency members (e.g., *banana,* lower left) or were low-frequency members (e.g., *guava,* lower right). M. C. Anderson et al. reasoned that if retrieval-induced forgetting depended on the degree to which unpracticed competitors interfered during practice, more retrieval-induced forgetting should occur for high-frequency than for low-frequency exemplars. Furthermore, retrieval-induced forgetting for low-frequency exemplars could be negligible if those items were sufficiently noninterfering. These predictions follow if one assumes high-frequency items to be more interfering than low-frequency items, given the former's stronger pre-experimental associations to the taxonomic category.

Figure 7 also depicts the results of this experiment. Data for each condition appear in the relevant node and are reported here as the difference in percent correct recall between that condition and its corresponding baseline. The positive numbers for practiced items (on the left side of each diagram) indicate the extent to which retrieval practice facilitated recall above baseline performance. The numbers for unpracticed items (on the right side of each diagram) indicate to what extent, if at all, recall of these items was inhibited by retrieval practice on a competitor (with negative numbers indicating inhibition). Unlike the facilitation that occurred for practiced items in all four conditions, the inhibition for unpracticed competitors occurred only when those competitors were high-frequency members of their categories (in upper left and lower left diagrams), with no impairment observed for low-frequency members (upper and lower right diagrams). Thus, consistent with the suppression view, episodic retrieval-induced forgetting occurs only if the target item interfered during the previous retrieval of competitors. Retrieval practice on any set of competitors per se is not sufficient to produce the forgetting, contrary to a pure occlusion account of the effect.

3. Localization of the Impairment to the Item

The greater impact of retrieval practice on high-taxonomic-frequency items favors a suppression-based account over a competition-based account of episodic retrieval-induced forgetting. However, rather than demonstrating suppression, this dependence of impairment on interference might reflect unlearning of the episodic associations linking categories and impaired exemplars, triggered by the intrusion of inappropriate competing responses during retrieval practice. M. C. Anderson and Spellman (1995) addressed this alternative account by examining whether retrieval-induced forgetting is cue independent.

According to the suppression hypothesis, the representations of unpracticed competitors are suppressed during retrieval practice. That is, practicing retrieval of *orange* to the cue *fruit* suppresses the representation of *banana* itself but not the *fruit–banana* association. If the *banana* representation is indeed suppressed, inhibition for *banana* should be measurable when that item is cued by associated retrieval cues other than *fruit,* such as *monkey.* Thus, whereas concurrent interference might be initiated because items share a common retrieval cue, the resulting suppression of interfering items should result in forgetting that generalizes to other cues. M. C. Anderson and Spellman (1995) referred to this predicted property of suppression models as *cue-independent forgetting,* and to the use of a cue such as *monkey* to assess inhibition as the *independent probe method.*

M. C. Anderson and Spellman (1995) examined whether the forgetting observed in the retrieval-practice paradigm exhibited cue independence, using the independent probe method. People followed the retrieval-practice procedure described previously, except that sometimes pairs of practiced and unpracticed categories were related to each other and sometimes they were unrelated. Figure 8 illustrates typical materials from the related and unrelated conditions of one of their experiments. In the related condition (A), people studied the categories *red* and *food,* and performed retrieval practice (indicated by a "+") on some items from one of those categories, for instance, items such as *red–blood.* Though it was never mentioned to the people in the experiment, the nonpracticed items of the *red* study category could also be categorized as *food* and some members of the *food* category could also be categorized as *red,* as shown by the dotted lines linking these items to their related categories. In the unrelated condition (B), categories were not related to one another, replicating the standard retrieval-practice paradigm. The new relations between the practiced and unpracticed categories in the related condition enabled M. C. Anderson and Spellman to test the property of cue independence.

Suppose that impairment of within-category items such as *tomato* results from their suppression when they interfere with *blood* during *red–blood* practice. M. C. Anderson and Spellman (1995) reasoned that if this were so, then *radish* might also be suppressed if, by virtue of its prior semantic association to the *red* category (dotted line), it also interferes with the practice of *blood.* If suppression truly affects item representations, the effects on *radish* should be observable even if *radish* is tested with the independent cue *food.* However, if *tomato*'s impairment results from associative unlearning, the ability to recall *radish* to the cue *food* should remain unaffected, because any impairment caused by practicing *red–blood* should be specific to testing via the unlearned *red–radish* association.

Results of this experiment are depicted in Figure 8 in the nodes for the exemplars in each condition, in terms of the percentage of items correctly

A

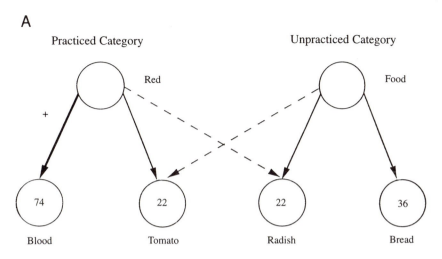

B

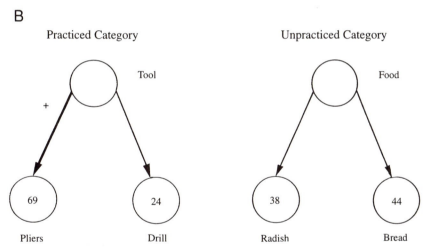

FIGURE 8   Design and results of an experiment by M. C. Anderson and Spellman (1995). Copyright © 1995 by the American Psychological Association. Adapted with permission. (A) The related condition, in which the studied category that was practiced (*red*) and the unpracticed category (*food*) are similar to one another. These categories are similar in that each has members that are categorizable as members of the other category (the figure illustrates this with dotted lines that denote the pre-existing semantic relationships between an item and the other studied category in which it did not appear). (B) The unrelated condition in which the practiced and unpracticed categories are not similar to one another. Note that the items receiving retrieval practice in these two conditions, *blood* and *pliers*, are denoted by a "+" next to the link for each of these items. Results are reported in the nodes for each condition in terms of the percentage of items correctly recalled. The cross-category inhibition of *radish* caused by doing retrieval practice on *blood* may be observed by comparing performance on *radish* in the related condition (A, *top right*) to *radish* in the unrelated condition (B, *bottom right*).

recalled on the final category cued-recall test. The items in the unpracticed category of the unrelated condition (B, *right*) serve as the baseline against which within-category impairment of *tomato* and the between-category impairment of *radish* can be measured in the related condition. As can be seen, retrieval practice on *red–blood* impaired recall of *red–tomato* (A, *left*) on the final recall test, relative to baseline items (i.e., *radish* in the unrelated condition; B, right diagram), replicating the basic retrieval-induced forgetting effect. More important, practicing *red–blood* impaired recall of *radish* to *food* in the related condition, which can be seen by comparing performance for that item to the *radish* baseline in the unrelated condition. Because *radish* was tested under the independent cue *food*, impaired recall of that item cannot be attributed to associative unlearning of the *red–radish* link during the practice of *red–blood*. This cross-category inhibition was observed across three experiments using different materials.

These findings clearly support the view that the retrieval-induced forgetting observed in the retrieval-practice paradigm exhibits the property of cue independence predicted by models attributing impairment to suppression. These findings resemble other phenomenon of cross-cue impairment discussed in previous sections of this chapter, such as output interference and retroactive interference in the A–B, C–D paradigm (both of which also hinge on training or testing procedures requiring retrieval of interfering items). Unlike those previous findings, however, the M. C. Anderson and Spellman (1995) study used a within-subjects baseline against which to measure cross-cue impairment of items like *food–radish*. This difference has the important implication that the present cross-cue impairment may not be explained in terms of competition for a general contextual cue. If participants' ability to recall *food–radish* were impaired because retrieval practice of *red–blood* increased the competition for the experimental context cue, within-subject baseline items should have suffered, as well. As such, there should have been no difference in people's recall performance between the baseline condition and *food–radish* (see M. C. Anderson & Spellman, 1995, for an elaboration of this reasoning). Thus, these findings provide clear evidence for cross-cue impairment that is not predicted by unlearning.

4. Durability of the Impairment

Because the consequences of activation and suppression are generally assumed to be fairly brief (e.g., less than a second), one might wonder whether such processes could underlie long-term forgetting from episodic memory. For example, the retrieval-induced forgetting observed in the retrieval-practice paradigm might reflect impairment that either (1) extends for only a brief period after retrieval practice, or (2) stems entirely from output interference, arising at test, because stronger practiced items tend to be retrieved before unpracticed competitors. If either of these possibilities characterized episodic retrieval-induced forgetting, such effects could not form the basis of long-term forgetting.

The first possibility—that retrieval-induced forgetting endures for only a brief period after retrieval practice—cannot by itself be true for the simple reason that all of the studies reviewed here have employed retention intervals of 20 min between retrieval practice and the final recall test. We thus turn to the possibility that the impaired recall of unpracticed competitors reflects the fleeting consequences of output interference at the time of test. The contribution of output interference has been assessed by M. C. Anderson et al. (1994), who demonstrated that impairment still occurred on a final recall test when the output order of items within a category was controlled. In this study, unpracticed competitors were always tested prior to stronger practiced competitors through the use of stem cues that uniquely identified each exemplar (e.g., *fruit–a___*) within the experiment. M. C. Anderson and Spellman (1995) observed similar findings, demonstrating that cross-category impairment of items like *food–radish* (see previous section) still occurred on a category-cued recall test when participants were cued to recall the unpracticed category prior to the practiced category. These findings show that retrieval-induced forgetting endures for at least 20 min, rendering it plausible that the mechanisms of retrieval produce the enduring character of episodic recall failure.

G. Retrieval as the Internal Focus of Attention

The findings just reviewed support the notion that retrieval processes in both episodic and semantic memory employ active suppression processes. This suppression causes deficits in the ability to use the affected information on subsequent tasks, which, in the case of episodic memory, may be quite enduring. Thus, such processes might seem quite undesirable. However, several authors (M. C. Anderson et al., 1994; M.C. Anderson & Spellman, 1995; R. A. Bjork, 1989; R. A. Bjork & Bjork, 1992; Dagenbach & Carr, 1994b; Hasher & Zacks, 1988; Keele & Neill, 1978; Neill, 1989; Zacks & Hasher, 1994) have argued for the functional utility of suppression processes as well (see the previous section on directed forgetting for a related discussion). In this section, we consider this functionality in the context of computational models of retrieval in situations that require selective attention. Such considerations have led to the novel claim that retrieval might best be viewed as the internal focus of selective attention, a claim that we hereafter refer to as the *attentional focusing view*. This view suggests a broader approach to understanding why phenomena as diverse as fact retrieval, lexical access, and episodic recollection might share common mechanisms underlying interference.

1. Selective Retrieval and Selective Attention

Most people would agree that attention can be shifted from objects in the external world to objects in the internal world, such as images, facts, or episodes generated on the basis of past experience. For example, to recollect what you had for dinner last evening requires that you cease reading so that attention may be refocused to the mental representation of last evening's dinner. Focusing attention in this manner is likely to bring the contents of that experience into awareness, allowing it to serve as a basis for the requested recollection. When characterized in this manner, the process of accessing particular items of prior knowledge can be viewed as selective attention toward an object that is no longer present in the external world. M. C. Anderson and Spellman (1995) identified these cases of selective retrieval as requiring what they called *conceptually focused selective attention*, thereby highlighting their similarity to cases of perceptually focused selective attention. This similarity is shown in Figure 9, which is taken from M. C. Anderson and Spellman (1995).

Figure 9A depicts the real-world perceptual problem of focusing attention on one piece of fruit in a nearly full fruit bowl. In this figure, the representations of the several fruits receive activation in parallel from per-

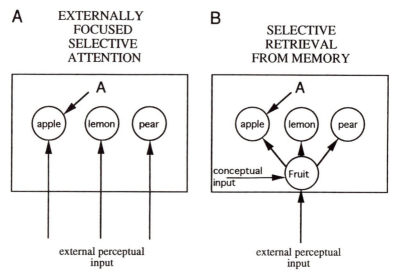

FIGURE 9   A schematic illustration of the relationship between selective attention (A) and selective retrieval from memory (B). In selective attention, attention ("A" in figure) isolates the representation of one fruit (apple) from amongst many fruits activated by external perceptual input. In memory retrieval, attention ("A") isolates the representation of one fruit (apple) from amongst many fruits activated by a retrieval cue (*fruit*), itself activated either by other concepts or by the external world.

ceptual input. Now, consider Figure 9B, which depicts the problem of focusing attention on one fruit among many present in long-term memory. In this figure, the representations of these fruits receive activation in parallel from a shared retrieval cue (which, in turn, may have been activated either by external perceptual input or by activation from other internal conceptual representations). In either case, selectively attending to one of the fruits entails the isolation of its representation from those of its competitors. According to this characterization, the primary differences between selective attention and selective retrieval are: (1) whether the competing representations' activations are conceptually or perceptually initiated; and (2) whether the output of attention is a consciously experienced memory or a consciously experienced percept. In both cases, proper task performance demands the selection of a single representation from among a set of active competitors. If we regard this function of selection as basic to selective attention, then selective retrieval can be regarded as conceptually focused selective attention.

Viewing retrieval as conceptually focused attention has interesting implications for work in both attention and memory. First, the evidence we have reviewed on interference effects in memory would bear on the question of whether attentional selection is achieved via facilitatory or inhibitory processes. Although most theorists agree that attention must somehow facilitate to-be-attended representations, the existence of inhibitory processes for deactivating distracting items is controversial (see Dagenbach & Carr, 1994b, for a collection of papers examining the status of inhibitory processes in cognition). To the extent that memory retrieval can be regarded as conceptually focused attention, data supporting the operation of suppression processes in retrieval and in perceptual selection tasks mutually reinforce each other, suggesting the broader conclusion that suppression achieves attentional selection.

Recent work with the negative-priming paradigm supports such a relation between memory retrieval and perceptually focused selective attention (for excellent reviews of negative priming, see Fox, 1995; Houghton & Tipper, 1994; May, Kane, & Hasher, 1995; Neill, Valdes, & Terry, 1994). In one version of this paradigm (Tipper, 1985), people are presented two line drawings of familiar objects, one in red, the other in green, and are asked to respond to the red one (the target) and to ignore the green one (the distractor). Reaction time to respond to a target on a critical trial, called the probe, is examined as a function of that probe's relation to the immediately preceding trial, called the prime. As might be expected, response times are faster to a target on the probe trial if it had also appeared as a target on the prime trial, relative to a condition in which the two trials are entirely unrelated. More provocative is the finding that response times to the target on the probe trial are longer when that stimulus had been ignored (i.e., was a distractor) on the prime trial. Interestingly, this latter effect, called negative priming, can under some circumstances persist through the presentation of other unrelated items between the prime and probe trials (DeSchepper & Treisman, 1996; Tipper, Weaver, Cameron, Brehaut, & Bestedo, 1991).

The negative-priming paradigm provides a clear test of the situation depicted in Figure 9A, in which attention must be directed to a single item among many activated in a parallel by perceptual input. Thus, the finding that focusing attention to a target percept (i.e., the red item) slows subsequent response times to ignored items (i.e., the green item) supports the hypothesis (Neill, 1977; Tipper, 1985) that attention employs active suppression processes to overcome interference. However, other accounts exist (Lowe, 1979; Park & Kanwisher, 1994). One such account, offered by Neill and Valdes (1992) and Neill, Valdes, Terry, and Gorfein (1992), is analogous to the notion of response competition reviewed in the present chapter. According to this approach, people encode the stimulus that they are supposed to ignore (which we will call the A stimulus) and associate it with the thought "no response," because they understand that they are to respond only to the target item. When that A distractor stimulus appears later as a target, people are assumed spontaneously to retrieve the "no response" feature associated with that A stimulus, which causes competition for the retrieval of the current task-relevant response to A. The extent to which such spontaneous retrievals occur should vary with factors influencing the retrievability of the prime distractor, such as delay and similarity. Although both the suppression and occlusion hypotheses easily accommodate many of the same findings, each accounts for some effects that the other has trouble explaining. Because of this, Fox (1995) and Milliken, Tipper, and Weaver (1994) have argued that both mechanisms are likely to contribute to the negative-priming effect. If these conclusions are correct, the phenomena of negative priming converge with those reviewed in the present chapter, concerning the role of attentional suppression in memory retrieval.

The attentional focusing view of memory retrieval suggests an intriguing perspective on the behavioral causes of forgetting that differs from traditional analyses. Specifically, this view implies that our experiences of retrieval failure may be linked to the very mechanisms that allow us effectively to direct cognition to particular objects in both the external and internal worlds. To understand the implications of this view, consider how semantic memory is used to mediate intelligent behavior, such as reasoning and communication. Because these activities demand prolonged sequential access to very specific referents in memory, they should entail an ongoing barrage of inhibitory suppression that renders access to even well-established conceptual representations volatile. In the case of episodic memory, the elaborate and incidental recollections that occur throughout the day should influence the subsequent accessibility of the episodic representations activated during those recollections. Thus, whereas classical views of interference have emphasized the role of learning as the primary cause of forgetting, the attentional focusing view emphasizes issues of cognitive control related to the retrieval and use of information, once acquired.

2. Comparisons to Previously Postulated Interference Mechanisms

Although the attentional focusing view of memory retrieval is a relatively new approach to interference effects, many of its aspects resemble components of classical interference theory. We now turn to a discussion of some of the specific relations between the attentional focusing view and three components of classical interference theory: occlusion, unlearning, and response-set suppression. We suggest that the attentional focusing view validates many of the intuitions behind these classical proposals, while at the same time questioning the historical emphasis on associative learning as a cause of forgetting.

a. Occlusion

The occlusion approach assumes that competition, if sufficiently strong, blocks the retrieval of otherwise intact memory items long enough for search efforts to be abandoned. Although the attentional focusing view also assumes that competition impedes recall, the nature of the impediment differs from that in occlusion. In the attentional focusing account, although retrieval competition causes the slowing of recall, it does not directly cause forgetting, as in occlusion; rather, it triggers the need for conceptually focused selective attention. That is, competition among items sharing a cue impedes target retrieval only until inhibitory control processes reduce interference from those competing items, at which point the target will be retrieved.

But how can the attentional focusing view explain the subjective experience of occlusion and its apparent relation to retrieval failure? Such experiences might arise in two ways. First, the retrieval target might be so weakly represented in memory that retrieval failure would occur regardless of whether perseverations of competitors accompanied the experience. To the extent that only partial target information, in the form of a few of the target's featural attributes, is available in memory, items sharing those attributes will tend to be recalled during attempts to retrieve the target. Second, suppression mechanisms might fail to exclude nontarget competitors from consciousness during an initial retrieval, perhaps because of distraction or because those competitors are especially strong. To the extent that retrieval of nontargets entails the (accidental) suppression of the desired item, such intrusions should impair target memory. After being suppressed a first time, the likelihood that suppression will occur again should increase, especially when we consider the increased accessibility of the intruded item. Thus, although the experience of occlusion surely occurs, the attentional focusing view ascribes little role to it as a mechanism of retrieval failure, independent of the suppression that would accompany this experience. Strong evidence for this view comes from M. C. Anderson et al.'s (1994) demonstration (see previous section on retrieval-induced forgetting in episodic memory) that associative strengthening of items via retrieval practice fails to impair competing items if they were unlikely to have been suppressed during that retrieval practice.

b. Unlearning

The conditions and causes of forgetting proposed in the attentional focusing account are quite similar to those proposed in the classical unlearning hypothesis (Melton & Irwin, 1940). According to the unlearning account of retroactive interference in the A–B, A–D paradigm, responses previously learned in List 1 intrude inappropriately during the learning of new responses in List 2. Such intrusions lead to the extinction of the stimulus–response associations linking the A cues to the older intruding B responses, impairing later memory for the A–B pairing. The attentional focusing view emphasizes competitor interference as a prerequisite of impairment, as does unlearning and occlusion.

The unlearning and attentional focusing approaches also both assume that competitor interference triggers a special process by which interfering items are impaired directly, increasing the effectiveness of subsequent retrievals of newly learned information. The attentional focusing account differs from the unlearning proposal, however, in the locus of the impairment and in the mechanisms by which impairment occurs. First, in unlearning, forgetting stems from decrements in cue–target associations, whereas in attentional focusing, impairment is localized to the target item itself. As illustrated in our discussion of the research addressing cue-independent forgetting (M. C. Anderson & Spellman, 1995), impairment associated with memory retrieval generalizes to other cues in a way not predicted by the unlearning hypothesis. Second, the unlearning proposal attributes forgetting to decrements in associative bonds caused by a general learning process, invoked by feedback on whether a retrieved item is appropriate or inappropriate. The attentional focusing view, on the other hand, ascribes forgetting to the reversible suppression of target items caused by an inhibitory control process. This control process reduces interference from competing items, but gives no special importance to the appropriateness of the retrieved item. (That is, suppression of competing items occurs whether a person overtly recalls the target or accidentally intrudes a distractor.) Thus, whereas the present view agrees with the functional conditions proposed in the unlearning hypothesis, it attributes forgetting to inhibitory control processes rather than to associative learning mechanisms.

c. Response-Set Suppression

Aspects of the attentional focusing view also bear strong resemblance to the response-set suppression hypothesis (Postman et al., 1968). This classical hypothesis attributes a portion of the recall impairment observed in retroactive interference to the suppression of the whole set of intrusive responses from List 1, during acquisition trials on a new set of responses in List 2. According to the response-set suppression hypothesis, the representations of intrusive items are impaired, in reversible fashion, by a control process (i.e., a selector mechanism), functioning to enhance performance in a more current activity. Thus, both the attentional focusing view and response-set suppression emphasize the item representation as the locus of effect and the role of inhibitory control processes in producing impairment.

The attentional focusing view differs from response-set suppression in two respects, however. First, according to Postman et al.'s (1968) classical view, the suppression process is directed at the entire set of List 1 responses and not to any particular item. Although intrusions of particular List 1 items trigger the selector mechanism, the consequent suppression impairs all List 1 items, irrespective of whether they intrude. The attentional focusing account differs in that suppression is directed at individual competitors as a function of whether they compete with target retrieval. Second, the response-set suppression process was construed as a way of shifting response sets, triggered in response to intrusions (see R. A. Bjork, 1989; R. A. Bjork & Bjork, 1992; Zacks & Hasher, 1994, for related functional proposals). In attentional focusing, inhibition occurs as part of the retrieval process, instead of after it, assisting in the isolation of the target item in memory. Nevertheless, even with these differences, the present attentional focusing proposal captures several aspects of response-set suppression, in the context of a theory that considers the on-line dynamics of retrieval.

V. RELATED RESEARCH AREAS

As should be clear from the findings covered in the present chapter, interference effects occur in a broad range of memory paradigms. Because interference is so ubiquitous, space limitations prevent us from covering data from all of the experimental paradigms in which such effects have been studied. Nonetheless, we mention here briefly several areas of research likely to be of interest to many readers, providing references to pertinent sources.

A. Generalizability of Interference Research

The first area concerns whether generalizations about interference as studied with verbal materials apply to other modes of knowledge, and also to other subject populations. Although the present review has focused primarily on interference phenomena in human verbal memory, interference effects in long-term memory have been demonstrated in other knowledge domains, including people's memory for visual stimuli (see, e.g., Chandler, 1989; 1991; Deffenbacher, Carr, & Leu, 1981), for motor skills (Hicks & Cohn, 1975; Hicks & Young, 1973; D. Lewis, McAllister, & Adams, 1951; D. Lewis, Shepard, & Adams, 1949; McAllister & Lewis, 1951; see Adams, 1987, p. 50, for discussion); and for facts accessed during cognitive skills such as mental arithmetic (Campbell, 1987, 1990, 1991; Campbell & Clark, 1989; Campbell, 1995). The basic phenomena and principles of interference studied in human memory also appear to characterize performance in studies of animal learning that employ Pavlovian conditioning paradigms (see Bouton, 1993, for review). Unfortunately, a discussion of how interference effects in these domains relate to those observed in verbal memory is beyond the scope of the present chapter.

   Much of the work reported thus far has focused on interference as it occurs in normal populations. However, a great deal of recent work has examined characteristics of interference in special populations in which the management of interference through inhibitory processes may be a crucial issue. For instance, deficits in the ability to inhibit interfering representations have been proposed to underlie cognitive changes associated with normal aging (Gerard, Zacks, Hasher, & Radvansky, 1991; Hartman & Hasher, 1991; Hasher, Stolzfus, Zacks, & Rympa, 1991; Hasher & Zacks, 1988; Kane, Hasher, Stolzfus, Zacks, & Connelly, 1994; McDowd, & Filion, 1992; McDowd, Oseas-Kreger, & Filion, 1994; see also Light, Chapter 13, this volume, for a thorough review of this proposal), and with several clinical syndromes, including schizophrenia (Beech, Powell, McWilliams, & Claridge, 1989; Cohen & Servan-Schreiber, 1992) and frontal lobe dysfunction (Fuster, 1989; Luria, 1966; Mishkin, 1964; Shimamura, 1994). The ability to inhibit extraneous information has even been proposed as an important dimension of general intelligence (Dempster, 1991). The general hypothesis in each of these cases is that the many cognitive deficits observed in these special populations may reflect a more basic deficit in the utilization of attentional inhibition. If these populations suffer from a generalized deficit in the ability to inhibit activated representations, they should exhibit exaggerated susceptibility to interference in both attention and memory tasks. At present, there appears to be promising support for a general, exaggerated susceptibility to interference in these populations, but further work must be done before this characteristic can be confidently attributed to impaired inhibitory processes (see Dagenbach & Carr, 1994b, Dempster & Brainerd, 1994, for collections of reviews of inhibitory processes).

B. The Misinformation Effect in Eyewitness Memory

A second area of research concerns how people's memory reports for the details of a crime event might be affected by encoding misleading information after the original event has been witnessed. Research on this topic began with the classic series of studies by Loftus and colleagues (Loftus, 1975, 1977, 1979a; Loftus, Miller, & Burns, 1978; Loftus & Palmer, 1974) using what has come to be known as the *misinformation procedure*. In a typical version of this procedure, people first view a series of photographic slides depicting a crime event such as a traffic accident or a theft. People then receive additional information about the crime, often in the form of a narrative summarizing the relevant events and details. For participants in the *misled* condition, one of these details is altered, and is thus inaccurate. For example, if the previous slides depicted a car passing a stop sign, the narrative might state that the car had passed a yield sign. People in the *control* condition receive the same narrative, except that the crucial detail is omitted (or in many studies, described in neutral terms, like "sign" instead of "stop sign"). Of crucial interest is whether, on a final recognition test, people select the correct slide on a critical trial in which the originally viewed slide (e.g., of a car passing a stop sign) is paired with a distractor altered to be consistent with the misleading detail (e.g., a slide depicting the same car passing a yield sign).

Numerous studies using this procedure have demonstrated that people receiving misinformation in the intervening narrative select the previously viewed slide significantly less often than do people not receiving misinformation (see Loftus & Hoffman, 1989, for a thorough listing of these studies). For example, in a study by Loftus et al. (1978), misled participants selected the correct slide only 42% of the time, whereas participants in the control condition correctly selected the appropriate slide 75% of the time (numbers estimated from Figure 2 in Loftus et al., 1978). Thus, presenting verbal misinformation after an original event seems substantially to impair people's memory for that event, much like the impairment observed in the classical retroactive interference procedure (compare to Figure 3A). Two aspects of the misinformation effect seem especially striking, especially when considering its relationship to retroactive interference. First, the deficit caused by a single incidental exposure to misinformation appears dramatic: Performance drops from a high level (75%) to worse than would be expected if people were guessing randomly between the two slides (42%). Second, this deficit occurs on a recognition accuracy test, even though retroactive interference is often reduced or even absent on such tests. Based on these considerations and on participants' high confidence when selecting the incorrect slide (Loftus et al., 1978; Tversky & Tuchin, 1989), Loftus has argued that misleading information permanently alters the memory trace for the original event (Loftus, 1975, 1979a, 1979b, 1981; Loftus & Loftus, 1980; Loftus et al., 1978).

Recent work has challenged this memory alteration view, however. Critics argue that misleading information has no effect on people's *memory* for the previously viewed events (McCloskey & Zarragoza, 1985a, 1985b; Zaragoza & Koshmider, 1989; Zaragoza & McCloskey, 1989; Zaragoza, McCloskey, & Jamis, 1987). Rather, decreased overall performance in the misled condition is seen to arise from a select subset of participants in that condition—namely, those participants who, for reasons unrelated to the encoding of misinformation, forgot the initially seen detail and who thus instead selected the altered slide based on their recollection of the misinformation. Although the issues are complex, many authors agree that such response bias or *misinformation acceptance* (Belli, 1989) contributes to the deficit caused by the misinformation procedure (see Belli, 1989; Loftus & Hoffman, 1989). Recent discussion has focused on whether misinformation acceptance is itself an interesting phenomenon (for arguments in favor see Loftus & Hoffman, 1989), whether accessibility is impaired beyond this bias (for supportive evidence see Belli, 1989; Bekerian & Bowers, 1983; Chandler, 1989; Christiannsen & Oschalek, 1983; Tversky & Tuchin, 1989; but see also Zaragoza et al., 1987), and, if so, whether impairment reflects failure to recollect the information in the original event (Chandler, 1991) or confusion over its source (Lindsay, 1990; Lindsay & Johnson, 1988). As discussion of this effect evolves, it is interesting to see that many of the central issues faced by theorists from the classical interference era (e.g., the issue, highlighted in the present chapter, of whether forgetting is produced by unlearning or response competition) have reemerged as pivotal to this debate and its implications for eyewitness memory (see Chandler & Fisher, Chapter 14, this volume, for further discussion of eyewitness memory).

C. Interference on Direct and Indirect Tests of Memory

A third and fairly recent area of research concerns whether interference effects occur on indirect memory tasks. Most of the tasks employed in both classical and modern studies of interference have been direct memory tasks, that is, tasks designed to tap what is now referred to as explicit memory. Direct memory tasks direct participants to make explicit reference to their particular study experience with the prior item to perform the task (e.g., free recall, cued recall, and recognition tests). Over the last decade, considerable attention has been given to how performance on such tasks might differ from performance on tasks that measure memory for a prior episode without actually asking a person to try to recollect that episode consciously (see Kelley & Lindsay, Chapter 2, this volume; Roediger & McDermott, 1993; Schacter, 1987). Often, research on this topic directly compares performance on indirect and direct tests as follows: People in both conditions study a list of words and then participate in a test of their memory for those words. In a commonly used paradigm, word stems (e.g., *car___*, for *carrot* or *ank__*, for *ankle*) are used as the retrieval cues. In the direct memory test, people are instructed to use each stem as a cue for retrieving a word they had just studied; in the indirect memory test, people are told, without reference to the prior study list, that they should complete the stem with the first word that comes to mind. In both tests, the benefits of prior study are revealed when people are more likely to complete the stem with a studied word than with a nonstudied word.

Considerable data now exist showing that many variables affect performance on direct and indirect tests in different and sometimes opposite ways (see the earlier mentioned reviews). Might these varieties of memory also be differentially susceptible to interference effects of the sort reviewed in the present chapter? The study most relevant to our present coverage was reported by Graf and Schacter (1987), who had people study paired associates in what corresponds to an A–B, A–D paradigm. In Graf and Schacter's experiment, people studied four different new responses to an A stimulus during A–D learning (rather than the customary one). For example, people first studied a pair such as *hen–carrot*, followed later by *hen–pond*, *hen–tree*, *hen–zipper*, and *hen–money*. In the control condition, the stimulus *hen* appeared only in the *hen–carrot* pair. Memory for response members of these paired associates was assessed in two ways, corresponding to the direct and indirect cued-recall methods described previously, except that each stem appeared beside a studied stimulus term (e.g., *hen–car___*). When people were explicitly instructed to retrieve the previously studied item that fit the stem cue, they suffered massive retroactive interference: Stem completion for the studied word was far worse when four other response terms had been studied with that stimulus than when only the cued response itself had been studied. Remarkably, people suffered no retroactive interference in the corresponding indirect memory test! Although a similar dissociation between retroactive interference effects in direct and indirect memory tests has been reported with word lists involving the presentation of individual words rather than paired associates (Jacoby, 1983), other studies using lists of individually presented words have obtained retroactive interference for both indirect and direct tests (see Roediger & McDermott, 1993, for review). One might also question the generality of Graf and Schacter's findings on the basis of the abundance of classical interference findings demonstrating retroactive interference in the MFR test (see previous section on paired associated methodology), which demands only that the subject recall the first verbal response that comes to mind. Nevertheless, the Graf and Schacter (1987) results provide tantalizing, though isolated, evidence that the kinds of interference mechanisms discussed in the present chapter may somehow be short-circuited by indirect memory tests (see, however, related work on directed forgetting in implicit memory: Basden et al., 1993; R. A. Bjork & Bjork, 1991; MacLeod, 1989; Paller, 1990). This intriguing finding clearly merits additional experimental scrutiny.

VI. SUMMARY AND CONCLUSIONS

The function of memory is never so conspicuous and astonishing as when it fails us. One cannot help but wonder how the events of our past—events from the best of times and from the worst of times, events that have shaped our characters and that verify our continued existence—fade to oblivion; or how a concept once well mastered and useful deteriorates into confusion and misunderstanding; or how the name of a friend whom we have known for many years eludes us, even if only momentarily. Such failures abound in daily experience, and sometimes with great consequence, motivating the abundant experimental research that has been devoted to their explanation. In the present chapter, we reviewed research on what many theorists agree is one of the most potent and pervasive factors underlying these experiences: interference.

Interference refers to the impaired ability to remember an item when it is similar to other items stored in memory. Interest in interference was initiated at the turn of the century, when G. E. Mueller and Pilzecker (1900) reported the first empirical study of retroactive interference. This observation ultimately led to a program of research lasting seventy years, the primary focus of which was to explain the substantial forgetting associated with interference. A core advance coming out of this classical era was a simple characterization of the basic situation of interference as competition between items sharing a common retrieval cue. According to this idea, attaching additional memory "responses" to a particular "stimulus" reduces recall performance on target items because those additional items compete with targets upon presentation of their shared stimulus. This core idea permeates modern theoretical work in a variety of domains, although the terms used to characterize competition may vary in each case. Indeed, the last twenty years have illustrated that these elementary dynamics apply to a variety of cognitive tasks in which one must select between multiple concurrently activated mental representations, such as: (1) trying to retrieve a specific episode from our past; (2) trying to retrieve facts that we encoded into semantic memory; (3) performing the seemingly effortless task of retrieving a single word's meaning, spelling, or pronunciation; (4) trying to select, for additional analysis, an object from among other objects in our perceptual environment; and (5) trying to retrieve sequentially the information needed to form a coherent sentence or argument or to solve a problem.

Many theories have been proposed to explain why associating additional items to a retrieval cue might render those items more susceptible to interference. In general, theories addressing this question may be divided into three categories, defined by the locus of the memory representation thought to play the greatest role in causing interference: theories attributing forgetting to changes in (1) the cues that people use to retrieve targets in memory; (2) the associations linking retrieval cues to targets; and (3) the targets themselves. Classical interference factors such as response competition and unlearning (comprising the Two-Factor Theory, Melton & Irwin, 1940) emphasized the role of associative learning processes, fitting our experience of forgetting into the general mold of learning theories prevalent during that era. Late in the development of the classical interference period, additional factors such as variable-stimulus encoding (E. Martin, 1968, 1971) and response-set suppression (Postman et al., 1968) were proposed, in which forgetting was attributed to changes in the retrieval cue and the memory target representations, respectively. Unfortunately, although these later theories of interference have considerable plausibility, they have not received the attention given to associative interference theories, in part, because the focus of memory research shifted from interference shortly after their development (see Wheeler, 1995, for a similar perspective). Since the end of the classical interference era, theories of interference have focused primarily on mechanisms of response competition (specifically, occlusion), reflecting a general disenchantment with unlearning and a belief that interference is best conceived as retrieval inhibition, that is, the failure to retrieve otherwise available memory items.

In the final section of this chapter, we presented a recent perspective on the causes of memory interference that casts our experiences of forgetting in a very different light. According to this perspective, our tendency to forget is intimately linked with the very mechanisms that allow focused memory retrieval to occur. That is, forgetting of target items derives not from learning interfering information per se, but from the selective retrieval of that interfering information after it has been acquired. Selectively retrieving related items harms our later recall of critical target memories by means of an active suppression process that inhibits those critical targets; although this suppression process helps to overcome competition exerted by these critical items, it has the side effect of impairing the retrieval of those targets when they later become relevant. Because inhibitory control processes are thought to be triggered in situations much like those we face in situations requiring selective attention, it is argued that retrieval should be regarded as a case of conceptually focused selective attention. We argued herein that this view validates many of the intuitions underlying classical theories of forgetting, while questioning the widespread assumption that forgetting derives in any direct way from associative learning. Rather, our many losses—of memories of past experiences, of our friends' names, or of our comprehension of concepts with which we once were adept—are seen as costs of the very mechanisms that enable us to direct cognition to internal thoughts and to the external environment.

Acknowledgments

The authors would like to thank Mike Ciranni, Chad Dodson, and Arthur Shimamura for commenting on early drafts of this chapter, and Elizabeth Bjork, Bob Bjork, C. C. Chandler, and Henry Roediger for help with the final version. Writing of this paper was supported by postdoctoral Grant 94-21 to M. C. Anderson by the McDonnell-Pew foundation, and by Grant MH48757 to Arthur Shimamura from the National Institute of Mental Health.

References

Adams, J. A. (1987). Historical review and appraisal of research on the learning, retention and transfer of human motor skills. *Psychological Bulletin, 101,* 41–74.

Anderson, J. R. (1974). Retrieval of propositional information from long-term memory *Cognitive Psychology, 6,* 451–474.

Anderson, J. R. (1976). *Language, memory and thought.* Hillsdale, NJ: Erlbaum.

Anderson, J. R. (1983). *The architecture of cognition.* Cambridge: Harvard University Press.

Anderson, M. C., & Bjork, R. A. (1994). Mechanisms of inhibition in long-term memory: A new taxonomy. In D. Dagenbach & T. Carr (Eds.), *Inhibitory processes in attention, memory, and language* (pp. 265–325). San Diego: Academic Press.

Anderson, M. C., Bjork, R. A., & Bjork, E. L. (1994). Remembering can cause forgetting: Retrieval dynamics in long-term memory. *Journal of Experimental Psychology: Learning, Memory, and Cognition, 20,* 1063–1087.

Anderson, M. C., & Spellman, B. A. (1995). On the status of inhibitory mechanisms in cognition: Memory retrieval as a model case. *Psychological Review, 102,* 68–100.

Anderson, R. C., & Watts, G. H. (1971). Response competition in the forgetting of paired associates. *Journal of Verbal Learning and Verbal Behavior, 10,* 29–34.

Balota, D. A., Ferraro, F. R., & Connor, L. T. (1991). On the early influence of meaning on word recognition: A review of the literature. In P. Schwanenflugel (Ed.), *The psychology of word meanings* (pp. 187–222). Hillsdale, NJ: Erlbaum.

Barnes, J. M., & Underwood, B. J. (1959). "Fate" of first-list associations in transfer theory. *Journal of Experimental Psychology, 58,* 95–105.

Basden, B. H., Basden, D. R., & Gargano, G. J. (1993). Directed forgetting in implicit and explicit memory tests: A comparison of methods. *Journal of Experimental Psychology: Learning, Memory, and Cognition, 19,* 603–616.

Beech, A., Powell, T., McWilliams, J., & Claridge, G. (1989). Evidence of reduced "cognitive inhibition" in schizophrenia. *British Journal of Clinical Psychology, 28,* 110–116.

Bekerian, D. A., & Bowers, J. M. (1983). Eyewitness testimony: Were we misled? *Journal of Experimental Psychology: Learning, Memory, and Cognition, 9,* 139–145.

Belli, R. F. (1989). Influences of misleading postevent information: Misinformation interference and acceptance. *Journal of Experimental Psychology: General, 118,* 72–85.

Bjork, E. L., Bjork, R. A., & Glenberg, A. (1973, November). *Reinstatement of interference owing to to-be-forgotten items.* Paper presented at the meeting of the Psychonomic Society, St. Louis, MO.

Bjork, E. L., Bjork, R. A., & White, S. (1984, November). *On the induced recovery of proactive interference.* Paper presented at the meeting of the Psychonomic Society, San Antonio, TX.

Bjork, R. A. (1970). Positive forgetting: The noninterference of items intentionally forgotten. *Journal of Verbal Learning and Verbal Behavior, 9,* 255–268.

Bjork, R. A. (1972). Theoretical implications of directed forgetting. In A. W. Melton & E. Martin (Eds.), *Coding processes in human memory* (pp. 217–235). Washington, DC: Winston.

Bjork, R. A. (1989). Retrieval inhibition as an adaptive mechanism in human memory. In H. L. Roediger & F. I. M. Craik (Eds.), *Varieties of memory and consciousness: Essays in honour of Endel Tulving* (pp. 309–330). Hillsdale, NJ: Erlbaum.

Bjork, R. A., & Bjork, E. L. (1991). *Dissociations in the impact of to-be-forgotten information on memory.* Paper presented at the 99th Annual Convention of the American Psychological Association, San Francisco.

Bjork, R. A., & Bjork, E. L. (1992). A new theory of disuse and an old theory of stimulus fluctuation. In A. F. Healy, S. M. Kosslyn, & R. M. Shiffrin (Eds.), *Essays in honor of William K. Estes: Vol. 1. From learning theory to connectionist theory* (pp. 35–67). Hillsdale, NJ: Erlbaum.

Bjork, R. A., & Woodward, A. E., (1973). Directed forgetting of individual words in free recall. *Journal of Experimental Psychology, 99,* 22–27.

Blaxton, T. A., & Bookheimer, S. Y. (1993). Retrieval inhibition in anomia. *Brain and Language, 22,* 221–237.

Blaxton, T. A., & Neely, J. H. (1983). Inhibition from semantically related primes: Evidence of a category-specific retrieval inhibition. *Memory & Cognition, 11,* 500–510.

Bouton, M. E. (1993). Context, time and memory retrieval in the interference paradigms of Pavlovian learning. *Psychological Bulletin, 114,* 80–99.

Bower, G. H., Thompson-Schill, S., & Tulving, E. (1994). Reducing retroactive interference: An interference analysis. *Journal of Experimental Psychology: Learning, Memory, and Cognition, 20,* 51–66.

Brown, A. S. (1979). Priming effects in semantic memory retrieval processes. *Journal of Experimental Psychology: Human Learning and Memory, 5,* 65–77.

Brown, A. S. (1981). Inhibition in cued retrieval. *Journal of Experimental Psychology: Human Learning and Memory, 7,* 204–215.

Brown, A. S. (1991). The tip of the tongue experience: A review and evaluation. *Psychological Bulletin, 109,* 204–223.

Brown, J. (1968). Reciprocal facilitation and impairment in free recall. *Psychonomic Science, 10,* 41–42.

Brown, R., & McNeill, D. (1966). The tip-of-the-tongue phenomenon. *Journal of Verbal Learning and Verbal Behavior, 5,* 325–337.

Burgess, C., & Simpson, G. B. (1988). Cerebral hemispheric mechanisms in the retrieval of ambiguous word meanings. *Brain and Language, 33,* 86–103.

Bushell, C. (in press). Dissociated identity and semantic priming in Broca's aphasia: How controlled processing produces inhibitory semantic priming. *Brain and Language.*

Campbell, J. I. D. (1987). Network interference and mental multiplication. *Journal of Experimental Psychology: Learning, Memory, and Cognition, 13,* 109–123.

Campbell, J. I. D. (1990). Retrieval inhibition and interference in cognitive arithmetic. *Canadian Journal of Psychology, 44,* 445–464.

Campbell, J. I. D. (1991). Conditions of error priming in number-fact retrieval. *Memory & Cognition, 19,* 197–209.

Campbell, J. I. D. (1995). Mechanisms of simple addition and multiplication: A modified network-interference theory and stimulation. *Mathematical Cognition, 1,* 121–164.

Campbell, J. I. D., & Clark, J. M. (1989). Time course of error priming in number fact retrieval: Evidence for excitatory and inhibitory mechanisms. *Journal of Experimental Psychology: Learning, Memory, and Cognition, 15,* 920–929.

Carr, T. H., & Dagenbach, D. (1990). Semantic priming and repetition priming from masked words: Evidence for a center-surround attentional mechanism in perceptual recognition. *Journal of Experimental Psychology: Learning, Memory, and Cognition, 16,* 341–350.

Ceraso, J., & Henderson, A. (1965). Unavailability and associative loss in RI and PI. *Journal of Experimental Psychology, 70,* 300–303.

Ceraso, J., & Henderson, A. (1966). Unavailability and associative loss in RI and PI: Second try. *Journal of Experimental Psychology, 72,* 314–316.

Chandler, C. C. (1989). Specific retroactive interference in modified recognition tasks: Evidence for an unknown cause of interference. *Journal of Experimental Psychology: Learning, Memory, and Cognition, 16,* 341–350.

Chandler, C. C. (1991). How memory for an event is influenced by related events: Interference in modified recognition tests. *Journal of Experimental Psychology: Learning, Memory, and Cognition, 17,* 115–125.

Chandler, C. C., & Gargano, G. J. (1995). Item-specific interference caused by cue-dependent forgetting. *Memory & Cognition, 23,* 701–708.

Christiannsen, R. E., & Oschalek, K. (1983). Editing misleading information from memory: Evidence for coexistence of original and postevent information. *Memory & Cognition, 11,* 467–475.

Coe, W. C., Basden, B. H., Basden, D., & Fikes, T. (1989). Directed forgetting and posthypnotic amnesia: Information processing and social contexts. *Journal of Personality and Social Psychology, 56,* 189–198.

Cohen, J. D., & Servan-Schreiber, D. (1992). Context, cortex and dopamine: A connectionist approach to behavior and biology in schizophrenia. *Psychological Review, 99,* 45–77.

Conway, A. R. A., & Engle, R. W. (1994). Working memory and retrieval: A resource dependent inhibition model. *Journal of Experimental Psychology: General, 123,* 354–373.

Crowder, R. G. (1976). *Principles of learning and memory.* Hillsdale, NJ: Erlbaum.

Dagenbach, D., & Carr, T. H. (1994a). Inhibitory processes in perceptual recognition: Evidence for a center-surround attentional mechanism. In D. Dagenbach & T. Carr (Eds.), *Inhibitory processes in attention, memory, and language* (pp. 327–358). San Diego: Academic Press.

Dagenbach, D., & Carr, T. H. (Eds.). (1994b). *Inhibitory processes in attention, memory, and language.* San Diego: Academic Press.

Dagenbach, D., Carr, T. H., & Barnhardt, T. M. (1990). Inhibitory semantic priming of lexical decisions due to failure to retrieve weakly activated codes. *Journal of Experimental Psychology: Learning, Memory, and Cognition, 16,* 328–340.

Dagenbach, D., Carr, T. H., & Wilhelmson, A. (1989). Task-induced strategies and near-threshold priming: Conscious influences on unconscious perception. *Journal of Memory and Language,* 412–443.

Davis, J. C., & Okada, R. (1971). Recognition and recall of positively forgotten items. *Journal of Experimental Psychology, 89,* 181–186.

Deffenbacher, K. A., Carr, T. H., & Leu, J. R. (1981). Memory for words, pictures, and faces: Retroactive interference, forgetting, and reminiscence. *Journal of Experimental Psychology: Human Learning and Memory, 7,* 299–305.

Dempster, F. N. (1991). Inhibitory processes: A neglected dimension of intelligence. *Intelligence, 15,* 157–173.

Dempster, F. N., & Brainerd, C. J. (Eds.). (1994). *New perspectives on interference and inhibition.* New York: Academic Press.

DeSchepper, B., & Treisman, A. M. (1996). Visual memory for novel shapes: Implicit coding without attention. *Journal of Experimental Psychology: Learning, Memory, and Cognition, 22,* 27–47.

Epstein, W. (1972). Mechanisms of directed forgetting. In G. H. Bower (Ed.), *The psychology of learning and motivation: Advances in research and theory* (Vol. 6, pp. 147–191). New York: Academic Press.

Epstein, W., Massaro, D. W., & Wilder, L. (1972). Selective search in directed forgetting. *Journal of Experimental Psychology, 94*, 18–24.

Epstein, W., & Wilder, L. (1972). Searching for to-be-forgotten material in a directed forgetting task. *Journal of Experimental Psychology, 95*, 349–357.

Erdelyi, M. H. (1985). *Psychoanalysis: Freud's cognitive psychology.* New York: W. H. Freeman.

Erdelyi, M. H. (1993). Repression: The mechanism and the defense. In D. M. Wegner & J. W. Pennebaker (Eds.), *Handbook of mental control* (pp. 126–148). Englewood Cliffs, NJ: Prentice-Hall.

Erdelyi, M. H., & Goldberg, B. (1978). Let's not sweep repression under the rug: Towards a cognitive psychology of repression. In J. F. Kihlstrom & F. J. Evans (Eds.), *Functional disorders of memory* (pp. 355–402). Hillsdale, NJ: Erlbaum.

Estes, W. K. (1955). Statistical theory of spontaneous recovery and regression. *Psychological Review, 62*, 369–377.

Estes, W. K. (1972). An associative basis for coding and organization in memory. In A. W. Melton & E. Martin (Eds.), *Coding processes in human memory* (pp. 161–191). New York: Wiley.

Fox, E. (1995). Negative priming from ignored distractors in visual selection: A review. *Psychonomic Bulletin & Review, 2*, 145–173.

Fuster, J. M. (1989). *The prefrontal cortex: Anatomy, physiology, and neuropsychology of the frontal lobe.* New York: Raven Press.

Geiselman, R. E., & Bagheri, B. (1985). Repetition effects in directed forgetting: Evidence for retrieval inhibition. *Memory & Cognition, 13*, 57–62.

Geiselman, R. E., Bjork, R. A., & Fishman, D. L. (1983). Disrupted retrieval in directed forgetting: A link with posthypnotic amnesia. *Journal of Experimental Psychology: General, 112*, 58–72.

Geiselman, R. E., MacKinnon, D. P., Fishman, D. L., Jaenicke, C., Larner, B., Shoenberg, S., & Swartz, S. (1983). Mechanisms of hypnotic and non-hypnotic forgetting. *Journal of Experimental Psychology: Learning, Memory, and Cognition, 9*, 626–635.

Gelfand, H., & Bjork, R. A. (1985, November). *On the locus of retrieval inhibition in directed forgetting.* Paper presented at the meeting of the Psychonomic Society, Boston.

Gerard, L., Zacks, R. T., Hasher, L., & Radvansky, G. A. (1991). Age deficits in retrieval: The fan effect. *Journal of Gerontology, 46*, 131–136.

Gillund, G., & Shiffrin, R. M. (1984). A retrieval model for both recognition and recall. *Psychological Review, 91*, 1–67.

Graf, P., & Schacter, D. L. (1987). Selective effects of interference on implicit and explicit memory for new associations. *Journal of Experimental Psychology: Learning, Memory, and Cognition, 13*, 45–53.

Greenberg, S., & Wickens, D. D. (1972). Is matching performance an adequate test of "extinction" effects on individual associations? *Psychonomic Science, 27*, 227–229.

Hartman, M., & Hasher, L. (1991). Aging and suppression: Memory for previously relevant information. *Psychology and Aging, 6*, 587–594.

Hasher, L., Stolzfus, E. R., Zacks, R. T., & Rympa, B. (1991). Age and inhibition. *Journal of Experimental Psychology: Learning, Memory, and Cognition, 17*, 163–169.

Hasher, L., & Zacks, R. T. (1988). Working memory, comprehension and aging: A review and a new view. In G. Bower (Ed.), *The psychology of learning and motivation: Advances in research and theory* (Vol. 22, 193–225). San Diego: Academic Press.

Hicks, R. E., & Cohn, D. M. (1975). Lack of proactive inhibition in a psychomotor task at two different retention intervals. *Journal of Motor Behavior, 7*, 101–104.

Hicks, R. E., & Young, R. K. (1973). Effect of amount of interpolated learning and length of retention interval upon retroactive inhibition in a serial search task. *Journal of Experimental Psychology, 100,* 297–301.

Holmes, D. S. (1990). The evidence for repression: An examination of sixty years of research. In J. L. Singer (Ed.), *Repression and dissociation: Defense mechanisms and personality styles* (pp. 85–102). Chicago: University of Chicago Press.

Horton, K. D., & Petruk, R. (1980). Set differentiation and depth of processing in the directed forgetting paradigm. *Journal of Experimental Psychology: Human Learning and Memory, 6,* 599–610.

Houghton, G., & Tipper, S. P. (1994). A model of inhibitory mechanisms in selective attention. In D. Dagenbach & T. Carr (Eds.), *Inhibitory processes in attention, memory, and language* (pp. 53–112). San Diego: Academic Press.

Jacoby, L. L. (1983). Perceptual enhancement: Persistent effects of an experience. *Journal of Experimental Psychology: Learning, Memory, and Cognition, 9,* 21–83.

Johnson, H. M. (1994). Processes of successful intentional forgetting. *Psychological Bulletin, 116,* 274–292.

Johnson-Laird, P. N. (1983). *Mental models: Towards a cognitive science of language, inference, and consciousness.* Cambridge: Harvard University Press.

Jongeward, R. H., Woodward, A. E., & Bjork, R. A. (1975). The relative roles of input and output mechanisms in directed forgetting. *Memory & Cognition, 3,* 51–57.

Joordens, S., & Besner, D. (1994). When banking on meaning is not (yet) money in the bank: Explorations in connectionistic modeling. *Journal of Experimental Psychology: Learning, Memory, and Cognition, 20,* 1051–1062.

Kane, M. J., Hasher, L., Stolzfus, E. R., Zacks, R. T., & Connelly, S. L. (1994). Inhibitory attentional mechanisms and aging. *Psychology and Aging, 9,* 103–112.

Karchmer, M. A., & Winograd, E. (1971). Effects of studying a subset of familiar items on recall of the remaining items: The John Brown effect. *Psychonomic Science, 25,* 224–225.

Keele, S. W., & Neill, W. T. (1978). Mechanisms of attention. In E. C. Carterette & P. Friedman (Eds.), *Handbook of perception IX* (pp. 3–47). New York: Academic Press.

Kihlstrom, J. F. (1977). Models of posthypnotic amnesia. In W. E. Edmonston (Ed.), *Conceptual and investigative approaches to hypnosis and hypnotic phenomena* (Vol. 296, pp. 284–301). New York: New York Academy of Sciences.

Kihlstrom, J. F. (1980). Posthypnotic amnesia for recently learned material: Interactions with "episodic" and "semantic" memory. *Cognitive Psychology, 12,* 227–251.

Kihlstrom, J. F. (1983). Instructed forgetting: Hypnotic and non-hypnotic. *Journal of Experimental Psychology: General, 112,* 73–79.

Kihlstrom, J. F., & Barnhardt, T. M. (1993). The self-regulation of memory: For better and for worse, with and without hypnosis. In D. M. Wegner & J. W. Pennebaker (Eds.), *Handbook of mental control* (pp. 88–125). Englewood Cliffs, NJ: Prentice-Hall.

Kihlstrom, J. F., & Evans, F. J. (1979). Memory retrieval processes in posthypnotic amnesia. In J. F. Kihlstrom & F. J. Evans (Eds.), *Functional disorders of memory* (pp. 179–218). Hillsdale, NJ: Erlbaum.

Lewis, C. H., & Anderson, J. R. (1976). Interference with real world knowledge. *Cognitive Psychology, 8,* 311–335.

Lewis, D., McAllister, D. E., & Adams, J. A. (1951). Facilitation and interference in performance on the Modified Mashburn Apparatus: I. The effects of varying the amount of original learning. *Journal of Experimental Psychology, 41,* 247–260.

Lewis, D., Shephard, A. H., & Adams, J. A. (1949). Evidence of associative interference in psychomotor performance. *Science, 110,* 271–273.

Lewis, M. Q. (1971). Categorized lists and cued recall. *Journal of Experimental Psychology, 87,* 129–131.

Lindsay, D. S. (1990). Misleading suggestions can impair eyewitnesses' ability to remember event details. *Journal of Experimental Psychology: Learning, Memory, and Cognition, 16,* 1077–1083.

Lindsay, D. S., & Johnson, M. K. (1988). The eyewitness suggestibility effect and memory for source. *Memory & Cognition, 17,* 349–358.

Loftus, E. F. (1975). Leading questions and the eyewitness report. *Cognitive Psychology, 7,* 560–572.

Loftus, E. F. (1977). Shifting human color memory. *Memory & Cognition, 5,* 696–699.

Loftus, E. F. (1979a). *Eyewitness testimony.* Cambridge: Harvard University Press.

Loftus, E. F. (1979b). The malleability of memory. *American Scientist, 67,* 312–320.

Loftus, E. F. (1981). Mentalmorphosis: Alterations in memory produced by the mental bonding of new information to old. In J. Long & A. Baddeley (Eds.), *Attention and performance IX* (pp. 417–434). Hillsdale, NJ: Erlbaum.

Loftus, E. F., & Hoffman, H. G. (1989). Misinformation in memory: The creation of new memories. *Journal of Experimental Psychology: General, 118,* 100–104.

Loftus, G. R., & Loftus, E. F. (1974). The influence of one memory retrieval on a subsequent memory retrieval. *Memory & Cognition, 2,* 467–471.

Loftus, E. F., & Loftus, G. R. (1980). On the permanence of stored information in the human brain. *American Psychologist, 35,* 409–420.

Loftus, E. F., Miller, D. G., & Burns, H. J. (1978). Semantic integration of verbal information into a visual memory. *Journal of Experimental Psychology: Human Learning and Memory, 4,* 19–31.

Loftus, E. F., & Palmer, J. E. (1974). Reconstruction of automobile destruction: An example of the interaction between language and memory. *Journal of Verbal Learning and Verbal Behavior, 13,* 585–589.

Lowe, D. G. (1979). Strategies, context, and the mechanism of response inhibition. *Memory & Cognition, 7,* 392–389.

Luce, R. D. (1959). *Individual choice behavior.* New York: Wiley.

Luria, A. R. (1966). Disturbances of higher cortical functions with lesions of the frontal regions. In *Higher cortical functions in man* (pp. 218–295). London: Tavistock.

MacLeod, C. M. (1975). Long-term recognition and recall following directed forgetting. *Journal of Experimental Psychology: Human Learning and Memory, 1,* 271–279.

MacLeod, C. M. (1989). Directed forgetting affects both direct and indirect tests of memory. *Journal of Experimental Psychology: Learning, Memory, and Cognition, 15,* 13–21.

Marcel, A. J. (1980). Conscious and preconscious recognition of polysemous words: Locating the selective effects of prior verbal context. In R. S. Nickerson (Ed.), *Attention and performance VIII* (pp. 435–457). Hillsdale, NJ: Erlbaum.

Martin, D. W., & Kelly, R. T. (1974). Secondary task performance during directed forgetting. *Journal of Experimental Psychology, 103,* 1074–1079.

Martin, E. (1968). Stimulus meaningfulness and paired-associate transfer: An encoding variability hypothesis. *Psychological Review, 75,* 421–441.

Martin, E. (1971). Verbal learning theory and independent retrieval phenomena. *Psychological Review, 78,* 314–332.

May, C. P., Kane, M. J., & Hasher, L. (1995). Determinants of negative priming. *Psychological Bulletin, 118,* 35–54.

McAllister, D. E., & Lewis, D. (1951). Facilitation and interference in performance on the Modified Mashburn Apparatus: II. The effects of varying the amount of interpolated learning. *Journal of Experimental Psychology, 41,* 356–363.

McCloskey, M., & Bigler, K. (1980). Focused memory search in fact retrieval. *Memory & Cognition, 8,* 253–264.

McCloskey, M., & Zaragoza, M. (1985a). Misleading postevent information and memory for events: Arguments and evidence against memory impairment hypotheses. *Journal of Experimental Psychology: General, 114,* 1–16.

McCloskey, M., & Zaragoza, M. (1985b). Postevent information and memory: Reply to Loftus, Schooler, and Wagenaar. *Journal of Experimental Psychology: General, 114,* 381–387.

McDowd, J. M., & Filion, D. L. (1992). Aging, selective attention, and inhibitory processes: A psychophysiological approach. *Psychology and Aging, 7,* 65–71.

McDowd, J. M., Oseas-Kreger, D. M., & Filion, D. L. (1994). Inhibitory processes in selective attention and aging. In F. N. Dempster & C. J. Brainerd (Eds.), *New perspectives on interference and inhibition in cognition* (pp. 363–400). New York: Academic Press.

McGeoch, J. A. (1936). Studies in retroactive inhibition: VII. Retroactive inhibition as a function of the length and frequency of presentation of the interpolated lists. *Journal of Experimental Psychology, 19,* 674–693.

McGeoch, J. A. (1942). *The psychology of human learning.* New York: Longmans, Green.

McGovern, J. B. (1964). Extinction of associations in four transfer paradigms. *Psychological Monographs, 78*(16, Whole No. 593).

Melton, A. W., & Irwin, J. M. (1940). The influence of degree of interpolated learning on retroactive inhibition and the overt transfer of specific responses. *American Journal of Psychology, 3,* 173–203.

Melton, A. W., & von Lackum, W. J. (1941). Retroactive and proactive inhibition in retention: Evidence for a two-factor theory of retroactive inhibition. *American Journal of Psychology, 54,* 157–173.

Mensink, G. J. M., & Raajmakers, J. G. W. (1988). A model of interference and forgetting. *Psychological Review, 95,* 434–455.

Merryman, C. T. (1971). Retroactive inhibition in the A–B, A–D paradigm as measured by a multiple-choice test. *Journal of Experimental Psychology, 91,* 212–214.

Merryman, C. T., & Merryman, S. S. (1971). Stimulus encoding in the A–B', AX–B and the A–B'r, AX–B paradigms, *Journal of Verbal Learning and Verbal Behavior, 10,* 681–685.

Meyer, A. S., & Bock, K. (1992). The tip-of-the-tongue phenomenon: Blocking or partial activation? *Memory & Cognition, 20,* 715–726.

Milliken, B., Tipper, S. P., & Weaver, B. (1994). Negative priming in a spatial localization task: Feature mismatching and inhibition of distractor location. *Journal of Experimental Psychology: Human Perception and Performance, 20,* 624–646.

Mishkin, M. (1964). Perseveration of central sets after frontal lesions in monkeys. In J. M. Warren & K. Akert (Eds.), *The frontal granular cortex and behavior* (pp. 219–237). New York: McGraw-Hill.

Mueller, C. W., & Watkins, M. J. (1977). Inhibition from part-set cueing: A cue-overload interpretation. *Journal of Verbal Learning and Verbal Behavior, 16,* 699–710.

Mueller, G. E., & Pilzecker, A. (1900). Experimentalle Beitrage zur Lehre vom Gedachtnis. *Zeitschrift fur Psychologie, 1,* 1–300.

Myers, J. L., O'Brien, E. J., Balota, D. A., & Toyofuku, M. L. (1984). Memory search without interference: The role of integration. *Cognitive Psychology, 16,* 217–242.

Neely, J. H. (1976). Semantic printing and retrieval from lexical memory: Evidence for facilitatory and inhibitory processes. *Memory & Cognition, 4,* 648–654.

Neely, J. H., Schmidt, S. R., & Roediger, H. L. (1983). Inhibition from related primes in recognition memory. *Journal of Experimental Psychology: Learning, Memory, and Cognition, 9,* 196–211.

Neill, W. T. (1977). Inhibitory and facilitatory processes in selective attention. *Journal of Experimental Psychology: Human Perception and Performance, 3,* 444–450.

Neill, W. T. (1989). Lexical ambiguity and context: An activation-suppression model. In D. S. Gorfein (Ed.), *Resolving semantic ambiguity* (pp. 63–83). New York: Springer-Verlag.

Neill, W. T., & Valdes, L. A. (1992). Persistence of negative priming: Steady state or decay? *Journal of Experimental Psychology: Learning, Memory, and Cognition, 18,* 565–576.

Neill, W. T., Valdes, L. A., & Terry, K. M. (1994). Selective attention and the inhibitory control of cognition. In F. N. Dempster & C. J. Brainerd (Eds.), *New perspectives on interference and inhibition in cognition* (pp. 207–261). New York: Academic Press.

Neill, W. T., Valdes, L. A., Terry, K. M., & Gorfein, D. S. (1992). Persistence of negative priming: II. Evidence for episodic trace retrieval. *Journal of Experimental Psychology: Learning, Memory, and Cognition, 18,* 993–1000.

Nickerson, R. S. (1984). Retrieval inhibition from part-set cueing: A persisting enigma in memory research. *Memory & Cognition, 12,* 531–552.

Paller, K. A. (1990). Recall and stem-completion priming have different electrophysiological correlates and are modified differentially by directed forgetting. *Journal of Experimental Psychology: Learning, Memory, and Cognition, 16,* 1021–1032.

Park, J., & Kanwisher, N. (1994). Negative priming for spatial location: Identity mismatching, not distractor inhibition. *Journal of Experimental Psychology: Human Perception and Performance, 20,* 613–623.

Postman, L. (1971). Transfer, interference and forgetting. In J. W. Kling & L. A. Riggs (Eds.), *Woodworth and Schlosberg's: Experimental psychology* (3rd ed., pp. 1019–1132). New York: Holt, Rinehart & Winston.

Postman, L., & Stark, K. (1969). The role of response availability in transfer and interference. *Journal of Experimental Psychology, 79,* 168–177.

Postman, L., Stark, K., & Fraser, J. (1968). Temporal changes in interference. *Journal of Verbal Learning and Verbal Behavior, 7,* 672–694.

Postman, L., & Underwood, B. J. (1973). Critical issues in interference theory. *Memory & Cognition, 1,* 19–40.

Raaijmakers, J. G. W., & Shiffrin, R. M. (1981). Search of associative memory. *Psychological Review, 88,* 93–134.

Radvansky, G. A., & Zacks, R. T. (1991). Mental models and the fan effect. *Journal of Experimental Psychology: Learning, Memory, and Cognition, 17,* 940–953.

Ratcliff, R., Clark, S. E., & Shiffrin, R. M. (1990). The list-strength effect: I. Data and discussion. *Journal of Experimental Psychology: Learning, Memory, and Cognition, 16,* 163–178.

Ratcliff, R., & Murdock, B. B., Jr. (1976). Retrieval processes in recognition memory. *Psychological Review, 83,* 190–214.

Reason, J. T., & Lucas, D. (1984). Using cognitive diaries to investigate naturally occurring memory blocks. In J. E. Harris & P. E. Morris (Eds.), *Everyday memory actions and absentmindedness* (pp. 53–70). London: Academic Press.

Reder, L. M. (1982). Plausibility judgments vs. fact retrieval: Alternative strategies for sentence verification. *Psychological Review, 89,* 250–280.

Reder, L. M., & Anderson, J. R. (1980). A partial resolution of the paradox of interference: The role of integrating knowledge. *Cognitive Psychology, 12,* 447–472.

Reder, L. M., & Ross, B. H. (1983). Integrated knowledge in different tasks: The role of retrieval strategy on fan effects. *Journal of Experimental Psychology: Learning, Memory, and Cognition, 9,* 55–72.

Reder, L. M., & Wible, C. (1984). Strategy use in question-answering: Memory strength and task constraints on fan effects. *Memory & Cognition, 12,* 411–419.

Reitman, W., Malin, J. T., Bjork, R. A., & Higman, B. (1973). Strategy control and directed forgetting. *Journal of Verbal Learning and Verbal Behavior, 12,* 140–149.

Richardson, J., & Stanton, S. K. (1972). Some effects of learning to a set of components on stimulus selection. *American Journal of Psychology, 85,* 519–533.

Roediger, H. L. (1973). Inhibition in recall from cueing with recall targets. *Journal of Verbal Learning and Verbal Behavior, 12,* 644–657.

Roediger, H. L. (1974). Inhibiting effects of recall. *Memory & Cognition, 2,* 261–269.

Roediger, H. L. (1978). Recall as a self-limiting process. *Memory & Cognition, 6,* 54–63.

Roediger, H. L., & McDermott, K. B. (1993). Implicit memory in normal human subjects. In F. Boller & J. Grafman (Eds.), *Handbook of neuropsychology* (Vol. 8, pp. 63–131). New York: Elsevier.

Roediger, H. L., & Neely, J. H. (1982). Retrieval blocks in episodic and semantic memory. *Canadian Journal of Psychology, 36,* 213–242.

Roediger, H. L., Neely, J. H., & Blaxton, T. (1983). Inhibition from related primes in semantic memory retrieval: A reappraisal of Brown's (1979) paradigm. *Journal of Experimental Psychology: Learning, Memory, and Cognition, 9,* 478–489.

Roediger, H. L., & Schmidt, S. R. (1980). Output interference in the recall of categorized and paired associate lists. *Journal of Experimental Psychology: Human Learning and Memory, 6,* 91–105.

Roediger, H. L., Stellon, C., & Tulving, E. (1977). Inhibition from part-list cues and rates of recall. *Journal of Experimental Psychology: Human Learning and Memory, 3,* 174–188.

Roediger, H. L., & Tulving, E. (1979). Exclusion of learned material from recall as a post-retrieval operation. *Journal of Verbal Learning and Verbal Behavior, 18,* 601–615.

Rudy, J. W. (1974). Stimulus selection in animal conditioning and paired-associate learning: Variations in the associative process. *Journal of Verbal Learning and Verbal Behavior, 13,* 282–296.

Rundus, D. (1973). Negative effects of using list items as recall cues. *Journal of Verbal Learning and Verbal Behavior, 12,* 43–50.

Schacter, D. L. (1987). Implicit memory: History and current status. *Journal of Experimental Psychology: Learning, Memory, and Cognition, 13,* 501–518.

Schneider, N. G., & Houston, J. P. (1968). Stimulus selection and retroactive inhibition. *Journal of Experimental Psychology, 77,* 166–167.

Shimamura, A. P. (1994). Memory and frontal lobe function. In M. S. Gazzaniga (Ed.), *The cognitive neurosciences* (pp. 803–814). Cambridge: MIT Press.

Simpson, G. B., & Kang, H. (1994). Inhibitory processes in the recognition of homograph meanings. In D. Dagenbach & T. Carr (Eds.), *Inhibitory processes in attention, memory, and language* (pp. 359–382). San Diego: Academic Press.

Slamecka, N. J. (1968). An examination of trace storage in free recall. *Journal of Experimental Psychology, 76,* 504–513.

Slamecka, N. J. (1972). The question of associative growth in the learning of categorized materials. *Journal of Verbal Learning and Verbal Behavior, 11,* 324–332.

Slamecka, N. J. (1975). Intralist cueing of recognition. *Journal of Verbal Learning and Verbal Behavior, 14,* 630–637.

Smith, A. D. (1971). Output interference and organized recall from long-term memory. *Journal of Verbal learning and Verbal Behavior, 10,* 400–408.

Smith, E. E., Adams, N., & Schorr, D. (1978). Fact retrieval and the paradox of interference. *Cognitive Psychology, 10,* 438–464.

Springer, S. P., & Deutsch, G. (1993). *Left brain, right brain* (4th ed.). New York: W. H. Freeman.

Timmins, W. K. (1974). Varying processing time in directed forgetting. *Journal of Verbal Learning and Verbal Behavior, 13,* 539–544.

Tipper, S. P. (1985). The negative priming effect: Inhibitory priming and ignored objects. *Quarterly Journal of Experimental Psychology, 37A,* 571–590.

Tipper, S. P., Weaver, B., Cameron, S., Brehaut, J. C., & Bastedo, J. (1991). Inhibitory mechanisms of attention in identification and localization tasks: Time course and disruption. *Journal of Experimental Psychology: Learning, Memory, and Cognition, 17,* 681–692.

Todres, A. K., & Watkins, M. J. (1981). A part-set cueing effect in recognition memory. *Journal of Experimental Psychology: Human Learning and Memory, 7,* 91–99.

Tulving, E. (1972). Episodic and semantic memory. In E. Tulving & W. Donaldson (Eds.), *Organization of Memory* (pp. 381–403). New York: Academic Press.

Tulving, E., & Arbuckle, T. Y. (1963). Sources of intratrial interferences in paired-associate learning. *Journal of Verbal Learning and Verbal Behavior, 1*, 321–334.

Tulving, E., & Thomson, D. M. (1973). Encoding specificity and retrieval processes in episodic memory. *Psychological Review, 80*, 352–373.

Tversky, B., & Tuchin, M. (1989). A reconciliation of the evidence on eyewitness testimony: Comments on McCloskey and Zaragoza (1985). *Journal of Experimental Psychology: General, 118*, 86–91.

Tzeng, O. J., Lee, A. T., & Wetzel, C. D. (1979). Temporal coding in verbal information processing. *Journal of Experimental Psychology: Human Learning and Memory, 5*, 52–64.

Underwood, B. J. (1948). 'Spontaneous recovery' of verbal associations. *Journal of Experimental Psychology, 38*, 429–439.

Watkins, M. J. (1975). Inhibition in recall with extralist "cues." *Journal of Verbal Learning and Verbal Behavior, 14*, 294–303.

Watkins, M. J. (1978). Engrams as cuegrams and forgetting as cue-overload: A cueing approach to the structure of memory. In C. R. Puff (Ed.), *The structure of memory* (pp. 347–372). New York: Academic Press.

Wegner, D. M. (1994). Ironic processes of mental control. *Psychological Review, 101*, 34–52.

Wegner, D. M., & Pennebaker, J. W. (1993). *Handbook of mental control.* Englewood Cliffs, NJ: Prentice-Hall.

Weiner, B. (1968). Motivated forgetting and the study of repression. *Journal of Personality, 36*, 213–234.

Weiner, B., & Reed, H. (1969). Effects of instructional sets to remember and to forget on short-term retention: Studies of rehearsal control and retrieval inhibition (repression). *Journal of Experimental Psychology, 79*, 226–232.

Wetzel, C. D., & Hunt, R. E. (1977). Cue delay and the role of rehearsal in directed forgetting. *Journal of Experimental Psychology: Human Learning and Memory, 3*, 233–245.

Wheeler, M. A. (1995). Improvement in recall over time without repeated testing: Spontaneous recovery revisited. *Journal of Experimental Psychology: Learning, Memory, and Cognition, 21*, 173–184.

Whitlow, J. W. (1984). Effects of precuing on focused search in fact retrieval. *Journal of Experimental Psychology: Learning, Memory, and Cognition, 10*, 733–744.

Wickelgren, W. A. (1976). Memory storage dynamics. In W. K. Estes (Ed.), *Handbook of learning and cognitive processes: Vol. 4: Attention and memory* (pp. 321–362). Hillsdale, NJ: Erlbaum.

Williams, R. F., & Underwood, B. J. (1970). Encoding variability: Test of the Martin hypothesis. *Journal of Experimental Psychology, 86*, 317–324.

Woodward, A. D., & Bjork, R. A. (1971). Forgetting and remembering in free recall: Intentional and unintentional. *Journal of Experimental Psychology, 89*, 109–116.

Zacks, R. T., & Hasher, L. (1994). Directed ignoring: Inhibitory regulation of working memory. In D. Dagenbach & T. Carr (Eds.), *Inhibitory processes in attention, memory, and language* (pp. 241–264). San Diego: Academic Press.

Zaragoza, M. S., & Koshmider, J. W. (1989). Misled subjects may know more than their performance implies. *Journal of Experimental Psychology: Learning, Memory, and Cognition, 15*, 246–255.

Zaragoza, M. S., & McCloskey, M. (1989). Misleading postevent information and the memory impairment hypothesis: Comment on Belli and reply to Tversky and Tuchin. *Journal of Experimental Psychology: General, 118*, 92–99.

Zaragoza, M. S., McCloskey, M., & Jamis, M. (1987). Misleading postevent information and recall of the original event: Further evidence against the memory impairment hypothesis. *Journal of Experimental Psychology: Learning, Memory, and Cognition, 13*, 36–44.

Monitoring and Controlling Our Memories

Distributing and Managing the Conditions of Encoding and Practice

Frank N. Dempster

"Practice makes perfect" is, in itself, hardly a reliable guide to successful learning. Mere repetition over the course of days or even weeks is no guarantee of long-term learning. How many Americans, despite weeks of concentrated practice, can recall more than the opening phrase of the Preamble to The Constitution, which has just 52 words? Yet most of us can still remember the "Pledge of Allegiance" or an evening prayer we once recited daily for years.

What, then, are the most effective ways of distributing and managing the conditions of encoding and practice? Research suggests that the effectiveness of repetition depends on a number of factors, including the time interval between repetitions, the frequency of repetitions, and even the form of the repetition, that is, whether it is in the form of an additional study opportunity or presentation (i.e., a review) or a test. A review provides an additional encoding opportunity, whereas a test provides retrieval practice. In this chapter, research on the effects of encoding practice and retrieval practice is reviewed, and the theoretical and educational implications of such research are examined. It is concluded that the effects of spaced practice, in particular, provide important insights into the basic mechanisms of learning and memory. Moreover, spaced repetitions have considerable potential for enhancing student achievement.

I. ENCODING PRACTICE

Several findings concerning the effects of reviews, or additional opportunities to study, deserve special attention. First, with total study time constant, two or more opportunities to study the same material are more effective than a single opportunity. For example, in a study conducted early in the century, Edwards (1917) had one group of elementary school children study a history or arithmetic lesson for $6\frac{1}{2}$ min continuously and another group for 4 min on one occasion and for $2\frac{1}{2}$ min several days later. Overall, the group given the opportunity to study the material twice performed about 30% better on the achievement measure than did the group that did not receive a review.

More recent research has found that an opportunity to review previously presented material may affect not only the quantity of what is learned, but also the quality. For example, Mayer (1983) found that repeated presentations of a science passage resulted in a hefty increase in recall of conceptual principles, but did little to promote the recall of technical details. Thus, reviews may do more than simply increase the amount learned; they may shift the learner's attention away from the verbatim details of the material being studied to its deeper conceptual structure. In general, additional study opportunities enable a learner to use increasingly more sophisticated encoding strategies based on knowledge obtained in previous encounters with the material, thereby affecting what is learned (see also Amlund, Kardash, & Kulhavy, 1986; Bromage & Mayer, 1986; Kiewra, Mayer, Christensen, Kim, & Risch, 1991).

Another important finding about reviews is that the amount of learning following two reviews that occur close together in time (massed) often is only slightly better than that following a single study opportunity. Thus, massed reviews, such as reviews that occur just a few hours apart, may be entirely uneconomical when evaluated in terms of additional learning. Much more effective are reviews that are spread out or distributed over lengthier periods of time. This phenomenon, known as the "spacing effect," is one of the most robust and dependable phenomena yet documented by behavioral scientists (Dempster, 1988; Hintzman, 1974; Melton, 1970). In fact, two spaced presentations are often about twice as effective as two massed presentations, and this advantage tends to increase as the frequency of review increases.

The spacing effect was known as early as 1885. With himself as the subject, Ebbinghaus noted that for a single 12-syllable series, 68 immediately successive repetitions had the effect of making possible an errorless recital after 7 additional repetitions on the following day. However, the same effect was achieved by only 38 distributed repetitions spread over 3 days. Mainly on the basis of this finding, Ebbinghaus concluded that "with any considerable number of repetitions a suitable distribution of them over a space of time is decidedly more advantageous than the massing of them at a single time" (Ebbinghaus, 1885/1913, p. 89). Soon after, the spacing effect gained formal recognition in the form of Jost's Law, which states that "If two associations are of equal strength but of different age, a new repetition has a greater value for the older one" (McGeoch, 1943, p. 140).

As might be expected, these two developments in the nineteenth century were followed by a flurry of related research in the early 1900s, addressing the general problem of the "economy of distributing work and rest periods" (see Ruch, 1928, for review). Although interpretation of the results of these studies (Dearborn, 1910; Perkins, 1914) is complicated by other potentially confounding variables and by relatively primitive statistical procedures, the results tend, in general, to confirm the earlier work of Ebbinghaus and Jost.

Since then, the spacing effect has been documented in dozens of studies, many of which were conducted in the 1930s, the 1970s, and the early to mid-1980s (Bruce & Bahrick, 1992). More recently, interest in the spacing effect has become strong again, and there is little reason to believe that it will not continue to be an intellectually active area (see Dempster, 1988, for review). Thus, the spacing effect is neither just a historical curiosity nor a johnny-come-lately. Fads come and go in psychology, but research on the spacing effect has withstood the test of time and significance; it continues to yield new discoveries and ideas relevant to other areas of psychology.

Another remarkable feature of spaced repetitions is the sheer size of the effect. Whereas many of the traditional learning variables studied in the laboratory have relatively weak effects, two spaced presentations often are about twice as effective as two massed presentations (Bahrick & Phelps, 1987; Dempster, 1987; Underwood, 1970), and the difference between them tends to increase as the frequency of repetition increases (Underwood, 1970). Moreover, longer retention intervals tend to favor the spacing of repetitions more than do short retention intervals (Austin, 1921; Bahrick & Phelps, 1987; Glenberg & Lehmann, 1980; Young, 1966, cited in Melton, 1970). For example, Bahrick and Phelps (1987) retested subjects who previously had learned and relearned foreign language vocabulary words after an interval of eight years, a retention interval much longer than those typically used in learning research. The interval between the subjects' successive relearning sessions had been either 30 days, 1 day, or 0, and they found this intersession interval to have a robust effect on retention, with the recall probability associated with the 30-day interval about 2.5 times the probability associated with the zero interval. For subjects that had been in the two shortest intersession interval conditions, even words that had been reviewed seven times or more were almost always forgotten eight years later.

The spacing effect is also truly remarkable in the scope of its application. Unlike many learning phenomena, it is not confined to one or two paradigms or stimulus domains. It has been found in virtually all traditional verbal learning tasks, including paired-associate learning, free recall, recognition memory, and in the distracter paradigm (see reviews in Hintzman, 1974; Melton, 1970). To-be-remembered materials have included nonsense syllables (Ebbinghaus, 1885/1913), words (Glenberg & Lehmann, 1980), sentences (Rothkopf & Coke, 1966), pictures (Hintzman & Rogers, 1973), and faces (Cornell, 1980; Goldstein, Chance, & Otto, 1987).

In addition, the spacing effect has been found in a variety of tasks with clear classroom analogies. In fact, several early demonstrations of the spacing effect reviewed by Ruch (1928) were, as he put it, "intended for schoolroom application" (p. 20). One of the most interesting of these effects from an educational perspective was reported by Pyle (1913), who had a group of third graders drilled in addition, either twice a day for 5 days (once in the morning and once in the afternoon) or once a day for 10 days. Their improvement in recall of addition facts, which was decidedly in favor of the latter instructional method, provided perhaps the earliest experimental confirmation of William James's (1901) advice to teachers and students that it is better to repeat an association on many days than again and again on just a few days (p. 129).

Spacing effects also have been demonstrated in the learning of science and mathematics concepts and in rule-learning tasks. In one study, the meanings of a series of scientific terms were learned much more effectively when repetitions were spaced than when they were massed (Reynolds & Glaser, 1964). In another study, arithmetical rules presented on a computer monitor were learned better when reviews occurred 1 and 7 days after the initial presentation than when they occurred 1 and 2 days following original learning (Gay, 1973, Experiment 2).

Another focus of spacing research has been vocabulary learning and, here too, substantial spacing effects have been reported (Bahrick & Phelps, 1987; Dempster, 1987). In a study by Dempster (1987), for example, 38 uncommon English words and their definitions were presented three times, either with each repetition of any given word separated by every other word (i.e., each repetition was separated by 37 other words) or with each repetition massed in succession. In three experiments in which spaced versus massed presentations were evaluated in this manner, spaced presentations yielded substantially higher levels of vocabulary learning than did massed presentations. In some cases, in fact, the number of word meanings recalled was 50–100% greater under spaced conditions than under massed conditions.

Finally, spacing effects have been demonstrated repeatedly in a variety of text processing tasks (Dempster, 1986; English, Wellborn, & Killian, 1934; Glover & Corkill, 1987; Kraft & Jenkins, 1981; Krug, Davis, & Glover, 1990). For example, Dempster (1987) found that 2 readings of a text separated by a 48-hour interval or a 30-min interval was significantly more effective than 2 readings of a text separated by 30 and 5 min. Also, English et al. (1934) found that 4 readings of a text at 3-hour intervals were associated with better learning than 4 consecutive unspaced readings. Similarly, Glover and Corkill (1987) observed the spacing effect (0 lag vs. a 30-min lag) in subjects' memory for paragraphs they had read as well as for brief lectures they had heard. Because students spend so much time reading and listening to lectures, these findings would appear to have considerable practical significance.

Although the spacing effect is one of the most dependable phenomena in the history of learning research, certain failures to obtain the effect suggest that it is subject to several not fully understood boundary conditions. Specifically, four sorts of boundary conditions are suggested. First, under certain circumstances, spaced presentations are no better than (Austin, 1921), and sometimes even worse than (Gordon, 1925), massed presentations in tests of immediate recall. For example, Austin found that massed readings (e.g., five times in one day) of text material proved as effective as spaced readings (e.g., daily for five days) in tests of immediate recall, whereas the spaced readings were much more effective in delayed tests, particularly if they came two to four weeks after learning. Second, it has been found that massed practice often is more efficient for certain simple, isolated skills, such as writing the products of number pairs as rapidly as possible (Thorndike, 1916).

Third, while most spacing effects are robust, much of the massed versus distributed practice research that has focused on perceptual motor skills tasks and lists of nonsense syllables has yielded weak effects of spacing (Underwood, 1961). Fourth, spacing effects have failed to materialize in certain incidental learning tasks. These include various implicit perceptual tasks, such as word fragment completion tasks that rely primarily on perceptual or data-driven processes for their completion and implicit cued-memory tasks that encourage graphemic processing (see Challis, 1993, for review).

As might be expected, the history of research on the spacing of presentations also includes some puzzling discrepancies. For example, Toppino and Gracen (1985) conducted a series of nine experiments on spacing in standard verbal learning tasks and failed to replicate the spacing effects reported in a study by Glenberg (1979). Another inconsistent set of findings in the spacing literature pertains to the effects of paraphrasing. Recently, two studies have shown that the spacing effect can be eliminated if paraphrased rather than verbatim versions of the repeated materials are used (Dellarosa & Bourne, 1985; Glover & Corkill, 1987; Krug et al., 1990). In addition, Dellarosa and Bourne found that a change in the speaker's voice at the time of repetition also eliminated the effect. By contrast, a much older study using similar paraphrased repetitions (e.g., "The ghosts who protect the men in war are offered melons" versus "Melons are offered to the ghosts who protect the men in war") found that changing the phrasing of a sentence when it is repeated did not remove the depressing effect resulting from massed repetition (Rothkopf, 1966).

Also puzzling is a study by Toppino and DiGeorge (1984) who found that the spacing effect did not apply to preschool-age children, even though it was present in the recall of first graders. This finding conflicts with the findings of Rea and Modigliani (1987) and Toppino (1991) who, in two more recent developmental studies, obtained spacing effects for every age group tested, including preschool-age children. This anomaly is even more striking when viewed from the perspective of research with even younger children, as spacing effects have also been demonstrated with infant subjects (Cornell, 1980; Vander Linde, Morrongiello, & Rovee-Collier, 1985). The cause of the discrepant results, however, is far from clear as there is no reason to believe that Toppino and DiGeorge's results are doe to sampling error or to a methodological flaw. Thus, one cannot rule out the possibility that their results are replicable under a highly specific set of conditions. Nevertheless, research as a whole indicates that subjects of all ages, including the elderly (Balota, Duchek, & Paullin, 1989), are subject to spacing effects.

Finally, the results of a number of studies seem to suggest that beyond a certain lag interval, further increases in lag are not always associated with further increases in learning. For example, whereas English et al. (1934) found that 4 readings of a text at 3-hour intervals were associated with better learning than 4 consecutive unspaced readings, readings at 3-hour intervals were no different than readings at either 1- or 3-day intervals. Similarly, Lyon (1914), Peterson, Ellis, Toohill, and Kloess (1935), and Sones and Stroud (1940) reported essentially no differences in retention between groups with rereading reviews spaced 1 and 7, 1 and 9, and 1 and 17 days, respectively, after original learning. These findings were later corroborated by Ausubel (1966) and by Gay (1973).

On the other hand, these findings stand in sharp contrast to spacing effects under long-lag conditions with traditional verbal learning material (Glenberg & Lehmann, 1980) and in vocabulary learning (Bahrick & Phelps, 1987). It may be that under certain lengthy lag conditions the usual benefits of spaced repetitions do not obtain because the results of initial processing efforts have been forgotten (see Lyon, 1914; Sones & Stroud, 1940, for earlier discussions of this hypothesis).

II. RETRIEVAL PRACTICE

One of the complexities of research is that the act of measurement often has an effect on what is measured. In physics, for example, procedures designed to pinpoint the location of a single quantum of light may actually alter its behavior. Memory is no exception: It is affected not only by additional study opportunities but also by tests, even though they may be designed simply to assess the individual's state of knowledge about a subject. As Lachman and Laughery (1968) put it, "Test[s] . . . though they be designed to measure changes in the state of the human memory system have profound and perhaps residual effects on the state of that system" (p. 40).

Research on learning—specifically research on the effectiveness of tests—has made it abundantly clear that tests do more than simply test; they also promote learning, even when no corrective feedback is provided and when there are no further study opportunities (Allen, Mahler, & Estes, 1969; R. C. Anderson & Biddle, 1975; Donaldson, 1971; Gates, 1917; Hogan & Kintsch, 1971; Izawa, 1971; Jones, 1923–1924; Lachman & Laughery, 1968; Nungester & Duchastel, 1982; Petros & Hoving, 1980; Raffel, 1934; Rea & Modigliani, 1985; Rothkopf, 1966; Runquist, 1983, 1986; Slamecka & Katsaiti, 1988; Spitzer, 1939, Wheeler & Roediger, 1992). In many cases, the effect has been strong. For example, Jones (1923–1924) found that the retention test scores of previously tested students was twice that of untested students. In other words, taking a test can confer substantial benefits on the retention of the same material tested on a later date, even when no corrective feedback is provided and when there are no further study opportunities. In addition, the beneficial effects of tests on later retention are not simply due to the fact that retrieval may provide an additional presentation of the target material (Carrier & Pashler, 1992). Thus, the effectiveness of tests cannot be explained in terms of an additional encoding opportunity.

The "test-spacing effect" refers to the fact that spaced tests are more effective than massed tests, especially if the interest intervals are of an expanding nature (Landauer & Bjork, 1978; Modigliani, 1976; Rea & Modigliani, 1985; Whitten & Bjork, 1977). In a study of name learning, for example, a pattern of increasing intervals between successive tests, in which subjects attempted to write the last names of fictitious characters in response to their first names, was superior to a pattern of uniform spacing (Landauer & Bjork, 1978).

In a related study, Rea and Modigliani (1985) investigated the effect of tests on the retention of grade-appropriate multiplication facts and spelling lists. In the massed uniform condition, the subjects received four evenly spaced tests occurring relatively close together in time; whereas, in the expanded condition, the interval between each of the successive tests increased by roughly 50%. Following the fourth test, a final test was administered. For multiplication facts, retention in the expanded condition was almost twice that in the massed condition. For spelling lists, a more modest, but still significant, difference in the same direction was obtained. Furthermore, expanded testing was equally beneficial for children of all ability levels.

Research on testing has revealed a number of other conditions that either diminish or heighten the effects of tests, whether massed or spaced. First, tests are normally most effective if the material to be learned is first tested relatively soon, but not immediately after its presentation (R. C. Anderson & Biddle, 1975; Modigliani, 1976; Spitzer, 1939). This phenomenon is nicely illustrated in a study by Spitzer (1939), who tested the entire sixth grade population of 91 elementary schools in Iowa. Each child read a highly factual article and then was tested one or more times at various intervals. An especially significant outcome, from a practical perspective, was that students whose initial test had occurred 1 and 7 days after reading scored 15 to 30% higher on a final test 2 weeks later than did students whose initial test had occurred 14 or 21 days following reading.

Second, information tested but not recalled at the first opportunity is not as likely to be recalled later as is information that was tested and remembered (R. C. Anderson & Biddle, 1975; Jones, 1923–1924; Modigliani, 1976; Runquist, 1986). Thus, the so-called "potentiating effect" of test trials applies mainly to test questions with successful outcomes. Nevertheless, even items that were not recalled on an earlier test may be recalled on a later test, a phenomenon known as "reminiscence" (Wheeler & Roediger, 1992). Finally, tests do not just slow the rate of forgetting from test to test. Remarkably, tests may also result in net improvements in recall across tests, a phenomenon first reported by Ballard (1913) and now known as "hypermnesia." Hypermnesia has been reported in many situations, particularly those in which overall levels of performance are fairly high (see Payne, 1987, for review). Although most studies of hypermnesia have used simple learning materials taught in the laboratory, there have been several demonstrations of the phenomenon using more realistic materials acquired in naturalistic settings (Bahrick & Hall, 1993; Brown, 1923; Hermann, Buschke, & Gall, 1987). In the study by Bahrick and Hall (1993), for example, robust hypermnesia effects were obtained for three types of educationally relevant content—namely, foreign language vocabulary, general knowledge, and names of portraits of famous individuals.

Third, the facilitating effects of tests are greater for repeated questions than for new items (R. C. Anderson & Biddle, 1975; Nungester & Duchastel, 1982; Rothkopf, 1966; Runquist, 1986; Sones & Stroud, 1940). For instance, Rothkopf (1966) had college students study a lengthy selection from a book on marine biology, followed by questions on the passage. On a later test, these students performed substantially better than a control group on repeated items and modestly better on new items (an indirect effect), even though knowing the answer to one question should not have given the answer to another. As R. C. Anderson and Biddle (1975) noted, however, the aggregate indirect benefit is likely to be greater than the direct benefit. "Only the points of information about which . . . questions are asked could be directly affected, whereas presumably every point in the text could be indirectly influenced" (p. 92).

III. THEORETICAL IMPLICATIONS

A satisfactory theory of learning should answer the kinds of questions a curious lay person would normally ask about everyday learning and remembering. Surely, some of those questions would pertain to the role of practice in learning. Indeed, as Hilgard and Bower (1975) noted, these are the very same questions that tend to give rise to theories of learning. Thus, the effects of repetitions on memory, whether in the form of additional study opportunities or tests, should be fertile soil for constructive inquiry into the mechanisms of learning.

A. Spacing Effects

Much of the theoretical work on encoding practice has focused on spacing effects, yet the theoretical picture that emerged was for many years rather confused, despite numerous attempts at clarification. In his highly influential review, Hintzman (1974) considered five theories of the spacing effect, which he later classified under two general headings: encoding variability theories and deficient-processing theories (Hintzman, 1976).

1. Encoding Variability Theories

Encoding variability theories appear to owe much to the work of Bower (1972) and Martin (1972), who fostered the notion that contextual variations had much explanatory power. The basic assumption is that there are a number of different ways in which to-be-remembered information can be encoded and, as the number of different encodings increases, the number of potentially effective retrieval routes increases. Further, it is assumed that as the spacing between presentations increases, the number of different subjective contexts in which the information is encoded also increases (see also McFarland, Rhodes, & Frey 1979).

As Hintzman (1974) noted, one of the original problems with encoding variability theory is that the nature of the contextual elements involved was not worked out in sufficient detail; however, later work has resulted in more exact specification of the elements involved (Glenberg, 1979). Glenberg proposed that automatic encoding variability processes are responsible for the spacing effect in free recall because free recall should depend to a great degree on contextual cues. During study, contextual information is assumed to be encoded automatically, with more varied contextual information being encoded with spaced, as opposed to massed, repetitions.

More recently, a similar hypothesis has been offered by Greene (1989) as part of a two-process account of the spacing effect. This account comports with the absence of spacing effects on certain cued-recall tasks, which are assumed to be less dependent on contextual information than free-recall tasks. Furthermore, it is consistent with several recent experiments that failed to find spacing effects in free recall of lists containing items of high interstimulus semantic similarity, presumably because subjects do not have to rely on contextual cues to retrieve items (Kahana & Greene, 1993). Rather, it is assumed that subjects can use the feature shared by all the items as a retrieval cue (e.g., animal names).

Nevertheless, there is still a major problem with the theory—namely, the assumption that a change in context benefits recall. In some cases, in fact, changes in context have been associated with poorer recall. For example, Murdock and Babick (1961) repeated a single word in a constantly changing context and found no benefits whatsoever from repetition. More recently, Postman and Knecht (1983) investigated the encoding variability hypothesis by systematically increasing the number of explicit contexts in which the to-be-remembered item was embedded. They found that recall levels were actually lower following variable encoding than after constant encoding. Finally, Dempster (1987) found that, whereas spaced presentations yielded significantly better vocabulary learning that did massed presentations, there was no independent effect of a manipulation designed to affect the number of retrieval routes to the word meanings. Here again, and in a related study (Dempster, 1989), contextual change during presentation tended to be associated with poorer recall.

In short, encoding variability theory, even in its most sophisticated form—namely, component-levels theory (Glenberg, 1979)—cannot be considered a general explanation for the spacing effect. For the most part, it is only in highly contrived situations, as when a homograph is presented in different contexts, that differences in favor of the different-encoding condition occur (Hintzman, 1974; Postman & Knecht, 1983).

2. Deficient-Processing Theories

Deficient-processing theories postulate that massed repetitions receive less processing than their spaced counterparts and that recall is a function of the amount or quality of processing the information receives. At the time of Hintzman's (1974) writing, four mechanisms had been advanced to account for variations in processing, two of which can be considered involuntary (consolidation and habituation) and two voluntary (rehearsal and attention). Since then, another involuntary deficient-processing hypothesis has been advanced, namely, the accessibility or reconstruction hypothesis.

The consolidation hypothesis (Landauer, 1969) proposes that the transfer of information from a relatively transient state in memory to a more permanent retrievable state in memory takes time, and that this process can be interrupted if a repetition of the to-be-remembered information occurs prior to "consolidation." Thus, if two repetitions are massed, the total amount of consolidation will be less than if the two repetitions are spaced. The consolidation hypothesis seems remarkably similar to the much older perseveration hypothesis that was originally advanced by Muller and Pilzecker (1900) to account for the facts of retroactive inhibition. In fact, the two hypotheses, at least as they apply to the spacing effect, seem identical. There is, however, still no evidence for consolidation–perseveration beyond the facts they are invoked to explain. In addition, the time course for consolidation has be estimated to range from 15 s to 1 hour (Baddeley, 1976). According to that estimate, these hypotheses would not provide an adequate account of spacing effects either when the spacing interval was very short, as in many studies, or when the intervals in question were relatively long (Bahrick & Phelps, 1987).

The habituation hypothesis has the same problems as the consolidation hypothesis. For example, Hintzman, Summers, and Block (1975) concluded that habituation would have to asymptote in less than 2.2 s for the habituation hypothesis to be supported. If this were true, there would be no difference between spacing intervals greater than 2.2 s, contrary to actual findings. Unlike the consolidation hypothesis, however, it attributes deficient registration to a mechanism that adapts or "turns off" for a short period following registration. Under massed conditions, then, assuming that the spacing interval is less than the time needed for recovery from habituation, a repetition would receive something less than full processing.

Another problem with the habituation hypothesis is that it seems to predict that massed repetition would lead to slower responses to the second occurrence of an item than to the first, as responses to the second occurrence would be "inhibited." Research has demonstrated, however, just the opposite (Rose, 1984). Although Hintzman (1974) found this hypothesis intriguing, it has been largely ignored.

The rehearsal hypothesis received some early support in a study by Rundus (1971) who found that spaced items received more rehearsals than massed items during the spacing interval, which, of course, is longer under spaced conditions than under massed conditions. Because frequency of rehearsal is often directly related to recall, one could argue that a differential amount of rehearsal underlies spacing effects. However plausible, the rehearsal hypothesis has not fared well overall. Most decisively, manipulations that should have affected rehearsal, such as an interpolated task (Bjork & Allen, 1970) and complex, difficult-to rehearse visual stimuli (Hintzman & Rogers, 1973), have not had the effects on memory that the rehearsal hypothesis predicts. Moreover, the fact that spacing effects have been found with very young children (Cornell, 1980; Rea & Modigliani, 1987; Toppino, 1991; Vander Linde et al., 1985), who are not inclined to rehearse spontaneously (Ornstein & Naus, 1978), is inconsistent with the rehearsal hypothesis.

In view of these difficulties, Greene (1989) concluded that rehearsal is only one of several processes underlying spacing effects and that the type of task for which rehearsal is most applicable is cued recall. In a series of experiments, Greene (1989, 1990) reported that on various cued-memory tasks (e.g., recognition, frequency discrimination), spacing effects occurred with intentionally learned material but not with incidentally learned material. According to his account, spaced repetitions in an intentional learning condition receive more rehearsal activity than massed repetitions because spaced repetitions are less familiar than massed repetitions. In comparison, subjects in an incidental learning condition would not use a voluntary rehearsal strategy because they would see no value in rehearsing items (Greene, 1989, 1990).

As Challis (1993) pointed out, however, Greene's (1989, 1990) interpretation of his findings is open to question. Several studies suggest that the manipulation of intentionality may lead subjects to engage in various types of processing and that the occurrence of spacing effects on cued-memory tests depends not so much on intentionality per se, but rather on the level or type of processing carried out on the stimuli (Craik & Lockhart, 1972). Furthermore, Challis (1993) found that the spacing of repetitions improved performance on cued-memory tests (a frequency judgment test and graphemic cued-recall test) when items were studied in an intentional or an incidental–semantic condition but not in an incidental–graphemic condition. If intentionality is the key to spacing effects on cued-memory tasks, spacing effects should have occurred only in the intentional condition. If, on the other hand, the occurrence of spacing effects on cued-memory tests depends on semantic processing as opposed to shallow processing, then Challis's (1993) findings would be expected. In short, these data undermine Greene's (1989) account of spacing effects in cued-memory tasks and suggest that these effects are due to an involuntary mechanism that promotes semantic (i.e., deep) processing.

The final deficient-processing theory considered by Hintzman (1974, 1976) was the voluntary-attention hypothesis. According to this account, the subject chooses to pay less attention to repetitions when they are massed than when they are spaced. In 1974, Hintzman ranked this hypothesis just behind the habituation hypothesis as the one most likely to be correct, largely because there was no decisive evidence against it and because of some evidence in its favor. For example, Elmes, Greener, and Wilkinson (1972) compared the free recall of words that occurred either immediately following massed repetitions or following spaced repetitions of other words and found that their recall was better following massed repetitions. This result suggests that subjects treat the massed repetition as a rest opportunity that enables them to devote more attention, and thus more processing resources, to the next word on the list.

Since then, the attention hypothesis has received further support. In a study by Dempster (1986), college students responded to a questionnaire administered following a recall test of a twice-read passage, with the two readings spaced either 30 or 5 min apart. The questionnaire consisted of 10 items, each followed by a 10-point rating scale, which was designed to elicit self-reports of various cognitive and affective states and processes during reading and testing. Included were questions concerning levels of attention, interest, anxiety, rehearsal, and changes of interpretation (subjective context) from one reading to the next. Group differences emerged on only two of the items: specifically, one asking the subjects to indicate how "interested" they were during the second reading and one asking them to indicate how much "attention" they paid during the second reading. In both cases, the average ratings of students in the spaced condition (those who also did best on the recall test) were higher than those in the massed condition. Moreover, a correlational analysis, applied to the scores of both groups combined, revealed a significant correlation between recall and only one of the questionnaire items (i.e., the attention paid during the second reading). Those who reported having paid more attention tended to have learned more from the text. These findings dovetail nicely with those of Magliero (1983) who found that pupil size associated with the second of two repeated items increases as the spacing between presentations increases. Because pupil size is a well-accepted measure of attention and is known to vary directly with amount of processing, this finding also suggests that differences in attention underlie at least some spacing effects.

Why should spaced presentations receive more attention than massed presentations? The voluntary-attention hypothesis assumes that processing effort can be allocated in a flexible way at the subjects' discretion. Thus, there must be something about the subjects' beliefs, expectations, or preferences that are affected by the spacing between repetitions. One possibility, suggested by the work of Zechmeister and Shaughnessy (1980), is that massed presentations inspire a false sense of knowing or confidence. In this study, college students rated the likelihood of recall of individual words presented for free-recall learning. They found that the students were more confident they would remember material repeated under massed conditions than under spaced conditions, even though they remembered significantly less under massed conditions.

Another possibility, suggested by Dempster's (1986) findings, is that subjects somehow find spaced repetitions more interesting than massed repetitions, perhaps because they seem less redundant and thus more informative than massed presentations. To the extent that interest has an affective component, this explanation is consistent with the results of an earlier study that found a tendency for subjects to judge spaced words as more "pleasant" than massed words (Elmes, Dye, & Herdelin, 1983).

There are, however, a number of difficulties with the voluntary-attention hypothesis, regardless of the specific mechanisms postulated. First, certain manipulations that should have induced subjects to attend to massed presentations have failed to attenuate the spacing effect (Hintzman, 1976). Second, substantial spacing effects have occurred in certain incidental learning tasks (Challis, 1993; Rowe & Rose, 1977; Shaughnessy, 1976) and with preschool-aged children (Rea & Modigliani, 1987; Toppino, 1991)—circumstances in which voluntary control processes should not have been much of a contributing factor. Finally, the very generality of the spacing effect seems to be an argument against a purely voluntary process. How reasonable is it to assume that the same or similar voluntary processes would operate under all sorts of task conditions with so many different subject populations?

In view of these considerations, the key to understanding most spacing effects may lie in the operation of an involuntary mechanism that controls attention. Since Hintzman's (1974) review, a growing number of researchers have suggested that the accessibility of previous encodings may be crucial to the explication of the spacing effect. A variety of formulations that share this theme have been proposed (Cuddy & Jacoby, 1982; Dellarosa & Bourne, 1985; Dempster, 1988; Glover & Corkill, 1987; Jacoby, 1978; Rea & Modigliani, 1987; Rose, 1980, 1984). The basic idea is that when a unit of information is repeated, an attempt is made to retrieve the previous encoding of that item. If the spacing between occurrences is relatively short, the results of the previous encoding(s) will be more accessible than if the spacing between repetitions is relatively lengthy. Thus, the subject will need to devote more attention or processing effort to spaced repetitions than to massed repetitions.

To date, efforts to test the "accessibility" or "reconstruction" hypothesis have led to mixed results. In one study (Glenberg & Smith, 1981), the repetition was in a modality different from that of the first presentation and a different orienting question was used during each presentation. Because these manipulations should have made the original encodings more difficult to retrieve, it was assumed that the repetition required constructive processing, regardless of the spacing interval. However, the spacing effect on a test of recall was not attenuated. In most studies using paraphrased repetitions, however, spacing effects have been eliminated (Dellarosa & Bourne, 1985; Glover & Corkill, 1987), as would be predicted by the accessibility hypothesis. Glover and Corkill (1987), for example, found that students who read paraphrased versions of a text or listened to paraphrased versions of a lecture in a massed condition recalled as much as their counterparts did in a spaced condition. Presumably, paraphrased versions of the same material do not permit easy retrieval of the prior encoding because they differ in surface structure. Thus, full encoding processes occur even under massed conditions.

In two other studies, the accessibility of memory traces was operationally defined in terms of the time needed to respond to a question that accompanied the repetition. Whereas Maskarinec and Thompson (1976) found no effect of spacing on reaction time, Rose's (1984) findings were generally consistent with the reconstruction hypothesis, which predicts that longer reaction time to questions should occur under spaced conditions.

Obviously, findings based on these sorts of manipulations are open to a variety of interpretations. For example, the effects of paraphrasing are consistent with both the rehearsal hypothesis and the voluntary-attention hypothesis, just as some of the findings consistent with these hypotheses are also congruent with the accessibility hypothesis. Accordingly, much of the appeal of the accessibility hypothesis rests upon data that are difficult to reconcile with voluntary-process explanations. These include spacing effects in certain incidental learning tasks (Challis, 1993), spacing effects in very young children (Rea & Modigliani, 1987; Toppino, 1991), including infants (Vande Linde et al., 1985), and the sheer ubiquity of spacing effects. Together these findings render voluntary-process explanations of the spacing effect implausible, at least to the extent that it can be considered the root cause of most spacing effects. By contrast, the performance of preschoolers in spacing experiments suggests that the most fundamental mechanisms underlying spacing effects are hard-wired into the memory system and operate relatively automatically. This, of course, does not preclude the possibility that in some situations the effect may be augmented or otherwise influenced by voluntary processes (see also Toppino, 1991).

If spacing effects are due to an involuntary process, then why are spacing effects not more persistent than they actually are? One possible explanation is offered by Challis (1993) who argues that semantic processing plays a critical role in some spacing effects and that, if learning conditions invite only shallow processing, there will be little value in spaced repetitions. In support of this view, he reports data showing that spaced repetitions failed to improve performance in an incidental–graphemic study condition. Clearly, though, this basic idea could be expanded to accommodate the absence of spacing effects in tasks involving simple perceptual motor skills (Thorndike, 1916; Underwood, 1961), and the weak effects of spacing with lists of nonsense syllables (Underwood, 1961). In effect, this is a levels-of-processing (Craik & Lockhart, 1972) approach to spacing effects; spacing effects will emerge only if spaced repetitions receive a deeper level of processing than massed repetitions. By this account, it is not so much the amount as it is the quality of additional processing a repetition receives that is critical.

B. Testing Effects

The effects of tests on learning have also received a great deal of theoretical attention, particularly in recent years. Nevertheless, relatively few studies have been conducted to determine why a test given between an initial learning episode and a final test enhances a subject's memory. Unlike spacing effects, which have spawned a number of clearly distinguishable hypotheses, testing effects have inspired only two, namely, the amount of processing hypothesis (see also Glover, 1989) and the retrieval hypothesis.

1. Amount of Processing Hypothesis

The simplest explanation for the effects of intervening tests is that tests improve memory performance by increasing the amount of processing devoted to particular items. An intervening test merely causes subjects to process information for an additional time prior to a final test, thereby improving final test performance. In short, test trials act primarily as additional study trials.

There are, however, at least four problems with this hypothesis. First, retrieving an item from memory when tested has beneficial effects for later retention above and beyond the effects due merely to studying the item (Carrier & Pashler, 1992). Second, there is some evidence that experimental conditions affect repetitions in the form of presentations and tests differently, suggesting that they have differential effects on learning. For example, Sones and Stroud (1940) provided seventh-graders with either a test or a review at various intervals following the reading of an article. Forty-two days after the reading, a multiple-choice retention test was administered. For subjects who had received a prior test, performance on the final retention test decreased as the interval between the original reading and the prior test increased. By contrast, the effect of the review on final retention was independent of the interval between the original reading and the review.

A third difficulty with the amount of processing hypothesis is that once some to-be-learned information is stored in memory, as indicated by a correct response to a test, further test trials tend to enhance performance more than further study trials (Brainerd, Kingma, & Howe, 1985; Halff, 1977; Nungester & Duchastel, 1982), even when the test questions and review statements contain the same content (Bruning, 1968). This is especially likely if the subject has achieved a high level of initial learning (Nungester & Duchastel, 1982). Finally, test-spacing effects seem to call for a more sophisticated explanation than that afforded by the amount of processing hypothesis. As it now stands, this hypothesis seems to lead to the straightforward prediction that massed tests should be just as effective as spaced tests.

2. Retrieval Hypothesis

In broad terms, the retrieval hypothesis suggests that it is the processing engendered by acts of retrieval that accounts for the effects of intervening tests, not merely the amount of processing. Intuitively, this notion is appealing because tests normally afford fewer retrieval cues than additional study opportunities. Furthermore, Glover (1989) found that an intervening free-recall test had a more facilitative influence on a final test than an intervening cued-recall test and that an intervening cued-recall test had a larger effect on the final test than did an intervening recognition test. This pattern of results was obtained whether the final test was free recall, cued recall, or recognition. Thus, the effectiveness of an intervening test was an inverse function of the availability of retrieval cues, just as the retrieval hypothesis would predict. According to Glover (1989), these findings suggest that it is the number and completeness of retrieval events that set the parameters of testing effects.

The retrieval hypothesis also provides a better account of test-spacing effects than does the amount of processing hypothesis. Basically, the same reconstruction or accessibility argument advanced to explain spacing effects can be extended to spaced retrieval practice. According to this argument, massed retrieval practice is less effective than spaced retrieval practice because memory traces corresponding to previous encounters with the target information will be less accessible under spaced conditions. Thus, full retrieval processes are more likely to occur on spaced tests than on massed tests (Glover, 1989).

The specifics of the retrieval hypothesis come in a variety of forms. Some have suggested that retrieval attempts may provide general practice or create a retrieval context that will be similar to that during later retrieval attempts and thus boost the likelihood of correct retrieval at a later date (Landauer & Bjork, 1978; Runquist, 1983). This account is difficult to reconcile with the fact that the beneficial effects of prior testing apply mainly to items that were successfully retrieved on that test. On the other hand, this account helps to explain the indirect effects of tests as well as reminiscence and hypermnesia. Indeed, indirect effects are most likely to obtain when the to-be-remembered material is related topically or semantically (R. C. Anderson & Biddle, 1975; Runquist, 1986). Under these circumstances, the benefits of general retrieval practice might be expected to extend to items that were not previously tested, or tested but not successfully retrieved.

Other accounts assume that the beneficial effect of retrieval occurs not at a global level, but rather at the level of individual items. The act of retrieval may either strengthen existing "retrieval routes" to the representation of the item in memory (Birnbaum & Eichner, 1971; Bjork, 1975) or result in the creation of new routes (Bjork, 1975). It is assumed that these new routes will increase the total number of retrieval routes to the representation of an item in memory and, thus, raise the probability of correct recall on a later test.

Each of these versions of the retrieval hypothesis can be directly extended to account for the superiority of test trials over study trials (see also Carrier

& Pashler, 1992). In the former case, retrieval routes that will prove useful later are more likely to be strengthened by an earlier retrieval than by an earlier study opportunity. In the latter case, the creation of new retrieval routes should be more likely to occur during retrieval than during study. As noted earlier, however, there is little evidence that multiple retrieval routes are a sufficient condition of improved recall (Postman & Knecht, 1983).

In addition to the retrieval routes versions of the retrieval hypothesis, it has been proposed that intervening tests have their effect on subsequent retrieval by "unitizing" the set of items retrieved (Glover, 1989). According to this perspective, the activation pathways among retrieved items are strengthened (see also J. R. Anderson, 1990). On subsequent test, then, the set of items previously retrieved have stronger links to one another, and the retrieval of any one member of the set increases the likelihood of retrieving any other member of the set. Although the unitizing version of the retrieval hypothesis focuses on the relations between items, rather than on individual items per se, it—like the retrieval route versions—applies only to previously retrieved items. In fact, each of these versions is seriously challenged by indirect effects, reminiscence, and hypermnesia.

There are, however, a number of models of retrieval that suggest potential explanations of reminiscence, and thus hypermnesia, although, as Roediger and Wheeler (1993) note, reminiscence is still largely a puzzle some eighty years after it was first discovered. These include models that describe memory search in terms of sampling with replacement (Rundus, 1973) or in terms of a recursive sampling from a pool of responses (Estes, 1955). Both models provide a general account of how items not retrieved on an earlier test may "recover" over time. One way of adding specificity to these models is to assume that recall tests cause output interference. As a consequence, some items are blocked at retrieval by the successful retrieval of other items. As time passes, new items are sampled from memory, including some that were interfered with earlier (see also Madigan 1976; Smith & Vela, 1991). (For further discussions of retrieval processes and interference effects in memory, see Roediger and Guynn, Chapter 7, and Anderson and Neely, Chapter 8, this volume.)

IV. EDUCATIONAL IMPLICATIONS

Given the long and eventful history of research on the effects of encoding and retrieval practice, one might assume that their implications for classroom practice would already be well known, at least among psychologists. This however, does not appear to be the case. For example, even those who have studied spacing effects from a theoretical perspective are unlikely to be aware of much of the more applied research, especially studies that were conducted around the turn of the century (A. M. Glenberg, personal communication, September 1987). Furthermore, the ahistorical character of applied research (Dempster, 1988) makes if difficult to apprcciate the range of school-like situations in which spacing effects have been found effective. In addition, there is little evidence of any serious effort to disseminate the results of research on reviews and tests to the educational community. In a recent sampling of practitioner-oriented textbooks suitable for use in teacher education programs, I found either little or no mention of the spacing effect, and I was able to find even less on the benefits of tests for learning (Gage & Berliner, 1992; Good & Brophy, 1990; Tuckman, 1992; Woolfolk, 1990). Tests are regarded mainly as instruments for making decisions about grading and pacing, not as a means of promoting learning (see also Dempster & Perkins, 1993).

As might be expected then, spacing effects have not yet captured the attention of teachers, teacher educators, or curriculum specialists, and they are not widely exploited in the classroom. For example, review—a prerequisite to the spacing of presentations—is not a common practice in the classroom. In a study of the effectiveness of an experimental mathematics teaching program, the teachers summarized the previous day's lesson only about 25% of the time, and homework was checked only about 50% of the time (Good & Grouws, 1979). Many topics, it seems, are presented just once (Armbruster & Anderson, 1984). Clearly, review is a teaching function that could be done more frequently in most classrooms (Dempster, 1991).

As to the use of spaced reviews in textbooks, the situation appears to be much the same. In a survey of mathematics textbooks, the use of a distributed method of presentation, with frequent use of spaced review, is clearly the exception rather than the rule (Stigler, Fuson, Ham, & Kim, 1986). In part, this may be due to the fact that the spacing effect is not intuitively obvious (Bjork, 1979; Dempster, 1988). Students tend to be more confident they will remember materials presented under massed conditions than under spaced conditions (Zechmeister & Shaughnessy, 1980). Thus, it is not surprising that cramming—"a heavy burst of studying immediately before an exam following a long period of neglect"— is the rule rather than the exception among students (Sommer, 1968). Even experienced educators, when judging the instructional effectiveness of text passages, tend to rate prose in which the repetition of information is massed as better than those in which it is spaced (Rothkopf, 1963).

Research also suggests that many, if not most, courses of instruction offer far less than optimal testing patterns. It is not unusual, for example, for postsecondary classes to have only two (a midterm and a final) or three tests in a term and relatively few of these appear to be cumulative, which, of course, would allow for distributed retrieval practice. Tests also are not an integral part of teachers' regular instruction at the elementary level, even though a particular subject may be taught three to five times a week. In one survey, fourth and sixth grade mathematics teachers reported having administered an average of about 18 curriculum-embedded tests per year or approximately 1 test every 2 weeks (Burry, Catteral, Choppin, & Dorr-Bremme, 1982). Worse, it appears that teachers test more frequently in mathematics than in reading and that grade level and amount of testing are inversely related (Yeh, 1978). Thus, there are reasons to believe that tests also are underutilized in the classroom in terms of their potential for improving learning (see also Dempster & Perkins, 1993).

Unfortunately, many educators have convinced themselves that "repetitive practice" stifles creativity, and they identify such practice with something called "rote learning." It is partly because of this belief that teachers avoid recycling curricular units via either reviews or tests throughout the term. Besides, recycling is not tidy; it does not let teachers teach a unit and dust off their hands quickly with a nice sense of completion (see also Dempster, 1993).

Arguably, the beneficial effects of an increase in the use of spaced reviews and tests in the classroom would extend beyond their effects on learning. Recall that distributed reviews and tests have been found to be more "attention grabbing" than similar massed events (Dempster, 1986; Magliero, 1983; Zechmeister & Shaughnessy, 1980). Thus, spaced repetitions are likely to promote student time-on-task, a highly valued classroom behavior. In addition, research suggests that students will find spaced repetitions an interesting and agreeable classroom practice (Burns, 1970; Dempster, 1986; Elmes et al., 1983). Burns (1970), for example, reported that his sixth grade pupils found review questions spaced throughout instruction both "useful" and "interesting." In short, the use of frequent spaced reviews and tests should help students develop and sustain positive attitudes toward school and learning (see also R. C. Anderson & Biddle, 1975, p. 128).

Also on the benefits side of the ledger, if indeed reviews and tests have differential effects on learning, reviews and tests may be used to serve two different learning-related purposes in the classroom. For material that is not well learned, reviews may be more productive than tests. But when degree of original learning is high, a test may result in significantly better retention than an equivalent amount of time spent in review (Nungester & Duchastel, 1982). As Sones and Stroud (1940) noted:

> Since testing reviews are more effective when placed in early positions, the effectiveness of such reviews should vary directly with the degree to which the material is originally learned. Moreover, for material that is well learned, recall, as in the form of a test, should be more productive than relearning, as in rereading.
>
> *(p. 675)*

These considerations raise the question of how best to put into practice the results of research on reviews and tests. It would appear that spaced reviews and tests can be successfully incorporated into a variety of instructional activities, including asking questions about concepts and skills taught in previous lessons, assigning and checking homework, and having students prepare a written summary of previous lessons. By distributing homework exercises concerning a particular topic across a number of weekly assignments, for example, students will receive repeated, spaced exposures to the same educational objective. The same result, of course, can be achieved by frequent, spaced (e.g., daily, weekly) reviews. Furthermore, reviews do not have to be verbatim (Dellarosa & Bourne, 1985; Krug et al., 1990). For example, Krug et al. (1990) found that a massed, repeated reading of a paraphrased version of an essay was more effective than a massed, repeated reading of a verbatim version of the essay.

The use of questions in the classroom may be a particularly advantageous way of translating research on the potentiating effect of tests into practice. Process-outcome research (reviewed in Brophy and Good, 1986) indicates a positive relationship between frequency of academic questions addressed to students and size of gain in student achievement. Moreover, the largest achievement gains were seen in classes where most, perhaps 75%, of the teachers' questions were answered correctly (as the results of testing would predict) and most of the rest yielded partially correct or incorrect answers rather than no responses at all.

More specifically, questions aimed at specific educational objectives should be repeated according to a pattern of increasing intervals between successive questions. Questions administered soon after the material is introduced are likely to have a favorable outcome, engender feelings of success and accomplishment, and strengthen the information sufficiently to survive a somewhat longer interval. An example of just this sort of application has been reported by Siegel and Misselt (1984), who conducted a study in which college students were taught foreign language vocabulary using a computer-assisted instruction program. When a student made an error, he or she received corrective feedback and then the missed item was programmed to reappear according to an expanded-ratio practice schedule. For example, the first retesting of a missed item might occur after an interval of three intervening items; if that test had a successful outcome, the third test would occur after an interval of six intervening items, and so forth. If at any time during practice an item was missed, the entire procedure was reset. Posttest performance revealed that the use of this procedure was successful. Unfortunately, most programs developed for use with computers are modeled after the traditional flash card drills and tend not to be guided by investigations of sequences of events that might be optimal for efficient and effective learning (Dempster & Perkins, 1993). As Siegel and Misselt (1984) point out, their procedure could be expanded to guide instruction in a variety of areas, including spelling, arithmetic, and concept learning.

Ideally though, both encoding and retrieval practice aimed at fostering the learning and retention of specific educational objectives should occur over an extended period of time. As several studies have shown, material acquired and maintained this way is virtually permanent (Bahrick & Hall, 1991; Bahrick & Phelps, 1987; Power, 1993). Retention losses are much less affected by individual-difference variables, such as aptitude and achievement, than they are by characteristics of the curriculum and instruction schedules (Bahrick & Hall, 1991). The kinds of school-based changes that should help to prevent retention losses are cumulative capstone review courses and cumulative reexamination at the end of a lengthy program of study (Bahrick & Hall, 1991; Conway, Cohen & Stanhope, 1992).

V. SUMMARY AND CONCLUSIONS

Research with direct implications for distributing and managing the conditions of encoding and practice has had a long and distinguished history, involving some of psychology's foremost contributors, including Ebbinghaus, Melton, Postman, Thorndike, and Underwood. The fruits of their research are in many ways remarkable: the effects of distributed practice, in the form of reviews and tests, are among the most dependable, robust, and ubiquitous phenomena in the entire psychological literature. Furthermore, distributed encoding and retrieval practice is one of the keys to effective learning. Information that is practiced at spaced intervals over a lengthy period of time, such as the "Pledge of Allegiance," is likely to be both effectively learned and highly resistant to forgetting.

Although the effects of spaced presentations on encoding are better known than the effects of tests on learning (Bruce & Bahrick, 1992), there are indications that this gap is closing. One indicator is that the spacing effect and test-spacing effects are increasingly becoming understood in terms of the same psychological mechanism—namely, retrieval processes mediated, in part, by the accessibility of previously encoded information. Encoding trials are not retrieval trials; however, both are heavily influenced by retrieval operations. In general terms, the assumption is that repetitions are effective to the extent that (1) they engender successful retrieval of the results of earlier processing, and (2) that the effort and level of processing involved in a successful retrieval operation increase with spacing. To some extent, therefore, further developments in the area of spaced presentations should inform research on testing.

A second indicator is that repetitions, in the form of either presentations or tests, have clear and verifiable implications for the classroom. Moreover, their potential for improving learning and retention is vast. Frequent distributed practice will help students maintain and develop concepts and skills introduced earlier in a sequence, and it will give them the time needed to find appropriate and meaningful ways of integrating information from a variety of sources. Even insights seldom occur without repeated exposure to relevant material over a relatively lengthy period. Anyone who has arrived at a profound understanding of something will recognize the importance of distributed practice and the sense of accomplishment it affords. Sustained involvement in an area of inquiry—what Isaac Newton reportedly referred to as "patient thought"—is the key to success in a wide variety of endeavors.

References

Allen, G. A., Mahler, W. A., & Estes, W. K. (1969). Effects of recall tests on long-term retention of paired associates. *Journal of Verbal Learning and Verbal Behavior, 8,* 463–470.

Amlund, J. T., Kardash, C. A. M., & Kulhavy, R. W. (1986). Repetitive reading and recall of expository text. *Reading Research Quarterly, 21,* 49–58.

Anderson, J. R. (1990). *Cognitive psychology and its implications* (3rd ed.). New York: W. H. Freeman.

Anderson, R. C., & Biddle, W. B. (1975). On asking people questions about what they are reading. In G. H. Bower (Ed.), *The psychology of learning and motivation: Advances in research and theory* (Vol. 9 pp. 90–132). New York: Academic Press.

Armbruster, B. B., & Anderson, T. H. (1984). Structures of explanation in history textbooks or so what if Governor Stanford missed the spike and hit the rail? *Journal of Curriculum Studies, 16,* 181–194.

Austin, S. D. M. (1921). A study in logical memory. *American Journal of Psychology, 32,* 370–403.

Ausubel, D. P. (1966). Early versus delayed review in meaningful learning. *Psychology in the Schools, 3,* 195–198.

Baddeley, A. D. (1976). *The psychology of memory.* New York: Basic Books.

Bahrick, H. P., & Hall, L. K. (1993). Long intervals between tests can yield hypermnesia: Comments on Wheeler and Roediger. *Psychological Science, 4,* 206–207.

Bahrick, H. P., & Hall, L. K. (1993). Long intervals between tests can yield hypermnesia: Comments on Wheefer and Roediger. *Psychological Science, 4,* 206–207.

Bahrick, H. P., & Phelps, E. (1987). Retention of Spanish vocabulary over 8 years. *Journal of Experimental Psychology: Learning, Memory, and Cognition, 13,* 344–349.

Ballard, P. B. (1913). Oblivescence and reminiscence. *British Journal of Psychology Monograph Supplement, 1,* 1–82.

Balota, D. A., Duchek, J. M., & Paullin, R. (1989). Age related differences in the impact of spacing, lag, and retention interval. *Psychology and Aging, 4,* 3–9.

Birnbaum, I. M., & Eichner, J. T. (1971). Study versus test trials and long-term retention in free-recall learning. *Journal of Verbal Learning and Verbal Behavior, 10,* 516–521.

Bjork, R. A. (1975). Retrieval as a memory modifier: An interpretation of negative recency and related phenomena. In R. L. Solso (Ed.), *Information processing and cognition: The Loyola Symposium* (pp. 123–144). Hillsdale, NJ: Erlbaum.

Bjork, R. A. (1979). Information-processing analysis of college teaching. *Educational Psychologist, 14,* 15–23.

Bjork, R. A., & Allen, T. W. (1970). The spacing effect: Consolidation or differential encoding? *Journal of Verbal Learning and Verbal Behavior, 9,* 567–572.

Bower, G. H. (1972). Stimulus-sampling theory of encoding variability. In A. W. Melton & E. Martin (Eds.), *Coding in human memory* (pp. 85–124). New York: Winston.

Brainerd, C. J., Kingma, J., & Howe, M. L. (1985). On the development of forgetting. *Child Development, 56,* 1103–1119.

Bromage, B. K., & Mayer, R. E. (1986). Quantitative and qualitative effects of repetition on learning from technical text. *Journal of Educational Psychology, 78,* 271–278.

Brophy, J., & Good, T. (1986). Teacher effects. In M. Wittrock (Ed.), *Third handbook of research on teaching* (pp. 328–375). New York: Macmillan.

Brown, W. (1923). To what extent is memory measure by a single recall trial? *Journal of Experimental Psychology, 6,* 377–382.

Bruce, D., & Bahrick, H. P. (1992). Perceptions of past research. *American Psychologist, 47,* 319–328.

Bruning, R. H. (1968). Effects of review and testlike events within the learning of prose material. *Journal of Educational Psychology, 59,* 16–19.

Burns, P. C. (1970). Intensive review as a procedure in teaching arithmetic. *Elementary School Journal, 60,* 205–211.

Burry, J., Catteral, J., Choppin, B., & Dorr-Bremme, D. (1982). *Testing in the nation's schools and districts: How much? What kinds? To what ends? At what costs?* (CSE Report No. 194). Los Angeles: University of California, Center for the Study of Evaluation.

Carrier, M., & Pashler, H. (1992). The influence of retrieval on retention. *Memory & Cognition, 20,* 633–642.

Challis, B. H. (1993). Spacing effects on cued-memory tests depend on level of processing. *Journal of Experimental Psychology: Learning, Memory, and Cognition, 19,* 389–396.

Conway, M. A., Cohen, G., & Stanhope, N. (1992). Very long-term memory for knowledge acquired at school and university. *Applied Cognitive Psychology, 6,* 467–482.

Cornell, E. H. (1980). Distributed study facilitates infants' delayed recognition memory. *Memory & Cognition, 8,* 539–542.

Craik, F. I. M., & Lockhart, R. S. (1972). Levels of processing: A framework for memory research. *Journal of Verbal Learning and Verbal Behavior, 11,* 671–684.

Cuddy, L. J., & Jacoby, L. L. (1982). When forgetting helps memory: An analysis of repetition effects. *Journal of Verbal Learning and Verbal Behavior, 21,* 451–467.

Dearborn, W. F. (1910). Experiments in learning. *Journal of Educational Psychology, 1,* 373–388.

Dellarosa, D., & Bourne, L. E. (1985). Surface form and the spacing effect. *Memory & Cognition, 13,* 529–537.

Dempster, F. N. (1986). *Spacing effects in text recall : An extrapolation from the laboratory to the classroom.* Unpublished manuscript, University of Nevada, Las Vegas.

Dempster, F. N. (1987). Effects of variable encoding and spaced presentations on vocabulary learning. *Journal of Educational Psychology, 79,* 162–170.

Dempster, F. N. (1988). The spacing effect: A case study in the failure to apply the results of psychological research. *American Psychologist, 43,* 627–634.

Dempster, F. N. (1989). *Do sentence contexts facilitate vocabulary learning? Additional comparisons.* Unpublished manuscript, University of Nevada, Las Vegas.

Dempster, F. N. (1991). Synthesis of research on reviews and tests. *Educational Leadership, 48,* 71–76.

Dempster, F. N. (1993). Exposing our students to less should help them learn more. *Phi Delta Kappan, 74,* 432–437.

Dempster, F. N., & Perkins, P. G. (1993). Revitalizing classroom assessment: Using tests to promote learning. *Journal of Instructional Psychology, 20,* 197–203.

Donaldson, W. (1971). Output effects in multitrial free recall. *Journal of Verbal Learning and Verbal Behavior, 10,* 577–585.

Ebbinghaus, H. (1913). *Memory* (H. A. Ruger & C. E. Bussenius, Trans.). New York: Teachers College. (Original work published 1885) (Paperback ed., New York: Dover, 1964).

Edwards, A. S. (1917). The distribution of time in learning small amounts of material. In *Studies in psychology: Titchener commemorative volume* (pp. 209–213). Worchester, MA: Wilson.

Elmes, D. G., Dye, C. J., & Herdelin, 'N. J. (1983). What is the role of affect is the spacing effect? *Memory & Cognition, 11*, 144–151.

Elmes, D. G., Greener, W. I., & Wilkinson, W. C. (1972). Free recall of items presented after massed- and distributed- practice items. *American Journal of Psychology, 85*, 237–240.

English, H. B., Wellborn, E. L., & Killian, C. D. (1934). Studies in substance memorization. *Journal of General Psychology, 11*, 233–260.

Estes, W. K. (1955). Statistical theory of spontaneous recovery and regression. *Psychological Review, 62*, 145–154.

Gage, N. L., & Berliner, D. C. (1992). *Educational psychology* (5th ed.). Boston: Houghton Mifflin.

Gates, A. I. (1917). Recitation as a factor in memorizing. *Archives of Psychology, 6*, 1–104.

Gay, L. R. (1973). Temporal position of reviews and its effect on the retention of mathematical rules. *Journal of Educational Psychology, 64*, 171–182.

Glenberg, A. M. (1979). Component-levels theory of the effects of spacing of repetitions on recall and recognition. *Memory & Cognition, 7*, 95–112.

Glenberg, A. M., & Lehmann, T. S. (1980). Spacing repetitions over 1 week. *Memory & Cognition, 8*, 528–538.

Glenberg, A. M., & Smith, S. M. (1981). Spacing repetitions and solving problems are not the same. *Journal of Verbal Learning and Verbal Behavior, 20*, 110–119.

Glover, J. A. (1989). The "testing" phenomenon: Not gone but nearly forgotten. *Journal of Educational Psychology, 81*, 392–399.

Glover, J. A., & Corkill, A. J. (1987). Influence of paraphrased repetitions on the spacing effect. *Journal of Educational Psychology, 79*, 198–199.

Goldstein, A. G., Chance, J. E., & Otto, J. (1987, November). *Enhanced face recognition memory after distributed viewing*. Paper presented at the annual meeting of the Psychonomic Society, Seattle.

Good, T. L., & Brophy, J. E. (1990). *Educational psychology* (4th ed.). New York: Longman.

Good, T. L., & Grouws, D. A. (1979). The Missouri mathematics effectiveness project. *Journal of Educational Psychology, 71*, 355–362.

Gordon, K. (1925). Class results with spaced and unspaced memorizing. *Journal of Experimental Psychology, 8*, 337–343.

Greene, R. L. (1989). Spacing effects in memory: Evidence for a two-process account. *Journal of Experimental Psychology: Learning, Memory, and Cognition, 15*, 371–377.

Greene, R. L. (1990). Spacing effects on implicit memory tests. *Journal of Experimental Psychology: Learning, Memory, and Cognition, 16*, 1004–1011.

Halff, H. M. (1977). The role of opportunities for recall in learning to retrieve. *American Journal of Psychology, 90*, 383–406.

Hermann, D. J., Buschke, H., & Gall, M. B. (1987). Improving retrieval. *Applied Cognitive Psychology, 1*, 27–33.

Hilgard, E. R., & Bower, G. H. (1975). *Theories of learning* (4th ed.). Englewood Cliffs, NJ: Prentice-Hall.

Hintzman, D. L. (1974). Theoretical implications of the spacing effect. In R. L. Solso (Ed). *Theories in cognitive psychology: The Loyola Symposium* (pp. 77–99). Potomac, MD.: Erlbaum.

Hintzman, D. L., (1976). Repetition and memory. In G. H. Bower (Ed.), *The psychology of learning and motivation: Advances in research and theory* (Vol. 10, pp. 47–91). New York: Academic Press.

Hintzman, D. L., & Rogers, M. K. (1973). Spacing effects in picture memory. *Memory & Cognition, 1*, 430–434.

Hintzman, D. L., Summers, J. J., & Block, R. A. (1975). What causes the spacing effect? Some effects of repetition, duration, and spacing on memory for pictures. *Memory & Cognition, 3*, 287–294.

Hogan, R. M., & Kintsch, W. (1971). Differential effects of study and test trials on long-term recognition and recall. *Journal of Verbal Learning and Verbal Behavior, 10*, 562–567.

Izawa, C. (1971). The test trial potentiating model. *Journal of Mathematical Psychology, 8*, 200–224.

Jacoby, L. L. (1978). On interpreting the effects of repetition: Solving a problem versus remembering a solution. *Journal of Verbal Learning and Verbal Behavior, 17*, 649–667.

James, W. (1901). *Talks to teachers on psychology: And to students on some of life's ideals.* New York: Holt.

Jones, H. E. (1923–1924). The effects of examination on permanence of learning. *Archives of Psychology, 10*, 21–70.

Kahana, M. J., & Greene, R. L. (1993). Effects of spacing on memory for homogeneous lists. *Journal of Experimental Psychology: Learning, Memory, and Cognition, 19*, 159–162.

Kiewra, K. A., Mayer, R. A., Christensen, M., Kim, S. I., & Risch, N. (1991). Effects of repetition on recall and note-taking: Strategies for learning from lectures. *Journal of Educational Psychology, 83*, 120–123.

Kraft, R. M., & Jenkins, J. J. (1981). The lag effect with aurally presented passages. *Bulletin of the Psychonomic Society, 17*, 132–134.

Krug, D., Davis, T. B., & Glover, J. (1990). Massed versus distributed repeated reading: A case of forgetting helping recall? *Journal of Educational Psychology, 82*, 366–371.

Lachman, R., & Laughery, K. L. (1968). Is a test trial a training trial in free recall learning? *Journal of Experimental Psychology, 76*, 40–50.

Landauer, T. K. (1969). Reinforcement as consolidation. *Psychological Review, 76*, 82–96.

Landauer, T. K., & Bjork, R. A. (1978). Optimum rehearsal patterns and name learning. In M. M. Gruneberg, P. E. Morris, & R. N. Sykes (Eds.), *Practical aspects of memory* (pp. 625–632). New York: Academic Press.

Lyon, D. O. (1914). The relation of length of material to time taken for learning and the optimum distribution of time. *Journal of Educational Psychology, 5*, 85–91, 155–163.

Madigan, S. (1976). Reminiscence and item recovery in free recall. *Memory & Cognition, 4*, 233–236.

Magliero, A. (1983). Pupil dilations following pairs of identical words and related to-be-remembered words. *Memory & Cognition, 11*, 609–615.

Martin, E. (1972). Stimulus encoding in learning and transfer. In A. W. Melton & E. Martin (Eds.), *Coding processes in human memory* (pp. 59–84). Washington, DC: Winston.

Maskarinec, A. S., & Thompson, C. P. (1976). The within list distributed practice effect: Tests of the varied context and varied encoding hypotheses. *Memory & Cognition, 4*, 741–746.

Mayer, R. E. (1983). Can you repeat this? Qualitative effects of repetition and advanced organizers on learning from science prose. *Journal of Educational Psychology, 75*, 40–49.

McFarland, C. E., Rhodes, D. D., & Frey, T. J. (1979). Semantic-feature variability and the spacing effect. *Journal of Verbal Learning and Verbal Behavior, 18*, 163–172.

McGeoch, J. A. (1943). *The psychology of human learning.* New York: Longmans Green.

Melton, A. W. (1970). The situation with respect to the spacing of repetitions and memory. *Journal of Verbal Learning and Verbal Behavior, 9*, 596–606.

Modigliani, V. (1976). Effects on a later recall by delaying initial recall. *Journal of Experimental Psychology: Human Learning and Memory, 2*, 609–622.

Muller, G. E., & Pilzecker, A. (1900). Experimentelle beiträge zur lehre vom gedächtnis [Experimental contributions to the study of memory]. *Zeitschrift für Psychologie, Erganzunosband, 1*, 1–288.

Murdock, B. B., Jr., & Babick, A. J. (1961). The effect of repetition on the retention of individual words. *American Journal of Psychology, 74*, 596–601.

Nungester, R. J., & Duchastel, P. C. (1982). Testing versus review: Effects on retention. *Journal of Educational Psychology, 74*, 18–22.

Ornstein, P. A. (1978). *Memory development in children*. New York: Wiley.

Ornstein, P. A., Naus, M. J. (1978). Rehearsal processes in children's memory. In P. A. Ornstein (Ed.), *Memory development in children* (pp. 69–99). Hillsdale, NJ: Erlbaum.

Payne, D. G. (1987). Hypermnesia and reminiscence in recall: A historical and empirical review. *Psychological Bulletin, 101*, 5–27.

Perkins, N. L. (1914). The value of distributed repetitions in rote learning. *British Journal of Psychology, 1*, 253–261.

Peterson, H. A., Ellis, M., Toohill, N., & Kloess, P. (1935). Some measurements of the effects of reviews. *Journal of Educational Psychology, 26*, 65–72.

Petros, T., & Hoving, K. (1980). The effects of review on young children's memory for prose. *Journal of Experimental Child Psychology, 30*, 33–43.

Porter, A. (1989). A curriculum out of balance: The case of elementary school mathematics. *Educational Researcher, 18*, 9–15.

Postman, L., & Knecht, K. (1983). Encoding variability and retention. *Journal of Verbal Learning and Verbal Behavior, 22*, 133–152.

Power, D. (1993). Very long-term retention of a first language without rehearsal: A case study. *Applied Cognitive Psychology, 7*, 229–237.

Pyle, W. H. (1913). Economical learning. *Journal of Educational Psychology, 3*, 148–158.

Raffel, G. (1934). The effect of recall on forgetting. *Journal of Experimental Psychology, 17*, 828–838.

Rea, C. P., & Modigliani, V. (1985). The effect of expanded versus massed practice on the retention of multiplication facts and spelling lists. *Human Learning, 4*, 11–18.

Rea, C. P., & Modigliani, V. (1987). The spacing effect in 4- to 9-year-old children. *Memory & Cognition, 15*, 436–443.

Reynolds, J. H., & Glaser, R. (1964). Effects of repetition and spaced review upon retention of a complex learning task. *Journal of Educational Psychology, 55*, 297–308.

Roediger, H. L., III, & Wheeler, M. A. (1993). Hypermnesia in episodic and semantic memory: Response to Bahrick and Hall. *Psychological Science, 4*, 207–208.

Rose, A. J. (1980). Encoding variability, levels of processing, and the effects of spacing of repetitions upon judgments of frequency. *Memory & Cognition, 8*, 84–93.

Rose, A. J. (1984). Processing time for repetitions and the spacing effect. *Canadian Journal of Psychology, 38*, 537–550.

Rothkopf, E. Z. (1963). Some observations on predicting instructional effectiveness by simple inspection. *Journal of Programmed Instruction, 3*, 19–20.

Rothkopf, E. Z. (1966). Learning from written instructive materials: An exploration of the control of inspection behavior by test-like events. *American Educational Research Journal, 3*, 241–249.

Rothkopf, E. Z., & Coke, E. V. (1966). Variations in phrasing and repetition interval and the recall of sentence materials. *Journal of Verbal Learning and Verbal Behavior, 5*, 86–89.

Rowe, E. J., & Rose, R. J. (1977). Effects of orienting task, spacing of repetitions, and list context on judgments of frequency. *Memory & Cognition, 5*, 505–512.

Ruch, T. C. (1928). Factors influencing the relative economy of massed and distributed practice in learning. *Psychological Review, 35*, 19–45.

Rundus, D. (1971). Analysis of rehearsal processes in free recall. *Journal of Experimental Psychology, 89*, 63–77.

Rundus, D. (1973). Negative effects of using list items as recall cues. *Journal of Verbal Learning and Verbal Behavior, 12*, 43–50.

Runquist, W. N. (1983). Some effects of remembering on forgetting. *Memory & Cognition, 11*, 641–650.

Runquist, W. N. (1986). The effect of testing on the forgetting of related and unrelated associates. *Canadian Journal of Psychology, 40*, 65–76.

Shaughnessy, J. J. (1976). Persistence of the spacing effect in free recall under varying incidental learning conditions. *Memory & Cognition, 4,* 369–377.

Siegel, M. A., & Misselt, A. L. (1984). Adaptive feedback and review paradigm for computer-based drills. *Journal of Educational Psychology, 76,* 310–317.

Slamecka, N. J., & Katsaiti, L. T. (1988). Normal forgetting of verbal lists as a function of prior testing. *Journal of Experimental Psychology: Learning, Memory, and Cognition, 14,* 716–727.

Smith, S. M., & Vela, E. (1991). Incubated reminiscence effects. *Memory & Cognition, 19,* 168–176.

Sommer, R. (1968). The social psychology of cramming. *Personnel and Guidance Journal, 9,* 104–109.

Sones, A. M., & Stroud, J. B. (1940). Review with special reference to temporal position. *Journal of Educational Psychology, 31,* 665–676.

Spitzer, H. F. (1939). Studies in retention. *Journal of Educational Psychology, 30,* 641–656.

Stigler, J. W., Fuson, K. C., Ham, M., & Kim, M. S. (1986). An analysis of addition and subtraction word problems in American and Soviet elementary mathematics textbooks. *Cognition and Instruction, 3,* 153–171.

Thorndike, E. L. (1916). Notes on practice, improvability and the curve of work. *American Journal of Psychology, 27,* 550–565.

Toppino, T. C. (1991). The spacing effect in young children's free recall: Support for automatic-process explanations. *Memory & Cognition, 19,* 159–167.

Toppino, T. C., & DeMesquita, M. (1984). Effects of spacing repetitions on children's memory. *Journal of Experimental Child Psychology, 37,* 637–648.

Toppino, T. C., DiGeorge, W. (1984). The spacing effect in free recall emerges with development. *Memory & Cognition, 12,* 118–122.

Toppino, T. C., & Gracen, T. F. (1985). The lag effect and differential organization theory. *Journal of Experimental Psychology: Learning, Memory, and Cognition, 11,* 185–191.

Tuckman, B. W. (1992). *Educational psychology: From theory to application.* Fort Worth, TX: Harcourt Brace Jovanovich.

Underwood, B. J. (1961). Ten years of massed practice on distributed practice. *Psychological Review, 68,* 229–247.

Underwood, B. J. (1970). A breakdown of the total-time law in free-recall learning. *Journal of Verbal Learning and Verbal Behavior, 9,* 573–580.

Vander Linde, E., Morrongiello, B. A., & Rovee-Collier, C. (1985). Determinants of retention in 8-week-old infants. *Developmental Psychology, 21,* 601–613.

Wheeler, M. A., & Roediger, H. L., III. (1992). Disparate effects of repeated testing: Reconciling Ballard's (1913) and Bartlett's (1932) results. *Psychological Science, 3,* 240–245.

Whitten, W. B., II, & Bjork, R. A. (1977). Learning from tests: Effects of spacing. *Journal of Verbal Learning and Verbal Behavior, 16,* 456–478.

Woolfolk, A. E. (1990). *Educational psychology* (4th ed.). Englewood Cliffs, NJ: Prentice-Hall.

Yeh, J. P. (1978). *Test use in schools.* Washington, DC: U.S. Department of Health, Education and Welfare, National Institute of Education.

Zechmeister, E. B., & Shaughnessy, J. J. (1980). When you know that you know and when you think that you know but you don't. *Bulletin of the Psychonomic Society, 15,* 41–44.

CHAPTER 10

Mnemonic Methods to Enhance Storage and Retrieval

Francis S. Bellezza

I. INTRODUCTION

In an often–told myth, the poet Simonides of Ceos chanted a lengthy poem during a banquet held to honor its host, the nobleman Scopas of Thessaly. The poem included a passage in praise of the twin gods Castor and Pollux. Afterward, Scopas derisively told the poet that he must seek half of his fee from the twin gods, Castor and Pollux, to whom he had devoted half of his poem. A little later, Simonides received a message that two young men wished to see him outside. When he left, the roof of the banquet hall fell killing all inside. The corpses were so mangled that relatives could not identify the bodies, but Simonides remembered the places at which the guests had been sitting and was able to identify the dead. This experience suggested to the poet the principles of the method of loci, which he is said to have invented (Yates, 1966).

I repeat this staple of mnemonic lore to emphasize some points not often mentioned in its retelling; points I discuss in more detail later. First, Simonides's recall of the guests at the banquet was not an example of the use of the method of loci. A key aspect of the success of any mnemonic device, including the method of loci, is to implement the mnemonic strategy during learning. Simonides did not use any mnemonic strategy to learn the guests' places during the banquet; he later just happened to remember the places. Second, Simonides's memories were based on perceptions formed by looking at the guests around him, not on visual images contrived during learning. Creating visual images based on imagination, not on immediate perception, is another important aspect of mnemonic learning. Finally, Simonides was a poet, not a farmer, laborer, or cook. We should, perhaps, not be surprised that an exceptional person was the discoverer of mnemonic devices. But, as it turns out, even those individuals known in history as especially proficient mnemonists seem to have possessed special talents. Does this mean even casual users of mnemonic devices have to have special abilities? Fortunately, special abilities seem not to be required, but it may be that not everyone can excel in the use of mnemonic devices. Mnemonic procedures and materials do appear to be valuable in classroom teaching, but there is some question as to how effective self-initiated mnemonic strategies are for all learners (Pressley, Scruggs, & Mastropieri, 1989; Richardson, 1987). I make these points to demonstrate that the story of Simonides of Ceos does not provide much insight into the essentials of mnemonic learning, but the popularity of this story among writers suggests how widespread are the misunderstandings regarding the nature and effectiveness of mnemonic devices (Higbee, 1979, 1988; J. R. Levin, 1981). What are needed are more incisive and more extensive analyses of the operation of mnemonic devices.

There have been a number of reviews of the research on various aspects of mnemonic devices (Bellezza, 1981, 1983; Higbee, 1988; Mastropieri & Scruggs, 1991; Paivio, 1971, chap. 6; Pressley, Levin, & Delaney, 1982) to which the interested reader is referred. In this chapter, I do not offer a general review, but selectively focus on three topics that I consider to be of current importance in the study of mnemonic devices: the types of mnemonic devices and the nature of their operation; mnemonic devices in the framework of associative network theories; and mnemonic devices in the classroom. Because of this focus, I do not discuss a number of important topics in mnemonics research, such as the value of mnemonic devices for the aged (Vrehaeghen, Marcoen, & Goossens, 1992; Yesavage, Lapp, & Sheikh, 1989) or for the brain injured (Cook, 1989; Richardson, 1992). Also, I do not discuss a variety of factors that can affect learning performance but do not deal directly with the strategic manipulation of available knowledge. As argued later, I consider the strategic manipulation of available knowledge for the acquisition of new knowledge to be the essential act in using mnemonic devices. The factors neglected include the manner in which material is presented, such as the number of repetitions (Bellezza & Young, 1989), the spacing of repetitions (Glenberg, 1976), the use of pictures versus words (Paivio, 1971), the number of study versus test trials (Tulving, 1967), the effects of generated information (Slamecka & Graf,

1978), and effects of anxiety reduction (Higbee, 1988). Other topics not discussed involve how information is rehearsed, such as elaborative versus maintenance rehearsal (Craik & Lockhart, 1972), the spacing of rehearsal (Bjork, 1988), the manner in which self-testing and review take place, as in the PQ4R procedure (Thomas & Robinson, 1972), and the degree of matching between the environment in which new information is learned and the environment in which it is recalled (Smith, Glenberg, & Bjork, 1978). Strategies used solely during remembering can affect recall performance (Fisher, Geiselman, & Amador, 1989), but my focus is on mnemonic strategies or induced mnemonic procedures that occur during learning.

Through focusing on only three topics, I hope to explain what mnemonic devices are and why they sometimes work and sometimes do not. I also hope to show that mnemonic devices activate knowledge already in memory, and this knowledge must be similar in certain ways to the information to be learned. This knowledge may have been memorized by a mnemonist not for its own sake but for the sole purpose of benefiting later learning. The learner may activate existing knowledge using a mnemonic strategy, but sometimes a teacher can do so by presenting the learner mnemonic aids. I argue that the effective use of many mnemonic devices requires a high level of skill resulting from a good deal of practice, a point often overlooked by those prescribing mnemonic devices to struggling students. Yet, I believe that learning using mnemonic devices represents an important psychological phenomenon that has been too much ignored by researchers in learning and memory. The study of mnemonic devices can contribute both to advancements in learning theory and to the development of effective instructional techniques.

II. A TAXONOMY OF MNEMONIC DEVICES

Mnemonic devices can be divided into two broad categories, encoding mnemonics and organizational mnemonics, with some subcategories within each (Bellezza, 1981). In both types of mnemonic devices, mental cues, often in the form of visual images, are created to make information retrievable. In some types of organizational mnemonics, the mnemonist must first memorize a set of mental cues, which then become part of the mnemonist's repertory of memory locations to be used as needed. New information can be associated to these cues and thus be remembered.

Encoding mnemonics also use mental cues. These mental cues, however, are different from organizational cues in that they are created during learning to be substitutes for material that is low in imagery and meaningfulness. These more memorable substitutions must be semantically or phonetically similar to the material to be learned and are memorized to represent that information in memory (Bellezza, Day, & Reddy, 1983). Often, both encoding mnemonics and organizational mnemonics are used concurrently when memorizing a set of information.

A. Organizational Mnemonics

The classic mnemonic device is the method of loci (method of locations) mentioned earlier. It was first described in Roman books on rhetoric, but it may have originated centuries earlier (Patten, 1990; Yates, 1966). When using the method of loci, the mnemonist must have prememorized the images of a sequence of locations. Next, if the set of information to be memorized is not already a list of words, but, for example, a text, it must be reduced to a sequence of essential words that represents an outline of the text. Each word is then associated to its corresponding location using visual-imagery mediation. The important point is that the loci organize information by providing a ready-made memory structure for it, and within the structure are a number of places, like distinctive containers, for the items of information to be stored. This process allows the items to be recalled in a specific order: recall from Locus 1, then from Locus 2, and so on. Hence, the method of loci not only enables a great deal of information to be recalled, but imposes a serial organization on it. Sometimes this organization is not necessary, as when recalling a grocery list, but sometimes it is, as when the method of loci is used to memorize the names of the presidents of the United States in the order in which they served in office.

A mnemonic procedure similar to the method of loci is the pegword mnemonic. Rather than using images of physical locations as mental cues, images of familiar objects are used as cues. The well-known rhyme "One is a bun, two is a shoe, three is a tree, four is a door, five is a hive, six is sticks, seven is heaven, eight is a gate, nine is a fishing line, and ten is a hen" (Miller, Galanter, & Pribram, 1960) represents a way of remembering ten pegwords, so later a list of ten items can be memorized by associating them with the pegwords. There are other system for generating and memorizing hundreds of pegwords (Bellezza, Six, & Phillips, 1992; Higbee, 1988).

1. Multiple Use versus Single Use

The method of loci and the pegword mnemonic can be used repeatedly. When a new list of words is memorized, it typically is stronger in memory than any list of words learned previously using the mnemonic; that is, there is much more retroactive interference than proactive interference among the lists (Bellezza, 1982a; see also Anderson & Neely, Chapter 8, this volume, for a discussion of interference effects in memory retrieval), although when the retention interval becomes long, items from old lists may intrude (Bower & Reitman, 1972). In addition to multiple-use mnemonics, there are organizational mnemonics that are single-use mnemonics. The rhyme "Thirty days has September, April, June, and November, . . ." is useful for recalling the days in each month. Sometimes these single-use mnemonics are not very good at cuing responses but are good at ordering information already well known (Bellezza, 1981). For example, the first letter of each word in the sentence "My very excellent mother just served us nice pie" is the first letter of the name of each planet according to its distance from the sun. Single-use mnemonics can also remind us of how much information needs to be remembered. The letters in the word *homes* remind us that there are five Great Lakes and indicate the first letter in each of their names. The sentence "I'm no wimp" reminds us that eight states surround the Great Lakes and gives us the first letter of the name of each state.

2. Intrinsic versus Extrinsic Cuing

The method of loci and pegword mnemonics rely on extrinsic cues that have been prememorized and are then associated to the material to be learned. If any to-be-remembered word is forgotten using either of these mnemonics, the mnemonist can simply move to the next loci or pegword and continue recalling. But lists of words can be memorized without using loci or pegwords. A list of words can be incorporated into a story and remembered using the story mnemonic (Bower & Clark, 1969; Drevenstedt & Bellezza, 1993). The link mnemonic is similar to the story mnemonic in that a visual image is used to link Word 1 to Word 2, a second visual image is used to link Word 2 to Word 3, and so on until $N-1$ visual images have been used to link the N words in the list.

A difficulty with the story and link mnemonics is that they rely on intrinsic cuing (Bellezza, 1981). In the link mnemonic, for example, before Word N can be recalled, Word $N-1$ must be recalled. Therefore, if any one word in the list is forgotten, recall of the rest of the words is adversely affected. A chain is only as strong as its weakest link, so if any link in the chain of images is forgotten, then it may not be possible to recall any of the words following in the chain. Like the link mnemonic, the story mnemonic also relies on intrinsic cues but is useful if multiple lists must be memorized. The story themes made up for various lists are different and depend on the particular words in the list for their unique content. The hierarchical structure of the particular story created provides the mental cues necessary for recall of the presented words (Thorndyke, 1977). If some words are forgotten, then parts of the hierarchy of the story acting as mental cues may not be retrieved, resulting in the inability to recall some words occurring in the list.

The intrinsic cuing of the story mnemonic can be improved by extrinsic cuing. Bellezza et al. (1992) found that when using the story mnemonic to memorize a list of 40 words, recall could be improved by structuring the story so that each successive set of 10 list words was elaborated in one of four predetermined locations (campus, beach, downtown, park). Hence, the extrinsic cuing provided by the method of loci combined with the instrinsic cuing of the story mnemonic resulted in optimal recall (see also Battig & Bellezza, 1979, Experiments 2 & 3).

B. Encoding Mnemonics

For some kinds of information, such as number or abstract concepts, it is difficult to create mental representations that will be remembered. Encoding mnemonics are procedures that generate memorable representations, whereas organizational mnemonics organize those representations in memory. Forming a visual image representing the referent of a word can be considered an encoding mnemonic, although a very simple one. If we form a visual image of a dog for the word *dog,* and associate that image to a locus or pegword, we later can remember the image of a dog and use the image as a mental cue for the word *dog.* Hence, the image of a dog is the mental cue for the word *dog.* Mnemonists, however, typically have to use encoding mnemonics in a more complex manner, and much of the skill of an expert mnemonist is the ability to create encodings or substitutions for information that is difficult to remember, such as faces and last names (Lorayne, 1975).

The need to memorize a list containing low-imagery words represents a common situation where an encoding mnemonic is necessary. For example, in a course in American history, the battles of the American Revolution may have to be memorized. To do this using the method of loci, each successive battle is associated with its corresponding locus. But how can one form an image of, say, the Battle of Saratoga, when one has no distinct image of it? One way is to use an encoding mnemonic based on semantic associations. If one is familiar with Saratoga Springs, then one could use the image of a spring of water and associate this image with the image of the corresponding locus. When later recalling the list, one would first remember the image of a spring of water, which then must act as a mental cue for the Battle of Saratoga. Natural memory would be used for this last step, rather than artificial memory (memory based on art). The image of a spring of water should remind the learner of Saratoga Springs, which, in turn, is a substitute for the Battle of Saratoga. These associations operating during learning should likely result in the same associations during recall and remind one of the Battle of Saratoga.

If, however, one has no meaningful association to the word *Saratoga,* phonetic associations to the word can be used to create a substitute representation. This imageable mental cue for the battle can then be associated with the mental cue of its corresponding locus. One could substitute for the word

Saratoga the two words *Sara* and *toga* and form the image of some familiar person named Sara wearing a toga and leading troops into battle. Here the image of Sara in a toga leading troops is a substitute for the Battle of Saratoga, and this is the image that will be recalled from the image of its locus. This image of Sara must then act in recall as a mental cue for the Battle of Saratoga. The effectiveness of semantic versus phonetic substitutions has been compared by Bellezza et al. (1983) who found semantic associations to have some superiority over phonetic associations for novice subjects.

An often-heard complaint from those desiring to learn mnemonic techniques is that they cannot remember the names of the people they meet. It is very difficult to learn to associate names and faces, although techniques for doing this are available (Lorayne, 1975; McCarty, 1980). Effectively encoding a person's name and associating it with some distinctive feature of that person's face requires a great deal of skill, and, apparently, no research studies have been performed that have trained people to a high level of proficiency in this skill. Meeting a large group of people and coming up with imageable substitutions for names, such as Auerbach, Ettinger, Tate, and Sussman, and associating the substitution to the appropriate face, all in a minute or two, is no easy feat.

Using encoding mnemonics to memorize numbers also requires a good deal of skill, but a fair amount of research has been performed on this topic (see Bellezza et al., 1992, for a summary). The remarkable subject, SF, studied by Chase and Ericsson (1981) was able to recall about 80 digits after they were presented to him once at the rate of one digit per second. This level of proficiency had required about 250 hours of practice. SF was an amateur runner and used an encoding mnemonic of his own devising in which he changed short strings of digits into times for various kinds of track events, such as 411 is a slow mile. He also encoded some of these strings into dates (1939 was the start of World War II) and ages (85 is old). Most people are not capable of developing their own mnemonic techniques for encoding numbers, but a traditional mnemonic, popularized by Gregor von Feinaigle in 1813, is available—namely, the digit–consonant mnemonic by which numbers can be encoded into imageable words. The words are then memorized and, when later recalled, translated back into the original numbers. This procedure is described in books on mnemonics (e.g., Higbee, 1988; Lorayne & Lucas, 1974) and involves treating each digit as a consonant sound, as shown in Table 1. Vowel sounds, along with the sounds for *w, h,* and *y,* have no digit equivalents and can be added anywhere among the consonant sounds to make imageable words.. For example, the number 0123456789 can be encoded as *Satan my relish coffee pie* (Bower, 1978).

The digit–consonant mnemonic is useful for purposes other than memorizing long strings of digits, which most of us do not have to do. For

TABLE 1   The Digit–Consonant Mnemonic

Digit	Consonant sound	Mnemonic aid
0	z, s, soft c	z is the first sound in *zero*
1	t, th, d	t and d have one downstroke
2	n	n has two downstrokes
3	m	m has three downstrokes
4	r	4 ends with the sound r
5	l	L is Roman numeral for 50
6	ch, j, or soft g	a 6 looks like a backword j
7	k, hard c, hard g, or qu	an uppercase K is made up of two 7s
8	f, v, or ph	an 8 looks like a handwritten f
9	p, b	9 and p are mirror images

example, the mnemonic can be used to generate and memorize 100 peg-words for use as a pegword mnemonic. The number 01 can be coded as *soda,* 02 as *swan,* 03 as *seam,* and so on up to 98 as *beef,* 99 as *pipe,* and 100 as *outhouses* (Higbee, 1988). These substitutions are also useful for remembering historical dates (Bellezza, 1982b). For example, the start of Prohibition was 1919, a date that can be translated as *tap tub.* So, one can form the image of beer barrels being hammered and associate this image with the word Prohibition. Hitler became Chancellor of Germany in 1933, so one can think of Hitler being sworn into office wrapped in *tape* like a *mummy.* Often, the century is already known and only the last two digits of the year have to be remembered.

C. Mental Cues and Their Properties

To relate mnemonic devices to general human learning, I rely on a theoretical framework that develops the notion of mnemonic devices as mental cues (Bellezza 1981, 1986b, 1987; Bellezza & Buck, 1988; Bellezza & Hoyt, 1992). In the mental-cuing framework, using a mnemonic device involves the formation and association of mental representations of the to-be-remembered information. To illustrate this process of mental cuing, consider the use of the method of loci for memorizing a list of words. An image of each successive word is combined with the image of its corresponding prememorized locus. Forming a visual image of the to-be-remembered word is the process of elaboration traditionally favored by mnemonists, though verbal elaboration may also be effective (E. Hunt & Love, 1972; Paivio, 1971). The loci provide mental cues for the words to be learned, and location images become associated to the word images, though the loci are not physically present when learning takes place. They exist only in the mind of the mnemonist. For recall, the mnemonist mentally reviews the images of the loci so that the cognitive context surrounding the original learning of each list word can be accessed though the use of these location images. This process typifies cue-based remembering (Tulving, 1974; Watkins, 1979). Mental cues are necessary for recall because of the principle of encoding specificity (Tulving & Thomson, 1973; for a discussion of the role of encoding specificity in retrieval processes and eyewitness memory, respectively, see Roediger & Guynn, Chapter 7, and Chandler & Fisher, Chapter 14, this volume); that is, for previously presented information to be recalled, the cognitive context and processes defining the event in its time and place must first be remembered (see also Reddy & Bellezza, 1983). The activation during recall of the image of a locus can be thought of as activation of the context accompanying learning.

The mnemonist images successive locations during learning, which means that the images of the locations, possibly hundreds of them, must be organized and available in memory. In the articles on mental cuing cited earlier, it was proposed that these mental cues must have four properties to support learning and remembering. These are the so-called ABCD properties (Bellezza & Hoyt, 1992) of associability, bidirectionality of association, constructibility, and discriminability. In many situations, a mental cue needs all four of these properties in order to support recall.

1. Constructibility

The property of constructibility refers to the reliability with which the same mental cues can be generated from memory at both learning and recall. Because of the principle of encoding specificity (Tulving & Thomson, 1973), each mental cue must be present both at learning and at recall to serve as a prompt for the information to be remembered when it must be recalled. Mental cues that are constructible are easily retrievable from memory during the two critical times in the learning process: during study and during recall. Constructibility depends on how well this cuing information is organized in memory and how reliably it can be remembered. If the mental cues are well organized in memory, then at recall the cues can be systematically generated in the same manner as they were during learning. The notion of constructibility suggests that a set of mnemonic cues, such as those used in the method of loci, is really a knowledge structure in memory (Galambos, Abelson, & Black, 1986). The method of loci depends on the mnemonist having a knowledge structure in memory representing real (or sometimes imaginary) physical locations.

2. Associability

Not only do mental cues, such as loci, have to be reliably generated, but these mental cues must be easily associated to the new information being learned. The greater the number of features, attributes, and associations activated in memory as part of the mental cue, the more associable the cue will be, as asserted by the associative probability hypothesis of Underwood and Schulz (1960). Mental cues in the form of visual images are easily associated to new information. For this reason, the classical mnemonic procedures placed great emphasis on creating vivid visual images to facilitate memorization (Patten, 1990; Yates, 1966, pp. 9–10). Although visual imagery seems to be best, mental cues representing meaningful and familiar words can also provide context to which new information can be linked. These links can be formed using verbal or linguistic elaborations (Paivio, 1971). Mental cues that represent concrete objects or locations are more associable than mental cues represented by abstract words. Therefore, in the method of loci visual images of locations, or sometimes objects in locations, are the mental cues. Associability and constructibility are distinct properties. The numbers 1 to 100 provide a very constructible set of mental cues, but for most people they are not associable.

3. Discriminability

To support recall, mental cues, like physical cues in the environment, must be discriminable from one another. Bellezza (1986a), for example, showed that a set of word lists presented on the same visual background are more poorly recalled than when each list is presented on a separate and distinct visual background. Though unrelated to the meaning of the words, the distinct visual backgrounds acting as mental cues helped keep the word lists discriminable in memory. In classical times, the aspiring orator mastered the method of loci so he could memorize his speeches, and he often used images from a public building as a source for his loci. However, some images, such as the spaces between repeated columns, were not considered good loci because their resemblance to one another caused confusion (Yates, 1966, p. 9). If the mental cues cannot be discriminated easily during learning, then too much new information may become associated to essentially the same cue, resulting in interference from cue overload (Watkins, 1979), with too many associative links fanning off the same cue (Anderson, 1976). As a result, all the information associated to the cue cannot be retrieved. The management and organization of memory involves optimizing the load on memory cues (Watkins, 1979).

How can the factors of associability and discriminability be separated experimentally? The associability of a mental cue can be assessed by including it in a set of cues with no other cues similar to it. For example, the mental image of the familiar word *child* is an associable cue to which new information can be easily associated when no mental cue similar to a child is also being used. On the other hand, the mental cue represented by the familiar word *interest* is abstract and would be low in associability for most people, regardless of the other mental cues used. In contrast to the property of associability, the discriminability of a cue is dependent not only on the number of its attributes but also on the number of attributes it shares with the other cues being used. For example, the image of an infant and that of a baby share many features and may not be discriminable enough for both to be maximally effective as mental cues, though both are high in associability. Hence, the mental representations of *infant* and *baby* should not both be used as mental cues at the same time. Nondiscriminable cues in memory may become functionally identical, with cue overload the result.

4. Bidirectionality of Associations

When using an organizational mnemonic, such as the method of loci, to memorize a grocery list, first an image is created of each locus and then the image of each locus is combined with its corresponding item. The to-be-remembered information can later be recalled by first thinking of the mnemonic cue followed by the information; the bidirectionality of the mnemonic association is not important. But when using an encoding mnemonic, it is important for the associations created between a mental cue and new information to be bidirectional. The reason for this is as follows: In the earlier example of an encoding mnemonic being used to encode the Battle of Saratoga into a visual image of Sara wearing a toga and leading troops into battle, the image formed acts as a mental cue elicited by or derived from the words *Battle of Saratoga*. The directional association formed during learning can be represented: Battle of Saratoga → Sara wearing toga. However, when recall takes place, the image of Sara in a toga is recalled first, and this must result in the mnemonist remembering the words *Battle of Saratoga;* that is, Sara wearing toga → Battle of Saratoga. The association must operate not only in the direction of list word to substitution, but also in the opposite direction of substitution to list word. Mental cues in the form of visual images usually result in bidirectional associations (Mastropieri, Scruggs, Bakken, & Brigham, 1992; Paivio, 1971, pp. 276–285).

III. MNEMONIC DEVICES AND ASSOCIATIVE NETWORKS

Mnemonic devices have traditionally been interpreted in terms of associations, and this approach continues to be productive, as when discussing the ABCD properties of mental cues. However, associative theories have become more sophisticated, and their refinements have resulted in some insights into the manner in which mnemonic devices operate. A number of current models of learning and memory assume that the structure of memory is made up of links and nodes to represent declarative knowledge. The nodes may represent concepts, as in the models of Collins and Loftus (1975) and the ACT* model of Anderson (1976, 1983), or the nodes may also represent more primitive features, as in the parallel distributed processing (PDP) models of Rumelhart and McClelland (1986). In some associative models, the links connecting these nodes carry activation that, if present, is positive or excitatory in nature (Collins & Loftus, 1975; Anderson, 1976, 1983) or may be either excitatory or inhibitory (Rumelhart & McClelland, 1986). Other processes may be operating in the memory system in addition to activation. Procedural knowledge may be incorporated in the production rules of the ACT* model in which activation is transferred between nodes not directly linked (Anderson, 1976, 1983). Production rules can also create new nodes and links as well as new rules. In these associative network frameworks, mnemonic devices can be considered strategies by which existing associations are used to facilitate the learning of new information. That is, mnemonic devices are strategies for promoting proactive facilitation. I outline below the processes by which this may occur.

A. Encoding Mnemonics and Elaboration

Consider a college student who is a subject in a psychological experiment. When a single list word, such as *dog,* is presented, its representation in memory is activated. Also, other nodes linked to that word may be activated, depending on the memory structure and the processing strategy of the perceiver (R. R. Hunt & Einstein, 1981), with the strategy used determining the degree to which the subject searches semantic memory for meaningful instantiations of the word (Craik & Tulving, 1975). Another important process, however, also occurs. The spatiotemporal information representing the event in memory is new because the event of being in an experiment is new, so new associations involving this information may be formed. These context associations enable the subject to associate the mental representation of the list word with a memory of the particular episode he or she is experiencing (Tulving, 1972).

If new associations involving context information are of the same kind as associations among concepts, then episodic memory can be thought of as part of a memory system that includes both episodic and semantic memory (Anderson & Ross, 1980), rather than as a separate memory system (Tulving, 1985). One difference between episodic and semantic representations in memory is that when an episodic memory is retrieved, context information associated with it is also retrieved. With respect to the example of imaging *dog,* however, an association is not automatically formed between the representation of the list word and the context information representing the larger event of participating in a psychological experiment. The strength of context associations depends on the cognitive strategy used to process the list word (Navon-Benjamin, 1990; Zacks, Hasher, Alba, Sanft, & Rose,

1984). If one assumes that episodic and semantic memory are part of the same memory system, then repeating episodes or events strengthens their unvarying attributes in memory and causes them to become part of semantic memory. In this view, then, the residue of repeated information from similar episodes forms semantic memory. According to Jost's Laws, old associations profit more from repetition and decay less rapidly than new associations (Youtz, 1941). In contrast to this strengthening, the unique context information associated with each individual event occurs only once and, therefore, suffers from decay; consequently, it becomes difficult to retrieve (McClelland & Rumelhart, 1985; Watkins & Kerkar, 1985).

Context information plays an important role when recalling information learned employing a multiple-use organizational mnemonic, such as the method of loci. If the loci have been used many times and the retention interval of the most recent list is short, then the context the learner experiences at recall is more similar to the context of the most recent list than to lists learned farther back in time. The context information constrains recall to the most recent list, thereby reducing proactive interference but creating retroactive interference (Bellezza, 1982a). For some remarkable mnemonists like Shereshevsky, context information endures in memory, and years later details of events can be successfully recalled (Luria, 1968, pp. 18–19). Most people, however, tend to combine similar events into one representation in memory, thus causing interference among the differing contexts associated with each particular event (Bellezza & Young, 1989). Shereshevsky somehow managed to avoid this interference, but his failure to categorize events had some unsatisfactory consequences. When memorizing word lists containing many words from the same taxonomic categories, he tended not to notice the relationship among the words. Also, when viewing the same face from different angles, he tended to think it was a different person (Luria, 1968, p. 64). Luria believed that this sensitivity to the uniqueness of each event diminished Shereshevsky's ability to think using abstract concepts (Luria, 1968, Chap. 5).

Consider now a mnemonist who is trying to memorize a list of presented word pairs. One of the simplest problems using a mnemonic strategy is to associate two words so that if one word is later presented, the other word can be recalled. If the word pair presented is *comb–hair* or *horse–saddle,* a pre-existing link can be activated in semantic memory. As indicated earlier, however, new associations must also be formed between the word pair and the context information regarding the time and place of this learning event. Though the association *horse–saddle* may be part of semantic memory, for it to become part of an event in episodic memory, the pair *horse–saddle* must also become associated with spatial–temporal context information (Hayes-Roth, 1977) representing a particular learning experience of the mnemonist. For when the cue word *horse* is later presented as a recall cue, the mnemonist cannot simply search semantic memory for the strongest association to *horse,* which may be the word *cow.* Rather, he or she must incorporate into the search the constraint that the information being searched for was part of a particular event (Anderson & Bower, 1974), namely, the previous laboratory presentation of word pairs. Because of the large number of associations in memory, constraints based on spatiotemporal context information are very important for retrieving the information desired. Context information is not different from any other type of constraining information used in memory retrieval (Norman & Bobrow, 1979). For example, Rubin and Wallace (1989) have discussed the importance of rhyming constraints in some mnemonics and how they can greatly improve the probability of recall.

Unlike the example of *horse–saddle* given earlier, in many learning situations associations must be formed using words seemingly unrelated. If the mnemonist is presented the word pair *bull–mint,* no pre-existing direct link between the two words may be immediately available in semantic memory. Because no link between the words *bull–mint* is activated, memory is searched with the goal of finding some indirect way of linking these words (Miller et al., 1960), such as both words being linked to a third concept (Bellezza & Poplawsky, 1974). The nature of this search—for example, whether it is based on phonetic or semantic associations—depends on the strategy used by the mnemonist. Any mediating concepts activated are experienced as elaborations by the mnemonist (Anderson & Reder, 1979), and this information becomes associated with the temporal–spatial information identifying the learning event. Some of these mediators involve the activation of both perceptual and semantic information stored in memory. For example, the mnemonist may form a mental picture of a bull eating mint leaves in a pasture. This image makes use of the semantic information in memory that a bull is an herbivore and that mint is an edible plant, and these categories are schematically related (Day & Bellezza, 1983). In addition, stored perceptual information depicting a bull and mint plants is activated in memory. Or, the mnemonist may create verbal elaborations by forming the sentence "Ferdinand the bull liked to sniff mint." In both these cases, declarative knowledge in memory is activated and context tagged, having the effect of linking the words in the pair and associating the pair to the experienced event.

The imagery or verbal elaborations are mediators (Bellezza, 1986b; Montague, 1972) for learning the pair and provide the basis for the proactive facilitation that can result from the retrieval of information already in memory that is somehow related to the information to be remembered. The finding and activating of an indirect path between two nodes in the associative network is more effective than creating a new and direct, albeit weak, link, because the context information enables the existing knowledge used to associate *bull* and *mint* to form a separate event distinct from other information in memory regarding the concepts bull and mint. The incorporation of this context information into the representation of the event reduces proactive and retroactive interference. Of course, if the words *bull* and *mint* occur together repeatedly, a direct association would be formed between them, such as for the frequently occurring pairs *soap–water* and *dog–cat*. If *bull–mint* repeatedly occurred, that set of unique context information defining one occurrence of the pair obviously could not be repeated, and the associations between the pair and the multiple contexts would suffer from interference. If the pair *bull–mint* occurs only once, the associations connecting the words *bull* and *mint* gradually decay following the event, as do the associations involving the list and context information associated with the learning experience. The associations between the words *bull* and *mint* may thus become too weak to be useful. Their existence in memory, however, may be detectable by sensitive memory measures, such as the method of savings (Nelson, 1978).

Often, mnemonic techniques must be used on material more difficult than the word pair *bull–mint*. When teaching learning-disabled school children to associate each of the 50 states with its capital (Mastropieri et al., 1992), many of the elaborations suggested to the children were based on semantic or phonetic similarity. Consider, for example, that the capital of Alaska is Juneau. How can prior knowledge be used to associate these two words? The encoding for the city Juneau was presented to the children as "Do you know?" and the encoding for Alaska was "I'll ask her." Because the two expressions "Do you know?" and "I'll ask her" are more easily associated than Juneau and Alaska, they act as related mental cues for the words *Juneau* and *Alaska*. The substitution of a mental cue for each word was based on phonetic similarity rather than semantic similarity. The two substitutions, however, are semantically related expressions. Notice also that in this example, little visual imagery is used. This type of mnemonic procedure does not eliminate the need for some learning to occur; it only reduces, by the use of proactive facilitation, the amount of learning that is needed. When the child is queried about the capital of Alaska, he or she must remember to encode Alaska as "I'll ask her." The statement "I'll ask her" can be associated with many things in memory, but the child understands that the associations are constrained by the goal of retrieving a state capital, so memory search is limited to information related to the event of recently learning state capitals in class using mnemonic techniques. What should be retrieved is "Do you know?" which the child then has to remember to decode into Juneau. In all mnemonic procedures, natural memory must always supplement artificial memory based on mnemonic art.

B. Organizational Mnemonics and Memory Schemas

Encoding mnemonics ensure that a meaningful or imageable mental cue or symbol exists for each piece of information to be memorized. Organizational mnemonics organize these symbols in memory. When these symbols are recalled, they act as mental cues for the information to be remembered. Sometimes a number of mental symbols must be assembled and associated to remember one item. For example, the image of a locus retrieves a mental image of Sara in a toga that, in turn, reminds the mnemonist of the Battle of Saratoga. Another example is using the mnemonic described above to recall that Juneau is the capital of Alaska. Just as some of the psychological theory involving associative networks and the process of elaboration helps explain the mechanics of encoding mnemonics, research on the manner in which information is organized in memory helps us understand organizational mnemonics. I have suggested elsewhere (Bellezza, 1987) that organizational mnemonics are knowledge structures in memory that mediate learning much as some kinds of schemas do. I make this point because schema-based learning is often considered to be a natural form of learning (Anderson, Spiro, & Anderson, 1978; Schank & Abelson, 1977), whereas learning using mnemonic devices has been considered to be unnatural. Yet, the two are similar in their manner of operation (Bellezza & Reddy, 1978). Both mnemonic devices and memory schemas enhance learning by a process of proactive facilitation; that is, making use of the strength of old associations and relations whenever possible. Context information enables the learner to keep distinct, to some extent, each instantiation of the schema or mnemonic device.

Under certain conditions, usually involving the perception of a specific set of environmental stimuli, a schema will become active in memory. Schema-based learning can be thought of as filling slots in the activated schema using information perceived and appropriate to the schema; that is, providing values for arguments or variables in the activated generic representation of a commonly encountered object or event (Brewer & Nakamura, 1984; Rumelhart, 1980; Schank & Abelson, 1977). This slot-filling process instantiates the schema so that a particular instance of the schema, a representation of the event, is stored in memory. But memory schemas can be represented by links and nodes, and the process of schema instantiation can be thought of as the activation of the links and nodes representing the schema, along with the creation of some new links (Anderson, 1983; Galambos et al., 1986; McClelland & Rumelhart, 1985; Thorndyke & Hayes-Roth, 1979). An idea common to both memory schemas and organizational mnemonics is that the activation of a well-organized knowledge structure in memory provides mental cues to which new information can be associated (Bellezza, 1987). But are memory schemas and organizational mnemonics

TABLE 2   Similarities and Differences between Organizational Mnemonics and Memory Schemas

Characteristics of knowledge structures	Similarities	Differences
Acquisition	Acquired over time	Deliberate versus nondeliberate learning
		Degree of abstraction from experience
Structure	Hierarchical organization	Dual-purpose versus single-purpose
		Level of abstraction in representation
Activation	Single-structure activation	Automatic versus deliberate activation
Function	Set of mental cues	Guide behavior versus not guide behavior
	Four properties of mental cues	Bandwidth size
		Capacity to infer missing information
		Existence of co-occurrence constraints

the same kind of memory structure exhibiting the same kind of learning? The answer is no, although there are a number of similarities between them. Their similarities and differences are described next and summarized in Table 2.

1. Acquisition

The mental cues of organizational mnemonics, such as 100 loci for the method of loci, and the content of many memory schemas are represented as sets of declarative knowledge that are *acquired over time* as the result of repeated exposure or study. Just how fast an organizational mnemonic or schema is acquired depends on a number of factors, but it is not typically after one encounter (but see Ahn, Brewer, Mooney, 1992). When thought of as a network, the links and nodes of schemas and organizational mnemonics are strengthened as a subassembly in a larger associative network.

One difference is that mnemonic devices are typically the result of *deliberate learning,* whereas most memory schemas are not. A second difference is that a schema in memory is often *abstracted* from the experience of similar events, not identical events (Brewer & Nakamura, 1984). An organizational mnemonic is usually learned as a stereotyped set of mental cues.

2. Structure

Memory schemas are *organized hierarchically* (Rumelhart, 1980). Mnemonic devices can also be nested, as when mental cues created by encoding mnemonics involving item substitutions become associated to the mental cues of an organizational mnemonic.

However, only memory schemas can be *dual-purpose structures*. For example, a cognitive map can function either as a schema to represent the structure of the physical environment or as an organizational mnemonic. Knowledge of one's house, for example, can function as either a memory schema or a source of locations to be used as the method of loci (Bellezza & Hoyt, 1992). Hence, schemas involving physical locations can be used interchangeably as cognitive maps or as loci in the method of loci. Organizational mnemonics, however, function only as organizational mnemonics.

Another difference is that the content of memory schemas can vary in their *level of abstraction* (Rumelhart, 1980), whereas to be effective the mental cues comprising a mnemonic device typically include the pictorial representations of physical objects or physical locations.

3. Activation

Because of the capacity limitations of conscious memory, only a *single structure* can be active at any time. For example, one cannot have both the house schema and the automobile schema active in memory at the same time. Similarly, as organized sets of declarative knowledge, only one set of mnemonic cues at a time can be active in conscious memory. Reddy and Bellezza (1986) found that subjects using a pegword mnemonic could memorize randomly selected nouns better than nouns taken from the same taxonomic category, apparently because the category words to be learned activated other category words in memory that interfered with imaging the pegwords.

There are differences, however, in the manner in which memory schemas and mnemonic devices are activated. Memory schemas are *automatically activated* in memory by events in the environment or by language communicated to the learner. The top-down processing that follows is also usually unintentional. On the other hand, the decision to implement a mnemonic device results from the learning strategy of the user. Hence activation and implementation of a mnemonic procedure depends on the user's continuing intent.

4. Function

When a schema is activated in memory, some of its component parts provide *mental cues* to which new information can be associated. For example, when visiting a particular restaurant for the first time, the generic restaurant schema is activated and information regarding this particular restaurant becomes associated with declarative-knowledge components within the restaurant schema (Bellezza & Bower, 1982). A schema, therefore, can act as an organizational mnemonic, and its components must have the necessary *properties of mental cues* for the instantiation of the schema to be remembered. These mental cues are derived from the declarative-knowledge components of the schema and must have the properties of associability, bidirectionality, constructibility, and discriminability to preserve the representation of the instantiating event in memory. Bellezza (1988) has suggested that, in general, the constructibility of mental cues associated with memory schemas is surprisingly low and that the specific representation of any object, activity, or event schema varies from one activation to the next. This low schema constructibility suggests that the recall of a particular schema instantiation should be inferior to recall based on a mnemonic device.

But there are a number of differences in the manner in which memory schemas and mnemonic devices function. Some schemas, called scripts (Schank & Abelson, 1977), not only enable a person to comprehend events in our culture, such as taking a commercial airline flight, but also serve to *guide behavior* when participating in these events. A mnemonic device, conversely, is not a guide for motor or for social behavior.

Organizational mnemonics, like the method of loci, have broad *bandwidths* and can be used to store a wide variety of information in memory. Most memory schemas can process only a semantically restricted range of information for which they are appropriate (Bellezza & Bower, 1982).

An organizational mnemonic, like the method of loci, cannot be used to *infer information* that was not presented during learning or was forgotten. A memory schema, such as that for a baseball game, can be used to infer missing information, however, because of its narrow bandwidth.

Once one piece of information is instantiated in a schema, it *constrains co-occurring information*. For example, in the restaurant script, one cannot eat a Big Mac and then later call a waiter. In an organizational mnemonic, however, the information associated to one locus does not constrain what information can be associated with another locus.

IV. MNEMONIC DEVICES IN EDUCATION

Although belief in the value of mnemonic devices in the classroom is not universal (Hall, Wilson, & Patterson, 1981; Hall, 1991; Shepherd & Gelzheiser, 1987), a number of researchers have defended this use of mnemonic procedures (e.g., Higbee, 1978; J. R. Levin, 1981) and have proposed that they become a regular part of classroom procedures (Bower, 1973; Mastropieri & Scruggs, 1991; Scruggs & Mastropieri, 1990b). In this section I look at some aspects of the use of mnemonics in the classroom and comment on related issues needing further study.

A. Why Memorizing Is Necessary

Memorization seems necessary in the early stages of learning about a topic. Vocabulary must be memorized to understand and speak a second language, technical terms must be memorized to begin to read in the sciences, proper nouns must be memorized to understand writings in history and geography, and so on. American education, however, has traditionally emphasized the learning of useful techniques and skills rather than the memorization of factual information. Educational theorists have stressed the teaching of knowledge-free thinking and problem-solving procedures. It may be, however, that these cognitive processes cannot be taught to students who do not already possess extensive knowledge (Glaser, 1984; Kyllonen, Tirre, & Christal, 1991). A major component of thinking seems to be the possession of accessible and usable declarative knowledge. We know that comprehension of what we read and observe depends on the activation of organized knowledge structures in memory, often called schemas (Brewer & Nakamura, 1984; Rumelhart, 1980) with the knowledge in them used to make inferences, draw conclusions, and retain new information. As discussed above, schematic knowledge, as mnemonic images, provides mental cues that support remembering. The knowledge on which schemas are based is built up slowly at first, but as more knowledge is organized in memory, learning and comprehension can take place quickly (Galambos et al., 1986). Ahn et al. (1992) have discussed how a new schema can be formed by one experience, but only if there is adequate background information available in memory. Some critics of our educational system have argued that students in primary and secondary schools do not learn enough basic information about our culture to function effectively as informed citizens or even as competent adults. Hirsch (1987), for example, provided a list of approximately 4700 words, dates, and phrases that every literate American should know. If one does not know this information, would memorizing Hirsch's basic information using mnemonic devices correct the problem? Or does already possessing this knowledge simply provide evidence of one's good education? That is, having Hirsch's list of information available in memory may be an indicator of other knowledge, with the list not representing the knowledge itself. Yet, even if Hirsch's list does not represent precisely what a citizen or student should know, memorizing the information in the list using mnemonic devices would, perhaps, be a good way to start acquiring the corpus of knowledge at issue.

B. Elaboration and Irrationality

Mnemonic devices seem to help learning, but such learning often depends on the formation of bizarre, ridiculous, and fantastic associations that do not represent actual events. Lorayne and Lucas (1974) suggest that images be ridiculous, impossible, crazy, illogical, or absurd, not logical or sensible. The anonymous Roman book on rhetoric, *Ad Herennium* (circa 86–82 B.C.) proposed much the same thing. Since the first appearance of handbooks on memorizing, authors have emphasized the formation of bizarre images (see also Yarmey, 1984). Is it wise to fill young minds with strange and artificial images that may not reflect reality?

There may be other reasons not to use bizarre imagery. First, the effectiveness of bizarre imagery in learning has not been strongly supported by research. Early research indicated that bizarre images, compared to common ones, might actually reduce the retention of information. More recent research has shown bizarre imagery to help retention but only under special circumstances (Einstein & McDaniel, 1987). Second, emphasis on irrational images contradicts our traditional notion that we should remember by first comprehending the information; that is, by fitting it into our scheme of reality in some logical way. The suggestion that we use absurd images suggests that we give up our attempts at understanding. It may be that the mnemonist remembers but does not understand, as was the case for the unfortunate mnemonist Shereshevsky (Luria, 1968).

It seems reasonable that we not abandon attempts to understand what we wish to remember, but we should acknowledge that mnemonic devices can play a role as a supplement to natural learning. Even if a student understands why Juneau is the capital of Alaska, and, indeed, understands some of the historical, geographic, and cultural reasons why each of the 50 state capitals were named as they were, the student may still need help remembering the 50 state and capital pairs. Similarly, even though a student may have some understanding of the historical, geological, and geographic reasons why the five divisions of the Paleozoic period in geology are named the Cambrian, the Ordovician, the Silurian, the Devonian, and the Permian, he or she may still profit from using a mnemonic device to remember them.

Even though mnemonic elaborations may seem bizarre and irrational, they should be used if they promote learning. Mnemonic procedures capitalize on those associations accessible in memory at the time learning takes place and are similar in some way to the material being learned. If the new information being learned activates a schema already existing in memory, then the mnemonic elaborations may actually involve schema instantiation. But in many cases the learner has very little information available in memory relevant to the information being learned and therefore must rely on mnemonic elaborations that may appear to be bizarre. The fact that these bizarre elaborations occur indicates that there exist remote associations in memory based on previous learning that can aid in interrelating new information.

As I discuss below, mnemonic learning, even if it appears bizarre, may be most useful as a way of getting information into memory when children do not have much of a relevant knowledge base. The mnemonic structure can act as early scaffolding for building a more permanent knowledge structure. With continued learning, the scaffolding will be forgotten as the student relies on more relevant associations when remembering. As is discussed below, mnemonic elaborations, though sometimes bizarre, may be provided to the learner in the form of drawings or verbal descriptions. The greatest benefits of mnemonic devices may eventually occur in the classroom where, under a teacher's guidance, effective mnemonic procedures are implemented so both remembering and comprehension will be optimized.

C. Using Mnemonic Devices in Education

Research is presently under way developing and testing mnemonic procedures in the classroom, including techniques for children with learning disabilities (Scruggs & Mastropieri, 1990a). Some of the most valuable of the mnemonic techniques used are variations of the keyword mnemonic.

1. The Keyword Mnemonic

The keyword mnemonic was first seriously evaluated as a procedure to study the acquisition of second-language vocabulary among college students (Atkinson, 1975). In its simplest form, the keyword mnemonic consists of two parts; a phonetic link connecting the word to be learned with the keyword, and an imagery link connecting the keyword with the meaning of the word (Pressley et al., 1982). For example, to learn the Spanish word *carta,* meaning postal letter, a keyword is created that is an English word, sounds like the word to be learned, and is high in imagery and meaningfulness. The keyword for *carta* might be *cart.* Thus, the phonetic link, carta → cart, is formed. Next, a visual image is created of the referent of the keyword *cart* interacting with the meaning of the word *carta.* For example, one might form a mental picture of a large postal letter being pushed in a grocery cart. This step connects the keyword with the meaning of the word to be learned using an imagery link. These two links can be represented as follows: carta → (phonetic link) → cart → (imagery link) → postal letter. Now, when the word *carta* is later heard or read, one should think of the keyword *cart,* which should elicit the image of a postal letter being pushed in a cart, which should give the meaning of *carta.* The keyword provides a memory mediator connecting the new word with its meaning.

The keyword method has also been evaluated as a procedure for teaching college students English vocabulary (Sweeney & Bellezza, 1982). Of possibly greater potential, however, is the use of the keyword mnemonic to teach grade school students and learning-disabled students a variety of information related to various classroom topics, such as the meanings of abstract English words, meanings of word parts, foreign language vocabulary, physical science, history, social studies, life sciences, spelling, and mathematics (Mastropieri and Scruggs, 1991). There is evidence that learning new vocabulary using the keyword method results in better word comprehension compared to the usual way of learning (Pressley, Levin, & Miller, 1981). Also, M. E. Levin and Levin (1990) have found that students learning the hierarchical plant classification system using a mnemonic procedure performed better on related problem solving, analogical reasoning, and syllogistic reasoning tasks than did students learning the classification system in the traditional manner. Next, I discuss how these mnemonic devices have been implemented in the classroom.

2. Mnemonic Strategies versus Mnemonic Materials

Encoding mnemonics result in visual imagery or verbal elaborations that act as mental cues for recalling information low in imagery or in meaningfulness. In a number of experiments, students have been instructed to form mental pictures to make the material presented to them more memorable. In other experiments, school children have been provided with actual pictures so that they can form their images from what they see rather than from what they can imagine. Presentation of such teacher-supplied pictures has enhanced learning for children with learning disabilities (Mastropieri & Scruggs, 1991), just as college students have been aided by experimenter-supplied code words when using the digit–consonant mnemonic to memorize numbers (Patton, D'Agaro, & Gaudette, 1991). The general rule seems to be that when the encoding task is easy, it is better for the learner to generate the mnemonic representation. If the encoding is difficult for the learner, externally provided mnemonic words or pictures may be of better mnemonic quality and therefore more memorable than the encodings the learner can generate on his or her own. Of course, these presented words or pictures activate their corresponding representations in the memory of the learner. Often, the problem with generating one's own mnemonic is not that the learner does not have some useful elaborations in memory for the information presented, but it is that these elaborations cannot be easily retrieved by the learner and may be too weak or inaccessible to be activated without a strong external cue.

Mnemonic procedures can be used in a number of ways in classroom work. First, students can be taught to create their own mnemonic devices so that they can *spontaneously* use them in their course work as needed. This procedure has been used in courses on study skills for college students, and even grade school children with slight learning disabilities have been taught with modest success to generalize mnemonic procedures to new material (Fulk, Mastropieri, & Scruggs, 1992; Scruggs & Mastropieri, 1992). Second, mnemonic procedures can be *induced* by instructing students before a particular set of material is presented to use a mnemonic strategy to remember it. With young and learning–disabled children, this strategy is necessary because these students will not spontaneously use mnemonic devices and must be instructed to do so. Finally, the mnemonic elaboration can be *imposed* by the teacher upon the student by visually presenting the elaboration, such as presenting a detailed picture or drawing that will both encode the information and organize it in memory (M. E. Levin & Levin, 1990); that is, these pictures activate mental cues for both encoding the information and organizing it.

As an example of the latter procedure, Mastropieri and Scruggs (1991, p. 73) provided a drawing of a farm with a sign over the entrance reading *FARM-B*. Five piles of dirt are pictured on this farm with the keyword *dirt* representing, as a similar-sounding substitute, the word *vertebrate*. On one pile of dirt is a fish representing *fish,* on a second pile is a frog wearing a bib representing *amphibian,* on a third pile of dirt are tiles with an alligator on them representing *reptile,* on a fourth is a camel representing *mammal,* and on a fifth pile is a bird representing *bird.* The word *bib* is a substitute for the word *amphibian, tiles* for *reptile,* and *camel* for *mammal.* In addition, *FARM-B* is a first-letter mnemonic for the words *fish, amphibian, reptile, mammal,* and *bird* representing the five kinds of vertebrates. Mnemonics of this kind have been shown to double, at least, the amount of information retained by regular students (M. E. Levin & Levin, 1990) and by learning–disabled students (Scruggs & Mastropieri, 1992). Even the most imaginative and knowledgeable grade school student would have trouble creating the *FARM-B* mnemonic. But once it is presented to students, they can understand it and use it. Hence, it is important to draw a distinction between *mnemonic strategies* in which the learner creates the mental cues and *mnemonic materials* that are presented to students to elicit the mental cues. Carefully constructed mnemonic materials can have beneficial effects on learning even when students are not always capable of creating such mental cues on their own.

D. Issues for Further Research

In spite of the seemingly artificial nature of mnemonic learning, mnemonic devices are based on the same cognitive structures and processes as are other types of learning. I tried to outline my reasons for this conclusion in the discussion earlier regarding the necessary properties of mnemonic cues and regarding the relation between organizational mnemonics and memory schemas. Also, becoming proficient with mnemonic devices is related to the general issue of skill learning. The use of some mnemonic devices requires a great deal of skill (Staszewski, 1990). Though based on accepted principles of learning, mnemonic devices have been proposed as special techniques for optimizing memorizing. If this proposal is taken seriously, a number of questions can be raised regarding how mnemonic devices should be evaluated, how often they should be used, with what material should they be used, who should use them, and so on. Most of these questions have no answers, but I now try to address some relevant aspects of a few of these questions.

1. Evaluating Mnemonic Devices

Most of the research done on mnemonic devices—although often inspired by the achievements of experts—has used novices as subjects. In a typical experiment, these novices are provided brief training in a mnemonic device and their memory performance is then compared to a control group. These novices often show an advantage when memorizing small amounts of specially selected information and when trained and tested under the tutelage of a teacher or experimenter. The superiority in performance of the mnemonic over the control group, while real, may be modest in size. But it can be argued that when evaluating the effectiveness of a mnemonic device, an hour, or even less, of instruction does not usually result in an adequate test of that procedure. We should not judge the effectiveness of a mnemonic device based only on the performance of beginners, just as we would not evaluate the effectiveness of a new mechanical tool by testing its effectiveness when operated by novices with only an hour or so of training. The memory structures and processes that novices use may be different from those of mnemonic experts. Furthermore, in some studies it was discovered that novices could not actually implement the mnemonic procedure they were reputedly using and being tested on (see Bellezza, 1981, 1983, for further discussion).

The difference between novices and experts may cause the factor level of skill to interact with other factors in experiments on mnemonic devices. For example, the value of bizarre imagery may be different for novices and experts. Expert mnemonists, some of whom are stage performers, have so much information stored mnemonically that it becomes important for them to reduce interference in memory by using bizarre, that is, unusual, imagery. Furthermore, because expert mnemonists have a much wider repertory of possible images and elaborations than does the novice, they may be able to generate bizarre images with minimal effort and great speed (Ericsson & Staszewski, 1989). For the novice, however, a bizarre image may not be so easily generated; rather, the typical and the mundane may be what springs most quickly to mind. But a mundane image may be effective, because the novice does not have as much information mnemonically stored as the expert; therefore, a common image may be discriminable enough to support later recall.

As another example, consider trying to determine the effectiveness of the digit–consonant mnemonic, a fairly complex mnemonic procedure. (See Table 1 and the discussion of the digit–consonant mnemonic above.) Experts endorse the digit–consonant mnemonic, but research results have been mixed when using novices with, at most, a few hours of training. But even when well-trained mnemonists learned strings of 80 digits, repetition of the same pair of digits in a string created some interference during recall (Bellezza et al., 1992). This interference occurred because these practiced mnemonists, in the course of their training, had memorized only one substitute word for each of the digit pairs from 00 to 99. Can we conclude, then, that the digit–consonant mnemonic can work only with digit strings of a size of approximately 80? The conclusion may not be correct. First, note that this problem of interference would not be detected if shorter strings were being memorized, as a novice would be doing, because repetitions of digit pairs would be infrequent. This emphasizes the point that mnemonic procedures cannot be adequately evaluated using novices. More important, a more expert mnemonist than the ones used by Bellezza et al. would have a larger number of substitute words for each pair of digits and could use a different substitute word each time the pair reappeared. In this way the problem of interference would be reduced. It is possible that other mnemonic procedures and associated visual-imagery procedures are different for novice, practiced, and expert mnemonists, so any conclusions regarding the effectiveness of a mnemonic device should be conditional on the proficiency of the participants being tested.

2. Individual Differences in Mnemonic Proficiency

The effectiveness of mnemonic devices increases with practice, just as practice aids any other skill (Ericsson, Krampe, & Tesch-Römer, 1993), or so it seems. But many expert mnemonists have been individuals unusual in background and in ability, and their mnemonic performance may have been the result of both practice and special talents. For example, Shereshevsky reported experiencing synesthesia, by which the stimulation of one sensory modality resulted in sensations in his other modalities, thus aiding him in remembering (Luria, 1968). The mnemonist, VP, who seemed not to rely on visual imagery, memorized the map of his native city of Riga when he was 5 years old (Hunt & Love, 1972), and a contemporary mnemonist, Jerry

Lucas, reports that, since the age of 8, he has memorized words both in their original spelling, as *shell,* and with their letters alphabetized, as *ehlls* (Lorayne & Lucas, 1974). Lucas did not use a mnemonic to do this, he just remembered the two spellings. These examples suggest that we may be misled if we use the performance of experts as an indication of what students of average or below average memorizing ability will achieve, even with prolonged practice.

Yet, expertise, whatever its causes, is needed for the broadly applied, continuing, spontaneous, and successful use of mnemonic devices. Even if ability determines the ultimate level of performance, how long would it take the average person to become adept in any of these mnemonic techniques? We simply do not know, although it might be comparable to other acquired skills (Ericsson et al., 1993). The studies that have provided long periods of practice used somewhat unusual subjects. For example, SF, the subject observed by Chase and Ericsson (1981), had abilities and intelligence average for a college student. Yet, he was both highly motivated and also skilled in developing mnemonic strategies on his own. Although some investigators have proposed that analyzing the performance of mnemonic experts enables us to train average people to high levels of skill (Ericsson & Chase, 1982), one wonders how well randomly selected college students would perform after longer periods of practice. We do not really know if skill level is determined primarily by practice or to what degree individual differences in performance increase or decrease with practice. It is unfortunate that the course of development of mnemonic devices of the kind discussed in this chapter has not been more carefully studied (Payne & Wenger, 1992).

Individual differences in the effectiveness of mnemonic devices occurs even among novice users who differ in ability (Kyllonen et al., 1991). Mnemonic devices have been found to be effective for high-ability army recruits but not for middle- or low-ability recruits (Griffith & Actkinson, 1978). Careful development of the learning procedure, however, such as by more training and study time, can often result in improved mnemonic learning for all ability levels (Pressley, Johnson, & Symons, 1987). Yet, spontaneous use of mnemonic devices seems to occur only for high-ability individuals (Scruggs, Mastropieri, Jorgensen, & Monson, 1986). The conclusion can be tentatively drawn that not all mnemonic devices are successful for all types of learners, although some mnemonic procedures will be helpful for all. It follows from this conclusion that a basic problem with mnemonic instruction books written by experts is that they may be of relatively little use to a large number of interested novices, for they do not provide instruction and exercises for a variety of levels of ability and skill. Neither do they provide realistic estimates of how much practice is necessary for the average learner to move from one level of performance to the next.

3. Mnemonic Devices and Interference

A distinction has been made between single-use and multiple-use mnemonic devices (Bellezza, 1981). Multiple-use mnemonic devices are organizational devices, such as the method of loci and the pegword mnemonic, that can be used at different times to memorize different sets of information. The most recently learned list is easily remembered if the retention interval is short (Bellezza, 1982a). Unlike multiple-use mnemonic devices, single-use or ad hoc mnemonics are designed to remember only one set of information of the kind found in semantic memory rather than in episodic memory. These mnemonics are useful in educational settings because single-use mnemonic devices minimize interference. They can be organizational mnemonics, such as "On old Olympic towering top a Finn and German viewed a hop," in which the first letter of each successive word provides the first letter of the name of each successive cranial nerve. (For an elaborate example from psychology, see Short, Workman, Morse, & Turner, 1992.) But most of the single-use mnemonic devices developed for classroom use emphasize encoding mnemonics that are variations on the keyword mnemonic.

The variations of the keyword mnemonic developed by researchers working in the classroom seem to be very effective (Mastropieri & Scruggs, 1991). However, these researchers do not deal with the problems experienced by students who are using the keyword mnemonic, or other mnemonic devices, regularly to learn large amounts of information. The students typically used to test the effectiveness of the keyword mnemonic have not had to use the same or similar keywords for memorizing other sets of material. The elaborations used for each item are typically distinct enough from others in the set to prevent confusions from occurring; that is, these mnemonic elaborations function as discriminable mental cues. There remains, however, the question of how much information can be learned at one time without students getting mnemonic mediators confused with one another. Lesson plans for grade school and high school students seem to deal with about 10 pieces of information at a time (Mastropieri & Scruggs, 1991). If mnemonic procedures are used more frequently in the classroom, students may be learning many sets of information at the same time, and the increased number of mnemonic images may be less discriminable than the 10 or so keyword elaborations currently used in research studies. This similarity among mnemonic cues may result in a decrement in memory performance, as reported by Bellezza et al. (1992) and discussed earlier.

Mastropieri and Scruggs (1991, p. 14), for example, provided the example of learning the word *grotto* by using the keyword *auto* and the mnemonic image of an auto driving into a cave to associate the word *grotto* with the meaning of cave. In another lesson, they used *car* as the keyword for *cardiac* with the mnemonic image of a car in the shape of a heart (Mastropieri and Scruggs, 1991, p. 26). This keyword associates the word *cardiac* with the meaning of heart. If the student is using the keyword mnemonic to remember the meaning of both *grotto* and *cardiac* at the same time, though taught in different classes, the meanings of the two words may become confused. The image of an auto driving into a cave may be confused or combined with the image of a car in the shape of a heart. This potential problem of mental-cue discriminability in the design of classroom materials may require further research if mnemonic devices begin to play a major role in classroom instruction.

This problem of nondiscriminable elaborations may be particularly acute for learning-disabled students who have a small knowledge base in which distinct mental cues must be activated (Pressley et al., 1987). When a picture or verbalization is presented to a student as part of a keyword mnemonic, it is effective only if it activates some representation in memory. If a mnemonic aid is presented that is not familiar and understood by the student, it will not be remembered. Even when creating mnemonic materials for the average student, limitations may exist as to how extensively mnemonic aids can be used. Individual differences in the content of students' knowledge bases may make it difficult for the teacher to create a large number of distinct mnemonic cues that all students in a classroom understand well enough to recall. Here is a situation in which it would be advantageous for each student to create his or her own mnemonic and thereby make use of the idiosyncrasies of his or her knowledge base. But as mentioned earlier, creating effective mnemonic elaborations is a skill that is difficult for some students to achieve. Therefore, an imposed mnemonic presented by the teacher must be one that will activate discriminable mediating information in the memories of all students.

One possible solution to this problem may be to practice a lesson until the material in it is learned to the extent that the aids are no longer needed. Then, the total number of mnemonic mediators being used at any one time will be limited to the current lesson. By implementing this procedure, one assumes that the mnemonic devices have value as temporary memory aids and their use in this manner is better than learning new information without them. I discuss this matter next.

4. Mnemonic Devices as Temporary Memory Aids

To deal with the problem of interference, whether it is manifested in confusion among mnemonic cues being used concurrently or in later learned mnemonic cues interfering with earlier learned ones, teaching procedures may be designed in which mnemonic devices are used only in the first phase of the learning process. As learning progresses and the newly learned items are repeatedly used, these mnemonic structures, like those examples of the keyword mnemonic that have been discussed earlier, drop out and a new organization in memory begins to connect the terms and concepts. This apparently occurred when Atkinson and Raugh (1975) had college students learn successive sets of Russian vocabulary words. With continued practice in retrieving new information, an associative network was formed in memory that included the information to be learned but no longer included the now-redundant keyword and its associated elaborations. In any learning situation, continued use of the keyword mnemonic may result in the keyword no longer being needed for recall. Learning the keyword can be followed by other types of learning experiences, and the growing memory network should reflect the organization of the subject matter as it is determined by classroom discussion, by reading, and, we hope, by life experiences.

If the keyword eventually drops out, why use it at all? Mnemonic devices may be helpful in the initial learning process, because they support recall and aid in the generation of responses (Wittrock, 1974). Experiments have shown that repeatedly presenting information is not as important to learning as trying to recall it (Tulving, 1967). As the mnemonically learned material is repeatedly retrieved from memory, associations will be formed among the components to be learned, and the artificial mnemonic elaborations will gradually become less necessary for remembering. In the previously described example of the mnemonic *FARM-B,* after a number of recalls, the students will remember simply that there are five types of vertebrates: fish, amphibians, reptiles, mammals, and birds. The mnemonic elaboration will not be used unless it is needed, and with practice it will be needed less and begin to be forgotten. In addition, students will continue to learn new facts about fish, amphibians, reptiles, mammals, and birds that will further interrelate these concepts. The mnemonic elaborations may be considered as the context material of early learning that will be forgotten as new, more meaningful associations are formed. The evidence from paired-associate learning seems to indicate that mnemonic mediators are forgotten as learning improves (Atkinson & Raugh, 1975; Bellezza, 1981). (I confess, however, that I still use the mnemonic Spring–Ahead/Fall–Back to change my clocks.) If we make the assumption that learning proceeds most rapidly when repeated responding by the learner is based on the retrieval of knowledge structures from memory, then mnemonic devices may play the important role of providing an early scaffolding of knowledge by which the new information can be associated. But these knowledge structures will not only be modified, fine-tuned, and made more efficient as they are used, as are memory schemas (Rumelhart & Norman, 1978), but may be completely replaced by later knowledge.

V. CONCLUSIONS

The study of mnemonic devices can make important contributions to the study of human memory. Analyzing their operation requires us to think about steps in the learning process that are normally performed automatically and taken for granted. When using a mnemonic device, the learner must elaborate new information to an unusual extent. The learner often must search memory for an information, no matter how bizarre, that will relate what he or she is trying to remember to what is already known. The elaborations later function as mental cues for the recall of the new information. As explained above, these mental cues must have certain properties to support new learning. Mnemonic devices represent artificial learning only in the sense that any learning using a deliberate strategy is the exercise of an art.

On the other hand, mnemonic learning is natural in many of the same ways that schema-base learning is natural, and both enhance learning by facilitating positive transfer from existing knowledge to the acquisition of new knowledge; that is, both mnemonic devices and memory schemas utilize existing knowledge structures in memory.

Mnemonic devices may play a large role in the classrooms of the future, but we must recognize that use of mnemonic procedures is a skill that must be developed in the learner. A number of mnemonic devices have been demonstrated to be effective in the classroom and laboratory, but their effectiveness depends on the expertise and ability of the learners tested. A distinct set of skills may have to be developed in teachers both for training students to use mnemonic strategies and for creating special mnemonic materials. Teachers must learn how to activate appropriate information in the memories of their students by using specially designed materials to initiate the development of useful knowledge structures. Current research provides reasons to be optimistic.

References

Ahn, W., Brewer, W. F., & Mooney, R. J. (1992). Schema acquisition from a single example. *Journal of Experimental Psychology: Learning, Memory, and Cognition, 18,* 391–412.

Anderson, J. R. (1976). *Language, memory, and thought.* Hillsdale, NJ: Erlbaum.

Anderson, J. R. (1983). *The architecture of cognition.* Cambridge: Harvard University Press.

Anderson, J. R., & Bower, G. H. (1974). A propositional theory of recognition memory. *Memory & Cognition, 2,* 406–412.

Anderson, J. R., & Reder, L. M. (1979). An elaborative processing explanation of depth of processing. In L. S. Cermak & F. I. M. Craik (Eds.), *Levels of processing in human memory* (pp. 385–403). Hillsdale, NJ: Erlbaum.

Anderson, J. R., & Ross, B. H. (1980). Evidence against a semantic-episodic distinction. *Journal of Experimental Psychology: Human Learning and Memory, 6,* 441–465.

Anderson, R. C., Spiro, R. J., & Anderson, M. C. (1978). Schemata as scaffolding for the representation of information in connected discourse. *American Educational Research Journal, 15,* 433–440.

Atkinson, R. C. (1975). Mnemotechnics in second-language learning. *American Psychologist, 30,* 821–828.

Atkinson, R. C., & Raugh, M. R. (1975). An application of the mnemonic keyword method to the acquisition of a Russian vocabulary. *Journal of Experimental Psychology: Human Learning and Memory, 1,* 126–133.

Battig, W. F., & Bellezza, F. S. (1979). Organization and levels of processing. In C. R. Puff (Ed.), *Memory organization and structure* (pp. 311–346). New York: Academic Press.

Bellezza, F. S. (1981). Mnemonic devices: Classification, characteristics, and criteria. *Review of Educational Research, 51,* 247–275.

Bellezza, F. S. (1982a). Updating memory using mnemonic devices. *Cognitive Psychology, 14,* 301–327.

Bellezza, F. S. (1982b). *Improve your memory skills.* Englewood Cliffs, NJ: Prentice-Hall.

Bellezza, F. S. (1983). Mnemonic-device instruction with adults. In M. Pressley & J. R. Levin (Eds.), *Cognitive strategy research: Psychological foundations* (pp. 51–73). New York: Springer-Verlag, 1983.

Bellezza, F. S. (1986a). A mnemonic based on arranging words on visual patterns. *Journal of Educational Psychology, 78,* 217–224.

Bellezza, F. S. (1986b). Mental cues and verbal reports in learning. In G. H. Bower (Ed.), *The psychology of learning and motivation: Advances in research and theory* (Vol. 20, pp. 237–273). New York: Academic Press.

Bellezza, F. S. (1987). Mnemonic devices and memory schemas. In M. McDaniel & M. Pressley (Eds.), *Imaginal and mnemonic processes* (pp. 34–55). New York: Springer-Verlag.

Bellezza, F. S. (1988). Reliability of retrieving information from knowledge structures in memory: Scripts. *Bulletin of the Psychonomic Society, 26,* 11–14.

Bellezza, F. S., & Bower, G. H. (1982). Remembering script-based text. *Poetics, 11,* 1–23.

Bellezza, F. S., & Buck, D. K. (1988). Expert knowledge as mnemonic cues. *Applied Cognitive Psychology, 2,* 147–162.

Bellezza, F. S., Day, J. C., & Reddy, B. G. (1983). A comparison of phonetic and semantic encoding mnemonics. *Human Learning, 2,* 49–60.

Bellezza, F. S., & Hoyt, S. K. (1992). The self-reference effect and mental cuing. *Social Cognition, 10,* 51–78.

Bellezza, F. S., & Poplawsky, A. J. (1974). The function of one-word mediators in the recall of word pairs. *Memory & Cognition, 2,* 447–452.

Bellezza, F. S., & Reddy, B. G. (1978). Mnemonic devices and natural memory. *Bulletin of the Psychonomic Society, 11,* 277–280.

Bellezza, F. S., Six, L. S., & Phillips, D. S. (1992). A mnemonic for remembering long strings of digits. *Bulletin of the Psychonomic Society, 30,* 271–274.

Bellezza, F. S., & Young, D. R. (1989). The chunking of repeated events in memory. *Journal of Experimental Psychology: Learning, Memory, and Cognition, 15,* 990–997.

Bjork, R. A. (1988). Retrieval practice and the maintenance of knowledge. In M. M. Gruneberg, E. P. Morris, & R. N. Sykes (Eds.), *Practical aspects of memory: Current research and issues* (pp. 396–401). New York: Wiley.

Bower, G. H. (1973). Educational applications of mnemonic devices. In K. O. Doyle (Ed.), *Interaction: Readings in human psychology* (pp. 201–210). Lexington, MA: Heath.

Bower, G. H. (1978, February). Improving memory. *Human Nature,* pp. 65–72.

Bower, G. H., & Clark, M. C. (1969). Narrative stories as mediators for serial learning. *Psychonomic Science, 14,* 181–182.

Bower, G. H., & Reitman, J. S. (1972). Mnemonic elaboration in multilist learning. *Journal of Verbal Learning and Verbal Behavior, 11,* 478–485.

Brewer, W. F., & Nakamura, G. V. (1984). The nature and functions of schemas. In R. S. Wyer & T. K. Srull (Eds.), *Handbook of social cognition* (Vol. 1, pp. 119–160). Hillsdale, NJ: Erlbaum.

Chase, W. C., & Ericsson, K. A. (1981). Skilled memory. In J. R. Anderson (Ed.), *Cognitive skills an their application* (pp. 141–189). Hillsdale, NJ: Erlbaum.

Collins, A. M., & Loftus, E. F. (1975). A spreading-activation theory of semantic memory. *Psychological Review, 82*, 407–428.

Cook, N. M. (1989). The applicability of verbal mnemonics for different populations: A review. *Applied Cognitive Psychology, 3*, 3–22.

Craik, F. I. M., & Lockhart, R. S. (1972). Levels of processing: A framework for memory research. *Journal of Verbal Learning and Verbal Behavior, 11*, 671–684.

Craik, F. I. M., & Tulving, E. (1975). Depth of processing and the retention of words in episodic memory. *Journal of Experimental Psychology: General, 104*, 268–294.

Day, J. C., & Bellezza, F. S. (1983). The relation between visual-imagery mediators and recall. *Memory & Cognition, 11*, 251–257.

Drevenstedt, J., & Bellezza, F. S. (1993). Memory for self-generated narration in the elderly. *Psychology and Aging, 8*, 187–196.

Einstein, G. O., & McDaniel, M. A. (1987). Distinctiveness and the mnemonic benefits of bizarre imagery. In M. McDaniel & M. Pressley (Eds.), *Imaginal and mnemonic processes* (pp. 78–102). New York: Springer-Verlag.

Ericsson, K. A., & Chase, W. G. (1982). Exceptional memory. *American Scientist, 70,* 607–615.

Ericsson, K. A., Krampe, R. T., & Tesch-Römer, C. (1993). The role of deliberate practice in the acquisition of expert performance, *Psychological Review, 100*, 363–406.

Ericsson, K. A., & Staszewski, J. J. (1989). Skilled memory and expertise: Mechanisms of exceptional performance. In D. Klahr & K. Kotovsky (Eds.), *Complex information processing* (pp. 235–267). Hillsdale, NJ: Erlbaum.

Fisher, R. P., Geiselman, R. E., & Amador, M. (1989). Field test of the cognitive interview: Enhancing the recollection of actual victims and witnesses of crime. *Journal of Applied Psychology, 74*, 722–727.

Fulk, B. M., Mastropieri, M. A., & Scruggs, T. E. (1992). Mnemonic generalization training with learning disabled adolescents. *Learning Disabilities Research and Practice, 7*, 2–10.

Galambos, J. A., Abelson, R. P., & Black, J. B. (1986). *Knowledge structures.* Hillsdale, NJ: Erlbaum.

Glaser, R. (1984). Education and thinking. The role of knowledge. *American Psychologist, 39*, 93–104.

Glenberg, A. M. (1976). Monotonic an nonmonotonic lag effects in paired-associate an recognition memory. *Journal of Verbal Learning an Verbal Behavior, 15*, 1–16.

Griffith, D., & Actkinson, T. R. (1978). Mental aptitude and mnemonic enhancement. *Bulletin of the Psychonomic Society, 12*, 347–348.

Hall, J. W. (1991). More on the utility of the keyword method. *Journal of Educational Psychology, 83*, 171–172.

Hall, J. W., Wilson, K. P., & Patterson, R. J. (1981). Mnemotechnics: Some limitations of the mnemonic keyword method for the study of foreign language vocabulary. *Journal of Educational Psychology, 73*, 345–357.

Hayes-Roth, B. (1977). Evolution of cognitive structures and processes. *Psychological Review, 84*, 260–278.

Higbee, K. L. (1978). Some pseudo-limitations of mnemonics. In M. M. Gruneberg, P. E. Morris, & R. N. Sykes (Eds.), *Practical aspects of memory* (pp. 147–154). New York: Academic Press.

Higbee, K. L. (1979). Recent research on visual mnemonics: Historical roots and educational fruits. *Review of Educational Research, 49*, 611–629.

Higbee, K. L. (1988). *Your memory: How it works and how to improve it* (2nd ed.). New York: Paragon House.

Hirsch, E. D. (1987). *Cultural literacy.* Boston: Houghton Mifflin.

Hunt, E., & Love, T. (1972). How good can memory be? In A. W. Melton & E. Martin (Eds.), *Coding processes in human memory* (pp. 237–260). Washington, DC: Winston.

Hunt, R. R., & Einstein, G. O. (1981). Relational an item-specific information in memory. *Journal of Verbal Learning and Verbal Behavior, 15,* 559–566.

Kyllonen, P. C., Tirre, W. C., & Christal, R. E. (1991). Knowledge and processing speed as determinants of associative learning. *Journal of Experimental Psychology: General, 120,* 57–79.

Levin, J. R. (1981). The mnemonic '80s: Keywords in the classroom. *Educational Psychologist, 16,* 65–82.

Levin, M. E., & Levin, J. R. (1990). Scientific mnemonomies: Methods for maximizing more than memory. *American Educational Research Journal, 27,* 301–321.

Lorayne, H. (1975). *Remembering people.* New York: Stein & Day.

Lorayne, H., & Lucas, J. (1974). *The memory book.* New York: Ballantine.

Luria, A. R. (1968). *The mind of a mnemonist* (L. Solotaroff, Trans.). New York: Basic Books.

Mastropieri, M. A., & Scruggs, T. E. (1991). *Teaching students ways to remember.* Cambridge: Brookline Books.

Mastropieri, M. A., Scruggs, T. E., Bakken, J. P., & Brigham, F. J. (1992). A complex mnemonic strategy for teaching states and their capitals: Comparing forward and backward associations. *Learning Disabilities Research and Practice, 7,* 96–103.

McCarty, D. L. (1980). Investigation of a visual imagery mnemonic device for acquiring face-name associations. *Journal of Experimental Psychology: Human Learning and Memory, 6,* 145–155.

McClelland, J. L., & Rumelhart, D. E. (1985). Distributed memory and the representation of general and specific information. *Journal of Experimental Psychology: General, 114,* 159–188.

Miller, G. A., Galanter, E., & Pribram, K. H. (1960). *Plans and the structure of behavior.* New York: Holt, Rinehart & Winston.

Montague, W. E. (1972). Elaborative strategies in verbal learning and memory. In G. H. Bower (Ed.), The *psychology of learning and motivation: Advances in research and theory* (Vol. 6, pp. 225–302). New York: Academic Press.

Navon-Benjamin, M. (1990). Coding of temporal order information: An automatic process? *Journal of Experimental Psychology: Learning, Memory, and Cognition, 16,* 117–126.

Nelson, T. O. (1978). Detecting small amounts of information in memory: Savings for non-recognized items. *Journal of Experimental Psychology: Human Learning and Memory, 4,* 453–468.

Norman, D. A., & Bobrow, D. G. (1979). Descriptions: An intermediate stage in memory retrieval. *Cognitive Psychology, 11,* 107–123.

Paivio, A. (1971). *Imagery and verbal processes.* New York: Holt, Rinehart & Winston.

Patten, B. M. (1990). The history of memory arts. *Neurology, 40,* 346–352.

Patton, G. W., D'Agaro, W. R., & Gaudette, M. D. (1991). The effect of subject-generated and experimenter-supplied code word on the phonetic mnemonic system. *Applied Cognitive Psychology, 5,* 135–148.

Payne, D. G., & Wenger, M. J. (1992). Improving memory through practice. In D. J. Herrmann, H. Weingartner, A. Searleman, & C. McEvoy (Eds.), *Memory improvement: Implications for memory theory* (pp. 187–209). New York: Springer-Verlag.

Pressley, M., Johnson, C. J., & Symons, S. (1987). Elaborating to learn and learning to elaborate. *Journal of Learning Disabilities, 20,* 76–91.

Pressley, M., Levin, J. R., & Delaney, H. D. (1982). The mnemonic keyword method. *Review of Educational Research, 52,* 61–91.

Pressley, M., Levin, J. R., & Miller, G. E. (1981). How does the keyword method affect vocabulary comprehension and usage? *Reading Research Quarterly, 16,* 213–226.

Pressley, M., Scruggs, T. E., & Mastropieri, M. A. (1989). Memory strategy research in learning disabilities: Present and future directions. *Learning Disabilities Research, 4,* 68–77.

Reddy, B. G., & Bellezza, F. S. (1983). Encoding specificity in free recall. *Journal of Experimental Psychology: Learning, Memory, and Cognition, 9,* 167–174.

Reddy, B. G., & Bellezza, F. S. (1986). Interference between mnemonic and categorical organization in memory. *Bulletin of the Psychonomic Society, 24,* 169–171.

Richardson, J. T. (1987). Social class limitations on the efficacy of imagery mnemonic instructions. *British Journal of Psychology, 78,* 65–77.

Richardson, J. T. (1992). Imagery mnemonics and memory remediation. *Neurology, 42,* 283–286.

Rubin, D. C., & Wallace, W. T. (1989). Rhyme and reason: Analyses of dual retrieval cues. *Journal of Experimental Psychology: Learning, Memory, and Cognition, 15,* 698–709.

Rumelhart, D. E. (1980). Schemata: The building blocks of cognition. In R. Spiro, B. Bruce, & W. Brewer (Eds.), *Theoretical issues in reading comprehension* (pp. 33–58). Hillsdale NJ: Erlbaum.

Rumelhart, D. E., McClelland, J. L., and the PDP Research Group (Eds.). (1986). *Parallel distributed processing: Explorations in the microstructure of cognition: Vol. 1. Foundations.* Cambridge: MIT Press.

Rumelhart, D. E., & Norman, D. A. (1978). Accretion, tuning and restructuring: Three modes of learning. In J. W. Cotton & R. Klatzky (Eds.), *Semantic factors in cognition* (pp. 37–53). Hillsdale, NJ: Erlbaum.

Schank, R., & Abelson, R. (1977). *Scripts, plans, goals, and understanding: An inquiry into human knowledge and structures.* Hillsdale, NJ: Erlbaum.

Scruggs, T. E., & Mastropieri, M. A. (1990a). Mnemonic instruction for students with learning disabilities: What it is and what it does. *Learning Disability Quarterly, 13,* 271–280.

Scruggs, T. E., & Mastropieri, M. A. (1990b). The case for mnemonic instruction: From laboratory research to classroom applications. *Journal of Special Education, 24,* 7–32.

Scruggs, T. E., & Mastropieri, M. A. (1992). Classroom applications of mnemonic instructions: Acquisition, maintenance, and generalization. *Exceptional Children, 58,* 219–229.

Scruggs, T. E., Mastropieri, M. A., Jorgensen, C., & Monson, J. (1986). Effective mnemonic strategies for gifted learners. *Journal for the Education of the Gifted, 9,* 105–121.

Shepherd, M. L., & Gelzheiser, L. M. (1987). Strategies and mnemonics go to school. In H. L. Swanson (Ed.), *Memory and learning disabilities: Advances in learning and behavior disabilities* (Suppl. 2, pp. 245–262). Greenwich, CT: JAI.

Short, D. D., Workman, E. A., Morse, J. H., & Turner, R. L. (1992). Mnemonics for eight DSM-III-R disorders. *Hospital and Community Psychiatry, 43,* 643–644.

Slamecka, N., & Graf, P. (1978). The generation effect: Delineation of a phenomenon. *Journal of Experimental Psychology: Human Learning and Memory, 14,* 592–604.

Smith, S. M., Glenberg, A., & Bjork, R. A. (1978). Environmental context and human memory. *Memory & Cognition, 6,* 342–353.

Staszewski, J. J. (1990). Exceptional memory: The influence of practice and knowledge on the development of elaborative encoding strategies. In W. Schneider & F. E. Weinart (Eds.), *Interactions among aptitudes, strategies, and knowledge in cognitive performance* (pp. 252–285). New York: Springer-Verlag.

Sweeney, C. A., & Bellezza, F. S. (1982). Use of the keyword mnemonic in learning English vocabulary words. *Human Learning, 1,* 155–163.

Thomas, E. L., & Robinson, H. A. (1972). *Improving reading in every class: A sourcebook for teachers.* Boston: Allyn & Bacon.

Thorndyke, P. W. (1977). Cognitive structures in comprehension and memory of narrative discourse. *Cognitive Psychology, 9,* 77–110.

Thorndyke, P. W., & Hayes-Roth, B. (1979). The use of schemata in the acquisition and transfer of knowledge. *Cognitive Psychology, 11,* 82–106.

Tulving, E. (1967). The effects of presentation and recall of material in free-recall learning. *Journal of Verbal Learning and Verbal Behavior, 6,* 175–184.

Tulving, E. (1972). Episodic and semantic memory. In E. Tulving & W. Donaldson (Eds.), *Organization and memory* (pp. 381–403). New York: Academic Press.

Tulving, E. (1974). Cue-dependent forgetting. *American Scientist, 62,* 74–82.

Tulving, E. (1985). Memory and consciousness. *Canadian Psychology, 26,* 1–12.

Tulving, E., & Thomson, D. M. (1973). Encoding specificity and retrieval processes in episodic memory. *Psychological Review, 80,* 352–373.

Underwood, B. J., & Schulz, R. W. (1960). *Meaningfulness and verbal learning.* Philadelphia: Lippincott.

Verhaeghen, P., Marcoen, A., & Goossens, L. (1992). Improving memory performance in the aged through mnemonic training: A meta-analytic study. *Psychology and Aging, 7,* 242–251.

Watkins, M. J. (1979). Engrams as cuegrams and forgetting as cue overload: A cueing approach to the structure of memory. In C. R. Puff (Ed.), *Memory organization and structure* (pp. 347–372). New York: Academic Press.

Watkins, M. J., & Kerkar, S. P. (1985). Recall of a twice-presented item without recall of either presentation: Generic memory for events. *Journal of Memory and Language, 24,* 666–678.

Wittrock, M. C. (1974). Learning as a generative process. *Educational Psychologist, 11,* 87–95.

Yarmey, A. D. (1984). Bizarreness effects in mental imagery. In A. A. Sheikh (Ed.), *International review of mental imagery* (Vol. 1, pp. 57–76). New York: Human Sciences Press.

Yates, F. A. (1966). *The art of memory.* London: Routledge & Kegan Paul.

Yesavage, J. A., Lapp, D., & Sheikh, J. I. (1989). Mnemonics as modified for use by the elderly. In L. W. Poon, D. C. Rubin, & B. A. Wilson (Eds.), *Everyday cognition in adulthood and late life* (pp. 598–611). New York: Cambridge University Press.

Youtz, A. D. (1941). An experimental evaluation of Jost's laws. *Psychological Monographs, 53,* (1, Whole No. 238).

Zacks, R. T., Hasher, L., Alba, J. W., Sanft, H., & Rose, K. C. (1984). Is temporal order encoded automatically? *Memory & Cognition, 12,* 387–394.

CHAPTER 11

Metacognitive Processes

Janet Metcalfe

Socrates, in making his defense against the charge of corrupting the minds of his students—a crime for which he suffered death by hemlock—noted that he had always been accompanied by an internal voice that would monitor his planned words and actions. If the intended act was wrong, this monitor would prevent him from doing it:

> Perhaps it may seem odd that although I go about and give all this advice privately, quite a busybody, yet I dare not appear before your public assembly and advise the state. The reason for this is one which you have often heard me giving in many places, that something divine and spiritual comes to me, which Meletos put into the indictment in caricature. This has been about me since my boyhood, a voice, which when it comes always turns me away from doing something I am intending to do, but never urges me on. This is what opposes my taking up public business. And quite right too, I think; for you may be sure, gentlemen, that if I had meddled with public business in the past, I should have perished long ago and done no good either to you or to myself.
>
> *(Plato, 1984, p. 437)*

Socrates's inner voice is the earliest well-known example of a self-reflective consciousness—an internal monitor and control system. A similar self-monitoring consciousness figures in the musings of Descartes, emerging as "the thinker" whose existence cannot be doubted, even though all of the content of the thought is open to question. Descartes considered this "I" to be at the very center of his being and to be the essential primitive upon which all else is built—more fundamentally real than external reality. Self-reflection, monitoring, control processes, predictions about our future knowledge, judgments about the accuracy and goodness of our skills, along with the consciousness necessary for these judgments, are the areas of interest within the study of human metacognition.

An accumulating body of evidence points to the prefrontal cortex as a brain region of critical importance for these functions. This region is distinct from those areas responsible for the knowledge and operations upon that knowledge that are the object of reflection, though, of course, they are interconnected. As Nelson and Narens (1994) have pointed out, object-level functions of cognition, such as memory storage, retrieval, and applying the operations of problem solving, may be separable from metalevel functions that monitor and control the object-level functions. In the normal person these two levels, cognition and metacognition, interact in a complex manner. This interaction is critical not only for problem solving, planning, and for memory, but arguably for sensitive assessments of one's own and other people's wants and needs, and evaluation and control of one's own appropriate social behavior. Frontal lobe damage may sometimes result in selective breakdown of the metacognitive monitoring and control functions, sparing more basic level functions. Severe consequences ensue not only for judgments about and control of cognition, but also for the structure of the personality. Unlike other kinds of brain damage, which leave intact the personality and the person's sense of self, frontal damage can produce alterations, which, to the extent that we are able to know about the phenomenology of another person's sense of being, appear to go right to the core of the self.

Socrates had complete confidence in the accuracy of his monitor, apparently assuming it was infallible. Indeed, he interpreted the fact that this inner voice did not protest his punishment of death as the strongest possible argument that his impending death was really a good thing—and so consoled those who would mourn him. Socrates is not alone in believing in such introspections. However, despite people's trust in them, feelings of knowing, judgments of learning, and confidence assessments—all metacognitive judgments—are frequently prone to error, often of a systematic nature. A major research issue in the study of metacognition concerns the accuracy of these predictions and the informational basis and mechanisms that underlie their accuracy or inaccuracy. Errors can lead to the illusion of knowing, to the mistaken notion of having made progress in problem solving, to illusions of comprehension, or to faulty assessments of having adequately mastered the skill at hand. Insofar as our actions are based on these assessments, such illusions can lead to acutely maladaptive learning and performance strategies, and to judgments that, while extremely convincing to outside observers (most perniciously to juries), may be far wide of the mark.

In this chapter, several different domains of human cognition in which metacognitive processes are of importance are discussed. First, the roles of metacognitions in problem solving, both with routine and insight problems, are outlined, as are some of the controversies within this area. Then, metacognitive judgments in learning and skills acquisition are discussed, an area of particular importance because such judgments contribute heavily to our choice of teaching techniques and of teachers; thus, errors in judgments may have far-reaching effects. Next, metacognitive judgments within human memory are described, and theories (along with relevant data) of prospective and retrospective judgments about our memories are reviewed. Finally, some of the results of metacognitive impairments found in frontal lobe patients are presented. These patient studies underscore the critical nature of metacognitive judgments and control processes: their breakdown has devastating consequences for human cognition.

I. PROBLEM SOLVING

A. Routine Problems

The importance of metacognitions in steering people toward the correct solution in problem-solving situations is affirmed by the general problem solver (GPS) of Newell and Simon (1972) (perhaps the most influential model of problem solving), as well as by other artificial intelligence models such as those of Fahlman (1974), Sussman (1975), and the SOAR model of Laird, Newell, and Rosenbloom (1987). The GPS model is able to solve a wide variety of problems by successively modifying the starting representation of the problem in the direction of the goal representation by selecting operations within the problem space in such a way that the modifications attributable to those operations lead to results that increasingly approximate the final goal state. At every step, the similarities between the goal state and the state attained by the possible moves must by *monitored* and the direction of the "search" is guided by these metacognitive assessments. This monitoring/control process is central in the model; without it, the search process would flounder. Indeed, these metacognitions were needed to rescue the problem-solving model from what Newell considered to be beyond the realm of plausibility—the hopelessness of random search.

Simon and Reed (1976) and Newell and Simon (1972; see also Ericsson & Simon, 1984) studied subjects' protocols and measured reaction times during the solution of noninsight problems, such as the missionaries-and-cannibals problem. When, in order to solve the problem, subjects had to make a move that would decrease the apparent similarity of the resulting state to the goal state, they took an inordinately long time. Additionally, their verbal protocols revealed a reluctance to enact such seemingly regressive moves, consistent with the predictions of the model. Metcalfe and Wiebe (1987) provided supporting evidence for a problem-solving procedure like that used in the general problem solver. They asked subjects to make successive "warmth" ratings, or assessments of their nearness to problem solution. As long as the problems were routine multistep problems to which the general problem solver would apply—such as algebra problems, the Tower of Hanoi, or the missionaries-and-cannibals problem—subjects' warmth ratings increased over the solving interval in the predicted manner.

B. Insight Problems

Insight problems are more recalcitrant to a straightforward analysis. In this case, the goal state is not known; hence, the kind of analysis proposed by Newell and Simon (1972) is problematic. If the goal state is not known, then the method by which individuals direct themselves through the problem space to reach the unknown goal is mysterious. Some researchers have postulated that the goal is, in fact, intuited, perhaps in an unconscious or preconscious manner. For example, Polanyi (1962) discussed the role of metacognitions in creativity and the discovery of problem solutions in the following terms:

> The problem solver's success will depend ultimately on his capacity for sensing the presence of yet unrevealed logical relations between the conditions of the problem, the theorems unknown to him, and the unknown solution he is looking for. Unless his casting about is guided by a reliable sense of growing approximation to the solution, he will make no progress towards it. Conjectures made at random, even though following the best rules of heuristics, would be hopelessly inept and totally fruitless. The process of solving a mathematical problem continues to depend, therefore, at every stage on the same ability to anticipate a hidden potentiality which will enable the student first to see a problem and then to set out to solve it. Polya has compared a mathematical discovery consisting of a whole chain of consecutive steps with an arch, where every stone depends for its stability on the presence of others, and he pointed out the paradox that the stones are in fact put in one at a time. Again, the paradox is resolved by the fact that each successive step of the complete solution is upheld by the heuristic anticipation which originally evoked its invention: by the feeling that its emergence has narrowed further the logical gap of the problem.
>
> (pp. 128–129)

Unfortunately for Polanyi's speculation, when Metcalfe and Wiebe (1987) tested subjects for increasing feelings of approaching the solution on insight problems, supporting evidence did not emerge. Subjects were asked to report their feeling-of-warmth ratings every 10 sec while solving insight problems. Typically, subjects would jump from a low or zero warmth directly to the solution. Metcalfe and Wiebe interpreted these findings as indicating that insight problems phenomenologically are solved suddenly.

Smith (1994, 1995) has proposed a state in problem solving (and in memory tip-of-the-tongue states) that he called imminence. In such a state, the subject knows that he or she knows the solution even though the solution is still inchoate and cannot be articulated. Wallas (1926) (in describing the process of discovery reported by Poincaré) noted such a phenomenal state existing for a moment before the solution could be produced. A number of subjects in our insight experiments also, informally, reported such states, as did the experimenters themselves when they first tried the insight problems. Unfortunately, at the present time no empirical methodology for isolating the state of imminence exists. Until such a methodology is discovered or invented, our understanding of what may be a very important subprocess in problem solving is unlikely to progress.

1. Metacognitive Accuracy in Problem Solving

Feeling-of-knowing (FOK) judgments are assessments, made by an individual, of how likely it is that he or she will later be able to remember or solve the problems that he or she cannot solve or remember at the time the judgment is made. In routine problem solving (Metcalfe, 1986a) and in memory, these judgments of future cognitive performance are predictive of whether the subject actually will be able to remember or to solve the problems later. However, for insight problems, the metacognitive judgments are not predictive. The correlation between judgments and accuracy is near zero with this class of problem. Similarly, in routine problem solving, feelings of warmth (that is, assessments taken dynamically during the course of problem solving that indicate the subject's perceived nearness to the solution) increase in a smooth way until the correct solution is produced; whereas, in insight problem solving, there is little if any increase until the moment of correct solution, indicating that subjects do not know when they are about to produce the solution. In fact, in contrast to the idea that strong feelings of approaching solution forecast the correct production of the solution, several experiments with insight problems have revealed the counterintuitive finding that when subjects did increase their warmth rating during the solving interval, they were more likely to produce an error of commission (Metcalfe, 1986b).

This "illusory premonition" effect might have occurred because subjects successively convinced themselves that a fairly good answer was good enough. Simon (1979) has called such a problem-solving strategy "satisficing." It may work well for problems where solutions are not clear-cut. In the real world, for example, where perfection is rare, one must frequently settle for a solution that is "good enough." With insight problems, however, a solution that is not quite right is a mistake. Consider the following question: "You are a museum curator and a suspicious-looking person comes in and offers to sell you an ancient-looking bronze coin marked 544 B.C. You have accepted coins from unsavory people before, but this time you immediately call the police. Why?" The answer that bronze had not been invented in 544 B.C., while perhaps having some feeling of plausibility, is not good enough to qualify as the solution for the insight problem. Before offering such a commission error, subjects frequently exhibit a high and incrementally increasing pattern of warmth ratings. These high ratings seem to be attributable to the subjects convincing themselves that such an answer is acceptable. During this self-deception process, they further increase their warmth ratings. Although this explanation is plausible, and enjoys some empirical support—for example, when asked to guess, subjects give higher ratings than when instructed to inhibit guessing—there may be alternative explanations. We do not yet know the generality of this finding or whether it occurs in domains other than insight problem solving. The finding that inordinately high presolution warmth predicts mistakes rather than correct solutions is a metacognitive illusion that may have practical consequences and deserves further study.

2. Catastrophic Process or Failure of Access to Consciousness?

There are (at least) two viable hypotheses for why correctly solved insight problems do not show incrementally increasing metacognitive (feelings-of-warmth) ratings. First, perhaps the metacognitions accurately reflect the underlying process, and the process is spontaneous, that is, nothing happens to the content of the representation until it suddenly shifts to the new organization. This perspective is consistent with the metaphors used by Gestalt psychologists likening insight to a perceptual reorganization, such as that seen in reversals of a Necker cube or in multistable ambiguous figures such as Boring's wife/mother-in-law figure. There is no incremental or piecemeal process whereby the figure undergoes a gradual realignment; rather, the reorientation happens synchronously and spontaneously over the whole figure. Alternatively, the processes underlying insight may not be spontaneous; rather, they may gradually approximate the solution, but this progress may not be open to conscious inspection. So, either the process is not incremental, or it is incremental but the metacognitive monitor cannot see it. Although some attempts have been made to tease apart these two possibilities (Bowers, Regehr, Balthazard, & Parker, 1990), the results are not yet definitive.

II. LEARNING

Metacognition in learning and training situations determines how much time and effort will be invested, what kind of training procedures will be practiced, and the praise that the trainee will bestow on the trainer. As Jacoby, Bjork, and Kelley (1994) have pointed out, it may be equally important to educate *subjective* experience as to educate objective experience. Bjork (1994) has documented a number of factors that lead to immediate and positive performance results and to introspective satisfaction, but that fail to result in adequate long-term performance. In such cases, our metacognitions may be misleading.

It is well known, for example, that massed practice has an immediate beneficial effect on performance, but that this effect fades rapidly. Spaced practice, on the other hand, shows less immediate efficacy, but promotes better learning for the long run (Bahrick, 1979; Dempster, 1990; Glenberg, 1992). One might expect, then, that people trained under massed practice and asked for their assessment of the technique (immediately at the end of training) would be well pleased. Those trained under spaced practice should be poorly satisfied, even though eventual performance favors them. Baddeley and Longman (1978) have demonstrated just this effect with British postal workers who were taught a keyboard skill under relatively massed or relatively spaced conditions. Immediate satisfaction was found to be a poor predictor of eventual performance.

Similarly, Jacoby and Kelley (1987) converted a task that was intrinsically very difficult (solving anagrams) into one that was ostensibly easy, by providing the solutions to the anagrams. When subjects were asked for their ratings of objective difficulty, the subjects who were given the unsolved anagrams thought that they were more difficult than did the people given the solutions. People who had to solve the anagrams themselves, rather than being provided with the answers, were not only more accurate at assessing the overall difficulty of the problems for other people, but also were more accurate at assessing which particular anagrams were objectively easy or difficult.

Dunlosky and Nelson (1992) provided a third variation on the theme that immediate but transient fluency may produce systematic biases in judgments of learning. They varied the time between initial study of a cue–target pair and subjects' judgments of learning, in which subjects were presented with the cue from the cue–target pair and asked for an assessment of whether they would be able to retrieve the target 10 min later. These judgments of learning were made either immediately after the study presentation or at a delay. The delayed judgments were more accurate at predicting eventual performance than were the immediate judgments. In another condition in the experiment, subjects were provided with the target as well as the cue before making the judgment, and, in this case, the judgments were inaccurate regardless of the interval. Spellman and Bjork (1992) proposed that subjects base their judgments of learning on the heuristic of the ease of immediate target access. Tasks or manipulations that violate what may often be a fairly strong correlation between this ease of immediate access and the goodness of later performance will reveal an illusion of knowing. The converse is also possible, of course. Some manipulations, for example, extremely difficult conditions of practice, or, possibly, subthreshold conditions of presentation, could produce an illusion of not-knowing in which the subjects would believe that they had had little benefit from a prior experience when, in fact, they had benefited substantially from that prior learning incident (see Bjork, 1994, for review).

Bjork (1994) pointed out that even though metacognitive judgments can mispredict later performance, those judgments on the part of the students are often the basis of their evaluations of the value of the learning experience. Thus, judgments of learning, rather than eventual performance, are frequently used to evaluate teaching procedures, and such evaluations may be used to reward or punish the teacher. A problem ensues when student satisfaction is high, even though eventual performance will be poor, or when satisfaction is low despite the fact that eventual performance will be good, as may frequently be the case. The result is a selection bias favoring ineffective training procedures and teachers over those producing better long-term results (but at the cost of less immediate satisfaction in their students). The pain we may need to endure to allow us to reap later gains in performance may be of a metacognitive nature.

III. MEMORY

A. Prospective Judgments

Predictive metacognitions about later memory performance have been intensively investigated (Blake, 1973; Gruneberg & Monks, 1974; Hart, 1965, 1967; Leonesio & Nelson, 1990; Metcalfe, 1986a; Nelson, Leonesio, Shimamura, Landwehr, & Narens, 1982; Schacter, 1983). In fact, metacognition was first advanced as a phenomenon amenable to scientific study by the work of Hart (1965) on metamemory. Hart devised a paradigm for studying people's knowledge about their future states of knowing that has come to be known as the recall, judge, recognize (RJR) paradigm. In the RJR paradigm, subjects are presented with a series of questions and asked to provide the answers. Often these questions target general information, though sometimes they are directed toward newly learned information. For example, a subject might be asked to say what color topaz turns when it is heated, or who was the first prime minister of Canada. Typically, feeling-of-knowing judgments (about how likely it is that the subject will be able later to remember the answer) are requested for only those questions to which the subject cannot recall the answer. The feeling-of-knowing judgment can be expressed as a numerical value indicating how likely it is that the subject deems that he or she will be able to choose the correct answer when given an *n*-alternative forced-choice test. Alternatively, subjects may express their feeling of knowing by the rank ordering of the unrecalled questions with respect to one another. After having made these judgments, subjects are then given a multiple choice test—the criterion task. The correspondence between the judgments and the memory performance on the criterion task is computed in the form of a correlation coefficient, often a nonparametric gamma correlation (Nelson & Narens, 1980). In the following sections, I refer to this correspondence between the ranking of particular items and later performance on those items as *micrometacognition*. To the extent that highly ranked questions are actually those for which the subject later correctly recognizes the answer, and lowly ranked questions are those for which the subject later fails to recognize the correct answer, micrometacognition is accurate.

Logical and Methodological Constraints

The goodness of the correspondence between the ranking of the questions and the later recognition or nonrecognition of the answers is logically independent of the overall goodness of recognition. There is no statistical constraint forcing a correspondence between the two measures. For example, one could correctly recognize the answers to very few questions, but if it happened that those few were the questions to which one had given high rankings in the judgment phase of the experiment, then the micrometacognitive gamma correlation would be high. Such a situation occurs with some amnesic patients. Alternatively, one could imagine a situation in which one would choose the correct answer to most of the recognition questions, but if the few for which one failed to select the correct response had been ranked very highly, one would exhibit poor micrometacognition. So, even though there is no necessary link between the goodness of memory and the goodness of metamemory as measured by the feeling of knowing, one might ask the empirical question: do those people who have good metacognitions tend to have good memories? If there is a correspondence, then perhaps metacognitions contribute to the memory processes themselves.

Good metacognitive skills may underlie our ability to remember events or to solve problems. Indeed, if the term metacognition is construed to encompass knowledge about which memorial or problem-solving strategies might prove effective in enhancing later performance, then it is plausible to expect a positive correlation between this kind of knowledge and later memory performance, at least on tasks that are amenable to conscious inter-vention (i.e., on explicit memory and problem-solving tasks, but not on implicit tasks; for a discussion of the distinction between explicit and im-plicit memory, see Kelley & Lindsay, Chapter 2, this volume). Furthermore, Reder (1987) and Reder and Ritter (1992) have suggested that one of the functions of metacognitive judgments is to provide subjects with salient information about whether it would be worthwhile to exert the effort to attempt to retrieve. According to this rationale, metacognitive judgments have a causal impact upon whether retrieval is attempted. If follows that there should be a correspondence between later success and judgment mag-nitude, because the judgment itself, by this notion, mediates effort (and perhaps other processes) on the memory task. Despite some supporting evidence for the idea that metacognitions may be related to memory perfor-mance, there is also evidence that the correspondence is neither necessary for all people (Shimamura & Squire, 1986) nor general across task domains (Metcalfe, Schwartz, & Joaquim, 1993; Schwartz & Metcalfe, 1992; Met-calfe, 1986a).

Micrometacognitive accuracy is also distinct from the mean of the feel-ing-of-knowing ratings given on the judgment task. A person might believe that he or she would correctly remember the answers to very few questions and, hence, give very low values on the judgment task overall, but still have the ordering substantially correct. In this case, one would know which items one would know and, hence, have a high gamma. At the same time, one's mean feeling-of-knowing rating might be low.

Micrometacognitive accuracy, as measured by the gamma correlations, is also distinct from the correspondence between a subject's mean feeling-of-knowing rating and the subject's mean proportions correct on the criterion test, that is, calibration (Yates, 1990). For example, a person's ratings on individual problems in the set might vary from an estimated chance of success of 50% (for the problem estimated least likely to get correct) to 90% (for the problem considered mostly likely to get correct), with an average of 70% over the entire set. This person could exhibit near zero or even nega-tive gamma correlations, indicating poor micrometacognitive accuracy, if the problems to which he or she assigned the highest ratings were the ones he or she later got wrong, and the ones assigned the lowest ratings were the ones he or she later got right. Even so, the person could show excellent calibration, that is, no under- or overconfidence, if the average rating were 70%, and it turned out that he or she got 70% correct overall. These two kinds of metacognition, which I call here micrometacognition and calibra-tion, though conceptually distinct, have sometimes been conflated.

Normal college-aged subjects tested using the RJR paradigm with gener-al information questions show gamma correlation coefficients (micro-metacognitive accuracy) of around .5; they are good, though not perfect, at predicting what they will know, even though, at the time of making the judgments, they ostensibly do not have the answers available. Much research has focused on how this prediction accuracy is accomplished; that is, on the nature of the judgment process and the information on which it is based. Three views, discussed below, have emerged: the target-retrievability hypothesis, the cue-familiarity hypothesis, and the accessibility account.

B. Theories of Feeling of Knowing in Memory

1. The Target-Retrievability Hypothesis

According to the target-retrievability hypothesis, people are able to make accurate judgments about their future knowledge even though the accessible knowledge may be insufficient to allow articulation, because they nevertheless know the answer or some part of the answer. Thus, people make accurate feeling-of-knowing judgments because they really do know what they will later know, despite the fact that they cannot express it as a recall response.

Hart (1965) was one of the first to propose this idea, saying that recall was a more difficult task than recognition and, hence, recall required more information to reach threshold than did recognition. He thought that the threshold for feeling-of-knowing judgments might be somewhere between those for recall and recognition. Since the time of Hart's research, investigators of human memory have concluded that the distinction between recall and recognition is much more complex than a simple threshold difference would suggest. Many experiments have shown that recall can sometimes be superior to recognition, in contrast to the predictions of a threshold theory of the two tasks. A simple strength-plus-differential-thresholds model of memory has proven far too simple to account for these and many other lines of data. On memory grounds, then, the simple threshold difference cannot be the whole story. Recently, however, a more complex target-retrievability theory, one not suffering from these problems, has come to the fore. Thus, despite criticisms of Hart's initial proposal, the target-retrievability hypothesis is enjoying something of a resurgence of interest.

Burke, MacKay, Worthley, and Wade (1991) recently offered a linguistically based model of the *tip-of-the-tongue (TOT) phenomenon* (i.e., the feeling that recall is imminent). In this model (MacKay, 1982), there is a semantic level of representation that is distinct from the articulatory phonemic level. Most importantly, from the perspective of a dissociation between knowledge and output, which presumably is the basis for the tip-of-the-tongue feeling and for accurate feelings of knowing, there are connections that may fail between the semantic and phonemic level. A person might have excellent knowledge at the semantic level but some confusion or breakdown might exist at the articulatory/phonemic level, or in the connections between one level and another. A recognition test, but not a recall test, allows circumvention of the articulatory requirements hard hit by the missing connections. If the person were able to directly monitor the knowledge base at the semantic level for the items that could not be articulated, he or she would be able to produce accurate feeling-of-knowing ratings. This model has been applied to TOT states, providing some insights about a dissociation between these two levels of representation and their role in provoking TOTs. Burke et al. (1991) argued that the model applies especially well to older patients, in whom the connections between the semantic and phonemic levels may be particularly fragile.

Two lines of evidence offer support for the general target-retrievability hypothesis, whether it is due to a threshold difference in tasks or to a possible dissociation of two levels of representation. First, the finding that metacognitive judgments are accurate lends credibility to this hypothesis. If subjects give high ratings because they really do know what they will know, then it falls out immediately that the ratings will and should be accurate. The second line of evidence that supports the target-retrievability hypothesis is the finding that people often report being in tip-of-the-tongue states. Moreover, these TOT states are highly correlated with high feelings of knowing, and, when in such states, subjects are sometimes able to provide partial information that is accurate. For example, A. S. Brown (1991), R. Brown and McNeill (1966), and Koriat and Lieblich (1974) reported that people in TOT states are able to report phonemic or orthographic information, such as the first letter or the number of syllables of the to-be-remembered word. Blake (1973) showed that partial recall of three-letter trigrams was positively correlated with feeling-of-knowing ratings. Schacter and Worling (1985) showed that subjects could better remember the affective valence of unrecalled items that had been given high feeling-of-knowing ratings than those given lower ratings. Although these studies might be criticized as being merely correlational, the results are nevertheless suggestive.

Several experiments, not impeachable by this "correlational" criticism, were reported by Schwartz and Metcalfe (1992). Target retrievability was manipulated. In some experiments, following Slamecka and Graf (1978), subjects either read or generated a rhyming word to the cue word or read an unrelated word. The generated words were more retrievable than the read or unrelated words both in the recall test and in the recognition test, which was based only on the unrecalled words. In other experiments, target retrievability was manipulated by target priming, that is, by facilitative effects attributable to presentation of the target word in an ostensibly unrelated context. In three of the four experiments, the feeling-of-knowing judgments were unaffected by the target-retrievability manipulation. This did not appear to be a simple null effect because other experimental variables were able to alter the feeling-of-knowing ratings. In one experiment, though—where the target words were primed—an effect that might have been due to target retrievability (though the authors interpreted this finding differently) was found.

Moreover, in addition to Schwartz and Metcalfe's (1992) nonsupportive study, many studies that have been interpreted as supporting the target-retrievability hypothesis are actually ambiguous as to whether the observed effect was due to partial knowledge of the unrecalled target or, instead, to increased familiarity of the cue. In these studies, some variable, such as level of processing (Lupker, Harbluk, & Patrick, 1991), study time, or number of repetitions (Nelson et al., 1982), is shown to influence the recallability of targets and also the magnitude of the feeling-of-knowing judgments. Although it is tempting to infer that target retrievability was responsible for the increased feeling-of-knowing values, such a conclusion is not justified. The manipulation may have had its effect, instead, because it secondarily altered the familiarity of the cues. To show that target retrievability was the sole contributing factor, one needs to hold the familiarity of the cues constant. In those studies that have done this (Jameson, Narens, Goldfarb, & Nelson, 1990; Metcalfe et al., 1993; Schwartz & Metcalfe, 1992, with one exception discussed earlier), no effect of target retrievability has been observed. These results are unfavorable for the target-retrievability hypothesis (cf., Narens, Jameson, & Lee, 1994).

2. The Cue-Familiarity Hypothesis

According to the cue-familiarity hypothesis, feeling-of-knowing judgments are not based on the unrecalled target itself but, rather, on the familiarity of the cue that is present at the time the judgment is made. There are two versions of the cue-familiarity hypothesis, developed independently and for different reasons.

Reder (1987; Miner & Reder, 1994) proposed that subjects in a memory situation make a very fast preretrieval assessment of whether the to-be-remembered information actually exists in memory, based on the familiarity of the cue. If the cue is sufficiently familiar, the subject assumes that the likelihood is high that the target information exists in memory, and therefore further efforts to retrieve it may be warranted. If the familiarity of the cue is low, then this serves as a signal for the subject to avoid initiating what may be an extensive and unproductive memory search. The cue-familiarity assessment is also thought to underlie the person's feeling-of-knowing judgment.

Metcalfe (1993a, 1993b) proposed an alternate cue-familiarity mechanism for feelings of knowing. In Metcalfe's model of human episodic memory (Metcalfe, 1990, 1991; Metcalfe Eich, 1982), the basic memory system requires a monitoring and control device to maintain stability. The monitor assesses the familiarity or novelty of the information being processed and sends a feedback signal that controls the weighting of the information coming into memory. If information is novel, it is given a high weighting; if it is old and familiar, it is given a low weighting. Metcalfe proposed that the novelty or familiarity feeling itself is available to the conscious inspection of the subject, and that it serves as the basis for the feeling-of-knowing judgment. In the RJR paradigm, in which the judgments are made only on those items for which subjects cannot recall the targets, it is assumed that the judgments are based on the familiarity of the cue because that is all that is available. However, this view does not preclude the possibility that subjects might use the accessibility of the target for some judgments if that target information were available, as it is in the judgment-of-learning paradigm described earlier. Thus, this view is compatible with the ease-of-accessibility heuristic proposed by Bjork (1994; Kelley & Lindsay, 1993) for judgments of learning.

Evidence favoring the cue-familiarity heuristic has been provided by a sequence of studies in which the familiarity of the cue was manipulated in a manner independent of target retrievability. Reder (1987) primed keywords in the cue and found that feeling-of-knowing judgments responded to this manipulation. For example, subjects might have seen the words *North Star* in a priming task prior to the general information test. This exposure increased feeling of knowing to the question: "What is the name of the North Star?" even though it did not influence the probability that the subject would be able to choose "Polaris."

In an arithmetic problem experiment, Reder and Ritter (1992) found that exposure to parts of a problem, even though not in the correct configuration relevant to the requested answer, influenced subjects decisions about whether to retrieve the answer versus to work out the solution. For example, exposure to the numbers 63 and 84 in the experimental sequence, even if these two were not grouped together in the form 63×84, nevertheless led people to choose to retrieve the answer rather than to work it out. Reder argued that the belief that the answer was known in memory, which she likened to a feeling of knowing, was attributed to the familiarity of the terms in the problem or cue. It could not have been attributable to knowledge of the answer because the answer had not been presented.

Metcalfe et al. (1993) used a classic interference-theory paradigm to contrast the target-retrievability to the cue-familiarity hypotheses. An A–B/A–B condition, in which both the cue and target were repeated, provided maximal positive transfer and thus best target retrieval. An A–B/A–D condition, in which the cue but not the target was repeated, resulted in negative transfer and worst target retrieval. An A–B/C–D condition, in which the cue was presented only once, resulted in target retrieval that was moderate, but better than that for the A–B/A–D condition. According to the target-retrievability hypothesis, feeling-of-knowing magnitudes should be related to memory for the targets; thus, the A–B/A–B condition should have produced the highest ratings, the A–B/C–D condition should have produced ratings in the middle, and the A–B/A–D condition should have produced the lowest ratings. In contrast, according to the cue-familiarity hypothesis, the magnitude of the feeling-of-knowing judgments should vary with the assessed familiarity of the cues, or, in the present experiment, with the number of repetitions of the cue. Thus, the A–B/A–B and the A–B/A–D conditions should have both produced high, and roughly equal, feeling-of-knowing ratings, whereas the A–B/C–D condition should have produced lower feeling-of-knowing ratings. The results closely followed the predictions of the cue-familiarity hypothesis.

Although the various findings described here provide compelling evidence for the cue-familiarity hypothesis, the accuracy of the feeling-of-knowing judgments seems problematic for this hypothesis. Criticisms of the hypothesis based on judgment accuracy, however, may be unwarranted. In Reder's theory, for example, one would expect a positive correlation between judgment and memory because the judgment determines whether a memory search will be enacted. If no search is enacted, it is self-evident that memory will be poor. But even leaving a direct causal mechanism aside, there are reasons why cue familiarity might be a good predictor of target recognition. In the real world, cues and targets are often experienced in synchrony. One learns at the same time that "the name of the songwriter for The Band, prior to their breakup" (cue) was "Robbie Robertson" (target), or that "the first person to set foot on the moon" (cue) was "Armstrong" (target). Those cues to which people are frequently exposed and that gain their interest occur in tight conjunction with frequent exposure to their targets. The feeling-of-knowing gamma correlation might be reflecting little more than this correlation in the world.

Indeed, Glenberg, Wilkinson, and Epstein (1982) have shown that people assign high feelings of knowing to domains in which they have expertise, regardless of the questions being asked. This is a reasonable general strategy. If you are a basketball aficionado, give the basketball questions a high rating. Even if you cannot retrieve the answer immediately, you will likely be able to eliminate irrelevant lures on a recognition test and, thus, have a good chance of guessing (or perhaps genuinely recognizing) the answers. In low-familiarity domains, (Indonesian history, say) such a strategy is less likely to produce favorable results, and so it would be wise to assign low feeling-of-knowing ratings. Furthermore, if the locus of the correlation between feeling-of-knowing judgments and target-recognition accuracy is attributable to a correlation between cue familiarity and target familiarity in the world, then one would expect this correspondence to be much less pronounced in cases of new learning, and it is (Metcalfe et al., 1993; Schwartz & Metcalfe, 1992).

3. The Accessibility Account

Recently, Koriat (1993, 1994) proposed a third theory of feeling-of-knowing judgments that he dubbed the accessibility heuristic. This heuristic resembles the target-retrievability hypothesis insofar as the subjects are assumed to base their judgments on retrieved information, not on the mere familiarity of the cue. However, Koriat makes the important point that much of the time subjects do not know whether the information they retrieve is correct or incorrect. Thus, according to the accessibility heuristic, the feeling-of-knowing judgment is a direct function of *all* of the information retrieved. Furthermore, individual elements of that information may be weighted by their speed of access. For example, because fast access presumably indicates strong or good information that is likely to be correct, such retrieved information is assigned a higher feeling-of-knowing rating in the theory. Slower access is presumably a marker of less good information; thus, such information is assigned a lower value.

To illustrate this view and why the positive feeling-of-knowing correlation results, Koriat performed an experiment in which subjects were given four unrelated consonants to remember. After a short distractor, they were asked to recall as many of the four as possible and to give a feeling-of-knowing judgment assessing the probability that they would be able to choose the correct string of four letters in a multiple-choice test. The multiple-choice test was constructed such that, if one knew no letters, one would have to guess (and the guessing probability was explicitly stated to the subject); if one knew one letter, half of the alternatives could be eliminated; with two letters, the remaining alternatives could be halved again; and so on. Feeling-of-knowing ratings increased with the amount of partial information (i.e., the number of letters) subjects were able to retrieve on the first recall test. These ratings, of course, also provided a good predictor of the later recognition performance, as the number of letters recalled would be a very good predictor of how easy it would be to eliminate alternatives on the multiple-choice test.

A number of the predictions of the accessibility heuristic overlap with those of both the target-retrievability and the cue-familiarity hypothesis. One major difference, however, concerns the phenomenology of the judgments. Whereas the accessibility heuristic assumes that the subject makes a very deliberate and calculated assessment of the odds given the situation at hand, the cue-familiarity view assumes that the subject bases his or her rating on a more intuitive *feeling*—more like a hunch than a calculation.

C. Retrospective Judgments

1. Confidence

After subjects have provided a memory response, they are sometimes asked to report on their confidence concerning that answer. This confidence may sometimes be given as a numerical rating, but sometimes, as in witness testimony in court cases, it is conveyed more indirectly by means of the strength of the language and the body language the witness exhibits. Confidence in response is important because it influences both how the rememberer will act on his or her memories, and how believable he or she will be. Lavrakas and Bickman (1975) found that prosecutors value the confidence with which witnesses express their remembrance of the crime perpetrator as the most important aspect of their testimony. In a study (W. M. O'Barr, in Loftus, 1979) in which apparent confidence was manipulated by the strength of the language (weak language being modified by hedges, such as "possibly," "perhaps," "I think,"—to indicate low confidence; and strong language being direct and simple—to indicate high confidence), a mock jury was clearly swayed in favor of the apparently more confident witness. As Loftus (1979) pointed out, and several studies have verified, there is nothing more convincing to a jury than a witness who confidently points a finger and states: "That is the person who did it." Despite our belief in the veridicality of the highly confident remembrances of others, such confidence can sometimes be unwarranted.

Oskamp (1965) conducted a study in which psychiatrists and psychiatric residents were given either a small or a large amount of information about a hypothetical patient. However, the information given (about childhood events, etc.) was nondiagnostic of the situation about which they were asked to make predictions. Nevertheless, the increase in irrelevant information provoked a proportional increase in confidence, despite the chance levels of the performance. Mere exposure to information, regardless of the quality of that information, apparently led to an illusion of knowing and an increase in confidence. Such spurious increases in confidence might also be expected in well-rehearsed witnesses, who have repeated their (possibly false) remembrances many times in preparation for a trial. The halo of confidence that such a witness exudes might well be convincing to a jury.

Weingardt, Leonesio, and Loftus (1994) investigated people's confidence in implanted (incorrect) information. Subjects viewed a crime and then later received the suggestion that some details of the original event were different from what they had originally experienced. They were then given a two–alternative forced–choice recognition test as well as a confidence judgment task for the original detail versus the misleading suggestion. Misled subjects were highly confident about their incorrect responses. In fact, their confidence was sometimes higher on the errors than on the correct responses. The relation between confidence and accuracy that one might intuitively expect (and which is sometimes found, Murdock, 1974) can break down.

Gigerenzer, Hoffrage, and Kleinbolting (1991) have proposed a model to explain why people frequently show overconfidence about their likelihood of successfully answering an individual item, but nevertheless fairly accurately assess the overall probability of success when they are asked how many questions they answered correctly over an entire pool. Gigerenzer et al. propose that people use a combination of what they call local mental models (LMM) and probabilistic mental models (PMM) as the basis for making confidence judgments. To illustrate, suppose that a person were asked to judge his or her confidence about the correctness of his or her answer (say "a") to a question like "Who was the artist who painted 'Afternoon at La Grande Jatte'?" where the possible answers were (a) Seurat, or (b) Monet. The person would first use the LMM, which means that he or she would try to give the direct solution to the problem, or to retrieve the answer directly from memory. If able to do that, he or she would give the answer with 100% confidence. (Errors in direct retrieval contribute to overconfidence.) Failing direct retrieval, the person would then construct a reference class (PMM) from memory—say, the class of all painters, or perhaps the class of all French impressionist painters—and then address cues toward his or her memory that might serve to indicate whether Seurat or Monet would be more likely to have painted this particular work. To the extent that the person is able to retrieve the subsidiary cues that allow inference, and to the extent that he or she feels that these cues are diagnostic and point in the direction of the answer chosen, the person's confidence increases. According to the PMM theory, these are the very same cues that would lead to a particular choice in the first place, so memory performance and confidence should be linked.

From this account, it is somewhat puzzling why overconfidence, rather than plain veridicality, should occur. The answer seems to be that there is a biased sampling of questions in the general information pool that is used in the experiments. Under biased conditions, the person's normal PMM, which might a priori be expected to produce the correct probability or confidence estimate if the sampling were random, produces overconfidence because the experimental sampling is selected to be more difficult than the ordinary sample in memory on which the PMM is constructed. This biased-sampling explanation of the overconfidence effect is, however, controversial. Griffin and Tversky (1992) found overconfidence even under conditions where the exemplars from the reference class (pairs of states of the United States) were selected randomly.

To address the issue of why a person may show overconfidence on the individual judgments, but yet show accuracy if asked how well he or she did on the whole test, Gigerenzer et al. (1991) assume that to assess performance on the entire test the person retrieves the set of all such tests that one has taken as the reference class, then answers with respect to this class. So, if, in the past, one has gotten about 70% correct, one would say 70%. Gigerenzer et al. (1991) gave an example of two friends, both wine tasters, who play a game of bringing one another bottles of wine and guessing the region from which the wine came. The judgment on a particular bottle will be based on the cues presented by the wine, and so these judgments will be made with considerable confidence. However, each knows that the other is not using a random sample, but rather is intentionally trying to trick the other. This knowledge will be taken into account when the friends make a prediction of the frequency of correctness over the course of, say, a year. Thus, the subjective prediction for the entire year will be lower than the average of the individual confidences over the same year. (If the friends were actually using a random sampling of wines, this strategy of taking the supposedly biased nature of the sample into account could result in apparent underconfidence.)

It is clear that the nature of human memory is of fundamental importance in this theory of confidence about one's memory. As Gigerenzer et al. (1991) note: "PMM theory proposes a frequentist interpretation of degrees of belief: Both confidence and frequency judgments are based on memory about frequency." Given the crucial nature of memory for frequency in this theory, it is surprising that the authors do not mention the empirical studies of memory for frequency. Testable predictions would almost certainly result from inclusion of the systematic biases shown in the data about memory for frequency within the theoretical framework. The frequentist theory also hinges critically on people being able to isolate reference domains and retrieve probabilities about the relevance of particular cues in just the manner needed to account for the data. One would, therefore, like to have some independent evidence that people can do this, and, when they do, that the patterns of performance take the form required by the theory. To say that the judgment of confidence in one's memory retrieval is based on how good one's memory retrieval is has a circular feeling, and so evaluation of this theory must await further empirical investigation of the details of the proposed mechanisms.

Griffin and Tversky (1992) presented an alternate theory of confidence, including confidence about one's answers to general information questions. They propose that these judgments are based on (1) the strength or extremity of the available evidence and (2) its weight or credibility. Typically the first of these two factors is overemphasized and the second underemphasized in the judgment. Overconfidence results when the strength of the evidence is high and the weight is low; underconfidence results when the strength is low but the weight is high. Such an analysis can be straightforwardly applied to certain situations, such as confidence concerning judgments about the success of a job applicant based on letters of recommendation. The strength of the evidence is mirrored in the warmth of the letter, whereas the weighting is given by the credibility of the letter writer and the extent of his or her knowledge of the applicant. Typically, Griffin and Tversky argue, the warmth of the letter will be the main factor influencing the judgment, with the credibility of the source contributing insufficiently to the assessment. This means that candidates with very strong letters from people who do not know them very well, or from people who write very strong letters for everyone, will be overly valued. Candidates with only moderately strong letters from people who know them extremely well, or, alternatively, who tend to write devastating letters for most people, will tend to be undervalued. This analysis extends to general information questions by allowing that the salience of the retrieved information relates to the strength (which is primary in determining the judgments), and the diagnosticity of the information relates to the weighting (which is undervalued in the confidence assessment). The theory predicts conditions of overconfidence and underconfidence in a number of situations and in keeping with much data.

2. Hindsight

In addition to overconfidence in the correctness of their responses, people very frequently exhibit a second type of bias in their retrospective judgments. If they are provided with the correct answers, they behave as if they had known these answers all along (Fischhoff, 1975). Furthermore, remembrances of their earlier incorrect answers are biased in the direction of the correct answers. Possibly as a result of hindsight bias, people are unable to reinstate or remember the troubling uncertain state of mind that they experienced prior to solution. After the fact, everything seems easy and obvious, regardless of the difficulties and uncertainty at the time. This bias has an indisputably negative pedagogical impact. Once a problem is solved, it is remembered as being easy. This hindsight bias necessarily results not so much in a lack of sympathy for the struggling problem solver, but a lack of real memory for the difficulties of the process.

IV. COGNITIVE NEUROSCIENCE OF MONITORING AND CONTROL

Converging evidence implicates the frontal lobes as being of critical importance for human metacognition: monitoring, control, and self-reflection. Injury to the prefrontal cortex is sometimes seen to have a devastating effect on this kind of judgment process. This locus of brain damage can also impact on the individual's personality, sense of self, and feelings about the soundness and familiarity of the environment and people in it (Stuss, 1991; Weinberger, Berman, & Daniel, 1991).

Many researchers have characterized frontal lobe damage as critically implicating a breakdown in monitoring and control. For example, Jouandet and Gazzaniga (1979) described the frontal lobes as functioning to guide behavior toward immediate or distant goals. Damasio (1985) argued that the frontal lobes are fundamental for coherent organization, for artistic endeavors, and for the planning of future actions. Norman and Shallice (1986) proposed that the frontal lobes function as a supervisory system, monitoring and controlling nonroutine thought and action.

An example of the kinds of difficulties frontal lobe patients have in problem solving is illustrated by a protocol reported by Luria (1976) of patient Sar, 10 days after surgical removal of a tumor from the left prefrontal cortex. Luria gave him the following problem: "A boy is 5 years old. In 15 years' time his father will be 3 times as old as his son. How old is the father now?" The patient replies:

> "How old is the father now . . . well that is an easy calculation. The 5-year-old lad will be big, he is growing, and he will catch up to his father. But after 15 years he will be 20 . . . how much older will the father be than his son? Let's work it out. It is of course a simple calculation . . . the son is 5 years old . . . the father . . . in 15 years' time he will be 20! This problem is solved. How old is the father now?" L: "Do you mean to say that in 15 years the father will be 20?" S: "No, the son . . . the son will then . . . now let us calculate . . . evidently a minimum of 20 years. Everything goes normally but I simply make mistakes in my plan . . . the son is now 5 years old. The father's age we don't know . . . when I add 15 years that makes the son 20 years old . . . presumably the same thing happens to the father, and so when I start to work it out I see that the minimum for the father is 25 years . . . and why not, he could have married at 18 years . . . he could have done so . . . but then the position is complicated because he could not have done so under certain conditions of life if he had married later. But suppose he married later, we then have to consider how old the father was when the son was 5." L: "Well solve it!" S: "Well, the son is 5 years old . . . in 15 years' time . . . when 15 years has gone past—the son will be 20 . . . what we want to know is, how much longer will the father have to live when the son is 15 years older . . . then the father must calculate how many years . . . how many? 15 years— that's a long time . . . if the son is 20 years old we have another question, how long can the father calculate in a day . . . and he might have married at 18 years and at 20 years of age."
>
> *(Luria, 1976, p. 324)*

A frontal deficit of metacognition is also seen in paradigms other than problem solving. Frontal lobe impairments are thought to be implicated in Korsakoff amnesia (a form of memory deficit resulting from thiamine deficiency associated with alcohol abuse). Shimamura and Squire (1986) tested several groups of amnesic and nonamnesic patients using variants of the classic RJR paradigm. Feeling-of-knowing predictions were correlated with later recognition using the standard gamma correlations. When the original level of memory performance was equated, only the Korsakoff amnesics, but not other kinds of amnesics (such as those with impaired memory resulting from electroconvulsive therapy), showed a deficit in their meta-cognitions. Other patients may have had poor memory, but even so, they knew what they would know and what they would not know. The Korsakoff patients' predictive accuracy, in contrast, was close to zero. The selectivity of the result argues against theories claiming that the metacognitive judgments rely on memory retrieval, or that metamemory is secondary to basic memory. Because the memory impairments were dissociable from the metamemory performance, different, though possibly interacting, systems are implicated for the two functions.

Janowsky, Shimamura, and Squire (1989) extended these findings by investigating metamemory processes with pure frontal patients who suffered no medial-temporal damage or diencephalic damage associated with memory impairments. Unfortunately, their sample included only seven patients, three of whom had right frontal damage and, thus, a priori might not be expected to show any impairments on a verbal task. Nevertheless, a small selective deficit on the feeling-of-knowing task was shown by this group, when the criterion task was given at a delay. Because these patients were free of memory deficits, it would appear that memory and monitoring of memory are distinct processes.

Frontal patients do sometimes show memory impairments, however. The deficits are considered by most researchers to be distinct from those exhibited in temporal lobe amnesias. In particular, the deficits of frontal patients seem to be secondary to organizational impairments, to confabulation, to capture by distractions, and to temporal transpositions. It is tempting to speculate that these memory impairments are secondary to monitoring and control deficits, rather than to a failure of a basic storage and retrieval system. Organizational and strategic processes are, of course, fundamental to optimal high-level memory performance, and they, in turn, depend on strategic control processes. But perhaps strategically based metalevel deficits can and should be separated from more basic-level processes of trace storage and retrieval. Frontal lobe patients often do well at simple memory tasks, such as recognition and paired-associate learning. These same patients may fail at story recall and comprehension—preseverating over particular story elements sometimes in an echolalic manner, losing track of order, intruding events from outside the story line, seeming to fail at keeping track of their output, or at monitoring and controlling their remembrances.

Luria (1976) gave an example of what he called a disturbance of "goal-directed activity," or what we might call monitoring and control, in the immediate recall of a story, "The Lion and the Mouse," by bilateral frontal patient Kork. The story was:

> "A lion was asleep and a mouse ran over his body. The lion awoke and caught the mouse. The mouse begged him to let her go. The lion laughed and let her go. Next day, a hunter caught the lion and tied him with a rope to a tree. The mouse came up stealthily, gnawed through the rope, and set the lion free."

Kork's immediate repetition of this was:

> "A few days later the mouse saw . . . that the mouse had fallen into a net set by the hunter . . . she ran to . . . (looks at the tape recorder) recognizes the telephone number that she must dial . . . (looks at the bed) so as to put the hunter on the same bed . . . well the mouse recognized this telephone number and chased the hunter away . . .". L: "Have you finished?" K: "No, I shall soon . . . it takes a little time . . . the mouse of course thinks, I must be quick and set free . . . the mouse . . . I must set the hunter free quickly . . . from prison . . . and so . . . some time passes . . . he thinks . . . Aha, I must set him free quickly . . . and so . . . some time passes . . . etc. etc."
>
> *(p. 339)*

V. CONCLUSION

From the intensive research that has been devoted to metacognition over the past 10 years, certain areas of consensus have emerged. First, it appears that people's metacognitions provide the basis for action. People's metacognitions as to whether they are approaching solution in problem solving guides the course of the process. The feeling that the person will know the answer to a memory question in the future motivates the person to attempt the retrieval. The judgment that a skill has been learned releases the person to go to a concert or engage in some other activity rather than persist further with the learning of the skill. The expression of confidence in one's remembrances is convincing to oneself and to one's peers concerning the veridicality of the remembrance. Given that people do believe and act on their metacognitions, the question arises as to whether these judgments result from privileged access to one's future knowledge states, implying that such trust in these states in invariably justified.

A negative answer to the question of privileged access is emerging. Instead, metacognitive judgments appear to be heuristically determined. The precise nature of the heuristics serving as the basis for various judgments is being hotly debated. Examples of some of the heuristics are the accessibility heuristic and the cue-familiarity heuristic in feeling-of-knowing judgments, the ease of access heuristic in judgments of learning, and the representativeness heuristic in confidence judgments. The study of heuristics leads in a natural way to investigation of the errors and systematic biases, not only because the nature of errors allows the testing of predictions based on the heuristics, but also because these investigations pinpoint areas where psychologists are likely to be able to make a real contribution to the educating of these critical introspections. But this emphasis on the errors and biases, while natural, given the current theoretical perspective, may distract us from appreciating the fact that these metacognitions, regardless of their mechanistic basis, are often good predictors of later performance and provide a useful, if sometimes imperfect, guide for our cognitive behavior.

Such an appreciation of the positive repercussions of normal human metacognition is inescapable upon examination of frontal lobe patients who appear to suffer a breakdown of these supervisory/metacognitive functions. These patients, while often exhibiting intact basic-level cognitive skills, lack the ability to plan and to carry out a plan if one is given to them. They lack the ability to monitor and control their actions and their cognitions. The difficulties of these patients, both in the lab and in their daily lives, underline the importance of our normal metacognitive abilities. Even given a high level of cognitive abilities, intact memory storage and retention, intact IQ as measured by a variety of tests, adequate basic-level computational skills, and unimpaired perception, the patient who has lost these most central metacognitive abilities and the attendant goal directedness does, indeed, appear to drift about like a rudderless ship. The irony is that often, though not always, such patients are unaware of their loss.

Acknowledgment

This research was supported by National Institute of Mental Health Grant MH48066 and by a grant from the James S. McDonnell Foundation to the author.

References

Baddeley, A. D., & Longman, D. J. A. (1978). The influence of length and frequency of training session on the rate of learning to type. *Ergonomics, 21,* 627–635.

Bahrick, H. P. (1979). Maintenance of knowledge: Questions about memory we forgot to ask. *Journal of Experimental Psychology: General, 108,* 296–308.

Bjork, R. A. (1994). Memory and metamemory considerations in the training of human beings. In J. Metcalfe & A. P. Shimamura (Eds.), *Metacognition: Knowing about knowing* (pp. 185–206). Cambridge: MIT Press.

Blake, M. (1973). Prediction of recognition when recall fails: Exploring the feeling-of-knowing phenomenon. *Journal of Verbal Learning and Verbal Behavior, 12,* 311–319.

Bowers, K. S., Regehr, G., Balthazard, C. G., & Parker, K. (1990). Intuition in the context of discovery. *Cognitive Psychology, 22,* 72–110.

Brown, A. S. (1991). A review of the tip of the tongue experience. *Psychological Bulletin, 109,* 204–223.

Brown, R., & McNeill, D. (1966). The "tip-of-the-tongue" phenomenon. *Journal of Verbal Learning and Verbal Behavior, 5,* 325–337.

Burke, D., MacKay, D. G., Worthley, J. S., & Wade, E. (1991). On the tip of the tongue: What causes word finding failures in young and older adults? *Journal of Memory and Language, 30,* 542–579.

Damasio, A. R. (1985). The frontal lobes. In K. M. Heilman & E. Valenstein (Eds.), *Clinical neuropsychology* (2nd edition). New York: Oxford University Press.

Dempster, F. N. (1990). The spacing effect: A case study in the failure to apply the results of psychological research. *American Psychologist, 43,* 627–634.

Dunlosky, J., & Nelson, T. O. (1992). Importance of the kind of cue for judgments of learning (JOL) and the delayed-JOL effect. *Memory & Cognition, 20,* 374–380.

Ericsson, K. A., & Simon, H. A. (1984). *Protocol analysis: Verbal reports as data.* Cambridge: MIT Press.

Fahlman, S. E. (1974). A planning system for robot construction tasks. *Artificial Intelligence, 5,* 1–49.

Fischhoff, B. (1975). Hindsight is not equal to foresight: The effects of outcome knowledge on judgment under uncertainty. *Journal of Experimental Psychology: Human Perception and Performance, 1,* 288–299.

Gigerenzer, G., Hoffrage, U., & Kleinbolting, H. (1991). Probabilistic mental models: A Brunswickian theory of confidence. *Psychological Review, 98,* 506–528.

Glenberg, A. M. (1992). Distributed practice effects. In L. R. Squire (Ed.), *Encyclopedia of learning and memory* (pp. 138–142) New York: Macmillan.

Glenberg, A. M., Wilkinson, A. C., & Epstein, W. (1982). The illusion of knowing: Failure in the self-assessment of comprehension. *Memory & Cognition, 10,* 597–602.

Griffin, D., & Tversky, A. (1992). The weighing of evidence and the determinants of confidence. *Cognitive Psychology, 24,* 411–435.

Gruneberg, M. M., & Monks, J. (1974). Feeling of knowing and cued recall. *Acta Psychologica, 38,* 257–265.

Hart, J. T. (1965). Memory and the feeling-of-knowing experience. *Journal of Educational Psychology, 56,* 208–216.

Hart, J. T. (1967). Memory and the memory-monitoring process. *Journal of Verbal Learning and Verbal Behavior, 6,* 685–691.

Jacoby, L. L., Bjork, R. A., & Kelley, C. M. (1994). Illusions of comprehensions and competence. In D. Druckman & R. A. Bjork (Eds.), *Enhancing human performance III* (pp. 57–80). Washington, DC: National Academy Press.

Jacoby, L. L., & Kelley, C. M. (1987). Unconscious influences of memory for a prior event. *Personality and Social Psychology Bulletin, 13,* 314–336.

Jameson, K. A., Narens, L., Goldfarb, K., & Nelson, T. O. (1990). The influence of near-threshold priming on metamemory and recall. *Acta Psychologica, 73,* 55–68.

Janowsky, J. S., Shimamura, A. P., & Squire, L. R. (1989). Memory and metamemory: Comparisons between frontal lobe lesion and amnesic patients. *Psychobiology, 17,* 3–11.

Jouandet, M., & Gazzaniga, M. S. (1979). The frontal lobes. In M. S. Gazzaniga (Ed.), *Handbook of behavioral neurobiology* (pp. 25–60). New York: Plenum Press.

Kelley, C. M., & Lindsay, D. S. (1993). Remembering mistaken for knowing: Ease of retrieval as a basis for confidence in answers to general knowledge questions. *Journal of Memory and Language, 32,* 1–24.

Koriat, A. (1993). How do we know what we know? The accessibility model of feeling of knowing. *Psychological Review, 100,* 609–639.

Koriat, A. (1994). Memory's knowledge of its own knowledge: The accessibility account of the feeling of knowing. In J. Metcalfe & A. P. Shimamura (Eds.), *Metacognition: Knowing about knowing* (pp. 115–135). Cambridge: MIT Press.

Koriat, A., & Lieblich, I. (1974). What does a person in a "TOT" state know that a person in a "don't know" state doesn't know. *Memory & Cognition, 2,* 647–655.

Laird, J., Newell, A., & Rosenbloom, P. (1987). SOAR: An architecture for general intelligence. *Artificial Intelligence, 33,* 1–64.

Lavrakas, P. J., & Bickman, L. (1975) *What make a good witness?* Paper presented at the meeting of the American Psychological Association, Chicago. Reported in Loftus (1979).

Leonesio, R. J., & Nelson, T. O. (1990). Do different metamemory judgments tap the same underlying aspects of memory. *Journal of Experimental Psychology: Learning, Memory, and Cognition, 16,* 464–470.

Loftus, E. F. (1979). *Eyewitness testimony.* Cambridge: Harvard University Press.

Lupker, S. J., Harbluk, J. L., & Patrick, A. S. (1991). Memory for things forgotten. *Journal of Experimental Psychology: Learning, Memory, and Cognition, 17,* 897–907.

Luria, A. R. (1976). *The neuropsychology of memory.* Washington, D.C.: Winston.

MacKay, D. G. (1982). The problems of flexibility, fluency, and speed-accuracy trade-off in skilled behavior. *Psychological Review, 89,* 483–506.

Metcalfe, J. (1986a). Feeling of knowing in memory and problem solving. *Journal of Experimental psychology: Learning, Memory, and Cognition, 12,* 288–294.

Metcalfe, J. (1986b). Premonitions of insight predict impending error. *Journal of Experimental Psychology: Learning, Memory, and Cognition, 12,* 623–634.

Metcalfe, J. (1990). Composite holographic associative recall model (CHARM) and blended memories in eyewitness testimony. *Journal of Experimental Psychology: General, 119* 145–160.

Metcalfe, J. (1991). Recognition failure and the composite memory trace in CHARM. *Psychological Review, 98,* 529–553.

Metcalfe, J. (1993a) Novelty monitoring, metacognition and control in a composite holographic associative recall model: Implications for Korsakoff amnesia. *Psychological Review, 100,* 3–22.

Metcalfe, J. (1993b). Monitoring and gain control in an episodic memory model: Relation to P300 event-related potentials. In A. Collins, M. Conway, S. Gathercole, & P. Morris (Eds.), *Theories of memory* (pp. 327–354). Hillsdale, NJ: Erlbaum.

Metcalfe, J., Schwartz, B. L., & Joaquim, S. G. (1993). The cue familiarity heuristic in metacognition. *Journal of Experimental Psychology: Learning, Memory, and Cognition, 19,* 851–861.

Metcalfe, J., & Wiebe, D. (1987). Intuition in insight and non-insight problem solving. *Memory & Cognition, 15,* 238–246.

Metcalfe Eich, J. (1982). A composite holographic associative recall model. *Psychological Review, 89,* 627–661.

Miner, A. C., & Reder, L. M. (1994). A new look at feeling of knowing: its metacognitive role in regulating question answering. In J. Metcalfe & A. P. Shimamura (Eds.), *Metacognition: Knowing about knowing.* (pp. 47–70). Cambridge: MIT Press.

Murdock, B. B., Jr. (1974). *Human memory: Theory and data.* Potomac, MD: Erlbaum.

Narens, L., Jameson, K. A., & Lee, V. A. (1994). Subthreshold priming and memory monitoring. In J. Metcalfe & A. P. Shimamura (Eds.), *Metacognition: Knowing about knowing* (pp. 71–92). Cambridge: MIT Press.

Nelson, T. O., Leonesio, R. J., Shimamura, A. P., Landwehr, R. S., & Narens, L. (1982). Overlearning and the feeling of knowing. *Journal of Experimental Psychology: Learning, Memory, and Cognition, 8,* 279–288.

Nelson, T. O., & Narens, L. (1980). A new technique for investigating the feeling of knowing. *Acta Psychologica, 46,* 69–90.

Nelson, T. O., & Narens, L. (1994). Why investigate metacognition? In J. Metcalfe & A. P. Shimamura (Eds.), *Metacognition: Knowing about knowing* (pp. 1–26). Cambridge: MIT Press.

Newell, A., & Simon, H. A. (1972). *Human problem solving.* Englewood Cliffs, NJ: Prentice-Hall.

Norman, D., & Shallice, T. (1986). Attention to action: Willed and automatic control of behavior. In R. J. Davidson, G. E. Schwartz, & D. Shapiro (Eds.), *Consciousness and self-regulation* (Vol. 4). New York: Plenum Press.

Oskamp, S. (1965). Overconfidence in case-study judgments. *Journal of Consulting Psychology, 29,* 261–265.

Plato (1984). *Great dialogues of Plato* (W. H. D. Rouse, Trans.; E. H. Warming & P. G. Rouse, Eds.). New York: Mentor, Penguin Books.

Polanyi, M. (1962). *Personal knowledge.* Chicago: University of Chicago Press.

Reder, L. M. (1987). Strategy selection in question answering. *Cognitive Psychology, 19,* 90–138.

Reder, L. M., & Ritter, F. E. (1992). What determines initial feeling of knowing? Familiarity with question terms, not with the answer. *Journal of Experimental Psychology: Learning, Memory, and Cognition, 18,* 435–452.

Schacter, D. L. (1983). Feeling of knowing in episodic memory. *Journal of Experimental Psychology; Learning, Memory, and Cognition, 9,* 39–54.

Schacter, D. L., & Worling, J. R. (1985). Attribute information and the feeling of knowing. *Canadian Journal of Psychology, 39,* 467–475.

Schwartz, B. L., & Metcalfe, J. (1992). Cue familiarity but not target retrievability enhances feeling-of-knowing judgments. *Journal of Experimental Psychology: Learning, Memory, and Cognition, 18,* 1074–1083.

Shimamura, A. P., & Squire, L. R. (1986). Memory and metamemory: A study of the feeling-of-knowing phenomenon in amnesic patients. *Journal of Experimental Psychology: Learning, Memory, and Cognition, 12,* 452–460.

Simon, H. A. (1979). *Models of thought.* New Haven, CT: Yale University Press.

Simon, H. A., & Reed, S. K. (1976). Modeling strategy shifts in a problem-solving task. *Cognitive Psychology, 8,* 86–97.

Slamecka, N. J., & Graf, P. (1978). The generation effect: Delineation of a phenomenon. *Journal of Experimental Psychology: Human Learning and Memory, 4,* 592–604.

Smith, S. M. (1994). Frustrated feelings of imminent recall: On the tip of the tongue. In J. Metcalfe & A. P. Shimamura (Eds.), *Metacognition: Knowing about knowing* (pp. 27–46). Cambridge: MIT Press.

Smith, S. M. (1995). Getting into and out of mental ruts: A theory of fixation, incubation, and insight. In R. Sternberg & J. Davidson (Eds.), *The nature of insight* (pp. 229–252). Cambridge: MIT Press.

Spellman, B. A., & Bjork, R. A. (1992). When predictions create reality: Judgments of learning may alter what they are intended to assess. *Psychological Science, 3,* 315–316.

Stuss, D. T. (1991). Disturbance of self awareness after frontal system damage. In G. P. Prigatano & D. L. Schacter (Eds.), *Awareness of deficit after brain injury* (pp. 63–83). New York: Oxford University Press.

Sussman, G. J. (1975). *A computational model of skill acquisition.* New York: Elsevier.

Wallas, G. (1926). *The art of thought.* New York: Harcourt Brace.

Weinberger, D. R., Berman, K. F., & Daniel, D. G. (1991). Prefrontal cortex dysfunction in schizophrenia. In H. S. Levin, H. M. Eisenberg, & A. L. Benton (Eds.), *Frontal lobe function and dysfunction* (pp. 275–287). New York: Oxford University Press.

Weingardt, K. R., Leonesio, R. J., & Loftus, E. L. (1994). Viewing eyewitness research from a metacognitive perspective. In J. Metcalfe & A. P. Shimamura (Eds.), *Metacognition: Knowing about knowing* (pp. 157–184). Cambridge: MIT Press.

Yates, J. F. (1990). *Judgment and decision-making.* Englewood Cliffs, NJ: Prentice-Hall.

Differences across Individuals

CHAPTER 12

Individual Differences in Memory

Douglas A. Bors
Colin M. MacLeod

Outside of our laboratories we will all admit to—indeed, sometimes even marvel at—the striking differences in memory that exist among people. Within the "normal" range, we are impressed when a friend remembers all of the lyrics to a song or knows the answers to a wide variety of trivia questions. With respect to more exceptional individuals, we find it difficult to imagine what it would be like to be learning disabled and unable to recall a phone number, or to be a mnemonist who can remember hundreds of names after a brief round of introductions. If not always this dramatic, individual differences in memory are still always important.

> We cannot possibly have a good theory of the processes involved in remembering, either in a short-term or a long-term sense, unless we have procedures for assessing the status and change of such processes within individuals. As long as we throw possible within-individual and between-individual differences together in a measurement, we have no way to think clearly about the effects of variables in experiments . . . the sooner our experiments on human memory and human learning consider the differences between individuals in our experimental analyses of component processes in memory and learning, the sooner we will have theories and experiments that have some substantial probability of reflecting the fundamental characteristics of those processes.
>
> *(Melton, 1967, pp. 249–250)*

Time and again, psychologists have called for a greater integration of individual differences into the development of our research and theorizing about psychological processes (Cronbach, 1957; Sargent, 1942). Although this request may have been made less often in the field of memory, it nevertheless has been made forcefully on occasion (Melton, 1967; Underwood, 1975). Techniques have even been proposed to decipher individual differences within experiments (Battig, 1979; Kareev, 1982), so that experimental psychologists will not have to calculate the dreaded correlation coefficient. Yet, rarely do cognitive psychologists examine or even consider individual differences, unless those differences are so obvious that they can no longer be treated as "error variance."

In fact, over the last one hundred years or so, a considerable body of work has accumulated relevant to the question of individual differences in memory, particularly over the past twenty-five years. Our goal in this chapter is to survey that work, especially the most recent research, attempting to draw out the basic principles and to demonstrate the relevance of these variations over people to theoretical development in the study of memory. To do so, we have chosen the most obvious organization, the one seen most frequently in introductory and cognitive texts. We first discuss individual differences in working memory and then turn to individual differences that are more related to long-term memory, concluding with a discussion of expertise that ties together many of the ideas in the two larger sections.

This organization is not meant to imply any structural distinction between working memory and long-term memory, though some individual differences work clearly supports such a distinction (Geiselman, Woodward, & Beatty, 1982). Rather, in addition to providing a convenient way to divide the labor between co-authors, it reflects the fact that there are two main ways to study individual differences. First, one can attempt to relate some intellectual ability measure (a test) to some cognitive process measure (a task), hopefully with the goal of evaluating a theory. This has been called the "cognitive correlates" approach (Pellegrino & Glaser, 1979). Second, one can delve into a cognitive task, attempting to identify different ways that different subjects perform that task, hopefully to shed light on the basic processes beneath. This has been labeled the "cognitive components" approach. In writing this chapter, we noticed an interesting feature of the work on individual differences in memory: The research on working memory largely uses the correlates approach, whereas the research on long-term memory primarily relies on the components approach. Thus, this distinction provided an additional rationale for our chosen organization. We begin, then, with working memory.

I. WORKING MEMORY

Although the architecture of memory was conceptualized differently at the time, interest in individual differences in working memory goes back over one hundred years. Because it is impossible to be fully comprehensive and to do justice to the entire corpus in any one review, we have restricted ourselves to three realms of research that reflect the field's theoretical development in the area of working memory: memory span, information processing tasks, and working memory capacity.

A. Memory Span

Ebbinghaus (1885/1913) discovered that he could reliably learn to repeat in order lists of up to seven nonsense syllables after only a single study period, whereas lists of greater lengths required repeated exposures. From Ebbinghaus's pioneering serial learning experiments emerged a task initially called mental span, then later referred to as memory span. Surprisingly, despite continuing research interest, our understanding of performance on this modest task is still far from complete. In a standard forward memory span experiment, subjects are presented with a list of verbal items (typically from three to nine digits or letters) and then are immediately asked to recall the items in their presented order. Quite quickly, a more difficult modified version of the task was produced: Backward memory span required subjects to recall the items in reverse order of presentation. Though some researchers have varied the display of the stimuli, the form of the required response, or the method of scoring, the task has remained essentially the same over the past century.

Almost immediately, researchers began pursuing the question of whether memory span was connected to other individual differences in cognitive performance, usually more global measures of aptitude and achievement. Investigations, such as that of Jacobs (1887), found the forward memory spans of both boys and girls in the top of their classes to be greater than those of their cohorts at the bottom. Others found the memory spans of "idiots" (mentally retarded) to be inferior to those of normals (Galton, 1887). Pondering such findings, Oliver Wendell Holmes (1871) was one of the first to speculate on the implications, referring to memory span as a simple mental "dynamometer" that could have applications in education. Burnham (1888–1889), in one of the early reviews of research on memory, proposed that memory span "should be used as a test for cerebral fatigue" (p. 609) and called for investigation into the links between memory performance and general intellectual powers.

This early work did not go unnoticed by those occupied with constructing the first intelligence (IQ) tests. The memory span task was understood to be indexing a simple yet central ability. Thus, Binet and Henri (1895) held that it assessed an important individual difference fundamental to other higher order abilities. Since Binet developed his first instrument for identifying children who would not benefit from standard instruction, memory span has remained a constituent of most individual tests of intelligence and mental status exams. And even as recently as 1977, Bachelder and Denny suggested constructing a general model of intelligence with memory span as the cornerstone. Its historical popularity has no doubt been based on the fact that it is uncomplicated to administer, simple to score, and easy to understand—or so it has been assumed.

Blankenship's (1938) review of the memory span literature highlighted several findings pertinent to individual differences. Critical for any task regarded to be a measure of individual difference is its stability. Blankenship's review of reported reliabilities revealed that the coefficients for six visual digit-span studies ranged from .68 to .93 and the coefficients for six auditory digit-span studies ranged from .28 to .80, leading him to conclude that "the test is one that shows surprisingly high reliability" (p. 7). When he examined memory span's relation to IQ, however, what he discovered was quite startling. The four correlations he found between forward digit-span and measures of intelligence (.03, .21, .16, and .18) clearly were less impressive than what would have been expected in light of the earlier studies and the weight Binet and others had put on the task. In contrast, the single study of reverse memory span that he reviewed produced a correlation of .75 with intelligence. In terms of sex differences, Blankenship located nine studies reporting the superiority of females on various memory span tasks, six studies reporting no differences between males and females, and five studies reporting some superiority of males on the task. Understandingly, he concluded that no judgment concerning sex differences in memory span could be made.

More recently, Miller and Vernon (1992) reported forward digit-span split-half reliability coefficients of .75 (auditory) and .66 (visual) and forward letter-span reliability coefficients of .26 (auditory) and .73 (visual). They assumed that the low reliability for the auditory forward letter-span task was connected to the fact that several of the letters used in the test were phonetically similar, thus producing interference. Roznowski (1993) found moderate test–retest reliability coefficients for both forward (.44) and backward (.50) digit spans.

Further research regarding reliability has also supported the belief that individual differences in memory span are consistent across stimulus materials and sensory modalities. Brener (1940) found that subjects whose memory spans were the longest for visually presented material tended to be those who had the longest spans for orally presented material as well. He also found that those subjects who performed well on memory span tasks with digits also performed well on tasks with letters, patches of color, words, and common geometrical shapes. Jensen (1971) affirmed the reliability of memory span across sensory modalities. He reported a strong relation between performances on visually and orally presented material (digits), and asserted that the two conditions were perfectly related when the correlations were corrected for attenuation. A factor-analytic study conducted by MacKenzie (1972) provided confirmation for the across-material reliability. Others have reported significant correlations between memory span tasks using digits and words (Cantor, Engle, & Hamilton, 1991) and between tasks using letters and words (Palmer, MacLeod, Hunt, & Davidson, 1985). But the idea that there is a single important process or mechanism that dominates performance on all types of memory span tasks has been challenged somewhat in a recent study by Miller and Vernon (1992). Although they found a matrix of positive correlations among the forward digit- and letter-span tasks presented both orally and visually, the strength of the coefficients was notably less impressive than those found in the referenced studies presented earlier. The within-modality but across-material correlations were .40 and .42; the within-material but across-modality correlations were .30 and .11; and the across-modality and across-material correlations were .19 and .17.

The latest version of the WAIS-R, presently the most popular IQ test, corroborated the relations between tests of memory span, other tests of cognitive abilities, and overall IQ. Of central importance, research on the WAIS-R again demonstrated that memory span (Digit Span) was a reliable measure of individual differences. The test–retest reliability coefficients across adult age groups ranged from .70 (ages 16–17) to .89 (ages 25–34), with an average of .83 (Wechsler, 1981, p. 30). Additionally, Digit Span was moderately correlated with the other subtests ($r = .43$) and with overall Full Scale scores (.58). One reason for the higher correlations between digit span and intelligence (Full Scale score) in comparison to the studies reviewed by Blankenship may be the fact that the Digit Span score on the WAIS-R is based on the subject's performance on both forward and backward digit-span tasks.

There is also evidence, however, challenging the long-held belief that memory span is of fundamental importance, or that it is at least predictive of psychometric measures of aptitude and achievement. For example, Rohwer (1967) failed to find a significant difference in digit span between two groups of children whose mean IQ differed by 18 points. Correlations between a modified version of forward digit span and Scholastic Aptitude Test (SAT) scores were found by Chiang and Atkinson (1976) to be near zero. In his commentary on the WAIS, Matarazzo (1972) concluded that memory span, as administered on the WAIS-R, although a useful diagnostic instrument for certain forms of organic disorder and mental impairment, is a poor measure of intelligence (p. 204). In his opinion, what justified the retention of digit span on the WAIS was its power to differentiate at lower levels of intelligence. Recently, Miller and Vernon (1992) correlated aural and visual forward memory span (digit and letters) tests with the ten subsets of the Multidimensional Aptitude Battery (MAB). The 40 coefficients ranged from −.02 to .27 with a mean of .12. Still other researchers have reported mixed results. Palmer et al. (1985) found memory span (words) to be moderately correlated with both the Nelson–Denny (reading comprehension) test (.44) and IQ (.24), whereas the correlations between memory span (letters) and the two tests were considerably smaller, .17 (Nelson–Denny) and .09 (IQ).

Other researchers continue to report substantial correlations between memory span tasks and tests of aptitude or achievement. For example, Jensen and Figueroa (1975) found both forward and especially backward digit span to be correlated with IQ. Dempster and Cooney (1982) reported two experiments where memory span correlated with assorted measures of aptitude and achievement. Digit span correlated positively with SAT scores ($r = .65$) and with College Entrance Examination Boards tests ($r = .68$). In neither experiment, however, did digit span correlate significantly with the Nelson–Denny Reading Rate Test. Yet the Nelson–Denny Vocabulary Test was significantly correlated with memory span in both experiments (.66). Finally, to further muddle the picture, whereas the correlation between memory span and the Nelson–Denny Reading Comprehension Test was nonsignificant in the first experiment (.30), it was significant in the second (.50).

Recent research does little to clear things up. Cantor et al. (1991) found memory span for words (.35), but not memory span for digits (.04), to be significantly correlated with the Scholastic Aptitude Tests (Verbal). In a test–retest study, Roznowski (1993) reported small to moderate (but significant) correlations between forward and backward digit-span tasks and scores on the American College Testing Program examination.

Regardless of its relation, or lack thereof, with aptitude and achievement, several explanations for individual differences in memory span itself have been offered. Historically, the most prevalent explanations have focused on the encoding of the stimulus list, contending that memory span reflects an individual's ability to group or *chunk* the individual items in the list (Blankenship, 1938; Estes, 1974; Hunt & Lansman, 1975). Although there are numerous data demonstrating that these and other strategic variables affect memory span performance, there is evidence that calls into question their role as sources of individual differences. A study by Lyon (1977) has been influential in this regard. In the first experiment, subjects were tested at two different rates of item presentation: 1/s (standard rate) and 3/s. At a rate of 3/s, subjects have sufficient time to recognize the digit and generate its linguistic code, but, unlike in the 1/s condition, there is not enough time to rehearse preceding items. If individual differences in memory span are the result of rehearsal or chunking strategies, then performance on the task with the faster rate of presentation should be a poor predictor of performance on the task at the standard rate. Lyon (1977, p. 406) found, however, that the correlation between performances on the two tasks was .82 (.95 when corrected for attenuation), indicating that individual differences are probably based on other factors.

In the second experiment, in addition to being tested again in the standard condition, Lyon presented subjects with the items temporally grouped by threes and told them to chunk the items into three-digit numbers (e.g., four hundred twenty-seven). If grouping and chunking are responsible for the individual differences, then a task where these variables were held constant should be unrelated to performance in the standard condition. The .85 correlation between these two conditions again suggested that other factors are responsible for individual differences. Additionally, a study by Dempster and Zinkgraf (1982), where degree of chunking was indexed by the serial position of errors, supported Lyon's conclusion by finding no significant correlations between chunking and memory span.

Reflecting theoretical developments that accompanied the cognitive revolution, other explanations for the individual differences in memory span have stressed the subject's ability to identify items (Huttenlocher & Burke, 1976) or proficiency at encoding the order of items (Martin, 1978). Hoping to narrow the field of suspects, Dempster (1981) carried out an extensive review of the relevant literature. Like others, he also concluded that— although strategic variables such as rehearsal, grouping, and chunking influence performance and are related to age—it has not been convincingly demonstrated that any of these strategic factors are responsible for within-age individual differences in memory span. In his opinion, item ordering and, in particular, item identification were good candidates as possible sources of individual differences in memory span. In support of the item-identification hypothesis, Dempster pointed to research revealing a relation between how quickly subjects could name items of particular type (digits or letters) and the average memory span. For example, digits are named faster than words and yield greater average memory spans than do words; words are named faster than pictures and yield greater average memory spans than do pictures (Mackworth, 1963). No one, however, appears to have reported a within-material correlation between naming speed and memory span.

In summary, with respect to individual differences, memory span has received immense attention, far more than any other memory task. We can safely say that there is a reliably identified common factor relating memory span tasks across both sensory modalities and stimulus material. Furthermore, there are established individual differences in this factor that are at least moderately stable. Yet, the nature of this factor remains undetermined. The historically popular explanations for these individual differences are at best questionable, and the more recent hypotheses (item ordering and item identification) require further testing before any conclusions can be drawn concerning their veracity. Finally, because of the continuing contradictory character of the empirical findings, we must conclude that memory span's relation to aptitude and achievement remains equivocal.

Before leaving this section, brief mention should be made of a related task, *span of apprehension*. Although the evidence is sparse, the account appears to be analogous to that for memory span. In a span-of-apprehension task, subjects again must immediately recall items in order; however, all items in the list are presented simultaneously for a brief period, usually 100 ms. With respect to reliability, Palmer et al. (1985) reported that span of apprehension for letters correlated with span of apprehension for words (.59). Regarding span of apprehension's relation to aptitude and achievement, they found that scores on the Nelson–Denny (reading comprehension) test correlated .05 and .31 with span of apprehension for letters and words, respectively. Scores on the Raven Progressive Matrices correlated .15 and .17 with the two span-of-apprehension tasks. Finally, with respect to the Palmer et al. study, of note is the fact that memory span and span of apprehension were unrelated. This result suggests that whatever process or mechanism is responsible for the individual differences in memory span apparently is not responsible for the individual differences in span of apprehension, differences that themselves remain to be explained.

B. Information Processing Approaches

With the cognitive revolution of the 1960s and 1970s came the development of a host of information processing paradigms for researching memory. Psychologists concerned with individual differences in aptitude and achievement began employing many of these paradigms in their investigations in what came to be called the "cognitive correlates" approach (Pellegrino & Glaser, 1979). Typically, researchers would correlate performance on these information processing tasks with scores on standardized psychometric tests, in the hope of revealing the basic cognitive processes responsible for the individual differences on the more complex tasks found on tests of aptitude and achievement. Note that some of these information processing tasks are concerned with measuring the movement of information in and out of long-term memory and therefore are discussed in the second half of this chapter.

Some of the first and most ambitious cognitive correlates studies were carried out by Hunt and colleagues (Hunt, Frost, & Lunneborg, 1973; Hunt, Lunneborg, & Lewis, 1975). One of the short-term memory (STM) information processing measures that was thought to be promising was Sternberg's (1966) STM scanning task. Here, a subject is presented with a list of items (the memory set), usually digits or letters. The subject is then asked to determine, as quickly as possible, whether a probe item was in the memory set. The number of items in the memory set is varied from trial to trial, typically ranging from one to seven digits or letters. Error rates usually are very low, so response latency is used as the dependent measure. Latencies have been discovered to be a linear function of the size of the memory set. The slop across memory set sizes (scanning time) has been construed as the time required by a subject to access a single item in STM, which could prove to be implicated in general intelligence or aptitude in specific domains, such as reading comprehension.

Unfortunately, the results have been less than compelling. Although Hunt et al. (1973) did report that the mean scanning time of 8 high-verbal subjects was shorter than the mean scanning time of 8 low-verbal subjects, they failed to find a relation between scanning time and quantitative ability. Chiang and Atkinson (1976) found scanning time to correlate with neither the verbal nor the mathematical portions of the SAT. The findings from more recent studies are somewhat less equivocal. Miller and Vernon (1992) found scanning time to have small but consistently negative correlations ($r = -.12$) with the 10 subtests of the MAB. Similarly, Roznowski (1993) has reported weak negative correlations between scanning time and ACT (composite) scores of $-.15$ on one occasion and $-.07$ with the same subjects on a subsequent occasion. In summary, if scanning time is related to performance on aptitude tests, it likely accounts for only an extremely small proportion of the variance.

Although scanning time may not be a good predictor of individual differences in aptitude and achievement, it has been suggested that there are moderately reliable individual differences in scanning time itself. Chiang and Atkinson (1976), after testing subjects on three consecutive days, found test–retest correlations of .28 (Day 1/Day 2) and .78 (Day 2/Day 3). They concluded that there were reliable individual differences in scanning time, but that a large number of trials were required for stability to be established. In support of Chiang and Atkinson's conclusion. Roznowski and Smith (1993) found moderate to strong correlations among scanning times for different stimulus materials (digits, letters, words, and symbols) over a week. Further, subjects' median latencies were significantly correlated across the two occasions for the four different stimulus materials: numbers (.74), letters (.68), words (.63), and symbols (.51). The important question, however, concerns the stability of the scanning times across occasions. The across-occasion correlations were .05 (numbers), .33 (letters), .21 (words), and .30 (symbols). These test–retest correlations suggest that individual differences in scanning time probably reflect state factors rather than trait differences.

Another, albeit less studied, information processing task has been the visual search task (search). Here, a single item—a digit, letter, or word—is first presented to serve as the target for which the subject must search. This target is then followed by the simultaneous presentation of one to seven items, the set of items through which the subject must search. Subjects indicate, as quickly as possible, whether the search set includes the target. As in the scanning task, the dependent measure is response latency (search time).

Chiang and Atkinson (1976) reported test–retest correlations of .29 (Day 1/Day 2) and .70 (Day 2/Day 3). Again, they concluded that there were reliable individual differences in search time, but that a large number of trials were required to establish stability. The correlations between the slope across search set sizes and SAT scores were mixed: .34 (Verbal) and −.05 (Math). Palmer et al. (1985) found search speed for letters and words to be correlated .07 and .20, respectively, with the Nelson–Denny reading comprehension test. The relation was somewhat stronger with IQ (.28 and .19). Palmer et al. did find, however, that search speed for letters and words was highly correlated (.70).

Another measure investigated in Hunt et al.'s (1973) seminal study was the Brown–Peterson task. In this task, subjects are presented with a consonant trigram (e.g., BXN) and then must count backward for a brief period as a rehearsal-preventing activity. The duration of this number-counting retention interval varies over trials from 1 to 30 s. Hunt et al. (1973) found that subjects with high qualitative abilities demonstrated consistently better performance at all retention intervals, and interpreted this result as suggesting that high-quantitative subjects were more resistant to interference. Earlier, Borkowski (1965) had discovered a greater decline in STM over increasing retention intervals for low-IQ than for high-IQ subjects. His conclusion was that susceptibility to proactive interference is related to IQ. Subsequent studies comparing the performances of retarded and normal subjects have suggested that susceptibility to proactive interference is linked to both reading abilities and IQ (Farnham-Diggory & Gregg, 1975). The obvious question is whether this link applies to individual differences within the "normal" range. In a study of university students, Dempster and Cooney (1982) found that although susceptibility to proactive interference was not predictive of mathematical ability, it was implicated in individual differences in verbal ability, particularly with respect to high-level reading skills (meaning) but not necessarily with low-level skills (knowledge of grammar and rate of decoding).

In summary, research on working memory using the cognitive correlates approach has not yet made the hoped-for impact. The prospect of revealing the basic working memory processes responsible for the individual differences in aptitude and achievement remains just that: a prospect. In fact, researchers operating within a cognitive correlates approach appear to have shifted their attention to working memory capacity, the topic to which we now shift our focus.

C. Working Memory Capacity

Most contemporary approaches to memory distinguish between an STM storage buffer, as exemplified by simple immediate recall tasks such as memory span, and a "mental scratch pad" where processing is carried out (Baddeley, 1986). Working memory (WM) can be seen as this scratch pad, a sort of librarian of the memory system. In a typical WM experiment (Daneman & Carpenter, 1980), subjects read a series of unrelated sentences aloud with the goal of remembering the last word in each sentence (targets). Subjects then recall these targets, with the number correctly recalled deemed to reflect that subject's WM capacity. Over the past decade, a growing number of researchers concerned with individual differences have concentrated their efforts around this paradigm.

Individual differences in WM capacity have been discovered to correlate with various measures of aptitude and achievement. For example, WM capacity has been found to predict performance on problem-solving and abstract-reasoning tasks (Anderson, 1983; Baddeley & Hitch, 1974; Kyllonen & Christal, 1990), to correlate with tests of general intelligence (Daneman & Tardiff, 1987; Larson & Alderton, 1992), and to be implicated in the acquisition of procedural skills (Woltz, 1988). Most frequently, however, WM capacity has been examined with regard to its relation to reading comprehension (Daneman & Carpenter, 1980; Swanson, 1992).

Daneman and Carpenter (1980, 1983) were among the first to articulate a theory explaining the basis of individual differences in WM capacity. They, like Baddeley, considered WM to be the arena where information is processed and the partial or completed products are temporarily stored. Additionally, WM is seen as a "bottleneck," having a limited amount of attentional resources for accomplishing these tasks. Using the WM task just described, Daneman and Carpenter (1980) measured the residual WM capacity the subject had for storage after the processing demands were met. In this and a subsequent study (Daneman & Carpenter, 1983), the number of final target words recalled was found to be positively correlated with scores on the Verbal SAT (.49). Daneman and Carpenter argued that individual differences in processing efficiency were responsible for the correlation between WM capacity and reading comprehension.

A similar position has been advanced by Salthouse (1992). He has contended that individual differences in WM capacity are the result of individual differences in the rates at which subjects activate stored information. In a later study, Carpenter and Just (1989) reported that subjects with large WM capacities spent less time reading the sentences than did subjects with smaller WM capacities. Further, large-capacity subjects spent more time staring at the target words than did subjects with smaller capacities. These findings were viewed as confirmation for the hypothesis that individual differences in processing efficiency were the crucial factor. As pointed out by Engle, Cantor, and Carullo (1992), however, because subjects with larger WM capacities also had higher IQs than did subjects with smaller capacities, it might be that larger capacity subjects more effectively allocated their limited resources; that is, could it be that strategy—not processing speed or efficiency—is responsible for individual differences in WM capacity?

Turner and Engle (1989) demonstrated that the correlation between WM capacity and reading comprehension is not restricted to tasks requiring subjects to read sentences. In addition to the standard sentence-reading condition, they had subjects confirm the products of simple mathematical operations, each followed by a target word. Individual differences in WM capacity resulting from this latter condition correlated equally as well with reading comprehension scores as did individual differences in capacity resulting from the standard procedure. Turner and Engle (1989), along with others (Cantor et al., 1991), interpreted these and similar results as suggesting that individual differences in WM capacity are the product of general capacity differences, rather than the consequence of individual differences in processing efficiency. A vexing additional finding in the Turner and Engle (1989) study was that only WM capacities resulting from moderately difficult processing tasks were significantly correlated with comprehension. This potentially complicating finding is yet to be elucidated.

There has been some suggestion that performance on WM capacity tasks and memory span tasks reflect a single underlying process or mechanism (Engle, Nations, & Cantor, 1990; LaPointe & Engle, 1990). Cantor et al. (1991) reported that memory span (words) and WM capacity (words) were both moderately correlated with SAT (Verbal) scores: .35 and .42, respectively. Contradicting the suggestion of a common process or mechanism, however, was the finding that the two tasks loaded on different factors.

Although there is yet to be a test of the stability of performance on WM capacity tasks, the consistent correlations indicate to us that the task produces reliable individual differences. Unfortunately, as was the case regarding memory span, the source of the individual differences in WM capacity is as yet undetermined. This is also true with respect to the cause for the correlations between WM capacity and reading comprehension and between WM capacity and IQ. We are certain, though, that the WM capacity paradigm will continue to receive attention from psychologists concerned with individual differences.

D. Summary

As we have seen, psychologists have taken great interest in individual differences in working memory. The paradigms used by these investigators have paralleled the theoretical evolution in the field. Moreover, explorations of individual differences in working memory have contributed to that evolution. Furthermore, in our view, converging evidence from both memory span and working memory capacity experiments indicates that the nature of the established individual differences can be captured in a single word: capacity. Presently, priority is being given to locating the source or sources of these capacity differences.

II. LONG-TERM MEMORY

Intuitively, individual differences might seem to be more plausible in working memory than in long-term memory. Seen as the "mental scratch pad" where the rapid manipulation of information is carried out, as well as an early "bottleneck" in the memory system, any variations in working memory ability would have profound implications that would echo throughout the memory system. If working memory is the librarian and long-term memory is the library, then the obvious place to look for differences in efficiency would be in the active entity, the librarian. And we have seen that there are individual differences in working memory, though perhaps not as sweeping nor as dramatic as one might have anticipated. But to continue the analogy, libraries also differ in their contents, organization, and operation. We will now consider whether corresponding variations can be isolated uniquely in long-term memory.

We have organized this half of the chapter along quite familiar lines: encoding, storage, and retrieval. We begin by focusing on how the different amounts and kinds of knowledge that people possess influence their ability to acquire new knowledge. We then move to how that knowledge is organized in long-term memory. From there, we examine the recent work differentiating implicit from explicit remembering. Finally, we turn to how people differ in their ability to retrieve knowledge from long-term memory.

A. Knowledge and Learning

Without question, people differ in the ways they go about acquiring information (Gagné, 1967; Ackerman, Sternberg, & Glaser, 1989). Educational psychologists have invested vast amounts of research effort in studying the different ways people learn (Cronbach & Snow, 1977). There are differences in ability and in approach, as well as in capacity and in knowledge (Resnick & Neches, 1984). Indeed, learning *style* is important: Some learners emphasize overall comprehension and are conclusion oriented, leading them to engage in deep processing; others concentrate on specific details and are description oriented, causing them to do more surface processing (Schmeck, 1983). The implications of such strategies are profound, but we cannot capture that huge literature here. Instead, having provided a few leads to the applied literature, we now highlight studies done within a cognitive, theoretical framework.

1. General Knowledge and Fact Learning

A plausible hypothesis about learning might be expressed as "the more you know, the more you can learn and remember." Is this true? There is, in fact, evidence that it is. Over four experiments, Kyllonen, Tirre, and Christal (1991; see also Kyllonen & Tirre, 1988) consistently found that the extent of factual knowledge an individual already possessed (indexed by a standard vocabulary test) predicted both that individual's rate of learning and ultimate retention test score in paired associate learning. Indeed, the greater the study time available in paired associate learning, the more impact knowledge differences had. In contrast, measures like simple and choice response time, as well as access time to physical and name codes in long-term memory (see also Posner, Boies, Eichelman, & Taylor, 1969), contributed little to this prediction. Kyllonen et al. (1991) also showed that subjects who search long-term memory faster perform much better than slower subjects when study time is limited, but that this advantage vanishes as study time increases.

Could this advantage for individuals with more knowledge be due not to the knowledge difference itself but to some correlated variable, such as the likelihood of using mnemonic techniques? When Kyllonen et al. gave all subjects a "minicourse" in mnemonics to try to level the playing field, both high-knowledge and low-knowledge subjects showed improved learning, but the difference between them remained at least as large. They concluded from their series of studies that high-knowledge individuals learn better "because knowledge is the essential material used in generating elaborations and forming links" (p. 75).

Kyllonen et al. (1991) also hastened to add that familiarity with mnemonic techniques did influence learning, a fact nicely illustrated in a study by Wang (1983; see also Mandler & Huttenlocher, 1956). Wang showed that subjects who learned paired associates faster were those who could quickly produce more "elaborations" (mnemonic-based associations) during acquisition. In addition, fast learners were more consistent in using a given elaboration during study; this consistency led to a greater likelihood of a match between study and test conditions, thereby providing a further boost from transfer-appropriate processing (Morris, Bransford, & Franks, 1977). Indeed, the slow learners were even at a disadvantage if they used the same techniques as fast learners because they did not use them as effectively. When Wang provided the elaborations generated by slow versus fast learners to another group of subjects, the subjects in this new group learned faster using the elaborations produced by the fast learners. It is also relevant here that individuals low in intellectual ability are more sensitive to the quality of the instruction they receive than are those high in intellectual ability (Cronbach & Snow, 1977).

On the issue of mnemonics, Karis, Fabiani, and Donchin (1984) conducted a particularly interesting study. They explored the von Restorff effect, the well-known phenomenon that a word that stands out from its surroundings (in their case by the different size of its font) is especially well learned. Subjects who reported little in the way of mnemonics use, and therefore presumably learned mostly by rote, showed overall poor recall but a very strong von Restorff effect. Intriguingly, the magnitudes of their P300 components in simultaneously recorded event-related brain potentials correlated well with individual word recall. In marked contrast, subjects who made extensive use of organizational mnemonics recalled more of the words and did not produce a von Restorff effect. In their case, P300 did not correlate with later recall. Karis et al. interpreted this pattern of individual differences as evidence that the initial encoding was dominant in later recall for those who failed to use mnemonics but that, for those who did employ mnemonics, the elaborated encoding overruled the initial encoding during recall.

2. General Knowledge and Skill Learning

We have highlighted the learning of facts, or declarative information, but there is also the issue of skill (or procedural) learning. If Humphreys (1979, p. 115) is on the right track, and general intelligence consists of "acquiring, storing in memory, retrieving, combining, comparing, and using in new contexts information and conceptual skills," then both facts and skills are relevant. Ackerman (1986, 1987, 1988, 1990) has been carrying out an extensive and comprehensive series of studies on individual differences and skill learning.

One of the frequently encountered ideas in the skill learning literature is that skills are highly specific. Ackerman (1990) tackled this issue head on by obtaining ability profiles of subjects and then having them repeatedly practice several clerical tasks as well as simple and choice RT tasks. The goal was to relate performance on these tasks—and changes in performance with practice—to performance on the learning of a criterion task, in the form of an air traffic controller "simulation." He observed that performance on the information processing measures showed consistent patterns of correlation with the criterion air traffic task, and apparently shared even more in common as practice progressed. These findings contradict the idea that all skills are necessarily specific and again highlight the role of individual differences in learning.

3. Specific Knowledge

So far, we have examined how breadth of knowledge influences learning, but only at a general level. We now turn to how the extent of knowledge of a particular topic influences further learning related to that topic—the question of domain-specific learning (see Resnick & Neches, 1984, for overview). Voss and colleagues tackled this question in the domain of baseball. In the first study, Chiesi, Spilich, and Voss (1979) demonstrated that people high in baseball knowledge were better able than people low in baseball knowledge to recognize newly acquired information about baseball and to notice important changes between study and test. Furthermore, high-knowledge individuals needed less information to support recognition, they could better predict upcoming information, and they could better recall the order of events, presumably because they related them more successfully.

Spilich, Vesonder, Chiesi, and Voss (1979) provided an explanatory context. They had subjects listen to and then summarize the text of a fictional baseball game. High-knowledge subjects produced larger chunks of information, augmented the actually presented information with more plausible inferences, and more accurately ordered the information. Voss, Vesonder, and Spilich (1980) extended this analysis to the case where subjects generated their own text and recalled it two weeks later. High-knowledge individuals produced more detailed texts and more closely attended to the sequence of events and critical changes as events progressed. These differences in the generation of the text reappeared in recall. When given texts produced by other subjects and later asked to recall them, high-knowledge subjects remembered much more than low-knowledge subjects if the text had originated with a high-knowledge subject, but there was little difference if the text had been generated by a low-knowledge subject.

Taken together, this work can be interpreted as evidence that the high-knowledge individuals more consistently tied events to the goal structure and kept the important information in working memory, strategies that are important during both acquisition and remembering. Other research dovetails nicely with this interpretation. As one illustration, Lee-Sammons and Whitney (1991), using the WM capacity paradigm discussed earlier, showed that high-span individuals were more able than low-span individuals to recall information from a text when the subjects were forced to change perspectives between reading and recalling the text. They argued that low-span subjects were more constrained by the perspective they had taken during initial reading, relying on that perspective to help compensate for their reduced working memory capacity. Perhaps the high-span individuals also had higher knowledge; certainly the working memory findings are quite consistent between the two lines of research and mesh with other work in that domain (see, e.g., Daneman & Tardiff, 1987).

We could go on. For example, Curtis and Glaser (1981) found that individuals with larger vocabularies and more knowledge about word meanings tended to obtain higher scores on tests of verbal aptitude when those tests included verbal analogies. Clearly, knowledge—both general and specific—makes learning and remembering easier, and therefore individuals with higher knowledge have a significant edge. A possible reason can be gleaned from the "paradox of the expert": If forgetting is due to interference among related concepts in memory, how is it that an expert in a particular domain can overcome this problem? Smith, Adams, and Schorr (1978) suggested that we all overcome this problem by integrating our knowledge such that related ideas are linked and therefore support, rather than compete with, each other.

B. Organization of Long-Term Memory

Underwood, Boruch, and Malmi (1978) conducted what is still probably the largest investigation of individual differences in episodic memory. Using 200 subjects and 28 tasks, they identified five episodic memory factors based on a factor analysis. These factors seemed very much to be sets of similar tasks—free recall on one, paired associates and serial tasks on another, memory span on a third, verbal discrimination on a fourth, and frequency and recognition on a fifth—rather than suggesting deeper process overlap. Underwood et al. concluded that the rate of forming associations during learning was the critical determinant of individual differences in episodic memory performance. In passing, we note two interesting aspects of the Underwood et al. study: First, given our prior discussion of chunking in working memory and our upcoming coverage of clustering in long-term memory, it is comforting that organization did not relate to any of the other episodic memory measures; second, the absence of a deeper relation underlying the tests does conflict with some of the more recent evidence, such as the Kyllonen and Tirre (1988) finding of a .53 correlation between a general knowledge factor and an associative learning factor.

Geiselman et al. (1982) took a similar tack, studying individual differences in episodic memory using both behavioral (several measures of recall) and physiological (heart rate, galvanic skin response, and eye movements) indices. Like Underwood et al. (1978), they argued that the critical determinant of success in remembering occurred during learning, and they identified rehearsal, coupled with the "intensity" or effort that subjects put into acquisition, as crucial. Enhanced recall from long-term memory was held to be due to effective use of semantic rehearsal strategies and extra effort, whereas effort made little contribution to immediate recall from working memory. Overall, they interpreted their individual-differences evidence as supporting a dissociation between working memory and long-term memory.

1. Episodic Memory

If Landauer's (1986) estimate that we store 10^9 facts in memory is anywhere near correct, then organization is essential. No doubt, this need for organization is true both in episodic memory, which contains our autobiographical knowledge, and in semantic memory, where our general knowledge is held (Tulving, 1972). Tulving (1962) showed that, even for a list of nominally unrelated words, subjects organize those words and tend to recall them in consistent patterns, though the patterns differ over individuals. Such subjective organization is very reminiscent of the idea of chunking in memory span: both can be indexed by the degree to which people consistently cluster words. Do people differ in how they cluster or in the benefits they accrue from clustering in episodic memory?

The results obtained by S. C. Brown, Conover, Flores, and Goodman (1991) offer some insight into this question. They grouped their subjects according to the degree of clustering they showed in their free recall of categorized words, and then examined several aspects of the performance of the high and low clusterers. Overall, subjects recalled the most instances of each category when given category names and allowed to exhaust recall within each category; they showed worst performance when given category cues at random and allowed to recall only one instance each time a cue appeared; and their free recall fell between these two extremes. The really noteworthy aspect of these results, however, was that this pattern held for both high and low clusterers and that high clusterers showed a constant advantage regardless of how they were cued. This advantage was not due to differential study or to inherent list organization: High clusterers continued to outperform low clusterers (1) whether categories were blocked or random during study, and (2) even for lists made up of unrelated words (where, surprisingly, high clusterers did not show more subjective organization). Brown et al. concluded that clustering was essentially a symptom of general ability differences among subjects, consistent with the evidence reviewed in the section on knowledge and learning. From our perspective, although clustering clearly affects performance on episodic memory tasks, it does not appear to be the source of individual differences, much as was the case with memory span.

2. Semantic Memory

How we arrange information in semantic memory should also be crucial, governing how quickly and reliably we can access it. This topic seems ripe for studies of individual differences, yet there has been surprisingly little work on the topic. Loftus and Loftus (1974) made a provocative beginning by showing that advanced psychology graduate students possess a superior organization of psychology by subarea. Coltheart and Evans (1981) delved more into the mainstream work on semantic memory. Following Rips, Shoben, and Smith (1973), they investigated how subjects represented instances of a single category, birds. Each subject generated 20 birds (e.g., robin, swan) and 20 dimensions of "birdness" (e.g., predatory, water dwelling), and then rated each bird he or she had provided on each of his or her dimensions. There was wide variation both in the birds and in the dimensions, but an individual subject's ratings predicted both (1) subsequent response latency to judge the degree to which each bird fit each dimension, and (2) subsequent amount of priming in a categorization task when a target bird was preceded by a nearby or a distant bird. To our knowledge, there has been no effort to follow up or to extend the Coltheart and Evans (1981) study.

The other approach to individual differences in semantic memory is the correlational approach, most recently used by Roznowski (1993). She showed that the best predictor ($r = .32$) of scores on the ACT was a subject's time to verify sentences of the type used in the classic Collins and Quillian (1969) studies of semantic memory (e.g., "a sparrow has wings"). Second best ($r = .26$) was the Clark and Chase (1972) sentence–picture verification task, arguably also a semantic memory task. All of the other response time measures—simple and choice reaction time, Sternberg memory scanning, and mental rotation—failed to predict test performance. Such findings are in accord with the notion that knowledge, here viewed in terms of rapid access to semantic memory, is a critical component in individual differences in long-term memory.

A number of correlational studies have tried to ascertain the degree to which semantic and episodic memory share processes or structure. The general conclusion seems to be that there is relatively little overlap, providing some reassurance for theories of independent memory systems (Tulving, 1983). In their large factor-analytic study, Underwood et al. (1978) found little correlation between their three measures of semantic memory— word frequency, vocabulary, and spelling—and their numerous measures of episodic memory. Similarly, Cohen (1984) showed that free recall of words and subject-performed tasks correlated quite highly ($r = .61$, episodic), that production of category-cued and letter-cued words correlated highly ($r = .70$, semantic), but that the members of these two sets were only modestly correlated, in the range of $r = .36$. Cohen suggested two specific factors and a more general one.

C. Implicit versus Explicit Remembering

In the past decade or so, a new distinction has emerged to command the lion's share of attention in episodic memory research. This is the contrast between explicit remembering, done with awareness, and implicit remembering, done without awareness (see Graf & Schacter, 1985; see also Kelley & Lindsay, Chapter 2, this volume for a review of differences between explicit and implicit memories). Much of the now quite substantial literature has sought to demonstrate dissociations between the two ways of remembering, an enterprise that has been quite successful (Roediger & McDermott, 1993). Only very recently has any attention been paid to whether there are individual differences in implicit remembering and, if so, to how those differences might relate to differences in explicit remembering.

Reber, Walkenfeld, and Hernstadt (1991) examined implicit versus explicit learning using one task from each domain. The implicit measure was Reber's artificial grammar task (subjects implicitly learn the rules by which letters are combined into strings and then demonstrate their learning by choosing grammatically correct strings); the explicit measure was a series-completion problem-solving task (subjects explicitly work out the pattern in a series of letters and then choose the appropriate completion). The principle findings were as predicted: There was substantially smaller individual differences in the implicit task as compared to the explicit task, and IQ correlated better with the implicit measure ($r = .69$) than with the explicit measure ($r = .25$). Furthermore, performance on the explicit and implicit tasks was only weakly correlated ($r = .32$). These observations are all in keeping with the idea that implicit and explicit memory are dissociable.

Perruchet and Baveux (1989) adopted Underwood's (1975) logic of using individual-differences data to test theories. They examined correlations between performance on two explicit tests—recall and recognition—and four implicit tests—clarification (a word embedded in a gradually disappearing mask), fragment completion, perceptual identification, and anagram solution—to assess the degree of dependence between the two types of remembering. Recall and recognition were quite highly correlated with each other ($r = .50$), whereas the correlations among the four implicit tests were considerably smaller (all $rs = .30$ or lower). Moreover, clarification and fragment completion were at least as well correlated with the explicit measures as they were with each other or with the other two implicit measures. Overall, it was clear that the evidence was not as supportive of independence between implicit and explicit remembering as might have been hoped. (See also Kelley and Lindsay, Chapter 2, this volume, for a discussion of correlations within and between measures of explicit and implicit memory.) Further work of this sort, where individual-differences patterns are used to help evaluate more global theories, is needed.

Woltz and Shute (1993) investigated individual differences in the hallmark measure of implicit remembering, repetition priming (the facilitation in processing the second occurrence of a piece of information). Working with impressive sample sizes (342 and 250 in Experiments 1 and 2, respectively), they explored a semantic comparison task in which subjects had to judge whether word pairs were related or unrelated over a series of trials in which pairs could reappear. The advantage due to reprocessing a pair was moderately correlated over 30–90 min in Experiment 1 ($r = .46$), indicating that subjects who benefited more from repetition at one point in time also did so at other points within that range. However, this relation virtually disappeared in Experiment 2 when performance at 30 s was correlated with that at 8 days ($r = .14$). Perhaps the decline in relation between Experiments 1 and 2 occurred because the very short and very long lags in Experiment 2 essentially amounted to correlating working memory with long-term memory, whereas the more intermediate lags in Experiment 1 all corresponded to long-term memory.

Additionally, Woltz and Shute (1993) looked at the degree to which repetition priming could predict fact learning. Are the subjects who show larger benefits from repetition also those who learn facts better? In Experiment 1, they found a moderate relation between repetition priming and paired-associate learning ($r = .33$), considerably better than the relation between repetition priming and either a two-choice reaction-time task ($r = .15$) or a letter arithmetic working memory task ($r = .24$), in which the subject must treat letters as standing for digits (e.g., A = 1, B = 2, etc.). This ability of repetition priming to predict explicit learning held up ($r = .35$) in Experiment 2 when the learning task switched to learning computer programming concepts. Basically, Woltz and Shute found that the implicit measure predicted the explicit measure within individuals, leading them to conclude that "declarative learning may involve more passive, implicit memory processes" (p. 356). It is worth noting that this kind of result, contrary to the supportive evidence in the previous section, presents a challenge for those who wish to claim that implicit and explicit remembering are broadly dissociated.

Woltz (1988, 1990) had previously shown that repetition priming also predicts procedural learning, and that the pattern of relation between these two types of implicit learning was independent of the relation between repetition priming and tasks measuring working memory capacity or semantic knowledge. Taken together, Woltz's studies demonstrate that what is learned from a single exposure to a piece of information can predict how learning will proceed in quite disparate settings.

D. Retrieval from Long-Term Memory

One of the best known research programs in individual differences has been that of Hunt and colleagues (see Hunt, 1978, for an overview). In their early studies (Hunt et al., 1973, 1975), the focus was on the manipulation of information in working memory, which we have already discussed. Gradually, though, the emphasis shifted to the retrieval of information from long-term memory (Hunt, 1978; Hunt, Davidson, & Lansman, 1981), where results proved to be less equivocal. The major finding that emerged from this work hinged on Posner's letter identification task (Posner et al., 1969), in which subjects had to determine as rapidly as possible whether two letters had the same name. On trials when they did, the letters could be physically identical (AA) or name identical (Aa). Whereas subjects' response times are always longer to Aa pairs than to AA pairs, Hunt's studies repeatedly showed that subjects higher in verbal ability showed a smaller difference between name and physical identity response times. This result was taken as evidence of a rapid and probably automatic process of decoding information from long-term memory that differed among individuals.

From the work using individual letters, investigators went on to study the processing of words. Goldberg, Schwartz, and Stewart (1978) used physically identical (*deer–deer*), phonologically identical (*deer–dear*), and semantically related (*deer–elk*) words, and found that the difference between subjects who were high versus low in verbal ability increased as the required comparison became more abstract and semantic. Hunt et al. (1981; see also Hogaboam & Pellegrino, 1978) looked at two semantic tasks—time to verify whether a single instance belonged to a category and time to verify whether two instances belonged to the same category—plus a word version of the Posner et al. (1969) task, all as a function of verbal ability. They consistently observed small but reliable correlations in the range of .25 to .30, leading them to conclude that "the process of accessing overlearned material is one of the important individual-differences variables that underlies skilled verbal performance" (p. 608). Although the differences between skilled and less skilled subjects were small in all of these studies, multiplying them many times over in situations such as reading (Palmer et al., 1985) would certainly make their impact an important one. When the most basic processes differ, the echoes throughout the system are likely to be loud and long.

E. Summary

In discussing individual differences in long-term memory, we have sketched three principal differences. First, people vary in how much they know, which has serious ramifications for learning, whether the learning is declarative or procedural. Those who know more learn better, whether the knowledge and learning are in a specific domain or more global. Second, individuals vary reliably and systematically in how the knowledge they possess is organized in memory. Third, there are consistent differences in retrieval speed for well-known information in long-term memory, and these are related to measures of intellectual ability, most notably verbal ability. Where our single-word summary of research on individual differences in working memory was capacity, the single word for long-term memory is clearly knowledge.

III. EXPERTISE IN REMEMBERING

We turn finally to an examination of expert and exceptional memories. Extraordinary memory ability is popularly thought to be something with which an individual must be born, but research suggests that this is not true. As Ericsson (1992, pp. 166–167) put it, "experts' superior memory is limited to meaningful information from their domains of expertise and can be viewed as the result of acquired skills and knowledge specific to each domain."

Probably the best known work on expertise in memory is that of Chase and Simon (1973), pursuing the pioneering research on expert chess layers begun by de Groot (1965). The most striking difference between beginners and experts was that experts faced with a 5-s exposure to the playing board of a chess game in progress could recall the locations of all of the 24 or so pieces, whereas novices could reproduce only about 4 locations accurately. This advantage, however, appeared only when the pieces were in actual game positions: With randomly located pieces, recall by the experts fell to that of the novices. Similar results have been obtained in a variety of games and sports (Ericsson, 1992). The strong suggestion is that chess experts can create larger chunks of information based on their superior knowledge of the game.

How does one develop an expert memory in a domain? Certainly one must acquire a lot of knowledge about the topic, but that knowledge must also be efficiently organized and readily retrievable. In studying physics experts versus novices solving physics problems, Chi, Feltovich, and Glaser (1981) showed that the experts identify the problems as members of conceptual groups, whereas the novices categorize by surface similarities. It appears that experts bring to bear their knowledge and rapidly integrate it, something novices do not do even when they possess the relevant knowledge. This rapid retrieval is the real hallmark of expertise.

A. Mnemonists

The individuals we have just been discussing have excellent memories for a particular specialty area, but are otherwise quite normal in their memory skills. There is, however, another group of individuals whose exceptional feats of memory are even more startling. These individuals are mnemonists, and they have always fascinated memory researchers and laypeople alike (E. Brown & Deffenbacher, 1975). Whereas the experts just discussed excel because of rapid retrieval of knowledge in a particular specialty area, mnemonists appear to excel because of the techniques they have learned by dint of extensive practice (Higbee, 1988; see also Bellezza, Chapter 10, this volume, for a discussion of mnemonic methods).

The best known mnemonist was Shereshevski, Luria's (1968) famous subject S. Luria studied S for 30 years, documenting his amazing feats of recollection and identifying three primary techniques that S used, often in combination. First, S produced vivid and detailed images. He then coupled this imagery ability with two mnemonic strategies: the method of loci (locating images in familiar places) and narrative chaining (weaving images into a story). The combined use of these techniques permitted him to acquire vast amounts of information quickly and to remember that information in virtually flawless detail for a very long time.

Other famous mnemonists have been reported as case studies; Bower (1973) and Thompson (1992) summarize these. We consider just one other here to show the breadth of tactics used by mnemonists. Hunt and Love (1972) studied VP, an expert chess player with a phenomenal memory for facts. Unlike S, VP used verbal associations to accomplish his feats, and clearly had practiced these extensively. Perhaps the most amazing fact about VP was a coincidence: He and S were from the same town in the then Soviet Union!

Finally, there are individuals who use mnemonics to memorize amazing amounts of information of one type. The best known of these are two individuals who memorize numbers. Rajan (described in Thompson, 1992) has learned vast lengths of numbers, including pi to over 30,000 decimal places. He does this by methodically organizing digits into chunks and placing them in an imagined matrix. In addition to helping him be a rapid learner, his use of this scheme permits him to rapidly recover portions of the matrix. Ericsson and Chase (1982) studied a subject who began with a normal digit span and then gradually increased his span with practice until he could rapidly encode numeric strings over 80 digits long. A runner, his tactic was to relate the numbers to running times and then to group them hierarchically.

These individuals illustrate the three main elements of superior memory (Ericsson & Chase, 1982). First, as it is encoded, the information must be elaborated with existing knowledge to give it meaning. This elaboration facilitates the second step, which involves consciously attaching cues to the to-be-remembered information during study so that these cues will be available later to aid retrieval. And third, both the mnemonic skill itself and the information being acquired must be practiced heavily or overlearned. There are, no doubt, a variety of ways to implement these steps, as the various mnemonists illustrate, but these steps do appear to be the fundamental building blocks of exceptional memory.

B. Imagery

A domain where individual differences are often discussed is that of visual imagery. There is a large body of evidence that people vary in the vividness, speed, frequency, and extent of their ability to image (Ernest, 1977) (indeed, some apparently do not image at all), but the degree to which this variation predicts memory performance is less clear. Thus, Katz (1983, p. 39) argued that "clear-cut and consistent relationships do not tend to emerge when variations in imagery level are used to predict task performance," although Paivio (1983) cited several situations that conflict with this conclusion. Perhaps the best summary statement about individual differences in imagery is one offered by Katz (1983, p. 53): "one might characterize high imagers as those who are more sensitive to the tasks that can be solved by imagistic means." If you have good imagery, you look for places to use it.

Reading about S's fantastic imagery ability brings to mind the question of eidetic imagery. Haber and Haber (1964) examined imagery ability in 150 children shown pictures to remember. Half of them showed some imagery, but about 8% showed a very unusual pattern of eye movements and reports of color that suggested an exceptional ability. Later, Leask, Haber, and Haber (1969) developed the "fusion" test of eidetic imagery where two meaningless pictures are mentally superimposed to produce an interpretable picture. Individuals who could do so were considered to be eidetic, and it was shown that such individuals were very likely to be under 6 years old (see also Haber, 1979). Thus, eidetic ability is unlikely to have much to do with the popular notion of "photographic memory" attributed to but rarely observed in adults (Crowder, 1992).

IV. CONCLUSION

At the outset, we argued that research on individual differences in memory is valuable in terms of broadening our understanding of memory processes and in terms of providing an additional testing ground for our theories. We have tried to illustrate both of these merits by showing that individual differences exist in working memory and especially long-term memory, and that sensitivity to these differences informs our overall understanding of memory.[1] The extent of the individual differences in long-term memory

---

[1] In examining the literature to prepare this chapter, we made every effort to locate reliable, consistent sex differences in memory. We found none. Almost invariably, analyses of sex differences appear to be afterthoughts in the memory literature, at best subsidiary goals in studies conducted for other reasons. Thus, we agree with the conclusion Maccoby and Jacklin (1974, p. 59) reached after their review of the literature: "it clearly cannot be said that either sex has a superior memory capacity, or a superior set of skills in the storage and retrieval of information, when a variety of contents is considered. Nor does existing evidence point to a difference in choice of mnemonic strategies."

may point to the importance of "top-down" strategic elements in the use of memory. Of course, like any good research, answering one question immediately opens up others. If individuals who have more and better organized knowledge in long-term memory benefit from this difference, we must begin to ask how this difference arose in the first place. Doing so will help us not only in furthering our understanding of how people differ in their memory abilities, but also in deciphering the basic structure and processes of memory.

Acknowledgments

Because contributions were equivalent, order of authorship is alphabetical. Preparation of this chapter was supported by Grant A7459 from the Natural Sciences and Engineering Research Council of Canada to Colin M. MacLeod. Address correspondence to either author at Division of Life Sciences, University of Toronto, Scarborough Campus, Scarborough, Ontario M1C 1A4 CANADA (e-mail: bors or macleod@lake.scar.utoronto.ca).

References

Ackerman, P. L. (1986). Individual differences in information processing: An investigation of intellectual abilities and task performance during practice. *Intelligence, 10,* 101–139.

Ackerman, P. L. (1987). Individual differences in skill learning: An integration of psychometric and information processing perspectives. *Psychological Bulletin, 102,* 3–27.

Ackerman, P. L. (1988). Determinants of individual differences during skill acquisition: Cognitive abilities and information processing. *Journal of Experimental Psychology: General, 117,* 288–318.

Ackerman, P. L. (1990). A correlational analysis of skill specificity: Learning, abilities, and individual differences. *Journal of Experimental Psychology: Learning, Memory, and Cognition, 16,* 883–901.

Ackerman, P. L., Sternberg, R. J., & Glaser, R. (1989). *Learning and individual differences.* San Francisco: W. H. Freeman.

Anderson, J. R. (1983). *The architecture of cognition.* Cambridge: Harvard University Press.

Bachelder, B. L., & Denny, M. R. (1977). A theory of intelligence: II. The role of span in a variety of intellectual tasks. *Intelligence, 1,* 237–256.

Baddeley, A. D. (1986). *Working memory.* Oxford: Clarendon Press.

Baddeley, A. D., & Hitch, G. (1974). Working memory. In G. H. Bower (Ed.), *The psychology of learning and motivation: Advances in research and theory* (Vol. 8, pp. 47–90). London: Academic Press.

Battig, W. F. (1979). Are the important "individual differences" between or within individuals? *Journal of Research in Personality, 13,* 546–558.

Binet, A., & Henri, V. (1895). La psychologie individuelle. *L'Année Psychologique, 2,* 411–465.

Blankenship, A. B. (1938). Memory span: A review of the literature. *Psychological Bulletin, 35,* 1–25.

Borkowski, J. G. (1965). Interference effects in short-term memory as a function of level of intelligence. *American Journal of Mental Deficiency, 70,* 458–465.

Bower, G. H. (1973). Memory freaks I have known. *Psychology Today, 7,* 64–65.

Brener, R. (1940). An experimental investigation of memory span. *Journal of Experimental Psychology, 26,* 467–482.

Brown, E., & Deffenbacher, K. (1975). Forgotten mnemonists. *Journal of the History of the Behavioral Sciences, 11,* 342–349.

Brown, S. C., Conover, J. N., Flores, L. M., & Goodman, K. M. (1991). Clustering and recall: Do high clusterers recall more than low clusterers because of clustering? *Journal of Experimental Psychology: Learning, Memory, and Cognition, 17,* 710–721.

Burnham, W. H. (1888–1889). Memory, historically and experimentally considered. *American Journal of Psychology, 2,* 568–622.

Cantor, J., Engle, R. W., & Hamilton, G. (1991). Short-term memory, working memory, and verbal abilities: How do they relate? *Intelligence, 15,* 229–246.

Carpenter, P. A., & Just, M. A. (1989). The role of working memory in language comprehension. In D. Klahr & K. Kotovsky (Eds.), *Complex information processing: The impact of Herbert A. Simon* (pp. 31–68). Hillsdale, NJ: Erlbaum.

Chase, W. G., & Simon, H. A. (1973). The mind's eye in chess. In W. G. Chase (Ed.), *Visual information processing* (pp. 215–281). New York: Academic Press.

Chi, M. T. H., Feltovich, P. J., & Glaser, R. (1981). Categorization and representation of physics problems by experts and novices. *Cognitive Science, 5,* 121–152.

Chiang, A., & Atkinson, R. C. (1976). Individual differences and inter-relationships among a select set of cognitive skills. *Memory & Cognition, 4,* 661–672.

Chiesi, H. L., Spilich, G. J., & Voss, J. F. (1979). Acquisition of domain-related information in relation to high and low domain knowledge. *Journal of Verbal Learning and Verbal Behavior, 18,* 257–273.

Clark, H. H., & Chase, W. G. (1972). On the process of comparing sentences against pictures. *Cognitive Psychology, 3,* 472–517.

Cohen, R. L. (1984). Individual differences in event memory: A case for nonstrategic factors. *Memory & Cognition, 12,* 633–641.

Collins, A. M., & Quillian, M. R. (1969). Retrieval time from semantic memory. *Journal of Verbal Learning and Verbal Behavior, 8,* 240–247.

Coltheart, V., & Evans, J., St. B. T. (1981). An investigation of semantic memory in individuals. *Memory & Cognition, 9,* 524–532.

Cronbach, L. J. (1957). The two disciplines of scientific psychology. *American Psychologist, 12,* 671–684.

Cronbach, L. J., & Snow R. E. (1977). *Aptitudes and instructional methods: A handbook for research on interactions.* New York: Irvington.

Crowder, R. G. (1992). Eidetic imagery. In L. Squire (Ed.), *Encyclopedia of learning and memory* (pp. 154–156). New York: Macmillan.

Curtis, M. B., & Glaser, R. (1981). Changing conceptions of intelligence. *Review of Research in Education, 9,* 111–148.

Daneman, M., & Carpenter, P. A. (1980). Individual differences in working memory and reading. *Journal of Verbal Learning and Verbal Behavior, 19,* 450–466.

Daneman, M., & Carpenter, P. A. (1983). Individual differences in integrating information between and within sentences. *Journal of Experimental Psychology: Learning, Memory, and Cognition, 9,* 561–583.

Daneman, M., & Tardiff, T. (1987). Working memory and reading skill reexamined. In M. Coltheart (Ed.), *Attention and performance XII* (pp. 491–508). London: Erlbaum.

de Groot, A. D. (1965). *Thought and choice in chess.* The Hague: Mouton.

Dempster, F. N. (1981). Memory span: Sources of individual and developmental differences. *Psychological Bulletin, 89,* 63–100.

Dempster, F. N., & Cooney, J. B. (1982). Individual differences in memory span, susceptibility to proactive interference, and aptitude/achievement test scores. *Intelligence, 6,* 399–416.

Dempster, F. N., & Zinkgraf, S. A. (1982). Individual differences in digit span and chunking. *Intelligence, 6,* 201–213.

Ebbinghaus, H. (1885/1913). *Memory: A contribution to experimental psychology.* New York: Columbia University, Teachers College.

Engle, R. W., Cantor, J., & Carullo, J. J. (1992). Individual differences in working memory and comprehension: A test of four hypotheses. *Journal of Experimental Psychology: Learning, Memory, and Cognition, 18,* 972–992.

Engle, R. W., Nations, J., & Cantor, J. (1990). Is "working memory capacity" just another name for word knowledge? *Journal of Educational Psychology, 82,* 799–804.

Ericsson, K. A. (1992). Experts' memories. In L. Squire (Ed.), *Encyclopedia of learning and memory* (pp. 166–170). New York: Macmillan.

Ericsson, K. A., & Chase, W. G. (1982). Exception memory. *American Scientist, 70,* 607–615.

Ernest, C. H. (1977). Imagery ability and cognition: A critical review. *Journal of Mental Imagery, 1,* 181–216.

Estes, W. K. (1974). Learning theory and intelligence. *American Psychologist, 29,* 740–749.

Farnham-Diggory, S., & Gregg, L. W. (1975). Short-term memory function in young readers. *Journal of Experimental Child Psychology, 19,* 279–298.

Gagné, R. M. (1967). *Learning and individual differences.* Columbus, OH: Merrill.

Galton, F. (1887). Notes on prehension in idiots. *Mind, 12,* 79–82.

Geiselman, R. E., Woodward, J. A., & Beatty, J. (1982). Individual differences in verbal memory performance: A test of alternative information-processing models. *Journal of Experimental Psychology: General, 111,* 109–134.

Goldberg, R. A., Schwartz, S., & Stewart, M. (1977). Individual differences in cognitive processes. *Journal of Educational Psychology, 69,* 9–14.

Graf, P., & Schacter, D. L. (1985). Implicit and explicit memory for new associations in normal and amnesic subjects. *Journal of Experimental Psychology: Learning, Memory, and Cognition, 11,* 501–518.

Haber, R. N. (1979). Twenty years of haunting eidetic imagery: Where's the ghost? *Behavioral and Brain Sciences, 2,* 583–629.

Haber, R. N., & Haber, R. B. (1964). Eidetic imagery: I. Frequency. *Perceptual and Motor Skills, 19,* 131–138.

Higbee, K. L. (1988). *Your memory: How it works and how to improve it* (2nd ed.). New York: Prentice-Hall.

Hogaboam, T. W., & Pellegrino, J. W. (1978). Hunting for individual differences in cognitive processes: Verbal ability and semantic processing of pictures and words. *Memory & Cognition, 6,* 189–193.

Holmes, O. W. (1871). *Mechanisms in thought and morals.* Boston: Osgood.

Humphreys, L. G. (1979). The construct of general intelligence. *Intelligence, 3,* 105–120.

Hunt, E. (1978). Mechanics of verbal ability. *Psychological Review, 85,* 109–130.

Hunt, E., Davidson, J., & Lansman, M. (1981). Individual differences in long-term memory access. *Memory & Cognition, 9,* 599–608.

Hunt, E., Frost, N., & Lunneborg, C. (1973). Individual differences in cognition: A new approach to intelligence. In G. Bower (Ed.), *The psychology of learning and motivation: Advances in research and theory* (Vol. 7, pp. 87–122). New York: Academic Press.

Hunt, E., & Lansman, M. (1975). Cognitive theory applied to individual differences. In W. K. Estes (Ed.), *Handbook of learning and cognitive processes* (Vol. 1, pp. 81–110). Hillsdale, NJ: Erlbaum.

Hunt, E., & Love, T. (1972). How good can memory be? In A. W. Melton & E. Martin (Eds.), *Coding processes in human memory* (pp. 237–260). Washington, DC: Winston.

Hunt, E., Lunneborg, C., & Lewis, J. (1975). What does it mean to be high verbal? *Cognitive Psychology, 7,* 194–227.

Huttenlocher, J., & Burke, D. (1976). Why does memory span increase with age? *Cognitive Psychology, 8,* 1–31.

Jacobs, J. (1887). Experiments on prehension. *Mind, 12,* 75–79.

Jensen, A. R. (1971). Individual differences in visual and auditory memory. *Journal of Educational Psychology, 62,* 123–131.

Jensen, A. R., & Figueroa, R. A. (1975). Forward and backward digit span interaction with race and I.Q.: Predictions from Jensen's theory. *Journal of Educational Psychology, 67,* 882–893.

Kareev, Y. (1982). Minitypologies from within-subjects designs: Uncovering systematic individual differences in experiments. *Journal of Verbal Learning and Verbal Behavior, 21,* 363–382.

Karis, D., Fabiani, M., & Donchin, E. (1984). "P300" and memory: Individual differences in the von Restorff effect. *Cognitive Psychology, 16,* 177–216.

Katz, A. N. (1983). What does it mean to be a high imager? In J. C. Yuille (Ed.), *Imagery, memory, and cognition: Essays in honor of Allan Paivio* (pp. 39–63). Hillsdale, NJ: Erlbaum.

Kyllonen, P. C., & Christal, R. E. (1990). Reasoning ability is (little more than) working memory capacity?! *Intelligence, 14,* 389–433.

Kyllonen, P. C., & Tirre, W. C. (1988). Individual differences in associative learning and forgetting. *Intelligence, 12,* 393–421.

Kyllonen, P. C., Tirre, W. C., & Christal, R. E. (1991). Knowledge and processing speed as determinants of associative learning. *Journal of Experimental Psychology: General, 120,* 57–79.

Landauer, T. K. (1986). How much do people remember? Some estimates of the quantity of learned information in long-term memory. *Cognitive Science, 10,* 477–493.

LaPointe, L. B., & Engle, R. W. (1990). Simple and complex word spans as measures of working memory-memory capacity. *Journal of Experimental Psychology: Learning, Memory, and Cognition, 16,* 118–1133.

Larson, G. E., & Alderton, D. L. (1992). The structure and capacity of thought: Some comments on the cognitive underpinnings of g. In D. K. Detterman (Ed.), *Current topics in human intelligence* (Vol. 2, pp. 141–146). Norwood, NJ: Ablex.

Leask, J., Haber, R. N., & Haber, R. B. (1969). Eidetic imagery in children: II. Longitudinal and experimental results. *Psychonomic Monograph Supplements, 3* (3, Whole No. 35).

Lee-Sammons, W. H., & Whitney, P. (1991). Reading perspectives and memory for text: An individual differences analysis. *Journal of Experimental Psychology: Learning, Memory, and Cognition, 17,* 1074–1081.

Loftus, E. F., & Loftus, G. R. (1974). Changes in memory structure and retrieval over the course of instruction. *Journal of Educational Psychology, 66,* 315–318.

Luria, A. R. (1968). *The mind of a mnemonist.* New York: Basic Books.

Lyon, D. R. (1977). Individual differences in immediate serial recall: A matter of mnemonics? *Cognitive Psychology, 9,* 403–411.

Maccoby, E. E., & Jacklin, C. N. (1974). *The psychology of sex differences.* Stanford, CA: Stanford University Press.

MacKenzie, A. J. (1972). A factor analysis of modified memory span tests. *Australian Journal of Psychology, 24,* 19–30.

Mackworth, J. F. (1963). The relation between visual image and post-perceptual immediate memory. *Journal of Verbal Learning and Verbal Behavior, 2,* 75–85.

Mandler, G., & Huttenlocher, J. (1956). The relationship between associative frequency, associative ability and paired-associate learning. *American Journal of Psychology, 69,* 424–428.

Martin, M. (1978). Memory span as a measure of individual differences in memory capacity. *Memory & Cognition, 6,* 194–198.

Matarazzo, J. D. (1972). *Wechsler's measurement and appraisal of adult intelligence.* New York: Oxford University Press.

Melton, A. W. (1967). Individual differences and theoretical process variables: General comments on the conference. In R. M. Gagné (Ed.), *Learning and individual differences* (pp. 238–252). Columbus, OH: Merrill.

Miller, L. T., & Vernon, P. A. (1992). The general factor in short-term memory, intelligence, and reaction time. *Intelligence, 16,* 5–29.

Morris, C. D., Bransford, J. D., & Franks, J. J. (1977). Levels of processing versus transfer appropriate processing. *Journal of Verbal Learning and Verbal Behavior, 16,* 519–533.

Paivio, A. (1983). The empirical case for dual coding. In J. C. Yuille (Ed.), *Imagery, memory, and cognition: Essays in honor of Allan Paivio* (pp. 307–332). Hillsdale, NJ: Erlbaum.

Palmer, J., MacLeod, C. M., Hunt, E., & Davidson, J. E. (1985). Information processing correlates of reading. *Journal of Memory and Language, 24,* 59–88.

Pellegrino, J. W., & Glaser, R. (1979). Cognitive correlates and components in the analysis of individual differences. In R. J. Sternberg & D. K. Detterman (Eds.), *Human intelligence: Perspectives on its theory and measurement* (pp. 61–88). Norwood, NJ: Ablex.

Perruchet, P., & Baveux, P. (1989). Correlational analyses of explicit and implicit memory performance. *Memory & Cognition, 17,* 77–86.

Posner, M. I., Boies, S., Eichelman, W., & Taylor, R. (1969). Retention of visual and name codes of single letters. *Journal of Experimental Psychology Monographs, 79* (1, Pt. 2).

Reber, A. S., Walkenfeld, F. F., & Hernstadt, R. (1991). Implicit and explicit learning: Individual differences and IQ. *Journal of Experimental Psychology: Learning, Memory, and Cognition, 17,* 888–896.

Resnick, L. B., & Neches, R. (1984). Factors affecting individual differences in learning ability. In R. J. Sternberg (Ed.), *Advances in the psychology of human intelligence* (Vol. 2, pp. 275–323). Hillsdale, NJ: Erlbaum.

Rips, L. J., Shoben, E. J., & Smith, E. E. (1973). Semantic distance and the verification of semantic relations. *Journal of Verbal Learning and Verbal Behavior, 12,* 1–20.

Roediger, H. L., III, & McDermott, K. B. (1993). Implicit memory in normal human subjects. In H. Spinnler & F. Boller (Eds.), *Handbook of neuropsychology* (Vol. 8). Amsterdam: Elsevier.

Rohwer, W. D. (1967). *Social class differences in the role of linguistic structures in paired-associate learning: Elaboration and learning proficiency* (Basic Research Project No. 5-0605, Contract No. OE 6-10-273). Washington, DC: U.S. Office of Education.

Roznowski, M. (1993). Measures of cognitive processes: Their stability and other psychometric and measurement properties. *Intelligence, 17,* 361–388.

Roznowski, M., & Smith, M. L. (1993). A note on some psychometric properties of Sternberg task performance: Modifications to content. *Intelligence, 17,* 389–398.

Salthouse, T. A. (1992). Influence of processing speed on adult age differences in working memory. *Acta Psychologica, 79,* 155–170.

Sargent, S. S. (1942). How shall we study individual differences. *Psychological Review, 49,* 170–182.

Schmeck, R. R. (1983). Learning styles of college students. In R. F. Dillon & R. R. Schmeck (Eds.), *Individual differences in cognition* (Vol. 1, pp. 233–279). New York: Academic Press.

Smith, E. E., Adams, N., & Schorr, D. (1978). Fact retrieval and the paradox of interference. *Cognitive Psychology, 10,* 438–464.

Spilich, G. J., Vesonder, G. T., Chiesi, H. L., & Voss, J. F. (1979). Text processing of domain-related information for individuals with high and low domain knowledge. *Journal of Verbal Learning and Verbal Behavior, 18,* 275–290.

Sternberg, S. (1966). High speed scanning in human memory. *Science, 153,* 652–654.

Swanson, H. L. (1992). Generality and modifiability of working memory among skilled and less skilled readers. *Journal of Educational Psychology, 84,* 473–488.

Thompson, C. P. (1992). Mnemonists. In L. Squire (Ed.), *Encyclopedia of learning and memory* (pp. 421–424). New York: Macmillan.

Tulving, E. (1962). Subjective organization in free recall of "unrelated" words. *Psychological Review, 69,* 344–354.

Tulving, E. (1972). Episodic and semantic memory. In E. Tulving & W. Donaldson (Eds.), *Organization and memory* (pp. 381–403). New York: Academic press.

Tulving, E. (1983). *Elements of episodic memory.* Oxford: Oxford University Press.

Turner, M. L., & Engle, R. W. (1989). Is working memory capacity task dependent? *Journal of Memory and Language, 28,* 127–154.

Underwood, B. J. (1975). Individual differences as a crucible in theory construction. *American Psychologist, 30,* 128–134.

Underwood, B. J., Boruch, R. F., & Malmi, R. A. (1978). Composition of episodic memory. *Journal of Experimental Psychology: General, 107,* 393–419.

Voss, J. F., Vesonder, G. T., & Spilich, G. J. (1980). Text generation and recall by high-knowledge and low-knowledge individuals. *Journal of Verbal Learning and Verbal Behavior, 19,* 651–667.

Wang, A. Y. (1983). Individual differences in learning speed. *Journal of Experimental Psychology: Learning, Memory, and Cognition, 9,* 300–311.

Wechsler, D. (1981). *Manual for the Wechsler Adult Intelligence Scale—Revised.* New York: Psychological Corporation.

Woltz, D. J. (1988). An investigation of the role of working memory in procedural skill acquisition. *Journal of Experimental Psychology: General, 117,* 319–331.

Woltz, D. J. (1990). Decay of repetition priming effects and its relation to retention from text: A study of forgetting. *Learning and Individual Differences, 2,* 241–261.

Woltz, D. J., & Shute, V. J. (1993). Individual difference in repetition priming and its relationship to declarative knowledge acquisition. *Intelligence, 17,* 333–359.

CHAPTER 13

Memory and Aging

Leah L. Light

How differently do different individuals behave in this respect! One obtains and reproduces well; another, poorly. And not only does this comparison hold good when different individuals are compared with each other, but also when different phases of the existence of the same individual are compared: morning and evening, youth and old age, find him different in this respect.

Ebbinghaus, 1964

The belief that memory declines in old age is widespread (Ryan, 1992). Indeed, adults over 60 report more memory problems in everyday life than do young adults (Cutler & Grams, 1988; Ryan, 1992) and experience less perceived control over their own memory functioning (Dixon & Hultsch, 1983). Such beliefs are not groundless. Older adults perform less well than young adults on standardized neuropsychological tests that tap memory (LaRue, 1992; Smith et al., 1991) as well as on laboratory tests of free recall, cued recall, and recognition (Craik & Jennings, 1992; Light, 1991). Although health is a factor in both memory complaints and performance, complaint frequency increases with age even when health status is statistically controlled (Cutler & Grams, 1988). Similarly, negative correlations of performance with age are found even when health is partialled out (Arbuckle, Gold, Andres, Schwartzman, & Chaikelson, 1993; Hultsch, Hammer, & Small, 1993; Perlmutter & Nyquist, 1990; Salthouse, Kausler, & Saults, 1990).

Age-related declines in memory cannot be attributed to the artificiality of laboratory tasks because older adults perform more poorly than young adults on more ecologically valid tasks. For instance, older adults have poorer memory for prose (Zelinski & Gilewski, 1988), for information on simulated medicine labels (Morrell, Park, & Poon, 1989), and for activities they have performed (Kausler & Lichty, 1988). They score lower on batteries of task designed to reflect everyday life (West, Crook, & Barron, 1992). Their memory is poorer for names and faces of people (Bahrick, 1984; Cohen & Faulkner, 1986; Maylor, 1990), for theme songs of television programs they have watched (Maylor, 1991), for the layout of museum exhibits through which they have walked (Uttl & Graf, 1993), for buildings on the major thoroughfares of towns in which they have lived for long periods (Rabbitt, 1989), for the appearance of common objects such as coins and telephones (Foos, 1989), and for the circumstances under which they learn about political events of national significance (Cohen, Conway, & Maylor, 1994).

The ubiquity of these declines in performance argues strongly for the reality of age-related changes in memory. This chapter examines four accounts of the nature of memory impairment in old age. These range from the view that poorer memory in old age arises from inefficient encoding and/or retrieval strategies that are subject to remediation by appropriate interventions to less optimistic views that declining memory is the result of irreversible age-related changes in basic mechanisms underlying cognition, such as reductions in working memory capacity, reduced processing speed, and impaired inhibition. The four classes of hypotheses considered are that age-related decrements in memory are attributable to (1) failures of strategic processing, (2) deficits in semantic processing, (3) problems in the utilization of context, and (4) changes in basic mechanisms underlying all aspects of cognition.

I. FAILURES OF STRATEGIC PROCESSING

The term "metamemory" refers to a broad domain of intuitions about how memory works. These include knowledge of the memory demands imposed by various tasks or situations, the strategies that are effective in improving memory in these situations, memory monitoring (self-knowledge about current memory use, contents, and states), and memory self-efficacy. Memory declines in old age could arise from erroneous beliefs about the nature of memory or the strategies appropriate to particular tasks, failure to use task-appropriate strategies spontaneously, or inefficient monitoring of encoding or retrieval processes.

Although such hypotheses have been the focus of considerable research activity (Burke & Light, 1981; Craik & Jennings, 1992), the evidence for them is not strong. For instance, young and older adults have very similar beliefs about the properties of memory tasks. In one study, Loewen, Shaw, and Craik (1990) found no reliable age differences in response to questions about how easy it would be to remember material varying in degree of interest, familiarity, relatedness, concreteness, personal significance or involvement, or bizarreness. Thus, it is unlikely that older people have difficulty in remembering new material because they have faulty understanding of tasks demands and, therefore, do not carry out effective encoding or retrieval operations. Even if older adults do have correct beliefs about the strategies that enhance memory performance, there are reasons for expecting that they might nonetheless engage in such strategies less often. These are (1) disuse, (2) diminished attentional capacity, and (3) reduced feelings of self-efficacy in memory tasks.

A. Disuse

According to the disuse perspective, the lives of older adults involve fewer demands on memory than the lives of younger adults, with a concomitant reduction in the role played by mnemonic strategies in later life. Age differences in laboratory memory tasks are, on this view, exacerbated by comparisons of young students with older nonstudents, these being the two groups that constitute the "convenience samples" of most researchers in cognitive aging. Several predictions follow from the disuse perspective, none of them confirmed by the available evidence.

First, when asked about the strategies they use in everyday life in questionnaire studies, young and older adults claim similar frequencies of use for various strategies, though there may be greater reliance on internally based mnemonics in the young and on external memory aids in the old (Dixon & Hultsch, 1983; Perlmutter, 1978). Second, age differences in memory are found when young students are compared to old students or when young nonstudents are compared to older nonstudents (Parks, Mitchell, & Perlmutter, 1986; Salthouse, Kausler, & Saults, 1988a). Even within academic circles, where demands on memory might be thought to continue into later life, age differences are found: professors in their 60s have poorer recall and recognition than graduate students in their 20s (Perlmutter, 1978). Third, the disuse perspective predicts that people who continue to be active in their domains of expertise should continue to have memory demands in those domains and, therefore, should have preserved memory for domain-relevant material. The data, however, suggest otherwise. Age differences in domain-relevant memory have been observed for chess (Charness, 1981), bridge (Charness, 1987), and aviation (Morrow, Leirer, & Altieri, 1992). Graphic design is a field that places a high emphasis on generation of visual images in the context of verbal material; yet younger graphic designers outperform older graphic designers when both are trained in the method of loci, a mnemonic technique involving imagery (Lindenberger, Kliegl, & Baltes, 1992). Finally, if strategies are less likely to be used or are used ineffectively by the old because of disuse, extended practice should eradicate age differences. However, even very long term strategy training does not eliminate age-related differences. After 38 sessions of practice with the method of loci in one study, the discrepancy between young and older adults' performance was greater than at the start of practice (Baltes & Kliegl, 1992).

B. Diminished Attentional Capacity

One hypothesized consequence of increasing age is a reduction in attentional capacity (see later discussion). It is possible that older adults engage less often in efficient self-initiated encoding and retrieval strategies because strategies are excessively attention demanding. That is, less frequent use of effective strategies, or choice of strategies different from those used by the young, could be an adaptation to reduced processing resources (Craik, 1977; Hasher & Zacks, 1979). If so, it should be possible to "repair" the production deficiency of older adults by guiding their encoding via orienting tasks and by using less effort-demanding tests of retention (e.g., recognition rather than recall) to assess memory (Craik, 1983, 1986). A similar position has been espoused by Bäckman (1989) who argued that it is possible to compensate for the limitations in older adults' self-initiated processing by experimenter-provided support (e.g., specific instructions on how to encode, orienting tasks that guide encoding, cued recall or recognition rather than free recall), by taking advantage of certain inherent task properties (e.g., multimodal and contextually rich encoding environments or extended study opportunities), and by cognitive support systems (use of tasks based on prior knowledge or semantic memory).

There are both empirical and conceptual obstacles to accepting this position. On the empirical level, it has not yet been shown for either young or older adults that strategy choice depends on attentional capacity. More critically, both the production deficiency and compensation approaches predict interactions of age with variables that affect encoding and retrieval. That is, conditions that constrain encoding or provide more environmental support for retrieval should differentially benefit older adults. Furthermore, strategy differences should give rise to qualitative as well as quantitative differences in performance across age. Generally speaking, however, qualitative differences are not observed. Experimental manipulations that benefit the old also benefit the young. For instance, in a recent meta-analysis, Verhaeghen and Marcoen (1993a) plotted the recall probability of older adults as a function of the recall probability of young adults in the same experimental condition. A quadratic function accounted for 83% of the variability in the older adults' recall in 154 experimental conditions from 91 studies. Similarly, older adults' performance on individual items on list recall, paired associate learning, and prose memory are well predicted from young adults' scores on those same items (Rubin, 1985; Stine & Wingfield, 1988; Verhaeghen & Marcoen, 1993b).

Interactions of age with variables that purportedly affect encoding or retrieval are also not consistently observed. Extensive discussion of this point may be found elsewhere (Burke & Light, 1981; Craik & Jennings, 1992; Light, 1991). Here, the focus is on the notion of retrieval support. Data-driven memory tests afford more retrieval support than do conceptually driven tests (Jacoby, 1983; Srinivas & Roediger, 1990). That is, performance on data-driven tests depends on the physical similarity between the materials studied and the test items and is relatively insensitive to the effects of orienting tasks, whereas performance on conceptually driven tasks is less dependent on the physical similarity between study and test items and shows levels of processing effects. Recall and recognition are primarily (but not exclusively) conceptually driven tasks. They are also direct measures of memory in that they require deliberate recollection of previously experienced events. Another large class of tasks measures memory indirectly by permitting the effects of prior experiences to be manifested in behavior when there has been no solicitation of deliberate recollection. Many, though not all, indirect measures of memory are data driven. Craik (1983) hypothesized that the magnitude of age-related differences in memory should be greater for tasks that require self-initiated constructive operations and offer little environmental support for retrieval and smaller or nonexistent for tasks that provide substantial environmental support. One way of construing Craik's hypothesis is that age differences should be smaller on data-driven than on conceptually driven memory tests. Recognition presumably affords more retrieval support than does recall and, indeed, age differences appear to be smaller for the former than for the latter (Craik & McDowd, 1987; La Voie & Light, 1994). Moreover, age differences on data-driven indirect measures of memory are smaller than those on recognition and recall (La Voie & Light, 1994). Thus, there is evidence in support of the general idea that age differences in memory can be reduced by increasing retrieval support. However, as discussed later, other hypotheses can also accommodate these findings. Further, some aspects of the environmental support hypothesis lack experimental confirmation.

In Craik's (1983) formulation of the environmental support hypothesis, amount of environmental support afforded by a memory task and need for self-initiated constructive operations were treated as alternative ways of describing the same construct, with amount of environmental support negatively correlated with need for self-initiated retrieval activity. However, these two factors can be separated experimentally. It is possible to equate the amount of environmental support across tasks while varying processing requirements by using the same stimuli for direct and indirect memory tests. For instance, the first three letters of words can be used in word–stem completion and in cued recall. In the former, the instructions simply ask subjects to complete the stems with the first English word that comes to mind; if the probability of completing the stem with a target word increases after targets are studied, repetition priming is said to have occurred. Because word–stem completion is in effect a word association task, no self-initiated retrieval operations are required, or (to be more precise) no deliberate recollection is requested. In cued recall, on the other hand, people are asked to use the stems as retrieval aids. Young and older adults typically do not differ in word–stem completion performance but do differ in cued recall (Light & Singh, 1987; Park & Shaw, 1992; but see Chiarello & Hoyer, 1988).

Similarly, it is possible to hold intention to remember constant within a task while varying retrieval support. Park and Shaw (1992) varied the number of letters available as clues for cued recall and word–stem completion from two to four and also varied the type of orienting task (semantic vs. nonsemantic). Although the age difference for priming in word–stem completion was not reliable, age differences favoring the young were found for cued recall. Increasing the number of letters in the cues improved performance for both tasks, but the benefit accruing from greater retrieval support was the same across age. If anything, and contrary to prediction, increasing the number of letters in the word stem was more helpful to the young than to the old in cued recall. Also contrary to prediction, guiding encoding via semantic processing increased the difference in cued recall performance between young and old. These contrasts between direct and indirect memory tests indicate that it is intention to remember, rather than extent of environmental support, that governs age differences in memory.

Construing the environmental support hypothesis as predicting larger age differences on conceptually driven tasks than on data-driven tasks also leads to the prediction of larger priming effects in the young on conceptually driven indirect memory tasks. To address this issue, Light and Albertson (1989) compared young and older adults in an exemplar generation task. After studying a long list of words in which members of several taxonomic categories were embedded, people were asked to generate members of categories, some of which had been represented in the study list and some of which were new. Because this task does not solicit deliberate recollection, it constitutes an indirect measure of memory, with the magnitude of priming evaluated by comparing the likelihood that target words are generated as associates to the category name when they are on the study list and when they are not. Because the test cues (category names) were conceptually rather than physically similar to the target items and were not present in the study list, the task was conceptually driven rather than data driven. Contrary to expectation, young and older adults showed similar levels of priming in this task, though younger adults remembered more words when the category names were offered as retrieval cues for recall. This set of results provides another demonstration that holding the extent of retrieval support constant eliminates age differences in one class of tasks but not in another.

On the conceptual level, the production deficiency approach also runs into difficulties. Although the production deficiency hypothesis as originally formulated by Craik (1977, 1983, 1986) lends itself to straightforward predictions, and the links are fairly clearly drawn between the hypothesized processing impairments and the operations involved in testing the hypothesis, the compensation version of the hypothesis (Bäckman, 1989) is less tightly linked to either processes or operations. For instance, older adults are less impaired on paired-associate learning tasks when stimulus and response terms are pre-experimentally associated than when they are unrelated (LaRue, 1992; Salthouse, 1991b). Treating relatedness of pairs as a form of compensation, however, does not help us to understand why this is the case. The compensation framework may have practical implications (e.g., for memory training or rehabilitation), but it does not provide sufficient theoretical machinery to help us understand *why* memory is less good in old age.

C. Memory Self-Efficacy

If older adults believe their ability to remember is poor, either because they have observed changes in their own performance over time or because of cultural stereotypes about cognition in old age, they may reduce their efforts to remember (Berry, 1989). They then remember less, experience further feelings of reduced self-efficacy, try less hard to remember, and so on. Some, but not all, aspects of this argument have received empirical support. As noted earlier, there is solid evidence for a reduced sense of mastery on memory tasks in old age (Dixon, 1989). There is also evidence that self-efficacy beliefs correlate with performance on memory tasks (Zelinski, Gilewski, & Anthony-Bergstone, 1990), though the correlations are not high. However, there is little evidence that self-efficacy beliefs bear a causal relation to performance on memory tasks; rather, the evidence suggests that self-efficacy beliefs are influenced by performance, rather than the other way around (Hertzog, Dixon, & Hultsch, 1990).

It might be expected that lower self-efficacy for memory would cause older adults to systematically underestimate how much they can remember, but there is no consistent evidence for this prediction. Older adults are at least as good as younger adults in assessing feelings of knowing, such as are involved in predicting recognition of currently unrecallable information (Butterfield, Nelson, & Peck, 1988). Younger and older adults do not differ much, if at all, in their ability to predict how much they will be able to remember when asked on an item–by–item basis as items are studied, or in postdicting the correctness of responses after they have been made (Devolder, Brigham, & Pressley, 1990; Rabinowitz, Ackerman, Craik, & Hinchley, 1982). Still, absence of an age effect in memory monitoring is not necessarily inconsistent with the self–efficacy hypothesis. Older adults could be as accurate as young adults in estimating their recall or recognition even if they have set their performance goals unnecessarily low.

One way to demonstrate an effect of memory self–efficacy on performance would be to change people's beliefs about their memory ability and then to examine their memory test scores. If memory ability remains constant across age, but negative expectations drive performance downward, increasing confidence in memory should improve recall, presumably by encouraging appropriate strategy use. Lachman, Weaver, Bandura, Elliott, and Lewkowicz (1992) assigned older adults to one of five training conditions: cognitive restructuring to promote adaptive beliefs about memory; memory skills training; both cognitive restructuring and memory skills training; practice on memory tasks; and a control group. Beliefs about memory ability and control were indeed influenced by cognitive restructuring. Moreover, people exposed to memory skills training were more likely to respond that they were using new strategies in the criterion tasks than were other groups. However, all groups showed equivalent performance increases from pretest to posttest. In other words, neither changes in memory self–efficacy nor reports of increased strategy use translated into differential gains in performance.

D. Summary

The present literature review offers little support for views that strategic failures are responsible for the memory declines seen in old age. Beliefs about the memory demands of different situations are similar across age. There are no great age-related differences in the use of mnemonic techniques in young and old or in the benefits gained from experimentally provided guidance at encoding or retrieval. Young and older adults are equally good at memory monitoring. Although older adults have lower estimates of self–efficacy in the domain of memory, there is no reason to believe that age-related declines in memory are the consequence of reduced self–efficacy. Perhaps the most striking negative finding is the absence of cross–over interactions in which the young perform better than the old on some tasks but less well on others. The lack of such interactions argues for a deficit in one or more fundamental processes, rather than for differences in strategy use.

II. SEMANTIC DEFICIT HYPOTHESIS

Although the use of deliberate encoding and retrieval strategies is known to improve memory in the laboratory, such strategies are not often used in real life (Intons-Peterson & Fournier, 1986). Rather, memory is more likely to be the by-product of routine encoding processes such as are involved in language comprehension. Hence, any change in the memory structures that represent knowledge about language or the world at large or in the processes involved in natural language understanding would be expected to have negative consequences for memory in old age. For instance, Craik and Byrd (1982) have hypothesized that in old age "an attenuation or shrinkage in the richness, extensiveness, and depth of processing operations at both encoding and retrieval" occurs, such that "older subjects' encodings will contain less associative and inferential information" and "an encoded event is less modified by the specific context in which it occurs for the older person and that this difference leads to a less distinctive (and thus less memorable) encoding of the event" (p. 208).

These claims have been tested within the framework of network theories of memory (Anderson, 1983). In such theories, factual knowledge, both semantic and episodic, is organized in networks consisting of nodes (which stand for features, concepts, or propositions), with the nodes being connected by associative pathways. When a concept is encountered, its node is activated. Activation also spreads along associative pathways to related nodes, making them more available for further cognitive processing. Because both episodic and semantic information are represented in the same network, spreading activation serves as the retrieval mechanism for both. This activation can be either automatic or attentional (effortful), with automatic processes having rapid rise times and immunity from the influence of expectations, and attentional processes having slow rise times and being driven by expectations (Neely, 1977). Activation processes have been implicated in perception of words in spoken and written form (McClelland & Rumelhart, 1981), in determining the syntactic structure of sentences (Tanenhaus, Dell, & Carlson, 1987), and in deriving meanings of single sentences and discourses (Kintsch, 1988). Activation of pragmatic or general world knowledge embodied in schemata is necessary for making inferences, for establishing the topic of a discourse, and for determining the antecedents of anaphors. Thus, age-related differences in either knowledge organization or in activation could produce comprehension difficulty and, ultimately, memory impairment in old age. Four hypotheses are evaluated here: (1) that older adults' encodings are less rich, extensive, and deep; (2) that older adults' encodings contain less associative or inferential content; (3) that older adults' encodings are more general; and (4) that deficits in episodic memory arise from deficits in encoding.

A. Richness, Extensiveness, and Depth of Encoding

Network models provide an interpretation for the concepts of "rich," "extensive," and "deep" processing. Anderson (1983) suggests that deep or elaborative encodings involve greater numbers of associative pathways between nodes, with elaboration involving activation of schemata embodying general world knowledge. Such encodings may be thought of as "richer." "Extensiveness" may similarly be treated in terms of the number of pathways activated during encoding. Age-related deficits in encoding could result from differences in either the content or the organization of knowledge in young and older adults (i.e., in the pattern of connections in the network) or from changes in the nature of activation. The evidence, however, suggests that young and older adults share the same system of meanings for concepts and pragmatic information and that there is little difference in the amount of activation, extent of activation, or rate of spread of activation across age (Light, 1992).

The strongest evidence for stability in the organization of semantic memory in old age comes from word-association tasks. In free-association tasks, the instructions are to give the first word that comes to mind when a stimulus word is presented. According to network models, this should be the word whose concept has the most shared properties with the stimulus or whose semantic distance is the smallest. In controlled-association tasks, the instructions place restrictions on the nature of the response. For instance, the response may be a superordinate, or a physical characteristic of an object, or an action that can be performed with the object. Here, network models would assume that there is a compound stimulus consisting of the word and the type of response to be produced. Activation from this compound stimulus may converge automatically on an appropriate response, or, alternatively, all properties of the stimulus concept may be activated and the concept associated with the pathway labeled with the correct relation selected as the response.

Both free- and controlled-association tasks provide evidence that semantic organization is similar across age. In free-association tasks, the nature of the response given varies little with age. Thus, young and older adults both produce predominantly paradigmatic (e.g., *light* to *heavy*) rather than syntagmatic (e.g., *burden* to *heavy*) responses (Burke & Peters, 1986; Lovelace & Cooley, 1982). The degree of specificity of responses in word-association tasks is also similar across age. For instance, Lovelace and Cooley asked young and older adults to free associate to groups of three words. The triads could consist of words that belonged to the same category, that shared a sensory property, or both. For both age groups, triads belonging to the same category evoked mostly superordinate terms as responses and property triads evoked adjectival responses. Similarly, when Nebes and Brady (1988) asked young and older adults to produce three types of responses to words referring to objects (a characteristic action, a distinctive physical feature, a general associate), the percentage of acceptable responses did not differ reliably across age (see also Stine, 1986). Young and older adults also have very similar frequencies of producing particular items when generating members of categories or properties of words (Howard, 1979, 1980). Finally, in free-association tasks, neither young nor older adults are likely to produce words that represent sensory characteristics of objects or words that are phonemically similar to the stimulus (Burke & Peters, 1986). Assuming that response frequency reflects the strength of associations between concepts, the results of these studies argue that the strengths of various types of associations do not vary across age. In particular, there is no indication that older adults encode words more shallowly, that is, in terms of phonological features or surface characteristics of objects, rather than in terms of semantic relationships.

Studies of semantic priming in lexical decision tasks, word naming tasks, and judgments of semantic relatedness offer scant support for the existence of age-related differences in either the extent or breadth of activation when type of associate is varied (Howard, McAndrews, & Lasaga, 1981; Ober, Shenaut, Jagust, & Stillman, 1991) or when strength of association between prime and target is varied (Balota & Duchek, 1988; Nebes, Boller, & Holland, 1986). In category judgment tasks, latencies are equally affected by exemplar typicality in young and older adults (Nebes et al., 1986). In lexical decision and naming tasks, the extent of priming is assessed by comparing latencies when the target is preceded by a related prime to latencies when the target is preceded by a neutral or unrelated prime. Varying stimulus onset asynchrony permits evaluation of the rate at which activation spreads. Facilitation at short prime-to-target intervals is believed to arise from automatic processes, while longer prime-to-target intervals permit the participation of attentional mechanisms. There is little evidence for reduced benefits or costs in old age when latencies following related and unrelated primes are compared to latencies following neutral primes (Bowles & Poon, 1985; Burke, White, & Diaz, 1987; Howard et al., 1981; Madden, 1989). Although there have been some exceptions (Balota, Black, & Cheney, 1992; Howard, Shaw, & Heisey, 1986), the majority of studies have found similar facilitation across age over a wide range of prime-to-target intervals (Balota &

Duchek, 1988; Bowles, 1994; Burke et al., 1987; Madden, 1989). Benefits are believed to reflect a mix of automatic and attentional processes, while costs are thought to be the product solely of attentional processes.

Thus, these results are generally inconsistent with reduced contributions of either automatic or attentional components of activation. Indeed, recent meta-analyses suggest that the extent of priming is, if anything, greater in the old than in the young, though the precise relationship between magnitude of priming in the young and in the old is at present disputed (Laver & Burke, 1993; Lima, Hale, & Myerson, 1991; Myerson, Ferraro, Hale, & Lima, 1992). Laver and Burke, however, note that older adults have had more practice with semantically associated words, thereby increasing the strength of their connections relative to younger adults, and that because nodes in a semantic network are richly interconnected, summation of priming may mask deficits in semantic priming. They also point out that the paradigms used to examine semantic priming do not limit the time available for responding. Older adults have generally longer response times, providing more opportunity for activation to spread from prime to target and (possibly) inflating the observed magnitude of semantic priming. In addition, based on studies of primed picture naming, Bowles (1994) has suggested that slowing of activation in older adults may not be evident in the onset of either facilitation or inhibition, but that the offset of inhibition by primes may be delayed in older adults, a result consonant with reduced spread of activation.

B. Encoding and Storing Inferences

Models of discourse comprehension assume that inferences based on activation of general world knowledge are needed for understanding and that certain kinds of inferences are made on-line during discourse comprehension (McKoon & Ratcliff, 1992). According to the semantic deficit hypothesis, older adults ought to show less evidence of on-line construction of inferences. However, when comprehension is examined during or very shortly after a sentence is read, young and older adults do not differ in how readily they draw inferences about the presuppositions of implicit causality inherent in some verbs (Light, Capps, Singh, & Albertson Owens, 1994); about the instruments with which verbs are used (Burke & Yee, 1984); about the properties of nouns relevant in particular sentence contexts (Burke & Harrold, 1988); about the topic of a metaphor (Light, Albertson Owens, Mahoney, & La Voie, 1993); about the instantiation of general terms (Light, Valencia-Laver, & Zavis, 1991); about the antecedents of pronouns (Light et al., 1994; Light & Capps, 1986); or about the antecedents of noun-phrase anaphors (Light & Albertson, 1988; Zelinski, 1988; but see Hasher & Zacks, 1988, for evidence that older adults may be slower here).

Studies that do report age differences in the likelihood of drawing inferences typically do not use on-line procedures. For instance, some studies have used implicational cues for recall (Till, 1985; Light et al., 1993), but these confound processes operating at storage with those operating at retrieval, and hence are not informative about encoding. Age-related differences are also obtained when some information must be held in memory until other facts needed to draw an inference are presented (Cohen, 1979, 1981; Hasher & Zacks, 1988; Light & Albertson, 1988; Light & Capps, 1986; Morrow et al., 1992). Forgetting of relevant information, inability to activate previously presented information when subsequent relevant information is given, and/or problems in combining related facts not presented in orders that foster integration may all contribute to problems in generating inferences. Such findings, however, do not constitute evidence that failure to draw inferences on-line produces impoverished semantic encoding or poorer memory.

Another way to examine the role of general world knowledge is to vary the likelihood that relevant schematic information is activated. Schemata are believed to guide expectations about the contents of discourse, to facilitate perception of individual words, to aid in the integration of old and new information, and to serve as frameworks for retrieval (Sanford & Garrod, 1981; Sharkey, 1986). The knowledge embodied in schemata appears to be remarkably consistent across age in a large variety of domains. For instance, when people are asked to generate a sequence of actions that are typically performed in carrying out an activity such as getting up in the morning, the production frequencies of particular actions are very similar across age. Correlations between age groups are also high when people are asked to rate how typical or necessary an act is for completing an activity (Hess, 1985; Light & Anderson, 1983; see Light, 1992, for review). The question here is whether such shared schemata are equally available for comprehension and equally represented in the episodic memories of young and old. The evidence strongly suggests that they are. For instance, the availability of particular schemata influences the rates of intrusions in recall and false alarms in recognition to the same extent in young and old, suggesting that schema-relevant inferences have been stored (Arbuckle, Vanderleck, Harsany, & Lapidus, 1990; Light & Anderson, 1983; Radvansky, Gerard, Hasher, & Zacks, 1990; Zelinksi & Miura, 1988). When asked to read a passage from the perspective of a homebuyer or a burglar, young and old are similar in the extent to which they remember perspective-relevant rather than perspective-irrelevant information (Hess & Flannagan, 1992). Hess (1985; Hess, Donley, & Vandermaas, 1989) has reported interactions between age and typicality of script actions such that recall and recognition differences are larger for atypical than for typical actions. This effect most likely reflects older adults' problems in establishing contextual links to atypical actions rather than age differences in the activation of scripts during comprehension.

C. General Encoding

Rabinowitz, Craik, and Ackerman (1982) have suggested that reduced attentional resources might limit the extent to which older adults form distinctive, contextually specific encodings of new information. On this hypothesis, older adults would be expected to encode events "in the same old way" from one occasion to the next. In terms of network models, when older adults encountered a concept, the pattern of activation would not depend on the specifics of the situation but only on the strengths of pre-existing associations. The general encoding hypothesis arises from encoding-specificty experiments modeled after those of Thomson and Tulving (1970), who presented subjects with both weakly and strongly associated word pairs to study and then tested them with either strong or weak associates as retrieval cues. Targets from both strongly and weakly associated pairs were better recalled when there was a match between study and test cues. Also, targets in the weak–weak condition were better recalled than those in the weak–strong condition, suggesting that strength of prior association is less critical than compatibility of study and test cues in terms of activation at retrieval. Rabinowtiz, Craik, and Ackerman (1982) observed this pattern of results for their young subjects, but their older subjects' recall was the same in the weak–weak and weak–strong conditions. They took this finding to mean that older adults' encodings are not as distinctive and that core meanings of words are activated regardless of the context. However, these original findings have not always been replicated (Park, Puglisi, Smith, & Dudley, 1987; Puglisi, Park, Smith, & Dudley, 1988), and the interaction of age and encoding context has sometimes disappeared when signal detection indices of memory are used (Hess, 1984). Moreover, finding that the match between input and test cues is less important for older adults when pairs are weakly associated may simply be a manifestation of the greater difficulty that older adults have in acquiring new connections, rather than an indication that their encodings are less contextually specific.

Evidence form other sources is more difficult to interpret. If older adults' encodings depend only on the strength of pre-existing associations, one might expect their responses to have greater consistency when word-association tests are repeated after an interval. The data, however, suggest either that there are no age differences in test–retest consistency (Burke & Peters, 1986) or that, if anything, the responses of older adults are more variable from occasion to occasion (Brown & Mitchell, 1991). If older adults' encodings are more "general," they might also be expected to be less variable across subjects than those of young adults. Variability has been defined in a number of ways, including the number of different responses given to a word, the number of unique responses generated, and the proportion of subjects producing the most common response. Age differences in the number of different associates or more unique associates are typically not found when education or verbal ability is equated across age (Burke & Peters, 1986). Most studies also find little difference across age in the proportion of people producing the most common response in their own age group or in the proportion producing the most common response in previously published norms (Burke & Peters, 1986; Howard, 1979, 1980).

There have also been claims that, under some circumstances, the properties produced by older adults are less stable across situations and also less variable across subjects, that is, less distinctive. Mäntylä and Bäckman (1990) asked people to generate a set of associations that in their experience constituted a good description of the meaning of the target. Not only were the responses of the old less likely to be repeated on a second occasion, but also they were higher in intersubject overlap and lower in number of different responses. Also, when subjects were given their own associates as cues, the old recalled fewer targets, but all of the variability in recall across subjects could be accounted for by degree of intrasubject overlap (see also Mäntylä, 1993). Mäntylä and Bäckman reconciled the apparent discrepancy between their results and those of previous studies of word associations by noting that the goal of prior studies was to examine the first responses people produced without thinking too much about the targets (i.e., automatically), whereas their subjects were asked to give good descriptions after evaluating the targets. This argument seems unsatisfactory as a complete account, however, because some of the studies reporting similar variability across age involved controlled association tasks in which evaluation of the responses was needed. In addition, Micco and Masson (1992) asked judges to evaluate clues to the identity of a target that were generated by young and old in an interpersonal communication task on dimensions of contextual appropriateness, idiosyncrasy, and associative strength. The responses of younger adults were judged as conveying the relation between the target and context better and as more likely to be generated if one wrote down the first words that came to mind when presented with a target. On the other hand, clues generated by young and old were not discriminable in terms of idiosyncratic responding. If the responses of older adults are more general, we might have expected them to be considered less idiosyncratic and higher in associative strength to the target, but this was not the case.

Finally, it should be noted that encoding specificity is typically studied in the context of list-learning experiments with emphasis placed on strategic encoding. The argument is that production of good encodings requires attentional capacity, which is reduced in old age. To my knowledge, however, the relation between quality of encoding (e.g., specificity, intersubject overlap, stability across time) and individual-difference measures of attentional capacity or other processing resources has not been the subject of empirical inquiry, so there is no evidence one way or another on this point. Moreover, on-line studies of language comprehension afford little support for reduced encoding specificity in old age. As discussed earlier, on-line studies suggest no age differences in instantiation of general terms with contextually appropriate exemplars, selection of contextually dictated referents for pronouns, or activation of contextually specific aspects of word meaning. Studies of word recognition and naming (Cohen & Faulkner, 1983; Nebes et al., 1986) and studies of immediate memory for sentences (Wingfield, Poon, Lombardi, & Lowe, 1985) find that older adults are at least as sensitive as younger adults to constraints imposed by prior syntactic and semantic context.

D. Encoding and Memory

In network models of memory, spreading activation is the mechanism of retrieval for both semantic and episodic information (Anderson, 1983). If older adults' memory problems were due to age-related changes in spreading activation, studies examining memory for words involved in semantic priming tasks should show reduced priming in the old whenever they perform less well in recall or recognition. Studies that have included both priming tasks and subsequent tests of retention, however, simply do not show this pattern. Younger adults score higher on recall and recognition than older adults despite age invariance in magnitude of semantic priming in lexical decision (Burke et al., 1987; Burke & Yee, 1984; Howard, 1983; Howard et al., 1983; Howard, Shaw, and Heisey, 1986; Madden, 1986) and in category judgment tasks (Mitchell & Perlmutter, 1986; Shaw, 1991). Mitchell (1989) found that recall and recognition of pictures used in a naming task were poorer in older adults, although repetition priming was constant across age in the picture-naming task itself. Finally, when correlations between the magnitude of priming and the accuracy of subsequent recall were examined in several of the studies enumerated above, they were not found to be reliable. In short, there is no support for the hypothesis that deficient comprehension, as indexed by semantic priming, is the cause of age-related differences in memory.

E. Summary

There is, on balance, no strong evidence that deficits in language comprehension underlie memory problems in old age. The structure of knowledge revealed by word-association responses is remarkably constant across age.

The rate and breadth of spreading activation shown in semantic priming tasks is fairly constant across age, though (contrary to the semantic deficit hypothesis) the magnitude of semantic priming may be greater in the old than in the young. Although the literature is not altogether consistent on this point, there is considerable evidence for encoding specificity in the old as well as in the young, especially in situations involving natural language comprehension. Under conditions that do not tax working memory, older adults demonstrate sensitivity to linguistic context by drawing pragmatic inferences based on word meanings and/or general world knowledge. Finally, attempts to find correlations between tasks that tap spreading activation and episodic memory have not succeeded. Yet, young and older adults do differ in memory.

III. SPARED ACTIVATION AND IMPAIRED PROCESSING OF CONTEXTUAL INFORMATION

Current accounts of memory often distinguish between processes that depend on familiarity, activation, or perceptual fluency, and those subserved by memory for new associations, either associations between events experienced simultaneously or between events and the environmental contexts in which they occurred (Gillund & Shiffrin, 1984; Humphreys, Bain, & Pike, 1989; Jacoby & Dallas, 1981; Mandler, 1980). In particular, activation, familiarity, or perceptual fluency mechanisms have been posited to underlie repetition priming, and context-dependent processes to underlie recall and recognition (Graf & Mandler, 1984; Jacoby & Dallas, 1981). The importance of contextual information in determining the accuracy of memory is also recognized by single-process theories that emphasize the contribution of similarity between current experiences and memorial representations of earlier events (Eich, 1985; Hintzman, 1988). In addition, reality monitoring, the discrimination between fact and fantasy, requires memory for such contextual details as perceptual information, spatiotemporal information, thoughts and feelings, and cognitive operations carried out as an event is experienced (Johnson, Foley, Suengas, & Raye, 1988).

Several lines of evidence suggest that there is relative sparing of activation processes in old age and that age-related deficits in recall and recognition are due to reduced efficiency in the acquisition or utilization of contextual information (Balota, Duchek, & Paullin, 1989; Light, Singh, & Capps, 1986; Rabinowitz, 1984). As discussed earlier, studies of semantic priming in lexical decision and word naming show no effect of age on the extent or breadth of semantic activation. Here, evidence showing that memory for context is reduced in old age, while repetition priming is spared, is reviewed.

A. Memory for Contextual Information

Studies that require the reporting of nonsemantic aspects of events provide evidence that contextual information is less available in old age (see Spencer and Raz, 1995, for a meta-analysis). Older adults are less good at remembering whether information was presented auditorily or visually (Kausler & Puckett, 1981a; Lehman & Mellinger, 1984, 1986; Light, La Voie, Valencia-Laver, Albertson Owens, & Mead, 1992; McIntyre & Craik, 1987), in upper- or lowercase letters (Kausler & Puckett, 1980, 1981a), by a man or a woman (Ferguson, Hashtroudi, & Johnson, 1992; Kausler & Puckett, 1981b; Schacter, Kaszniak, Kihlstrom, & Valdiserri, 1991), or in a particular color (Park & Puglisi, 1985). They are less accurate in remembering whether they saw a word or generated it from a clue (Mitchell, Hunt, & Schmitt, 1986; Rabinowitz, 1989), in remembering whether they studied a word in the most recent list or in an earlier list (Kliegl & Lindenberger, 1993), in assessing whether they learned a fact in an experimental setting or knew it before (Janowsky, Shimamura, & Squire, 1989; McIntyre & Craik, 1987), in deciding whether a word was thought or spoken (Hashtroudi, Johnson, & Chrosniak, 1989), in judging whether an act was planned or imagined or actually carried out (Cohen & Faulkner, 1989), in monitoring whether an act has already been performed (Koriat, Ben-Zur, & Sheffer, 1988), and in remembering which of two orienting tasks they used for particular items during encoding (Brigham & Pressley, 1988). Finally, there is an extensive literature documenting poorer memory for temporal and spatial memory in the old (see Kausler, 1990, for review).

In addition to results from studies soliciting deliberate recollection of contextual information, several other findings are consistent with impairment of context-dependent relative to familiarity-based processes. Older adults are more susceptible to the effects of misleading information after witnessing a series of events (Cohen & Faulkner, 1989). Also, they are more likely than young adults to call a previously seen nonfamous name or face "famous" when it is repeated (Bartlett, Strater, & Fulton, 1991; Dywan & Jacoby, 1990). Both of these findings suggest that perceptual fluency or activation processes are operating normally but that source monitoring is less good in the old. Rated familiarity predicts false alarms in face memory for old, but not young, adults (Bartlett & Fulton, 1991), again suggesting a greater reliance on activation-based mechanisms in the old. When asked whether they remember the circumstances of original encounter or only "know" that an item they have recognized or recalled was previously studied, the proportion of "know" judgments remains constant or increases with age, whereas the proportion of "remember" judgments declines (Mäntylä, 1993; Parkin & Walter, 1992).

Finally, Jennings and Jacoby (1993) used opposition methodology to obtain separate estimates of familiarity and intentional recollection within a single paradigm. In one experiment, a list of nonfamous names was first read to subjects who were then tested with a mixed list of old and new nonfamous names and new famous names. They were first asked to choose the famous names and were told that all the old names were really the names of famous people, so that if they remembered reading a name earlier, they could be sure it was famous. In a second test, they were told that all of the old names were in reality nonfamous and thus they should avoid choosing as famous any name they remembered reading earlier. These two tests, the inclusion test and the exclusion test, pit familiarity and recollection against each other. Estimated recollection—taken as the difference in the probabilities of responding "famous" on the two tests—was higher in the young, but there was no difference across age in estimates of the contribution of familiarity, a result consistent with sparing of activation in the old.

B. Indirect Measures of Memory

Two broad classes of indirect measures of memory have been investigated: item priming tasks involving memory for words or objects that have pre-existing memory representations, and associative priming tasks involving memory for new connections or for novel stimuli for which there are no previously existing memory representations (Graf & Schacter, 1985). Item priming tasks include word fragment completion, word stem completion, lexical decision, homophone spelling, rereading, and perceptual identification under impoverished conditions. In these tasks, repetition priming is said to occur if a word fragment or stem is more likely to be completed with a recently studied word, if a decision that a string of letters is a word is more rapid after a recent exposure to that word, if a homophone presented auditorily is more likely to be spelled in accordance with a particular meaning (e.g., *cell* rather than *sell*) after being studied in a context that biases that meaning, if words are read more rapidly the second time they are encountered, or if identification of a visually degraded or briefly presented word is enhanced by prior presentation.

Studies of anterograde amnesia strongly implicate the involvement of the hippocampus and its associated structures in deliberate recollection (Squire, 1992). Even amnesic patients who show severe deficits in recall and recognition may show normal or near-normal item priming, though impaired priming has been reported (see Ostergaard & Jernigan, 1993; Bowers & Schacter, 1993, for reviews). Age-related changes in the hippocampus that could be responsible for problems in deliberate recollection have also been well documented (Ivy, MacLeod, Petit, & Markus, 1992). On this view, repetition priming is supported by other brain structures. For instance, Tulving and Schacter (1990) have argued for the existence of a presemantic representation system with a posterior cortical location that operates independently from the hippocampus and its related structures. Sparing of repetition priming in the old would then argue for the relative immunity of such a system from the effects of aging (Schacter, Cooper, & Valdiserri, 1992). In any event, the choice of whether to interpret dissociations in terms of processes or in terms of memory systems is most likely a matter of difference in perspective, reflecting a preference for a cognitive or a neuropsychological approach to theorizing (Shimamura, 1993).

Age differences are usually, though not always, unreliable in studies of item priming. Nonsignificant age differences in item priming have been reported for word fragment completion (Light et al., 1986), word stem completion (Dick, Kean, & Sands, 1989; Java & Gardiner, 1991; Light & Singh, 1987; Park & Shaw, 1992), perceptual identification of degraded or briefly presented words and pictures (Hashtroudi, Chrosniak, & Schwartz, 1991; Light et al., 1992; Light & Singh, 1987; Russo & Parkin, 1993), lexical decision (Moscovitch, 1982), category judgments (Rabbitt, 1982, 1984), homophone spelling (Howard, 1988), word naming (Light & Prull, 1995), anagram solution (Java, 1992), picture naming (Mitchell, 1989; Mitchell, Brown, & Murphy, 1990), and generation of category exemplars (Isingrini, Vazou, & Leroy, 1995; Light & Albertson, 1989). Some studies, however, have found age differences in these same tasks (Abbenhuis, Raaijmakers, Raaijmakers, & van Woerden, 1990; Chiarello & Hoyer, 1988; Davis et al., 1990; Hashtroudi et al., 1991; Howard, 1988; Hultsch, Masson, & Small, 1991; Rose, Yesavage, Hill, & Bower, 1986). These differences are nonetheless not as consistently obtained as age differences in recall and recognition. Many of the studies cited above also included direct measures of memory, and these measures generally revealed significant effects of age.

The overall pattern of findings, then, suggests that performance on item priming tasks is spared in old age relative to performance on direct measures of memory. This pattern is readily interpretable in terms of contemporary two-process models of memory that claim that activation, familiarity, or perceptual fluency mechanisms underlie repetition priming phenomena, and that context-dependent operations are critical for recall and recognition (Graf & Mandler, 1984; Jacoby & Dallas, 1981). On this view, repetition priming requires only the activation of an already extant memory representation during encoding, whereas recall and recognition require more elaborative processing of contextual information at that time. The sparing of repetition priming in old age, together with the decline in deliberate recollection, implies that activation processes are intact but processing of contextual information is compromised. Further support for this position comes from the finding that the increment in performance from word stem completion or exemplar generation to cued recall is greater in the young than in the old (Light & Albertson, 1989; Light & Singh, 1987; Park & Shaw, 1992).

Also, as noted above, age differences in recall appear to be greater than those in recognition, which is widely held to depend more on familiarity than does recall.

In studies of associative priming, the goal is to determine whether a new representation has been formed for a novel stimulus, such as a nonword, or a new association has been made between pairs of previously unrelated words. The experimental question is whether performance is improved by maintaining the original pairing at test. For instance, after studying the word pairs *jail–strange* and *balance–chair,* word stem completion may be tested for intact items (*jail–str____*, *balance–cha____*) and for re-paired items (*jail–cha____*, *balance–str____*). Association formation is inferred if previously studied words appear more often as completions for intact than for recombined pairs (Graf & Schacter, 1985). There are reasons for predicting that associative priming, unlike item priming, should show systematic age differences. Although early reports suggested that associative priming is intact in anterograde amnesia, later studies have not replicated this result (see Bowers and Schacter, 1993, for review). To the extent that memory deficits in normal aging are similar in kind (though not in degree) to those in anterograde amnesia, reduced associative priming in old age might be expected. Older adults are also particularly impaired on direct memory tests that require formation of new connections. For example, age differences in paired-associate learning are larger for unrelated than for related words pairs (see, e.g., La Rue, 1992; Salthouse, 1991b, for reviews of the neuropsychological and experimental evidence). Two-process theories cannot, without further assumptions about association formation, account for the development of new connections, though once these have been formed, activation mechanisms can explain associative priming. To the extent that older adults have greater difficulty in establishing new connections, indirect measures of memory should show age-related impairments when formation of new connections is required (MacKay & Burke, 1990). Finding age invariance in associative priming would suggest that formation of new associations is not age sensitive. Age differences in recall and recognition of new associations would then signal problems in context-dependent retrieval processes but not in acquisition. A memory systems approach would also predict that older adults should be impaired on associative priming.

Studies that compare the size of associative priming effects in young and older adults are less numerous than those dealing with item priming. In some, age-related differences in associative priming have been found (Howard, 1988; Howard, Fry, & Brune, 1991; Howard, Heisey, & Shaw, 1986; Moscovitch, Winocur, & McLachlan, 1986). In others, however, age-related differences have not been reliable (Hasher & Zacks, 1988; Howard, Heisey, & Shaw, 1986; Howard et al., 1991; Light, La Voie, & Kennison, 1995; Moscovitch et al., 1986; Nilsson, Bäckman, & Karlsson, 1989; Rabinowitz, 1986; Schacter, Cooper, & Valdiserri, 1992). Howard (1988; Howard et al., 1991) has suggested that factors conducive to finding reliable age effects in associative priming include single presentations, long study-to-test delays, test order (backward vs. forward associations), and less elaboration–inducing study conditions. There is evidence that elaborative encoding of items is a necessary condition for associative priming to be obtained (Graf & Schacter, 1985). Howard and colleagues (Howard, Heisey, & Shaw, 1986; Howard et al., 1991) have found less associative priming in the old than in the young in word stem completion and item recognition under conditions when study times were limited or when there was but a single study opportunity. On the other hand, there have been reports of similar levels of associative priming in young and old after a single study trial (Hasher & Zacks, 1988; Moscovitch et al., 1986; Rabinowitz, 1986). Thus, the evidence is ambiguous with regard both to the magnitude of associative priming across age and to the conditions under which age differences in associative priming will be observed.

Although age-related differences in repetition priming tend to be small and unreliable in individual studies, they do, on the whole, favor young adults, and, when age differences are aggregated across studies in a meta-analysis, the effect size for repetition priming is reliably greater than zero for verbal materials (La Voie & Light, 1994; but see Mitchell, 1993, for a different conclusion for pictorial materials). Nonetheless, the effect size for repetition priming is also reliably smaller than that for either recognition or recall. Moreover, the effect size does not differ for item and for associative priming. As Jacoby (1991) has observed, repetition priming tasks are not "factor pure." They may involve a mix of processes and are subject to contamination by an intrusion of deliberate recollection. Young adults perform better on tasks involving deliberate recollection than do older adults and may, therefore, be more likely to notice that studied items recur on the indirect memory test; having noticed this, they may use this information to either guess or produce list members (see Ratcliff, McKoon, & Verwoerd, 1989, on issues of response bias in repetition priming), thereby creating a small age difference favoring the young in repetition priming.

C. Summary

Although the evidence is generally consistent with relative sparing of activation processes and concomitant impairment of context-dependent processes, some findings do not fit quite as neatly as they might. First, the conclusion that context-dependent mechanisms are impaired in old age rests partly on findings from studies that directly queried memory for contextual details of events. These studies involved direct measures of memory for context and findings of age differences are the norm. However, when Light et al. (1992) used an indirect measure of memory for context (the extent to which changes of modality from study to test negatively impact on repetition priming), young and old were equally affected by the match between study and test modalities. This pattern suggests that there may be a general age deficit in memory that encompasses both target information and contextual information, but only when memory for that information is tested directly.

Second, if reduced recall and recognition result from problems in memory for contextual information, one might suppose that age differences in retrieval of contextual detail would disappear when young and old are equated on target memory. However, they do not invariably do so (Ferguson et al., 1992; Kliegl & Lindenberger, 1993; Mäntylä & Bäckman, 1992; Russo & Parkin, 1993; Schacter et al., 1991). Of course, equating young and old on recognition for targets does not guarantee equal contributions from familiarity and context-dependent processes across age; familiarity or activation mechanisms could still play a greater role in the performance of the old. Third, it is not clear that all activation processes are intact in old age. Older adults experience increased word-finding problems, suggesting a deficit in transmission of activation from concepts to orthographic or phonological information (Burke, MacKay, Worthley, & Wade, 1991). Fourth, finding a significant effect size for repetition priming tasks is troublesome because it means that the dissociation between direct and indirect measures of memory is only partial. That is, rather than there being age equivalence on one type of memory measure coupled with age differences on another, age differences of varying magnitudes are found on the two classes of tasks (Shimamura, 1993). This pattern raises the possibility that a single process is affected in old age, and that the apparently greater discrepancy in the performance of young and old on direct measures of memory relative to indirect measures arises from differences in task difficulty or from differences in the way processes map onto performance in the two classes of tasks.

IV. RESOURCE DEFICIT HYPOTHESIS

Navon (1984) defined the concept of processing resources as "any internal input essential for processing (e.g., locations in storage, communication channels) that is available in quantities that are limited at any point in time" (p. 217). Both attention and working-memory capacity readily fit this definition. Although it is unclear whether speed of processing should itself be deemed a processing resource or whether the speed of carrying out mental operations depends on the amount of attention or working-memory capacity that is allocated to some task, speed is generally treated as a processing resource by cognitive aging researchers (Salthouse, 1988b). The thesis is that age-related impairments in cognition are mediated by changes in one or more fundamental processes that participate in a variety of cognitive domains. Hasher and Zacks (1988) have added efficiency of inhibitory processing to the list, arguing that many aspects of cognitive decline in old age can be explained by increased difficulty in operations that regulate the entrance of task-relevant and task-irrelevant thoughts to working memory and their maintenance therein. In this section I review evidence that age-related deficits in memory and in memory-dependent domains, such as reasoning, are mediated in whole or in part by changes in attention, working memory, inhibition, and/or processing speed.

A. Reduced Attentional Capacity

The assumptions underlying both the attentional and working-memory deficit accounts of memory impairment in old age are that tasks vary in the extent to which they require processing resources, that resource capacity can be treated as a stable, traitlike attribute of individuals, and that, on average, older people have less processing resources (attentional or working-memory capacity). Given these assumptions, predictions about memory and aging are straightforward. First, when the optimal strategies required for storage or retrieval exceed attentional capacity, older adults should resort to less optimal strategies. As previously discussed, however, evidence for differential strategy use in young and old is at best limited. Second, those aspects of memory that are effortful should be selectively impaired in old age, whereas those that are automatic (requiring little or no attentional capacity) should be age invariant. Hasher and Zacks (1979) have specifically proposed that memory for temporal, spatial, and event frequency information should be stable across the adult years. The evidence, however, suggests that these attributes of events are not in fact coded automatically (Jonides & Naveh-Benjamin, 1987; Naveh-Benjamin, 1987, 1990) and that, like memory for other contextual information, memory for temporal, spatial, and frequency information is age sensitive (Light, 1991). Third, when two tasks must be carried out simultaneously, the performance of older adults should suffer more than that of younger adults relative to single-task conditions. It is to this third claim that I now turn.

Early studies of age-related differences in memory in divided-attention tasks focused on a single paradigm, dichotic listening, and yielded inconsistent results (Somberg & Salthouse, 1982). Subsequent studies have also yielded mixed outcomes with respect to whether older adults experience greater decrements when asked to remember under dual-task than under single-task conditions (see Salthouse, Fristoe, Lineweaver, and Coon, 1995, for a discussion of methodological issues that have plagued this research). For instance, Salthouse, Rogan, and Prill (1984) found greater divided-attention costs for the old when two memory span tasks were combined, but Baddeley, Logie, Bressi, Della Sala, and Spinnler (1986) reported no age difference in the disruptive effects of combining a tracking task and a span task. Also, the effects of divided attention in working-memory tasks appear to be similar in young and old (Gick, Craik, & Morris, 1988; Morris, Craik, & Gick, 1989). Despite these inconsistencies, however, a recent meta-analysis (Kieley, 1990) found a large average effect size for a collection of divided-attention studies, including most of those mentioned earlier.

Much of the research on divided attention, memory, and aging has centered on short-term memory paradigms. Few studies have examined the effects of divided attention on long-term recall or recognition, and the results of these tend to be ambiguous. Recall is generally viewed as more attention demanding than recognition because recall affords less retrieval support. Consonant with this view, Craik and McDowd (1987) found greater absolute (though not relative) costs for the old associated with cued recall than with recognition. Macht and Buschke (1983) also reported greater slowing of responses in a secondary task during recall for the old, suggesting increased attentional demands on retrieval in the old. A similar result has been reported by Mellinger, Lehman, Happ, and Grout (1990). On the other hand, Park, Smith, Dudley, and La Fronza (1989) did not observe an interaction between age and divided attention during recall. Nor did Light and Prull (1995) find greater costs of divided attention for study in older adults on either inclusion or exclusion tests of recognition memory. Similarly, when Tun, Wingfield, Stine, and Mecsas (1992) had subjects divide attention between listening to 15-word sentences for recall and performing a continuous recognition task with picture stimuli, they did not find the cost of divided attention on picture recognition accuracy to be greater for the old than for the young. Still, responses on the picture-recognition task were slowed more for the old in the divided-attention condition. This interaction could reflect greater demands on processing the sentences for recall and/or deciding whether pictures were old or new, or, because there was no pressure to respond rapidly, may simply reflect stylistic differences across age in deciding when to respond.

Studies addressing the question of whether encoding information for later retrieval entails a greater attentional burden in old age have also yielded inconsistent outcomes, with some reporting larger effects of divided attention for the old (Park et al., 1989; Puglisi et al., 1988) and others not obtaining reliable interactions between attentional status and age (Park, Puglisi, & Smith, 1986; Park et al., 1987). In a dual-task study, Tun (1989) found neither an effect on recall of divided attention during study of prose passages nor any indication of greater slowing on a secondary task during prose reading, arguing against increased attentional demands on encoding in the old. Evidence from other paradigms involving on-line semantic processing is consonant with this conclusion. Sentence verification latencies are not differentially slowed in the old by adding a memory load or by increasing the size of a memory load (Morris et al., 1989; Morris, Gick, & Craik, 1988); nor do the old take relatively longer to make semantic rather than nonsemantic encoding decisions during list study, despite the fact that their subsequent recall performance is worse (Duchek, 1984).

In sum, the evidence from divided-attention studies permits no firm answers to questions of whether either encoding or retrieval operations impose proportionally greater attentional demands on the old than on the young. The absence of coherent findings in these areas further damages the hypothesis that memory deficits in old age are due to inadequate self-initiated processing. According to this view, reduced attentional capacity is responsible for problems in self-initiated encoding and retrieval operations, and older adults would be expected to show greater divided attention costs for both types of processing.

B. Working Memory Capacity

Baddeley (1986) described working memory as "a system for the temporary holding and manipulation of information during the performance of a range of cognitive tasks such as comprehension, learning, and reasoning" (p. 34). Accordance to Baddeley, working memory consists of a central executive that "has attentional capacities and is capable of selecting and operating control processes" (p. 71), along with a set of slave systems that have specialized storage functions. The view taken by cognitive aging researchers is that lower capacity in the central executive constrains performance in the elderly by limiting ability to store and/or manipulate information.

Investigations of the role of working memory in age-related decrements in cognition have used either a within-context approach, in which capacity limitations are inferred from performance on tasks not specifically designed for this purpose, or an out-of-context, or individual-differences approach, in which indices of working memory are used as predictors of performance in such domains as memory for text, reasoning, or spatial integration (Salthouse, 1990). Examples of within-context assessment are numerous. Light, Zelinski, and Moore (1982) have argued that working-memory limitations explain why older adults have difficulty in integrating information across several premises, even when these premises can be recognized accurately. Light and Capps (1986) found that older adults had no difficulty in identifying the antecedents of referentially ambiguous pronouns unless working memory was taxed by inserting intervening material between a sentence containing the pronoun and a sentence containing its antecedent. Similarly, backgrounding information by shifting the topic of a discourse affects the young less than the old in an anomaly-detection task (Light & Albertson, 1988), and inserting material between two contradictory statements in a prose passage differentially impairs the ability of older adults to identify the inconsistencies in what is asserted by the text (Zabrucky, Moore, & Schultz, 1993). In these cases, age-related impairments in performance may be attributed to difficulties in maintaining relevant information in working memory. Older adults also have more difficulty imitating left-branching sentences, remembering prose passages containing many left-branching sentences, and judging the grammaticality of complex left-branching sentences (Kemper, 1986; Norman, Kemper, & Kynette, 1992; Pye, Cheung, & Kemper, 1992); the presence of left-branching clauses also has a greater impact on running memory span in older adults (Norman, Kemper, Kynette, Cheung, & Anagnopolous, 1991). Left-branching sentences are more complex syntactically than right-branching sentences and comprehending them is thought to tax working memory more.

In a series of studies using within-context methodology, Salthouse and colleagues have systematically varied task complexity by manipulating the number of identical mental operations that must be carried out and/or the amount of information that must be retained in working memory. Such manipulations include the number of stimulus frames containing line segments to be integrated into a figure or the number of segments per frame (Salthouse, 1987; Salthouse & Mitchell, 1989; Salthouse, Mitchell, & Palmon, 1989), the number of folds of a piece of paper that must be kept track of before a hole is punched and the appearance of the unfolded paper is tested (Salthouse, 1992b; Salthouse, Mitchell, Skovronek, & Babcock, 1989), the number of premises presented in a verbal reasoning task (Salthouse, 1992b, 1992c; Salthouse, Legg, Palmon, & Mitchell, 1990; Salthouse, Mitchell, Skovronek, & Babcock, 1989), and the number of cube faces that need to be examined to determine whether all faces on two cubes are the same (Salthouse & Skovronek, 1992). In each case, older adults were more adversely affected by increased complexity, suggesting that age-related performance declines are mediated by reductions in working-memory capacity.

A number of findings suggest that older adults are particularly impaired in their ability to maintain information from prior mental operations in a form that permits subsequent computation. For instance, in studies in which the number of premises relevant to solving a verbal reasoning problem or determining the appearance of an unfolded piece of paper is varied so that either one or all premises are relevant, the complexity effect is the same regardless of number of relevant premises or folds (Salthouse, Mitchell, Skovronek, & Babcock, 1989), suggesting that the difficulty of maintaining even one piece of relevant information in working memory increases with age. Also, older adults request more redundant information in cube comparison and matrix reasoning tasks (Salthouse, 1993a; Salthouse & Skovronek, 1992), though this result could simply reflect greater cautiousness in the old. Evidence from more direct assessment of the availability of prior information from earlier operations is more mixed. In some studies, older adults have impaired memory for prior information as tested by recognition probes during problem solution (Salthouse, 1993a; Salthouse & Mitchell, 1989), though this result is not always obtained (Salthouse, 1992c; Salthouse, Mitchell, & Palmon, 1989; Salthouse & Skovronek, 1992). Possibly, passive maintenance of information in working memory is not affected, but maintenance of information in a state amenable to further processing is selectively influenced by aging. Salthouse, Mitchell, and Palmon (1989) presented young and older adults with two successive frames of line segments, with segments either added or deleted in the second frame, and then required a judgment of whether the figure shown in a third frame was consistent with the operations performed on the first two. In some conditions, the second frame preserved a "memory" of the first frame by showing the relevant segments in dotted or full lines. These copy conditions are formally equivalent to a recognition test, yet there was an age difference in these conditions but not in a simple two-frame match/nonmatch recognition test. The old may thus have special problems when storage and processing must be carried out simultaneously, a hallmark of working memory.

Despite these impressive successes, not all within-context assessments of working memory have produced the predicted outcomes. Some variables that would be expected to affect performance do not. Increasing propositional density of sentences of a constant length (a manipulation that also increases syntactic complexity) does not differentially impair gist recall in the old (Stine, Wingfield, & Poon, 1986). Varying the size of a concurrent memory load affects sentence verification latencies to the same extent in young and old (Morris et al., 1988, 1989). Neither the number of variables that must be tracked nor the number of operations performed on them interacts with age in numeric or spatial tasks (Salthouse, Babcock, & Shaw, 1991). Nor does adding a mental operation to a simple storage task increase the magnitude of the age difference in a working-memory task (Babcock & Salthouse, 1990), though this result could be interpreted as implicating storage loss as the major determinant of decreased working memory in old age.

The goals of out-of-context assessments of working memory are twofold: to establish measures of individual differences in working memory and to determine whether working memory mediates age-related differences in other cognitive domains. Age-related differences have been obtained on numerous indices of working-memory capacity including digit span, sentence span, and several types of computation span (see Salthouse, 1990, for review). More important, partialling out measures of working-memory capacity leads to an attenuation of age-related differences in memory for televised news (Stine, Wingfield, & Myers, 1990), reading comprehension (Norman et al., 1992), memory for prose (Morrow et al., 1992; Stine & Wingfield, 1990; but see J. T. Hartley, 1986; Light & Anderson, 1985, for negative results), sentence memory (Stine & Wingfield, 1987), memory for spatial locations (Cherry & Park, 1993), appropriate use of pronouns in recall (Pratt, Boyes, Robins, & Manchester, 1989), verbal reasoning (Salthouse, 1992b, 1992c; Salthouse, Mitchell, Skovronek, & Babcock, 1989), mental paper folding (Salthouse, 1992b; Salthouse, Mitchell, Skovronek, & Babcock, 1989), matrix reasoning (Salthouse, 1993a), geometric analogies (Salthouse, 1992b), problem solving (Charness, 1987), and procedural assembly tasks (Morrell & Park, 1993). In most studies, however, age differences remain even when working-memory capacity is partialled out, suggesting that factors other than working memory also play a role in cognitive declines in old age. It is also possible that there is no single working memory entity, but rather a number of different working memories that are domain specific (Turner & Engle, 1989). If so, the relatively small attenuations of age and performance correlations found when working memory measures are partialled out could be due to mismatches between the domains tapped by the individual-difference measures and cognitive tasks (Hultsch, Hertzog, & Dixon, 1990; Morrell & Park, 1993).

C. Inhibition Deficit Hypothesis

Hasher and Zacks (1988) have proposed that older adults do not have reduced working-memory capacity, but rather have a deficit in the inhibitory mechanisms that regulate the *contents* of working memory. Inhibitory processes are important in restricting entrance into working memory to task-relevant ideas and in suppressing those task-irrelevant ideas that do gain admittance. According to this view, the contents of working memory may differ in young and old, with older adults being more likely to entertain thoughts that are off the goal path, such as personally relevant thoughts, contextually inappropriate interpretations of words or phrases subject to multiple interpretation, and daydreams. Such task-irrelevant contents of memory may arise either because of the presence of irrelevant material in the task environment or because of a broader activation of material relevant to target information. Whatever its origin, the presence of task-irrelevant material is compatible with reduced memory for target information and impaired comprehension when successive parts of a discourse must be integrated.

In the last few years, considerable evidence has accrued in support of the reduced inhibition hypothesis. Older adults have increased difficulty in rejecting distracting information. For instance, they are more susceptible to the Stroop effect (Cohn, Dustman, & Bradford, 1984; Comalli, Wapner, &

Werner, 1962) and show less reduction with practice of Stroop-like inhibition in a mental arithmetic task (Rogers & Fisk, 1991). Older adults are slowed more in a speeded categorization task when target words in one category are flanked by distractors from the competing category (Shaw, 1991). They are also slowed more than young adults in reading passages in which the text is interspersed with distracting material, especially when the distracting material is meaningfully related to passage contents, although it is not clear whether this slowing is accompanied by a greater reduction in memory for the contents of the passages (Connelly, Hasher, & Zacks, 1991). Similarly, search through memory is disproportionately slowed in the old when memorized propositions share concepts with the target proposition; that is, the fan effect is enhanced in old age, suggesting greater sensitivity to interference from competing material in memory (Gerard, Zacks, Hasher, & Radvansky, 1991). Older adults also have difficulty in suppressing irrelevant (disconfirmed) information and in abandoning inferences that are no longer consistent with the contents of a passage (Hamm & Hasher, 1992; Hartman & Hasher, 1991). In studies of directed forgetting, older adults appear to be less able to suppress the processing of items they have been instructed to forget (Zacks, Radvansky, & Hasher, 1996).

Several studies have now examined inhibitory processing in variations of the Tipper paradigm. In this paradigm, two competing stimuli are presented, with subjects instructed to select one and ignore the other. If, on the next trial, a previously ignored distractor becomes the target, responding is slowed, at least in young adults; this outcome is known as "negative priming." In contrast to young adults, older adults show either reduced negative priming, or, in some cases, positive priming (Hasher, Stoltzfus, Zacks, & Rypma, 1991; McDowd & Oseas-Kreger, 1991; Stoltzfus, Hasher, Zacks, Ulivi, & Goldstein, 1993). In these studies, older adults demonstrate reduced inhibition based on the *identity* of the distracters. There is evidence, however, that inhibition based on the *location* of distractors is preserved in old age (Connolley & Hasher, 1993). Moreover, some studies have reported similar levels of negative priming based on identity of distractors (Kramer, Humphrey, Larish, Logan, & Strayer, 1994; Sullivan & Faust, 1993).

Thus, the inhibition hypothesis enjoys considerable empirical support. There are, nonetheless, areas in which it fares less well. It is not clear how general a problem older adults have with respect to inhibitory functioning. For instance, Plude and Doussard-Roosevelt (1989) found no special disadvantage of increasing number of distractors for older adults in a visual search task when the target was defined by a single feature, though the old suffered more when the target was defined by a conjunction of features. Older adults may have more difficulty in ignoring irrelevant auditory stimuli but not irrelevant visual stimuli (McDowd, Oseas-Kreger, & Filion, 1995). And, contrary to expectation, older adults do not show reduced costs associated with invalid cues for the location or identity of a target (see A. A. Hartley, 1992, for review).

More specific claims with respect to the contents of working memory also lack universal support. Daydreaming and task-unrelated thoughts appear to become less, rather than more, frequent in old age (Giambra, 1989). Although older adults report better memory for thoughts and feelings surrounding an event than do young adults and recall more thoughts and feelings and less perceptual and spatial information than do young adults (Hashtroudi, Johnson, & Chrosniak, 1990), it has not been demonstrated that increased memory for thoughts and feelings is responsible for decreases in other aspects of memory. The evidence that does exist on this point is negative: older adults whose speech can be classified as consisting of a "series of loosely associated recollections increasingly remote from, relatively unconstrained by, and irrelevant to the present external contextual stimuli," do not remember less well than other older adults whose speech is not characterized as containing off-target verbosity (Gold, Andres, Arbuckle, & Schwartzman, 1988), despite the fact that off-target verbosity is predicted by scores on tasks thought to measure ability to inhibit task-irrelevant thoughts (Arbuckle & Gold, 1993). Intrusions in recall, which may be taken as indices of irrelevant working-memory contents, are sometimes found to be more frequent in old age (Stine & Wingfield, 1987) but not always (Light & Anderson, 1983; Perlmutter, 1978). A broader spread of activation of meanings should also result in less particularization of word meanings in context, but as noted earlier, this is not the case. Difficulty in rejecting less relevant information should lead to a flattening of the levels effect in prose recall in the old; that is, the old should show less difference in probability of remembering central points and details. However, a recent meta-analysis failed to find this outcome (Verhaeghen, Marcoen, & Goossens, 1993). Finally, if older adults are less able to inhibit target-irrelevant information, we might expect them to remember more contextual details about learning experiences than do young adults, but this does not occur.

D. Cognitive Slowing

Older adults respond more slowly than young adults in almost every task in which speed has been assessed, including rate of rehearsal during a memory task (Salthouse, 1980), rate of scanning in memory search tasks (Cerella, 1985; Fisk, McGee, & Giambra, 1988), and rate of responding in primary and secondary memory tasks (Waugh, Fozard, & Thomas, 1978). Indeed, the phenomenon of general slowing has given rise to the so-called "complexity hypothesis" that the latencies of the old are longer than those of the young by a constant proportion, though that proportion may not be the same for verbal and nonverbal domains (Hale, Lima, & Myerson, 1991;

Lima et al., 1991; Myerson et al., 1992). This slowing has been attributed to greater noise in the nervous system (Salthouse & Lichty, 1985), broken or attenuated neural connections (Cerella, 1990), weakened linkage strength between connections (MacKay & Burke, 1990), or an increase in the proportion of information lost at each step of processing (Myerson, Hale, Wagstaff, Poon, & Smith, 1990).

Some theorists have suggested ways in which deficits in transmission of activation in a network might account for important aspects of age-related memory declines without invoking the concept of attentional capacity. Slower transmission of activation can result in a smaller number of connected nodes being activated, so that memory traces are less elaborated (Salthouse, 1988a). Slowing of activation can lead to fewer nodes being simultaneously active, or, in other words, to reduced working-memory capacity (Salthouse, 1992a). MacKay and Burke (1990) have described mechanisms whereby transmission deficits can prevent the formation of new associations or cause activation failures in existing connections, resulting in retrieval failures such as the tip-of-the-tongue experience. Baddeley, Thomson, and Buchanan (1975) found that memory span is related to rate of pronunciation in the young and the same function appears to account for memory span in the old, as well (Kynette, Kemper, Norman, & Cheung, 1990). Interestingly, Myerson et al. (1990) noted that increasing the amount of time available for study cannot compensate for slowing of transmission, so that age-related differences in memory should not be eliminated by providing unlimited presentation time—and they are not (Craik & Rabinowitz, 1985).

Empirical efforts to demonstrate that memory declines in old age are due wholly or in large measure to cognitive slowing have used correlational techniques such as hierarchical regression or path analysis to determine whether age-performance correlations are attenuated when individual-difference measures of processing speed are controlled statistically. For instance, Salthouse (1985) used digit symbol substitution performance as an index of cognitive speed and examined the pattern of intercorrelations among age, speed, and performance on several measures of memory, including a number of span tasks, a supraspan task (eight trials on seven pairs of letters or digits), free recall of word lists, paired-associate learning, and spatial recall. In most cases, partialling out speed reduced the correlation between age and performance, at least somewhat. Similarly, Salthouse (1988b) reported that age-performance relationships on verbal and spatial memory tasks were mediated by cognitive speed as assessed by digit–symbol substitution performance. In neither case, however, did age-performance correlations drop to zero, as would be expected if slowing were the sole basis of age-related declines in memory; moreover, in a path analytic study that included a variety of measures of cognition, including some memory tasks, Salthouse, Kausler, and Saults (1988b) reported that in the great majority of cases, the magnitude of the direct path between age and performance exceeded that of the indirect (age–speed–performance) path.

Nevertheless, more recent studies have found substantial evidence for speed mediation of age–cognition relationships in tasks clearly identifiable as measures of memory, such as paired-associate learning and recall of lists or prose passages (Lindenberger, Mayr, & Kliegl, 1993; Salthouse, 1993b, 1994), as well as in other measures of cognition thought to have a memory component, such as verbal reasoning, solution of geometric analogies, matrix reasoning, and spatial ability (Hertzog, 1989; Lindenberger et al., 1993; Salthouse, 1991a, 1992b, 1993a; Schaie, 1989). To give just one example, Salthouse (1993b) found that statistically controlling for a composite measure of speed attenuated the age-related variance in a composite measure of cognition by 98.5% and in a composite measure of memory by 82.6%. The size of age-related differences in measures of working memory capacity is also reduced materially by controlling for variables reflecting the speed of simple perceptual comparison (Salthouse, 1988b, 1991a, 1992a, 1992b; Salthouse & Babcock, 1991; Salthouse & Coon, 1993).

Several points should be made at this juncture. First, studies that pit perceptual-speed and working-memory measures against each other as mediators of age-performance measures have found mixed outcomes. That is, statistically controlling speed does not always attenuate the amount of age-related variance more than controlling indices of working memory (Salthouse, 1991a, 1993b). Thus, it is not clear that one of these constructs does a better job of explaining age-related differences in cognition. Salthouse (1993b) has suggested that with more complex tasks, the influence of speed may operate via working memory, with reduced working memory in old age leading to problems in maintaining the availability of products of earlier operations for subsequent processing. There is also some evidence that the influence of speed is greater when the criterion measure is number of items correct in a given amount of time (e.g., on reasoning problems), but that working memory is more important when the proportion of attempted items successfully completed is considered.

Second, questions arise as to just which aspects of speed mediate age-related differences. It has become apparent that a single slowing parameter cannot describe the relationship between young and old latencies in all tasks or domains (Baron & Mattila, 1989; Cerella, 1985; Hale et al., 1991; Hertzog, Raskind, & Cannon, 1986; Lima et al., 1991; Myerson et al., 1992; Rogers & Fisk, 1991). Similarly, studies of time-accuracy functions indicate that old/young ratios for the amount of time needed to reach particular accuracy levels are not constant across tasks: tasks requiring coordinative as opposed to purely sequential processing are more affected by age (Kliegl, Mayr, & Krampe, 1994; Mayr & Kliegl, 1993). Whether slowing is greater in cognitive operations or in sensorimotor processes is also unclear. For instance, studies measuring both reaction time and electrophysiological indices of slowing (the P300) find that the functions relating young and old reaction times and young and old P300 measures are different (see Bashore, 1993, for review). It thus becomes crucial to ask which aspects of slowing play a role in age-related differences in cognition. Salthouse (1993b) has argued that perceptual rather than motor speed is the variable most responsible for mediating age differences in cognition and memory. He has also suggested that task-independent (general) measures of perceptual speed do a better job of capturing age-related variance than do task-specific measures of perceptual speed (Salthouse & Coon, 1993). In support of this suggestion, J. T. Hartley (1988) identified both a general slowness factor and a specific-process slowing factor—the former, but not the latter, appearing to be important in predicting discourse memory either for her whole sample of young, middle-aged, and older adults or for just the older sample.

E. Summary

Processing-resource approaches are appealing because they seek to identify deficits in basic mechanisms underlying not only memory but also other aspects of cognition. In this section, findings relevant to the hypotheses that memory changes in old age are due to reduced attentional capacity, smaller working-memory capacity, defective inhibitory processing, or general slowing have been reviewed. The picture with respect to attentional capacity is at best mixed, with some studies reporting larger divided-attention costs for old adults than for young adults on tasks thought to tap encoding or retrieval processes, and others reporting comparable costs for both age groups. A similar picture exists with respect to the inhibition-deficit hypothesis. Age differences are found in some, but not all, paradigms that purport to measure inhibitory mechanisms. Also, there are at present no good individual-difference measures of either attentional capacity or inhibition. The outlook is somewhat better for both the working-memory capacity and general slowing approaches. Measures of both of these constructs that reliably discriminate between young and older adults have been developed. More crucially, both working-memory capacity and speed appear to account for substantial proportions of the age-related variability in memory as well as in other areas of cognition, though it is as yet unknown whether one of these is more fundamental or whether both do an equally good job in explaining age differences.

V. CONCLUSION

Four accounts of the nature of age-related changes in memory have been considered in this chapter. A review of the literature turned up little support for the view that changes in the nature of encoding or retrieval strategies are responsible for reduced performance on memory tasks requiring deliberate recollection. Nor was there convincing evidence that deficits in semantic processing underlie age-related memory impairment. Although there is quite good evidence that older adults have poorer recollection of contextual information and there is reason to believe that familiarity or perceptual fluency mechanisms are relatively insensitive to aging, there are some obstacles to accepting the hypothesis that age deficits in recall and recognition are due solely to reduced efficiency of context-dependent processing. Whether young and older adults differ on indirect measures of memory remains an open question. At present, interest centers on investigating the role of basic mechanisms such as attention, working-memory capacity, inhibition, and processing speed in mediating age-related changes in memory.

Acknowledgment

Preparation of this chapter was supported by National Institute on Aging Grant R37 AG02452.

References

Abbenhuis, M. A., Raaijmakers, W. G. M., Raaijmakers, J. G. W., & van Woerden, G. J. M. (1990). Episodic memory in dementia of the Alzheimer type and in normal ageing: Similar impairment in automatic processing. *Quarterly Journal of Experimental Psychology, 42A,* 569–583.

Anderson, J. A. (1983). A spreading activation theory of memory. *Journal of Verbal Learning and Verbal Behavior, 22,* 261–295.

Arbuckle, T. Y., & Gold, D. P. (1993). Aging, inhibition, and verbosity. *Journal of Gerontology: Psychological Sciences, 48,* P225–P232.

Arbuckle, T. Y., Gold, D. P., Andres, D., Schwartzman, A., & Chaikelson, J. (1992). The role of psychosocial context, age, and intelligence in memory performance of older men. *Psychology and Aging, 7,* 25–36.

Arbuckle, T. Y., Vanderleck, V. F., Harsany, M., & Lapidus, S. (1990). Adult age differences in memory in relation to availability and accessibility of knowledge-based schemas. *Journal of Experimental Psychology: Learning, Memory, and Cognition, 16,* 305–315.

Babcock, R. L., & Salthouse, T. A. (1990). Effects of increased processing demands on age differences in working memory. *Psychology and Aging, 5,* 421–428.

Bäckman, L. (1989). Varieties of memory compensation by older adults in episodic remembering. In L. W. Poon, D. C. Rubin, & B. A. Wilson (Eds.), *Everyday cognition in adulthood and late life* (pp. 509–544). Cambridge: Cambridge University Press.

Baddeley, A. (1986). *Working memory.* Oxford: Clarendon Press.

Baddeley, A., Logie, R., Bressi, S., Della Sala, S., & Spinnler, H. (1986). Dementia and working memory. *Quarterly Journal of Experimental Psychology, 38A,* 603–618.

Baddeley, A. D., Thomson, N., & Buchanan, M. (1975). Word length and the structure of short-term memory. *Journal of Verbal Learning and Verbal Behavior, 14,* 575–589.

Bahrick, H. P. (1984). Memory for people. In J. E. Harris & P. E. Morris (Eds.), *Everyday memory, actions and absent-mindedness* (pp. 19–34). New York: Academic Press.

Balota, D. A., Black, S. R., & Cheney, M. (1992). Automatic and attentional priming in young and older adults: Reevaluation of the two-process model. *Journal of Experimental Psychology: Human Perception and Performance, 18,* 485–502.

Balota, D. A., & Duchek, J. M. (1988). Age-related differences in lexical access, spreading activation, and simple pronunciation. *Psychology and Aging, 3,* 84–93.

Balota, D. A., Duchek, J. M., & Paullin, R. (1989). Age-related differences in the impact of spacing, lag, and retention interval. *Psychology and Aging, 4,* 3–9.

Baltes, P. B., & Kliegl, R. (1992). Further testing of limits of cognitive plasticity: Negative age differences in mnemonic skill are robust. *Developmental Psychology, 28,* 121–125.

Baron, A., & Mattila, W. R. (1989). Response slowing of older adults: Effects of time-limit contingencies on single- and dual-task performances. *Psychology and Aging, 4,* 66–72.

Bartlett, J. C., & Fulton, A. (1991). Familiarity and recognition of faces in old age. *Memory & Cognition, 19,* 229–238.

Bartlett, J. C., Strater, L., & Fulton, A. (1991). False recency and false fame of faces in young adulthood and old age. *Memory & Cognition, 19,* 177–188.

Bashore, T. R. (1993). Differential effects of aging on the neurocognitive functions subserving speeded mental processing. In J. Cerella, J. Rybash, W. Hoyer, & M. L. Commons (Eds.), *Adult information processing: Limits on loss* (pp. 37–76). San Diego: Academic Press.

Berry, J. M. (1989). Cognitive efficacy across the life span: Introduction to the special series. *Developmental Psychology, 25,* 683–686.

Bowers, J., & Schacter, D. L. (1993). Priming of novel information in amnesic patients: Issues and data. In P. Graf & M. Masson (Eds.), *Implicit memory: New directions in cognition, development, and neuropsychology* (pp. 303–326). Hillsdale, NJ: Erlbaum.

Bowles, N. L. (1994). Age and rate of activation in semantic memory. *Psychology and Aging, 9,* 414–429.

Bowles, N. L., & Poon, L. W. (1985). Aging and retrieval of words in semantic memory. *Journal of Gerontology, 40,* 71–77.

Brigham, M. C., & Pressley, M. (1988). Cognitive monitoring and strategy choice in younger and older adults. *Psychology and Aging, 3,* 249–257.

Brown, A. S., & Mitchell, D. B. (1991). Age differences in retrieval consistency and response dominance. *Journal of Gerontology: Psychological Sciences, 46,* P332–P339.

Burke, D. M., & Harrold, R. M. (1988). Automatic and effortful semantic processes in old age: Experimental and naturalistic approaches. In L. L. Light & D. M. Burke (Eds.), *Language, memory, and aging* (pp. 100–116). New York: Cambridge University Press.

Burke, D. M., & Light, L. L. (1981). Memory and aging: The role of retrieval processes. *Psychological Bulletin, 90,* 513–546.

Burke, D. M., MacKay, D. G., Worthley, J. S., & Wade, E. (1991). On the tip of the tongue: What causes word finding failures in young and older adults? *Journal of Memory and Language, 30,* 542–579.

Burke, D. M., & Peters, L. (1986). Word associations in old age: Evidence for consistency in semantic encoding during adulthood. *Psychology and Aging, 1,* 283–292.

Burke, D. M., White, H., & Diaz, D. L. (1987). Semantic priming in young and older adults: Evidence for age constancy in automatic and effortful processes. *Journal of Experimental Psychology: Human Perception and Performance, 13,* 79–88.

Burke, D. M., & Yee, P. L. (1984). Semantic priming during sentence processing by young and older adults. *Developmental Psychology, 20,* 903–910.

Butterfield, E. C., Nelson, T. O., & Peck, V. (1988). Developmental aspects of the feeling of knowing. *Developmental Psychology, 24,* 654–663.

Cerella, J. (1985). Information processing rates in the elderly. *Psychological Bulletin, 98,* 67–83.

Cerella, J. (1990). Aging and information-processing rate. In J. E. Birren & K. W. Schaie (Eds.), *Handbook of the psychology of aging* (3rd ed., pp. 201–221). New York: Academic Press.

Charness, N. (1981). Aging and skilled problem solving. *Journal of Experimental Psychology: General, 110,* 21–38.

Charness, N. (1987). Component processes in bridge bidding and novel problem-solving tasks. *Canadian Journal of Psychology, 41,* 223–243.

Cherry, K. E., & Park, D. C. (1993). Individual difference and contextual variables influence spatial memory in younger and older adults. *Psychology and Aging, 8,* 517–526.

Chiarello, C., & Hoyer, W. J. (1988). Adult age differences in implicit and explicit memory: Time course and encoding effects. *Psychology and Aging, 3,* 358–366.

Cohen, G. (1979). Language comprehension in old age. *Cognitive Psychology, 11,* 412–429.

Cohen, G. (1981). Inferential reasoning in old age. *Cognition, 9,* 59–72.

Cohen, G., Conway, M. A., & Maylor, E. A. (1994). Flashbulb memories in older adults. *Psychology and Aging, 9,* 454–463.

Cohen, G., & Faulkner, D. (1983). Word recognition: Age differences in contextual facilitation effects. *British Journal of Psychology, 74,* 239–251.

Cohen, G., & Faulkner, D. (1986). Memory for proper names: Age differences in retrieval. *British Journal of Developmental Psychology, 4,* 187–197.

Cohen, G., & Faulkner, D. (1989). Age differences in source forgetting: Effects on reality monitoring and on eyewitness testimony. *Psychology and Aging, 4,* 10–17.

Cohn, N. B., Dustman, R. E., & Bradford, D. C. (1984). Age-related decrements in Stroop color test performance. *Journal of Clinical Psychology, 40,* 1244–1250.

Comalli, P. E., Jr., Wapner, S., & Werner, H. (1962). Interference effects of Stroop color-word test in childhood, adulthood, and aging. *Journal of Genetic Psychology, 100,* 47–53.

Connelly, S. L., & Hasher, L. (1993). Aging and the inhibition of spatial location. *Journal of Experimental Psychology: Human Perception and Performance, 19,* 1238–1250.

Connelly, S. L., Hasher, L., & Zacks, R. T. (1991). Age and reading: The impact of distraction. *Psychology and Aging, 6,* 533–541.

Craik, F. I. M. (1977). Age differences in human memory. In J. E. Birren & K. W. Schaie (Eds.), *Handbook of the psychology of aging* (pp. 384–420). New York: Van Nostrand-Reinhold.

Craik, F. I. M. (1983). On the transfer of information from temporary to permanent storage. *Philosophical Transactions of the Royal Society of London, Series B, 302,* 341–359.

Craik, F. I. M. (1986). A functional account of age differences in memory. In F. Klix & H. Hagendorf (Eds.), *Human memory and cognitive capabilities* (pp. 409–422). Amsterdam: Elsevier.

Craik, F. I. M., & Byrd, M. (1982). Aging and cognitive deficits: The role of attentional resources. In F. I. M. Craik & S. Trehub (Eds.), *Aging and cognitive processes* (pp. 191–211). New York: Plenum Press.

Craik, F. I. M., & Jennings, J. M. (1992). Human memory. In F. I. M. Craik & T. A. Salthouse (Eds.), *The handbook of aging and cognition* (pp. 51–110). Hillsdale, NJ: Erlbaum.

Craik, F. I. M., & McDowd, J. M. (1987). Age differences in recall and recognition. *Journal of Experimental Psychology: Learning, Memory, and Cognition, 13,* 474–479.

Craik, F. I. M., & Rabinowitz, J. C. (1985). The effects of presentation rate and encoding task on age-related memory deficits. *Journal of Gerontology, 40,* 309–315.

Cutler, S. J., & Grams, A. E. (1988). Correlates of self-reported everyday memory problems. *Journal of Gerontology: Social Sciences, 43,* S82–S90.

Davis, H. P., Cohen, A., Gandy, M., Colombo, P., VanDusseldorp, G., Simolke, N., & Romano, J. (1990). Lexical priming deficits as a function of age. *Behavioral Neuroscience, 104,* 288–297.

Devolder, P. A., Brigham, M. C., & Pressley, M. (1990). Memory performance awareness in younger and older adults. *Psychology and Aging, 5,* 291–303.

Dick, M. B., Kean, M.-L., & Sands, D. (1989). Memory for internally generated words in Alzheimer-type dementia: Breakdown in encoding and semantic memory. *Brain and Cognition, 9,* 88–108.

Dixon, R. A. (1989). Questionnaire research on metamemory and aging: Issues of structure and function. In L. W. Poon, D. C. Rubin, & B. A. Wilson (Eds.), *Everyday cognition in adulthood and late life* (pp. 394–415). Cambridge: Cambridge University Press.

Dixon, R. A., & Hultsch, D. F. (1983). Structure and development of metamemory in adulthood. *Journal of Gerontology, 38,* 682–688.

Duchek, J. M. (1984). Encoding and retrieval differences between young and old: The impact of attentional capacity usage. *Developmental Psychology, 20,* 1173–1180.

Dywan, J., & Jacoby, L. (1990). Effects of aging on source monitoring: Differences in susceptibility to false fame. *Psychology and Aging, 5,* 379–387.

Ebbinghaus, H. (1964). *Memory: A contribution to experimental psychology.* New York: Dover.

Eich, J. M. (1985). Levels of processing, encoding specificity, elaboration, and CHARM. *Psychological Review, 92,* 1–38.

Ferguson, S. A., Hashtroudi, S., & Johnson, M. K. (1992). Age differences in using source-relevant cues. *Psychology and Aging, 7,* 443–452.

Fisk, A. D., McGee, N. D., & Giambra, L. M. (1988). The influence of age on consistent and varied semantic-category search performance. *Psychology and Aging, 3,* 323–333.

Foos, P. W. (1989). Age differences in memory for two common objects. *Journal of Gerontology: Psychological Sciences, 44,* P178–P180.

Gerard, L., Zacks, R. T., Hasher, L., & Radvansky, G. A. (1991). Age deficits in retrieval: The fan effect. *Journal of Gerontology: Psychological Sciences, 46,* P131–P136.

Giambra, L. M. (1989). Task-Unrelated-Thought frequency as a function of age: A laboratory study. *Psychology and Aging, 4,* 136–143.

Gick, M. L., Craik, F. I. M., & Morris, R. G. (1988). Task complexity and age differences in working memory. *Memory & Cognition, 16,* 353–361.

Gillund, G., & Shiffrin, R. M. (1984). A retrieval model for both recognition and recall. *Psychological Review, 91,* 1–67.

Gold, D., Andres, D., Arbuckle, T., & Schwartzman, A. (1988). Measurement and correlates of verbosity in elderly people. *Journal of Gerontology: Psychological Sciences, 43,* P27–P33.

Graf, P., & Mandler, G. (1984). Activation makes words more accessible, but not necessarily more retrievable. *Journal of Verbal Learning and Verbal Behavior, 23,* 553–568.

Graf, P., & Schacter, D. L. (1985). Implicit and explicit memory for new associations in normal and amnesic subjects. *Journal of Experimental Psychology: Learning, Memory, and Cognition, 11,* 501–518.

Hale, S., Lima, S. D., & Myerson, J. (1991). General cognitive slowing in the nonlexical domain: An experimental validation. *Psychology and Aging, 6,* 512–521.

Hamm, V. P., & Hasher, L. (1992). Age and the availability of inferences. *Psychology and Aging, 7,* 56–64.

Hartley, A. A. (1992). Attention. In F. I. M. Craik & T. A. Salthouse (Eds.), *The handbook of aging and cognition* (pp. 3–49). Hillsdale, NJ: Erlbaum.

Hartley, J. T. (1986). Reader and text variables as determinants of discourse memory in adulthood. *Psychology and Aging, 1,* 150–158.

Hartley, J. T. (1988). Aging and individual differences in memory for written discourse. In L. L. Light & D. M. Burke (Eds.), *Language, memory, and aging* (pp. 36–57). New York: Cambridge University Press.

Hartman, M., & Hasher, L. (1991). Aging and suppression: Memory for previously relevant information. *Psychology and Aging, 6,* 587–594.

Hasher, L., Stoltzfus, E. R., Zacks, R. T., & Rypma, B. (1991). Age and inhibition. *Journal of Experimental Psychology: Learning, Memory, and Cognition, 17,* 163–169.

Hasher, L., & Zacks, R. T. (1979). Automatic and effortful processes in memory. *Journal of Experimental Psychology: General, 108,* 356–388.

Hasher, L., & Zacks, R. T. (1988). Working memory, comprehension, and aging: A review and a new view. In G. H. Bower (Ed.), *The psychology of learning and motivation: Advances in research and theory* (Vol. 22, pp. 193–225). New York: Academic Press.

Hashtroudi, S., Chrosniak, L. D., & Schwartz, B. L. (1991). Effects of aging on priming and skill learning. *Psychology and Aging, 6,* 605–615.

Hashtroudi, S., Johnson, M. K., & Chrosniak, L. D. (1989). Aging and source monitoring. *Psychology and Aging, 4,* 106–112.

Hashtroudi, S., Johnson, M. K., & Chrosniak, L. D. (1990). Aging and qualitative characteristics of memories for perceived and imagined complex events. *Psychology and Aging, 5,* 119–126.

Hertzog, C. (1989). Influences of cognitive slowing on age differences in intelligence. *Developmental Psychology, 25,* 636–651.

Hertzog, C., Dixon, R. A., & Hultsch, D. F. (1990). Relationships between metamemory, memory predictions, and memory task performance in adults. *Psychology and Aging, 5,* 215–227.

Hertzog, C., Raskind, C. L., & Cannon, C. J. (1986). Age-related slowing in semantic information processing speed: An individual differences analysis. *Journal of Gerontology, 41,* 500–502.

Hess, T. M. (1984). Effects of semantically related and unrelated contexts on recognition memory of different-aged adults. *Journal of Gerontology, 39,* 444–451.

Hess, T. M. (1985). Aging and context influences on recognition memory for typical and atypical script actions. *Developmental Psychology, 21,* 1139–1151.

Hess, T. M., Donley, J., & Vandermaas, M. O. (1989). Aging-related changes in the processing and retention of script information. *Experimental Aging Research, 15,* 89–96.

Hess, T. M., & Flannagan, D. A. (1992). Schema-based retrieval processes in young and older adults. *Journal of Gerontology: Psychological Sciences, 47,* P52–P58.

Hintzman, D. L. (1988). Judgments of frequency and recognition memory in a multiple-trace memory model. *Psychological Review, 95,* 528–551.

Howard, D. V. (1979). *Restricted word association norms for adults between the ages of 20 and 80* (Tech. Rep. NIA-79-2). Washington, DC: Georgetown University.

Howard, D. V. (1980). Category norms: A comparison of the Battig and Montague (1969) norms with the responses of adults between the ages of 20 and 80. *Journal of Gerontology, 35,* 225–231.

Howard, D. V. (1983). The effects of aging and degree of association on the semantic priming of lexical decisions. *Experimental Aging Research, 9,* 145–151.

Howard, D. V. (1988). Implicit and explicit assessment of cognitive aging. In M. L. Howe & C. L. Brainerd (Eds.), *Cognitive development in adulthood: Progress in cognitive development research* (pp. 3–37). New York: Springer-Verlag.

Howard, D. V., Fry, A. F., & Brune, C. M. (1991). Aging and memory for new associations: Direct versus indirect measures. *Journal of Experimental Psychology: Learning, Memory, and Cognition, 17,* 779–792.

Howard, D. V., Heisey, J. G., & Shaw, R. J. (1986). Aging and the priming of newly learned associations. *Developmental Psychology, 22,* 78–85.

Howard, D. V., Mc Andrews, M. P., & Lasaga, M. I. (1981). Semantic priming of lexical decisions in young and old adults. *Journal of Gerontology, 36,* 707–714.

Howard, D. V., Shaw, R. J., & Heisey, J. G. (1986). Aging and the time course of semantic activation. *Journal of Gerontology, 41,* 195–203.

Hultsch, D. F., Hammer, M., & Small, B. J. (1993). Age differences in cognitive performance in later life: Relationships to self-reported health and activity life style. *Journal of Gerontology: Psychological Sciences, 48,* P1–P11.

Hultsch, D. F., Hertzog, C., & Dixon, R. A. (1990). Ability correlates of memory performance in adulthood and aging. *Psychology and Aging, 5,* 356–368.

Hultsch, D. F., Masson, M. E. J., & Small, B. J. (1991). Adult age differences in direct and indirect tests of memory. *Journal of Gerontology: Psychological Sciences, 46,* P22–P30.

Humphreys, M. S., Bain, J. D., & Pike, R. (1989). Different ways to cue a coherent memory system: A theory for episodic, semantic, and procedural tasks. *Psychological Review, 96,* 208–233.

Intons-Peterson, M. J., & Fournier, J. A. (1986). External and internal memory aids: When and how often do we use them? *Journal of Experimental Psychology: General, 115,* 267–280.

Isingrini, M., Vazou, F., & Leroy, P. (1995). Dissociation of implicit and explicit memory tests: Effects of age and divided attention on category exemplar generation and cued recall. *Memory & Cognition, 23,* 462–467.

Ivy, G. O., MacLeod, C. M., Petit, T. L., & Markus, E. J. (1992). A physiological framework for perceptual and cognitive changes in aging. In F. I. M. Craik & T. Salthouse (Eds.), *The handbook of aging and cognition* (pp. 273–314). Hillsdale, NJ: Erlbaum.

Jacoby, L. L. (1983). Remembering the data: Analyzing interactive processes in reading. *Journal of Verbal Learning and Verbal Behavior, 22,* 485–508.

Jacoby, L. L. (1991). A process dissociation framework: Separating automatic from intentional uses of memory. *Journal of Memory and Language, 30,* 513–541.

Jacoby, L. L., & Dallas, M. (1981). On the relationship between autobiographical memory and perceptual learning. *Journal of Experimental Psychology: General, 110,* 306–340.

Janowsky, J. S., Shimamura, A. P., & Squire, L. R. (1989). Source memory impairment in patients with frontal lobe lesions. *Neuropsychologia, 27,* 1043–1056.

Java, R. I. (1992). Priming and aging: Evidence of preserved memory function in an anagram task. *American Journal of Psychology, 105,* 541–548.

Java, R. I., & Gardiner, J. M. (1991). Priming and aging: Further evidence of preserved memory function. *American Journal of Psychology, 104,* 89–100.

Jennings, J. M., & Jacoby, L. L. (1993). Automatic versus intentional uses of memory: Aging, attention, and control. *Psychology and Aging, 8,* 283–293.

Johnson, M. K., Foley, M. A., Suengas, A. G., & Raye, C. L. (1988). Phenomenal characteristics of memories for perceived and imagined events. *Journal of Experimental Psychology: General, 117,* 371–376.

Jonides, J., & Naveh-Benjamin, M. (1987). Estimating frequency of occurrence. *Journal of Experimental Psychology: Learning, Memory, and Cognition, 13,* 230–240.

Kausler, D. H. (1990). Automaticity of encoding and episodic memory processes. In E. A. Lovelace (Ed.), *Aging and cognition: Mental processes, self-awareness, and interventions* (pp. 29–67). Amsterdam: Elsevier.

Kausler, D. H., & Lichty, W. (1988). Memory for activities: Rehearsal-independence and aging. In M. L. Howe & C. J. Brainerd (Eds.), *Cognitive development in adulthood: Progress in cognitive development research* (pp. 93–131). New York: Springer-Verlag.

Kausler, D. H., & Puckett, J. M. (1980). Adult age differences in recognition memory for a nonsemantic attribute. *Experimental Aging Research, 6,* 349–355.

Kausler, D. H., & Puckett, J. M. (1981a). Adult age differences in memory for modality attributes. *Experimental Aging Research, 7,* 117–125.

Kausler, D. H., & Puckett, J. M. (1981b). Adult age differences in memory for sex of voice. *Journal of Gerontology, 36,* 44–50.

Kemper, S. (1986). Imitation of complex syntactic constructions by elderly adults. *Applied Psycholinguistics, 7,* 277–288.

Kieley, J. (1990). *A meta-analysis and review of aging and divided attention.* Unpublished manuscript, Claremont Graduate School, Department of Psychology, Claremont, CA.

Kintsch, W. (1988). The role of knowledge in discourse comprehension: A construction-integration model. *Psychological Review, 95,* 163–182.

Kliegl, R., & Lindenberger, U. (1993). Modeling intrusions and correct recall in episodic memory: Adult age differences in encoding of list context. *Journal of Experimental Psychology: Learning, Memory, and Cognition, 19,* 617–637.

Kliegl, R., Mayr, U., & Krampe, R. T. (1994). Time-accuracy functions for determining process and person differences: An application to cognitive aging. *Cognitive Psychology, 26,* 134–164.

Koriat, A., Ben-Zur, H., & Sheffer, D. (1988). Telling the same story twice: Output monitoring and age. *Journal of Memory and Language, 27,* 23–39.

Kramer, A. F., Humphrey, D. G., Larish, J. F., Logan, G. D., & Strayer, D. L. (1994). Aging and inhibition: Beyond a unitary view of inhibitory processing in attention. *Psychology and Aging, 9,* 491–512.

Kynette, D., Kemper, S., Norman, S., & Cheung, H. T. (1990). Adults' word recall and word repetition. *Experimental Aging Research, 16,* 117–121.

Lachman, M. E., Weaver, S. L., Bandura, M., Elliott, E., & Lewkowicz, C. J. (1992). Improving memory and control beliefs through cognitive restructuring and self-generated strategies. *Journal of Gerontology: Psychological Sciences, 47,* P293–P299.

La Rue, A. (1992). *Aging and neuropsychological assessment.* New York: Plenum Press.

Laver, G. D., & Burke, D. M. (1993). Why do semantic priming effects increase in old age? A meta-analysis. *Psychology and Aging, 8,* 34–43.

La Voie, D., & Light, L. L. (1994). Adult age differences in repetition priming: A meta-analysis. *Psychology and Aging, 9,* 539–553.

Lehman, E. B., & Mellinger, J. C. (1984). Effects of aging on memory for presentation modality. *Developmental Psychology, 20,* 1210–1217.

Lehman, E. B., & Mellinger, J. C. (1986). Forgetting rates in modality memory for young, mid-life, and older women. *Psychology and Aging, 1,* 178–179.

Light, L. L. (1991). Memory and aging: Four hypotheses in search of data. *Annual Review of Psychology, 42,* 333–376.

Light, L. L. (1992). The organization of memory in old age. In F. I. M. Craik & T. A. Salthouse (Eds.), *The handbook of aging and cognition* (pp. 111–165). Hillsdale, NJ: Erlbaum.

Light, L. L., & Albertson, S. (1988). Comprehension of pragmatic implications in young and older adults. In L. L. Light & D. M. Burke (Eds.), *Language, memory, and aging* (pp. 133–153). New York: Cambridge University Press.

Light, L. L., & Albertson, S. A. (1989). Direct and indirect tests of memory for category exemplars in young and older adults. *Psychology and Aging, 4,* 487–492.

Light, L. L., Albertson Owens, S., Mahoney, P. G., & La Voie, D. (1993). Comprehension of metaphors by young and older adults. In J. Cerella, J. Rybash, W. Hoyer, & M. L. Commons (Eds.), *Adult information processing: Limits on loss* (pp. 459–488). San Diego: Academic Press.

Light, L. L., & Anderson, P. A. (1983). Memory for scripts in young and older adults. *Memory & Cognition, 11,* 435–444.

Light, L. L., & Anderson, P. A. (1985). Working-memory capacity, age, and memory for discourse. *Journal of Gerontology, 40,* 737–747.

Light, L. L., & Capps, J. L. (1986). Comprehension of pronouns in young and older adults. *Developmental Psychology, 22,* 580–585.

Light, L. L., Capps, J. L., Singh, A., & Albertson Owens, S. A. (1994). Comprehension and use of anaphoric devices in young and older adults. *Discourse Processes, 18,* 77–103.

Light, L. L., La Voie, D., & Kennison, R. (1995). Repetition priming of nonwords in young and older adults. *Journal of Experimental Psychology: Learning, Memory, and Cognition, 21,* 327–346.

Light, L. L., La Voie, D., Valencia-Laver, D., Albertson Owens, S. A., & Mead, G. (1992). Direct and indirect measures of memory for modality in young and older adults. *Journal of Experimental Psychology: Learning, Memory, and Cognition, 18,* 1284–1297.

Light, L. L., & Prull, M. W. (1995). Aging, divided attention, and repetition priming. *Swiss Journal of Psychology, 54,* 87–101.

Light, L. L., & Singh, A. (1987). Implicit and explicit memory in young and older adults. *Journal of Experimental Psychology: Learning, Memory, and Cognition, 13,* 531–541.

Light, L. L., Singh, A., & Capps, J. L. (1986). Dissociation of memory and awareness in young and older adults. *Journal of Clinical and Experimental Neuropsychology, 8,* 62–74.

Light, L. L., Valencia-Laver, D., & Zavis, D. (1991). Instantiation of general terms in young and older adults. *Psychology and Aging, 6,* 337–351.

Light, L. L., Zelinski, E. M., & Moore, M. (1982). Adult age differences in reasoning from new information. *Journal of Experimental Psychology: Learning, Memory, and Cognition, 8,* 435–447.

Lima, S. D., Hale, S., & Myerson, J. (1991). How general is general slowing? Evidence from the lexical domain. *Psychology and Aging, 6,* 416–425.

Lindenberger, U., Kliegl, R., & Baltes, P. B. (1992). Professional expertise does not eliminate age differences in imagery-based memory performance during adulthood. *Psychology and Aging, 7,* 585–593.

Lindenberger, U., Mayr., U., & Kliegl, R. (1993). Speed and intelligence in old age. *Psychology and Aging, 8,* 207–220.

Loewen, E. R., Shaw, R. J., & Craik, F. I. M. (1990). Age differences in components of metamemory. *Experimental Aging Research, 16,* 43–48.

Lovelace, E. A., & Cooley, S. (1982). Free associations of older adults to single words and conceptually related word triads. *Journal of Gerontology, 37,* 432–437.

Macht, M. L., & Buschke, H. (1983). Age differences in cognitive effort in recall. *Journal of Gerontology, 38,* 695–700.

Mackay, D. G., & Burke, D. M. (1990). Cognition and aging: A theory of new learning and the use of old connections. In T. M. Hess (Ed.), *Aging and cognition: Knowledge organization and utilization* (pp. 213–264). Amsterdam: North-Holland.

Madden, D. J. (1986). Adult age differences in visual word recognition: Semantic encoding and episodic retention. *Experimental Aging Research, 12,* 71–77.

Madden, D. J. (1989). Visual word identification and age-related slowing. *Cognitive Development, 4,* 1–29.

Mandler, G. (1980). Recognizing: The judgment of previous occurrence. *Psychological Review, 87,* 252–271.

Mäntylä, T. (1993). Knowing but not remembering: Adult age differences in recollective experience. *Memory & Cognition, 21,* 379–388.

Mäntylä, T., & Bäckman, L. (1990). Encoding variability and age-related retrieval failures. *Psychology and Aging, 5,* 545–550.

Mäntylä, T., & Bäckman, L. (1992). Aging and memory for expected and unexpected objects in real-world settings. *Journal of Experimental Psychology: Learning, Memory, and Cognition, 18,* 1298–1309.

Maylor, E. A. (1990). Recognizing and naming faces: Aging, memory retrieval, and the tip of the tongue state. *Journal of Gerontology: Psychological Sciences, 45,* P215–P226.

Maylor, E. A. (1991). Recognizing and naming tunes: Memory impairment in the elderly. *Journal of Gerontology: Psychological Sciences, 46,* P207–P217.

Mayr, U., & Kliegl, R. (1993). Sequential and coordinative complexity: Age-based processing limitations in figural transformations. *Journal of Experimental Psychology: Learning, Memory, and Cognition, 19,* 1297–1320.

McClelland, J. L., & Rumelhart, D. E. (1981). An interactive activation model of context effects in letter perception: Part 1. An account of basic findings. *Psychological Review, 88,* 375–407.

McDowd, J. M., & Oseas-Kreger, D. M. (1991). Aging, inhibitory processes, and negative priming. *Journal of Gerontology: Psychological Sciences, 46,* P340–P345.

McDowd, J. M., Oseas-Kreger, D. M., & Filion, D. L. (1995). Inhibitory processes in cognition and aging. In F. M. Dempster & C. J. Brainerd (Eds.), *Interference and inhibition in cognition* (pp. 363–400). New York: Academic Press.

McIntyre, J. S., & Craik, F. I. M. (1987). Age differences in memory for item and source information. *Canadian Journal of Psychology, 41,* 175–192.

McKoon, G., & Ratcliff, R. (1992). Inference during reading. *Psychological Review, 99,* 440–466.

Mellinger, J. C., Lehman, E. B., Happ, L. K., & Grout, L. A. (1990). Cognitive effort in modality retrieval by young and older adults. *Experimental Aging Research, 16,* 35–41.

Micco, A., & Masson, M. E. J. (1992). Age-related differences in the specificity of verbal encoding. *Memory & Cognition, 20,* 244–253.

Mitchell, D. B. (1989). How many memory systems? Evidence from aging. *Journal of Experimental Psychology: Learning, Memory, and Cognition, 15,* 31–49.

Mitchell, D. B. (1993). Implicit and explicit memory for pictures: Multiple views across the lifespan. In P. Graf & M. Masson (Eds.), *Implicit memory: New directions in cognition, development, and neuropsychology* (pp. 171–190). Hillsdale, NJ: Erlbaum.

Mitchell, D. B., Brown, A. S., & Murphy, D. R. (1990). Dissociations between procedural and episodic memory: Effects of time and aging. *Psychology and Aging, 5,* 264–276.

Mitchell, D. B., Hunt, R. R., & Schmitt, F. A. (1986). The generation effect and reality monitoring: Evidence from dementia and normal aging. *Journal of Gerontology, 41,* 79–84.

Mitchell, D. B., & Perlmutter, M. (1986). Semantic activation and episodic memory: Age similarities and differences. *Developmental Psychology, 22,* 86–94.

Morrell, R. W., & Park, D. C. (1993). The effects of age, illustrations, and task variables on the performance of procedural memory tasks. *Psychology and Aging, 8,* 389–399.

Morrell, R. W., Park, D. C., & Poon, L. W. (1989). Quality of instructions on prescription drug labels: Effects on memory and comprehension in young and old adults. *Gerontologist, 29,* 345–354.

Morris, R. G., Craik, F. I. M., & Gick, M. L. (1989). Age differences in working memory tasks: The role of secondary memory and the central executive. *Quarterly Journal of Experimental Psychology, 41A,* 67–86.

Morris, R. G., Gick, M. L., & Craik, F. I. M. (1988). Processing resources and age differences in working memory. *Memory & Cognition, 16,* 362–366.

Morrow, D. G., Leirer, V. O., & Altieri, P. A. (1992). Aging, expertise, and narrative processing. *Psychology and Aging, 7,* 376–388.

Moscovitch, M. (1982). A neuropsychological approach to perception and memory in normal and pathological aging. In F. I. M. Craik & S. Trehub (Eds.), *Aging and cognitive processes* (pp. 55–78). New York: Plenum Press.

Moscovitch, M., Winocur, G., & McLachlan, D. (1986). Memory as assessed by recognition and reading time in normal and memory-impaired people with Alzheimer's disease and other neurological disorders. *Journal of Experimental Psychology: General, 115,* 331–347.

Myerson, J., Ferraro, F. R., Hale, S., & Lima, S. D. (1992). General slowing in semantic priming and word recognition. *Psychology and Aging, 7,* 257–270.

Myerson, J., Hale, S., Wagstaff, D., Poon, L. W., & Smith, G. A. (1990). The information-loss model: A mathematical theory of age-related cognitive slowing. *Psychological Review, 97,* 475–487.

Naveh-Benjamin, M. (1987). Coding of spatial location information: An automatic process? *Journal of Experimental Psychology: Learning, Memory, and Cognition, 13,* 595–605.

Naveh-Benjamin, M. (1990). Coding of temporal order information: An automatic process? *Journal of Experimental Psychology: Learning, Memory, and Cognition, 16,* 117–126.

Navon, D. (1984). Resources—A theoretical soup stone? *Psychological Review, 91,* 216–234.

Nebes, R. D., Boller, F., & Holland, A. (1986). Use of semantic context by patients with Alzheimer's disease. *Psychology and Aging, 1,* 261–269.

Nebes, R. D., & Brady, C. B. (1988). Integrity of semantic fields in Alzheimer's disease. *Cortex, 24,* 291–299.

Neely, J. H. (1977). Semantic priming and retrieval from lexical memory: Roles of inhibition-less spreading activation and limited-capacity attention. *Journal of Experimental Psychology: General, 106,* 226–254.

Nilsson, L.-G., Bäckman, L., & Karlsson, T. (1989). Priming and cued recall in elderly, alcohol intoxicated and sleep deprived subjects: A case of functionally similar memory deficits. *Psychological Medicine, 19,* 423–433.

Norman, S., Kemper, S., & Kynette, D. (1992). Adults' reading comprehension: Effects of syntactic complexity and working memory. *Journal of Gerontology: Psychological Science, 47,* P258–P265.

Norman, S., Kemper, S., Kynette, D., Cheung, H., & Anagnopolous, C. (1991). Syntactic complexity and adults' running memory span. *Journal of Gerontology: Psychological Sciences, 46,* P346–P351.

Ober, B. A., Shenaut, G. K., Jagust, W. J., & Stillman, R. C. (1991). Automatic semantic priming with various category relations in Alzheimer's disease and normal aging. *Psychology and Aging, 6,* 647–660.

Ostergaard, A. L., & Jernigan, T. L. (1993). Are word priming and explicit memory mediated by different brain structures? In P. Graf & M. E. J. Masson (Eds.), *Implicit memory: New ditions in cognition, development, and neuropsychology* (pp. 327–349). Hillsdale, NJ: Erlbaum.

Park, D. C., & Puglisi, J. T. (1985). Older adults' memory for the color of pictures and words. *Journal of Gerontology, 40,* 198–204.

Park, D. C., Puglisi, J. T., & Smith, A. D. (1986). Memory for pictures: Does an age-related decline exist? *Psychology and Aging, 1,* 11–17.

Park, D. C., Puglisi, J. T., Smith, A. D., & Dudley, W. N. (1987). Cue utilization and encoding specificity in picture recognition by older adults. *Journal of Gerontology, 42,* 423–425.

Park, D. C., & Shaw, R. J. (1992). Effect of environmental support on implicit and explicit memory in younger and older adults. *Psychology and Aging, 7,* 632–642.

Park, D. C., Smith, A. D., Dudley, W. N., & LaFronza, V. N. (1989). Effects of age and a divided attention task presented during encoding and retrieval on memory. *Journal of Experimental Psychology: Learning, Memory, and Cognition, 15,* 1185–1191.

Parkin, A. J., & Walter, B. M. (1992). Recollective experience, normal aging, and frontal dysfunction. *Psychology and Aging, 7,* 290–298.

Parks, C. W., Mitchell, D. B., & Perlmutter, M. (1986). Cognitive and social functioning across adulthood: Age or student status differences? *Psychology and Aging, 1,* 248–254.

Perlmutter, M. (1978). What is memory aging the aging of? *Developmental Psychology, 14,* 330–345.

Perlmutter, M., & Nyquist, L. (1990). Relationships between self-reported physical and mental health and intelligence performance across adulthood. *Journal of Gerontology: Psychological Sciences, 45,* P145–P155.

Plude, D. J., & Doussard-Roosevelt, J. A. (1989). Aging, selective attention, and feature integration. *Psychology and Aging, 4,* 98–105.

Pratt, M. W., Boyes, C., Robins, S., & Manchester, J. (1989). Telling tales: Aging, working memory, and the narrative cohesion of story retellings. *Developmental Psychology, 25,* 628–635.

Puglisi, J. T., Park, D. C., Smith, A. D., & Dudley, W. N. (1988). Age differences in encoding specificity. *Journal of Gerontology: Psychological Sciences, 43,* P145–P150.

Pye, C., Cheung, H., & Kemper, S. (1992). Islands at eighty. In H. Goodluck & M. Rochemont (Eds.), *Island constraints: Theory, acquisition, and processing* (pp. 351–370). Dordrecht, Netherlands: Reidel.

Rabbitt, P. M. A. (1982). How do old people know what to do next? In F. I. M. Craik & S. Trehub (Eds.), *Aging and cognitive processes* (pp. 79–98). New York: Plenum Press.

Rabbitt, P. M. A. (1984). How old people prepare themselves for events which they expect. In H. Bouma & D. G. Bouwhuis (Eds.), *Attention and performance. X: Control of language processes* (pp. 515–527). Hillsdale, NJ: Erlbaum.

Rabbitt, P. (1989). Inner-city decay? Age changes in structure and process in recall of familiar topographical information. In L. W. Poon, D. C. Rubin, & B. A. Wilson (Eds.), *Everyday cognition in adulthood and late life* (pp. 284–299). Cambridge: Cambridge University Press.

Rabinowitz, J. C. (1984). Aging and recognition failure. *Journal of Gerontology, 39*, 65–71.

Rabinowitz, J. C. (1986). Priming in episodic memory. *Journal of Gerontology, 41*, 204–213.

Rabinowitz, J. C. (1989). Judgments of origin and generation effects: Comparisons between young and elderly adults. *Psychology and Aging, 4*, 259–268.

Rabinowitz, J. C., Ackerman, B. P., Craik, F. I. M., & Hinchley, J. L. (1982). Aging and metamemory: The roles of relatedness and imagery. *Journal of Gerontology, 37*, 688–695.

Rabinowitz, J. C., Craik, F. I. M., & Ackerman, B. P. (1982). A processing resource account of age differences in recall. *Canadian Journal of Psychology, 36*, 325–344.

Radvansky, G. A., Gerard, L. D., Hasher, L., & Zacks, R. T. (1990). Younger and older adults' use of mental models as representations for text materials. *Psychology and Aging, 5*, 209–214.

Ratcliff, R., McKoon, G., & Verwoerd, M. (1989). A bias interpretation of facilitation in perceptual identification. *Journal of Experimental Psychology: Learning, Memory, and Cognition, 15*, 378–387.

Rogers, W. A., & Fisk, A. D. (1991). Age-related differences in the maintenance and modification of automatic processes: Arithmetic Stroop interference. *Human Factors, 33*, 45–56.

Rose, T. L., Yesavage, J. A., Hill, R. D., & Bower, G. H. (1986). Priming effects and recognition memory in young and elderly adults. *Experimental Aging Research, 12*, 31–37.

Rubin, D. C. (1985). Memorability as a measure of processing: A unit analysis of prose and list learning. *Journal of Experimental Psychology: General, 114*, 213–238.

Russo, R., & Parkin, A. J. (1993). Age differences in implicit memory: More apparent than real. *Memory & Cognition, 21*, 73–80.

Ryan, E. B. (1992). Beliefs about memory changes across the adult life span. *Journal of Gerontology: Psychological Sciences, 47*, P41–P46.

Salthouse, T. A. (1980). Age and memory: Strategies for localizing the loss. In L. W. Poon, J. L. Fozard, L. S. Cermak, D. Arenberg, & L. W. Thompson (Eds.), *New directions in memory and aging: Proceedings of the George A. Talland Memorial Conference* (pp. 47–65). Hillsdale, N. J.: Erlbaum.

Salthouse, T. A. (1985). *A theory of cognitive aging*. Amsterdam: North-Holland.

Salthouse, T. A. (1987). Adult age differences in integrative spatial reasoning. *Psychology and Aging, 2*, 254–260.

Salthouse, T. A. (1988a). Initiating the formalization of theories of cognitive aging. *Psychology and Aging, 3*, 3–16.

Salthouse, T. A. (1988b). The role of processing resources in cognitive aging. In M. L. Howe & C. J. Brainerd (Eds.), *Cognitive development in adulthood: Progress in cognitive development research* (pp. 185–239). New York: Springer-Verlag.

Salthouse, T. A. (1990). Working memory as a processing resource in cognitive aging. *Developmental Review, 10*, 101–124.

Salthouse, T. A. (1991a). Mediation of adult age differences in cognition by reductions in working memory and speed of processing. *Psychological Science, 2*, 179–183.

Salthouse, T. A. (1991b). *Theoretical perspectives on cognitive aging*. Hillsdale, NJ: Erlbaum.

Salthouse, T. A. (1992a). Influence of processing speed on adult age differences in working memory. *Acta Psychologica, 79*, 155–170.

Salthouse, T. A. (1992b). Why do adult age differences increase with task complexity? *Developmental Psychology, 28,* 905–918.

Salthouse, T. A. (1992c). Working-memory mediation of adult age differences in integrative reasoning. *Memory & Cognition, 20,* 413–423.

Salthouse, T. A. (1993a). Influence of working memory on adult age differences in matrix reasoning. *British Journal of Psychology, 84,* 171–199.

Salthouse, T. A. (1993b). Speed mediation of adult age differences in cognition. *Developmental Psychology, 29,* 722–738.

Salthouse, T. A. (1994). Aging associations: Influence of speed on adult age differences in associative learning. *Journal of Experimental Psychology: Learning, Memory, and Cognition, 20,* 1486–1503.

Salthouse, T. A., & Babcock, R. L. (1991). Decomposing adult age differences in working memory. *Developmental Psychology, 27,* 763–776.

Salthouse, T. A., Babcock, R. L., & Shaw, R. J. (1991). Effects of adult age on structural and operational capacities in working memory. *Psychology and Aging, 6,* 118–127.

Salthouse, T. A., & Coon, V. E. (1993). Influence of task-specific processing speed on age differences in memory. *Journal of Gerontology: Psychological Sciences, 48,* P245–P255.

Salthouse, T. A., Fristoe, N. M., Lineweaver, T. T., & Coon, V. E. (1995). Aging of attention: Does the ability to divide decline? *Memory & Cognition, 23,* 59–71.

Salthouse, T. A., Kausler, D. H., & Saults, J. S. (1988a). Investigation of student status, background variables, and feasibility of standard tasks in cognitive aging research. *Psychology and Aging, 3,* 29–37.

Salthouse, T. A., Kausler, D. H., & Saults, J. S. (1988b). Utilization of path-analytic procedures to investigate the role of processing resources in cognitive aging. *Psychology and Aging, 3,* 158–166.

Salthouse, T. A., Kausler, D. H., & Saults, J. S. (1990). Age, self-assessed health status, and cognition. *Journal of Gerontology: Psychological Sciences, 45,* P156–P160.

Salthouse, T. A., Legg, S., Palmon, R., & Mitchell, D. (1990). Memory factors in age-related differences in simple reasoning. *Psychology and Aging, 5,* 9–15.

Salthouse, T. A., & Lichty, W. (1985). Tests of the neural noise hypothesis of age-related cognitive change. *Journal of Gerontology, 40,* 443–450.

Salthouse, T. A., & Mitchell, D. R. D. (1989). Structural and operational capacities in integrative spatial ability. *Psychology and Aging, 4,* 18–25.

Salthouse, T. A., Mitchell, D. R. D., & Palmon, R. (1989). Memory and age differences in spatial manipulation ability. *Psychology and Aging, 4,* 480–486.

Salthouse, T. A., Mitchell, D. R. D., Skovronek, E., & Babcock, R. L. (1989). Effects of adult age and working memory on reasoning and spatial abilities. *Journal of Experimental Psychology: Learning, Memory, and Cognition, 15,* 507–516.

Salthouse, T. A., Rogan, J. D., & Prill, K. A. (1984). Division of attention: Age differences on a visually presented memory task. *Memory & Cognition, 12,* 613–620.

Salthouse, T. A., & Skovronek, E. (1992). Within-context assessment of age differences in working memory. *Journal of Gerontology: Psychological Sciences, 47,* P110–P120.

Sanford, A. J., & Garrod, S. C. (1981). *Understanding written language: Explorations of comprehension beyond the sentence.* Chichester, England: Wiley.

Schacter, D. L., Cooper, L. A., & Valdiserri, M. (1992). Implicit and explicit memory for novel visual objects in older and younger adults. *Psychology and Aging, 7,* 299–308.

Schacter, D. L., Kaszniak, A. W., Kihlstrom, J. F., & Valdiserri, M. (1991). The relation between source memory and aging. *Psychology and Aging, 6,* 559–568.

Schaie, K. W. (1989). Perceptual speed in adulthood: Cross-sectional and longitudinal studies. *Psychology and Aging, 4,* 443–453.

Sharkey, N. E. (1986). A model of knowledge-based expectations in text comprehension. In

J. A. Galambos, R. P. Abelson, & J. B. Black (Eds.), *Knowledge structures* (pp. 49–70). Hillsdale, NJ: Erlbaum.

Shaw, R. J. (1991). Age-related increases in the effects of automatic semantic activation. *Psychology and Aging, 6,* 595–604.

Shimamura, A. P. (1993). Neuropsychological analyses of implicit memory: History, methodology and theoretical interpretations. In P. Graf & M. E. J. Masson (Eds.), *Implicit memory: New directions in cognition, development, and neuropsychology* (pp. 265–285). Hillsdale, NJ: Erlbaum.

Smith, G., Ivnik, R. J., Petersen, R. C., Malec, J. F., Kokman, E., & Tangalos, E. (1991). Age-associated memory impairment diagnoses: Problems of reliability and concerns for terminology. *Psychology and Aging, 6,* 551–558.

Somberg, B. L., & Salthouse, T. A. (1982). Divided attention abilities in young and older adults. *Journal of Experimental Psychology: Human Perception and Performance, 8,* 651–663.

Spencer, W. D., & Raz, N. (1995). Differential effects of aging on memory for content and context: A meta-analysis. *Psychology and Aging, 10,* 527–539.

Squire, L. R. (1992). Memory and the hippocampus: A synthesis from findings with rats, monkeys, and humans. *Psychological Review, 99,* 195–231.

Srinivas, K., & Roediger, H. L., III. (1990). Classifying implicit memory tests: Category association and anagram solution. *Journal of Memory and Language, 29,* 389–412.

Stine, E. L. (1986). Attribute-based similarity perception in younger and older adults. *Experimental Aging Research, 12,* 89–94.

Stine, E. L., & Wingfield, A. (1987). Process and strategy in memory for speech among younger and older adults. *Psychology and Aging, 2,* 272–279.

Stine, E. A. L., & Wingfield, A. (1988). Memorability functions as an indicator of qualitative age differences in text recall. *Psychology and Aging, 3,* 179–183.

Stine, E. A. L., & Wingfield, A. (1990). How much do working memory deficits contribute to age differences in discourse memory? *European Journal of Cognitive Psychology, 2,* 289–304.

Stine, E. A. L., Wingfield, A., & Myers, S. D. (1990). Age differences in processing information from television news: The effects of bisensory augmentation. *Journal of Gerontology: Psychological Sciences, 45,* P1–P8.

Stine, E. L., Wingfield, A., & Poon, L. W. (1986). How much and how fast: Rapid processing of spoken language in later adulthood. *Psychology and Aging, 1,* 303–311.

Stoltzfus, E. R., Hasher, L., Zacks, R. T., Ulivi, M. S., & Goldstein, D. (1993). Investigations of inhibition and interference in younger and older adults. *Journal of Gerontology: Psychological Sciences, 48,* P179–P188.

Sullivan, M. P., & Faust, M. E. (1993). Evidence for identity inhibition during selective attention in old adults. *Psychology and Aging, 8,* 589–598.

Tanenhaus, M. K., Dell, G. S., & Carlson, G. (1987). Context effects and lexical processing: A connectionist approach to modularity. In J. L. Garfield (Ed.), *Modularity in knowledge representation and natural-language understanding* (pp. 83–110). Cambridge: MIT Press.

Thomson, D. M., & Tulving, E. (1970). Associative encoding and retrieval: Weak and strong cues. *Journal of Experimental Psychology, 86,* 255–262.

Till, R. E. (1985). Verbatim and inferential memory in young and elderly adults. *Journal of Gerontology, 40,* 316–323.

Tulving, E., & Schacter, D. L. (1990). Priming and human memory systems. *Science, 247,* 301–306.

Tun, P. A. (1989). Age differences in processing expository and narrative text. *Journal of Gerontology: Psychological Sciences, 44,* P9–P15.

Tun, P. A., Wingfield, A., Stine, E. A. L., & Mecsas, C. (1992). Rapid speech processing and divided attention: Processing rate versus processing resources as an explanation of age effects. *Psychology and Aging, 7,* 546–550.

Turner, M. L., & Engle, R. W. (1989). Is working memory capacity task dependent? *Journal of Memory and Language, 28,* 127–154.

Uttl, B., & Graf, P. (1993). Episodic spatial memory in adulthood. *Psychology and Aging, 8,* 257–273.

Verhaeghen, P., & Marcoen, A. (1993a). Memory aging as a general phenomenon: Episodic recall of older adults is a function of episodic recall of young adults. *Psychology and Aging, 8,* 380–388.

Verhaeghen, P., & Marcoen, A. (1993b). More or less the same? A memorability analysis on episodic memory tasks in young and older adults. *Journal of Gerontology: Psychological Sciences, 48,* P172–P178.

Verhaeghen, P., Marcoen, A., & Goossens, L. (1993). Facts and fiction about memory aging: A quantitative integration of research findings. *Journal of Gerontology: Psychological Sciences, 48,* P157–P171.

Waugh, N. C., Fozard, J. L., & Thomas, J. C. (1978). Retrieval time from different memory stores. *Journal of Gerontology, 33,* 718–724.

West, R. L., Crook, T. H., & Barron, K. L. (1992). Everyday memory performance across the life span: Effects of age and noncognitive individual differences. *Psychology and Aging, 7,* 72–82.

Wingfield, A., Poon, L. W., Lombardi, L., & Lowe, D. (1985). Speed of processing in normal aging: Effects of speech rate, linguistic structure, and processing time. *Journal of Gerontology, 40,* 579–585.

Zabrucky, K., Moore, D., & Schultz, N. R., Jr. (1993). Young and older adults' ability to use different standards to evaluate understanding. *Journal of Gerontology: Psychological Sciences, 48,* P238–P244.

Zacks, R. J., Radvansky, G., & Hasher, L. (1996). Studies of directed forgetting in older adults. *Journal of Experimental Psychology: Learning, Memory, and Cognition, 22,* 143–156.

Zelinski, E. M. (1988). Integrating information from discourse: Do older adults show deficits? In L. L. Light & D. M. Burke (Eds.), *Language, memory, and aging* (pp. 117–132). New York: Cambridge University Press.

Zelinski, E. M., & Gilewski, M. J. (1988). Memory for prose and aging: A meta-analysis. In M. L. Howe & C. J. Brainerd (Eds.), *Cognitive development in adulthood: Progress in cognitive development research* (pp. 134–158). New York: Springer-Verlag.

Zelinski, E. M., Gilewski, M. J., & Anthony-Bergstone, C. R. (1990). Memory Functioning Questionnaire: Concurrent validity with memory performance and self-reported memory failures. *Psychology and Aging, 5,* 388–399.

Zelinski, E. M., & Miura, S. A. (1988). Effects of thematic information on script memory in young and old adults. *Psychology and Aging, 3,* 292–299.

Memory for Real-World Events and Information

Retrieval Processes and Witness Memory

Carla C. Chandler
Ronald P. Fisher

Every day, we experience and form memories about dozens of events. Of these memories, a few may become important for criminal investigations. The amount that an eyewitness recalls, and the accuracy of recall and recognition, are major determinants of whether a case is solved. Although it is not feasible to change how witnesses encode criminal events, one can exert some control over the environment *after* the event occurs, including the cues in the retrieval environment. By understanding retrieval processes, we may eventually suggest procedures that the legal system could use to increase the amount that an eyewitness remembers and its accuracy.

In this chapter, we address several issues concerning retrieval and discuss their potential implications for eyewitness testimony. First, we discuss predictions made by the widely embraced encoding specificity principle (Thomson & Tulving, 1970; Tulving & Thomson, 1971). The encoding specificity principle asserts that an event will be remembered to the extent that the retrieval cues match the features stored in the memory trace. For example, reinstating the original emotional and physical context should increase the amount that witnesses recall as well as the accuracy of lineup identification, and it does. The theory also predicts that performance should increase if more cues are provided through repeated tests, and if witnesses can convey their responses in the same format (e.g., visual, tactile) in which

Memory

they encoded the event. (For an extensive discussion of encoding specificity and other principles that govern the retrieval of information from human memory, see Roediger & Guynn, Chapter 7, this volume.)

Second, we discuss why memory for an event can be reduced by experiencing related events (i.e., interference). Recent evidence (Chandler, 1991) questions the notion that the original trace is altered (Loftus, 1979) and suggests that related events interfere by affecting the retrieval process. Interference effects may be less pervasive than was once thought, occurring only if the related events are accessed during the retrieval process. Even if a related event is accessed, it does not interfere under some circumstances. (For a discussion of the varieties of possible interference mechanisms in human memory, see Anderson & Neely, Chapter 8, this volume.)

Third, we ask why people claim to remember objects that were only suggested to them. Are they responding to social demands, are they merely reporting whatever comes to mind, or are they misremembering where they saw the object? Requiring witnesses to make a decision about where they saw an object can improve performance (D. S. Lindsay & Johnson, 1989). However, encouraging witnesses to make such decisions may not help in circumstances where source judgments are error prone.

In Section IV, we describe evidence that retrieval requires mental resources (effort). Removing distractions should increase performance because all attentional resources can then be focused on retrieval. Effort would also be needed to use various strategies for recall, such as mentally reinstating the context and generating specific cues. Even when witnesses devote their full attention to retrieval, they do not spontaneously engage in these strategies. As a consequence, their performance improves when they are instructed to imagine the original context and to consider the source of a memory.

Finally, we discuss applied research. The Cognitive Interview, developed by Fisher and Geiselman (1992) is a technique that increases the number of correct details that witnesses recall in an interview. Techniques are also discussed that improve accuracy in lineup identification tests.

I. IMPLICATIONS AND EXTENSIONS OF THE ENCODING SPECIFICITY PRINCIPLE

Most memory theorists embrace the view that we store a variety of attributes about an event, including its meaning within a context, its sensory qualities, the environment in which the event occurred, and our thoughts and emotions at the time (Johnson, 1988; Tulving, 1983). The trace lies dormant, along with a vast number of traces for other events. Whether the event can be remembered depends on the cues that are used to search memory. A witness is more likely to remember an event if the cues match the trace than if the cues do not match the trace. Formally, the idea is known as the encoding specificity principle (Thomson & Tulving, 1970; Tulving & Thomson, 1973).

The encoding specificity principle has several implications for improving the quantity of eyewitness testimony. Providing cues that match what the witness encoded should increase the number of details that the witness can recall and recognize. Performance on the test should improve if the original meaning, sensory characteristics, emotional context, or environmental cues are reinstated. More details should be recalled if the investigator is sensitive to the witness's personal viewpoint or organization of the event. Also, more information may be elicited by allowing witnesses to respond in a format (e.g., visual, tactile) that they encoded. Because each cue provides a way of accessing the trace, each cue may elicit some additional information.

A. Context Reinstatement Effects

Several findings support the encoding specificity principle by showing that recall or recognition is better when some aspect of the original event is reinstated as a cue than when it is not. An experiment by Tulving and Thomson (1971) provides an example. The subjects learned a list of word pairs (e.g., *black–train*). Later, a recognition test provided pairs of words and the subjects were asked to circle each word in the pair if they recognized it. Recognition of *train* was higher when the original context word was provided as a cue (*black–train*) than when a different word was provided (*wedding–train*). Providing the original context word probably benefited recognition because it reinstated the semantic meaning that was encoded. In addition, a list of unrelated words is recalled more successfully when other kinds of context are reinstated. Context reinstatement effects have been found when the context is the person's affective state (Blaney, 1986; Bower, Gilligan & Montiero, 1981), drug state (for reviews see J. E. Eich, 1980; E. Eich, 1989), the speaker's voice (Fisher & Cuervo, 1983), or the room in which the words were learned (for reviews see R. A. Bjork & Richardson-Klavehn, 1989; S. M. Smith, 1988; and Roediger & Guynn, Chapter 7, this volume).

1. Witness Recall

One implication of the encoding specificity principle is that witnesses will recall more details if the original environment is reinstated either physically or mentally (S. M. Smith, 1979). A study by Geiselman, Fisher, MacKinnon, and Holland (1986, Experiment 2) supports this prediction. Witnesses saw a film of a crime and after 5 min were asked to recall all that they could about the film. Those who were asked to reinstate the original context recalled more details than those who were not given this instruction.

Instructing subjects to reinstate the original emotional and physical context also improves the quality of facial composite drawings (Davies & Milne, 1985). In the Photofit task, an interviewer provides a set of hairstyles, noses, eyes, and mouths that the witness can use to construct the composite. Davies and Milne's subjects first saw a woman search the experimental room for a calculator and then they returned after a week to make a Photofit composite drawing of the woman. Half of the subjects returned to the original room, and the other half returned to a different room. In each condition (same room, different room), half of the subjects were instructed to think of how they arrived at the experiment on the first day and how they felt during the experiment. To test the quality of the composite drawings, other subjects were then shown each composite and were asked to determine which of four photos represented the same individual. Composites were judged to be the target most often if the room and emotional context was reinstated (52 %) or if the emotional context was reinstated (49 %). Less effective composites were drawn if only the room was reinstated (40 %), or if neither the room nor the emotional context was reinstated (31 %).

2. Witness Recognition

Recognition of unfamiliar faces[1] can also be improved by reinstating the original environmental context (see Shapiro & Penrod, 1986, for a meta-analysis). Cann and Ross (1989) showed slides of unfamiliar faces in the presence of an odor (ammonium sulfide or cologne). Two days later, the subjects returned to a different room for a yes/no recognition test. Performance was more accurate (d') when the original odor was reinstated. Furthermore, reinstating the odor increased d' compared to a control group who smelled no odors at study or test. The distinctive odor provided a unique cue that aided recognition.

Dalton (1993) reported similar results using a within-subjects design. Dalton's subjects saw 24 unfamiliar female faces in Room A and the same number of faces in Room B. The rooms differed in size, contents, and odor. The faces were recognized more accurately (d') when the environmental cues at test matched the environmental cues at study. The effect was large, affecting recognition hits by 20% without affecting false positive rates. However, the environmental reinstatement effect was limited to faces that the subjects had never seen before. Environmental reinstatement effects were not found when the subjects had seen the nonfamous faces before the critical experiment began.

---

[1] Context reinstatement effects are usually not found in recognition tests if the targets are familiar but unrelated words (Eich, 1980, 1989; S. M. Smith, 1988). However, context reinstatement effects can be found in recognition tests if the targets are unfamiliar faces (Dalton, 1993).

Contextual reinstatement effects have also been found in a lineup identification test. For example, Gibling and Davies (1988) presented a videotape of a shoplifting incident in a supermarket. After a week, the witnesses returned to the lab. A Context Reinstatement group was asked how they had arrived at the lab on the day that they had seen the videotape. They were also shown slides of the empty supermarket and were encouraged to recall what had happened in each slide. A No Context group merely conversed with the experimenter. All of the witnesses were then asked to identify the culprit from a photospread of seven faces (the target, three similar faces, and three dissimilar faces). The culprit was identified more often when the original context was reinstated than when it was not (see also Cutler, Penrod, & Martens, 1987; Krafka & Penrod, 1985).

Physical reinstatement of the context is not always necessary to find contextual reinstatement effects. Mental reinstatement has also been found to improve performance in a lineup identification task. Malpass and Devine (1981b) staged a crime and then asked witnesses to view a lineup (culprit plus four foils) 5 months later. The culprit was identified more often when the subjects were told to visualize the room and the culprit (57%) than when they were not given these instructions (36%).

However, lineup identification is not always improved by mentally reinstating the environmental context. In studies that have used a retention interval of a week or less, no mental reinstatement effects have been found. For example, in S. M. Smith and Vela (1992), a confederate interrupted a class. The students attempted to identify the confederate from a lineup that was shown 1 to 7 days later. The students identified the confederate more often if the lineup was presented in the classroom rather than in a different room. Performance improved when the original environment was physically reinstated. However, performance was not affected by asking people mentally to recreate the original environment. Identifications that were made in a different room were equally inaccurate, regardless of whether or not the students were asked to imagine the classroom (see also Fisher, McCauley, & Geiselman, 1994).

B. Multiple Retrieval Cues

Another implication of the encoding specificity principle is that details that are not accessed by one cue may be accessed by another cue (Tulving, 1974; Tulving & Bower, 1974). Because several aspects of the event are stored (Bower, 1967; Wickens, 1970), there will be several cues that will match the trace. Because each cue has some probability of accessing the details that are stored, providing a variety of cues or a variety of tests should increase the number of details that are recalled.

An experiment by R. C. Anderson and Pichert (1978) highlights the point. Their subjects read a story about children playing hookey in a house. Some aspects of the house were relevant for homebuyers, while others were relevant for burglars. The subjects read the story from one perspective (e.g., a burglar) and were asked to recall the story 12 min later. Five minutes after the initial recall attempt, they were instructed to recall the passage from the original perspective (burglar) or from another perspective (homebuyer). When the subjects adopted a different perspective (homebuyer) in the second test, they recalled additional facts. Other researchers have reported similar findings (Fisher & Chandler, 1991; Tulving & Watkins, 1975).

As Tulving and Bower (1974, p. 289) pointed out, the value of additional retrieval cues depends on their informational overlap. Additional retrieval cues that access different information than the first retrieval cue will increase recall the most. Still, we can expect that any second recall attempt will elicit additional facts, as long as the retrieval cues differ somewhat. Even the same retrieval cue may elicit additional facts on a second test, because a nominally identical cue can be interpreted somewhat differently on two occasions.

Additional facts are often recalled during a second test that were not recalled during an initial test (for reviews see Payne, 1987; Roediger & Guynn, Chapter 7, this volume; Roediger, Wheeler, & Kajaram, 1993). Most studies have used lists of unrelated words, but a study by Scrivener and Safer (1988) found the same effect using a realistic film of a burglary. The witnesses recalled the event 3 times that day and again 2 days later. Each recall attempt uncovered details that had not been recalled earlier, without increasing the number of incorrect facts reported.

The literature suggests that people recover additional accurate details when they are interviewed a second time. Yet, the validity of such memories is often questioned. Often, the opposing attorney attempts to convince the jury that recollection decreases with the passage of time. If a witness did not recall the detail initially, then how could the witness recall it later? Perhaps the witness is remembering a detail that was suggested during the initial interview? We would like to point out that details recovered during later tests are not necessarily tainted. Indeed, witnesses normally report additional, accurate details during a second interview.

The point is illustrated by an experiment conducted by McCauley (1993) in which young children were interviewed twice about a game that they had played. The children were interviewed that same day and were interviewed again 2 weeks later. The subjects recalled a mean of 33 details in the first interview and an *additional* 8.5 details during the second interview. Details that were recalled during both interviews were most likely to be accurate (94% correct). However, accuracy was high for details that were recalled during only one of the interviews, regardless of whether those details were recalled during the first interview (88% correct) or during the second interview (78% correct). Thus, accuracy is not necessarily compromised by interviewing the witness more than once. On the contrary, a second interview can uncover additional details.[2]

C. Witness-Compatible Questioning

Another implication of encoding specificity is that what is encoded depends on the individual. Witnesses who view the same event encode the event somewhat differently from one another. In order to maximize recall, interviewers should tailor their questions to each witness's unique representation of the crime. Instead, police interviewers tend to question all witnesses in a uniform fashion, as if they were reading from a checklist (Fisher, Geiselman, & Raymond, 1987). For example, if a witness reported seeing an assailant from the rear, then the interviewer should concentrate on probing for details about the back of the assailant, as opposed to the universally adopted approach of focusing on facial characteristics.

D. Matching Input and Output Formats

An extension of the encoding specificity principle is that details that are encoded in one format (e.g., tactile, spatial, verbal) are best recalled in the same format. There are two reasons to make this prediction. First, the format itself is encoded, and the trace is more likely to be accessed by the same format cues than by different format cues. Fisher and Cunningham (in preparation) have found support for this idea. When blindfolded subjects touched objects, the objects were better recognized later when the test format was tactile rather than visual. However, when the subjects saw the objects rather than touched them, more of the objects were later recognized in a visual test than in a tactile test.

Second, events that occur in one format can be difficult to describe using another format. Leibowitz and Guzy (1990) found that verbal descriptions were often less accurate than responses made in a nonverbal format. For example, they asked people to describe the size of a dollar bill in inches (a verbal response) or by touching slips of paper and choosing the one that matched a dollar bill in size (a tactile response). The tactile responses were far more accurate than the verbal responses, presumably because the tactile cues matched the tactile experience that the subjects had with dollar bills (see also A. F. Smith, Jobe, & Mingay, 1991). Enabling people to respond in nonverbal formats (visual, tactile) should be particularly beneficial for respondents who have limited verbal skills, such as children and adults who

[2] Repeating a question within an interview may create social demands for the witness to change his or her answer. Witnesses, especially young children, may infer that the interviewer was not happy with their initial answer (Geiselman & Padilla, 1988; Poole & White, 1991). As a consequence, witnesses may change their answers, and accuracy will be compromised.

do not speak the same language as the interviewer. The general principle to be derived from these findings is that the output mode should be similar to the format in which the information is stored (see also Greenwald's, 1970, ideo-motor theory).

II. WHEN DO INTERFERENCE EFFECTS OCCUR AND WHY?

The preceding section established that retrieval is more likely when the retrieval cues match the trace. A mismatch between cues and the trace accounts for large amounts of forgetting. However, it may not be the only cause of forgetting. In addition, performance on a memory test is affected by the kind of events that occur between learning and the test. A target event (e.g., the name Robert Harris) is recalled or recognized more accurately if it is followed by dissimilar events (Lydia Garcia) rather than by similar events (Robert Knight). The effect is known as a "retroactive interference effect."

A witness is likely to encounter events similar to the crime (the target event). Some of the similar events occur naturally; others may be introduced during a police interview. For example, a witness who sees a robber may encounter similar-looking people on television or in the market, and may also see similar-looking people in a mugbook. As a result, the witness may be less likely to recall or recognize the target. Under what conditions will the related events interfere with performance and why?

One possibility is that the memory trace for the target is changed by exposing the witness to related events (Loftus, 1979, p. 117). If the trace is changed or altered, then the original information could never be recovered, a possibility that would have serious practical implications. If a memory trace can be changed, then witnesses should not be exposed to any related information before the critical test.

Another possibility is that a memory trace is not changed by learning about related events. Instead, related events interfere with retrieving the target. In other words, the trace for the target remains intact, but it may be difficult to retrieve. By changing the retrieval environment, it may be possible to recover the original information.

Finally, social factors may produce interference effects (McCloskey & Zaragoza, 1985). Consider an experiment performed by Loftus, Miller, and Burns (1978) in which the witnesses saw a car speed past a stop sign. The witnesses were then asked questions about the slides. A questionnaire either did not mention the sign (control group) or implied that there was a yield sign (experimental group). Later, when asked whether they had seen a stop sign or a yield sign, the control group chose the stop sign more often than did the experimental group. The experimental group may have selected the yield sign because the interviewer said that a yield sign had been shown (social demands). Also, if the witnesses had not encoded the sign, the experimental group may have chosen the yield sign because it was the most familiar alternative (response bias). Social demands and response bias do not exist for the control group, and so the control group was more accurate than the experimental group.

Social factors can also produce interference effects in a cued recall test (What type of road sign did you see?). Implying that a yield sign had been shown may create social demands to report a yield sign (an intrusion) and omit the correct response. Also, if the witnesses never encoded the stop sign, they may report the familiar yield sign (an intrusion).

The influence of social demands and response bias could be reduced by warning people that they have been exposed to misinformation and to report only what they witnessed. But interference effects would remain if the related event had altered the original trace or affected a retrieval process. By using designs that eliminate social demands and response bias, we can see if any interference effects remain that could be attributed to a changed trace or to retrieval problems (McCloskey and Zaragoza, 1985).

Table 1 defines four tests that eliminate social demands and response bias. Excluding the related item as a possible response eliminates any social demands or response bias to choose it. For example, a modified recognition test asks people to choose between the target and a *novel* item (McCloskey & Zaragoza, 1985). A matching recognition test requires people to match the original stimuli and responses. The related items are not alternatives on the test (Chandler, 1989, p. 257; 1993). In a cued recall test, a cue can be

TABLE 1   Designs that Eliminate Social Demands and Response Bias

Condition	Target	Related item	Test
			MODIFIED RECOGNITION
Control	Lake A	None	Did you see Lake A or Lake C?
Experimental	Fern A	Fern B	Did you see Fern A or Fern C?
			MATCHING RECOGNITION TEST
Control	Laura Anderson	None	Laura Harris
Experimental	Robert Harris	Robert Knight	Robert Anderson
			CUED RECALL
Control	note–criminal	non	note–cri _____
Experimental	child–apple	child–bicycle	child–app _____
			RECALL ALL RESPONSES
Control	soda–Sunkist	none	What type of soda? _____
Experimental	tool–hammer	tool–wrench	What type of tool? _____ _____

provided that can be completed only with the target response (Chandler & Gargano, 1995; Zaragoza, McCloskey, & Jamis, 1987). Finally, social demands and response bias can be eliminated by providing a cue and instructing the subject to recall *both* the target event and the related event (Belli, Lindsay, Gales, & McCarthy, 1994). Eliminating social demands and response bias allows us to ask how *memory* for the target is affected by related events.

A. Memory Traces Are Not Changed by Learning about Related Events

One theory of interference is that the related events change the trace for the target. It has been suggested that related information displaces the trace for the target event (Loftus & Loftus, 1980) or changes its features (Loftus, 1979, p. 117). A change in the trace would have serious implications because the original information could then never be recovered. If a trace can be changed, then witnesses should not be exposed to any related information before the critical test. Preliminary interviews would introduce related (or "leading") information and reduce accuracy in the courtroom. Showing mugshots would reduce accuracy in a lineup identification task. Furthermore, being exposed to related events would cast doubt on the accuracy of a witness's testimony. If the trace is changed, the witness may recall or recognize something that never happened.

Several studies show that the trace for an event (e.g., Fern A) is *not* changed irrevocably by seeing a related event (e.g., Fern B). While retroactive interference is found at short retention intervals, the effect is not found at longer retention intervals (Chandler, 1991, 1993). In Chandler's (1991) study, the subjects first rated nature pictures (e.g., Fern A) for complexity (1 = simple to 5 = complex). Some of these targets were followed by related pictures (e.g., Fern B) that were rated for pleasantness (1 = unpleasant to 5 = pleasant). The subjects were then asked whether they had seen the target or a novel picture (Fern A vs Fern C). Examples of pictures A, B, and C are shown in Figure 1. Targets that were followed by a related picture (Fern B) were less accurately recognized after 15 min, but not after 24 h.

Chandler (1993) reported a similar result using names and a matching recognition test. Target names (e.g., Robert Harris) that were followed by related names (e.g., Robert Knight) were matched less accurately after 5 min, but not after 30 min. At the longer retention interval, there was no interference to attribute to trace alteration. Some other mechanism must have caused the interference that was found at the shorter retention interval.

Some researchers have argued that a trace is only altered if a subsequent event directly contradicts it (see Belli, Windschitl, McCarthy, & Winfrey, 1992; Belli, Lindsay, Gales, & McCarthy, 1994). For example, the trace for

FIGURE 1   Fern A, Fern B, and Fern C are examples of the nature pictures used in Chandler's (1991) experiments. A given picture served equally often as the target, the related picture, and the novel alternative on the recognition test.

Bride A would be altered by seeing Bride B only if the subject believes that Brides A and B are the same person. However, Windschitl (in press) found evidence against alteration, even if the participants were told that Brides A and B were the same person. The participants rated target faces (Bride A) for attractiveness, and rated some additional faces (Bride B) for honesty. They were told that Bride A and Bride B were the same person (a direct contradiction) or that they were different people (no contradiction). A modified recognition test followed after a 45 min or a 48-hr retention interval. The instructions did not affect the pattern of results. An interference effect was found at the 45-min retention interval, which disappeared by the 48-hr retention interval. Furthermore, performance improved over time in the experimental condition, which could not have happened if Bride B had altered the trace for Bride A.

Another storage theory of interference contends that traces are collections of features that disintegrate over time, and that seeing related information speeds up the process (Belli, Windschitl, McCarthy, & Winfrey, 1992; see also Posner & Kosnick, 1966). Interference effects should be larger when there is more time for the trace to disintegrate. To test this prediction, Chandler (1993) presented target names (e.g., Robert Harris) that were followed by related names (e.g., Robert Knight) either *early* or *late* in a 30-

min retention interval. Showing the related name early would allow more time for the trace to disintegrate, and should produce the greatest interference effect. But the interference effect was larger when the related name was shown just before the matching test.

The above evidence suggests that related events do not change an existing trace, nor do they make it disintegrate. A memory trace would not be altered by interviewing the witness or showing mugshots. Instead, these related events influence the retrieval process.

B. Interference Effects Can Be Reduced by Selective Cues

According to retrieval theories, interference occurs only when the related trace is accessed. If the related trace is dormant, it will not interfere with memory for the target. The evidence is consistent with this idea. In experiments using word pairs (e.g., *child–apple*) as targets, a recently presented event (*child–bicycle*) interferes with recall (*child–app___*) more than less recent events (Chandler & Gargano, 1995). Likewise, Chandler (1993) found that target names (e.g., Robert Harris) were matched less accurately when related names (e.g., Robert Knight) were shown just before the test.

The idea that nonaccessed items do not interfere is supported by other findings in the literature. For example, people can recall more targets if the test instructions indicate that they will not have to recall other items. Epstein (1972, p. 156) describes an experiment in which two study lists were presented, and then the subjects were given special instructions for recall. More first-list words were recalled when the subjects were instructed to forget the second list compared to when they expected to recall the second list. Epstein contends that the instructions provided cues to search the first list selectively, such that words from the second list did not interfere.

In order for selective search to occur, there must be a cue that distinguishes the set to be recalled from the set to be ignored. For example, the subject might be asked to recall the first of two lists that were learned. "First list" versus "second list" is a cue that can be used to access one of the lists. Any cue that distinguishes between targets and nontargets can serve as a cue for selective search. For example, a particular environmental context can provide selective access to targets if the nontargets were learned in a distinctly different context.

Consistent with the idea of selective access, less interference is observed when the target and related events are learned in different environments rather than in the same environment (see R. A. Bjork & Richardson-Klavehn, 1989, p. 323; S. M. Smith, 1988, Table 2.4, for reviews). When the cues selectively access the targets, there is less interference.

Selective access could improve performance for two reasons. Instructing people to consider the original context provides a cue that would otherwise be ignored. As we discussed previously, performance can be improved by asking people to focus on the original emotional and environmental context. Selective access could also improve performance because the subjects are not reminded of memories that would otherwise interfere. There is evidence for both mechanisms.

1. Better Cues

First, there is evidence that reinstating contextual cues can improve performance in recall tests (Davies & Milne, 1985; Fisher & Quigley, 1991; Geiselman et al., 1986, Experiment 2; for an exception, see Fernandez & Glenberg, 1985) and face recognition tests (Cann & Ross, 1989; Dalton, 1993; Gibling & Davies, 1988; but see Fisher, McCauley, & Geiselman, 1994, for an exception).

Benefits of reinstating the original context (the temporal order of events) have been found even after a wrong decision has been made. Kroll and Timourian (1986) showed slides of a purse-snatching incident, followed by a questionnaire and an initial recognition test (target vs suggested item). The scene of the crime was then reinstated by showing slides in the original sequence or in random order, and then the subjects took the recognition test again. Those who had chosen the wrong item on the first test often chose the correct item on the second test, and did so more frequently after seeing the slides in sequential order (53% correct) than after seeing the slides in a random order (25% correct). A follow-up experiment by Kroll and Ogawa (1988, Experiment 2) found that the effect occurred even when no misleading information had been presented. Those subjects who chose incorrectly on the first test often chose the correct response on a subsequent test, and did so more frequently after a sequential return (57% correct) than after a random return (14% correct). Reinstating the original sequence of events improved memory for details.

2. Selective Cues May Reduce Access to Interfering Items

Another way that selective access can improve performance is by circumventing memories that would otherwise interfere. Experiments reported by Bekerian and Bowers provide evidence for this process. They showed slides depicting an auto accident, followed by misinformation and then a recognition test (target vs. suggested item). The misinformation was presented in a random order. On the recognition test, the questions duplicated the original sequence of slides or were presented in another random order. Performance was better when the test questions reinstated the sequence of the slides (Bekerian & Bowers, 1983). However, reinstating the original order of the slides did not improve performance when the misleading information was also presented in that same sequence (Bowers & Bekerian, 1984). Reinstating the original sequence did not improve performance when it cued memories of both the original and suggested events.

3. Selective Cues May Increase Access to Interfering Items

If retrieval cues selectively access memory for nontargets, this reduces the probability that the target will be recalled. An example of this principle is provided by Chandler, Gargano and Holt (in preparation). On Day 1 of the experiment, the subjects imagined events that were described in a story about a robbery (e.g., a man hid a calculator underneath the hammer in his toolbox). On Day 2, the subjects read the story again, but were warned that some of the details had been changed (e.g., a screwdriver had been substituted for the hammer in the first story). Their task was simply to imagine the events in the story. Then, immediately after reading the story on Day 2, they were asked to recall the objects from both stories (e.g., The man hid a calculator underneath a _____ or _____ in his toolbox). Recall of items from the first story was poor unless the subjects were told that this was the most important information to recall. In contrast, objects from the second story were recalled equally well regardless of instructions. These results suggest that people tend to selectively access recent events and that additional instructions or retrieval cues may be required to access less recent events.

4. Summary and Implications

The evidence suggests that interference effects can be reduced if the target is accessed selectively. For example, if a target is associated with unique emotional and contextual cues, it can be accessed selectively by reinstating these cues. The unique cues increase the likelihood of recalling the original event, in part because they do not cue memory for related events. In many cases, the emotional and environmental context at the scene of the crime are cues that are unique to the crime. Although witnesses have been exposed to related events (e.g., a police interview, mugshots), those events are likely to have occurred in a different emotional and environmental context. Asking eyewitnesses to remember what they felt and saw around the scene of the crime should help them to recall and recognize targets without interference from related events.

In some cases, however, a retrieval cue may activate both the trace for the crime and a trace for related events. In such cases, it is important to know why the interference effect occurs and what kind of errors to expect. Some theories of retrieval (cue-change and blocking theories) predict errors of omission, while others predict intrusions (feature recombination theories). Omissions and intrusions would reduce the chance of apprehending the correct individual. Intrusion errors would cast doubt on the validity of an eyewitness's report.

C. How Related Traces Affect Retrieval of a Specific Target

Many retrieval processes have been proposed to explain interference effects (M.C. Anderson & Bjork, 1994) and researchers are just beginning to contrast predictions and test them experimentally. There is now evidence for three retrieval processes.

1. A Related Event Can Change the Retrieval Cue

In Section I, we emphasized that recall is higher if the retrieval cue matches the trace for the target than if it does not. A related event may affect recall of the target event by priming features that become part of the retrieval cue. If the functional retrieval cue no longer matches the target, then the target should be omitted. For example, suppose that a target (e.g., The child ate the apple) brings to mind a young child. Later, a related event (e.g., The child rode the bicycle) brings to mind an older child. The retrieval cue *child–app____* brings to mind the older child because that meaning was primed recently. Because this functional retrieval cue does not match the trace for the target, the target is not recalled (Chandler & Gargano, 1995; Martin, 1972). On the other hand, if the related event emphasizes features that match the target (e.g., The child ate the cookies), then the retrieval cue matches the target, and recall is facilitated. Chandler and Gargano's (1995) results are consistent with both of these predictions.

The practical importance of such a cue-change process is that presenting wrong or irrelevant information during a recall test can reduce the number of targets recalled (omissions). Witnesses should recall less about what they saw (e.g., the back of the criminal, the criminal's stature and dress) if they are asked to recall something they did not see (e.g., the criminal's face).

2. A Related Item May Block the Target

Chandler and Gargano's (1995) study showed that a target (*child–apple*) is recalled *more often* if a related item (*child–orange*) is shown just before the test (*child–app____*). This happens because the related item primes features that are relevant to the target, and the retrieval cue begins to match the target. However, if the retrieval cue already matches the target, the related item can interfere with recognizing it.

Chandler and Gargano (in preparation) provided a retrieval cue that matched the context and semantic category of the target (*child–____*: apple, grape, banana, pear, peach). Presenting the item *child–orange reduced* recognition of *child–apple*. However, the effect was found only if the interfering item was shown recently. The finding is consistent with blocking theories, which claim that a recently formed trace for *child–orange* is stronger than the trace for the target. The strongest trace is sampled from memory, and is further strengthened by its retrieval, thereby reducing the chance of sampling the target (E. L. Bjork & Bjork, 1988; Roediger, 1974, 1978; Rundus, 1973).

In interviewing witnesses, the best results may be achieved by establishing a category (e.g., What was the culprit wearing on the upper body?). If the witness fails to recall, the investigator may obtain more information by asking more specific questions (was the culprit dressed formally or casually?). However, the investigator should avoid leading questions that introduce information that could block retrieval of the target. For example, asking the witness to describe the criminal's T-shirt could reduce the chance of recalling that the suspect was dressed in a formal jacket.

3. Recombinations of Features during Retrieval and Failing to Discriminate between Traces

An error of omission occurs if the target trace is not activated by the retrieval cues. Another type of error can occur if the retrieval cues activate traces of both the target and related events. According to feature recombination theories, the features from the two traces may recombine (Metcalfe, 1990; Metcalfe & Bjork, 1991; Reinitz, Lammers, & Cochran, 1992; see Hintzman, 1986, for a similar position). For example, suppose that Lynn has a large nose and a large mouth, and that Amy has a small nose and a small mouth. If both traces are activated, Lynn may be remembered as a person with a small nose and a large mouth. A feature recombination process can produce errors of intrusion.

Evidence for a recombination of features has been found in both recall and recognition tests. For example, Reinitz, Lammers, and Cochran (1992) asked people to study sentences of the form "The X saw the Y," and asked them to recall the sentences 15 min later. The most frequent errors in recall were conjunction errors (recalling the X from one sentence and the Y from another sentence). In addition, Reinitz et al. reported that people often recognized conjunction stimuli that recombined features from two studied items. The effects were found in recognizing nonsense words and human faces (see Reinitz, Morrisey, & Demb, 1994, for a similar result).

If features from two activated traces can recombine, can a person ever determine which features co-occurred? A traditional answer is that it is possible to discriminate one trace from another if the traces differ in temporal and contextual features. Chandler and Gargano (in preparation) recently found support for this prediction. People studied nature pictures (Fern A) and were given a forced-choice recognition test (Did you see Fern A or Fern C) 15 min later. Fern B interfered if it was presented in the study phase of the experiment, because it shared temporal and contextual features with the target. However, Fern B did not interfere if it was presented in the test phase, because unique temporal/contextual cues specified which features had co-occurred.

The implication of this research is that conjunction errors may happen in lineup identification and in recall. In lineup identification, intrusions may occur if the suspect possesses features that match two different memory traces. It is not known how frequently such intrusions occur. They may be infrequent because the criminal and mugshots are seen at different times and in different contexts. If the original context is reinstated before the lineup, a witness would activate traces formed at the crime scene but not traces that were formed at the police station, and no conjunction errors would be found. If both traces were activated, however, conjunction errors may occur. At short retention intervals, the context could be used to determine which features had co-occurred. But, at long retention intervals, there may be little contextual information left to discriminate between the traces.

In remembering objects, conjunction errors and discrimination problems may be found only with stimuli that have a rather arbitrary collection of features. For example, almost any shape of eyes, nose, and mouth can be combined to form a face. Conjunction errors would not be expected if the features are more interrelated, as with commonly known objects. For example, an apple and an orange would not be remembered as a fruit with a hard red shell and a soft interior. These stimuli show a pattern of interference effects that is more consistent with a blocking process (Chandler & Gargano, in preparation).

Another type of conjunction error may be more common. Witnesses may remember two events that occurred in different contexts as if they both occurred at the scene of the crime.

III. ATTRIBUTING AN ITEM TO A SOURCE

The preceding section established that recall and recognition of a target can be reduced by seeing a related event, at least under some circumstances. In addition to interference effects, people sometimes err by claiming that an object or event occurred at a wrong time or place (Davis & Sinha, 1950; Dodd & Bradshaw, 1980, Experiments 1 & 2). In other words, people sometimes attribute a familiar item to the wrong source. For example, Loftus (1975, Experiment 3) showed slides of an auto accident followed by questions about the slides. Some of the subjects were asked a question that implied a barn had been shown in the slides (How fast was the car going when it passed the barn?). A week later, the subjects were asked whether they had seen a barn in the slides. The subjects often claimed to have seen a barn if it had been suggested to them a week earlier. Schooler, Gerhard, and Loftus (1986) found that subjects would even describe details of the suggested objects when pressed to do so.

Why do people report having seen objects in the slides when the objects were only suggested to them? Perhaps they are responding to social demands to report the suggested item, even though they know that they did not see it in the slides. Intrusions that are caused by social demands might be reduced by telling people that the interviewer might be misinformed, or that the interviewer's questions may have contained some incorrect assumptions. Intrusions that occur because of memory retrieval processes should not be affected by such instructions.

Alternatively, there are two retrieval problems that could lead to such intrusions. One possibility is that people report whatever information comes to mind without assessing the source of the information (Jacoby & Kelley, 1987; Jacoby, Kelley & Dywan, 1989; D. S. Lindsay, 1993). Another possibility is that, although people consider the source of the information, they sometimes attribute the information to the wrong source (D. S. Lindsay, 1993). Support exists for both ideas.

A. Accuracy Improves When the Source Is Considered

When people make yes/no recognition decisions, they may not consider or use information about the source (D. S. Lindsay, 1993). Studies performed by D. S. Lindsay and Johnson (1989) suggest that accuracy improves when people are instructed to consider information about the source. Their subjects saw a complex scene that contained many objects, and then read a narrative that described the picture and suggested that additional objects were shown. Immediately thereafter, the subjects were asked to indicate whether each item had occurred in the picture (yes/no, Experiment 1), or whether they *remembered seeing the item in the picture* (yes/no, Experiment 2). Subjects often said that suggested items had been shown in the picture (Experiment 1), but claimed to have *seen them in the picture* less often (Experiment 2). The result could be explained by social demands. People may have claimed that the suggested items were in the picture because the narrative had been presented to them as being an accurate description of the slide (Experiment 1). Social demands would be reduced by asking subjects whether they remembered *seeing each item in the picture* (Experiment 2).

Another test, however, suggests that performance can be improved even more by requiring people to make source judgments. D. S. Lindsay and Johnson (1989) asked other subjects to indicate the source of each item (seen, read, both, new) and found that these instructions completely removed the tendency to say that the suggested items appeared in the slides (see also Zaragoza & Lane, 1994, Experiment 3). Perhaps performance was more accurate because the subjects considered their memory for perceptual details that they would not otherwise have retrieved. Retrieving such perceptual details would help them to identify the source of the item (picture or narrative).

B. Source Misattributions

When people are directly asked to make source judgments, their judgments are not always accurate. Generally, it has been found that greater featural similarity between events increases source misattributions (see, e.g., Johnson, 1988, for review of the findings; Underwood, 1977). For example, Carris, Zaragoza, and Lane (1992) showed slides followed by a narrative that described the slides. Later, the subjects indicated whether items had occurred in the slides, in the narrative, in both, or in neither. Source attributions were more accurate when the subjects had been instructed simply to read the narrative than when they had been asked to imagine the events in the narrative as they read. When people had imagined the suggested items, they were more likely to attribute such items to the slides.

Similar conclusions have been reached in studies that have examined source judgments in an interference paradigm. Source judgments are not affected if the target and related item are presented in different formats (e.g., a picture vs. a narrative). Zaragoza and Koshmider (1989) presented slides that contained targets (e.g., a Folgers jar, a hammer), followed by a narrative that described the slides. The narrative presented neutral information for some of the targets (e.g., coffee jar) and misinformation about other targets (the tool was a screwdriver). This manipulation did not influence the frequency with which people attributed the targets to the slides (a correct attribution), nor the frequency with which they attributed the misinformation to the slides (an incorrect attribution).

On the whole, people were able to judge whether they had seen an item or had only read about it. And they were able to do so both immediately (Zaragoza & Koshmider, 1989, Experiment 1) and after a day (Zaragoza & Koshmider, 1989, Experiment 2). These findings are encouraging from a practical standpoint. If people can make accurate source judgments, then encouraging them to make these judgments could determine whether they actually had witnessed something at the scene of the crime or whether it had been suggested to them.

Of course, there are limits to such a strategy. Any procedure that makes the original trace and subsequent traces more similar should increase source misattributions. For example, it is more difficult for people to determine whether they saw or imagined an object than it is to determine whether they saw or only read about an object (Carris et al., 1992; see Zaragoza & Lane, 1994, for similar findings).

As one might expect, it is also difficult to distinguish between two pictorially presented events. This point is illustrated in an experiment conducted by Chandler (1991, Experiment 4). The targets were nature pictures that people rated for complexity. Some of the targets (e.g., Fern A) were followed by related pictures (e.g., Fern B) that people rated for pleasantness. Fifteen minutes later, they were given a modified recognition test (target vs.

novel picture). After making their choice, they were asked to indicate whether they had rated the picture for complexity or pleasantness (a source judgment). For trials in which subjects chose the correct picture, the source judgments (complexity vs. pleasantness) were analyzed. The source judgments were more accurate if the target was unique (75% correct) than if the target was followed by a related picture (51% correct).

As with other interference effects, the related picture did not always interfere with source judgments. In another experiment, the related picture *preceded* rather than followed the target. Neither accuracy nor source judgments were affected by a related picture in that experiment. Source judgments were equally accurate for unique targets (68% correct) and for targets that were preceded by a related picture (67% correct). In the proactive design, the targets were more recent than the nontargets. It is possible that the subjects did not access the nontargets and so their source judgments were not affected by the related pictures.

Summary and Implications

The findings suggest that people may claim to have seen an object when, in fact, they have only heard or read about it. Such errors are more likely when related objects (e.g., a hammer and a wrench) are presented in a similar way (e.g., saw a hammer and imagined a wrench) than when they are presented in different ways (e.g., saw a hammer but read about a wrench). If the events were presented in different ways, source errors can be reduced by asking people to consider information about the source of the event (e.g., Did you see the event, hear about it, or read about it?).

IV. EFFORTFUL AND STRATEGIC RETRIEVAL PROCESSES

Remembering an event depends on the effort devoted to retrieval and a witness's retrieval strategies. Even if an event is potentially memorable, it may not be remembered if the witness is distracted. Also, witnesses do not spontaneously generate cues that would help them remember an event. By helping witnesses to generate relevant cues (cues that might match the memory trace), more details about the event can be recovered.

A. Retrieval Is an Attention-Demanding Process

There is evidence suggesting that recollection is not automatic; instead, it is an attention-demanding process. A study by Johnston, Greenberg, Fisher, and Martin (1970) measured performance on a motor tracking task as people tried to recall words or as they counted out loud (1, 2, 3, etc.). More errors were made on the motor tracking task when people tried to recall words than when they counted. Apparently, the recall task used some of the capacity that would otherwise have been devoted to the motor tracking task. Because attention (or capacity) is limited, anything that deflects attention away from retrieval should decrease performance in a memory test (see also Jacoby, Woloshyn, & Kelley, 1989).

A variety of distractions and concurrent tasks could reduce the amount that witnesses recall. For example, police often conduct interviews in a noisy work environment or leave their radios on while conducting the interview (Fisher, Geiselman, & Raymond, 1987). Frequently, witnesses must interpret grammatically complex questions, which leaves less capacity to devote to retrieval. Another problem is that police interviewers often ask about too many details in a single question (Fisher, Geiselman, & Raymond, 1987). For example, "Did he have any unusual markings, like scars or tattoos, or perhaps jewelry, maybe gold teeth, or was he unusually tall, or mean-looking?" Maintaining the question in working memory would leave less capacity to devote to recall (Baddeley, 1986).

B. Strategic Retrieval

Even when witnesses devote their full attention to recalling an event, they may not generate cues that could help them to recall. For example, they may not realize that imagining the original environment could help them recall the event. The problem is one of metamemory, defined as a person's knowledge or beliefs about how variables influence performance on a memory test (Nelson & Narens, 1990; Metcalfe, Chapter 11, this volume). If witnesses fail to use the strategy spontaneously, then interviewers might improve performance by providing the strategy.

1. Considering the Environmental Context and Source

Asking witnesses to reinstate the original context can improve their performance on recall and recognition tests, as discussed earlier. Furthermore, instructing subjects to consider information about the source can improve performance (D. S. Lindsay & Johnson, 1989). Witnesses, however, do not consider the source spontaneously. Either they do not realize that this strategy would be useful, or the strategy requires too much effort. In any case, performance can be improved by instructing witnesses to consider environmental context and source.

2. Memory for Details

Both general and detailed information is stored about complex events (Fisher & Chandler, 1991), and people may not generate cues that would help them to recall details about appearance. For example, a witness may recall that a burglar wore dark clothing, but may not go beyond this general description unless asked for more details. One technique used in Fisher and Geiselman's (1992) cognitive interview is to prompt witnesses for specific details (e.g., Try to imagine the clothing. What type of clothing was it? Describe how it fits and how it looks).

V. APPLIED RESEARCH IN EYEWITNESS TESTIMONY

How effectively have these retrieval principles been applied in witness tasks? Our analysis follows the two phases of a typical police investigation. Initially, witnesses are asked to describe the event during an interview. Later in an investigation, witnesses may be asked whether they recognize a suspect in a lineup or a photo array. To what degree has performance on these tasks been improved by our knowledge of retrieval processes?

A. Description (Recall) of the Event

In an effort to enhance the amount reported by witnesses, Fisher and Geiselman (1992) developed an interactive interview known as the Cognitive Interview (CI). In the CI, interviewers ask the witnesses to: (1) reinstate the environmental and emotional context; (2) recall from different personal perspectives; and (3) recall in different temporal orders (recall in forward order and in backward order). All of these instructions are based on the encoding specificity principle. By reinstating the environmental and emotional context, the witnesses are generating cues that match the memory trace and this should improve recall. By recalling the event from different perspectives and in different temporal orders, more cues are generated that might match the trace. In addition to these instructions, the witnesses are asked not to edit their recall. They are asked to report all correct details, whether they seem trivial, irrelevant, or out of temporal order.

To examine the effectiveness of the CI, Fisher and Geiselman (1992) conducted a series of laboratory studies that used the following procedure. Volunteer witnesses saw a film of a crime or a live innocuous event and then returned to the laboratory (usually 2 days later) where they were interviewed by professional law enforcement agents. The witnesses recalled 30 to 35% more details when the interviewers used a Cognitive Interview instead of their standard interview techniques. The number of erroneous details reported was the same for the CI and standard interviews (for reviews see Bekerian & Dennett, 1993; Fisher, McCauley, & Geiselman, 1994; Kohnken, Milne, Memon, & Bull, 1992). Furthermore, the success of the CI comes at little cost. In the studies just mentioned, the CI techniques were taught in about 30 min.

Most of the research on the CI cannot tell us which of the various components of the CI are responsible for the improved performance. However, Geiselman et al. (1986) compared the amount recalled by groups of subjects who were given different instructions during the interview. One group was given a standard police interview, a second group was asked to reinstate the environmental context, and a third group was asked to avoid editing their responses. Compared to the standard interview, more details were recalled by subjects who were instructed either to reinstate context or to avoid editing responses. The Geiselman et al. (1986) study did not include a group that recalled from different personal perspectives or a group that recalled in forward and backward order. So, the study cannot tell us whether these instructions are more effective than a standard interview.

However, a correlational analysis by Saywitz, Geiselman, and Bornstein (1992) suggests that each of the four techniques can increase the amount recalled. Children aged 7 to 11 witnessed an argument and were interviewed by detective 2 days later. The detectives were trained to use CI techniques, but not all of the sheriffs used all of the techniques. Each instruction was associated with higher recall, although the effect of changing perspectives was marginally significant.

Fisher and Geiselman revised their Cognitive Interview to address additional concerns that they had about the retrieval environment and communication. In addition to the techniques used in the original CI, the interviewers were told to avoid distracting the witness with a noisy environment or with complex questions. In an environment without distractions, the witness can devote full attention to retrieving details about the event. Also, the witness is asked to imagine an object or person before describing it. The revised CI also includes techniques that are intended to improve communication between the interviewer and the witness. For example, the interviewer is instructed to avoid interrupting the witness and to encourage the witness to work hard (see Fisher & Geiselman, 1992, for a full description of these techniques).

The effectiveness of the revised CI has been tested in two laboratory studies (Fisher, Geiselman, Raymond, Jurkevich, & Warhaftig, 1987; George, 1991) and in two field studies involving actual victims and witnesses of crimes (Fisher, Geiselman, & Amador, 1989; George, 1991). In the two field studies, more crime-relevant details were recalled in the revised CI than in a standard police interview. Furthermore, Fisher et al. found that accuracy was equally high in the two groups, as measured by the corroboration rates between witnesses (.94 with the revised CI and .93 with the standard interview). In the two laboratory studies, more correct information was recalled with the revised CI than with either a standard police interview or the original CI. The groups did not differ in the amount of incorrect information that they recalled.

The advantage of the revised CI over the original CI (Fisher, Geiselman,

Raymond, Jurkevich, & Warhaftig, 1987) indicates that at least one of the new instructions facilitates recall. However, the effectiveness of each additional technique in the revised CI will need to be tested experimentally in order to determine why the revised CI is more effective.

There is some evidence that the revised CI does not work solely by improving communication. Two studies have shown that witnesses recall more details when they are interviewed with the revised CI rather than a structured interview based on principles of communication (Kohnken, Thurer, & Zoberbier, 1994; Mantwill, Kohnken, & Aschermann, 1995). These findings make sense, given that recall increases when witnesses are instructed to reinstate context, to avoid editing responses (Geiselman et al., 1986; Saywitz et al., 1992), and to recall from different perspectives and in different orders (Saywitz et al., 1992). In addition, George (1991) reported that higher recall was associated with instructing witnesses to imagine the person/object before describing it. Other cognitive components of the revised CI have yet to be investigated.

B. Lineup Identification

Later in the police investigation, witnesses may be asked whether they recognize a suspect in a photo array or a live lineup. Several studies have asked whether reinstating the original context improves accuracy in a lineup identification task. Accuracy tends to be higher when the scene of the crime is physically reinstated than when it is not (S. M. Smith & Vela, 1992). The same effect occurs when the original context is reinstated by showing subjects slides that contain some of the original environmental cues (Gibling & Davies, 1988). However, the effect of imagining the original context is somewhat variable. Instructing subjects to imagine the original context sometimes increases accuracy (Malpass & Devine, 1981b), and sometimes the manipulation has no effect (Fisher, McCauley, & Geiselman, 1994; Smith & Vela, 1992). From the practical standpoint of improving accuracy, the physical context reinstatement effects are noteworthy.

Other ways of improving accuracy have been found by altering the nature of the lineup task. Typically, the witness is shown all of the members of the lineup simultaneously, a procedure that encourages witnesses to choose the person who *most resembles* the culprit. Wells (1993) called this procedure a relative judgment process, and he pointed out that it can produce false identifications when the lineup does not include the culprit. Wells suggested that a relative judgment process can be discouraged (1) by telling witnesses that the culprit may not be in the lineup and (2) by presenting the lineup sequentially (one member at a time). Consistent with Wells's idea, both techniques have been found to reduce false identifications without affecting the number of correct identifications.

By telling witnesses that the culprit may not be in the lineup, one counteracts demands for witnesses to select someone from the lineup. Demands to choose someone are great without this instruction. For example, the witness may reason that the police would not conduct a lineup unless they thought that they had apprehended the culprit. Because of social demands, the witness may select the person who most resembles the culprit. Telling witnesses that the culprit might not be in the lineup reduces false identifications without reducing correct identifications (Malpass & Devine, 1981a; for review see Wells, 1993).

Lineup identification is also less error prone when the members of a lineup are shown sequentially rather than simultaneously. In the sequential lineup procedure, the witness must decide whether a member of the lineup is the culprit before seeing the next person in the lineup. Witnesses do not know how many people will be shown in the lineup and are not allowed to select a member that they rejected earlier. They cannot go back through the lineup to choose the person who most resembles the culprit. Presenting the lineup sequentially instead of simultaneously reduces false identifications substantially in tests given immediately (R. C. L. Lindsay & Wells, 1985; R. C. L. Lea, & Fulford, 1991; R. C. L. Lindsay, Lea, Nosworthy, et al., 1991) and after a day (Sporer, 1993). Yet the sequential and simultaneous procedures produce the same percentage of correct identifications.

VI. SUMMARY AND ASSESSMENT

During the past few years, basic questions about retrieval have sparked the interest of both basic researchers and those concerned with improving the amount and accuracy of eyewitness testimony. What kinds of cues are effective? When will memory for an event be affected by related events? When will people misattribute an event to the wrong source? How is retrieval affected by attention and strategies? Although the goals of basic and applied research are somewhat different, basic researchers are interested in learning whether their laboratory findings generalize to different materials and situations, and applied researchers can look to laboratory findings to know which techniques might affect eyewitness testimony. Applied research can also lead to ideas that did not occur to those doing basic research.

As discussed in the first section of this chapter, the encoding specificity principle (Tulving, 1983) has been most fruitful in guiding efforts to improve eyewitness testimony. The principle states that recollection is more likely the more the cues match the trace, and it predicts many findings that generalize to situations that witnesses encounter. Instructing the witness to reinstate the original environmental and emotional context has been shown to improve the amount that they recall (Geiselman et al., 1986) and often improves performance in a lineup identification task. Witnesses also tend to recall more when more cues are provided that might match the trace. Witnesses tend to recall more when they are instructed to recall in different temporal orders (Saywitz et al., 1992) and when they are tested more than once (McCauley, 1993; Scrivener & Safer, 1988). Some recent research suggests that the performance of witnesses is also improved by testing them in the same format (e.g., visual, tactile) in which they encountered the event.

Because witnesses are often exposed to events that are related to the crime, it is important to know how this affects their performance. As reviewed in the second section of this chapter, the idea that such events can change the memory trace has not been supported by research. Instead, related events appear to reduce the probability of accessing or retrieving the trace. The evidence suggests that interference effects are found only when the retrieval cue activates the trace for the related event. Thus, we expect that interference effects will not often be found in witness testimony. Because witnesses encode the crime and related events in different contexts, they can use the scene of the crime as a cue selectively to access target events. Furthermore, some new results show that interference does not always occur even when the related events are highly accessible.

Another concern, discussed in Section III, is that witnesses may misattribute a familiar (or suggested) item to the scene of the crime. Laboratory experiments indicate that such errors can be reduced by instructing people to consider whether they saw the event or merely read about it (D. S. Lindsay & Johnson, 1989). The instructions probably work because they reduce social demands and because people can use their memory about source to discriminate between what they saw and what they read. However, it is more difficult to discriminate between memory for two events that are presented in the same format (e.g., both are imagined). More laboratory and applied research needs to be done to determine whether these conclusions will generalize to the parameters and stimuli that confront witnesses.

Last, as discussed in Section IV, retrieval is an effortful process that is influenced by retrieval strategies. Theoretically, distractions would reduce the resources that witnesses can devote to retrieval, lowering the amount that witnesses recall. Even when witnesses devote full attention to memory retrieval, they may not use strategies that could improve their performance. Either they do not realize that a strategy could improve their performance, or using it requires too much effort. Instructing witnesses to use strategies (e.g., think about the scene of the crime) may increase the number of details that are recalled and recognized.

We are optimistic that cognitive research will continue to have implications for understanding witness memory. In return, the tasks facing witnesses will continue to challenge the generality of our theories. Because of convenience, laboratory studies are still usually done using verbal stimuli and short retention intervals. Of course, witnesses are asked to remember unfamiliar names, unfamiliar faces, and actions, often at very long retention intervals. Applied research that uses such materials and retention intervals will continue to expand our scope.

Applied research also emphasizes the importance of factors outside of current theories. Some of these factors have implications for understanding human memory. For example, communication and social factors affect witnesses' performance. One of these factors, demand characteristics, can influence performance in some memory tests. Even researchers who are solely interested in memory processes cannot ignore it. As discussed in the preceding sections, social demands can account for interference effects in some tests, and why people report that they have seen an item when they have, in fact, only read about it. Social demands may encourage a relative judgment process in a lineup identification task. It is not known how much of these effects are attributable to social demands as opposed to memory processes.

Acknowledgments

This work was partially funded by grants to R. P. Fisher from the National Institute of Justice (#USDJ-85-IJ-CX-0053) and the National Science Foundation (SES-8911146). We thank Michelle McCauley for her assistance in collecting and analyzing data from several studies.

References

Anderson, M. C., & Bjork, R. A. (1994). Mechanisms of inhibition in long-term memory: A new taxonomy. In D. Dagenbach & T. Carr (Eds.), *Inhibition in attention, memory and language,* (pp. 265–325). San Diego: Academic Press.

Anderson, R. C., & Pichert, J. W. (1978). Recall of previously unrecalled information following a shift in perspective. *Journal of Verbal Learning and Verbal Behavior, 17,* 1–12.

Baddeley, A. D. (1986). *Working memory.* Oxford: Oxford University Press.

Bekerian, D. A., & Bowers, J. M. (1983). Eyewitness testimony: Were we misled? *Journal of Experimental Psychology: Learning, Memory, and Cognition, 9,* 139–145.

Bekerian, D. A., & Dennett, J. L. (1993). The cognitive interview technique: Reviving the issues. *Applied Cognitive Psychology, 7,* 275–298.

Belli, R. F., Lindsay, D. S., Gales, M. S., & McCarthy, T. T. (1994). Memory impairment and source misattribution in postevent misinformation experiments with short retention intervals. *Memory & Cognition, 22,* 40–54.

Belli, R. F., Windschitl, P. D., McCarthy, T. T., & Winfrey, S. E. (1992). Detecting memory impairment with a modified test procedure: Manipulating retention interval with centrally presented event items. *Journal of Experimental Psychology: Learning, Memory, and Cognition, 18,* 356–367.

Bjork, E. L., & Bjork, R. A. (1988). On the adaptive aspects of retrieval failure in autobiographical memory. In M. M. Gruneberg, P. E. Morris, & R. N. Sykes (Eds.), *Practical aspects of memory: Current research and issues* (Vol. 1, pp. 283–288). Chichester, England: Wiley.

Bjork, R. A. & Richardson-Klavehn, A. (1989). On the puzzling relationship between environmental context and human memory. In C. Izawa (Ed.) *Current issues in cognitive processes,* (pp. 313–344). Hillsdale, NJ: Erlbaum.

Blaney, P. H. (1986). Affect and memory: A review. *Psychological Bulletin, 99,* 229–246.

Bower, G. H. (1967). A multicomponent theory of the memory trace. In K. W. Spence & J. T. Spence (Eds.), *The psychology of learning and motivation: Advances in research and theory* (Vol. 1). New York: Academic Press.

Bower, G. H., Gilligan, S. C., & Montiero, K. P. (1981). Selectivity of learning caused by affective states. *Journal of Experimental Psychology: General, 110,* 451–472.

Bowers, J. M., & Bekerian, D. A. (1984). When will postevent information distort eyewitness testimony? *Journal of Applied Psychology, 69,* 466–472.

Cann, A., & Ross, D. (1989). Olfactory stimuli as context cues in human memory. *American Journal of Psychology, 102,* 91–012.

Carris, M., Zaragoza, M., & Lane, S. (1992). *The role of visual imagery in source misattribution errors.* Paper presented at the annual meeting of the Midwestern Psychological Society, Chicago.

Chandler, C. C. (1989). Specific retroactive interference in modified recognition tests: Evidence for an unknown cause of interference. *Journal of Experimental Psychology: Learning, Memory, and Cognition, 15,* 256–265.

Chandler, C. C. (1991). How memory for an event is influenced by related events: Interference in modified recognition tests. *Journal of Experimental Psychology: Learning, Memory, and Cognition, 1,* 115–125.

Chandler, C. C. (1993). Accessing related events increases retroactive interference in a matching recognition test. *Journal of Experimental Psychology: Learning, Memory, and Cognition, 19,* 967–974.

Chandler, C. C., & Gargano, G. J. (1995). Item-specific interference caused by cue-dependent forgetting. *Memory & Cognition, 23,* 701–708.

Chandler, C. C., & Gargano, G. J. (in preparation). Retrieval processes that produce interference in modified forced-choice recognition tests.

Chandler, C. C., Gargano, G. J., & Holt, B. C. (in preparation). How post-event information reduces recall for a target event.

Conrad, R. (1967). Interference or decay over short retention intervals? *Journal of Verbal Learning and Verbal Behavior, 6,* 49–54.

Cutler, B. L., Penrod, S. D., & Martens, T. K. (1987). Improving the reliability of eyewitness identification: Putting context into context. *Journal of Applied Psychology, 72,* 629–637.

Dalton, P. (1993). The role of stimulus familiarity in context-dependent recognition. *Memory & Cognition, 21,* 223–234.

Davies, G., & Milne, A. (1985). Eyewitness composite production: A function of mental or physical reinstatement of context. *Criminal Justice and Behavior, 12,* 209–220.

Davis, D. R., & Sinha, D. (1950). The influence of an interpolated experience upon recognition. *Quarterly Journal of Experimental Psychology, 2,* 132–137.

Dodd, D. H., & Bradshaw, J. M. (1980). Leading questions and memory: Pragmatic constraints. *Journal of Verbal Learning and Verbal Behavior, 19,* 695–704.

Eich, E. (1989). Theoretical issues in state dependent memory. In H. L. Roediger & F. I. M. Craik (Eds.), *Varieties of memory and consciousness,* (pp. 331–354). Hillsdale, NJ: Earlbaum.

Eich, E. (1980). The cue-dependent nature of state-dependent retrieval. *Memory & Cognition, 8,* 157–173.

Epstein, W. (1972). Mechanisms of directed forgetting. In G. H. Bower (Ed.), *The psychology of learning and motivation: Advances in research and theory* (Vol. 6, pp. 147–191). New York: Academic Press.

Fernandez, A., & Glenberg, A. M. (1985). Changing environmental context does not reliably affect memory. *Memory & Cognition, 13,* 333–345.

Fisher, R. P., & Chandler, C. C. (1991). Independence between recalling interevent relations and specific events. *Journal of Experimental Psychology: Learning, Memory, and Cognition, 17,* 722–733.

Fisher, R. P., & Cuervo, A. (1983). Memory for physical features of discourse as a function of their relevance. *Journal of Experimental Psychology: Learning, Memory, and Cognition, 9,* 130–138.

Fisher, R. P., & Cunningham, L. A. (in preparation). *Interaction between encoding and test formats in recognition of 3-dimensional objects.* Florida International University, Miami.

Fisher, R. P., & Geiselman, R. E. (1992). *Memory-enchancing techniques for investigative interviewing.* Springfield, IL: Thomas.

Fisher, R. P., & Quigley, K. L. (1991). Applying cognitive theory in public health investigations: Enhancing food recall. In J. Tanur (Ed.), *Questions about questions,* (pp. 154–169). New York: Sage Press.

Fisher, R. P., Geiselman, R. E., & Amador, M. (1989). Field test of the cognitive interview: Enhancing the recollection of actual victims and witnesses of crime. *Journal of Applied Psychology, 74,* 722–727.

Fisher, R. P., Geiselman, R. E., & Raymond, D. S. (1987). Critical analysis of police interview techniques. *Journal of Police Science and Administration, 15,* 177–185.

Fisher, R. P., Geiselman, R. E., Raymond, D. S., Jurkevich, L. M., & Warhaftig, M. L. (1987). Enhancing enhanced eyewitness memory: Refining the cognitive interview. *Journal of Police Science and Administration, 15,* 291–297.

Fisher, R. P., McCauley, M. R., & Geiselman, R. E. (1994). Improving eyewitness testimony with the cognitive interview. In D. Ross, J. D. Read, & M. Toglia (Eds.), *Adult eyewitness testimony: Current trends and developments* (pp. 245–269). London: Cambridge University Press.

Geiselman, R. E., Fisher, R. P., MacKinnon, D. P., & Holland, H. R. (1986). Enhancement of eyewitness memory with the cognitive interview. *American Journal of Psychology, 99,* 385–401.

Geiselman, R. E., & Padilla, J. (1988). Interviewing child witnesses with the cognitive interview. *Journal of Police Science and Administration, 16,* 236–242.

George, R. (1991). *A field and experimental evaluation of three methods of interviewing witnesses/victims of crime.* Unpublished manuscript, Polytechnic of East London, London.

Gibling, F., & Davies, G. (1988). Reinstatement of context following exposure to post-event information. *British Journal of Psychology, 79,* 129–141.

Greenwald, A. G. (1970). Sensory feedback mechanisms in performance control: With special reference to the ideomotor mechanism. *Psychological Review, 77,* 73–99.

Hintzman, D. L. (1986). "Schema abstraction" in a multiple-trace memory model. *Psychological Review, 93,* 411–428.

Jacoby, L. L., & Kelley, C. M. (1987). Unconscious influences of memory for a prior event. *Personality and Social Psychology Bulletin, 17,* 314–336.

Jacoby, L. L., Kelley, C. M., & Dywan, J. (1989). Memory attributions. In H. L. Roediger & F. I. M. Craik (Eds.), *Varieties of memory and consciousness,* (pp. 391–422). Hillsdale, NJ: Erlbaum.

Jacoby, L. L., Woloshyn, V., & Kelley, C. (1989). Becoming famous without being recognized: Unconscious influences of memory produced by dividing attention. *Journal of Experimental Psychology: General, 118,* 115–125.

Johnson, M. K. (1983). A multiple-entry, modular memory system. In G. H. Bower (Ed.), *The psychology of learning and motivation: Advances in research and theory* (Vol. 17, pp. 81–123). New York: Academic Press.

Johnson, M. K. (1988). Discriminating the origin of information. In T. F. Oltmanns & B. A. Maher (Eds.), *Delusional beliefs: Interdisciplinary perspectives,* (pp. 34–65). New York: Wiley.

Johnston, W. A., Greenberg, S. N., Fisher, R. P., & Martin, D. W. (1970). Divided attention: A vehicle for monitoring memory processes. *Journal of Experimental Psychology, 83,* 164–171.

Kohnken, G., Milne, R., Memon, A., & Bull, R. (1992). *A meta-analysis on the effects of the cognitive interview.* Paper presented at the 3rd European Congress on Psychology and Law, Oxford.

Kohnken, G., Thurer, C., & Zoberbier, D. (1994). The cognitive interview: Are the interviewers' memories enhanced, too? *Applied Cognitive Psychology, 8,* 13–24.

Krafka, C., & Penrod, S. (1985). Reinstatement of context in a field experiment on eyewitness identification. *Journal of Personality and Social Psychology, 49,* 58–69.

Kroll, N. E. A., & Ogawa, K. H. (1988). Retrieval of the irretrievable: The effect of sequential information on response bias. In M. M. Gruneberg, P. E. Morris, & R. N. Sykes (Eds.), *Practical aspects of memory: Current research and issues* (Vol. 1, pp. 490–495). Chichester, England: Wiley.

Kroll, N. E., & Timourian, D. A. (1986). Misleading questions and the retrieval of the irretrievable. *Bulletin of the Psychonomic Society, 24,* 165–168.

Leibowitz, H. W., & Guzy, L. (1990). *Can the accuracy of eyewitness testimony be improved by the use of nonverbal techniques?* Paper presented at the meeting of the American Psychology–Law Society, Williamsburg, VA.

Lindsay, D. S. (1993). Memory source monitoring and eyewitness testimony. In D. F. Ross, J. D. Read, & M. P. Toglia (Eds.), *Adult eyewitness testimony: Current trends and developments.* New York: Cambridge University Press.

Lindsay, D. S., & Johnson, M. K. (1989). The eyewitness suggestibility effect and memory for source. *Memory & Cognition, 17,* 349–358.

Lindsay, R. C. L., Lea, J. A., & Fulford, J. A. (1991). Sequential lineup presentation: Technique matters. *Journal of Applied Psychology, 76,* 741–745.

Lindsay, R. C. L., Lea, J. A., Nosworthy, G. J., Fulford, J. A., Hector, J., LeVan, V., & Seabrook, C. (1991). Biased lineups: Sequential presentation reduces the problem. *Journal of Applied Psychology, 76,* 796–802.

Lindsay, R. C. L., & Wells, G. L. (1985). Improving eyewitness identifications from lineups: Simultaneous versus sequential lineup presentation. *Journal of Applied Psychology, 70,* 556–564.

Loftus, E. F. (1975). Leading questions and the eyewitness report. *Cognitive Psychology, 7,* 560–572.

Loftus, E. F. (1979). *Eyewitness testimony.* Cambridge: Harvard University Press.

Loftus, E. F., & Loftus, G. R. (1980). On the permanence of stored information in the human brain. *American Psychologist, 35,* 409–420.

Loftus, E. F., Miller, D. G., & Burns, H. J. (1978). Semantic integration of verbal information into a visual memory. *Journal of Experimental Psychology: Human Learning and Memory, 4,* 19–31.

Malpass, R. S., & Devine, P. G. (1981a). Eyewitness identification: Lineup instructions and the absence of the offender. *Journal of Applied Psychology, 66,* 482–489.

Malpass, R. S., & Devine, P. G. (1981b). Guided memory in eyewitness identification. *Journal of Applied Psychology, 66,* 343–350.

Mantwill, M., Kohnken, G., & Aschermann, E. (1995). *Effects of the cognitive interview on the recall of familiar and unfamiliar events. Journal of Applied Psychology, 80,* 68–78.

Martin, E. (1972). Verbal learning theory and independent retrieval phenomena. *Psychological Review, 78,* 314–332.

McCauley, M. R. (1993). *Enhancing children's memory with the revised cognitive interview.* Unpublished master's thesis, Florida International University, Miami.

McCloskey, M., & Zaragoza, M. (1985). Misleading postevent information and memory for events: Arguments and evidence against memory impairment hypotheses. *Journal of Experimental Psychology: General, 114,* 1–16.

Metcalfe, J. (1990). Composite holograph associative recall model (CHARM) and blended memories in eyewitness testimony. *Journal of Experimental Psychology: General, 119,* 145–160.

Metcalfe, J., & Bjork, R. A. (1991). Composite models never (well, hardly ever) compromise: Reply to Schooler and Tanaka (1991). *Journal of Experimental Psychology: General, 120,* 203–210.

Nelson, T. O., & Narens, L. (1990). Metamemory: A theoretical framework and new findings. In G. Bower (Ed.), *The psychology of learning and motivation: Advances in research and theory* (Vol. 26, pp. 125–173). San Diego: Academic Press.

Payne, D. G. (1987). Hypermnesia and reminiscence in recall: A historical and empirical review. *Psychological Bulletin, 101,* 5–27.

Poole, D. A., & White, L. T. (1991). Effects of question repetition on the eyewitness testimony of children and adults. *Developmental Psychology, 27,* 975–986.

Posner, M. I., & Kosnick, A. W. (1966). On the role of interference in short-term retention. *Journal of Experimental Psychology, 72,* 221–231.

Reinitz, M. T., Lammers, W. J., & Cochran, B. P. (1992). Memory-conjunction errors: Miscombination of stored stimulus features can produce illusions of memory. *Memory & Cognition, 20,* 1–11.

Reinitz, M. T., Morrisey, J., & Demb, J. (1994). Role of attention in face encoding. *Journal of Experimental Psychology: Learning, Memory, and Cognition, 20,* 161–168.

Roediger, H. L., III. (1974). Inhibition effects of recall. *Memory & Cognition, 2,* 261–269.

Roediger, H. L., III. (1978). Recall as a self-limiting process. *Memory & Cognition, 6,* 54–63.

Roediger, H. L., III, Wheeler, M. A., & Rajaram, S. (1993). Remembering, knowing and reconstructing the past. In D. L. Medin (Ed.), *The psychology of learning and motivation: Advances in research and theory* (Vol. 30, pp. 97–134). New York: Academic Press.

Rundus, D. (1973). Negative effects of using list items as recall cues. *Journal of Verbal Learning and Verbal Behavior, 12,* 43–50.

Saywitz, K. J., Geiselman, R. E., & Bornstein, G. K. (1992). Effects of cognitive interviewing and practice on children's recall performance. *Journal of Applied Psychology, 77,* 744–756.

Schooler, J. W. Gerhard, D., & Loftus, E. F. (1986). Qualities of the unreal. *Journal of Experimental Psychology: Learning, Memory, and Cognition, 12,* 171–181.

Scrivner, E., & Safer, M. A. (1988). Eyewitnesses show hypermnesia for details about a violent event. *Journal of Applied Psychology, 73,* 371–377.

Shapiro, P. N., & Penrod, S. (1986). Meta-analysis of facial identification studies. *Psychological Bulletin, 100,* 139–156.

Smith, A. F., Jobe, J. B., & Mingay, D. J. (1991). Question-induced cognitive biases in reports of dietary intake by college men and women. *Journal of Health Psychology, 10,* 244–251.

Smith, S. M. (1979). Remembering in and out of context. *Journal of Experimental Psychology: Human Learning and Memory, 5,* 460–471.

Smith, S. M. (1988). Environmental context-dependent memory. In G. M. Davies & D. M. Thomson (Eds.), *Memory in context: Context in memory* (pp. 13–34). New York: Wiley.

Smith, S. M., & Vela, E. (1992). Environmental context-dependent eyewitness recognition. *Applied Cognitive Psychology, 6,* 125–139.

Sporer, S. L. (1993). Eyewitness identification accuracy, confidence, and decision times in simultaneous and sequential lineups. *Journal of Applied Psychology, 78,* 22–33.

Thomson, D. M., & Tulving, E. (1970). Associative encoding and retrieval: Weak and strong cues. *Journal of Experimental Psychology, 86,* 255–262.

Tulving, E. (1974). Cue-dependent forgetting. *American Scientist, 62,* 74–82.

Tulving, E. (1983). *Elements of episodic memory* (chap. 11). Oxford: Clarendon Press.

Tulving, E., & Bower, G. H. (1974). The logic of memory representations. In G. H. Bower (Ed.), *The psychology of learning and motivation: Advances in research and tehory* (Vol. 8). New York: Academic Press.

Tulving, E., & Thomson, D. M. (1971). Retrieval processes in recognition memory: Effects of associative context. *Journal of Experimental Psychology, 87,* 116–124.

Tulving, E., & Thomson, D. M. (1973). Encoding specificity and retrieval processes in episodic memory. *Psychological Review, 80,* 352–373.

Tulving, E., & Watkins, M. J. (1975). Structure of memory traces. *Psychological Review, 82,* 261–275.

Underwood, B. J. (1977). *Temporal codes for memories: Issues and problems.* Hillsdale, NJ: Erlbaum.

Wells, G. L. (1993). What do we know about eyewitness identification? *American Psychologist, 48,* 553–571.

Wickens, D. D. (1970). Encoding categories of words: An empirical approach to meaning. *Psychological Review, 77,* 1–15.

Windschitl, P. D. (in press). Memory for faces: Evidence of retrieval-based impairment. *Journal of Experimental Psychology: Learning, Memory, and Cognition.*

Zaragoza, M. S., & Koshmider, J. W., III. (1989). Misled subjects may know more than their performance implies. *Journal of Experimental Psychology: Learning, Memory, and Cognition, 15,* 246–255.

Zaragoza, M. S., & Lane, S. M. (1994). Source misattributions and the suggestibility of eyewitness memory. *Journal of Experimental Psychology: Learning, Memory, and Cognition, 20,* 934–945.

Zaragoza, M. S., McCloskey, M., & Jamis, M. (1987). Misleading postevent information and recall of the original event: Further evidence against the memory impairment hypothesis. *Journal of Experimental Psychology: Learning, Memory and Cognition, 13,* 36–44.

CHAPTER 15

The Long-Term Retention of Training and Instruction

Alice F. Healy
Grant P. Sinclair

Knowledge and skills, acquired during training, often are not reactivated for considerable time periods. Disuse can lead to skill deterioration, which, in the extreme, might mean that a skill is no longer functional when needed. Training procedures must be developed to maintain skills at functional levels over periods of disuse. Although there has been considerable research designed to develop training procedures for efficient acquisition of skills, relatively much less is known about training procedures or refresher techniques that lead to maintenance over time; see Naylor and Briggs (1961), Schendel, Shields, and Katz (1978), and Farr (1987) for valuable summaries of earlier research on long-term skill retention. In the present chapter, we review empirical results and theories from recent experimental research on long-term retention. From this research, we develop a set of guidelines to improve the conditions of training and instruction so as to facilitate long-term retention of knowledge and skills.

I. METHODOLOGICAL ISSUES

In this section, we review recent approaches to the study of long-term retention. We include a preliminary question concerning skill decay, a discussion of some groundbreaking work on long-term retention of knowledge, and some of the problems typically encountered in the training and subsequent assessment of skills. We then describe the new approach used in our research program for investigating training conditions and refresher techniques that contribute to skill maintenance over extended periods of disuse. These methodologies address a variety of skills, ranging from perceptual skills to motoric skills to higher level cognitive skills.

A. Decay of Skills

An important study by Geoffrey Loftus (1985a) addressed the crucial preliminary issue of how to measure the decay of knowledge and skills and how to compare decay rates for differing degrees of original acquisition (although the retention intervals actually considered by Loftus were not particularly long). More specifically, Loftus reviewed a study by Slamecka and McElree (1983) in which subjects learned verbal material to differing degrees of acquisition. Subjects were subsequently tested at retention intervals varying from 0 to 5 days. Slamecka and McElree found that the difference in performance levels on items learned to differing degrees of acquisition was as large after long retention intervals as after short retention intervals (i.e., there was not an interaction between retention interval and degree of acquisition). They concluded that decay from memory was independent of degree of acquisition. Loftus, however, re-examined the same data from a different perspective and reached the opposite conclusion. He assessed how much delay time was required for performance to fall from any given level (e.g., nine items recalled) to some lower level (e.g., four items recalled) for each degree of initial acquisition. Whenever such delay times differed as a function of degree of acquisition, the decay rates were classified as different. Because he found that it took more delay time for a drop from one level of performance to a lower level when the degree of initial acquisition was higher (i.e., the amount of overlearning was larger), he concluded that decay was slower under high-acquisition conditions than it was under low-acquisition conditions. This hypothesis was proposed originally by Jost (1897), who stated that "If two associations are now of equal strength but of different ages, the older one will lose strength more slowly with the further passage of time" (Woodworth & Schlosberg, 1954, p. 730). This work by Loftus not only provides an important measurement tool for assessing decay rate (see, however, Bogartz, 1990a, 1990b; Loftus, 1985b; Loftus & Bamber, 1990; Slamecka, 1985; Wixted, 1990, for a continuation of the debate about this issue), but also reaffirms the important rule that knowledge and skills can be acquired to differing degrees and that those differences will influence the extent to which the skills are maintained.

B. Retention of Knowledge

Important recent work on the retention of knowledge was conducted by Harry Bahrick and colleagues (Bahrick, 1979, 1984; Bahrick, Bahrick, & Wittlinger, 1975; Bahrick & Hall, 1991). Bahrick developed two different methods to evaluate the maintenance of knowledge and to assess the extent to which knowledge maintenance depends on periodic access to the learned material. The first method involves a cross-sectional statistical procedure to investigate the acquisition and maintenance of various types of knowledge over retention intervals much longer than those typically used in laboratory experiments. The advantage of this method is that it enables the investigator to study the effects of real-world intervals that would be impractical or impossible to examine in an experimental setting. This method requires that a large number of subjects be available who acquired the same knowledge at different times in the past. It also requires that the subjects be able to estimate both their degree of original acquisition of the material and their amount of rehearsal of the material during the retention interval. Subjects are then assigned to groups depending on when they acquired the knowledge, and a retention function is calculated based on their retention test performance. This retention function is then corrected, by means of multiple regression techniques, for factors contributing to the original level of acquisition and for the extent of rehearsal or practice during the retention interval. Bahrick et al. (1975) used this technique to study retention levels for names and faces from a yearbook of high school classmates. Retention was tested at intervals of up to approximately 50 years since high school graduation. The investigators found that in the absence of rehearsals, both names and faces were accessible, given the appropriate cues, even over a lifetime. Subsequently, Bahrick (1979) applied this technique to study the maintenance of knowledge about the names and spatial locations of buildings and streets within a university city by former residents of the city. He concluded from this investigation that spatial information was lost more rapidly than information about names but that the two types of information could be maintained with equal ease through subsequent visits to the city.

The cross-sectional study that has had the greatest impact on the literature is one involving the retention of Spanish learned in the classroom (Bahrick, 1984). Bahrick administered a large battery of tests of Spanish knowledge to more than 700 subjects whose last exposure to a course in Spanish ranged from 0 to almost 50 years ago. Subjects were also selected and grouped according to their final level of acquisition of Spanish. Questionnaires concerning the amount and recency of practice and exposure to Spanish were administered to the subjects to obtain estimates of the amount of rehearsal necessary to maintain the acquired Spanish knowledge over time. Rehearsal levels during the retention interval were found to be very low and unrelated to the level of knowledge retention. In contrast, reliable predictors of long-term retention were training level, mean grade in Spanish courses, and level of training in other Romance languages. The retention function indicated that memory level dropped for about 6 years to a stable asymptote and then remained constant for about 50 years, at which time it again started to decline (presumably because of neurological deterioration attributable to old age). Because very little rehearsal was reported by the subjects, Bahrick proposed that much of the knowledge originally learned was retained in a "permastore" and that it remained accessible for many years without periodic maintenance activities. Bahrick concluded that most of what influences the degree of long-term retention is determined by acquisition processes and not by rehearsal processes during the retention interval. This conclusion is reminiscent of one by Schendel et al. (1978), who reviewed the literature on the long-term retention of motor skill and argued that the level of original training is the single most important determinant of motor skill retention. Bahrick's conclusion must be viewed as tentative, however, because the rehearsal levels were very low in his study, and it is not known whether greater amounts of rehearsal during the retention interval would increase long-term retention (see discussion of Bahrick & Hall, 1991, later). This rich cross-sectional method is particularly attractive for investigating skill maintenance because it is applicable to skills learned outside the laboratory under ecologically realistic conditions.

Conway, Cohen, and Stanhope (1991) recently extended Bahrick's (1984) cross-sectional method to a new knowledge domain. They assessed the retention over a 12-year span of various types of general and specific information learned in a college-level cognitive psychology course. Conway et al. found that overall memory declined rapidly over the first 3 to 4 years and then stabilized at above-chance levels for the remaining 8 years. More specifically, they found that memory for the names of individual researchers presented throughout the course showed more rapid declines compared to memory for more general concepts, such as theories and models. Bahrick (1992) concluded: "The Conway et al. (1991) data confirm that retention of semantic memory can remain stable for many years, even in the absence of significant rehearsals" (p. 112; but see Hintzman, 1993, for a dispute of Bahrick's conclusion).

Using a different technique, Meiskey, Healy, and Bourne (1990) obtained similar results in a study of the long-term retention of algebra learned in a college classroom setting. They found that memory for specific rules (e.g., the quadratic formula) showed a significantly greater decline after a 6-month retention period compared to memory for more general procedures associated with the manipulation of algebraic equations (e.g., simplifying expressions). Overall, they found that although students did lose a small, but statistically reliable, amount of the information over the delay interval, they did learn and retain most of what they were taught during the semester (see also Semb & Ellis, 1994, for a review of classroom learning).

The second method developed by Bahrick (1979) to investigate the maintenance of knowledge is conducted completely in the laboratory and involves successive relearning sessions. In the original learning session, the information to be acquired is tested and repeated with a dropout technique to ensure that every item receives the same number of correct responses (although not necessarily the same number of study trials). Subsequent relearning sessions start with a test of all the items originally learned and then continue with the dropout technique employed in the original learning session. Among other materials, Bahrick applied this technique to the learning of English–Spanish vocabulary pairs. He systematically varied the intersession interval from 0 to 30 days, and he examined performance in the original learning session, in 2 or 5 subsequent relearning sessions, and in a final test session that occurred 30 days after the last relearning session. He found that the level of performance in the final test session depended more on the length of the earlier intersession intervals than on the level of performance reached in the last relearning session. Performance in the last relearning session was greatest when the interstimulus intervals were the shortest. However, performance in the final test session was greatest when the earlier interstimulus intervals were the longest (i.e., 30 days), so that they matched the interval between the last relearning session and the final test session. Bahrick concluded that for optimum maintenance of knowledge, practice should be spaced at intervals not much shorter than the interval separating practice from test, at least for intervals of up to 30 days.

In more recent studies, Bahrick and Phelps (1987) and Bahrick, Bahrick, Bahrick, and Bahrick (1993) investigated the maintenance of English–foreign word pairs and found that increasing the spacing between successive relearning sessions disturbed performance slightly during acquisition, but greatly increased long-term retention.

The most important point of Bahrick's (1979; Bahrick et al., 1993; Bahrick & Phelps, 1987) laboratory studies with respect to the maintenance of skills is that individuals who exhibit the same level of proficiency immediately after acquisition can differ substantially on tests of long-term retention, depending on their previous acquisition history (i.e., depending on the length of the intervals between practice or relearning sessions). As stated above, on the basis of his cross-sectional study, Bahrick (1984) concluded that most of what influences the degree of long-term retention is determined by acquisition, not rehearsal, processes. More recently, Bahrick and Hall (1991) investigated this point further in a real-world study spanning 50 years of memory for high school algebra and geometry by comparing subjects who had with those who had not subsequently taken college-level mathematics courses. Bahrick and Hall found that subjects who had proceeded to college-level mathematics (which required rehearsal of the high school mathematics) exhibited superior retention of high school algebra and geometry compared to that of subjects who had not proceeded on to college-level mathematics, even though the initial level of acquisition for the two groups was equivalent. Bahrick and Hall concluded that extending rehearsal over several years after initial learning can stabilize performance for up to a half century, whereas when the same content is acquired over a shorter period, or is not subsequently rehearsed, performance declines rapidly and continuously. This point is a refinement of Bahrick's (1984) earlier conclusion that retention is most influenced by acquisition processes, and not rehearsal processes. From these results of Bahrick and colleagues, we must reject the intuitive notion that criterion performance at the end of acquisition alone is a sufficient predictor of long-term retention, as we discuss in the following section on training and testing of skills.

C. Training and Testing of Skills

In an important recent review of methodologies used in the training and subsequent testing of skills, Schmidt and Bjork (1992; see also Bjork, 1994) discussed two problems typically encountered in skill training. The first, foreshadowed in Bahrick's (1979) study, is that performance assessment during the acquisition phase of training is not a reliable indicator of training efficiency and skill learning. Only posttraining retention and transfer testing, after an appropriate retention interval, can provide a true measure of learning and performance and of the effectiveness of any experimental manipulation designed to enhance training efficiency. Schmidt and Bjork argued that some training effects may affect performance temporarily, and such transitory effects must be allowed to dissipate before accurate measures can be obtained.

The second problem addressed by Schmidt and Bjork (1992) is that learning and retention are often viewed as different phenomena, and, thus, are typically measured separately with different methods. In contrast, Schmidt and Bjork maintained "that the effectiveness of learning is revealed by, or measured by, the level of retention shown" (p. 209). Based on this argument, they described two criteria by which the effectiveness of a training program can be appropriately assessed. The first criterion is posttraining performance: How well does the trainee perform after extended periods of disuse? The second criterion involves posttraining generalization: How well does the trainee perform under conditions that vary considerably from those experienced during the training period? It is important that the training conditions allow for subsequent *generalization* across varying conditions and environments.

Schmidt and Bjork (1992) reviewed three methodological manipulations that have been shown to enhance posttraining performance and generalizability of trained skills. The first involves varying practice schedules; the second involves the scheduling of feedback provided to the trainee; and the third involves the incorporation of variability into the practice sessions. Schmidt and Bjork showed that these three manipulations inhibit the rate of skill acquisition but facilitate retention and generalization. For each of these manipulations, Schmidt and Bjork provided examples of both motoric and verbal skills, as summarized in the following sections.

1. Scheduling of Tasks during Practice

Schmidt and Bjork (1992) reviewed several studies comparing blocked and random scheduling of tasks that yielded large effects on retention. With blocked scheduling, each task is learned separately, and learning for one task is completed before the trainee moves to another task. With random scheduling, the tasks are intermixed during acquisition, with the same task never being performed on two successive trials. For example, in an experiment by Shea and Morgan (1979), subjects were required to learn fairly difficult arm movement tasks, with each of three tasks involving different patterns. Subjects first learned the tasks according to either a blocked or a random task scheduling during acquisition, and were then tested 10 days later with either a blocked or a random test scheduling. Blocked scheduling always produced a faster rate of learning during acquisition, but, regardless of the type of test scheduling, random scheduling during acquisition resulted in the best performance at retention testing.

Landauer and Bjork (1978) provide good evidence for a random scheduling advantage in verbal tasks in their study of the *spacing effects* first described by Melton (1967); see also the studies by Bahrick and Phelps (1987) and Bahrick et al. (1993) reviewed earlier. In the study by Landauer and Bjork, subjects were presented with fictitious names during acquisition and were then tested on the names after a delay interval. Landauer and Bjork demonstrated that spacing repetitions of a given name (with the repetitions separated by presentations of different to-be-learned items) resulted in better long-term retention of the names than did presenting one name on five successive trials before moving to the next name. They also found that spacing repetitions was most effective when conducted in an expanding interval format in which the number of items separating repetitions of a particular name increased from one presentation of the name to the next.

Schendel et al. (1978) had concluded earlier that the distribution of practice (massed vs. spaced) did not appear to influence the retention of motor skills. This finding was in marked contrast to those just reviewed showing strong effects of practice scheduling. A possible explanation for this discrep-

ancy pertains to the conclusion of Bahrick (1979) that the spacing of learning sessions should be as long as the retention interval. In many of the
studies cited by Schendel et al., immediate trial repetitions were compared
to ones spaced only seconds apart. Retention was then tested after a relatively long delay interval (e.g., 1 month). Perhaps the spacing of the learning trials was too short relative to the retention interval to produce a detectable difference in retention (see Fendrich et al., 1988, for a discussion of this
point).

2. Scheduling of Feedback during Acquisition

Schmidt and Bjork (1992) also reviewed studies involving the feedback
presented to trainees during the acquisition phase. For example, Schmidt,
Young, Swinnen, and Shapiro (1989) trained subjects on a complex arm
movement task with a set time goal. Subjects received feedback concerning
movement-time errors in the form of a graph showing their performance on
each trial of a just-completed learning set. Three summary set sizes were
compared: 1, 5, and 15 trials per set. Performance during acquisition decreased as summary set size increased. However, after a 2-day retention
interval, test performance increased as set size increased; that is, spacing the
feedback resulted in better retention. Winstein and Schmidt (1990) obtained
similar effects in a study in which subjects received feedback after every trial
(100% condition) or after only one-half of the trials (50% condition). In
the latter condition, the feedback was *faded* across trials so that it was provided after every trial initially and then gradually withdrawn. Subjects exhibited similar learning performance in the two conditions, but the 50%
condition resulted in superior retention test performance after an extended
delay interval.

   With respect to verbal tasks, Schmidt and Bjork (1992) described a study
by Schooler and Anderson (1990) who showed that reducing the number of
feedback trials during the learning of a programming language decreased
acquisition performance but facilitated retention performance (see also
Krumboltz & Weisman, 1962; Schulz & Runquist, 1960, for related findings
in studies of paired-associate learning).

3. Variability of Practice

Schmidt and Bjork (1992) further discussed varying tasks on a single dimension during acquisition and the effect of this induced variation on a subject's
ability to perform similar but novel tasks during a subsequent test. For
example, Catalano and Kleiner (1984) required subjects to respond to a
moving visual target. Subjects in the constant practice condition trained at
one of four target speeds. Subjects in the variable practice condition trained
at all four speeds for the same total number of trials. All subjects were then

tested with a novel target speed outside of the range previously experienced during practice. Acquisition was superior in the constant practice condition, but subjects in the variable practice condition showed superior generalization performance during retention testing. Similarly, Kerr and Booth (1978) found that children who learned to toss bean bags at targets 2 and 4 ft away actually performed better at test with a 3-ft-distant target than did children who had practiced constantly at the 3-ft distance. Schmidt and Bjork (1992) also reviewed a verbal task involving the learning of novel concept words (Nitsch, 1977) that demonstrated that constant practice facilitated acquisition but variable practice facilitated generalizability.

4. Conclusions

Schmidt and Bjork (1992) concluded that a systematic alteration of practice, which encourages different types of information processing, may disturb performance during acquisition but can lead to better retention or transfer performance. Specifically, they concluded that random practice, reduced feedback, and variable practice are all effective ways of altering practice to facilitate the long-term retention or transfer of trained skills.

D. Features of Our Research Program

Our research program has been aimed at understanding and improving the long-term retention of knowledge and skills. Six features of our program, together, distinguish it from earlier research on retention of knowledge and skills (Healy et al., 1993, 1995):

1. As recommended by Schmidt and Bjork (1992), we have been explicitly concerned with optimizing performance after a delay interval rather than inferring superior retention from optimized performance during acquisition. Guided by Bahrick's (1984) concept of "permastore," we have sought to identify conditions of learning or characteristics of learned material that differentiate between items that do and do not achieve permanency in memory.

2. Relative to most other empirical programs investigating skill retention, we have used longer retention intervals, usually including tests after several weeks or months, and in some cases including intervals up to 1 or 2 years.

3. We have employed a combination of structural and analytic experimental techniques. In the structural approach, we aim to identify and describe the components of specific skills both during acquisition and after long periods of disuse. In the analytic approach, we experimentally investigate factors influencing and promoting retention in order to check hypotheses

concerning the characteristics that distinguish between permanent and non-permanent components of knowledge and skill.

4. We have conducted experiments over a wide range of different skills and paradigms, both because theoretical conclusions may rely on the specific nature of the tasks and because different processes crucial to retention may be highlighted in different tasks.

5. In contrast to traditional studies in which subjects were required to achieve a fixed criterion of performance mastery in terms of accuracy (e.g., achieve errorless performance; see Farr, 1987; Underwood, 1964, for criticisms of this approach), we have usually provided subjects with training for a fixed number of trials that allowed subjects to continue to practice beyond the point at which they achieved errorless performance.

6. Finally, rather than assessing retention exclusively by examining changes in the percentage of subjects who maintain an accuracy criterion as a function of delay, we have monitored aspects of the skill that reveal performance changes beyond those evident by assessing accuracy alone (especially when accuracy measures are near the ceiling), such as component response time measures and verbal protocols.

II. PROCEDURAL REINSTATEMENT

In our research (see, e.g., Healy et al., 1992), we found a set of tasks yielding very high levels of retention performance and another set of tasks yielding considerable forgetting across delay intervals. We were able to accommodate these two sets of findings within a single theoretical framework. According to this framework, long-term retention will be evident to the extent that the specific procedures acquired during study can be reinstated during retention testing. Note that we use the term "procedures" to refer to motoric, perceptual, and cognitive operations. In other words, in order to demonstrate durable retention across a delay interval, it is crucial that the procedures used during skill training are reinstated at the time of skill testing. In the present section, we clarify this theoretical framework and review research providing relevant evidence. First, we review studies with tasks yielding outstanding retention performance. Then we show how the procedural reinstatement framework can provide an account of the outstanding retention found with these tasks. We then review research with tasks yielding considerable forgetting over even relatively short retention intervals, and we show how the procedural reinstatement framework can also accommodate the considerable forgetting found with those tasks. Finally, we draw conclusions concerning the procedural reinstatement framework.

A. Studies Demonstrating Remarkable Memory

1. Target Detection

In our studies of target detection (Healy, Fendrich, & Proctor, 1990; see Proctor & Healy, 1995, for a review of studies on the acquisition and retention of skilled target detection), subjects were presented with computer terminal displays containing random letters or characters grouped to resemble words. Half of the displays contained the target letter and half did not. The subjects' task was to press a response button every time they detected a target. Both response accuracy and latency were recorded as dependent variables. The major independent variable was frame size (i.e., the number of letters in the display). Previous studies had shown that subjects generally responded less accurately and more slowly as frame size increased unless they had reached automaticity (W. Schneider & Shiffrin, 1977). Thus, to test the hypothesis that the degree of retention performance would be related to the degree of skill automaticity, we took the loss of the frame size effect with practice as an index of automaticity.

In Experiment 1, we compared 3 groups of subjects who received either 0, 2, or 4 sessions of detection training. Accuracy increased and response latencies decreased during acquisition. Also, the frame size effect was significantly smaller for the group receiving the most training, suggesting that, indeed, responding did become more automatic after extensive training. Importantly, comparisons of performance at the end of training with that after a 1-month delay showed no decrease in accuracy or speed for the 2 groups given training, suggesting essentially perfect retention of the detection skill over the delay interval.

In Experiment 2, we employed only 2 individuals who were given 12 days of practice on the detection task. Both individuals were called back 6 months later for a retention test, and one of the individuals was tested again 15 months after training. Large improvements in accuracy were evident during training, so that before the end of training both individuals attained essentially errorless performance, even with the largest frame size, and this maximal level of performance was maintained across the long retention intervals. A similar pattern was evident for response latencies. There were large improvements in performance with practice, but the functions for the different frame sizes did not completely converge, suggesting that the individuals became more automatic with practice but did not achieve full automaticity. Nonetheless, performance on the retention tests showed a remarkable degree of memory. Specifically, after 6 months one individual showed absolutely no forgetting, and although the other individual did show some loss on the first retention test, her response latencies after the 15-month interval were not different from those at the end of training (perhaps reflecting the power of spaced practice, as demonstrated, e.g., by Landauer & Bjork, 1978).

2. Mental Multiplication

We also found remarkable retention in a paradigm involving mental multiplication (Fendrich, Healy, & Bourne, 1993). In this task, we also examined whether retention was related to automaticity. Subjects were shown single-digit multiplication problems, like 2 × 6, and they responded either by typing the answers into the computer or by saying them aloud into a microphone. We report here only the results from Experiment 3, which involved 2 subjects who were given 11 training sessions with the typing response and a final training session with the oral response. The subjects were then re-tested with the oral response at retention intervals up to 14 months. On each training and testing session, the subjects were shown the full set of problems with single-digit operands. Individuals typically respond more slowly as the size of the operands increases (e.g., responses are typically slower to 8 × 9 than to 3 × 2). Hence, we used as our index of automaticity the function relating the speed of responding to the size of the multiplication column; we expected that as subjects' performance became automatic, this function would flatten.

During acquisition with the typing response, both subjects showed large effects of multiplication column, large decreases in response time as training progressed, but essentially no change in the effect of multiplication column with practice. Hence, the subjects improved at this skill, but performance did not become automatic by our index. As with the target detection task, subjects showed essentially no forgetting across long retention intervals, even though their performance had not become automatic by our criterion.

3. Data Entry

The third task in which subjects show amazing retention is a motor task involving data entry (Fendrich, Healy, & Bourne, 1991). Subjects were shown lists of digits and typed them using a computer keypad. In Experiment 1, subjects were given 2 days of training at entering lists of 10 3-digit numbers. One month later they were given a retention test in which they entered some of the old lists of digits along with some new lists. Also, subjects were asked to give a recognition rating for each digit list shown at the retention test. For half of the subjects, the rating for each list was given immediately after the list was entered on the keypad, and for the other subjects, the rating was made before the list was typed. We found that subjects' typing times significantly decreased as training progressed and changed very little over the 1-month delay interval. Also, we found that the response times on the retention test were significantly faster for the old lists than for the new lists. Most crucial are the results of the recognition test, which is an explicit, or direct, measure of memory in contrast to the implicit, or indirect, measure of response time (Graf & Shachter, 1985; Richardson-Klavehn & Bjork, 1988; see also Kelley & Lindsay, Chapter 2, this volume, for discussions of this distinction). We found that subjects had significant memory for the digit lists presented 1 month earlier by our direct as well as by our indirect measure. We found further that recognition was better when the test came after, rather than before, the subjects entered the numbers. Hence, typing the digit lists aided the subjects in making their recognition decisions. These results suggested to us that the memory processes reflected by the direct and indirect measures are not independent. This dependency was underlined by an analysis in which we examined the entry times contingent on whether or not the subjects correctly classified the digit lists on the recognition test. We found a significant difference in typing times between old and new digit lists only when those lists were correctly classified on the recognition test. Thus, evidence for reliable memory by the indirect measure was evident only when there was also reliable memory by the direct measure.

In a subsequent experiment, we sought to determine whether the remarkable retention we found was reflecting only a motor component of the data entry task or whether a perceptual component was involved, as well. To separate the motor and perceptual components, we used two different orientations of a number keypad (telephone and calculator). Subjects were trained on one keypad orientation and then switched to the other at the retention test 1 week later. We included new lists of digits as well as two different types of old lists on the retention test. The "old digit" lists included the same sequences of digits as shown during training but required new motor responses. In contrast, the "old motor" lists included new sequences of digits but ones that required the same sequence of motor responses. We found that subjects showed a significant advantage in response times relative to the new lists for both types of old lists, thereby locating the long-term priming at both the motoric and perceptual stages of processing.

B. Procedural Reinstatement Hypothesis

The three tasks just reviewed all provided evidence for strong long-term skill retention. Healy et al. (1992) considered what these three tasks had in common, so that we could generate a hypothesis concerning the factors responsible for durable retention. First, on the basis of the results from the target detection (Healy et al., 1990) and mental multiplication (Fendrich et al., 1993) studies, we ruled out the original hypothesis that durable retention is associated with automaticity. In those two tasks there was essentially perfect retention with little evidence that subjects' performance had achieved automaticity. Second, on the basis of the results from the data entry study (Fendrich et al., 1991), we ruled out the hypothesis that only indirect memory measures can reveal durable retention, because long-term retention was evident in that study using a direct as well as an indirect memory measure. In fact, the processes underlying the indirect and direct measures were shown to be interdependent. Third, on the basis of the results from the mental multiplication study (Experiment 3, Fendrich et al., 1993), we ruled out the hypothesis that only motor learning yields superior long-term retention (see, e.g., Naylor & Briggs, 1961). As mentioned previously, the 2 subjects in that study were tested using an oral response even though they had been trained with a typing response.

After ruling out these alternative hypotheses, Healy et al. (1992) concluded that the most important common feature shared by the three tasks is a major or overriding procedural component. In other words, procedural information (motoric, perceptual, and cognitive procedures involved in the performance of a skill) is well retained, whereas declarative information (facts or knowledge that can be declared) is quickly forgotten (see Anderson, 1983, for a discussion of the distinction between procedural and declarative information). This procedural reinstatement hypothesis is in agreement with Kolers and Roediger (1984), who proposed that the durability of memory depends critically on the extent to which learning procedures are reinstated at test. Tasks like target detection, mental multiplication, and data entry require the use of specific procedures, in contrast to other tasks that place a greater emphasis on declarative components, such as the standard list-learning experiments. In the traditional studies involving list learning, the procedures used by subjects to code the list in memory are not easily reinstated at the time of test because different mnemonic strategies are used for every list. If subjects use specific mnemonic procedures consistently to remember different lists, then they might also show superior retention. In fact, Ericsson and Chase (1982) trained a long-distance runner to retain lists of over 80 digits. He achieved this memory skill by consistently relating subsets of digits to familiar running times and dates. The procedures used by subjects in our three tasks during acquisition are easily reinstated on the retention test because the subjects are performing the same task at both times under exactly the same task demands. The procedural reinstatement hypothesis is consistent with both the theory of transfer-appropriate processing (Morris, Bransford, & Franks, 1977) and the encoding specificity principle (Tulving & Thomson, 1973), which postulate that memory performance will be best when the retrieval operations used on the retention test correspond to the encoding operations used during learning (see Schmidt & Bjork, 1992, for a similar conclusion; see also Roediger & Guynn, Chapter 7, this volume, for further discussion of how these principles and others govern retrieval of information from human memory).

Another experiment on data entry provided direct support for the importance of transfer-appropriate processing to skill retention (Gesi, Fendrich, Healy, & Bourne, 1989; Fendrich, Gesi, Healy, & Bourne, 1995). In this study, subjects were presented with 4–digit sequences on a computer screen. In one condition, the subjects simply read each sequence and pressed the space bar once for each digit in the sequence. In a second condition, they entered the sequence using the numeric keypad of the computer console, and, in a third condition, they entered the sequence using the horizontal number row on the console keyboard. One week after the training session, subjects were given a retention test. This test required them to enter old and new sequences using, in some cases, the number row and, in other cases, the keypad configuration. After entering each sequence, the subjects also made an old/new recognition decision. The theory of transfer-appropriate processing would predict that subjects' recognition would be most accurate for the sequences entered in the same way at acquisition and at test. Indeed, we found that subjects showed highest recognition scores for the sequences entered with the same key configuration at test as used at study. Interestingly, when old sequences were entered with a different keypad configuration at study and at test, subjects' recognition memory was no better than when they simply read the sequences at study. Entering the sequence at study aided explicit recognition only if the sequence was entered in the same way on the retention test.

C. Studies Demonstrating Considerable Forgetting

1. Memory for Numerical Calculations

In our work on memory for numerical calculations (Crutcher & Healy, 1989), we provided a more general test of the importance to memory of mental procedures. This work was based on a phenomenon known as the *generation effect,* which is the finding that people show better retention of learned material when it is self-produced, or generated, than when it is simply copied, or read (see, e.g., Slamecka & Graf, 1978). If the generation effect is due to the activation in the subjects of auxiliary mental procedures, then a task leading the subjects to perform such procedures without overt generation of an item may show equivalent retention to a generate task. Likewise, a task involving overt generation by the subjects but no auxiliary mental procedures may not result in any better retention than a reading task. Thus, according to this formulation, it is not essential that the subjects generate the stimulus, but it is essential that the subjects engage in mental procedures linking the stimulus to other information stored in memory.

To test this mental procedures hypothesis, we developed four tasks, which we called the "read," "generate," "verify," and "calculate" tasks. All subjects were exposed to all four tasks. For each task, they were shown single-digit multiplication problems on index cards and were required to say aloud the problems and answers. In the read task, the answers were presented with the problems; thus no multiplication operations (i.e., the relevant mental procedures) were required by the subjects. In the generate task, the answers were absent, so the multiplication operations had to be performed by the subjects themselves. The verify and calculate tasks were crucial for testing the mental procedures hypothesis. In the verify task, the subjects were given a problem with its answer but were required to verify that the answer was correct. In the calculate task, the subjects had to provide the answers to the problems, but they were told to use a calculator rather than perform the arithmetic themselves. After completing all the problems, subjects were asked to recall the answers to all the problems they had been shown. The mental procedures hypothesis yields the prediction that retention on the verify and generate tasks would be superior to that on the read and calculate tasks, because in the former two tasks the multiplication operations are performed by the subjects themselves, whereas in the latter two tasks the multiplication operations are not required by the subjects. In contrast, no difference is expected between the generate and verify tasks or between the calculate and read tasks because whether the answers are absent or present in the problems is not thought to be of much consequence. In agreement with this hypothesis, recall was greatly affected by whether or not the subjects performed the mental procedures themselves but not by whether they were shown the answers with the problems. The same pattern of results was found for recognition as well as for recall and for both immediate testing and testing after a 2-day or a 1-week delay.

This study, like most previous studies of the generation effect was limited to an examination of memory for episodes or events. In contrast, our more recent work (McNamara & Healy, 1995) extended this finding to memory for facts and skills, including multiplication skill.

In accordance with the procedural reinstatement framework, we proposed that a critical factor leading to a generation advantage for skill training is that stable cognitive strategies be developed during the training process. Multiplication is a skill for which most college students have already developed some cognitive strategies. For simple single-digit operand problems, no change in these strategies is expected as a result of training because they are deeply entrenched. In fact, answer retrieval might be automatic (see the section later on direct and mediated retrieval in mental arithmetic). In contrast, most college students have not developed stable cognitive strategies for more difficult multiplication problems with operands greater than 12. Thus, only for these difficult problems would a generation advantage be expected because the generate condition would be more apt than the read condition to promote the formation of new cognitive strategies.

We tested this prediction in Experiment 1 by comparing read and generate conditions of training on both easy (e.g., $40 \times 9 = 360$) and difficult (e.g., $14 \times 9 = 126$) multiplication problems. Subjects were given a pretest,

10 blocks of training in either a read or generate condition, and an immediate posttest on multiplication problems. In accord with our prediction, for both accuracy and correct response latency, a generation advantage was found only on the difficult problems in the posttest.

2. Foreign Vocabulary Learning

The arithmetic material studied in the previous experiment was already familiar to the subjects before training. In Experiment 2, McNamara and Healy (1995) extended this investigation to a situation in which subjects learned new material, namely word–nonword associations like those used in foreign vocabulary acquisition. Subjects were given a list of 30 word–nonword pairs to study for 10 min before training began. They were then administered a pretest, followed by 14 blocks of read or generate training over 2 days. During each block of training, subjects were shown the words one at a time. They were required to write down each word and the corresponding nonword. In the read condition, the nonwords were shown to the subjects before they wrote them down, whereas, in the generate condition, subjects first wrote a nonword response and then were shown the appropriate nonword equivalent. If their initial nonword response was incorrect, then the subjects were required to write the correct nonword after it was shown. Training on the second day was followed immediately by a posttest. Finally, subjects returned for a retention test after a 1-week delay. On all three tests (pretest, posttest, and retention test) subjects were shown the words and were required to provide the corresponding nonword equivalents.

As expected, there was no advantage for the generate training on the pretest, but a generation advantage was evident after training on both the posttest and the retention test. The results of this study have important implications for the many training situations that involve teaching new material, rather than improving the efficiency with which old material is retrieved. The generation advantage found originally in the context of memory for episodes or events does seem to extend to this more practical context (but see Carroll & Nelson, 1993) and to longer retention intervals.

Work on foreign vocabulary retention by Crutcher and Ericsson (1988; Crutcher, 1990) provides additional support for the hypothesis that the durability of memory depends on the extent to which encoding during learning is reinstated at test. Subjects in this study learned Spanish–English vocabulary pairs using the keyword method, in which subjects are given the Spanish word (e.g., *doronico*), a mediating keyword (e.g., *door*), and the English translation (e.g., *leopard*). The keyword is phonologically and/or orthographically related to the Spanish word, and subjects are instructed to form an interactive image linking the keyword and the English word (e.g., a leopard passing through a door). (See Bellezza, Chapter 10, this volume, for further analysis of the keyword method as a learning technique.)

In their initial experiments, Crutcher and Ericsson (1988; Crutcher, 1990) tested subjects on three tasks: (1) the keyword subtask, in which the stimulus was the Spanish word and the response was the keyword; (2) the English subtask, in which the stimulus was the keyword and the response was the English word; and (3) the full vocabulary task, in which the stimulus was the Spanish word and the response was the English word. In one experiment, 2 groups of subjects acquired the vocabulary items and were then tested immediately and after either a 1-week or a 1-month delay. Although there was little difference in performance among the three tasks on the immediate test, the keyword subtask showed the best performance after the delay, especially at the 1-month interval. This finding can be understood if the procedures used to generate the response from the stimulus are easier to reinstate at the test for the keyword subtask than for the English subtask. In fact, subjects given the Spanish word can easily use inferencing to generate the keyword because there are a limited number of words that are phonologically and/or orthographically related to the Spanish word. In contrast, subjects given the keyword cannot use inferencing to derive easily the English word because of the extremely large number of words that can possibly be linked with the keyword in an interactive image.

3. Recall of Temporal, Spatial, and Item Information

Another task domain showing rapid forgetting that can be understood in terms of the procedural reinstatement framework involves the recall by undergraduate students of information about their course schedules. Wittman (1989; Wittman & Healy, 1995) examined the retention of four different types of course schedule information—the actual title of the course ("what"), the instructor's name ("who"), the location of the class building on a campus map ("where"), and the class start time ("when"). In Experiment 1, Wittman tested 3 groups of subjects on each of 3 different occasions, with a 6-month retention interval separating the 3 tests on average. The testing made use of a cued recall procedure. Subjects were probed about courses taken during a particular test semester. Across subjects, each type of information was used equally often as a cue to recall the other three types of information. There was considerable forgetting of this course schedule information. The overall level of performance was quite low, and there was a large overall decrease in performance on the second and third tests relative to that on the first test. On all three tests, subjects' performance **was much better on the spatial, or where, information than on the other three types (but see Bahrick, 1979). In accordance with the procedural reinstatement framework, Wittman's explanation for the superiority of spatial** location recall in this case is that subjects learned this information by using procedures that were repeated throughout the semester: Subjects walked through the campus to the classroom each time the class was held. A similar type of procedural learning was not as readily available for the course title, instructor's name, or class start time.

To provide an initial test of this hypothesis, Wittman (1989) conducted a follow-up experiment in which subjects had to learn the four different types of course schedule information in the laboratory. Subjects were given a series of training trials followed by a pair of retention tests 1 week later and then another pair of tests after approximately 5 more weeks. In both tests, subjects were required to provide from memory the course title and the instructor's name. The tests differed in the type of temporal and spatial information required. In the map test, the subjects provided the order of their classes during the school week and the location of each class on the campus map. In contrast, in the class-listing test, subjects provided the start time of each course and the building name where the class was held. The map test was meant to mimic the procedures naturally used to retrieve course locations, whereas the class-listing test was meant to remove any procedural component from the recall of course locations.

Subjects showed overall forgetting of the course schedule information across the 6-week retention interval. Of most interest is the finding that the superiority of spatial information occurred only in the map test, which involved procedural memory. In fact, there was almost no sign of forgetting the spatial information on the map test over the 6-week retention interval. In the class-listing test, spatial information showed no superiority in retention at test and showed significant loss at retest. Thus, there was initial support for the hypothesis that the superiority of spatial memory is due to the fact that procedures are used to learn that information and reinstatement of these procedures is required at test.

The objective of a more recent follow-up experiment by King (1992; see also Healy et al., 1995) was to separate the procedural experience from the use of a map in order to elucidate the role of procedural knowledge in spatial memory superiority. Subjects' memory for fictitious course schedules was tested within two separate situations: one in which subjects had previous procedural experience of the campus and one in which subjects were without such experience. If the retention advantage of spatial information is due to procedural experience, then we would expect a retention advantage for spatial information only in the familiar condition in which subjects had previous procedural experience. Specifically, undergraduate students from two different universities participated as subjects. All subjects were unfamiliar with the other campus. Different fictitious course schedules were constructed, some based on the directory of classes from one university, and others based on the directory from the other university. The students assigned to schedules from their own campus were in the familiar condition, and those assigned to schedules from the other campus were in the unfamiliar condition. Wittman's (1989) cued recall testing procedure was employed here with a 1-month retention interval.

King (1992) found a significant degree of forgetting across the retention interval. Recall differed among the four types of information. The effect of information type was, however, modulated by familiarity. Performance was better for the familiar condition than for the unfamiliar condition, but only on spatial information. These results support the hypothesis that the spatial advantage is due to procedural experience, such as frequently walking through a university campus.

In these studies of memory for course schedules, the *who, what, where,* and *when* questions necessarily differed from each other along a number of dimensions other than whether they involved temporal, spatial, or item information. In a recently completed pair of laboratory experiments, Sinclair, Healy, and Bourne (1994) controlled for those other dimensions in an effort to determine whether there would be a spatial advantage under these more controlled conditions (Healy et al., 1995). Because there was no procedural component in these new experiments, no retention advantage for spatial information was predicted.

In Experiment 1, subjects learned a list of common nouns, each beginning with a different consonant from the alphabet. The words were presented one at a time in a vertical array on a computer terminal, with each word occurring in a different location within the array. At the termination of the list presentation, subjects recalled the words by writing them on a sheet of paper. Some subjects were given the words and required to recall them according to the temporal sequence of presentation, others according to their spatial location within the vertical field during presentation, and the remaining subjects chose the words that had been presented from a longer list including the critical words intermixed with similar distractor words. For all subjects, after each recall, another trial was started with the words being presented in the same order and locations, and this process continued until a criterion of perfect recall on three successive trials was achieved. Subjects returned after a 1-week delay and were asked to recall the words as they had during the first session. After an initial recall attempt, the presentation and recall trials were resumed and continued until the criterion was achieved again.

In Experiment 1, Sinclair et al. (1994) found that learning, as indexed by the number of trials to criterion, was most difficult in the spatial condition and least difficult in the item condition, and that first-session learning required more trials than did second-session relearning. There was also an interaction between information type and session. Although initial learning proceeded more slowly in the spatial condition than in the temporal and item conditions, relearning in the spatial condition was more similar to that in the other conditions.

It is likely that the higher degree of learning difficulty observed in the spatial condition of Experiment 1 was due partially to the subjects' inability to discriminate effectively one spatial location from another. Central locations contained no unique information to distinguish them from neighboring locations. Hence, in Experiment 2, a new array of two matrices replaced the vertical array used in Experiment 1. Each spatial location was unique and easily distinguishable from every other location within the new array. Whereas in Experiment 1 more trials were required to reach the criterion in the spatial condition than in the temporal condition, the opposite was found in Experiment 2. Simply changing the presentation array so that each of its component positions provided unique spatial information facilitated learning in the spatial condition. Also, as in Experiment 1, although initial learning proceeded at very different rates for the three types of information, their relearning was more similar. These findings place important constraints on the spatial memory superiority found for the retention of course schedule information. They are consistent with the procedural reinstatement framework used to explain the earlier finding, but they also point to the importance of other factors such as the distinctiveness of the spatial locations.

D. Conclusions

Although the procedural reinstatement framework is able to shed considerable light on the long-term maintenance of knowledge and skills, it is clear from the study of temporal, spatial, and item information just discussed that it can by no means account for all important retention phenomena, such as the effects of distinctiveness on learning. Nevertheless, it is interesting to note the wide variety of memory studies that fit into this framework and the remarkably large range of forgetting rates found in these studies. For example, information about course schedules was quickly forgotten, whereas there was virtually no forgetting over long retention intervals for the target detection skill.

III. GENERALIZABILITY AND SPECIFICITY OF TRAINING

In our experiments just reviewed, we have found remarkable retention of some trained skills, including those involving target detection, data entry, and mental multiplication. There was virtually no forgetting over long delay intervals in some cases. The procedural reinstatement framework provides an account for these findings by proposing that the procedures developed during skill acquisition are the same as those utilized during skill testing after the extended delays. In more recent research, we have found that for some durable skills, which show remarkable retention, the learning is highly specific and lacks generalizability. The procedural reinstatement framework is consistent with the high degree of specificity observed for these durable skills because the procedures that provide the basis for long-term retention of these skills would be expected to be very specific. We review next two areas of research related to these issues.

A. Mental Arithmetic

Some evidence documenting the specificity of skills comes from the mental arithmetic task discussed earlier (Fendrich et al., 1993). In one experiment, subjects were given three sessions of training on only half of the multiplication problems with single-digit operands, with the two halves of the problems differing only in operand order (e.g., 6 × 5 in one half and 5 × 6 in the other half). A retention test occurred 1 month later during which all subjects were shown the complete set of problems. In all four sessions, subjects responded by typing their answers on a computer keypad. We found a consistent advantage for the old relative to the new problems. Because the new problems differed from the old ones only in operand order, the observed old/new difference suggests that the information learned by the subjects during training was very specific.

In the next experiment, we addressed the question of whether practice with matching problems that have similar multiplication operations leads to any facilitation for problems that differ in operand order. The design was like that used in the last experiment except that subjects were exposed to only a quarter of the problems during acquisition. There were three types of problems in this experiment: old, reverse, and new. The reverse problems were the same as the old ones except that the order of the operands was reversed. New problems in this experiment contained new combinations of operands. We found a consistent advantage for the old relative to the other two types of problems and for the reverse relative to the new problems. This finding indicates that learning was specific but not totally so; that is, subjects did learn more than an association between the answer and the specific order of the operands.

In a follow-up study, Rickard, Healy, and Bourne (1994; see also Healy et al., 1993) trained subjects extensively to perform single-digit multiplication and division calculations. Three sessions of training were limited to a subset of problems in a single operand order, half of which were multiplication problems and half division problems. Immediately following training, subjects were tested on four versions of each of the training problems. One of these versions was the same as that used in acquisition (e.g., ____ = 4 × 7); the three others were transformed versions, serving as tests of transfer. The manipulations used to create transfer versions of training problems were: (1) a change of operand order (e.g., ____ = 7 × 4); (2) a change of operation (multiplication to division or division to multiplication, e.g., 28 = ____ × 7); and (3) both operand order and operation change (e.g., 28 = ____ × 4). One month later, subjects were given a test of retention in which all four versions of each problem were presented again.

At both the immediate and delayed tests, Rickard et al. (1994) found that any change in problem format at the posttest had a negative impact on performance. The degree of impact depended on the type of transformation made, but, in all cases, performance was worse on transfer problems than on training problems, suggesting that effects of training were specific to some extent to the problems used in training. In addition, performance on transfer problems provided a way to identify two processing components of the mental arithmetic task. One of these components was more concrete or perceptually based, corresponding to the particular digits and their order. The second component was more conceptual and related to the calculation required by the problem, either multiplication or division. A change between training and transfer in the calculation required by the problem had a more substantial negative impact on performance than did a change in the perceptually based component, such as a change in operand order.

B. Stroop Effect

More recent evidence from our laboratory for skill specificity involves the Stroop (1935) effect (Clawson, King, Healy, & Ericsson, 1993, 1995; see also Healy et al., 1995). In the Stroop color–word interference task, subjects name the color of the ink in which color words are presented, and the ink color and word do not correspond (e.g., for the word *blue* printed in orange ink, the subject responds with "orange"). The present study provided experimental subjects with 12 sessions of training on the Stroop task. Subjects were tested in a posttest after training and in a retention test after a month-long delay. There was a set of tests related to Stroop interference: one test each on word reading and on simple color-patch naming plus a Stroop test and a test with Stroop stimuli but requiring word reading responses ("reverse Stroop"). One index of specificity was provided by the use of two different color/word sets (pink, blue, orange; purple, green, red). Although the experimental subjects were *trained* on only one set (with training set counterbalanced across subjects), all subjects were *tested* on both sets. If there is specificity of training, then there should be less improvement on the untrained set than on the trained set.

Specificity of training was in fact observed and persisted across the 1-month delay. Subjects were faster on the trained set than on the untrained set when naming colors (i.e., in the Stroop test and in the color-patch naming test), but not when reading words (i.e., in the word reading test and the reverse Stroop test). For the word reading tests, reaction times were actually faster for the untrained set. This pattern can be understood by appreciating the fact that in the Stroop task subjects name colors and ignore words, so Stroop training may facilitate color naming responses but may suppress word reading responses.

Overall, what these effects of specificity suggest for training routines that are designed to optimize durability and transferability of training is that tasks used in training somehow must capture the variety of tasks eventually to be encountered.

IV. CONTEXTUAL INTERFERENCE

Some investigators (see, e.g., Rubin, 1985) have claimed that despite forgetting, no qualitative changes in performance occur as a function of delay; that is, the performance level declines, but the performance pattern is the same at both short and long retention intervals. This claim implies that it is not necessary to conduct experiments on long-term retention except possibly to establish quantitative decay functions. However, research on contextual interference has demonstrated that methods used to optimize acquisition performance may not be optimal for long-term retention or transfer. These results imply that retention is not completely predictable from acquisition and that it is essential to examine both acquisition and long-term retention. Specifically, it has been shown that certain methods that hinder performance during acquisition (such as the use of difficult materials or conditions of high interference) promote maximal long-term retention. As mentioned earlier in the section on methodological issues concerning the training and testing of skills, these findings concerning contextual interference have been obtained for different practice and feedback schedules as well as for variation in practice contexts (Schmidt & Bjork, 1992). We next review the early literature on contextual interference and then describe some new results on this topic from our own laboratory.

A. Intratask Interference

Battig (1972, 1979) proposed a principle that he labeled intratask interference or, later, contextual interference. According to this principle, the larger the interference at the time of learning the greater the subsequent long-term retention and transfer of what has been learned. In a review of research on this phenomenon, Fendrich et al. (1988) concluded that intratask interference effects are usually large. They reviewed a set of 12 studies, each of which included both a low- and a high-interference condition. Assume that maximum facilitation is an increase from the performance level in the low-interference condition to perfect performance; then the high-interference conditions averaged over 1/3 of the maximum facilitation possible. In other words, there were substantial improvements in retention and transfer in the high-interference conditions compared to the low-interference conditions. Fendrich et al. also distinguished between two distinct bases for interference found in previous studies: similarity (or confusability) of the items composing the learning unit (see, e.g., Pellegrino, 1972, who varied the formal similarity of paired-associate responses) and variations in the context in which the learning unit appears (see, e.g., Battig, 1972, who compared separation and mixing of paired-associate pairings and recall tests). Although not independently manipulating the learning unit and its context, some studies did combine these two factors (Johnson, 1964). Fendrich et al. speculated that the retention or transfer conditions might interact with the type of interference to determine the magnitude of the contextual interference effect. When context conditions are changed between the acquisition phase and the retention or transfer testing phases, then increased contextual variety should yield a large contextual interference effect (i.e., should show a strong facilitation of long-term retention and transfer). In contrast, when the learning unit is the same for the acquisition phase as for the retention and transfer testing phases, then high item similarity should yield a large contextual interference effect. These predictions await empirical verification but, if valid, would lead to the conclusion that a combination of both increased contextual variety and learning unit similarity would produce a contextual interference effect over a wider range of retention and transfer testing conditions than would either factor on its own.

One popular manipulation of contextual variability concerns the scheduling of practice trials on different tasks. There has been considerable work in both verbal and motor learning on the comparison of blocked and random acquisition trials. Battig (1966) found that randomly ordering the practice tasks, as opposed to practicing different tasks in separate blocks, hampered acquisition of a verbal learning task but facilitated its retention. As reviewed earlier in the section on methodological issues concerning the training and testing of skills, the same pattern was found to be present in motor learning tasks by Shea and Morgan (1979). Shea and Morgan's task, however, confounded practice schedule effects (blocked vs. random) with reaction-time paradigm effects (simple for blocked practice vs. choice for random practice). Lee and Magill (1983) devised three motor learning experiments that avoided this confounding yet yielded the same pattern of results. The reaction-time confounding was eliminated by using cued and uncued practice trials and also by adding a third serial practice group, which demonstrated performance similar to that of the random group at retention. Because the trials in the serial practice schedule were predictable, the retention disadvantage for blocked practice was attributed largely to the repetition of events rather than to their predictability.

B. Contextual Interference in Acquisition of Logic Rules

The contextual interference effect for random, as opposed to blocked, practice schedules was also demonstrated by Carlson and Yaure (1990) for the acquisition and retention of logic rules. A study recently completed in our laboratory by V. I. Schneider (1991; V. I. Schneider, Healy, Ericsson, & Bourne, 1995) pursued this investigation further. Schneider used a display consisting of four panels, only one of which was relevant on any given trial. A cue indicated which was the relevant panel on a given trial. The subjects' task was to decide whether or not the display in the relevant panel indicated an emergency and to respond by pressing one of two response keys ("Y" for an emergency and "N" for no emergency). Both response time and accuracy were measured. The relevant panel contained two lines of X's or O's in one of four combinations: XXX and XXX, XXX and OOO, OOO and XXX, OOO and OOO. Each panel involved a different logical rule on which the decision was to be made. The four rules were: AND, OR, NAND, and NOR. For the AND rule, an emergency was indicated only if both stimuli contained X's (i.e., XXX and XXX); for the OR rule, an emergency was indicated if one or the other or both stimuli contained X's (i.e., XXX and XXX; XXX and OOO; OOO and XXX). For the NAND rule, an emergency was indicated only if both stimuli did not contain X's (i.e., XXX and OOO; OOO and XXX; OOO and OOO). Finally, for the NOR rule, an emergency was indicated only if neither stimuli contained X's (i.e., OOO and OOO).

V. I. Schneider (1991) included one group of subjects given blocked practice, in which all trials within a block involved the same rule although the particular stimulus configuration varied randomly from trial to trial, and a second group given random practice, in which both the rule and the stimulus varied randomly from trial to trial. Following Lee and Magill's (1983) study with motor learning, Schneider also included in one of her experiments a third group of subjects who were presented the rules in a fixed serial order. Because the rules were presented in a fixed serial order, they were predictable, but because they changed from trial to trial, they had to be retrieved from memory on each trial. Thus, the serial group allowed Schneider to determine whether the unpredictability of the rules in the random group, rather than the need to retrieve them from memory, can explain the contextual interference effect. Unlike the study of motor learning by Lee and Magill (1983), repetition of events could not be a factor contributing to the effects in the present study of acquiring logic rules, because the particular stimulus configuration shown varied from trial to trial in each of the three conditions.

This experiment included a random test at the end of the acquisition phase, and this test was repeated after a delay interval of 1 week or 1 month, so that V. I. Schneider (1991) could determine whether the contextual interference effect would survive, disappear, or perhaps become magnified on a retention test. Results from the acquisition phase showed that the blocked practice schedule yielded the shortest correct response times, and the serial practice schedule yielded times midway between those of the blocked and random conditions, suggesting that both unpredictability and the need for rule retrieval contribute to contextual interference.

Although blocked practice led to superior performance during acquisition, it led to inferior performance, in terms of both the response times and the proportion of correct responses, during both the immediate test and the long-term retention test. The serial group's level of performance was intermediate between the blocked and random groups for both performance measures. V. I. Schneider (1991) also found no forgetting evident between the immediate and delayed tests; indeed accuracy improved for the blocked condition on the retention test relative to the immediate test, perhaps because the subjects received practice at rule retrieval during the immediate test, in which the rules were presented in a random order. Thus, these findings provided additional support for the contextual interference effect, and they suggest that the long-term benefit found for contextual interference in this cognitive task is attributable in part to the practice subjects received in retrieving the rules from memory. Although the rule information is declarative, it is the cognitive procedure involved in the retrieval of the rules that is crucial to retention test performance. Hence, these results are also consistent with the procedural reinstatement framework.

V. PART VERSUS WHOLE TRAINING AND TRAINING ORDER

In complex skills, which involve two or more subskills, should initial training include the entire set of subskills (i.e., the whole task) or only some of the subskills (i.e., part of the task)? For example, the skill of golf includes subskills involving the use of different golf clubs (e.g., drivers, irons, putter) and their respective swings. In this example, part training might involve work just on the driving range or on the putting green, whereas whole training would include all aspects of the game (i.e., playing a round of golf). Given the use of initial part training, should the training involve the easier or the more difficult subskills? On the basis of our own research, we have suggested that any conclusions concerning part–whole training are critically dependent on the nature of the whole task and on the characteristics of the component part tasks (Healy et al., 1993).

Early investigations of part versus whole training foreshadowed our findings. For example, Annett and Kay (1956) proposed that whole training is preferred when responses associated with the early subtasks of a skill do not affect success on subsequent subtasks of the skill. However, if early subtasks do influence performance on later subtasks, then part training can be more effective than whole training by reducing errors on earlier subtasks that could inhibit performance on subsequent subtasks. Naylor and Briggs (1963) compared whole training to progressive part training (in which the trainee practices the first subtask alone, then practices the first two subtasks together, then practices the first three subtasks together, etc.). They concluded that for skills with highly integrated subtasks whole training is best, but for skills with loosely integrated subtasks progressive part training is best. In a review of the part versus whole training literature, Stammers (1982) concluded that in training, one should begin with a preliminary attempt to use whole training, then use part training only if the whole training fails to provide the necessary acquisition rate in the preliminary attempt.

With respect to the ordering of tasks in part training, Seymour (1954) suggested that when a verbal skill contains both difficult and easy subtasks, beginning with the difficult tasks typically results in better performance. More recently, Pellegrino, Doane, Fischer, and Alderton (1991) found that in a visual discrimination task, subjects who first learned more difficult discriminations performed better than did subjects who first learned easier discriminations on a subsequent test that included both levels of discrimination. Pellegrino et al. suggested that subjects who began with the easier discriminations used only a loose discrimination net during initial learning, whereas subjects who began with the difficult discriminations had to construct a much finer discrimination net during the initial sessions that was useful for the subsequent sessions involving the whole set of stimuli. This research suggests that, contrary to intuition, part training is most effective if the learning begins with the more difficult subtasks or stimulus subsets.

A. Part versus Whole Training in Morse Code Reception

In work on Morse code reception recently conducted in our laboratory, Clawson (1992; Clawson, Healy, Ericsson, & Bourne, 1993) compared the effects of part and whole training on long-term retention. She also addressed the related question raised by Pellegrino et al. (1991) concerning whether any initial part training should include the easiest material or the most difficult material. She sought to determine whether the advantage for initially difficult training found for visual discrimination by Pellegrino et al. would also be found for Morse code training and whether it would continue to be evident on a delayed retention test.

In this study, subjects learned to receive 12 Morse code signals and to translate them to their letter equivalents. The set of 12 code–letter pairs was divided into 2 equal-sized subsets, one with easy and the other with difficult items. In Experiment 1, all subjects were given 3 sessions of training followed 1 month later by a retention session. The subjects were divided into three groups. Training in the first session was devoted exclusively to the easy subset of code–letter pairs in the "easy-first" group, to the difficult subset in the "difficult-first" group, and to the entire set of pairs in the "all-first" group. All subsequent sessions for all three groups of subjects involved the full set of pairs. During every session, training was preceded by a pretest and followed by a posttest covering all 12 code–letter pairs. Clawson (1992) found similar levels of improvement across the first 3 days of training for the 3 conditions. However, there was a difference among the groups on the retention pretest after the month-long delay interval. In contrast to the findings from Pellegrino et al. (1991), the difficult-first group showed a strong drop in accuracy at that point, whereas little forgetting was evident for the other two groups.

Experiment 2 explored this finding further by including only the easy-first and difficult-first training groups with more subjects in each group and an examination of response times as well as accuracy. Once again, there was a larger drop in accuracy in the retention pretest for the difficult-first group than for the easy-first group, but in this case the difference between training groups was found only on the easy pairs. Further, in that test there was slower responding for the difficult-first group than for the easy-first group on the easy pairs. However, on the difficult pairs in that test, the difficult-first group was faster than the easy-first group. Despite this one advantage for the difficult-first group, Clawson (1992) found performance after training was generally inferior when the difficult items were studied first, contrary to the findings of Pellegrino et al. (1991). Clawson explained this discrepancy between the two studies in terms of a difference in the initial mastery of the easy items. In Clawson's Morse code task the easy items were in fact quite challenging, with performance on them being only about 50% correct initially, whereas in the discrimination task of Pellegrino et al. the easy items were extremely easy, with performance at the ceiling in the initial training phase. When subjects must devote their initial training time to very easy or trivial items, they are not led to develop strategies that would help them with more challenging material presented subsequently. That is, easy-first part training may be advisable but only if that training is sufficiently demanding.

B. Part versus Whole Training of Tank Gunner Skills

Whether acquisition and retention benefit from part–whole training was also a focus of recently completed research in our laboratory by Marmie (1993; Marmie & Healy, 1995) on the training of tank gunner skills. In this study, subjects were engaged in a realistic, goal-directed simulation exercise in which the whole task was broken down into sequential component sub-tasks. Because of the complex nature of the training task, this study resem-bled an earlier one by Mané, Adams, and Donchin (1989), who compared part and whole training of the motor skills required for learning a video game. However, the subtasks in the study by Mané et al. were repetitive drills, whereas the subtasks in Marmie's tank gunner study were natural, meaningful, and goal directed on their own.

More specifically, subjects controlled tank gun turret movements via hand controls, aimed at threat targets with the aid of a sight, and fired by pressing either of two buttons under their index fingers. A threat target was destroyed when a shot struck its center of mass, resulting in a "kill." Mar-mie (1993) examined the proportion of kills and two different response-time measures: time to identify, which occurred when the subject brought the threat into the field of view, and time to fire after an identification had been made. The identification measure reflected the search component of the task. The time-to-fire measure reflected the more difficult combined com-ponents of sighting and firing.

Subjects were tested over 4 sessions, including 3 acquisition sessions and a retention session occurring after a 4-week delay. There were 2 groups of subjects. During the first 2 sessions, the part-training group practiced only the sighting and firing task subcomponents (which are indexed by the time-to-fire measure) while a simulated commander took over the searching component of the task. The whole-training group was trained on all 3 subcomponents of the task during the first 2 sessions. For both groups, the last 2 sessions involved the whole task, combining sighting and firing with searching (which is indexed by the time-to-identify measure). It is interest-ing to note that the type of part-task training used here was a backward-chaining segmentation procedure, in which the final segment of a task is practiced first; Wightman and Lintern (1985) found this type to be the most effective of the part-task methods.

During initial training, there was a substantial advantage in terms of the proportion of kills for the part-training group because the commander effi-ciently took over the searching component of the task. However, after the initial training period, there was no difference between the two training groups. Further, even though the part-training subjects received no practice on the search component of the task during the first two sessions, after the initial training they performed just as well as the whole training group on the time-to-identify measure. Most interesting were the results of the time-to-fire measure: the subjects given part training showed a large advantage on this measure in the second session of training, and that advantage was maintained even at the retention test.

Thus, initial part training on the difficult subtask did not hurt performance relative to whole training on any measure and improved performance on the measure reflecting the more difficult subtask. By comparing this finding to that obtained by Clawson (1992), who found a clear disadvantage for initial training on the difficult subcomponent of Morse code reception, it is clear that conclusions concerning differences between part and whole training depend crucially on the nature of the whole task and the characteristics of the component part tasks. Healy et al. (1993) attributed the disadvantage for the difficult-first condition in the Morse code study and the contrasting advantage for the similar condition in the tank gunner study to the fact that the difficult items in the Morse code reception task could not be mastered within the time allotted, whereas the sighting and firing subtasks of the tank gunner skill could. If one also considers the results of the study by Pellegrino et al. (1991), the conclusion follows that when training on only part of a task, one should focus on a component that is sufficiently complex to be engaging but not so complex to be impossible to master in the time allowed.

VI. AUTOMATICITY

Automatic processing occurs effortlessly, with no demands on attentional resources, whereas nonautomatic, or controlled, processing requires deliberate, conscious, and effortful uses of attention (W. Schneider & Shiffrin, 1977). The classification of a skill as automatic or controlled depends to a large extent on the degree of prior skill acquisition. Many skills require controlled processes in the initial stages of acquisition, but as the task becomes better and better learned, its attentional demands gradually decline (Logan, 1979) until it becomes fully automatic after extensive practice. Some of our earlier work on the long-term retention of trained skills (see Healy et al., 1992, and the section earlier on procedural reinstatement) was guided by a hypothesis that automatic processing leads to superior long-term retention. We provided tests for this hypothesis in the domains of target detection and mental multiplication. Although we did find superior long-term retention in these domains, we were unable to establish conclusively either (1) that subjects achieved an automatic level of processing, or (2) that the extent of automaticity was related to the level of long-term retention. Nevertheless, in more recent work discussed next, we have found that automaticity has important effects on skill training and retention.

A. Direct and Mediated Retrieval in Mental Arithmetic

Facts can be retrieved from memory either automatically by direct access or indirectly by some mediated route. For example, Bourne and Rickard (1991; see also Healy et al., 1993) found in a mental arithmetic task that sometimes answers were retrieved directly and other times indirectly and that this distinction had important consequences for performance. In one study, they gave subjects two sessions of practice on selected single-digit multiplication problems. After responding to each problem in the first two blocks of each session, subjects were asked whether the answer "popped into mind" directly or was retrieved through at least one consciously mediated step.

Bourne and Rickard (1991) found that across subjects about 18% of the problems were solved by mediation in the first two blocks of training, and they observed that when mediation was reported, the subjects were slower to respond with the correct answer, with the effects of mediation on response times for particular problems persisting throughout the entire experiment. They also reported both intrasubject and intraproblem stability in these data. If a particular problem was mediated in the first training session, it had a high probability of continuing to require mediation in the second training session, even though response times became faster with training. This finding was taken as a challenge for Logan's (1988) influential instance theory of automatization, which posits that increased learning leads to a transition from mediated to direct retrieval.

To investigate the transition from mediated to direct retrieval, Rickard (1994) developed a novel mental arithmetic task that initially requires the application of a general algorithm but that can be performed by retrieving answers directly from memory after sufficient practice (Healy et al., 1995). Adult subjects were given 90 blocks of training over 5 sessions on problems based on a novel, arbitrary operation symbolized by the pound sign (#). The pound operation was one in which the answer is equal to the second element plus the difference between the first and second elements, plus 1. For example, the answer to 7 # 15 is $15 + (15 - 7) + 1 = 24$.

During practice, subjects were probed on 1/3 of the trials to determine whether they used the algorithm that they were taught, retrieved the answer directly from memory, or used some other approach. On a retention test occurring 6 weeks later, subjects were probed after every trial. The strategy probing results from practice showed a transition from the algorithm to retrieval. By about Block 60, "direct" retrieval was the reported strategy on nearly all trials. When examining reaction time speedup, Rickard (1994) found large improvements with practice but a clear deviation from the usual power function (Logan, 1988). This finding suggested to Rickard that the power law might be strategy specific. To test this hypothesis, he performed additional reaction time analyses only for trials on which strategy probes were collected. Rickard found, in accordance with his hypothesis, that when the data were separated by strategy, they conformed to two linear but different (i.e., different in slope and intercept) power functions.

The reaction time results for the delayed test indicated a much greater loss in skill across the retention interval than had been observed in our previous work on simple arithmetic (see Fendrich et al., 1993; Rickard et al., 1994; and the sections earlier on procedural reinstatement and on generalizability and specificity of training). To investigate this finding further, Rickard (1994) plotted the reaction times on the delayed test separately by strategy and found that when retrieval was the reported strategy on the delayed test, the reaction times were almost exactly the same as on the immediate test. This result suggested that the only effect of the retention interval was to decrease the probability with which the automatic retrieval strategy was used, but not to change the time required to execute the automatic retrieval strategy when it was used.

B. Direct and Mediated Retrieval in Vocabulary Acquisition

In their earlier studies of vocabulary learning with the keyword method (see the section earlier on procedural reinstatement), Crutcher and Ericsson (1988; Crutcher, 1990) have shown that retrieval of English equivalents after original acquisition was virtually always mediated by retrieval of the keyword in working memory. For example, they showed that retrieval times for the full vocabulary task were substantially slower than those for either the keyword subtask or the English subtask. Also, retrieval accuracy on the full vocabulary task was a direct function of accuracy on the two subtasks.

Crutcher and Ericsson (1992; Crutcher, 1992) subsequently studied the effects of additional extended practice on retrieval. After initial acquisition and test, subjects practiced the full vocabulary task (*full practice* condition) for half of the items and the English subtask for the other half (*subtask practice* condition), with 80 practice trials for each item. Both the pretest and a posttest after extended practice included the full vocabulary task and the English subtask for all items. At the pretest, the English subtask was faster than the vocabulary task for both practice conditions, as in the study with limited practice. However, at the posttest, there was a crossover interaction: Items in the subtask practice condition were faster with the English subtask than with the full vocabulary task, but items in the full practice condition were faster with the full vocabulary task than with the English subtask, suggesting unmediated direct retrieval in that case.

Crutcher (1992) retested subjects after a 1-month delay (see Healy et al., 1995). Although recall performance was generally very high, a crossover interaction was evident: For items in the subtask practice condition recall was worse on the full vocabulary task, whereas for items in the full practice condition recall was worse on the subtask. Specifically, for items in the full practice condition, 99% were recalled correctly in the full vocabulary task and 95% in the English subtask. This result suggests that there was a loss of association between the Spanish word and the mediating keyword for a small percentage (i.e., 4%) of the items, which were thus retrieved directly. However, for most items (i.e., 95%), the keyword remained effective as a cue, suggesting that mediated retrieval was employed, despite the fact that the keyword had hardly been presented since the initial acquisition period and that only the direct association between the Spanish word and keyword had been practiced. On the basis of this finding and evidence from other experiments, Crutcher concluded that the original mediated encoding continues to influence retrieval after extended practice even when other evidence points to unmediated direct retrieval.

Based on the combined results from the mental arithmetic and vocabulary acquisition studies, we conclude that automatic retrieval can be very difficult to achieve in some circumstances (as in the study by Crutcher, 1992), but once achieved can have a profound effect on retention performance (as in the study by Rickard, 1994).

VII. CONCLUSIONS AND GUIDELINES

In this section, we present the practical implications of the research summarized in the earlier sections by providing 12 different guidelines concerning the conditions of training and instruction designed to improve the long-term retention of knowledge and skills. It should be noted that although these guidelines should facilitate long-term retention, they may also inhibit the rate of initial acquisition in some circumstances.

1. Periodic retrieval practice benefits retention after a long delay interval, especially when there is a large spacing between the successive practice attempts (Bahrick et al., 1993).

2. If more than one task is to be acquired, it is better to use random rather than blocked scheduling of the tasks during training (Landauer & Bjork, 1978; Shea & Morgan, 1979; Schmidt & Bjork, 1992).

3. It is best not to provide feedback after every trial but rather to give summary feedback or intermittent feedback that is gradually reduced across training (Schmidt & Bjork, 1992; Schmidt et al., 1989).

4. To ensure generalizability, training should maximize variability of practice (Catalano & Kleiner, 1984; Kerr & Booth, 1978; Schmidt & Bjork, 1992).

5. Superior performance on a retention test will result from the use of reinstatable procedures during learning; that is, the procedures used during training should be designed to match the procedures that will be required at test (Healy et al., 1992).

6. The well-known generation advantage can be extended from memory for episodes to memory for facts and skills (McNamara & Healy, 1995). Hence, active generation, as opposed to passive presentation, should be encouraged during training.

7. When possible, the information to be learned should be related to previous experience (King, 1992).

8. Learning spatial information can be facilitated by increasing the distinctiveness of the to-be-learned information (Sinclair et al., 1994).

9. Investigators should be wary of the fact that durable performance at test often occurs at the expense of generalizable performance, so that what is learned and retained is highly specific to the training situation (Clawson et al., 1995; Fendrich et al., 1993; Healy et al., 1993, 1995; Rickard et al., 1994).

10. A combination of both increased contextual variety and learning unit similarity should be used to promote best performance over a wide range of retention and transfer testing conditions (Battig, 1979; Fendrich et al., 1988; Schmidt & Bjork, 1992). The findings of Schneider (1991) suggest further that to optimize retention it is crucial that subjects receive practice retrieving the appropriate response procedures from memory during training.

11. It is best to focus initially on a maximally trainable component of a task (Clawson, 1992; Healy et al., 1993; Marmie, 1993; Pellegrino et al., 1991); that is, initial part training can be beneficial relative to whole training, but the choice of the initially trained part is crucial. If the task involves a trivial component that is not sufficiently demanding, then it is better to begin with a more difficult component. On the other hand, if the task involves a component that cannot be adequately mastered within the constraints of the training period, then it is better to begin with an easier component.

12. Although automaticity may be difficult to achieve in some cases (Crutcher, 1992) and is not always required for maximal long-term retention (Fendrich et al., 1993; Healy et al., 1990), training should promote automatic responding if speed of performance is crucial, because automaticity has been found to increase performance speed (Rickard, 1994).

Acknowledgments

Much of the research reported here from our laboratory was supported in part by Army Research Institute Contracts MDA903-86-K0155 and MDA903-90-K-0066 to the Institute of Cognitive Science at the University of Colorado, Boulder. We would like to thank Lyle Bourne, Deborah Clawson, Robert Crutcher, Anders Ericsson, David Fendrich, Antoinette

Gesi, Cheri King, William Marmie, Danielle McNamara, Timothy Rickard, Vivian Schneider, and William Wittman for their help with the research reported in this chapter from our laboratory and Katie Ricci and Robert Bjork for their helpful comments on an earlier version of this chapter. We are especially indebted to Lyle Bourne for his many valuable suggestions and comments about this chapter. Correspondence concerning this chapter should be sent to Dr. Alice F. Healy, Department of Psychology, University of Colorado, Boulder, CO 80309-0345.

References

Anderson, J. R. (1983). *The architecture of cognition*. Cambridge: Harvard University Press.

Annett, J., & Kay, H. (1956). Skilled performance. *Occupational Psychology, 30*, 112–117.

Bahrick, H. P. (1979). Maintenance of knowledge: Questions about memory we forgot to ask. *Journal of Experimental Psychology: General, 108*, 296–308.

Bahrick, H. P. (1984). Semantic memory content in permastore: Fifty years of memory for Spanish learned in school. *Journal of Experimental Psychology: General, 113*, 1–29.

Bahrick, H. P. (1992). Stabilized memory of unrehearsed knowledge. *Journal of Experimental Psychology: General, 121*, 112–113.

Bahrick, H. P., Bahrick, L. E., Bahrick, A. S., & Bahrick, P. E. (1993). Maintenance of foreign language vocabulary and the spacing effect. *Psychological Science, 4*, 316–321.

Bahrick, H. P., Bahrick, P. O., & Wittlinger, R. P. (1975). Fifty years of memory for names and faces: A cross-sectional approach. *Journal of Experimental Psychology: General, 104*, 54–75.

Bahrick, H. P., & Hall, L. K. (1991). Lifetime maintenance of high school mathematics content. *Journal of Experimental Psychology: General, 120*, 20–33.

Bahrick, H. P., & Phelps, E. (1987). Retention of Spanish vocabulary over 8 years. *Journal of Experimental Psychology: Learning, Memory, and Cognition, 13*, 344–349.

Battig, W. F. (1966). Facilitation and interference. In E. A. Bilodeau (Ed.), *Acquisition of skill* (pp. 215–244). New York: Academic Press.

Battig, W. F. (1972). Intratask interference as a source of facilitation in transfer and retention. In R. F. Thompson & J. F. Voss (Eds.), *Topics in learning and performance* (pp. 131–159). New York: Academic Press.

Battig, W. F. (1979). The flexibility of human memory. In L. S. Cermak & F. I. M. Craik (Eds.), *Levels of processing in human memory* (pp. 23–44). Hillsdale, NJ: Erlbaum.

Bjork, R. A. (1994). Memory and metamemory considerations in the training of human beings. In J. Metcalfe & A. P. Shimamura (Eds.), *Metacognition: Knowing about knowing* (pp. 185–205). Cambridge: MIT Press.

Bogartz, R. S. (1990a). Evaluating forgetting curves psychologically. *Journal of Experimental Psychology: Learning, Memory, and Cognition, 16*, 138–148.

Bogartz, R. S. (1990b). Learning-forgetting rate independence defined by forgetting function parameters or forgetting function form: Reply to Loftus and Bamber and to Wixted. *Journal of Experimental Psychology: Learning, Memory, and Cognition, 16*, 936–945.

Bourne, L. E., Jr., & Rickard, T. C. (July, 1991). *Mental calculation: The development of a cognitive skill*. Paper presented at the Interamerican Congress of Psychology, San Jose, Costa Rica.

Carlson, R. A., & Yaure, R. G. (1990). Practice schedules and the use of component skills in problem solving. *Journal of Experimental Psychology: Learning, Memory, and Cognition, 16*, 484–496.

Carroll, M., & Nelson, T. O. (1993). Failure to obtain a generation effect during naturalistic learning. *Memory & Cognition, 21*, 361–366.

Catalano, J. F., & Kleiner, B. M. (1984). Distant transfer in coincident timing as a function of variability of practice. *Perceptual and Motor Skills, 58*, 851–856.

Clawson, D. M. (1992). *Acquisition and retention of Morse code reception skills.* Unpublished master's thesis, University of Colorado, Boulder.

Clawson, D. M., Healy, A. F., Ericsson, K. A., & Bourne, L. E. (1993, April). *Acquisition and retention of Morse code reception: Part-whole training.* Paper presented at the Joint Annual Convention of the Western Psychological Association and the Rocky Mountain Psychological Association, Phoenix, AZ.

Clawson, D. M., King, C. L., Healy, A. F., & Ericsson, K. A. (1993). Specificity of practice effects in the classic Stroop color-word task. *Proceedings of the fifteenth annual conference of the cognitive science society* (pp. 324–329). Hillsdale, NJ: Erlbaum.

Clawson, D. M., King, C. L., Healy, A. F., & Ericsson, K. A. (1995). Training and retention of the classic Stroop task: Specificity of practice effects. In A. F. Healy & L. E. Bourne, Jr. (Eds.), *Learning and memory of knowledge and skills: Durability and specificity* (pp. 234–254). Thousand Oaks, CA: Sage.

Conway, M. A., Cohen, G., & Stanhope, N. (1991). On the very long-term retention of knowledge acquired through formal education: Twelve years of cognitive psychology. *Journal of Experimental Psychology: General, 120,* 395–409.

Crutcher, R. J. (1990). *The role of mediation in knowledge acquisition and retention: Learning foreign vocabulary using the keyword method* (Tech. Rep. No. 90-10). Boulder: University of Colorado, Institute of Cognitive Science.

Crutcher, R. J. (1992). *The effects of practice on retrieval of foreign vocabulary using the keyword method.* Unpublished doctoral dissertation, University of Colorado, Boulder.

Crutcher, R. J., & Ericsson, K. A. (1988, April). *A componential analysis of the keyword method.* Paper presented at the American Educational Research Association Convention, New Orleans, LA.

Crutcher, R. J., & Ericsson, K. A. (1992, November). *Mediation processes in memory retrieval before and after extended retrieval practice.* Poster presented at the 33rd Annual Meeting of the Psychonomic Society, St. Louis, MO.

Crutcher, R. J., & Healy, A. F. (1989). Cognitive operations and the generation effect. *Journal of Experimental Psychology: Learning, Memory, and Cognition, 15,* 669–675.

Ericsson, K. A., & Chase, W. G. (1982). Exceptional memory. *American Scientist, 70,* 607–615.

Farr, M. J. (1987). *The long-term retention of knowledge and skills: A cognitive and instructional perspective.* New York: Springer-Verlag.

Fendrich, D. W., Gesi, A. T., Healy, A. F., & Bourne, L. E., Jr. (1995). The contribution of procedural reinstatement to implicit and explicit memory effects in a motor task. In A. F. Healy & L. E. Bourne, Jr. (Eds.), *Learning and memory of knowledge and skills: Durability and specificity* (pp. 66–94). Thousand Oaks, CA: Sage.

Fendrich, D. W., Healy, A. F., & Bourne, L. E., Jr. (1991). Long-term repetition effects for motoric and perceptual procedures. *Journal of Experimental Psychology: Learning, Memory, and Cognition, 17,* 137–151.

Fendrich, D. W., Healy, A. F., & Bourne, L. E., Jr. (1993). Mental arithmetic: Training and retention of multiplication skill. In C. Izawa (Ed.), *Cognitive psychology applied* (pp. 111–133). Hillsdale, NJ: Erlbaum.

Fendrich, D. W., Healy, A. F., Meiskey, L., Crutcher, R. J., Little, W., & Bourne, L. E., Jr. (1988). *Skill maintenance: Literature review and theoretical analysis* (AFHRL-TP-87-73). Brooks AFB, TX: Training Systems Division, Air Force Human Resources Laboratory.

Gesi, A. T., Fendrich, D. W., Healy, A. F., & Bourne, L. E. (1989, April). *Episodic and procedural memory for digit sequences.* Paper presented at the Joint Annual Convention of the Western Psychological Association and the Rocky Mountain Psychological Association, Reno, NV.

Graf, P., & Schacter, D. L. (1985). Implicit and explicit memory for new associations in normal and amnesic subjects. *Journal of Experimental Psychology: Learning, Memory, and Cognition, 11,* 501–518.

Healy, A. F., Clawson, D. M., McNamara, D. S., Marmie, W. R., Schneider, V. I., Rickard, T. C., Crutcher, R. J., King, C. L., Ericsson, K. A., & Bourne, L. E., Jr. (1993). The long-term retention of knowledge and skills. In D. Medin (Ed.), *The psychology of learning and motivation: Advances in research and theory* (Vol. 30, pp. 135–164). New York: Academic Press.

Healy, A. F., Fendrich, D. W., Crutcher, R. J., Wittman, W. T., Gesi, A. T., Ericsson, K. A., & Bourne, L. E., Jr. (1992). The long-term retention of skills. In A. F. Healy, S. M. Kosslyn, & R. M. Shiffrin (Eds.), *From learning processes to cognitive processes: Essays in honor of William K. Estes* (Vol. 2, pp. 87–118). Hillsdale, NJ: Erlbaum.

Healy, A. F., Fendrich, D. W., & Proctor, J. D. (1990). Acquisition and retention of a letter-detection skill. *Journal of Experimental Psychology: Learning, Memory, and Cognition, 16,* 270–281.

Healy, A. F., King, C. L., Clawson, D. M., Sinclair, G. P., Rickard, T. C., Crutcher, R. J., Ericsson, K. A., and Bourne, L. E., Jr. (1995). Optimizing the long-term retention of skills. In A. F. Healy & L. E. Bourne, Jr. (Eds.), *Learning and memory of knowledge and skills: Durability and specificity* (pp. 1–29). Thousand Oaks, CA: Sage.

Hintzman, D. L. (1993). Twenty-five years of learning and memory: Was the cognitive revolution a mistake? In D. E. Meyer & S. Kornblum (Eds.), *Attention and performance XIV: Synergies in experimental psychology, artificial intelligence, and cognitive neuroscience—A silver jubilee* (pp. 359–391). Cambridge: MIT Press.

Johnson, R. B. (1964). *Recognition of nonsense shapes as a function of degree of congruence among components of a pretraining task.* Unpublished doctoral dissertation, University of Virginia, Charlottesville.

Jost, A. (1897). Die assoziationsfestigkeit in ihrer abhangigkeit von der verteilung der wieder holungen. *Zeitschrift fur Psychologie, 14,* 436–472.

Kerr, R., & Booth, B. (1978). Specific and varied practice of a motor skill. *Perceptual and Motor Skills, 46,* 395–401.

King, C. L. (1992). *Familiarity effects on the retention of spatial, temporal, and item information in course schedules.* Unpublished doctoral dissertation, Colorado State University, Ft. Collins.

Kolers, P. A., & Roediger, H. L. (1984). Procedures of mind. *Journal of Verbal Learning and Verbal Behavior, 23,* 425–449.

Krumboltz, J. D., & Weisman, R. G. (1962). The effect of intermittent confirmation in programmed instruction. *Journal of Educational Psychology, 53,* 250–253.

Landauer, T. K., & Bjork, R. A. (1978). Optimum rehearsal patterns and name learning. In M. M. Gruneberg, P. E. Morris, & R. N. Sykes (Eds.), *Practical aspects of memory* (pp. 625–632). London: Academic Press.

Lee, T. D., & Magill, R. A. (1983). The locus of contextual interference in motor-skill acquisition. *Journal of Experimental Psychology: Learning, Memory, and Cognition, 9,* 730–746.

Loftus, G. R. (1985a). Evaluating forgetting curves. *Journal of Experimental Psychology: Learning, Memory, and Cognition, 11,* 397–406.

Loftus, G. R. (1985b). Consistency and confoundings: Reply to Slamecka. *Journal of Experimental Psychology; Learning, Memory, and Cognition, 11,* 817–820.

Loftus, G. R., & Bamber, D. (1990). Learning-forgetting independence, unidimensional memory models, and feature models: Comment on Bogartz (1990). *Journal of Experimental Psychology: Learning, Memory, and Cognition, 16,* 916–926.

Logan, G. D. (1979). On the use of concurrent memory load to measure attention and automaticity. *Journal of Experimental Psychology: Human Perception and Performance, 5,* 189–207.

Logan, G. D. (1988). Toward an instance theory of automatization. *Psychological Review, 95,* 492–527.

Mané, A. M., Adams, J. A., & Donchin, E. (1989). Adaptive and part-whole training in the acquisition of a complex perceptual-motor skill. *Acta Psychologica, 71,* 179–196.

Marmie, W. R. (1993). *The long-term retention of a complex skill: Part-whole training of tank gunner simulation exercises.* Unpublished master's thesis, University of Colorado, Boulder.

Marmie, W. R., & Healy, A. F. (1995). The long-term retention of a complex skill: Part-whole training of tank gunner simulation exercises. In A. F. Healy & L. E. Bourne, Jr. (Eds.), *Learning and memory of knowledge and skills: Durability and specificity* (pp. 30–65). Thousand Oaks, CA: Sage.

McNamara, D. S., & Healy, A. F. (1995). A generation advantage for multiplication skill training and nonword vocabulary acquisition. In A. F. Healy & L. E. Bourne, Jr. (Eds.), *Learning and memory of knowledge and skills: Durability and specificity* (pp. 132–169). Thousand Oaks, CA: Sage.

Meiskey, L., Healy, A. F., & Bourne, L. E., Jr. (1990). Memory for classroom algebra. *On Teaching, 2,* 57–67.

Melton, A. W. (1967). Repetition and retrieval from memory. *Science, 158,* 532.

Morris, C. D., Bransford, J. D., & Franks, J. J. (1977). Levels of processing versus transfer appropriate processing. *Journal of Verbal Learning and Verbal Behavior, 16,* 519–533.

Naylor, J. C., & Briggs, G. E. (1961). *Long-term retention of learned skills: A review of the literature* (ASD-TR-61-390, AD-267 043). Wright-Patterson AFB, OH: Advanced Systems Division.

Naylor, J. C., & Briggs, G. E. (1963). Effects of task complexity and task organization on the relative efficiency of part and whole training methods. *Journal of Experimental Psychology, 65,* 217–224.

Nitsch, K. E. (1977). *Structuring decontexualized forms of knowledge.* Unpublished doctoral dissertation, Vanderbilt University, Nashville, TN.

Pellegrino, J. W. (1972). Effects of intralist response formal similarity upon paired-associate transfer and retroactive inhibition. *Journal of Experimental Psychology, 92,* 134–141.

Pellegrino, J. W., Doane, S. M., Fischer, S. C., & Alderton, D. (1991). Stimulus complexity effects in visual comparisons: The effects of practice and learning context. *Journal of Experimental Psychology: Human Perception and Performance, 17,* 781–791.

Proctor, J. D., & Healy, A. F. (1995). Acquisition and retention of skilled letter detection. In A. F. Healy & L. E. Bourne, Jr. (Eds.), *Learning and memory of knowledge and skills: Durability and specificity* (pp. 282–299). Thousand Oaks, CA: Sage.

Richardson-Klavehn, A., & Bjork, R. A. (1988). Measures of memory. *Annual Review of Psychology, 39,* 475–543.

Rickard, T. C. (1994). *Bending the power law: The transition from algorithm-based to memory-based performance.* Unpublished doctoral dissertation, University of Colorado, Boulder.

Rickard, T. C., Healy, A. F., & Bourne, L. E., Jr. (1994). On the cognitive structure of basic arithmetic skills: Operation, order, and symbol transfer effects. *Journal of Experimental Psychology: Learning, Memory, and Cognition, 20,* 1139–1153.

Rubin, D. C. (1985). Memorability as a measure of processing: A unit analysis of prose and list learning. *Journal of Experimental Psychology: General, 114,* 213–238.

Schendel, J. D., Shields, J. L., & Katz, M. S. (1978). *Retention of motor skills: Review* (Tech. Pap. No. 313). Alexandria, VA: U.S. Army.

Schmidt, R. A., & Bjork, R. A. (1992). New conceptualizations of practice: Common principles in three paradigms suggest new concepts for training. *Psychological Science, 3,* 207–217.

Schmidt, R. A., Young, D. E., Swinnen, S., & Shapiro, D. C. (1989). Summary knowledge of results for skill acquisition: Support for the guidance hypothesis. *Journal of Experimental Psychology: Learning, Memory, and Cognition, 15,* 352–359.

Schneider, V. I. (1991). *The effects of contextual interference on the acquisition and retention of logic rules.* Unpublished doctoral dissertation, University of Colorado.

Schneider, V. I., Healy, A. F., Ericsson, K. A., & Bourne, L. E., Jr. (1995). The effects of contextual interference on the acquisition and retention of logical rules. In A. F. Healy & L. E. Bourne, Jr. (Eds.), *Learning and memory of knowledge and skills: Durability and specificity* (pp. 95–131). Thousand Oaks, CA: Sage.

Schneider, W., & Shiffrin, R. M. (1977). Controlled and automatic human information processing: I. Detection, search, and attention. *Psychological Review, 84,* 127–190.

Schooler, L. J., & Anderson, J. R. (1990). The disruptive potential of immediate feedback. *Proceedings of the Cognitive Science Society* (pp. 702–708). Hillsdale, NJ: Erlbaum.

Schulz, R. W., & Runquist, W. N. (1960). Learning and retention of paired adjectives as a function of percentage occurrence of response members. *Journal of Experimental Psychology, 59,* 409–413.

Semb, G. B., & Ellis, J. A. (1994). Knowledge learned in school: What is remembered? *Review of Educational Research, 64,* 253–286.

Seymour, W. D. (1954). Experiments on the acquisition of industrial skills. *Occupational Psychology, 28,* 77–89.

Shea, J. B., & Morgan, R. L. (1979). Contextual interference effects on the acquisition, retention, and transfer of a motor skill. *Journal of Experimental Psychology: Human Learning and Memory, 5,* 179–187.

Sinclair, G. P., Healy, A. F., & Bourne, L. E., Jr. (1994). *The acquisition and long-term retention of temporal, spatial, and item information.* Manuscript submitted for publication.

Slamecka, N. J. (1985). On comparing rates of forgetting: Comment on Loftus (1985). *Journal of Experimental Psychology: Learning, Memory, and Cognition, 11,* 812–816.

Slamecka, N. J., & Graf, P. (1978). The generation effect: Delineation of a phenomenon. *Journal of Experimental Psychology; Human Learning and Memory, 4,* 592–604.

Slamecka, N. J., & McElree, B. (1983). Normal forgetting of verbal lists as a function of their degree of learning. *Journal of Experimental Psychology: Learning, Memory, and Cognition, 9,* 384–397.

Stammers, R. B. (1982). Part and whole practice in training for procedural tasks. *Human Learning, 1,* 185–207.

Stroop, J. R. (1935). Studies of interference in serial verbal reactions. *Journal of Experimental Psychology, 18,* 643–662.

Tulving, E., & Thomson, D. M. (1973). Encoding specificity and retrieval processes in episodic memory. *Psychological Review, 80,* 352–373.

Underwood, B. J. (1964). Degree of learning and the measurement of forgetting. *Journal of Verbal Learning and Verbal Behavior, 3,* 112–129.

Wightman, D. C., & Lintern, G. (1985). Part-task training for tracking and manual control. *Human Factors, 27,* 267–283.

Winstein, C. J., & Schmidt, R. A. (1990). Reduced frequency of knowledge of results enhances motor skill learning. *Journal of Experimental Psychology: Learning, Memory, and Cognition, 16,* 677–691.

Wittman, W. T. (1989). *A long-term retention advantage for spatial information learned naturally and in the laboratory.* Unpublished doctoral dissertation, University of Colorado, Boulder.

Wittman, W. T., & Healy, A. F. (1995). A long-term retention advantage for spatial information learned naturally and in the laboratory. In A. F. Healy & L. E. Bourne, Jr. (Eds.), *Learning and memory of knowledge and skills: Durability and specificity* (pp. 170–205). Thousand Oaks, CA: Sage.

Wixted, J. T. (1990). Analyzing the empirical course of forgetting. *Journal of Experimental Psychology: Learning, Memory, and Cognition, 16,* 927–935.

Woodworth, R. S., & Schlosberg, H. (1954). *Experimental psychology* (rev. ed.). New York: Holt, Rinehart & Winston.

Index